Revolution and the Word

EXPANDED EDITION

Revolution and the Word

The Rise of the Novel in America

Cathy N. Davidson

OXFORD

UNIVERSITY PRESS

2004

OXFORD
UNIVERSITY PRESS

Oxford   New York
Auckland   Bangkok   Buenos Aires   Cape Town   Chennai
Dar es Salaam   Delhi   Hong Kong   Istanbul   Karachi   Kolkata
Kuala Lumpur   Madrid   Melbourne   Mexico City   Mumbai   Nairobi
São Paulo   Shanghai   Taipei   Tokyo   Toronto

Copyright © 1986, 2004 by Oxford University Press, Inc.

Published by Oxford University Press, Inc.
198 Madison Avenue, New York, New York 10016

www.oup.com

Oxford is a registered trademark of Oxford University Press

The Library of Congress cataloged the original edition as follows:

Davidson, Cathy N., 1949—
Revolution and the word.
Bibliography: p.   Includes index.
1. American fiction—19th century—History and criticism.   2. Social history
in literature.   3. American fiction—18th century—History and criticism.
4. Literature and society—United States.   5. United States—
Civilization—1783–1865.   I. Title.
PS374.S67D38   1986   813'.009   86–5272

ISBN 0-19-517771-1; ISBN 0-19-514823-1 (pbk.)

1 3 5 7 9 8 6 4 2

Printed in the United States of America
on acid-free paper

To my teachers and students—past and future

Preface to the Expanded Edition

Introducing One's Past

When my editor at Oxford University Press asked if I would write a substantial introduction to a new edition of *Revolution and the Word*, reframing it for this generation of readers, I had to consider what that might involve. When it appeared in 1986, *Revolution and the Word* was one of the first books to focus on the coemergence of the new U.S. nation and the new literary genre of the novel. It was an ambitious book. It analyzed the role played by literary culture in the urgent political and social debates in the early Republic and examined the role of the novel in the everyday lives of men and women of varying social classes. It was comprehensive in scope (mapping the full range of U.S. fiction written between 1789 and 1820) and method (moving from archival documents and even marginalia to current literary theory and social history). And it proposed a new way of looking at literature—a "history of texts" approach that brought together history of the book, reception studies, social history, historical materialism, and poststructuralist critical theory (including deconstructive ways of reading texts and subtexts). Since then, myriad books and articles have taken up various of these topics. Reintroducing *Revolution and the Word* would require an unusual intellectual exercise: I would have to historicize my own work and respond to these responses.

The prospect of return was daunting, and made more so by the fact that in the intervening years I have concentrated on other intellectual areas and historical periods in my research and teaching. As new arguments, theories, and archives emerge, a responsible scholar rethinks one's own argument. I certainly have. So what would it mean, over fifteen years later, to reunite with a book to which I devoted the first decade of my academic career? I've never been to a class reunion, but I suspect the feelings aroused by such a conscious return to a previous era in one's life are not dissimilar to those I felt upon revisiting *Revolution and the Word*.

It has been a fascinating, if humbling, experience. To reread one's own work is to view one's earlier self through the lens of all that has transpired. It requires *contextualizing* one's own intellectual contribution within a specific critical moment. This is the opposite of nostalgia (which is memory without context). And it requires being receptive to (and again contextualizing) dozens of essays and books that take one's ideas as a launching pad for different ideas, and then translating those insights as well.

I have spent the last two years reading work specifically related to the history and culture of the early national period and the origins of American fiction while continuing to pursue wide-ranging interdisciplinary scholarly interests that are key to my current position as vice provost for interdisciplinary studies and co-founder of the John Hope Franklin Humanities Institute at Duke University. Putting these very different scholarly experiences together—specialized research in a foundational period in American political and cultural history and working to foster, institutionally, research across all of the departments and professional schools at a research university—has made me think about the intertwined networks of scholarship that contribute to any project. Writing the new introduction has made me think deeply once again about the scholars who influenced me during the decade in which I wrote *Revolution and the Word* as well as those whom I have read with excitement since the book's publication. And reading different critics read my book has in turn helped me read other critics—a circular process, but not a trivial one.

To that end, the new introduction does several things. It provides a reconsideration of an older set of critical assumptions; it posits a new framework for thinking about the postrevolutionary era of American culture in the light of new scholarship and theories; and it stands back and asks a series of questions about the ways theories, fields, disciplines, canons, and archives are constructed and interpreted. Rather than re-address questions already discussed in detail in *Revolution and the Word*, I have tried to give readers glimpses into the process of history-and theory-making that is at the heart of all scholarship. The new introduction, in part, makes visible the workings of culture that contribute to education (in the varied senses of that word)—not only in the early national period but in the present social, political, and intellectual climate.

WHO WERE THE CRITICS who most influenced me in the process of writing *Revolution and the Word*? Even a glimpse at the endnotes to the original edition shows there are too many to mention by name. However, those who most shaped my thinking in the 1970s and 1980s when I was doing archival research on early American writers, readers, publishers, and educators shared my fascination with the relationship between political movements and cultural forms. To encompass that wide topic, *Revolution and the Word* combines various kinds of analysis—literary and historical, theoretical and archival, aesthetic and material, formal and sociological, text-based and reception-based. It draws overtly from and combines two different understandings of "culture": what is often described as the "literary-moral" analysis of culture as well as the "anthropological explanation," which sees culture (in the succinct summary of Janice A. Radway) as "the whole way of life of a historically and temporally situated people."[1] Especially in part two, *Revolution and the Word* owes much to the formalist tradition of close reading that was promoted by the New Critics and that continues to have an array of diverse proponents today.[2] It is formalism motivated by the conviction—and here my chief influences are Mikhail Bakhtin and Fredric Jameson—that the novel as a genre can have political force that exceeds the specific politics of a given writer because its generic conventions allow multiple interpretations and different points of entry by a wide range of readers, including those with varying levels of literacy and education. The novel provides imaginative freedom that might not be otherwise available within a specific historical setting.[3] Reader-response and reception theory (which were influential in the early 1980s) were also important to the close readings I performed. I extended the work on reception by searching for communities of early American readers and constructing an ethnography of eighteenth-century readership from evidence in publishers' account books, lending library rosters, diaries, and letters. I found traces of readers in the marginalia or on the end papers of extant copies of the novels.[4]

Revolution and the Word embeds its aesthetic, generic, and formalist readings in the founding national moment of U.S. history and is thus indebted to research by myriad social historians of the early Republic. Conceptually, it owes a special debt to historical materialist and Marxist historians going back, in the American tradition, at least to Charles Beard's landmark work *An Economic Interpretation of the Constitution of the United States* (1913).[5] It is influenced by the work of British historians, especially E. P. Thompson and, even more so, by Raymond Williams (considered by many to be one of the founders of cultural studies, who himself moved continuously between literary criticism and social history).[6] In the final stages of preparing *Revolution and the Word* for publication, I found increasing affinities with new work emerging from the Birmingham school of cultural studies, in particular the writings of Stuart Hall and Dick Hebdige.[7] Poststructuralist theory influenced my reading of culture and my assessment of how culture is read, especially Roland Barthes on the aesthetics and semiotics of popular culture, Michel Foucault on power and knowledge, and Jacques Derrida on deconstruction. Derrida's practice of close reading for contradictory meanings within a single sentence or even word exploded the tired notion that reading produces one consistent and coherent interpretation or that one's affective engagement in a sensational plot corresponds to the didactic message advanced by the same text. Deconstruction was instrumental to my discussions of the way a seemingly conservative text could have radical underpinnings (or vice versa).

Revolution and the Word would not have asked the questions it did were it not for the monumental work of the feminist historians and literary scholars who preceded me. I was influenced by Nina Baym, Nancy Cott, Linda Kerber, Gloria Hull, Annette Kolodny, Mary P. Ryan, Jane Tompkins, and many others who are cited in *Revolution and the Word*.[8] I was as inspired by their methods as their content, particularly in their relentless search for traces of women's history in archives too often catalogued and collected patronymically. How do you track the accomplishments of a woman who disappeared once she took her husband's name? When I began *Revolution and the Word* in 1976, very little work by early American women writers had been collected by libraries and even less had been catalogued. One went to the historical society that held the papers of the author's father, and then one went to the historical society that held the papers of the author's husband(s) and sometimes even to the archive that held the work of an author's son. Often the author's own contribution was not indexed in the description of the holdings. Nor were there very many cross-listings to the woman's other contributions that might be included in papers under different male family names. The creation of the archive of women's history is a major contribution made by feminist historians. I remain proud that *Revolution and the Word* and a companion series I edited, the Oxford University Press Early American Women Writers Series, were part of that process.

By combining these various scholarly influences, I argue in *Revolution and the Word* for a "history of texts" approach to the conundrum of the relationship of texts to history. I propose a view of literature that elaborates the social, political, material, legal, and intellectual conditions in which writers write, readers read, and printers publish books. I argue that *as these conditions change* so does the reading of texts (whether literary or political texts). And since development is always "uneven" (a Marxist term taken up brilliantly and extended to gender by Mary Poovey), there is a circularity since different ways of reading also influence, symbiotically, social, political, material, legal, and intellectual conditions as well.[9] A book is more than what is caught on the printed page and larger than the space between its covers. So, in a way, a book (like its author) keeps evolving after its publication. New readers bring to the book the changing interests and tastes of their own critical moment.

That is true of any text whether it be an early American novel, the U.S. Constitution—or *Revolution and the Word*, for that matter. I may have sent my book out into the world on its own in 1986, but, in a sense, it has been evolving at the same time that I have because of the new interpretations subsequent readers bring to it. A specific example might be helpful here. Many of the first critics of *Revolution and the Word* saw it primarily as a book about the sentimental novel and a theory of women as readers and writers. This portion of the book is not the longest in terms of pages, but the book came out at the very height of debates on gender and was incorporated into those debates. Since then, different chapters of the book have been reprinted or translated. Interestingly, no one chose to reprint chapter 7, "The Picaresque and the Margins of Political Discourse," until 2002—which saw two reprintings on different continents. It is as if suddenly that chapter has piped up and is being heard in a fresh way, no doubt because of postcolonial theory as well as general political events that have made many think hard about the role of culture in moments of overheated radical and reactionary politics (including the role of culture in democratic governance, free speech, and the interpretation of national and international law).

Scholarship is not stable. Nor should it be. It is as much a result of social, cultural, and material conditions as any other form of expression. If it were otherwise, libraries would contain only a few shelves, with one book on each subject, and students could educate themselves by reading those books instead of paying tuition to attend college or graduate school. Professors would not be required to do original research but to spout what had been said before. But no generation rests comfortably with the wisdom of its teachers. "History of ideas" as a field is based on the assumption that ideas constantly change as they are discussed, that thinkers develop in debate with one another. There is no need for a "scorched earth" policy toward one's predecessors since it is a precondition of knowledge that we grow *when* we are challenged—a psychological truism as germane to intellectual exchange as it is to any other human relationship. The academic life is productive so long as we continue to understand knowledge as a process, not a product, to which we all differently contribute. In Foucault's terms, a scholar's work itself becomes an archive for future readers and other scholars. The archive itself—what is significant and what is not—changes over time.

Whether looking at early American studies at the present moment, at new developments in history of the book, or surveying significant developments in fields that have emerged or grown in prominence since the book's publication, I have tried in the new introduction to paint an overview of major intellectual movements in the last decade and a half without becoming embroiled in particular arguments. I see this as a synthetic overview of the contingencies of knowledge production for early American studies and for intellectual life more generally. Thus my new introduction includes discussions of metasubjects such as "What Is a Field?"

Do I appreciate *every* work that has "taken on" *Revolution and the Word* since its publication? Of course not! But I hope that the new introduction makes clear its general appreciation for the richness, variety, depth, and significance of interdisciplinary humanities in the past fifteen years. During the decade when I was editor of *American Literature*, it was my job to read approximately four hundred submissions a year, including some submissions that began with one of the arguments made in *Revolution and the Word*. I learned enormously from those essays and, by extension, from the many critics, historians, and theorists who have written about either the early national period or the emergence of different fictional forms in the new Republic.

MY NEW INTRODUCTION covers some of the same ground as *Revolution and the Word,* but with a different intellectual map and, indeed, with new theoretical compass points. Issues that were hotly contested and that seemed essential when I was writing (female literacy rates, for example) seem less pressing in the wake of fifteen years of research on virtually every aspect of women's expressive culture and social formation. New questions motivate my intellectual endeavors now (including the way the "separate spheres" model of male public and female private life continues to shape criticism and social life or the way racial assumptions permeate ideology even when there is no overt reference to race in a text).

There is also something of a shift in field focus between the new introduction and the original book. While I spent much of my time in writing *Revolution and the Word* in the archives, in the new introduction I have let the original archival discussions stand pretty much as they were in 1986. While an enormous amount of historical material has been brought to light in the past decades, my findings themselves have not changed (or been changed by other work) as significantly as my thinking about how to frame those findings. I have not found myself drawn to the archive to "redo" my past study. I'm allowing the original archival materials presented in *Revolution and the Word* to stand, with the invitation that others may interpret these materials anew. At this writing, I find myself most immersed in rethinking the relations of culture to politics in the light of a wealth of new theory—literary theory, anthropological theory, political economy, race theory, gender studies, cultural geography, social theory, world systems theory, postcolonial theory, political philosophy, critical legal theory, and on and on. The new introduction revisits *Revolution and the Word* and updates its theoretical implications.

Because of extensive analysis of nation building since the publication of *Revolution and the Word*, I also find myself returning to the relationship between the Constitution and the early novel. No doubt, there are other reasons, too, why I continue to find this aspect of *Revolution and the Word* compelling. The political use of the U.S. Constitution and arguments over the intentions of the Founding Fathers that have occurred in Congress and the Supreme Court throughout the 1990s and the early twenty-first century inspire me to revisit the points made in *Revolution and the Word* with new zeal.

In sum, *Revolution and the Word* in 2004 is a different book from what it was in 1986 because of the prodigious amount of research and writing that has taken place in those intervening years as well as changes in the larger society. In the pages to follow, I begin by reframing my discussion of the relationship of the new genre and the new nation in light of revisions in my own thinking about that relationship. I look at subfields such as sexuality studies and postcolonial studies that were nascent in the late 1970s and 1980s when I was writing but that have taken on major importance since. I also step back to look at more institutional issues of field and canon formation, interdisciplinarity, and future directions for the field. I see the following pages as a dialogue between myself as a critical reader writing in 2003 and the "author" of *Revolution and the Word* who in 1986 had not been able to avail herself of the riches in scholarship available to the present author.

WRITING THE ACKNOWLEDGMENTS to this edition of *Revolution and the Word* brings me special pleasure. The first edition of *Revolution and the Word* was dedicated to Russell B. Nye and Linda Wagner-Martin, colleagues who were also my mentors in my first tenure-track job at Michigan State University. Now, I dedicate this expanded edition to the thousands of students who, since I entered the profession, have challenged me to think ever more deeply over the years, beginning with my first doctoral student in early American studies, Dana D. Nelson. As is clear in the new introduction, Dana's work has inspired much of my own rethinking of early American studies. So has the work of myriad subsequent students, including four superb women currently completing their Ph.D.s at Duke University: Monique Allewaert, Lauren Coats, Nihad Farooq, and Eden Osucha. My wonderful colleague Priscilla Wald suggested I invite these four to take part in a seminar with the focus of rereading *Revolution and the Word* and several early American novels in preparation for writing this new introduction. Over the past decade, I've read dozens of books and articles that referenced, agreed, disagreed with, or charted new territory away from *Revolution and the Word*, but, until that seminar, I had not gone back to read my own book. These brilliant and generous Americanists made the process of return more rewarding because more challenging than it otherwise would have been. If they are indicative of their generation, the future of our profession is in good hands. Since then, Monique, Eden, and Nihad have all worked as research assistants on this new edition. I am particularly indebted to them for their insights and their scholarly care.

My coeditor at *American Literature*, Michael Moon, was part of an ongoing dialogue on American culture for a decade. I cannot thank him enough for the many lunches over which we discussed our "editorial philosophy." Srinivas Aravamudan, Houston Baker, Jamie Boyle, Larry Buell, Emory Elliott, Grant Farred, Fred Jameson, David Theo Goldberg, Inderpal Grewal, Larry Grossberg, Caren Kaplan, Karla Holloway, Ranji Khanna, Jill Lepore, Lisa Lowe, Wahneema Lubiano, Walter Mignolo, Chris Newfield, Charlotte Pierce-Baker, Jan Radway, Kristin Ross, Eve Kosofsky Sedgwick, Laurie Shannon, Hortense Spillers, and Robyn Wiegman are among the many colleagues with whom I've exchanged ideas about literature, politics, and culture in the course of writing the new introduction. Peter Lange has been a dynamic boss and spirited colleague during my years as an administrator; Nan Keohane has been an inspiring leader, in ways large and small. My friend and writing partner, Alice Kaplan, has read and commented with her usual intelligence, eloquence, and care on several drafts of the new introduction. It is almost miraculous to think that we have been reading and responding to one another's work for over a decade. Charles Davidson learned to spot duodecimos and to operate a microfilm printer in his youth, both of which contributed to the first edition of *Revolution and the Word*. He and his wife Susan Brown and their family now teach me as much as they may learn. Finally, I thank Ken Wissoker, who, in his attention to the new introduction, combined the skills and knowledge of a professional editor with his unequaled tenderness, support, and love for this author. It was my friend Bob Keohane who recently told me that, when he was still a preschool child, someone asked him what he wanted when he grew up, and he answered, "Love and happy work." Those are fine words to live by—and never to be taken for granted when achieved.

Notes

1. Janice A. Radway, introduction to the second edition of *Reading the Romance: Women, Patriarchy, and Popular Literature* (Chapel Hill: Univ. of North Carolina Press, 1991), p. 3. In her introduction, Radway notes that, because of the exceptionalist tendencies of American studies programs, she was not influenced by the British cultural studies traditions with which her work has clear affinities. Interestingly, for *early* Americanists, the influence of British scholarship and models tends to be very strong. As a student of early America, my primary texts were works by John Locke, David Hume, all of the major and minor British novelists, essayists, and poets, and the Scottish Common Sense philosophers. My scholarly models were also largely British and European—walking in the footsteps of E. P. Thompson rather than Vernon Parrington. My understanding of culture owes much to Raymond Williams, *Culture and Society, 1780–1950* (New York: Columbia Univ. Press, 1958).

2. For superb examples of formalist criticism (from Cleanth Brooks to Eve Kosofsky Sedgwick and Homi Bhabha), see Frank Lentricchia and Andrew DuBois, eds., *Close Reading: The Reader* (Durham: Duke Univ. Press, 2003).

3. Mikhail Bakhtin, *The Dialogic Imagination: Four Essays*, ed. Michael Holquist, trans. Caryl Emerson and Michael Holquist (Austin: Univ. of Texas Press, 1981), and Fredric Jameson, "Reification and Utopia in Mass Culture," *Social Text*, 1 (Winter 1979), 130–48, and *The Political Unconscious* (Ithaca: Cornell Univ. Press, 1981).

4. For an extended and comprehensive account of scholarly uses of marginalia in different fields, see H. J. Jackson, *Marginalia: Readers Writing in Books* (New Haven: Yale Univ. Press, 2000). Robert Darnton has made elegant interpretations of marginalia in a number of his contributions to the history of the book and reading. See especially *The Kiss of Lamourette: Reflections in Cultural History* (New York: Norton, 1990) and *The Great Cat Massacre and Other Episodes in French Cultural History* (New York: Penguin, 1984). See also Guglielmo Cavallo, Roger Chartier, and Lydia G. Cochrane, *A History of Reading in the West* (Amherst: Univ. of Massachusetts Press, 1999), and Chartier, *Forms and Meanings: Texts, Performances, and Audiences from Codes to Computer* (Philadelphia: Univ. of Pennsylvania Press, 1995).

5. Charles Beard, *An Economic Interpretation of the Constitution of the United States* (New York: Macmillan, 1913).

6. E. P. Thompson, *The Making of the English Working Class* (New York: Pantheon Books, 1963); Raymond Williams, *The Country and the City* (New York: Oxford Univ. Press, 1973), *Keywords* (New York: Oxford Univ. Press, 1976), and *The Long Revolution* (New York: Columbia Univ. Press, 1961).

7. Dick Hebdige, *Subculture: The Meaning of Style* (London: Methuen, 1979); Stuart Hall, "Cultural Studies and the Centre: Some Problematics and Problems," in *Culture, Media, Language: Working Papers in Cultural Studies, 1972–79* (London: Hutchinson, 1980), and "Cultural Studies: Two Paradigms," *Media, Culture and Society*, 2 (1980), 52–72.

8. Nina Baym, *Woman's Fiction: A Guide to Novels by and about Women in America, 1820–1870* (Ithaca: Cornell Univ. Press, 1978); Nancy F. Cott, *The Bonds of Womanhood: "Woman's Sphere" in New England, 1780–1835* (New Haven: Yale Univ. Press, 1977); Linda Kerber, *Women of the Republic: Intellect and Ideology in Revolutionary America* (Chapel Hill: Univ. of North Carolina Press, 1980); Gloria T. Hull, Patricia Bell Scott, and Barbara Smith, *All the Women Are White, All the Blacks Are Men, but Some of Us Are Brave* (New York: Feminist Press, 1982); Annette Kolodny, *The Lay of the Land: Metaphor as Experience and History in American Life and Letters* (Chapel Hill: Univ. of North Carolina Press, 1975); Mary P. Ryan, *Womanhood in America, from Colonial Times to the Present* (New York: New Viewpoints, 1975); and Jane Tompkins, *Sensational Designs: The Cultural Work of American Fiction, 1790–1860* (New York: Oxford Univ. Press, 1985).

9. Mary Poovey, *Uneven Developments: The Ideological Work of Gender in Mid-Victorian England* (Chicago: Univ. of Chicago Press, 1988).

Contents

Literature is a luxury. Fiction is a necessity.
—G. K. Chesterton

Introduction to the Expanded Edition

New Genre, New Nation

When I began the research for *Revolution and the Word* in the 1970s, two stereotypes prevailed about early American fiction. The first assumption was that it did not exist. This isn't true. Although most survey courses and anthologies of American fiction at the time began with James Fenimore Cooper's Leatherstocking Saga of the 1820s or sometimes with *Wieland* by Charles Brockden Brown, at least one hundred novels were produced in America between 1789 and 1820.[1] Novelists of the early national period read one another and often responded to one another's plots. Readers avidly sought out novels. Publishers and proprietors of lending libraries advertised novels prominently as a way to attract readers to buy or borrow other kinds of books. Nonfiction authors of advice books, primers, histories, tracts, or sermons took up novelistic techniques or even claimed to be novelists as a way to reach the wider novel-reading public.

The second stereotype countered by *Revolution and the Word* was equally specious (and contradictory of the first): that novels published in the early Republic were imitations, if not outright plagiarisms, of Anglo-European fiction. This claim is also wrong but not surprising. Many early American novelists borrowed plots as the structure on which to hang their own adaptations, translations, and co-optations, sometimes writing new endings, often undermining the class assumptions of their progenitors. When American novelists took up themes, characters, and ideas from writers such as Samuel Richardson or Henry Fielding (or, more often, William Godwin and Ann Radcliffe), they also responded to and thereby differentiated themselves from their forerunners, often translating the sophisticated English or European metropolis to American soil and talking back with impudence if not overt critique. *Revolution and the Word* argues that the task of the early American novelist was to find a distinctive voice despite the dominance of British and European traditions and against the demoralizing derision of Anglo-European arbiters of value and good taste.[2]

That the originality of postrevolutionary American literature was invisible to many elites in the 1790s and continued to be so to subsequent literary historians should not be surprising given what we have come to learn in the past decades about colonial and postcolonial societies (a subject I will take up at length later in this introduction). However, to recall America's humble colonial origins takes a tremendous act of imagination given the dominance of the United States on the world scene throughout the twentieth and twenty-first centuries. As the historian Bernard Bailyn has summarized recently:

> The American founders were provincials—living on the outer borderlands of an Atlantic civilization whose heartlands were the metropolitan centers of England, France, the Netherlands, and Spain. The world they were born into was so deeply provincial, so derivative in its culture, that it is difficult for us now to imagine it as it really was—difficult for us to reorient our minds to that small, remote world. . . . Language can mislead us. The vocabulary of politics in eighteenth-century America was metropolitan, transcultural, European if not universal; but the reality of the Americans' lives, the political and social context in North America, was parochial.[3]

The urge to ape the imperial language is yet another feature of those attempting to express their legitimacy. No wonder then that derivativeness and plagiarism are two standard accusations leveled against postcolonial artists—now as in 1789 New England. Indeed, these two erroneous assumptions—that the early American republic produced no novels *and* that its novels were derivative—summarize the chief dismissals of postcolonial culture more generally.[4] For this is the optic through which dominant culture views the artistic productions of its colonies (or, indeed, of its most marginalized subcultures): If it's not about us, it doesn't exist; if it is about us, that's *all* it is.

Not only did the American novel exist as a definable, distinctive literary form, but also, *as a genre,* the novel played a significant role in shaping provincial and parochial identities and communities of the postrevolutionary era into the evolving entity that would become the United States of America. But it did not do so by championing the kind of "universalism" Bailyn ascribes to the Founding Fathers and their political documents. Most novelists were closer to what Grant Farred has defined as the "vernacular intellectual" in that they could both contribute to the nationalist agenda and also redefine that agenda for an audience only partially included in what Bailyn calls the "universalist" rhetoric of the Founding Fathers.[5] Vernacular form has significant overlap (in address and audience) with mainstream culture and at the same time accrues vernacular power from its articulation of its separation from the overarching national ("universal") culture.

The early American novel soon became the single most popular literary genre of its day. Circulating libraries boasted about (and exaggerated) the number of "novels" they stocked in order to draw in new members. One reason, I argue, for the popularity of early American novels was the way they coupled sensational plots with problems that were very much part of the nation-building enterprise (diffuse, varied, and often disharmonious) engaged in by Americans across the spectrum of class, region, religion, ethnicity, race, occupation, age, and gender in the 1790s.

Yet the nationalist agenda of the novel differs from the form codified and ratified in the founding political documents of the new nation and in particular the U.S. Constitution. To simplify a difference detailed in *Revolution and the Word*, novels tended to exemplify a range of energies and impulses expressed throughout the early national period but that did not survive in the final document ratified as the U.S. Constitution—including a political role for women.[6] Popular history—and especially our legal system's continual reference back to Constitutional precedence—has made the Constitution a monument, not the result of a process, representing only a fraction of those living in what would become the United States, that was sometimes divisive, contentious, and even cynical. Popular history and political polemic preserve an image of valiant revolution against an oppressive power, culminating in the creation of a unified new America proud of a Constitution that has stood for over two hundred years.

The transition was hardly so seamless. Fearing continuing riot, insurrection, and counterrevolution, the Constitutional Convention convened behind locked doors, enacted its compromises in secret, sealed its deliberations for fifty years, and emerged with one final document (although it was signed by only thirty-nine of those present, with Rhode Island never being represented in the final deliberations). Due to fears of rebellion, Madison's notes on the convention were to be kept secret until all the men who participated in the convention had died.[7]

The novel operated (to speak metaphorically) among the populace milling outside those locked doors, a populace whose very existence challenged and thus influenced what happened within. In the minds of many of America's leaders, the novel was more closely allied with the Whiskey Rebellion and Shays's Rebellion ("the American Revolution's final battle") than with the Constitutional Convention.[8] Rereading early American novels, understanding the role the novel played in debates on literacy and public education, allow us to see the variety of political and social topics at issue in the early national period. The novels reveal the contest over the shape the new nation should take, who might be the nation's paradigmatic heroes and heroines, and who was being left out of the picture in the official version of America's new "representative democracy."

In undertaking to write *Revolution and the Word*, I was intrigued by a form so popular and yet so feared (including by some early U.S. presidents). Certainly a form purported to agitate the young, arouse female sexual desire, and inspire the headstrong to political radicalism couldn't be all bad! Why was Charlotte Temple—a penniless and pregnant British schoolgirl who was educated and misled by a French teacher, seduced by a British soldier, and abandoned on American soil—*the* single most popular fictional figure of the early national period? For what did the "seduced and abandoned" heroine stand in the social psyche of early America? *Revolution and the Word* argues that a community of readers (men and women) turned to the novel as a way of participating in national debates on a range of problems that were both included and overlooked in the nation's founding documents. Novels addressed ideas (such as abolitionism and female suffrage) that did not survive the secretive and partisan process of compromise, codification, and ratification that resulted in adoption of the final draft of the Constitution. Novels, in a sense, were the rough drafts for a range of problems vital to everyday life, both in and out of the public sphere.

Societies are characterized by conflict. Democracy is the system and structure that facilitates nonviolent conflict and debate. Without disagreement, there is no democracy. Nor can you have democracy without free speech. Defending dissent is a lesson in democracy—a lesson in how it is possible to criticize without disloyalty, oppose without treason. Opposition to one aspect of a ruling party's policies does not mean one wants the collapse of "the government." If government is of, by, and for the people, then dissent is the opposite of tyranny, the antithesis of disloyalty. Dissent is democracy in action.[9]

The novel is the paradigmatic democratic form. Conflict (of desire, motive, agency, principles) is the basis of fictional plot. The novel is not only *about* conflict—as is the case with democracy, without conflict there is no novel. In the early American novel what is especially notable (vis-à-vis the British novel and similar to fiction produced in other postrevolutionary societies) is how individual conflict becomes a metonym for national conflict and private vice a synonym for corruption of the polity. If the truism of the British novel is that it mirrors Enlightenment interest in individualism, the countering truism of the early American novel is that individual action is inseparable from the national: thus the abundance of prefaces, dedications, and other overt addresses in early novels that underscore the collective (or even national) significance of seduction, picaresque aimlessness, or gothic horror (to name the three major genres of early American fiction addressed in *Revolution and the Word*).

Novelists continued to "amend" the idea of the nation throughout the early national period. Nor were their additions always well accepted. Given the significance of the written word during the eighteenth-century Enlightenment, the rapid rise of the unruly genre of the novel caused anxiety to many who were attempting to create a stable, unified nation in the aftermath of the War of Independence.[10] Free speech and dissent may be hallmarks of democracy—but that does not mean they are always welcome by those in positions of power. Rambunctious in its plots and expansive in its audience, the novel moved in a different direction from that adopted by many political leaders. Specifically, the new U.S. Constitution translated the Revolutionary principle of "equality" into a circumscribed and limited form of representative democracy, circumscribed in order to serve the larger goal of "unity." It further attempted to constrain what John Adams referred to as "democratic despotism" with a codified and centralized government characterized by careful checks and balances among executive, legislative, and judicial branches.[11] By contrast, the novel imagined an unbridled version of the nation, featuring a vivid and diverse cast of characters whose wild adventures over the raw American landscape (and beyond) and whose excessive affect spoke to America's tumultuous heart.

Given all of the different forms available to early American authors and the censure of fiction by many social arbiters, *why* did they choose to write novels rather than other kinds of books—and why did so many Americans choose to read them? I argue that the generic possibilities of fiction offered an opportunity to expand the public sphere in the face of what Dana D. Nelson has called the "de-politicizing logic of U.S. Constitutional nationalism."[12] The Constitution centralized authority as a way of restraining, channeling, and even suppressing local expressions of democracy. Its proponents extolled its ability to encode a restricted and selectively representative form of democracy (namely, republicanism) and cast other examples of democratic political expression as anarchic, divisive, unpatriotic, and potentially violent.[13] But what about those who were not represented or who believed in a less restrictive form of democracy? I argue that the novel provided an alternate public forum on democracy, based on a different cast of characters and texts with a seemingly limitless range of meanings and interpretations. Generically, the form encouraged the practice and underscored the importance of fanciful interpretation at the moment of nation building when the dominant, Madisonian political impulse went in the opposite direction. If politicians succeeded in restraining postrevolutionary energies with definitive rules of governance, novelists polemically or satirically exposed inconsistencies at the heart of the national self-image. More to the point, they saw their critique as patriotic, a vital contribution to the national identity.

The novel's popularity lay in its ability to address the widest possible demographic of readers—Federalists and anti-Federalists, liberals and republicans. One reason the novel faced censure from many social arbiters was precisely because of its wide appeal. The line between novels and schoolbooks was a fine one, and the novel addressed the marginally literate who educated themselves outside the privileged traditions and values of the elite colleges. As is still the case today, the same novel might function as a light entertainment for the aristocrat or as a "primer" for the serving girl, a guidebook to social mobility. Novelists viewed the genre's popular appeal and diverse audience as an opportunity to carry a message directly to the people. The decision to write a novel was an ideological choice (no matter what the specific ideology of a given author) because the ability to appeal to individuals without any mediation (by a preacher or an elected representative) was in and of itself a political topic in the early national period. Distributed through booksellers, circulating libraries, reading groups, or itinerant book peddlers, early American novels were read in the farthest reaches of the country, including in the unnamed territories, and fell into the hands of unknown and anonymous readers, many of whom continued to believe in the revolutionary aspirations to equality and freedom.

Understanding how the genre defined itself and reached its readership parallel with the creation of the United States helps us to delineate contending forces in the early Republic that are often erased in the heroic historiography of nation building. As Houston A. Baker, Jr., has written so eloquently in *Blues, Ideology, and Afro-American Literature*:

> Black and white alike have sustained a literary-critical and literary-theoretical discourse that inscribes (and reinscribes) AMERICA as an immanent idea of boundless, classless, raceless possibility in America. The great break with a Europe of aristocratic privilege and division has been filled by virtuoso rifts on AMERICA as egalitarian promise, trembling imminence in the New World.[14]

By studying the early American novel and its readership, we see how many felt and expressed disappointment in the loss of the "American dream" even at the originating moment of the dream.

The "first American novel" (so it proclaimed itself) was published as a national event perfectly timed with other founding events—and it embodies the disharmonious "vernacular culture" that I have been describing. Specifically, the newly ratified Constitution of the United States went into effect on March 4, 1789, with its famous Preamble:

> We the people of the United States, in order to form a more perfect union, establish justice, insure domestic tranquility, provide for the common defense, promote the general welfare, and secure the blessings of liberty to ourselves and our posterity, do ordain and establish this Constitution for the United States.

In January 1789, *The Power of Sympathy*—advertised grandly as "THE FIRST AMERICAN NOVEL"—was published with a preamble of its own:

> To the young ladies of United Columbia, these volumes, intended to represent the specious causes and to expose the fatal consequences of seduction, to inspire the female mind with a principle of self complacency and to promote the economy of human life, are inscribed, with esteem and sincerity, by their friend and humble servant, The author.[15]

The textual parallels and contrasts between these two founding documents are fascinating in and of themselves. Audience, authorship, and purpose all differ. Instead of the presumed universal "we" of the Constitution (a "we" posited both as author and reader), there is a specified audience of "young ladies." Authorship (although anonymous) is also individualized: the "friend and humble servant." Instead of a more abstract call for a "more perfect union," the novel focuses on the "specious causes" and "fatal consequences" of seduction. The "domestic tranquility" of the Constitution is literalized, individualized, and privatized. The novel is less concerned with the promise of a calm nation-state in the aftermath of a revolution than it is with the disruptions of private, domestic space.

However, the world of the Founding Fathers and that of the Founding Novel turn out not to be as divergent as they might seem to a contemporary reader. In fact, if mapped by a Venn diagram, the area of overlap would be significant, a fact that would have been known by any New Englander in 1789 who read the newspapers or heard the local gossip about the notorious scandal among America's ruling class. Twenty-three-year-old William Hill Brown wrote *The Power of Sympathy* as a *roman à clef.* In it, he accused his neighbor, Perez Morton ("Martin" in the novel), of seducing Fanny Apthorp, the beautiful young sister of Morton's wife (the poet Sarah Wentworth Apthorp Morton)—an affair that, by the standards of the time, was considered to be incestuous. Morton was one of Boston's wealthiest and most prominent citizens. When Fanny became pregnant, Morton denied he was the father. Her subsequent suicide led to an investigation of Morton's behavior, an inquest, and an official coverup, culminating in a published (and false) exoneration penned by two even more famous Americans, Excellencies James Bowdoin and John Adams. William Hill Brown used the vehicle of the first American novel to gain justice—not in the court of laws but in the court of democratic and popular opinion. Public and private sphere merge in an extraordinary way in the plot of the novel and in the history of its publication. Brown left town soon after the publication of the novel; attempts were made to censor and withdraw *The Power of Sympathy* from circulation. By contrast, Perez Morton went on to become Speaker of the Massachusetts House of Representatives and the state's attorney general, while Bowdoin became governor and Adams the second president of the United States.

Thus the American novel begins. Born in scandal, the American novel was scandal-mongering too. Moralistic and sensational. Political and sentimental. As I argue throughout *Revolution and the Word*, it is not a contradiction within the world of the early American novel that *The Power of Sympathy* can be a seduction novel while also being a protest against slavery and a tract on improved public education, especially for women. While the Constitution and official political documents such as the *Federalist Papers* attempted to formalize and constrain the riot of American life in the aftermath of its Revolution, the novel—as a form—reminded early American readers of vaguer aspirations implicit in an earlier document, the Declaration of Independence: "We hold these truths to be self-evident, that all men are created equal, that they are endowed by their Creator with certain unalienable Rights, that among these are Life, Liberty and the pursuit of Happiness."

Indisputably, the novel as a genre was more inclusive in its audience and characters than was the new government. What is less clear is the specific political valence its populism entailed. Was the novel "liberal" (in our sense of the word or the very different eighteenth-century sense) or "conservative"? Neither. And both. Politically, it is impossible to characterize all of the early American novelists and their creations as one or the other, and, indeed, in any single novel one is likely to find a range of political positions, from progressive to reactionary, depending on the topic and sometimes even on what seems to be the *same* topic.[16] Yet even for those novelists who implicitly or explicitly espoused a conservative political position (some were overtly Federalist, some were even latent Royalists), the genre conventions sometimes undermined the politics. For example, S.S.B.K. Wood ("Madam Wood," as she was known) espoused socially conservative views on women, advocating an entirely submissive role for daughters and wives. Yet when she depicts such submissiveness in *Amelia; or, The Influence of Virtue* (1802), showing the virtuous Amelia repeatedly abused by a caddish husband, the specificity of harm done to a character with whom the reader empathizes makes the book seem less like advocacy for passivity than an argument for sturdy feminism of the Wollstonecraftian variety.

I am less interested in the explicit politics of specific early American novelists than I am with the range of characters (rich, poor, men, women, whites, Indians, immigrants, African Americans, etc.), the variety of experience (from seduction to cross-dressing to privateering), and the diversity of expression characteristic of the genre at this time. Early American novels were bold, assertive, declarative—episodic (even chaotic) in form, rebellious in affect (sentimental, sensational, frightening, or satirical). They walked on the dark side of the Enlightenment, exploring not just the middle class but also the lower classes, often focusing on the young or ill-educated, frequently focusing on females. As in *The Power of Sympathy*, young women were often misled or mistreated by the rich and powerful. These protagonists traveled in humbler social circles and could be motivated by love, patriotism, virtue, social climbing, sexuality, greed, despair, megalomania, corruption, deceit. Their ambitions (political, economic, social, sexual) often parodied the loftier aspirations of the nation as represented by its Founders or promulgated in political exhortations of the time.

Equally important, the complex class map drawn by the early American novel charted the different kinds of interactions among the social orders of the time, with egress in and out of the upper classes through the bedroom, kitchen, tavern, and back door. Along with freedom of religion, a fluid class structure was one of America's defining differences with England. "There is no class in America" has been a recurring theme from the nation's inception. Yet no one reading the body of fiction produced in the early Republic would find a representation of a classless society. On the contrary, early American novelists present (and often critique) the American version of a non-egalitarian class system.[17]

Although less precise in its social architecture than the upstairs and downstairs of late-eighteenth-century British fiction, class is a major determinant of social justice in numerous early American novels. On the most sinister level, black marketing, the slave trade, political campaigns, military actions, and the callous circulation of young women all expose social interconnections and dependencies among the classes. In political novels such as Hugh Henry Brackenridge's *Modern*

Chivalry (1792–1815), the representation of the public sphere is generally less divided between men and women than between upper and lower classes. Sometimes little more than a stone's throw separates the rabble from the elite, yet few manage to actually transcend that divide. Scenes of domesticity rarely cross class lines. Forms of address, networks of affiliation, friendship, and influence operate by rules so absorbed into the fabric of everyday life that they need not be spoken. Cross-class ambition and upward mobility simply underscore the obstacles of class that need to be overcome, whether exemplified by mythologized self-representations such as those by Benjamin Franklin in his evolving autobiography or by the novelist Charles Brockden Brown in his Gothic reprisal of the Frank-linesque rise from rags to riches in *Arthur Mervyn* (1799–1800). Passion—typically sexual—also both confuses and emphasizes class relations, with the inequality of gender doubled when the "wronged woman" is (quite typically in American as well as British fiction) a humble serving girl.

Early American novels, somewhere in their plots, typically provide class allegories, yet it is not entirely clear how those allegories were read, by whom, and to what social end. We know that the audience of the novel crossed class lines, extending from the very rich to those who were quite poor. The stereotypical way this happened was that the maid read the novels that she borrowed and returned to the local lending library for her mistress. Yet I am suggesting that a cross-class audience does not equate with "democratization." Given the indeterminacy of meaning in novels as well as their affective power, it is safe to say that, even when reading the same novel, mistress and maid probably did not draw the same class moral; while each may have been moved to sympathy, it is not at all clear that they felt the same range of sympathy for the same characters or savored the same sense of virtue rewarded at the novel's ending.[18]

We know from various sources that the popularity of certain novels, in particular *Charlotte Temple* and *The Coquette*, crossed class, gender, and regional lines. In one sense, one could say that this popularity contributed to the "shared national culture" that was vaunted as an ideal in the eighteenth century as it has been sporadically throughout American history. *Revolution and the Word* asks what we mean by that word *shared*. Is reading the same book sharing a culture? In some ways it is since it means a body of referents that individual readers can recognize. However, the meaning one makes of those references can vary radically depending upon the experiences and sympathies one brings to a text—and especially a text as open-ended (and stirring) as a novel. As Gayatri Spivak emphasizes, whenever one evokes a "shared national culture" the question must be asked: Shared by whom?[19] It further must be asked: And shared in what way?

Revolution and the Word attempts to answer that question on many levels, including by proposing the most complete ethnography we have to date of an early American readership: who bought novels and who borrowed them (at minimal expense) through the ever-expanding network of the nation's circulating libraries. From many different forms of evidence, *Revolution and the Word* also attempts to provide an affective account of early American reading. How did these early novel readers feel about the books they bought or borrowed? Did they find self-expression through the reading of novels that they did not find in the celebratory beginnings of the new nation?[20] *Revolution and the Word* raises questions about the outlines, bonds, relationships, and obligations of membership in both structured and loose settings, literary communities, and reading associations—ethnographic and interpretive questions of the kind asked, in a different context, by Elizabeth McHenry in her brilliant study of African American literary societies.[21]

In some cases, novels were a vehicle of dissent in a form easily recognizable as political in their form of engagement. These novels fit most neatly into the concept of a public sphere as defined by Jürgen Habermas and many Habermasian critics of the public sphere, most notably Michael Warner for the early national period. This world was defined largely as male, explicitly and implicitly.[22] Yet male and female worlds, public life and inner life, were not rigidly segregated as either eighteenth-century moral authorities or twentieth-century critics might believe. Later in this introduction, I will return to the gender assumptions embedded in discussions of the public sphere; here I will simply note that female as well as male novelists debated topics raised in the public sphere (and both—sometimes pseudonymously or anonymously—also addressed problems often relegated to the "private sphere"). Some novelists used the cover of satire, effusive language, or sensational plots to covertly address the contradictions in representative democracy. This was especially true after President John Adams attempted to control "mobocracy" by passing the draconian Alien and Sedition Acts of 1798 (which penalized myriad forms of written or oral protest, labeling them "malicious" and "seditious"). Sentimental, picaresque, and gothic novels provided one means to *allegorize* dissent—and evade legal persecution—under the protective cover of a genre considered "imaginary."

Using a variety of forms, methods, techniques, and plots, the early American novel expressed the multiple and contradictory aspirations of a postcolonial and postrevolutionary society while the official business of government was to create a "United States." Unruly forces had been stoked ("No taxation without representation!") to incite the American Revolution; now those energies had to be repressed, constrained, and contained. As Antonio Negri has recently argued, if revolutions are based on utopian dreams, constitutions are designed to prevent the anarchic imaginings that lead to revolution.[23]

Postrevolutionary America was not the tidy or unified world conjured up at historical theme parks, Fourth of July parades, or presidential inaugurations. Nor was it the egalitarian utopia sometimes attributed to our "origins," especially by Constitutional fundamentalists attributing omniscience retrospectively to the Founding Fathers. On the contrary, postrevolutionary America exhibited divisiveness, counterrevolutionary military and mob actions, and disappointed expectations—as well as the strong communal desire for order, an end of violence, widespread prosperity, and the creation of a truly representative democracy. How to achieve those ends; who would and would not be represented in the democracy; how prosperity could be decentralized; and who had claim to the label "American" were all vibrant topics of the early national period. They are the kinds of populist ideals expressed in virtually all postcolonial societies.[24] So where do we go to find traces of that heterogeneous version of the new Republic? The early American novel is one of the best sources. Decentralized, polyphonic, almost impossible to pin down, the novel echoed energies that many political leaders wanted to harness and voiced a disquiet that the new engine of government was designed to still. The coemergence of the American novel with the new nation reminds us that "nationalism" was a process, even a *contest*, about what shape thirteen colonies would assume in the wake of their successful revolt against England.

The United States as a Postcolonial Nation

An early essay that attempted to understand early American literature through the lens of postcolonial theory is Lawrence Buell's "American Literary Emergence as a Postcolonial Phenomenon" (1992). Buell notes: "As the first colony to win independence, America has a history that Americans have liked to offer as a prototype for other nations, yet which by the same token might profitably be studied by Americans themselves in light of later cases." He observes that there are "formidable barriers" to "analogizing between this country's literary emergence and even that of Canada or Australia, let alone West India or West Africa" and modestly describes himself as a novice in this comparative enterprise. He further warns of the suspicion of hypocrisy that might attach to anyone who describes America's expansionist years as "postcolonial rather than proto-imperial."[25] That distinction appears, in various forms, throughout much criticism of nationalism and postcolonialism written in the 1990s and the early twenty-first century. It is central to the essays in the landmark 1993 volume edited by Amy Kaplan and Donald Pease, *The Cultures of U.S. Imperialism*, as well as the forum in the *Journal of American History* generated by Ann Laura Stoler's "Tense and Tender Ties: Intimacies of Empire in North American History and (Post) Colonial Studies."[26]

If "postcolonialism" brings with it a specific implication of a release from prior colonial oppression, what does it mean to apply such a term to the nation that, for the past one hundred years, has been the dominant power on the globe? To do so entails risks in at least two directions. On the one hand, it is essential to remember that the whole project of coming to the New World was a form of "settler colonialism" based on the confiscation of land from its inhabitants, the eradication of the land claims of those people, territorialization, and the pacification and ultimately genocide against those inhabitants.[27] The process of settling the harsh New World was also accomplished by the capture and enslavement of Africans, countless numbers of whom died during the Middle Passage. Later in this introduction, in the section entitled "Race Studies," I will return to the interconnections among those factors—settler colonialism, genocide against indigenous peoples, and slavery (the intersection of postcolonial and race theory)—as well as their connections to imperialism and capitalism. The intertwined horrors of that foundational moment in the history of Western imperialism cannot be overstated.

On the other hand, one is remiss not to remember that the white settlers in the New World were also colonials who, in 1776, severed their relationship with Britain through violent revolution. It is essential that we try to understand the complex and ambiguous legacy of America's settler colonialism on behalf of an imperial power; its revolution against that imperial power; the larger context of world systems of imperialism, capital, and the trade in humans; and the equally significant context of widespread revolutionary actions within Europe itself (France, Geneva, Holland, Poland, Ireland, Naples, etc.) and the Caribbean (most notably, Haiti). This complex story of origins (with its contradictory narratives of power and powerlessness, isolation and global superiority) has had a formative impact on American ideology to the present, including on America's infinitely refreshable self-concept as the innocent and its self-appointed role as world crusader. Particular actions at home or abroad—throughout our history—have not disturbed the mythic identity.

THE INTERTWINED LEGACIES of colonialism and postcolonialism are not foregrounded in the original edition of *Revolution and the Word.* Indeed, the word "postcolonial" is not in its index, even though the creation of a culture in the wake of a revolution is its primary subject. I was doing research and writing in the 1970s and early 1980s, before the flourishing of postcolonial studies. Within a year of the publication of *Revolution and the Word,* two important books on the history of postcolonial theory appeared, the translation into English of Tzvetan Todorov's *The Conquest of America: The Question of the Other* and Gayatri Spivak's *In Other Worlds: Essays in Cultural Politics.* Although they are radically different kinds of studies, each addresses relationships of culture and the state under postcolonial conditions.[28]

Since the publication of *Revolution and the Word,* I have continued to think about the meaning of a postrevolutionary culture in the context of complex histories of colonialism and postcolonialism, throughout Canada, the Caribbean, and the Americas. As Dana Nelson has recently noted in a review essay, "From Manitoba to Pantagonia," most of the work on postcolonialism and the United States and on inter-American studies has not come from Americanists but from those working in other national traditions and in other languages. Indeed, perhaps because of the strong exceptionalist tradition of American studies, much of our scholarship has been insular. (It is a classic feature of American studies programs, for example, not to require languages other than English—despite the efforts of many scholars to expand the definition of "America" beyond those productions written in English.)[29] Personally, I find the move away from nation-based cultural studies toward theories of interactions, responses, networks, and interconnections extremely fruitful and find equally productive recent work on the cultural expression of subcultures and subalterns, a term that is disputed by many but that continues to signal the role of those disenfranchised within the nation-state or inhabiting the stateless world of the migrant "resident alien." Analyses of these problems run the gamut from world systems theory proposed by Immanuel Wallerstein, subaltern studies articulated and subsequently refined by Gayatri Spivak, cosmopolitanism as addressed by Homi K. Bhabha, European provincialism and ideological translation as addressed by Dipesh Chakrabarty, globalization and cultural movements as assessed by Arjun Appadurai, globalization from below as described by Walter Mignolo, and immigration and the mobilization (or immobilization) of culture as discussed by Lisa Lowe.[30] In my 1993 presidential address at the American Studies Association, I alluded to the potential of transnational American studies to move beyond naive "American exceptionalism" that has been the trap of American studies since its inception as a discipline.[31] Increasing numbers of scholars are taking up this challenge to exceptionalist thinking, looking more closely at the colonial/postcolonial legacies of the American past.

Many problems I address in *Revolution and the Word* are pertinent in the various histories of postcolonial societies and indigeneity, especially in Latin America (especially addressed by Mignolo) and South Asia (by Chakrabarty)— from literacy rates (and the debate over who could or should be allowed to read and at whose expense) to public education, to primitive book distribution networks, to the relationship between the official national rhetoric of self-definition and cultural forms that express alternative ideals. Without the benefit of the last fifteen years of postcolonial theory, *Revolution and the Word* proposed a "test case" for how those within a marginal and developing nation can use a marginal and nascent cultural form to represent aspirations, disappointments, ambitions, frustrations, and contradictions that get minimized in the official process of nation building.[32]

But the question remains: if postcolonial theory is fraught when applied to early U.S. culture, why apply it? What can we learn from explanations that map only crudely onto the complex and ambiguous case of America's postcolonial origins? I am arguing that postcolonial theory helps give us the insights and keywords necessary to foreground the diverse and discordant ideological and aesthetic productions shaping the nascent nation-state into what would become the

"United States of America." I am arguing, further, that this is a necessary *corrective* to nationalist accounts of those origins.

Postcolonial theorists understand state formation as a conflictual process—a process in which some opinions emerge triumphant, instantiated in the documents of government, while others persist to antagonize the new state (sometimes resulting in state-sanctioned acts of repression and retaliation). Postcolonial theory is antinationalist in its impulses if by "nationalism" we mean a unified, unitary, isolated state. It is thus useful in helping us to see which elements in the new Republic may have indigenous particularities and which are part of the process of postcolonial self-definition. Rethinking the early Republic as a postcolonial society can help us move beyond a jingoistic historiography that homogenizes the past, erasing its violence, minimizing its undemocratic features, and harmonizing its discord. Nostalgic versions of the early national period erase both the struggle and the compromise over the creation of the nation.

As I suggest throughout this introduction, it is a challenge *even for historians of the period* to remember the fledgling and contestatory origins of the most powerful nation on the globe. Let me use one recent example to make this point. David McCullough's Pulitzer Prize–winning best-seller, *John Adams*, clearly sets out to give stature and luster to America's second president, a president who has been overshadowed by his place between the towering figures of George Washington and Thomas Jefferson. It is perhaps with this popularizing objective in mind that McCullough passes over hastily and defensively the passage of the 1798 Alien and Sedition Acts during Adams's presidency. These laws made immigrants vulnerable to deportation and native-born citizens vulnerable to fines and imprisonment for speaking out against the U.S. government, and most specifically against the Federalist Party then in power. The Alien and Sedition Acts created a picture of an embattled new Republic cowering under the threat of British imperial power and dangerous French revolutionaries abroad, and the dangers of populist insurrections, Indian attacks, and slave revolts within its borders. The more immediate thrust of the Alien and Sedition Acts, however, was to ensure the destruction of Thomas Jefferson's Republican Party. The Republicans, after all, had expressed sympathy for the French revolutionaries—which is no doubt why the Federalist-controlled Congress passed the Sedition Act on July 14 (Bastille Day). After passage of the Alien and Sedition Acts, immigrants were deported and newspaper editors arrested for criticizing the president of the United States, conspiring to oppose any measure of the government, or intimidating officeholders through dissent and critique. Benjamin Franklin's grandson, Benjamin Franklin Bache, editor of the Philadelphia *Democrat-Republican Aurora*, was among the twenty-five editors and writers of Republican newspapers who were arrested and whose newspapers were shut down under the Alien and Sedition Acts. These have been called the most serious abrogation of the right of free speech prior to the McCarthy era in U.S. history. And they were passed by only the *second* president of the United States.

McCullough refers to these events only a few times in his enormous biography, using the word "infamous" but never describing how they were infamous, what the acts said, or how much they compromised the ideology of freedom that most Americans attribute to the Founders. I use this graphic example to underscore a tendency of history to celebrate origins. In contrast, postcolonial histories are predicated on a different model of historical scholarship, not teleological in impetus but explanatory in terms of complex networks of capital, domination, control, communication, and cultural production that do not start and stop at the borders of what comes to be defined (at least for a time) as a "nation." The explanatory thrust of postcolonial history and theory lies in their sophisticated and subtle explanation of the workings of power, not just of the dominating group but of subgroups ("subalterns"). Universalist or heroic history has to erase or minimize contradictions such as the second president of the United States passing the Alien and Sedition Acts. Most Americans have forgotten this controversial moment in our own nation's founding, just as they have forgotten that many Republicans in the new nation supported the French Revolution.[33] Indeed, the spectacularized differences between the "sane" American and "irrational" French Revolution in popular history are part of the same tendency to use history to justify the status quo.

It should be added that dissent triumphed over the Alien and Sedition Acts. The outcry against implementation of the Alien and Sedition Acts was so vehement that Jefferson won his bid for the presidency. By 1801, he had pardoned all those convicted of sedition. In 1802, the Republican-controlled Congress repaid fines levied against those convicted with interest and repealed the Naturalization Act. The remaining Alien and Sedition Acts were simply allowed to expire.

Why is it important to remember discord in the world of the Founding Fathers? One reason is because of the function nostalgic history serves in the present. It supplies a false teleology. The economic and political power of the United States from the late nineteenth century to the present is seen to be based on moral superiority, colonial expansionism, a mission on behalf of "Truth, Justice, and the American Way" (as Superman comics tell us). Critics from Perry Miller to Sacvan Bercovitch have analyzed the ideological embrace of moral superiority (the jeremiad) which is deep in the fiber of not only "America" but "Americanism."[34] On what is that boastful moralism based? Christopher Newfield argues eloquently, in *The Emerson Effect*, that "moderation"—not freedom, equality, free speech, dissent, difference, individualism, or separation of church and state—is the most consistent and foundational American value.[35] Paradoxically, although "freedom" has been America's most persistent rallying cry (the basis for its jeremiads), exercising freedom and articulating political differences have been castigated (and sometimes legally suppressed) throughout American history, including at its very beginning.

Nationalist history casts disagreement as "anti-American"—as dissent from an assumed, if unarticulated, consensus rather than as an invaluable contribution to a process that is innately and definitionally "democratic."[36] As the social philosopher Jacques Rancière notes, "consensus thinking conveniently represents what it calls 'exclusion' in the simple relationship between an inside and an outside. But what is at stake under the name of exclusion is not being-outside. It is the mode of division according to which an inside and an outside can be joined." Rancière argues that "exclusion" is the form of that division, but since exclusion from political process means that one is invisible (i.e. unrepresented), there is almost no way to characterize the excluded *except* by their exclusion. The excluded are outside of (and irrelevant to) the political debate of those inside. "The 'exclusion' referred to is the very absence of a representable barrier."[37] A statement such as "All men are created equal" begs the question of "all women" as well as of those men (typically, of color) who aren't. This is the problem of consensus arguments about America history, arguments that begin in foundational colonial and postcolonial moments, rendering a long American history of disagreement invisible by branding disagreement "un-American."

When viewing the ideological histories of other nations, including postcolonial states, one often encounters examples of political dissent treated as un-patriotic or even treasonous (conditions implicit in the labeling of certain forms of expression "un-American"). However, rarely does one find governmental suppression of political protest occurring simultaneously with an idealistic national commitment to the protection of free speech. In established capitalist democracies, it is almost inconceivable to label criticism of the ruling political party as antithetical to the nation. The most vituperative British member of Parliament, railing against the prime minister, is still British, maybe even definitively so *because* of the railing. He or she would rarely be called "un-British" or "anti-British." In considering the rich body of theory and history on nation building, it becomes clear that one of the *defining* features of Americans is the ease with which we pronounce other citizens "un-American" or "anti-American" for relatively mild protests against the status quo. In many democracies, this tendency in itself would be seen as antidemocratic and thus threatening. As Homi K. Bhabha notes, "nation" is a convenient epithet to express the authenticity of cultural locale. But what does "nation" really mean? Nationalism—like colonialism—is presented as seamless (not fragmented, fractured, and contradictory), perhaps because nationalism always risks breaking apart at its seams.

We always need to ask ourselves who is or is not allowed to speak in the name of the nation.[38] And, in the case of the United States, we have to ask, in historical terms, what it means when certain voices are excluded from the national registry, as it were. In virtually every postcolonial society seeking to establish some form of democratic rule, obscure, coercive, and secret processes are required to reach a compromise among factions in order to create systems of governance. But what does it mean when the compromise to create a government requires a jettisoning of the nation's core values of freedom and equality? What does it do to a nation, for example, to accept slavery in its founding documents? The acceptance of slavery was not a pat decision. Although it did not seem to bother most men at the Constitutional Convention that women were not represented in the new government, the topic of slavery caused consternation, bitterness, and argument that lasted for months and threatened to end the Convention without the creation of a constitution. What would such an early acquiescence on the principle of freedom and equality (principles that had fueled a revolution) mean to the moral fabric of the nation?[39]

The most important consequence of such an early and profound bartering away of a foundational principle of freedom is that compromise for the sake of national unity itself becomes the highest principle of the nation. Compromise on behalf of solidarity and nationhood supersedes freedom and equality and, indeed, all other principles. The argumentative logic of this elevation of compromise to the highest level of principle is that, without the unified nation, no other principles are possible. The logical inconsistency that is pushed aside is that, if those other principles have been forfeited already, why do we need the unified "United States" to protect them? That is the unaskable question. America *is* freedom, definitionally—so much so that it does not have to be always free and equal in order to support freedom. It only has to be "America."

Constitutional compromise solidified America's ambivalent ideology of freedom. Even the concept of "dissent" implies an overall consensus from which departure is (barely) tolerated. Yet dissent happens constantly (as witness the opposition to the Alien and Sedition Acts leading to Jefferson's victory). Unsuccessful dissent is forgotten or forever vilified. Successful dissent, in retrospect, is preserved as success, not as dissent. Its outcome becomes part of the national mythology of both compromise and freedom: the Revolutionary War itself, the abolitionist movement that led to a civil war to end slavery, late-nineteenth-century suffragist movements that resulted in women gaining the vote, labor movements that regulated safety and wages, opposition to McCarthyism, or the Civil Rights movement that ended legalized segregation are a few of the most prominent examples. The way history is told means that radical acts become mainstream when they succeed. Or to reverse that: to succeed is to have been right all along. But is the converse also true? Does failure to change the society mean one was wrong to try?

Revolution and the Word returns us to the exact moment when process, not product, was the topic at hand. Early American novels struggle with the regulation of private behavior in the face of public morality, the relationship between democratic representation and ignorance, the containment of political strife in a republic, and the reasonable articulation of social discord in the aftermath of a revolution and on the brink of creating a highly unstable new government. We must remember that newspapers in the early national period were partisan, frequently vicious, and sometimes bordering on the slanderous. The novel, while not specifically affiliated with political parties, candidly articulated a wide range of political and social opinions.

A number of postcolonial critics have argued about the novel's role in providing this form of "uncompromised" expression—raw, discordant, even cacophonous— in a postcolonial setting, beginning with Benedict Anderson's early work on the role of culture in nation building, *Imagined Communities: Reflections on the Origin and Spread of Nationalism*. Although many subsequent critics have built upon, challenged, or in other ways reacted to *Imagined Communities*, it is worth returning to this influential text to see the parallels between early American novels and the novels of colonial Mexico. Anderson analyzes the novel purported to be the first Latin American novel, José Joaquín Fernandez de Lizardi's *El Periquillo Sarniento* (1816).[40] He describes it as a "ferocious indictment of Spanish administration in Mexico." It is a picaresque novel; "the movement of a solitary hero through a sociological landscape of a fixity that fuses the world inside the novel with the world outside" allows the novelist to describe hospitals, prisons, schools, monasteries, cities, and remote villages. The picaro himself embodies, in Jean Franco's terms, "the parasitism and laziness" encouraged by the "Spanish government and education system."[41] In Anderson's formulation, this novel—through its extensive tour of the Mexican landscape in the context of Spanish political rule—helps constitute a "national imagination" for the readers of colonial Mexico.

I quote Anderson here because his description could apply, with little change in emphasis, to a number of novels in the postcolonial United States, most notably those I discuss in the chapter on "The Picaresque and the Margins of Political Discourse." Hugh Henry Brackenridge's sprawling, multivolume comic epic *Modern Chivalry*, for example, takes the American reader on the same kind of tour through cities teaming with impoverished immigrants or to the countryside populated by rude farmers, scheming politicians, religious fanatics, or displaced Indians. Brackenridge satirizes the new American democracy; the oppressive force here is no longer England (for colonial rule is no longer at issue) but the defects in postrevolutionary American democracy. Captain Farrago, arguably the novel's chief protagonist, provides the exceptionally ambiguous voice of quirky rationalism. Intriguingly, in this passage Captain Farrago sounds both like James Madison and like a critic of Madison:

> Why should I undervalue democracy; or be thought to cast a slur upon it; I that am a democrat myself. . . . *Nor is it democracy, that I have meant to expose; or reprehend, in any thing that I have said; but the errors of it: those excesses which lead to its overthrow.*

These excesses have shown themselves in all democratic governments; when it is that a *simple* democracy has never been able to exist long. An experiment is now made in a new world, and upon better principles; that of *representation and a more perfect separation, and near equipoise of the legislative, judicial, and executive powers.* But the balance of the powers, is not easily preserved. *The natural tendency is to one scale.* The demagogue is the first great destroyer of the constitution by deceiving the people. He is no democrat that deceives the people. He is an aristocrat.[42]

In this passage, Farrago's fear of democratic unrest is secondary to his apprehensions about the tendency toward aristocracy that he witnesses in the present U.S. government. And interestingly, Captain Farrago is the *conservative* voice in the novel. But this political positioning should not be surprising given that Brackenridge was an eccentric Princeton-educated classicist turned backwoods lawyer who served as a mediator at the Whiskey Rebellion, a rural insurrection of farmers mostly from rural Pennsylvania, and one of the first tests of federal authority. The farmers protested an excise tax levied by the U.S. government on the producers of whiskey. To quell the gathering mob, George Washington assembled a militia of nearly thirteen thousand men. Brackenridge was called in to mediate between the rebels and the militia, and to be a slippery spokesman for both sides and neither. His hero Captain Farrago similarly switches sides, often in reaction to the outlandish (but often charismatic and always shrewd) actions of his Irish servant, Teague O'Regan. But for Farrago, O'Regan could have been elected to the state legislature, ordained a Presbyterian minister, named chief of the Kickapoo Indians, or made a member of the august American Philosophical Society. To return to Anderson's formulation, with far more texture than one would ever find in one of the nation's founding documents, Brackenridge's hero and antihero, moving like a postcolonial Don Quixote and Sancho Panza over the American landscape, allow us to see the inner workings of a range of institutions—the new democratic government, the ministry, tribal governance, and academe. *Modern Chivalry* both reveals and helps to constitute a "national imagination" for the readers of the new United States.

The difference between the body of work Anderson analyzes and the novels described in *Revolution and the Word* is that the former are colonial novels and the latter are written in North America after a revolution from a colonial power. In intent and in political impact, early American novels may more closely resemble the nineteenth-century postrevolutionary Latin American novels that Doris Sommer calls "foundational fictions." Yet if those novels are designed to end conflict and promote unity, despite a range of opinions and disagreements evidenced in the plots, then we have another fascinating difference, for in early American novels it is not at all clear that unity is the end result—especially in novels where "union" is the explicit goal.[43] America's foundational fictions are, more typically, antifoundational.

Noteworthy in America's postcolonial novels is that England is rarely a site of nostalgia or reactionary longing (even for the most socially conservative American writers). On the other hand, England is hardly ever summoned up as a metaphor for evil oppression either. When England is represented negatively, it is typically because England *mirrors* problems in the new Republic. Colonial oppressor and new national government are interchangeable, as in Washington Irving's famous political jibe in "Rip Van Winkle" (1819) at "King" George Washington.

In the postcolonial American novels—as in the colonial and postcolonial Mexican and Latin American novels described by Anderson and Sommer—it is the role of the picaro/picara to keep moving as a way to evade the repressive operations of government but also individualist actions by those outside of government. It's a toss-up, really, between American mobocracy and autocracy. A very interesting case is Herman Mann's *The Female Review* (1797), loosely based on the story of Deborah Sampson, a young woman who cross-dressed as a man in order to fight in the Revolutionary War. In this novel, Deborah Sampson fears sexual exposure (and military demotion) every bit as much as she fears the Revolutionary War itself. Mann turns an incident in Revolutionary War history into a fascinating metaphor for the psychological violence of being a woman in the new Republic. She is free, handsome, even swashbuckling in drag, and she protects her false identity in order to hold on to the fiction of her freedom.[44] And part of the appeal of the best-selling American novel before the publication of *Uncle Tom's Cabin*, Susanna Rowson's *Charlotte Temple* (1791), is that its domestic tribulations are set against the backdrop of the American Revolution and its heroine is equally vulnerable in the Old Country and in the New. Seduced in England, impregnated on the passage over, and abandoned to die alone and penniless in America, Charlotte Temple is the archetypal postcolonial heroine. Her fate is an object lesson (albeit a negative one) in separation from parental authority and the requirements for both independence and survival.

Since Anderson, postcolonial studies, and particularly those focusing on nation building, have gone in many productive directions. Among them are comparative Americas studies (inter-American studies, hemispheric studies, circum-Atlantic studies, Pacific Rim studies), a rich area that highlights the different traditions within the Americas as well as interconnections between the Americas and other parts of the globe.[45] Understanding the processes of nation building in various countries throughout the Caribbean and the Americas helps us to understand which formations are typical and which site-specific. It also helps to counterbalance clichés about the "national character" and sort out the local from the universal.

I've learned especially from postcolonial studies to focus on indigenous voices and to make discriminations among the kinds of cultural productions within postcolonial societies, including multiply voiced forms of dissent, heterogeneous populations both within those colonizing and those colonized, and multiple meanings within the culture of the postcolonial state that carry the traces of those diverse populations. Their particular relevance to *Revolution and the Word* is in the way they shed light on mutually constitutive conditions of colonialism. The new United States was susceptible both to influences from European high culture and to what Mignolo calls "globalization from below"—the impact of the cultures and values of indigenous peoples as well as those who were brought by force or circumstance to the New World (slaves, indentured servants, political outcasts, the rural and urban poor, etc.).

The interplay of these diverse traditions created an "America" far more complex than we know from popular history. Another example from John Adams is useful. Adams, it will be recalled, was the attorney who defended the British soldiers who fired upon and killed five civilians in the Boston Massacre. In court, he argued that the British soldiers were justified in what they did because they were attacked not by respectable Americans but by an unruly and unrespectable mob led by Crispus Attucks (who was part African and part Native American). In Adams's memorable phrase, they were "a motley rabble of saucy boys, Negroes and mulattoes, Irish teagues and outlandish jacktars."[46] Six of the British soldiers who had fired upon the crowd were acquitted; the other two were found guilty of manslaughter. Their punishment was to be branded on their thumbs, and this miscarriage of justice became fodder for those seeking independence from England. Adams's role is not often remembered on patriotic occasions. And it is significant that history has "whitened up" the patriots who died during the Boston Massacre. It makes them New Englanders, even "Puritans," not multicultural, multinational dock workers in a system of global trade in which capital, goods, and human beings were exchanged. Postcolonial theory helps us to attend to different parts of this particular story—the attorney turned patriot turned Federalist president, the translation of a multiracial mob into storybook (white) American heroes that reinforces later discrimination against people of color. America was one destination on worldwide colonial trading circuits. Think about the Boston Tea Party. From where was that tea coming? Obviously from India, China, or Japan. What else was coming from those other ports on the colonial trading circuits?

In the years after the American Revolution, America began creating the unified myth of itself. Many have argued, however, that "myth" is the operative word in that equation. The early novel provides us with scraps that have not been homogenized by heroic histories. Rural, scattered, a nation of immigrants with different cultural and religious traditions, with poverty and homelessness, pestilence, and slavery, with vitriolic party politics as well as political corruption, with mobocracy and would-be aristocracy, and very little in the way of high culture, America had no urban center of population, power, and culture equivalent to London or Paris. America started in part as a refuge for English Puritans seeking a place to practice their religion without persecution. That's one part of the story. The other story is of thirteen dissimilar colonies and various territories representing different religious, ethnic, and linguistic traditions (German, French, Spanish, etc.). Some, but not all, of these were yoked together in a revolution against imperial England. Some, but not all, emerged as a small, shaky, contentious, and hybrid nation—part of a world system of global trading and colonization whose foundation was genocide and displacement of indigenous populations, piracy, indentured servitude, and enforced slavery. It is a story of a fledgling nation whose leaders often expressed insecurity and inferiority relative to the cultural and political hegemony of Europe (chiefly England) and superiority relative to the rest of the Americas (especially, but not exclusively, those portions that were predominantly nonwhite and non-British—the Caribbean and Central and South America). Revolutions, wars, slave revolts, and border disputes (such as the War of 1812 with Canada) caused anxieties.[47] An unstable world position became a powerful driver in shaping American ideology, including one that homogenized and unified America's story. Postcolonial theory helps us resuscitate a repressed America.

A Paradigm Shift: Subversion

If the absence of the word "postcolonial" in the index of *Revolution and the Word* reminds us that it was written in the 1970s and early 1980s, the intermittent presence of the word "subversion" similarly marks its time. That word, so prominent in the work of Michel Foucault as well as in the work of New Historicists, struck a chord with me as I tried to describe the novel's role in the early Republic.[48] In places, I argue that the novel undercut the status quo, providing a subversive voice in the nation.

In retrospect, subversion seems like a narrow way to describe the complex operations of the literary form in the contest over how to define and create that amorphous entity called a "nation." "Subversion" implies an undermining of something that is solid, fixed, overarching. It is a binary configuration: the novel versus the Founding Fathers (to put it in its most black-and-white formulation). Yet, as I argue in this new introduction, most of the individuals who wrote novels thought of themselves as patriots contributing to and improving the new nation, not subverting it. Susanna Rowson, for example, saw herself as part of a larger project of enfranchisement, inclusive in the audience she addressed in her novels, plays, histories, and textbooks (demographies of readers who were often outside the official political process). "Symbolic enfranchisement" might be a better description of Rowson's ambitions than "subversion." The novel did not operate outside the nation but had a powerful formative impact on what was in the process of solidifying itself into a nation.

While that understanding of the novel's cultural role is dominant in *Revolution and the Word*, the more narrow "subversive" role is also intermittently present.

Rereading at this distance, I would have to say that the models of power and influence I used in *Revolution and the Word* are inconsistent. This is partly because those models themselves were in flux at the time I was writing. The concept of subversion was being tested and debated. Can one subvert a nation and be part of the nation at the same time? What and who constitute "the nation"? Although I was not aware of it then, I had not fully resolved for myself the role of oppositionality within a culture.

Because *Revolution and the Word* was the first theoretical analysis of the early American novel, its paradigms became those against which other critics had to set their own theories, both of the novel and of the public sphere in the early national period.[49] And because "subversion" remained such a powerful construct throughout the mid-1980s and well into the 1990s, many critics defined their view of the novel as "more subversive" or "less subversive" than *Revolution and the Word* supposed.[50] These debates have been vigorous and significant, and have led to a clarification of the political dimensions of fiction.[51] Without the dialogue generated by these critics and the generous attentions they have paid to my work, I could not and would not be introducing this expanded edition of *Revolution and the Word*. At the same time, I admit that there are times in rereading *Revolution and the Word* and subsequent scholarship on the early American novels when I feel as if I'm at a gymnastic competition where the judges award or withhold points to early American novels based on the degree and dexterity of their subversion.

I have learned a tremendous amount from a post-Foucauldian generation of scholars who assess in a more nuanced way the dimensions of power and power relations, especially relationships between dominant and marginalized groups, between culture and subcultures.[52] To describe the novel as "subversive" carries with it the baggage of perfect authorial intentionality (mounting almost to omnipotence) as well as the misplaced idea that a novel (or any cultural form) is somehow outside and apart from the very forces that contribute to its creation and to which it contributes. Subversive of what? How do we extricate the multiple, convoluted, and inconsistent strands of protest, acquiescence, acceptance, resistance, coercion, cooptation, complicity, privilege, exclusion, and domination? Lora Romero's remarkable book *Home Fronts: Domesticity and Its Critics in the Antebellum United States* articulates some of the pitfalls of a binaristic model of power. She uses the example of gender and sentimentalism to address models of cultural power:

> The figure of the domestic woman has haunted us for over two centuries because of her utility for overstabilizing the analytic terms "ideology" and "opposition." No matter which side of the binarism contemporary criticism places her on, she still serves the same purpose she serves in domesticity itself: defining (either through her presence or renunciation) a literary space insulated from politics. The nineteenth century called this

> place "home." We call it either "high culture" or "the margins." And if we characterize a high cultural or a marginal literary tradition as "political," we mean only that it resists or demystifies some ideological construct external to it. . . . These debates proceed from the assumption that culture either frees or enslaves. There appear to be no other choices. We seem unable to entertain the possibility that traditions, or even individual texts, could be radical on some issues (market capitalism, for example) and reactionary on others (gender or race, for instance). Or that some discourses could be oppositional without being outright liberating. Or conservative without being outright enslaving. . . . If, following Foucault, we view hegemony not as a monolithic "structure" radiating from a single source but instead a web of "non-egalitarian and mobile" power relations, then we can better understand the incommensurability of political visions represented in early nineteenth-century texts—and perhaps temper our disappointment when we realize that authors have not done the impossible, that is, discovered the one key for the liberation of all humankind.[53]

This complicated notion of cultural work presents a less didactic model for the impact and responsibility of writers on the process of social change than I, at some points, advocate in the original preface and introduction to *Revolution and the Word*.

Romero's formulation reminds us that we do not have to praise or condemn a given writer or genre that isn't oppositional ("subversive") enough. Opposition is part of, contiguous with, and a contributor to "culture." Opposition cannot be outside of culture, nor can writers (or anyone else). For Romero, it is not the job of the critic to find instances of subversion or complicity since power relations themselves are always mobile. This formulation frees us from what Paul Ricoeur calls a "hermeneutics of suspicion" by which every action gets parsed out for its presumed political impurities. Other critics have also provided healthier models for criticism than the "subversive" or "oppositional."[54] Without belaboring this point, I point to Eve Kosofsky Sedgwick's brilliant essay "Paranoid Reading, Reparative Reading," which argues against paranoid reading practices that are ultimately both self-fulfilling and self-defeating.[55]

Sedgwick proposes a generous way of reading without giving up on the importance of political resistance. Similarly, my rethinking of "subversion" as a category is in no way a capitulation to those (Walter Benn Michaels is the primary example) who insist that nothing, after all, can ever be subversive. In several essays and books, Michaels has made variations on a theme: Those who criticize racism are elevating "race" to a category and are therefore (by definition, if unwittingly) racists themselves.[56] It's an argument whose main goal is provocation. It is a style of argument that is designed to stir more argument, to create the proverbial tempest in a teapot. Michaels evacuates the content and passion of dissent. He argues primarily from the form of anti-racist discourse, then generalizes and applies the same reductive formula to other scholarship that addresses gender, class, colonialism, and so forth. His premises are confused and sometimes even obfuscating, the logic leading to another typically tendentious conclusion. By reducing syllogism to tautology, Michaels begs the questions others strive to understand.

If subversion doesn't work as a category of analysis, neither does sophistry. If subversion has shortcomings as an action plan, it beats apathy. In some ways, I admit that I still value the affective role that words such as "subversion" and "opposition" perform since they insistently evoke a different tradition from the one of compromise and moderation that I have addressed earlier in this introduction and that, as I have emphasized, contribute to a complacent national history. For all the inherent theoretical contradictions and flaws in parsing out dissident elements of a culture whose ultimate shape has to be some articulation of all its elements, including the dissident, there is a power to resistance that I'm not prepared to give away. Like faith or even faith healing, oppositionality may well have a placebo effect. Yet who's to argue with the result if a placebo enacts productive and positive change?

Protest need not (and maybe *should* not) be logical but expressive and performative. The desire to change, disrupt, or even destroy aspects of one's society that one sees as immoral and intolerable is, after all, one impulse that structures a culture. The desire to move outside of one's culture deserves validation—so long as one accepts that the desire does not (and cannot) move the subject outside of his or her culture. And on certain occasions, these powerful desires do serve to fragment or even restructure a culture. For many, these bottom-line convictions inform the way we read our world.[57] The desire itself is cathartic *and* sometimes transformative. The ability to stir affect into action (individual or collective) has been a particular function of the artist not only in Western society but in many of the world's societies. I want to hold on to Melville's famously pure negation—"Saying 'no' in thunder!" It is the ultimate clarion call for writers, intellectuals, and anyone else who does not feel cozy within the State one cannot avoid inhabiting.

Sometimes I try to imagine what it must have been like living in postrevolutionary America, a thought experiment that, I realize, is ultimately a projection of my own lived condition in 2004 as much as it is a statement about the 1780s. History has preserved relatively little about Shays and his fellow farmers since part of the project of nation building is to exaggerate solidarity and downplay dissent.[58] It takes a leap of imagination to understand the levels of betrayal and disappointment experienced by those nine thousand desperate and destitute Massachusetts farmers in 1787 who marched on Springfield, Massachusetts. Most of them were veterans who left the army with worthless government certificates only to return to war-ravaged farms, harsh taxes, and the threat of debtor's prison. They staged a rebellion of their own, with the heroic battle cries of the Revolution ("No taxation without representation!") still ringing in their ears, led by Daniel Shays, who had fought in the battles of Lexington, Bunker Hill, Saratoga, and

Stony Point. One of the insurgents wrote, "I earnestly stepped forth in defense of this country, and liberty is still the object I have in view."

However, the officials in the new government did not agree. Governor James Bowdoin (the same man who defended Perez Morton, portrayed as the evil seducer "Martin" in *The Power of Sympathy*) joined with other Boston merchants who put up their own money to fund an army to attack the rebels. They stopped them at the government arsenal. Cannons killed four of the rebels and wounded twenty others. The rebels had never dreamed that they would be attacked by their fellow veterans. They retreated in horror, disarray, and bitter disillusionment. The former revolutionary Samuel Adams pronounced that while of course it had been fine to rebel against a king, anyone who "dares to rebel against the laws of a republic ought to suffer death." Shays himself escaped into Vermont (which was not then part of the union), but two hundred others were charged with treason. In April 1787, five of them were condemned to be hanged. Although Bowdoin was defeated in the intervening election, his successor, John Hancock, had to face the same problem of what to do with the rebels. His solution was to bring them to the gallows for public execution—and then reprieve them at the last moment.[59] What better example of the symbolics of governmental authority (in Foucault's sense) than this public exhibition of the "merciful" state granting a pardon to convicted rebels against the state?

Maybe "strategic subversion" has the same pitfalls as "strategic essentialism" as a philosophical category, but it should nonetheless be obvious that Daniel Shays and his rebels were doing *something* in opposition to the officially constituted government of the new nation. Popular history conjoins winning the Revolutionary War and ratifying the Constitution into one continuous and glorious moment, erasing what came between, minimizing the disparate voices, quieting dissent. Popular history ignores those "men and women who had to cope with a revolution that had failed them, one which in their judgment had merely shifted power from one set of 'plunderers' to another."[60] Local forms of popular culture (foremost, the novel) are one place where we find articulations of the inequality, poverty, disenfranchisement, abandonment, and betrayal lingering in a new nation.

Whatever the explicit political position of their authors, the novels in the early Republic assayed the social terrain of beggar maids, the rural poor, illiterate immigrants, indentured servants, slaves, spinsters, fallen women, unwed mothers, star-crossed lovers, wanton soldiers, cross-dressing soldiers, skilled artisans, itinerant laborers, female adventurers, brave explorers, schoolteachers, midwives, corrupt evangelists, devious aristocrats, corrupt politicians, wayward youths, stoic breadwinners, fierce matriarchs, pious ministers, angry mobs, devout pilgrims, heartsick lovers, seducers, suicides, prostitutes, pirates, proud Indians, entrepreneurial Irishmen, sympathetic Jews, wise mullahs, captives, confidence men, hucksters, even Catholics: a different constellation of "We the People."

Gender and Sexuality Studies

Revolution and the Word was researched, written, and published in the midst of an astonishing flourishing of feminist history, criticism, and literary theory. Americanists in particular were producing work of enormous range, depth, inventiveness, and profundity that would change forever the constructs by which future generations of scholars would view American culture and politics. Or so it was thought. In fact, in some contemporary books, one would think that the critical and social revolution often dubbed "Seventies Feminism" had never happened at all. Yet in other books (most often by either virulent antifeminists or by later generations of feminists) one would think that "Seventies Feminism" was something like a Satanic cult that had forever corrupted the minds of historians and literary critics.

I have put the term "Seventies Feminism" in quotation marks to signal that its existence in contemporary criticism is more monolithic than it was at the time. That said, however, I need to be clear that I wrote *Revolution and the Word* partly in reaction against aspects of "Seventies Feminism" that I found to be reductive—even though there would have been no *Revolution and the Word* without "Seventies Feminism." I wanted to understand everything I could about the role of the novel in the creation of the new Republic. That, to me, meant also analyzing the role of women in the creation of the American novel—as writers, readers, educators, and social critics. In this regard, my project was consonant with other feminist work of its day.

However, the more I read novels, newspapers, tracts, and private sources (such as letters and diaries), the less I was convinced that gender was *the* defining category of identity in the new Republic or, indeed, that any one category of identity trumped all the others. The attempt to factor gender into the analysis of the early American novel had a special weight given the tradition, since James Fenimore Cooper, of suggesting that serious writers were being drowned out by popular sentimental writers and that those terms were coded "male" and "female," respectively. My research persuaded me that those codes and equations were slippery and often false. Not all eighteenth- and nineteenth-century popular novels were sentimental; not all sentimental novels were popular; not all sentimental fiction was written or read by women. I discovered that all the material evidence available—extant lending-library rosters, subscription lists published in novels, and inscriptions found in extant copies of novels—suggested that men as well as women read even the most sentimental books.

Methodologically, my interest in documenting the readership of the early American novel as well as finding out more about early American writers led to a theoretical quandary. Given the weight of evidence, research, archives, and generalizations about male readers and writers—as well as the burdensome clichés about women—to amass the amount of evidence necessary to refute the

existing paradigms necessitated particularly energetic research to create and analyze a women's archive. As with a seesaw where all the weight is on one side,
it took a considerable effort to weight the opposite side enough for balance. Yet
how does one present so much evidence without tilting in the opposite direction
and seemingly writing a book *about* women—especially when that is exactly the
kind of gender segregation one has set out to dispel? There is no resolution to
this quandary. In any cultural narrative, more "back story" is required to displace
a generalization and to fill a gap than to support existing paradigms.

Revolution and the Word has much to say about women readers. Yet it is not a
book only about women. And, despite its attention to women, one of its convictions is that the "separate spheres" view of American culture attributed to the
late eighteenth and the nineteenth centuries did not operate consistently in the
world of early American fiction.[61] *Revolution and the Word* was both part of
the new feminist historiography of the early and mid-1980s and partly inspired
by my disagreement with some feminist critics who focused on women but who
may not have been as interested in the contiguous topics of gender and gender
relations.

Indeed, like "postcolonial," the word "gender" is not in the index of *Revolution
and the Word*. Gender was not yet a key term in the feminist debates but evolved,
largely in the late 1980s, in reaction to discussions of "woman" and "women"
that assumed as universal gender attributes that were race- or class-specific or
that were tacitly based on a normative heterosexuality. As with "subversion,"
"feminism" in 1986 was a term that was being debated with seriousness and
rigor—especially by scholars who defined themselves as feminists. The word
"gender" helped make a crucial distinction between that which was thought to
be biologically female and the range of cultural and social characteristics ascribed
to those who were biologically female. A range of other terms debated in the
1970s and 1980s (such as "domesticity" or "sentimentalism") carried excess cultural baggage precisely because of the myriad levels of confusion between the
biological and cultural.

My charge in *Revolution and the Word* was to try to parse out (and maybe even
straighten out) one part of this confusing debate. I was concerned with distinguishing the sentimental origins of the American novel from those origins that
were not in the sentimental tradition—and to see both in relationship to the
reading habits of women and men (mostly white, but not all middle class by any
means). I was also attempting to understand the role that women as well as men
played in the creation of the novel genre as writers, readers, printers (rarely
female), cultural arbiters, educators, or proprietors of lending libraries. True, the
American novel began with a sentimental novel, *The Power of Sympathy*. What
does it mean that *The Power of Sympathy* was written by a man, not a woman?
Its publishing history is itself an allegory in gender theory. Published anonymously, *The Power of Sympathy* was attributed throughout much of the nineteenth

century to a female author. Why? No doubt because it is dedicated to the "young ladies of United Columbia," because women characters play significant roles in the plot, and because sympathy and sentimentalism, over the course of the next century, were increasingly considered "female" (even though many nineteenth-century male writers—including Hawthorne and Melville on occasion—penned works that must be considered sentimental). That complex gender history is partly what makes *The Power of Sympathy* a fascinating beginning for American fiction and one that already complicates traditional gender bifurcations (male/political/public sphere v. female/sentimental/domestic sphere). Although some nineteenth-century commentators (although not as many as some late-twentieth-century feminist critics insist) divided the world into "separate spheres," there were always women and men who operated between, among, around, and outside of those spheres. As I have argued at length elsewhere, the spheres overlapped (again one thinks of a Venn diagram), but they were also irrelevant to masses of working-class women and men, to many African Americans (who continued to use the affective power of sentimentalism in slave narratives), immigrants, and many others.[62]

In certain instances, identification by gender and gender alone made a difference in women's experience. This was true in a number of biological areas (menses, childbirth, menopause) and in a number of legal areas (women—*all* women, regardless of age, economic status, race, or other factors—could not vote in early America). However, the range of behaviors, attitudes, stereotypes, and prejudices within even these gender-determined areas varies radically because of several other factors. Equally important, the egalitarian (or "feminist") response to socially and legally prescribed gender roles was as varied as the roles themselves, which is precisely why the novel was the perfect genre to portray a range of behaviors of women and men within a non-egalitarian legal system.

Illicit heterosexual behaviors were a favorite topic of early American novelists. Desire and destiny were interwoven in fascinating ways, with communities of men and women serving complex regulatory roles (as advisors, critics, and goads) within the world of sexual attraction and exchange. Intriguingly, the nuances and complexities of these sexual encounters varied greatly in their performance but typically ended in the solitary death of the heroine in childbirth. And here it didn't matter whether the women were penniless adolescents such as the hapless Charlotte Temple or educated, capable, middle-class women such as Eliza Wharton. I tend to see death-in-childbirth in narrative terms and also in philosophical terms as an expression of the ultimate frustration of eighteenth-century writers when it came to envisioning alternative models of female sexual expression and behavior.[63]

Every woman's movement from the late eighteenth century to the present has had to face the same contradiction between demanding equal legal or legislative treatment and advocating special consideration. Insisting that laws be changed, for example, to grant women the right to vote presumes that women are equal to men and that equal opportunity will rectify the past discrimination. However, the argument for special consideration implies that a long history of unequal opportunity (such as women not being admitted to colleges in the eighteenth century) necessarily means that women are less prepared than men for these equal opportunities. Activists who stress the need for special privileges emphasize the necessity for remedial training to compensate for a history of inequality. Special programs designed to encourage young girls to study math are one example of compensatory feminism. Some critics of feminism insist the movement is contradictory because of these two quite divergent philosophies that address the same problem of how female equality might be achieved.

I contend that this Catch-22, while applied in this case to women, has also been applicable over time to various minority groups seeking a voice within the political system as well as for colonized peoples seeking independence. "Equality" is a very difficult term to pin down. Different feminists have fought for a different range of rights and privileges based on different ranges of values—from "fairness" to "redress." Because of these differences, feminists have often been accused of being contradictory. What *do* women want? The answer varies with the circumstance and the specificities of the particular individual or group of women involved.

Most recently, the debates over affirmative action policies have conflated different ideas of equity. It might be useful here to unpack one strand of that controversy in order to understand the social, cultural, and economic content hidden in the seemingly straightforward notions of "equality." Briefly, universities have decided that racial diversity is one of many different kinds of diversity that are important to the collective social and educational experience for which students pay tuition. However, we know from past experience that if seemingly "equal" selection criteria are applied to all applicants, racial diversity is not always possible. This is because the seemingly objective measure of achievement scores (the baseline of "equal" admissions) is not objective at all but changes depending upon one's degree of preparation. One can even pay to take expensive crash-courses in how to take these tests, with higher test scores the promised (and statistically valid) result of finishing the course. Since black Americans live disproportionately in poverty and attend schools that are *substandard*, there is no way that their educational preparation ensures success on *standard-ized* tests (since the standard itself is based on a norm of educational achievement at American secondary schools). Equal admissions standards, given this complex history, yield inequal results that reflect and perpetuate inequalities in the larger society. "Race blind," when we unpack this history, is thus discriminatory or racist.

Why unpacking this affirmative action argument is useful in this context is because it shows how many assumptions about our culture are embedded in seemingly simple words. "Feminism" is one of those words that can mean so many things to so many people precisely because it carries centuries of divergent meanings. "Identity" is another such term. Since the publication of *Revolution and the Word*, dozens of important theorists have worked to understand the complexities of the identity terms we use casually and constantly in our everyday lives and in our scholarship. Different scholars have found a range of ways to negotiate between theories and applications, identity and acts, expression and performance (terms parsed with particular philosophical rigor in Judith Butler's *Gender Trouble*). "Essentialism," "antiessentialism," and "strategic essentialism" are all terms that work to differentiate between an identity category and the hidden assumptions embedded in that category. The importance of making or not making certain differentiations has been argued by critics such as Diana Fuss, Naomi Shor, Gayatri Spivak, and others. "Agency" and "affect" have both become central to these discussions. To test theories of universalism or foundationalism, some gender critics have insisted we need specificity and concentration on the local, while others (and I think particularly of Caren Kaplan and Inderpal Grewal) have insisted on the transnational. Gender critics have productively employed and deconstructed epistemological, ontological, psychological, psychoanalytic (Freud and Lacan as well as Julia Kristeva and other French feminists), sociological, and other disciplinary discourses and traditions while, even more recently, the critic Ranjana Khanna has used deconstructive methodologies of attentive and skeptical close reading to explore the tension between psychoanalytic assumptions and postcolonial conditions.[64]

It would be ludicrous to attempt to summarize in a few pages some of the most important feminist criticism of the late twentieth and early twenty-first century. Instead, I want to highlight two different ways of thinking about gender that go further than I did in 1986 to complicate the paradigms of unequal power. The first requires attending to multiple categories of identity at once and being attuned to the ways that a single person can move in and out of positions of power in different contexts. The categories, in other words, are not fixed, and, in one instance, personal wealth may have a greater impact than gender. In another, the privileges of whiteness may outweigh the limitations of gender. In still others, being a black female might be very different from being a white female. In each of these instances, the word "woman" can be significant or insignificant— and differently so in different circumstances.

To acknowledge the range of applications and significations of identity is by no means to evacuate the category of its power. Quite the contrary. I continue to argue that identity politics as a governing principle was central to the creation of the new nation and to its perpetuation. Citizenship, responsibilities, and rights have all been based on principles of inclusion or exclusion rooted in the blatant equation between "personhood" and such defining characteristics of identity as race or whether one was biologically male or female. Take, as a signal instance, voting rights. Who could and who could not vote in American history has been rooted, *fundamentally and foundationally*, in identity politics as legislated by the U.S. Constitution and upheld by the Supreme Court of the United States. It was only in the wake of the Civil War and the 1870 ratification of the Fifteenth Amendment to the Constitution that "the right to vote shall not be denied or abridged on the basis of race, color or previous condition of servitude." However, by 1876, two decisions by the Supreme Court—the Enforcement Act and the Force Act—severely limited the scope of the Fifteenth Amendment by removing federal troops that protected black voters in the South and by allowing states to enact fraudulent means—poll taxes, literacy tests, vouchers of "good character," and grandfather clauses (that allowed one to vote only if one's grandfather could)—to disenfranchise blacks again. By 1910, there was *de facto* disenfranchisement of nearly all black citizens in the South and virtually all black legislators had been removed from office. This did not change until passage of the 1965 Voting Rights Act.

Identity politics was equally at work for women. It was not until 1920 that female citizens (of any race) were enfranchised. For Asian American men and women, citizenship was also denied on the basis of identity until the 1943 repeal of the Chinese Exclusion Acts and the 1952 passage of the McCarran-Walters Act nullifying the racially exclusive language of the 1790 Act of the federal Bureau of Citizenship and Immigration, which restricted naturalization to "free, white person(s)." Further, a genealogy of Asian American voting rights might be extended to 1964, when racist restrictions on "Asian" immigration embedded in the Immigration and Naturalization Service quota system were removed. Finally, the right of U.S. citizenship (including the right to vote) was extended to Native Americans only in 1924. And, in cases similar to those in the Jim Crow South, many states instituted restrictions on or obstacles to voting for Native Americans that were upheld until challenged by a major lawsuit in 1947. It was not until 1975 that protections secured by the Voting Rights Acts were extended to Native Americans. In a representative democracy, that certain Americans were excluded from electoral representation because of gender, race, or national origin *is* identity politics (long before that phrase itself was coined). To say so is not just "politically correct" (another buzzword of the late twentieth century). It is historically accurate.[65]

The thirteen essays included in *No More Separate Spheres!* (a 2002 collection of essays that I coedited with Jessamyn Hatcher) represent different ways that feminist literary critics have complicated gender as a category of identity by taking into account other categories, including race, sexuality, class, region, and nationality. Amy Kaplan, for example, shows the ways white middle-class and upper-class women encouraged and enjoyed the fruits of imperialism in the first half of the nineteenth century by identifying their "femaleness" as part of the operation of "civilizing" power. She has coined the term "manifest domesticity" to underline the role these women played in support of "domestic policies" (values within the white middle-class home that reflected those values within the nation) that led to the subjugation of other nations, policies that also played out in the middle-class U.S. home where feminine virtue itself was defined in contrast to the "uncivilized" and nonwhite populations both at home and abroad. You-me Park and Gayle Wald deconstruct the "cult of domesticity" by attending to class and race. They show how differently domesticity signifies for the working-class women of color who clean the homes of middle-class women (of any race). "Working outside the home" takes on an ironic cast when one's work is tending someone else's home. Park and Wald destabilize the idea that the home is the sphere of "women" by examining the multiple forms of female labor required to support the bourgeois home. The educational training of immigrant girls as well as African American and Native American girls in the values of bourgeois domesticity enhanced their market value as domestics. In each of these essays, the focus isn't on "women" so much as the particular circumstances, limitations, and privileges enjoyed by certain women. Park and Wald replace "woman" as a category by asking "Which women?" When, why, and by what social and economic forces is such a sphere maintained, sustained, and retained?[66]

In *Revolution and the Word,* I argue that the didacticism of early American fiction was often aimed at improving social and legal conditions for women, but many of the same novels could also be critical of middle-class women for not taking their social responsibilities seriously enough. If men are sometimes cruel to women, so are women, a subtle way of complicating gender stereotypes. In addition, a number of the novels that advocated improved female education also addressed a range of "public" topics such as representative democracy, religious tyranny or hypocrisy, poor laws, the institution of slavery, unfair taxation, imitation of European fashions, the responsibilities of elected officials, immigration, military and maritime authority, and other controversies that dominated political discussion of the time. In other words, the novels may be "about" women—but women are about many things.

Gender is one of many subjects *Revolution and the Word* works to complicate by redefining what and who constituted the postrevolutionary public sphere. I argue that the novel—like newspapers, tracts, advice books, primers, poetic epics, and other forms of print culture—participated in the public sphere not only by extending the discussion of political and social problems to those who were not "at the table" as laws and policies were being formalized but also by translating the implications of the Declaration of Independence, Articles of Confederation, or Bill of Rights into everyday life situations. Novels challenged the very distinction between "private" and "public" life.

A second line of analysis out of gender studies that I find productive for reframing *Revolution and the Word* for a new generation of readers is the emphasis on pleasure, freedom, and mobility enjoyed even by those in circumstances that would seemingly preclude anything positive at all. Amid the palpable bitterness of tending someone else's house is there also a vicarious appreciation of luxury that well might be pleasurable and even empowering? If the choices are between factory work or domestic labor, are there emotional bonuses that come from recognizing one's own capability relative to the incapacities of the upper-class person who has gained her station due to inherited or marital wealth? What is the dividing line between her station and yours? Writers as diverse as Edith Wharton, Alice Childress, and Toni Morrison have all explored these topics— the upward mobility of the domestic worker as an inverted mirror of the precarious (and often joyless) wealth of the middle-class married woman. What, as scholars and readers, do we gain by coupling our training in *critical* thinking (in the sense of being quick to assay the negative, the powerless, the embattled) with sensitivity to pleasures obtainable even in the grimmest of worlds? Hard-won pleasures (Charlotte Temple's brief comfort by the fire, Eliza Wharton's eyes shining with freedom and triumph, however temporary) may, however, allow the reader to take away a more inspiring (and less depressing) message. Finding tidbits of optimism does not mean one is insensitive to oppression. On the contrary, operational optimism may well be a better spur to activism than is relentless critique. All of these possibilities have been explored by a range of critics interested in the powers of pleasure and the pleasure of power. In the succinct formulation of Robert Blair St. George, "power is creative as well as coercive."[67]

In *Revolution and the Word*, there are many places where I focus on women's pleasures—including the delicious pleasure of reading, the delight in education, and the joy of female friendship. *Revolution and the Word* was among the first books to attribute agency both to female protagonists (they are not simply passive in the face of men) and to the female reader (who could take away from the plot an inspiration to personal strength and power). However, in the last edition of *Revolution and the Word* my general view of the political and legal situation of women in the early Republic was relatively bleak. I tended to see the bad end of so many seduction novels as exemplifying the sense that there was "no way out" for the Republican woman.

While in no way denying the limited legal status and circumscribed political role of women in the new Republic, I am now inclined to view women in the postrevolutionary period as less *confined* than I held in 1986. I am persuaded by critics such as Christopher Castiglia that there are other ways of seeing agency, even in extremely restrictive settings. Castiglia looks for examples of women who are actors and agents despite what seem insuperable obstacles. He pays particular attention to the narratives of white women captured by Indians (who had typically been interpreted as the most passive victims) and sees the release from the demands of white female domesticity as liberating. He uses these examples of agency to show that, even in a society where legal and political definitions of women are severely constrained, women find ways to become social actors. His emphasis on women's abilities to imaginatively "transcend their captivities" applies to the heroines of seduction novels as well and is a good corrective to a more bleak definition of postrevolutionary women.[68]

Building on Castiglia, I would now posit a different way of seeing the fatal endings (such as the death in childbirth) of so many late-eighteenth-century novels. *Revolution and the Word* follows Fredric Jameson's work in understanding the ideological potentials of the novel *as a genre*. If the convention of the seduction novel genre is an unhappy ending, then one could say that it is the unhappy ending itself that permits the exploration of desire—like the corpse in a mystery novel: without it, there's no motivation for the plot. If the reader is forewarned by a dedication (*The Power of Sympathy* promises to "expose the fatal consequences of seduction") and knows the unhappy ending in advance, then that ending is pro forma—so expected—that one can ignore it, simply enjoying the unfolding plot, which is, after all, about a woman indulging her desires.

I like the idea that eighteenth-century readers understood that there was no way a novelist could explore female sexuality without expressing disapproval in the end. The preface and the last three or four pages of the novel provided enough moral improvement that the reader could enjoy the intervening two hundred pages guiltlessly. Seduction novels are *fixated* on female sexual expression— as every critic of the novel knew full well. I am suggesting that the fixity gave writer and reader alike narrative mobility. In other words, accepting the discourse conventions of an unhappy ending allowed the reader to indulge a guilty pleasure. There was freedom in the pro forma.

Were I to rewrite *Revolution and the Word* today, enriched by fifteen years of subsequent analysis of gender and sexuality studies, I would also pay more attention to the subtle ways that female-ness is transformed by class and race affiliations as well as by sexuality. Same-sex desire and homosociality are two rich areas still inviting more attention from scholars of early American fiction. Surprisingly, there has still not been enough analysis to date of the ways that the hostile heterosexual world encouraged a fertile world of female homosociality.[69] And there is certainly plenty of material. Cross-dressing novels such as Herman Mann's *The Female Review* (1797, mentioned earlier), which fictionalizes the real-life adventures of the soldier Deborah Sampson in the Revolutionary War, or the more picaresque tales of war-tossed, star-crossed lovers such as the anonymous *History of Constantius and Pulchera* (1794) become especially interesting in view of queer theory.[70] Both books need to be reread in light of excellent studies of female masculinity by scholars such as Judith Halberstam. Inevitably, the women-posing-as-men are universal sex objects, their cross-dressing proving to be an aphrodisiac to both male and female suitors. For there is no "opposite sex" for the cross-dressers—there's just sex![71] Virtually all of Charles Brockden Brown's work, beginning with *Alcuin* (1798), deserves rereading in light of queer theory.[72]

Many of his plots, rooted as they are in both sentimental and gothic fictional traditions, enact the rituals, codes, permissions, and prohibitions operating, in Sedgwick's evocative phrase, "between men."[73]

Libido runs high (for women and men) in these tales of cross-dressing. But then "running high" is what these novels are about. In these fantasies, the cross-dressing women enjoy physical adventures, make autonomous decisions, and act boldly and heroically. They travel. They fight. They love. And they are able to do so *because* they can pass as men. These are fantasies of freedom—with a set of men's clothes and a handsome swagger providing the passport to new adventures. At the end of these novels, the heroine typically returns to women's dress and sometimes even to marriage ever after. Yet the return to femaleness in the cross-dressing novels may well be as pro forma as the death-in-childbirth ending. The cross-dressing adventures (and not their termination) are what we read for. That's the fun and the freedom. The ending is, for what it is worth, all too conventional.

Race Studies

I wrote *Revolution and the Word* when race studies were at a vibrant, even heady, moment. Major work by Houston A. Baker, Jr., Henry Louis Gates, Jr., and Arnold Rampersad had either recently appeared or was being presented as papers at scholarly conferences, ensuring that African American literature would be both part of both the Americanist literary canon and an important subject with which literary theorists had to grapple.[74] There was enough excitement and maturity for debate. Sessions on black studies at meetings of the Modern Language Association were packed with hundreds of scholars learning a new literary history. The debates were especially trenchant when black feminist critics, including Hazel Carby, Gloria Hull, Deborah McDowell, bell hooks, and others, were at the podium to ensure that African American women writers were part of the interpretation of American and African American literature.[75]

Most of the work on race written in the decade when I was researching and writing *Revolution and the Word* focused on writers of color (creating a new canon), on images of African Americans in white-authored texts, or on the history and impact of slavery. *Revolution and the Word* was a product of its time in its emphasis on these aspects of race as well. In addition, in the late 1970s and 1980s, race studies typically meant *black* studies. At the time, few early black writers had been "discovered" except for poet Phillis Wheatley and the former slave Olaudah Equiano, so there was not yet a significant group of critics working on race in the early national period.

To date, we still do not know of any black-authored early American novels, although the canon of early black literature, especially of the Black Atlantic, has expanded significantly, with many critics specializing in this area, many texts now available, and significant controversies (always a sign of health) in the field.[76] Brilliant analyses of race in the last decade by critics such as Paul Gilroy, Wahneema Lubiano, and Robin Kelley (in a parallel fashion to work on gender) have also made more visible the ramifications of a system based on race in the entire social fabric of nationhood and nationalist ideology.[77]

Although it was still too early in the history of critical race studies to be able to understand systematically the operations of "race" (in its complex and varied applications) in the origins of American fiction, race is the focus of several discussions in *Revolution and the Word*. I note representations of blacks in several early American novels, including *The Power of Sympathy*, Tabitha Tenney's *Female Quixotism* (1801), *Modern Chivalry*, and, most powerfully, Royall Tyler's *The Algerine Captive* (1797).[78] If I were writing about race and early American fiction now, I would want to investigate divergent treatments of race in different white-authored texts, the network of assumptions supporting racial representations within those texts, the continuities of racial assumptions with other ideological formulations (about sexuality, for example), and, more generally, the contiguity of racialist assumptions undergirding seemingly opposite representations in a variety of different early novels. For example, the portrayal of African Americans in *Female Quixotism* is derogatory and offensive. What are the interconnections between racial attitudes in that novel and Tenney's representation of Dorcasina Sheldon's sentimental fantasies of upward mobility through a successful heterosexual union? What is the role of parody in maintaining the status quo on any number of levels? *Female Quixotism* is a novel ripe for a multipronged deconstruction.

Similarly, there are unresolved paradoxes even in an abolitionist text such as *The Algerine Captive*. Updike Underhill, the alternately clownish and serious protagonist of this picaresque and moralistic tale, is captured by Barbary pirates. Tyler works by a reversal of racial polarities: his protagonist, a white American who is enslaved by North Africans, assesses the conditions, morality, and pain of slavery. Lest the reader miss his point, Tyler explicitly applies the lessons learned in Algiers to America, underscoring the hypocrisy of a land founded on an ideology of freedom thriving on the slave trade and the subjugation and debasement of other human beings. For Tyler, to create a revolution on a rhetoric of equality and to ratify a Constitution founded on a compromise that accepted slavery was dramatic proof of a violation of American idealism at its founding moment. This is not to say that Tyler is a radical. While passionate on the topic of abolitionism, he also ends his novel with a plea for calm citizenship and national unity. What he poses (but does not resolve) for his readers is the core Constitutional problem of which should take precedence—the principle of equality (necessitating the abolition of slavery) or the principle of unity (necessitating the compromise that allowed slavery in several states).

Native Americans are also the focus of some discussions in *Revolution and the*

Word, but here, too, the focus is primarily on the representation of Indians in white-authored texts, with some historical attention to the treatment of Native Americans in the postrevolutionary era, in particular the genocidal history of American colonization of the New World.[79] What was not current in literary studies in the 1970s and 1980s (but which would have been invaluable to the history and theory I presented in *Revolution and the Word)* was an overarching comprehension of racism as a system and symptom that linked slavery, genocide, imperialism (including the Barbary pirates who profiteered off the underbelly of imperialism and the slave trade), capitalism, and modernity. As with the magnifying glass of critical race theory that exposes the fingerprints of racism where they were previously invisible, recent discussions of the attitudes and treatment of indigenous populations in the conquest of the "New World" expose the propagandistic functions of the literary tropes of the heroic Indian, the noble savage, and the barbaric savage.

In this regard, I am persuaded by insights by the world systems theorist Immanuel Wallerstein. In a succinct and magisterial essay written with Anibal Quijano, Wallerstein links "coloniality, ethnicity, racism, and the concept of newness itself" as the four building blocks upon which the new United States was created. Ethnicity, he argues, is the "inevitable cultural consequence of coloniality" because it delineates and enforces hierarchy within a society in flux with immigrants from many lands as well as with the indigenous peoples of that conquered land. Whether slavery for Africans, coerced agricultural labor (or genocide) for Native Americans, or indentured labor for working-class Europeans (valued according to a racialized ethnic hierarchy as well), ethnicity and racism reinforced a new value and class system in America. The specter of working-class riots and race riots within America, and the external example of the slave revolts in Haiti, helped America's ruling class gain acceptance for a new American state that fell far short of its most idealistic prerevolutionary articulations.[80] A number of historians and literary theorists, including Russ Castronovo, Eric Cheyfitz, Saidiya Hartman, Amy Kaplan, and Ann Laura Stoler, have also analyzed the continuous relationship between U.S. nationalism and imperialism—especially the American adaptation of slavery to colonial capitalism and then its exporting of racial supremacist thinking in its colonizing of other nations.[81]

Literary race studies have taken several forms in recent years that bear on *Revolution and the Word*. Deconstructing the term "race" has been one of the most interesting and compelling developments in critical race theory over the last decade. A first move seems, in retrospect, to be obvious but was not at the time: that "race" applies to everyone, not simply to people of color. Sometimes labeled as "whiteness studies" (a term that, personally, I find far more limited than the concept), these analyses of race by scholars including Eric Lott, David Roediger, and Robyn Wiegman understand its operations even in situations and texts where it seemingly has no place.[82] One of the most powerful analyses of whiteness comes from a surprising source—a critical book by the Nobel Prize–winning novelist Toni Morrison. Her now classic *Playing in the Dark: Whiteness and the Literary Imagination* observes and examines the roiling energy in certain white-authored texts—Poe, Melville, Cather, Hemingway—that occurs *before* any person of color enters the scene. She documents an infusion of prose polemic that has no logical cause and that becomes explicable only a few paragraphs or pages later when the black character finally enters the scene. *That*—the mysterious disturbance, barely noticeable, even subliminal—is the affective universe of unconscious racism. The precision with which Morrison zeroes in on the jolts in the prose style of these authors allows for a powerful theory of how freedom, individualism, innocence, and manhood in these texts depend on a black presence (configured, inevitably, as *not* free). She uses this textual sign as a metaphor for how race, racism, and racial tension operate throughout American society—including in situations where all participants are white.

Systems of racial coding, the workings of racism, the privileges of whiteness, and the complex intertwining of racial, sexual, gender, class, national, and other kinds of codifications have received much scholarly attention in the past decade.[83] Through profound reexaminations of how these assumptions are coterminous and mutually constitutive or in detailed analyses of one particular incident, law, or event, scholars studying race have made visible a system that American society conceals. They have focused on the creation of modern fields of study—from anthropology to medicine—to understand how racialist assumptions have shaped so profoundly the way we educate our culture to racism, embedding racist assumptions so deeply that it takes relentless excavation to find their origins.[84] Through these studies, we are redefining what race is and how much its assumptions permeate every aspect of American society.

As I have argued throughout this introduction, by accepting the bitter compromise over slavery in order to win the Southern support needed for creation and ratification of the Constitution, those Founders who were abolitionists made a moral choice for unity over conviction. At what should have been a glorious and triumphant moment, slavery became the law of the land and one race of humans deemed another less than human. The values, ideology, and social psychology of that compromise had an indelible effect on American culture and history, from the early national period to the present.

History of the Book

The "single field" that was most important in bringing the arguments of *Revolution and the Word* beyond the world of English departments was history of the book. I put the phrase "single field" in quotation marks to signal that the history of the book was neither singular nor a "field" if accounted for by any definition that includes departmental structures or traditional disciplines. History of the book largely comprises social historians and literature scholars, all of whom have a sense that there is something to be learned by what the other does if we are to comprehend the material and social factors influencing how books are written, circulated (sometimes in manuscript), printed, distributed, and read.[85] The complexities of such an enterprise cannot be comprehended by one field alone and, indeed, rarely by one person. Many of the most important contributions in history of the book are made not by one person but by collaborative teams of scholars.

Certainly, *Revolution and the Word* would have made a far less important contribution had I not been fortunate to receive a fellowship at the American Antiquarian Society (AAS) and to spend a summer with other scholars working in the AAS Program on the History of the Book. I count among the most revelatory moments of my academic career the day at AAS when I asked to see all copies of all editions of America's first best-seller, Susanna Rowson's *Charlotte Temple* (1791). Since AAS, like every major archive, must carefully control access to the fragile materials for which it serves as custodian (and especially popular nineteenth-century books that are literally turning to dust because of the quality of the paper and ink used in cheap editions), assembling all of the editions was an "occasion" at AAS. I'll never forget the excited crowd of scholars and professional librarians who assembled around the two book carts in which dozens of *Charlotte Temples* had been arranged in chronological order. At a glance, we were all seeing the history of the popular book in America—duodecimos, children's books, gilt-edged gift books, working-class story papers, even a scholarly edition of *Charlotte Temple* prepared in 1905 (and which, perhaps significantly, marked the last printing of the book for some sixty years). The material evidence before us on that cart suggested how one book can serve many audiences and a variety of social purposes, something literary critics can easily forget.[86] The experience became central to my "history of texts" approach. That approach combined many of the insights of French literary theory with work by social historians, including those in or influenced by the *Annales* school.[87]

The Program in the History of the Book in American Culture at AAS continues to provide fellowships, offer seminars, and support a wide-ranging network of scholars across disciplinary boundaries. Some of the most important work in book history has come from scholars affiliated with this program. To cite just a few in a wide range of such books: William J. Gilmore's *Reading Becomes a Necessity of Life: Material and Cultural Life in Rural New England, 1780–1835*, the excellent source book *Perspectives on American History: Artifacts and Commentary*, edited by Scott E. Casper, Joanne D. Chaison, and Jeffrey D. Groves, and *Reading Acts: U.S. Readers' Interactions with Literature, 1800–1950*, edited by Barbara Ryan and Amy M. Thomas. The five-volume compendium for which David D. Hall serves as the general editor promises to provide a thorough, canonical, and significant foundation for future research in history of the book in

America. At this writing, the impressive first volume has already made a contribution by taking a trans-Atlantic approach to early American book production and consumption.[88]

To the forms of archival research common to historians of the book, *Revolution and the Word* added theoretical concerns with epistemology. Because someone read a certain book, how do we know what they made of that book? I argued for a "history of texts" to signal that, even once we know all the material and sociological conditions of readership, we are still left with the particularity of the reading experience. If readers didn't find different ways of interpreting their texts, we would not need to teach or write about literature. The fact that a single text can generate multiple interpretations makes it clear that reading is as complex as human psychology. Yet the fact that thousands (or, in more recent times, millions) of readers may read the same text also has an impact on public culture. Reading is both a private and a public act. How do we understand what that act means? For contemporary culture, we can use ethnographic methods to determine how readers understand what they read. My challenge was to put together, from the scraps left by history, insights into reading from readers who had been dead for over two hundred years.[89]

I did so in any way I could, with the awareness that any one method has limitations. For example, a fundamental way that social historians understand the texture of lives in another era is by diaries and letters. Some historians take what is written in these forms, especially within a diary, as "true." My history of texts approach signals a certain skepticism—texts (*all* texts) must be interpreted. They are not transparent or univocal in their meaning. The challenge with personal forms is for the historian to judge "representativeness": How much does or doesn't an individual's responses reflect those of others in his or her society? What literary conventions are at work in an individual's expressiveness, shaping even what might seem like the unmediated communication between writer and diary? As I saw time and again in the diaries and letters I found, readers who love sentimental fiction, for example, often write and observe the world in the hyperbolic, exclamatory style of sentimental fiction. Personal accounts have gaps that the historian must fill in, and often those gaps are the most central (and inexpressible) events in a life. Nor are people always reliable witnesses or informants. My point in emphasizing these human qualities is not to undermine one of the few means by which historians can access the private record of past eras but to stress the continuities and codes mediating "private" and "public" expression in any era.

It was partly from my frustration with the limited array of tools in the social historian's took kit that I also began looking for and, eventually, collecting marginalia. For probably the first six or seven years of my research, I noted marginal remarks in novels almost as a hobby. I found words scribbled on end pages of novels or written in the margins interesting and often delightful, but it was quite late in the writing of *Revolution and the Word* that I realized I might actually be able to use them as "evidence." It was, once again, in the company of other historians of the book at the American Antiquarian Society that I found myself arguing that the telegraphed marginalia in hundreds of copies of novels could provide a sampling of book use and attachment that supplemented the insights in diaries, letters, and reviews of the time. It was refreshing to find that many scholars (especially those working on premodern traditions) had used marginalia as evidence, even though this was not common for Euro-Americanists working on post-Enlightenment topics. A number of recent exhibits of marginalia have examined the function of such scratchings, both for the individual writer and for later historians, whether in the ancient world or in the present.

A number of critics have taken up the controversy discussed in *Revolution and the Word* about the role of novel reading in the creation of the American polis. I argue for a continuity between private and public spheres in which some who were legally and politically excluded from U.S. politics could express opinions on the shape of public culture through the novels they wrote as well as the ones they bought and borrowed. As I note in *Revolution and the Word*, every early American novel somewhere in its plot addresses the topic of education, often with special attention to the education of women. Even the most sensational novels typically included a preface that made explicit the civic mission of the novel. Rather than seeing them as pro forma, I took these expressions seriously in *Revolution and the Word* and argued that the novel became a major space for the articulation of public values within the alternative political community created by the circulation of books and sometimes away from the more visible public culture of oratory (for example, in churches or political rallies).[90] Because of my interest in the circulation of ideas outside organized and hierarchical (top-down) communication networks, I realized that my history of texts approach would provide me with a new body of evidence as a conceptual framework for understanding the multiple aspects of print culture in material, legal, social, and psychological terms.

As I write this introduction, I'm not sure either a "history of the book" or a "history of texts" approach comprehends what is obviously one of the most important developments in the history of "print" since Gutenberg invented movable type.[91] I speak of digitization and the creation of electronic forms of print. It is as impossible today to anticipate what American literary studies will look like fifteen years from now as it would have been to imagine future intellectual developments from the vantage point of 1986 when *Revolution and the Word* first appeared—but it is absolutely certain that, whatever the future holds, it will be enhanced, challenged, facilitated, transformed, influenced, or in other ways changed by electronic access to a world of ideas and archives. In fact, the electronic media are so pervasive that we need to be thinking ahead to a "history of the archive" and not simply of "the book," or we need to extend the metaphor of "book" and "print" to include a variety of mediated digital forms, including Web sites, databases, and other electronic sources. Nor is it too early to do *critical* thinking about this glorious new medium of electronic databases and to apply the history of texts approach to digitization too: who is doing the digitizing, who has access, what is *not* being digitized, and who decides? Are there forms of evidence (such as marginalia) that are not part of the digital package? How do we both take advantage of the wealth of new materials and guard ever more zealously against a complacent sense that what has been digitized is somehow "complete."

It is not clear *what* influence new digitized materials will have on the study of early America, but, without a doubt, it is and will continue to have an ever greater impact. Scholars (and I am among them) who spent thousands of hours laboriously searching through archives or bent over a microform reader are astonished by resources such as the new "Digital Evans." This is a digitization of Charles Evans's famous *American Bibliography* (1955), which made available virtually every book, pamphlet, and broadside published in America from 1639 to 1800. Now, the Digital Evans gives us the same resource as a database with 36,000 works and 2,400,000 images available and searchable to anyone who is a member of a library that owns the database-driven Web site. In a matter of minutes, one can find every book that uses the word "woman" in its title, for example, or can search for the word "novel" in eighteenth-century publishers' account books. And we are clearly only at the beginning of this brave new world in scholarly digitization. I would not venture to predict what kinds of scholarship will be facilitated by these new tools—but I am completely comfortable predicting that the tools, now as ever, will have an irrevocable impact on future scholarship.

What Is a Field?

As the foregoing discussion has made clear, fields change. A work of historical research and literary scholarship may well answer certain quandaries, but the very act of formulating an answer makes visible new kinds of questions. Scholars take up those questions, and the answers they pose then reveal other areas of ignorance, confusion, or murkiness. And so it goes, until there is such a sophisticated and interconnected body of knowledge that we soon have what amounts to a new field. At the same time, when we return to the original work, there may be many areas that suddenly look new, that were never taken up and commented on, and that provide new grounds for analyses, research, and exploration.

What forces, influences, resources, politics, and transitions in the life of an academic discipline lead to the opening up of new areas of knowledge for examination? And when is there then enough material, conversation, organization, and controversy (for a field cannot exist without debate that defines its parameters) for a new field to emerge? Articles, books, panels at conferences, and then whole conferences begin to realign bodies of knowledge and networks of scholars. Next, someone creates a professional association (formal or informal). Course syllabi change, then courses are introduced and sometimes even become required as part of the core of a department's curriculum. Faculty members need to be hired to teach these courses. Graduate students decide to come work in a given department because of what is offered and who is teaching there. Gradually, balances that had tipped in one direction tilt in another.

In the 1980s and 1990s, many English departments added an introduction to critical theory as part of their graduate and sometimes undergraduate requirements. During that same time period, many colleges and universities added courses and (much less frequently) requirements in identity-based areas such as women's studies, gender studies, sexuality studies, ethnic studies, or race studies (terms that sometimes overlap and carry both specific and general meanings). Postcolonial studies is another area that has emerged since the 1990s. Job descriptions have appeared in forums such as the *MLA Job Information List* requiring expertise in these subfields, often in addition to training in an area designated by a more traditional period (medieval studies or the eighteenth century). What such overlapping job descriptions document is the way we have both the creation of subfields and paradigm shifts in the shape, emphases, interests, and objects of study within existing fields. The process is ever-evolving and, to my mind, as productive as it is unstoppable. The history of ideas throughout the West records these Kuhnian transformations, both subtle and cataclysmic, cyclical and epistemic.[92]

Whenever an original theory, an important book, a new discovery ("the first African American novel," etc.), or a different archive is identified, responsible scholars must circle back and reexamine some of our premises. It is virtually impossible to simply restore the old after a confrontation with the new. Returning to "traditional" areas of knowledge after a time of debate about the most fundamental disciplinary assumptions is not a return at all but a rediscovery precisely because of all we have learned on the journey back. For example, *Revolution and the Word*, as its title suggests, was always and intentionally focused on the interesting and not entirely coincidental fact that the novel took off as a literary form exactly as the nation was forming itself. That was the motivating argument of my book. Yet fifteen years of writing about colonial and postcolonial states and the culture produced in those states has made the whole idea of national formation far more complex and vexed. So while I spent a good deal of work unpacking certain definitional problems in gender theory and also in analyzing the disproportionate sense of exclusion or inclusion experienced by those who felt themselves marginalized (by class or race or gender or immigrant status), I spent less time defining the particular notion of "nation" embedded in founding documents and founding novels. That term seems less transparent to me now that it has been the subject of such scrupulous analysis, especially in relationship to such words as "state," "country," "continent," "colony," and "empire." Clearly as used in the *Federalist Papers*, the word "nation" variously designates a political entity, an ideology, a fiction of collectivity, a consortium of interested entities, a borderland within a far larger land mass occupied by different peoples or "staked" by different colonizing countries, and even a claim to some of those lands on the other side of those borders. Were I sitting down to write *Revolution and the Word* now, significantly more of the text would be spent explicating nationalism before I went on to analyze the representational role played by the nation's founding documents (whether the Constitution or the "first American novel"). Five years from now, however, nationalism might not be a key concern. It's impossible to know. And that's a good thing, for the condition of not-knowing is what keeps the intellectual life alive. If the academy were not responsive to changing social, political, and intellectual currents, it would be ossified and irrelevant, and, ultimately, it would fail in its pedagogical function of preparing students for the future. Intellectual dexterity—being able to shift directions because of pressing concerns—is, to my mind, the best feature of the modern university.

What shapes those changing "concerns and interests"? Indisputably, each generation of students is faced with different social, political, economic, scientific, and technological challenges and brings those concerns into the classrooms—in the questions they ask about what they read, in the papers they write, in the challenges they pose. As with other collaborative (rather than hierarchical) models of cultural change I've argued for in this introduction, in very real ways teachers are as influenced by their students' concerns as students are inspired by their professors' scholarship. Or at least for *good* teachers and students this is always a two-way process. Not to belabor the obvious, it should be underscored that even academics live in a world outside the academy as well as within. That world bears significantly on our intellectual lives (and vice versa).

In the years since the publication of *Revolution and the Word*, a number of events have brought us back to discussions about why the Constitution was constructed as it was and what, exactly, it means. Everything from the impeachment of President Bill Clinton to the election of George W. Bush without the popular vote and partly based on a controversial and shockingly rapid Supreme Court decision has encouraged new courses and books on democracy, representative government, separations of power, and the electoral college. Northwestern University Law School's Center on Wrongful Convictions has used DNA and other forms of scientific and forensic evidence to exonerate falsely accused prisoners on death row. The sociological work determining the racial basis of a disproportionate number of those false accusations has inspired extensive scholarship on the history, efficacy, and international attitudes toward the death penalty. Women's reproductive rights, affirmative action, and privacy are all areas of social and civil legislation currently gaining renewed attention by both grassroots political activists and by academics precisely because these areas are under increasingly conservative legal and political pressure. Global information systems and new international movements of capital (by NGOs, multinational corporations, or even terrorist networks) have had a direct impact on international studies and on political theories of globalization. And certainly the impact of the attack on the World Trade Center and the Pentagon, as well as the United States' unprecedented break with the traditions and imperatives of international law in order to declare war against Iraq, has meant that courses in Middle Eastern history, Islamic studies, and Arabic are attracting more students than ever before—and more job openings for faculty in those areas (even in a year that saw a 20 percent decline in the number of academic job listings in English departments and a 16 percent decline in other foreign language departments).[93] Military history is, once again, a "hot" field. So is international diplomacy.

My point, simply, is that the academy is continuous with and a contributor to other historical processes. The humanities, especially, are centrally placed to offer historical depth, theoretical insights, critical resistance, and comparative complexity to public policy debates. If the humanities, definitionally, are the study of what it means to be human—offered in the widest historical and international context—then it should be the role of the humanities to put policy in a clear and firm perspective, both historical and comparative. Conversely, social and political events have an impact on the shape of scholarship and on the definition of fields. I tend to be optimistic about this process and convinced that education *means* being responsive to the questions most on the minds of our students.

Yet change can also bring problems. The shifts in focus and emphasis can sometimes contribute to what Evelyn Brooks Higginbotham calls "academic amnesia," a process by which known histories are forgotten or repressed, especially histories by those occupying marginalized positions within the academy and within society at large. In a forthcoming study on the history of race in the twentieth century, Higginbotham finds that many ideas are left behind so completely that a new generation of scholars often researches the problem all over again, only to arrive once more at similar conclusions. Indeed, even the lament that subsequent generations find themselves reinventing the wheel was expressed in the 1930s by black historians surprised to find forgotten histories of black education, rebellion under slavery, and earlier biographies of forgotten black leaders of the nineteenth century. This loss of academic memory can be depressing if it seems that progressive scholarship is doomed to be forgotten (a complaint that has been made by feminist scholars and those working in sexuality studies as well as scholars of race). At other times, however, ideas move outward from academe to become commonsense notions in the culture at large and persist as part of the common knowledge even when their original scholarly traces are lost. Both processes—of loss and of influence—may well occur simultaneously.[94]

Perhaps the single most important change in humanistic disciplines since the

1986 publication of *Revolution of the World* is in the conscious and conscientious pursuit of and debate about interdisciplinarity in the humanities.[95] The sciences have favored an interdisciplinary or multidisciplinary model for both intellectual and material reasons at least since the end of World War II, but cross-disciplinary thinking has come more slowly in the humanities and interpretive social sciences.

During the 1970s and 1980s when I was writing *Revolution and the Word,* interdisciplinarity also met with a good deal of resistance—particularly between historians and literary scholars, but also *within* literature and history departments. In the most heated of these debates, historians (and traditionalist literary critics) dismissed the exciting developments in literary theory as "jargon" and intellectual hocus-pocus while literary theorists accused traditional historians of "positivism." In writing *Revolution and the Word,* my largest interdisciplinary ambition was methodological: I wanted to combine the most diligent archival research with poststructuralist theories of knowledge, to combine archive with Foucauldian in-terrogations of what is legitimated *as* an archive. In some forums, it was worth risking making these kinds of methodological leaps. In others, my attempts to combine history and theory were so unproductive (including the kind of name-calling noted earlier) that I often had to decide, in advance of presenting a paper at a scholarly gathering, what *outcome* I hoped for from the presentation. If debate was a worthy outcome, I combined my different interests. If, however, I hoped to test certain findings or theories in the most rigorous way, I quickly discovered that it worked best if I disaggregated my work. Often, when I was presenting a paper at a historical meeting, I would present my archival findings with nary a mention of Foucault. The result would inevitably be a rich discussion that would lead me to many new archival sources as well as debate on the minutia of my material that pushed me to ever-greater detail and accuracy. If I were presenting a paper at a congress of literary theorists, I did not often show overheads of the various "scrabblings" I'd discovered on the endpapers of dozens of duodecimos of *Charlotte Temple.* Talk of marbling, watermarks, and signatures would have led to glazed eyes, not exciting discussion that tested the limits of my own theoretical thinking.

During the ten years when I was presenting papers leading up to the publi-cation of *Revolution and the Word,* I was extremely excited by what I learned from specialized audiences. At the same time, it was depressing that the choice was, on two or three occasions (I do not mean to overstate the case), between with-holding certain of my arguments in order to have a productive conversation or of articulating my full vision of the subject and courting the all-too-common outcome of having discussion devolve into unproductive and often ad hominem debate. Sometimes it was entirely worthwhile entering the fray of debate. If it weren't for finding a number of brilliant and generous scholars working on the history of the book, I might have left the field feeling, simply, frayed.

Writing about interdisciplinarity, Lisa Lattuca has noted: "To the untrained eye the world is interdisciplinary—or, more accurately, nondisciplinary. In Western society, our attempts to understand it, however, are often discipline-based. In Cartesian fashion we use our analytic skills to divide the world into smaller and smaller units, hoping that in understanding the parts we will eventually understand the whole."[96] It is my conviction, however, that it doesn't work that way. One can understand ever more detailed parts without coming up with a whole picture. More to the point, only through interdisciplinary open-ness can one arrive at a whole that is, as the saying goes, *greater* than the sum of its parts. Although one can learn certain specific kinds of information and gain some precise insights from this division of the world into minute disciplinary parts, it demands greater *intellectual* rigor to take those findings and synthesize them into a larger, interdisciplinary whole. Rather than (as is the cliché) interdisciplinarity implying a loss of standards, I would insist that it ultimately requires a higher standard of accountability and precision, including being tested by those who do not share one's informing assumptions.

Part of my job in writing *Revolution and the Word* was to put together the specialized knowledge I was gaining from each scholarly field and find a way to present it such that it had value to both its "home" discipline and the other.[97] However, my real aim was combining these various specialized knowledges into a theory of the novel that took into account the relationship between texts and society, between real readers and theories of reading, and material and formalist literary analysis. Much of the introductory material in *Revolution and the Word* explicitly addresses the investments of literary theory in cultural history. Conversely, the introductory chapters argue for the light that can be shed on cultural and social history by reader-response criticism, poststructuralist examinations of power and knowledge, and deconstructive readings of texts and textuality that alert us to seemingly disparate and even opposite ideologies, plots, and structures that coexist within the same book.[98]

Making one field of study visible to another is only the first level of true interdisciplinarity. For years, even within an ostensibly interdisciplinary organization such as the American Studies Association, there were often panels that "looked like" history whereas others "looked like" literature. Disciplinary barriers have by no means vanished—universities still have departments of history and departments of literature—but more and more courses within each department *look* like courses that might be taught by the other, and more scholars are actually combining methodologies, theories, and practices from different fields in order to arrive at a larger understanding of a particular topic or area. The merging, influence, blending, and impact of one field on another is, to my mind, one of the most significant characteristics of the humanities in the contemporary American university and certainly was one of the chief motivating forces behind my writing *Revolution and the Word*. It continues to be a source of intellectual inspiration to me. In fact, as some literary scholars now lament the passing of high poststructuralist literary theory, I tend to see the matter differently. The insights of that theory have permeated the thinking of many of us, including many younger scholars who have accepted the insights of poststructuralist theory without being particularly aware of where those insights originated or how revolutionary they were thought to be in the 1970s and 1980s. To choose two of myriad examples: A decentered canon is a pretty banal notion when one's college and even high school syllabi already include minority writers, popular culture, media, and new media. Queer theory can seem less radical when its reappropriation of the invidious epithet "queer" has been picked up in the titles of popular television shows or when its academic proponents are quoted in a Supreme Court decision. Similarly, poststructuralism (including deconstruction) has influenced virtually every humanistic field and is also used casually in popular discourse about architecture, law, engineering, cooking, or fashion. The realms of archive (history), text (literature), and ethnography (anthropology) have become increasingly mixed and merged not only across the disciplines but within the very disciplines themselves.

As I have been suggesting, who decides what is or isn't central to a nation's culture was hotly debated in the early national period because it was assumed that cultural values and political life were contiguous. Intriguingly, the same issue became the focus of much national debate again throughout the 1980s and 1990s, partly in response to and in backlash against modestly successful efforts to expand the syllabus of the college core curriculum.[99] Books such as Allan Bloom's *The Closing of the American Mind* (1987) and E. D. Hirsh's *Cultural Literacy* (1987) fanned the flames of the Culture Wars (and climbed best-seller lists) by insisting that American culture was going to the dogs.[100] The "dogs" were defined widely and variously, as proponents and purveyors of mass culture as well as (incongruously) feminists, people of color, Marxists, Vietnam War protestors, and other radicals who were thought to be controlling the academy, changing the syllabi and required courses, replacing core courses in Western civilization with "politically correct" requirements for "diversity" and "Third World" culture. Under the Ronald Reagan and George H. W. Bush presidential administrations, highly politicized directors and governing boards for the federal agencies supporting American cultural production—the National Endowment for the Humanities and the National Endowment for the Arts—worked to stem the tide of "liberal" and "left" infiltration of the academy by supporting works that were purportedly of a higher moral value and that promoted a "shared national culture." Reviving interest in the "Great Books" of Western culture was seen as the antidote to both populism and multiculturalism. Returning to New Criticism (the critical formalism prominent between the 1940s and late 1960s) was the solution to poststructuralism.

Writing a book on early American novels that no one had heard of and arguing that these proposed an alternative to the constricted democratic principles offered by the Founding Fathers put me squarely in the "liberal" corner in what became known as the "Culture Wars," a term every bit as hyperbolic as the overheated and acrimonious discourse of the time. What intrigues me most in retrospect, however, is the resonance between questions raised by the Culture Wars and those by the Revolutionary War. In both, culture authorities (including teachers and scholars) were perceived to have the real and active power to change lives, influence opinion, and, ultimately, sway votes, thus determining the shape of the future. And at both time periods, a constellation of jumbled values were lumped under the rubric of culture. In the 1980s, there was heated debate over which books should be required reading for students; the grounds for inclusion of that list of books; and whether the list was based on intrinsic (formal) merit, traditional values, patriotic concerns, habit, or prejudice against (or on behalf of, said conservative critics) women, people of color, labor activists, Marxists, radicals, the aesthetic avant-garde, or popular culture.

The argument over "culture" in the 1980s was a stand-in for more concrete political activities that were labeled the "Reagan Revolution," the attempt by a popular president and his administration to roll back many of the social reforms enacted by Lyndon Johnson as part of the "Great Society" as well as by later presidents, especially in the aftermath of the Vietnam War. As with the censure of the novel, the "Culture Wars" and "canon debate" were terms deployed to make it seem as if there were clear sides (good and evil, traditional and radical, high culture and low), but the use of the terms was often slippery, subjective, and non-exclusive. One can believe, for example, that one should read African American writers *and* believe that popular culture is debased and unworthy of significant study. W. E. B. DuBois, Ralph Ellison, James Baldwin, Gwendolyn Brooks, or Toni Morrison are hardly writers one reads as light entertainments or for mindless escapism. Somehow pointing out these contradictions was less important than the polemical heat (and the headlines) that could be generated by, for example, accusing the Nobel Prize Committee of bowing to "political correctness" in choosing Toni Morrison as the recipient of its prize for literature.[101]

The real issue—in the early Republic as in the 1980s—was less the value of certain literary texts than the *power* of writers, artists, educators, and scholars to shape social attitudes: to determine a "national culture." The rhetoric in both the 1790s and the 1980s was hyperbolic because it was supposed that the stakes were the very highest: the definition of American society itself.[102]

Revolution and the Word was one of many scholarly studies of the 1980s thought to be changing the interpretation of our national culture and the canon of American literature. Most of the novels I discussed in *Revolution and the Word* were not in print when the book appeared or were only available in expensive or obscure editions. Making several of these novels available in classroom editions was an important side-benefit of the book. If there are now myriad articles and books on early American fiction, it is partly because the texts themselves are now accessible and frequently taught in undergraduate and graduate classes.

Many fields besides early American studies were transformed by projects dedicated to creating a new syllabus of American literature and making available as many new texts as possible. The Schomburg Library of Nineteenth-Century Black Women Writers, edited by Henry Louis Gates, the Rutgers University Press American Women Writers Series, or the monumental retrieval efforts by the Feminist Press were among the important series that expanded the canon. In addition to these republications of individual titles, the collaborative effort that led to the creation of the *Heath Anthology of American Literature* (1990), edited by Paul Lauter and many others, gave teachers a chance to redesign their American literature survey courses to include works that may have been widely esteemed in their day but, for one reason or another, had dropped off the literary map.[103] The availability of these new texts as part of the core teaching in undergraduate courses shaped the assumptions, the pedagogy, and the future scholarship of Americanists.

In early American studies, several new anthologies also have changed the shape of the field. Two massive anthologies, *The English Literatures of America, 1500–1800* (1997) and *The Literatures of Colonial America* (2001), remap early American literature in terms of colonial expansion in the New World.[104] The Longfellow Project started at Harvard by Marc Shell and Werner Sollors has produced *The Multilingual Anthology of American Literature: A Reader of Original Texts with English Translations* (2000), a great spur to transnational early American studies. Sharon M. Harris's *American Women Writers to 1800* (1996) is a splendid collection that is arranged chronologically within thematic categories such as "On Women's Education," which brings together everything from Zuni corn-grinding lessons to Judith Sargent Murray's long poem on female complacency and improved education. Ann Allen Shockley's *Afro-American Women Writers, 1746–1933* (1988) includes an impressive selection of early black women's writing.[105] Moira Ferguson's *Nine Black Women* (1998) collects writing by nineteenth-century writers from the United States, Canada, Bermuda, and the Caribbean. Equally exciting are Deirdre Mullane's *Crossing the Danger Water: Three Hundred Years of African-American Writing* (1993) and John Edgar Wideman's *My Soul Has Grown Deep: Classics of Early African-American Literature* (2001).[106] Alan R. Velie's *American Indian Literature* (1991) includes tales, songs, oratory, memoirs, poetry, and fiction, from pre-Columbian oral transmission to the present.[107] Arnold Krupat's anthology *Native American Autobiography* (1994) includes a section on "Traditional Lives" and a contrasting section on "Christian Indians" before the 1830 Indian Removal. These are among the many excellent new anthologies that have not only contributed to the field but changed the map of what constitutes "the field."

Taken together, all of these books, plus dozens of other reprints and anthologies published by various university and commercial presses, have transformed the shape of American literature, redirecting the questions one asks, posing new scholarly puzzles, demanding new literary histories. What is available to be read has a profound impact on the way one sees everything else. One's archive shapes one's reading of the archive. That works negatively as well. It is possible to continue in one's conception of the world by *not* reading, by retaining the paradigms and syllabus in which one was educated even after those intellectual structures have outlasted their usefulness. Whether to keep freshly reading or to preserve—as if it were a museum or a shrine—the archive of one's youth is a decision each scholar makes for herself or himself over the course of a career. Some find it exhilarating while others (in *any* generation) consider the new to be a "declension," personally and for the profession at large.

Change was at the root of the Culture Wars but with a difference: Now change itself was the subject of debate. Shouldn't we all, forever, be reading the same books in order to be unified as a nation? Aren't those who propose new texts and new ways of reading old texts destroying our culture? In 1991, I edited the section on "Beginnings to the Mid–Nineteenth Century" for the *Columbia History of the American Novel* edited by Emory Elliott.[108] When the book was published, the editors were all surprised to find that the words "New Views" had been added to the dust jacket without the foreknowledge or approval of any of us. It was as if someone in the publisher's head office, frightened by the hyperbole and upheaval of the Culture Wars, was afraid that the volume was too new, too radical to be an official "history." The force of those two words lay somewhere between a disclaimer and a "parental guidance" sticker on a rap album.

However, in 2003, the *Columbia History of the American Novel* looks pretty benign, even canonical. I doubt that any student reading it now finds it particularly shocking. So it goes. "Culture Wars? What were those about?" a first-year graduate student recently asked me. I smiled with delight at her casual use of the past tense. A lot of heat and fury, careers made and lost, took place over a process that is as inevitable as breathing. And perhaps that is exactly as it should be. If the intellectual life is important, then problems of content, importance, paradigms, methods, and theories all should be debated. Debate (even acrimonious debate) is part of the process by which new ideas are accepted. In the words of Martin Bernal, the author of the controversial *Black Athena*, any novel and significant insight or discovery goes through a four-stage process of being ignored, dismissed, attacked, and then eventually absorbed. In Bernal's verdict: "Attack is great progress."[109]

History is never still. Intellectual vitality requires that each new generation of students and scholars pose new questions. The answers evoke still other questions. Inevitably, every scholar in the course of a career has to make a decision whether to continue reading, thinking, growing, and changing. The bitterness of being passed by, overlooked, or shortchanged is, it seems to me, the personal price one pays for becoming stuck in the glowing paradigms of one's intellectual youth, as pristine (and remote) as a mosquito caught in amber.

Conclusion

In October 1999 I attended a conference on American studies at Vietnam National University in Hanoi. A delegation of American scholars joined Vietnamese colleagues for the first American studies conference ever held in the new capital of Vietnam. "American Studies Today" was organized by Jonathan Auerbach and Nguyen Lien. They also coedited the historic bilingual conference volume, *Tiếp Cận Đương Đại Văn Hoá Mỹ/Contemporary Approaches to American Culture.*[110]

The historical situation that led to this binational academic meeting gave special weight to the questions we asked repeatedly during our two days together. These were questions not about the past but about the future: How do you make a national culture after a revolution or any violent rupture in civil society overthrows an external (colonial) power? What cultural forms best serve the postrevolutionary and postcolonial goals of expressing, concretizing, and coalescing support for the values of a nascent and fragile nation-state? What are the profound effects of war on the creation of a subsequent national culture? And what influences carry over between national cultures? One feature of the conference recognized by all who were present was that Americans came as guests. Vietnamese scholars spoke with authority about both American and Vietnamese culture. They spoke of the lasting effect of American culture on Vietnam. However, what turned out to be the surprise of the conference for all was discovering that the Vietnamese scholars were not aware of influence in the other direction. In their preface, Nguyen Lien and Nguyen Ba Thanh note that "for the first time, we Vietnamese have come to realize the powerful influence [of the Vietnam War and Vietnamese resistance] on cultural movements that have brought about great changes in American academia and publishing and in other spheres of American life."[111] The Vietnamese scholars were, in their own historical context and moment, trying to rebuild intellectual life and, more specifically, to create an intellectual and cultural life suitable to their new nation—including by finding validation in the impact that they had exerted on the cultural life of the United States.

Again and again, the topics to which the Vietnamese returned during this conference were the ones raised in *Revolution and the Word* and central to the debates on national culture in the aftermath of the U.S. Revolutionary War. At one point, a Vietnamese scholar showed me the inexpensive textbook she had created for her students in her American studies course. It included a pirated excerpt from *Revolution and the Word.* Her self-published textbook was printed on inexpensive paper, the words crammed as closely together as possible. Instantly I was reminded of the cheap early American editions of popular tales such as *Charlotte Temple* or *History of Constantius and Pulchera* that had been pirated and circulated among the populace. Later, in the course of the conference, another Vietnamese scholar told me, much to my surprise, that *Revolution and the Word* is an important book in present-day Vietnam. She said scholars and students believe it addresses the problems they face in the aftermath of both the "American War" (their name for what we call the "Vietnam War") and their subsequent civil war, and as they struggle to create a unified nation. She explained that many of the debates on national culture in the aftermath of the U.S. Revolutionary War parallel debates in modern-day Vietnam about what constitutes a national culture. What is the relationship between literacy levels, education, and cultural life? What is advanced literacy in political and social terms, and who is granted access to "universal" literacy? How do you foster, subsidize, regulate, and promote an indigenous print culture—and how does the definition of the nation influence that cultural production? What is a government's obligations to its authors, and where is the line between promoting national literature and imposing standards for what does or does not constitute the "right" national image? Where does censorship (as well as more subtle cultural censure) come into the picture? How do the special circumstances of postrevolutionary society influence the definitions and regulation of intellectual property, copyright, patent, and tariff protection (to either encourage or minimize the importation of books and magazines from outside the new nation)? What is the role of a national educational system in the creation of postcolonial culture? A national system of libraries? Subsidized publishing? And how does one ensure access to national culture to an entire populace—including women, people of color, the indigent, various religious and ethnic groups, rural citizens, and those who may not share the values of the new nation? In Vietnam in 1999, as in the new United States in 1789, these were complex and intertwined subjects of vital significance.[112]

My discovery that *Revolution and the Word* was being studied as a blueprint for how to make a national culture in present-day Vietnam—as much as for what it said about the American past—brought home to me, in a literal fashion, the active role history plays in any society and the historian's role in creating (not just re-creating) history. My wish for present readers of *Revolution and the Word* is similar: that they remember that problems of culture and country never go away. We must attend to them now every bit as assiduously as did the first generation of Americans.

Part One

1 Introduction:
Toward a History of Texts

Throughout the first decade of the nineteenth century, Ethan Allen Greenwood, a rather pedantic young diarist, each day recorded both the weather and the title of the book he was reading. He sometimes observed that a particular work was "instructive" or "entertaining" and occasionally noted the library from which the volume was borrowed—the Adelphi Fraternity Library, the Social Friends Library, or the unnamed circulating library he joined in 1806. His meticulous account of his activities and expenses—whether living at home in Worcester County, Massachusetts, or at Dartmouth College or later in Boston, or whether traveling around the countryside as an itinerant painter—provides posterity with an unusually comprehensive portrait of "Ethan Allen Greenwood, His Life and Times." Looking over the record that he left, we can well imagine that we *know* this serious and sober, parsimonious and abstemious young man Franklinesquely working his way toward fame and fortune. But then we encounter a curious entry: "Rode out with the ladies. Returned and spent the evening agreeably. What I do not write here will not be forgotten."[1]

It is what is not written here that especially seizes our attention. As any semiotician knows, the omissions in a text are often as revealing as what that text explicitly tells. Yet it is difficult to formulate the rules whereby silence is admissible as historical evidence. What did go on between the lines in the diary, between Greenwood and the ladies? That question is pertinent to the historical record precisely because it is not answered in the autobiographical one. Nevertheless, whatever codes and considerations prompted Greenwood's circumspection are as much a part of his diary and a sign of his times as are the detailed lists of his various daily expenses.

I begin my study of the origins of American fiction with this enigmatic diary entry for two basic reasons. First, the lacuna in Greenwood's account reminds us that however familiar we are with a particular era or person, what we do not know may be just as telling as what we do. The public record always fictionalizes, at least to a degree, private life, and the interstices between the two allow "the expected fiction" to slide over into and to become "the real life." Nor can the known absence be simply read. Schooled as we may be in decoding silences (and especially so through recent reassessments of the possibilities of criticism), we have too often also been schooled in dismissing presence. Greenwood left out the details of that not-to-be-forgotten evening in a definite time and place. Before we can plumb his silence, we must sound a larger one—the historical moment in which he both wrote and did not write. Indeed, without a careful appraisal of those moments in which literature is written—or not written—the literary historian perpetuates essentially tautological arguments about the "rise of the novel," as proven by the observed rise of the novel, or the "origins of the American mind," as attested to by the chosen texts of that mind's originating.[2]

Each of those tautologies is also, it will be noted, a likely trap into which a book about the origins of American fiction well might stumble. But I hope to avoid such stumbling by keeping both traps clearly in mind and by working around them. What this book proposes is a way of reading texts in response to a specific set of circumstances that not only created both texts and ways of reading them but also that those texts, in turn, created. In other words, I am concerned, on one level, with the forces that shape *mentalités*—not the psychology of individual readers during a particular time (a naive goal and necessarily beyond reach) but the interpretive grid (lost but still largely recoverable) in and around which those readers read—"community assumptions," in Robert Escarpit's terminology.[3] This focus of my study is particularly indebted to the scholarship of *l'histoire du livre*, the multidisciplinary approach worked out by a number of historians (primarily Europeans and Americans working with European materials) who have attempted, in Robert Darnton's formulation, to decipher "the social and cultural history of communication by print" in order better to understand "how ideas were transmitted through print and how exposure to the printed word affected human thought and behavior during the last 500 years."[4] Lucien Febvre and Henri-Jean Martin formulated this approach most cogently with their *L'Apparition du livre* (1958), a monumental work whose impact in America is attested to by the establishment, in 1979, of the Center for the Book at the Library of Congress and, in 1980, the Program in the History of the Book in American Culture at the American Antiquarian Society.[5]

But for all the insights that I derive from reading, say, Carlo Ginzburg's remarkable account of Menocchio, a sixteenth-century Italian miller who taught himself to read and whose world was uniquely altered by his participation in print culture, I am concerned, of course, with texts other than those Menocchio happened upon and with other *possibilities* for meaning besides those that Menocchio might have perceived in the texts he read.[6] Ultimately, books are written for readers and not for any one reader, actual or implied or ideal. An individual reading of a work, no matter how detailed or persuasive, does not tell us the whole story of that text. Drawing, therefore, from reader-response critical theory, I suggest strategies by which texts may be deciphered in terms of the complex set of generic, stylistic, thematic, cultural, ideological, and literary expectations that readers bring to texts and that authors (themselves readers of the work that they are writing) play with and around in the creation of texts.[7] My focus on *mentalités* is balanced, then, by a second focus on the codes or rules of fictive discourse. This second focus is not in opposition to the first but is different from it. To summarize in one polyglot formulation, I have attempted to combine *l'histoire du livre* and *Rezeptionsästhetik*, using each methodology as a check and a balance to the other.[8] Instead of a history-of-the-book approach to early American fiction, I am more interested in what might be termed a history-of-texts approach (with that last term deliberately bearing its semiotic and perhaps even ahistorical connotations).[9]

I am also aware that this *histoire du texte* may satisfy neither the cultural historian nor the literary theorist. Yet how can we even presume to talk about books and readers without taking into account considerations about how books are made? A book is not simply a text waiting for a cunning reader to come upon it and decode it. A book is also an artifact, a product of the printer's art as well as the author's or, for that matter, the reader's. Conversely, how can we talk about the history of books without taking into account such concepts as genre, audience, implied authors, implied readers, and the strategies by which given texts operate within a given culture?[10] To trace out how the American novel originated in purely historical and sociological terms—the economics of early publication and distribution, the sociometrics of Federalist book buying—would be as dubious as to premise a literary interpretation of these same novels on the readers for whom they were first intended without knowing whether, on the simplest and most crucial level, those readers had access to novels, could afford them, or could even read them. It is simply too easy to perpetuate assumptions about the reader that neglect the inescapable fact that readers, as much as texts, operate within historical contexts. Having wisely revalued authors and texts, contemporary criticism still perpetuates its worst tendencies when it attempts to valorize an ostensibly historical reader who turns out to be mostly another apotheosis of the contemporary literary theorist.[11] Nor can we conveniently overlook the historicity of the writer. To subject an eighteenth-century American novel to a Derridean deconstruction that does not take into account the codes whereby it was originally constructed demonstrates, again, mostly the transubstantiations of the critic.

The writer has at least left the record of the work; readers, in many cases, left nothing at all. Partly to fill in this gap, a number of literary theorists have addressed themselves to constructing models of the reader. Stanley Fish's *Is There a Text in This Class?* emphasizes that all texts exist *in* the reader and within appropriate "interpretive communities."[12] Fish uses the readings of students as a paradigm of one such interpretive community. Yet the historical application of this contemporary community is necessarily limited, since students come to texts with the current presuppositions of apprentice literary critics, of tyros looking to impress their teacher. Similarly, when Jonathan Culler insists that what we need is a history of reception consisting essentially of a survey of published assessments of a given literary work and then a reconstruction of the codes that occasioned this multiplicity of interpretations, he necessarily (and by design) limits reception to an academic exercise—in both senses of that word.[13] What of the implied and actual readers envisioned by writers, the vast majority of whom do not write about what they read? The best model of that reader, to date, has been provided by Janice A. Radway in *Reading the Romance: Women, Partiarchy, and Popular Literature*. Radway has interviewed the readers of romance novels to reveal the surprisingly diverse functions served in their lives by fictions that critics have typically dismissed as simple, escapist fantasies.[14]

My problem, of course, is that my readers have been dead for almost two hundred years, so one can hardly interview them to reconstruct an early American interpretive community. Yet in diaries, in letters, and in the fiction itself there are accounts and versions of how the first novels in America were first read. Furthermore, in extant copies of the novels and in other kinds of books as well, readers have often left their marks.[15] Inscriptions and marginalia tell us something about how books were valued and how they were read. Wear and tear and the repairs of same—torn pages neatly handsewn back into the volume, dog-eared corners carefully trimmed, thumb papers (little tabs of vellum or wallpaper) secured in the spines of books to protect the print from smudging—constitute further evidence of worth and use. Book morphology also provides clues to at least the intended audience of books (and perhaps the actual audience since early publishers, as much as present ones, had to know their market to survive). American novels were not published as impressive folio or octavo volumes, which itself suggests fiction's relatively low social status. But we can discriminate beyond that obvious generalization, too. Was the novel published in a calf-bound duodecimo version with illustrative material and marbled endleaves or with paper covers and signatures printed on varying grades or colors of cheap paper? Other questions are also pertinent in reconstructing the interpretive community in which a volume first appeared. What size is the book? How large is the type? Which words are capitalized or italicized in the text? What is the relationship between text and visual material? Or between text and preliminary matter such as a dedication, a preface, or a subscription list bound within the volume? Prefatory material or any other such reading clues also serve as *reader* clues and indicate something of the gender, age, class, and level of literacy of the first audience to whom the book was addressed.

At this point an example can more concretely illustrate how seemingly nonliterary considerations still suggest the scope and nature of a particular work's use and appeal, the interpretive community to which the work appealed, how its appeal illuminates the sociological context in which it takes place, and how all of these factors together can contribute to a history of texts, an archaeology of reading. More specifically, by comparing a popular nonfiction book with early American novels, we can see the complex place novels inhabited in early American culture and some of the complicating factors in any projection of the novel-reading public. George Fisher's *The Instructor; Or, American Young Man's Best*

Within the illustration:

ARITHMETIC
NAVIGATION
MEASURING
ARCHITECTURE
GEOMETRY

Tis to y.e Press & Pen we Mortals owe. All hail ye great Preservers of these A.r.
All we believe & almost all we know, That raise our thoughts & Cultivate our

FIGURE 1. Frontispiece, George Fisher, *The Instructor; Or, American Young Man's Best Companion* (Worcester, Mass.: Isaiah Thomas, 1785). *Courtesy of the American Antiquarian Society.*

Companion, was first published in London in 1727, was imported to America soon thereafter, and was retitled *The American Instructor* and reprinted by Benjamin Franklin in 1748. The book was a steady seller in America until the second quarter of the nineteenth century. Designed as an adult self-help book, not a textbook or a children's book, this relatively sophisticated work instructs the reader on a wide variety of topics, ranging from calligraphy and other fine arts to practical advice on such matters as how to draw up deeds and to more esoteric information such as how to use a Gunter's-Line or Coggeshall's Sliding-Rule. Different editions vary the book's title and subtitle and include different descriptions of the contents, sometimes suggesting a commitment to further educational refinement, sometimes to artisanal application. Clearly, the book was never meant to be a trade manual.[16] Its frontispiece portrays a robed scholar in his study, surrounded by telescope, sundial, globes, weighty folios, and five boys—apparently ranging from early to late adolescence—all awaiting the scholar's wisdom. The legend beneath the engraving reads: "Tis to the Press & Pen we Mortals owe, / All we believe & almost all we know. / All hail ye great Preservers of these Arts, / That raise our thoughts & Cultivate our Parts." The community ("we Mortals," "All hail") here assumed and pictorialized is exclusively masculine. Learning is emblemized as the province of the socially prominent, of those who can afford education and its accoutrements. That ideal is more Old World than New, as is also the frontispiece of the scholar in his High Renaissance study (an illustration taken over from the English editions and published in most American versions of the book).

Considering the title and the frontispiece, it should not be surprising that nearly all of the fifty-three names I have found inscribed in different copies of this book are male (on a few occasions only first initals are given, but this form of book signing was seldom used by eighteenth-century women unless preceded by Mrs. or Miss). Even this highly informal survey suggests that, in the case of Fisher's book, a preponderantly masculine readership was not only implied by the text itself but may, in fact, have existed. But when we come to novels generalizations about the gender of the audience require further qualification and examination; one is also struck by how easily sociological factors elide into literary issues. In over one thousand extant copies of early American novels I have surveyed, women's signatures outnumber men's roughly two to one. Male names, however, actually outnumber female in the few subscription lists published with early American novels.[17] While these figures are both preliminary and impressionistic (I have by no means seen every extant copy of every novel nor is there anything statistically controlled about the sample of copies that happens to survive), they do seem to suggest a disparity between private book ownership (evidenced by signatures) and public endorsement of a book (as in a subscription list). Were women ashamed to subscribe to novels, which were often considered a licentious form of literature? Or is economics at issue here? Who could afford to buy books? What books were considered necessities and what extravagances? Were books considered more of a luxury for one sex than for the other? Who paid—at least publicly—for literature? "Gentlemen holding subscription papers for *Emily Hamilton*, a New Novel, are requested to return them immediately to this office," Isaiah Thomas, Jr., announced in the *Massachusetts Spy, or Worcester Gazette* on March 2, 1803, *assuming* that the subscribers to this novel—about women, implicitly for women, and written "By a Young Lady of Worcester County"—would be gentlemen.[18]

We know, from surviving eighteenth-century account books as well as from entries in numerous diaries of the time, that men did (or were credited with doing) most of the purchasing in the early national period. Seven transactions with the notoriously irresponsible William Rowson are recorded in Mathew Carey's account books, to cite one particularly graphic example, but none with Rowson's wife, Susanna, the first bestselling novelist in America and one of Carey's most profitable authors.[19] In short, the sociology of wage earning and spending is important here since in a social and economic context that privileged male buying and reading, *any* evidence of a female readership becomes a significant literary and sociological phenomenon. It should also be noted that women, in particular, flocked to the new lending libraries where they could rent novels far more cheaply than they could buy them. The clearer gender differentiation in the case of Fisher's self-help book highlights the complex case of fiction—and the ambiguous status of women as implied readers of early American fiction.

The gender of Fisher's interpretive community seems to be fairly clear-cut, but I hasten to emphasize that gender is not the only important factor in discovering readers. Fisher's book also illustrates the ways in which interpretive communities can be composed of readers with vastly different educational levels and, by extension, different class affiliations. The frontispiece of *The Instructor* suggests a book addressed to the young upwardly mobile professional of two hundred years ago. But inscriptions and marginalia suggest that Fisher's appeal may have extended far beyond wealthy or upper-middle-class American men (the majority of whom could read and write fluently by the middle of the eighteenth century). One E. J. Patterson, for example, in an 1800 edition, practiced printing a very crude series of numbers from one to nine on the inside flyleaf; while in a 1753 edition, Adam Orth neatly and clearly wrote his name (twice) on the endpapers, yet also practiced the most elementary addition problems taught in the book (such as how to carry the ten) and practiced writing his numbers. What, one wonders, was the relationship between elementary literacy and numeracy in early America and what class or regional factors may have influenced the acquisition of these different skills? Similar questions are raised by Joseph Langdon's signatures in a 1748 edition. Langdon wrote his name several times and on the inside front flyleaf, directly beneath his name, practiced "abcd." Were signatures learned first, before other elementary writing skills (a sequence that could have implications for the study of sign literacy, an issue discussed in chapter 4)? Or by George Duncan, who signed his name six times in the flyleaves of the book over a five-year period beginning in 1815, the successive signatures indicating increasing skill in the art of penmanship; or by an anonymous reader in an 1802 edition who used the endpapers to practice the geometric designs that constituted the preliminary exercises in the study of penmanship. What was the class, the educational level, and the age of Fisher's readers? These matters seem clear in the text itself but highly ambiguous when we assess the way actual readers made use of that text.

Other evidence also indicates that the readers of *The Instructor* were drawn from a range of social situations, possessed varying literary sophistication, and used the same text to very different ends. Thus one anonymous inscriber set down in haphazard fashion on one of the endpapers a crude and sloppy partial index ("Will 294," "Receipt for Black Ink 49") to presumably just those sections pertinent to this reader. In contrast, when John Blakey, an accomplished calligrapher, presented his friend John Sharples with a copy of the book on April 4, 1772, he included with the volume an elaborate, finely penned, and beautifully organized index to its entire contents. From such evidence, one can postulate a disparate community of male readers, some of whom used the book at a very elementary level, apparently to improve basic literacy and numeracy skills; some of whom used it as a convenient reference book (especially when hand-indexed to serve more efficiently an artisan or tradesman or busy gentleman); and some of whom presented it as a gift book—more a proper token of social esteem (and status) than a utilitarian reference guide. As different inscriptions indicate, the book could be given by one well-educated friend to another, but it could also be passed among a community of marginal writers and readers to be preserved and shared—as the different names and dates of an 1812 edition show—over the course of a quarter of a century and in a setting (frontier Michigan) seemingly worlds removed from the genteel world of Renaissance learning depicted by the volume's frontispiece but, no doubt, still inspired by this vision of tradition and status.[20] In view of the varied responses to the text, the frontispiece, too, is a text to be read and interpreted. It seems less a sign of the book's contents than a symbol of the reader's aspirations and an implicit promise (like a before-and-after ad) of the benefits to be gained by studying the volume. (You, too, can have youth eagerly attend to your words of wisdom!)

Such assessments of an interpretive community, although necessarily inconclusive, give us glimpses of how books were read in the new Republic. The issues, as already noted, are considerably more complex when it is a novel, not a textbook, that is the focus of investigation. None of Fisher's readers need look for a hidden political allegory behind his discussion of calculation. Furthermore, and as even *The Instructor* demonstrates, the same book can serve different demands of different readers possessed of different needs, skills, and experiences. These differences should be even greater with novels than with self-improvement books since novels necessarily leave so much more to the individual imagination. Nevertheless, by surveying inscriptions and marginalia (sometimes merely a partial signature, sometimes a miniature book review), by assessing book use, by considering book morphology as well as visuals of reading situations, by attending to clues offered up by the texts themselves, and by taking into account diaries and letters about the novel and the extensive recorded testimony denouncing the genre, one can construct an ethnography of the early American novel reader (and writer) that provides a "thick description" of the role of the novel in early American culture. This phrase (borrowed from Clifford Geertz) emphasizes the need not just to describe the "meaning particular social actions have for the actors whose actions they are" but for "stating, as explicitly as we can manage, what the knowledge thus attained demonstrates about the society in which it is found and, beyond that, about social life as such."[21]

The novel, I argue throughout this study, became the chapbook of the nineteenth century—that is, a cheap book accessible to those who were not educated at the prestige men's colleges, who were outside the established literary tradition, and who (as both Charles Brockden Brown and Helena Wells noted) for the most part read few books besides novels. Given both the literary insularity of many novel readers and the increasing popularity of the novel, the new genre necessarily became a form of education, especially for women. Novels allowed for a means of entry into a larger literary and intellectual world and a means of access to social and political events from which many readers (particularly women) would have been otherwise largely excluded. The first novels, I would also argue, provided the citizens of the time not only with native versions of the single most popular form of literary entertainment in America, but also with literary versions of emerging definitions of America—versions that were, from the first, tinged with ambivalence and duplicity.

Having suggested in the barest terms what the book intends, I will now as briefly indicate what it does not. Most obviously, I do not examine the early American novel in comparison with British models. Everyone knows that the first American fiction imitated earlier British originals, but we are not so sure just what that means. Did "the American novel" imitate "the British novel" (phrases that assume each national product was monolithic and the influence equally so)? Or did Charles Brockden Brown imitate William Godwin (implying a subservience of the apprentice author to the master writer)? Yet Godwin in his 1817 preface to *Mandeville* acknowledged his debt to Brown, and Brown was also credited with influencing Godwin's daughter, Mary, and her husband, Percy Bysshe Shelley, even though few studies of the Shelleys posit their debt to Brown. What should be clear from these preliminary observations is that there are unquestioned assumptions of cultural hegemony implicit in the conventional concept of imitation. Those assumptions may be correct, but they are as yet undemonstrated, and a full investigation of the whole matter would depend on a detailed study of precisely what British books were read in America, in what numbers, by whom, and how New World writers responded individually and collectively to Old World texts, individually and collectively.[22] It should also be remembered that the most popular writers in Britain at the time the American novel began were not Richardson, Fielding, and Sterne but Godwin, Robert Bage, Ann Radcliffe, and "Monk" Lewis and that the English novel most often listed in late eighteenth-century American booksellers' catalogues was Henry Brooke's *The Fool of Quality* (1766–1770).[23] No one, however, seems to wish to investigate in detail these particular authors.[24] Finally, and most important, any adequate study of the influence of English fiction on the emerging American novel would be at least as extensive as the present work. It is a different study from my own, and, I would suggest, until it is done, there is little to be gained either by reiterating or rejecting the conventional assumptions of influence and imitation.

Yet I must also emphasize that most books Americans read, even after the Revolution, still came from abroad, either imported directly or pirated by American printers from European originals. David D. Hall, John Seelye, and William Spengemann have each cogently argued, in different contexts, that it is both insular and ahistorical to develop a model of the "American mind" or an "American tradition" based solely on books written in America, and they are completely correct in doing so.[25] As every aspiring American novelist knew full well, he or she competed in a precarious market already flooded with European products. For example, Hocquet Caritat, with the 1804 catalogue for his New York library of fiction, could include only some forty American titles in a list of almost fifteen hundred works—despite what seems to have been his concerted effort to gather as many native novels as possible.[26] One cannot deny the omnipresence of European fiction. As will be clear throughout this study, early American novels contain numerous allusions to (and condemnations of) British novelists. But I must reiterate that I am leaving the European connections of American fiction to other scholars specifically interested in that topic.[27] My concern is with the ways in which a small body of Americans used the novel as a political and cultural forum, a means to express their own vision of a developing new nation.[28] Like writers in any country that has achieved independence through revolution, early American novelists faced the special task of creating literature *against* the overwhelming impact of their nation's residual Colonial mentality. How did they make an American fiction? What local issues were fictionalized, were considered significant enough to warrant the attention of novelist *and* reader? More theoretically, how does one make art in an inchoate land whose boundaries are all the more difficult to perceive *because* of a persistent imperial presence? These insistently political questions pervade early American novels and can be seen in myriad comments within the novels on the need for an indigenous art or the correlative need for an indigenous audience (the repeated argument that Americans should read and buy American books).

I do not assess how British fiction shaped American fiction and neither do I assess in any detail how the first novels might have shaped those that came after— Nathaniel Hawthorne, Herman Melville, Harriet Beecher Stowe, and the clear beginning of a "tradition" of American fiction. Whatever affinities these subsequent writers have with the early authors will be, for the most part, implicit in my discussion of the earlier writers and need not be validated by further discussion of the later ones.[29] At the same time, it would be naive to pretend that the present study has not been influenced by my own education in and to a tradition of nineteenth-century American fiction. As diverse commentators such as Michel Foucault, Clifford Geertz, and Edward Said have argued, any study of origins is necessarily compromised from the beginning by the fact that the historian already knows what it is that is to be explained.[30] A cultural given is *given* only on the terms whereby it is already possessed. It is that possession that proves old patents, not vice versa. Artifacts are always labeled by virtue of a whole history of past labeling; they carry their archaeology in their name. On some level, then, to trace origins is to repeat the name, and any foray into the ostensibly revelatory past is hopelessly grounded in the very present to be thereby explained. Indeed, hindsight, as much as foresight, is vision affronting time.

The objectivity of any retrospective vision is also compromised by the subjectivity of the "I" seeing. If we focus back through Edith Wharton and Nathaniel Hawthorne to more distant fictional foremothers and forefathers such as Hannah Webster Foster and Charles Brockden Brown, the perspective virtually predicts one of two only seemingly contradictory ends. The already valorized nineteenth-century authors can serve to valorize their eighteenth-century predecessors ("Here we see the seeds of . . ."). Or the still devalued eighteenth-century writers can serve to valorize further their nineteenth-century successors ("Not from this did Melville spring . . ."). In either case the governing impulse is the same. We search for roots not out of dispassionate curiosity about the past but because we know that the family tree ultimately produced "me."

The subjectivity (one might even say egotism) at the heart of all genealogical endeavors is, inevitably, part and parcel of the present volume.[31] My discussion, for example, owes a large debt to poststructuralist criticism, even though I have tried, as much as possible, to avoid what has already become the formulaic roll call of prominent theorists, the invocation of the Continental Muses that ensures their presence in the text. It will also be obvious that I am indebted to recent feminist critiques of gender and ideology; of, in Mary Jacobus's phrase, the "textuality of sexuality," and vice versa.[32] As a feminist and a sociological critic, my pulse naturally quickens when I discover an 1814 novel by Sarah Savage entitled *The Factory Girl* in which the heroine of the novel organizes her fellow workers into a study group. My biases are also, no doubt, evident in my disappointment with the assimilationism that is the end of such a beginning, although, given the time and place within which the book was written, published, and read, Christian forbearance and subservience of one's personal will to the demands of and for domestic tranquility are more likely conclusions for a heroine than the one I would have preferred. The point is, simply, that all etiologic studies assume a development that has already taken place, and the investigator inevitably posits origins congruent with the development that can be documented as following from those origins—the tautology of history, which is as inescapable as the historian's place *in* history. For any version of history *is* a version; implicit in that version are often complex hegemonic forces that have little to do with the subject under study and much to do with the historian. In sociological terms: "To understand the state of the socially constructed universe at a given time, or its change over time, one must understand the social organization that permits the definers to do their defining."[33]

All history is choice, discourse that begins with the very questions the historian chooses to ask (or not ask) of his or her own version of the past. Fiction cannot be simply "fit into its historical context," as if context were some Platonic pigeonhole and all that is dark or obscure in the fiction is illuminated when the text is finally slipped into the right slot. If we argue that history provides the context, then who or what, we must also ask, provides the history? Organizing a multiplicity of disparate data into a coherent structure, any history is itself necessarily a narrative. Historians tell their stories as much as do novelists, and through much the same means—by what they bring in and what they leave out, by how they structure their material and to what end.[34] One story (history) seeking to explain another (fiction) can only extend or circumambulate it. Nor can we really ever think of history or context as something that contains fiction. The early American novel, for example, did not sit around waiting for a favorable context in which it could flourish but instead immediately embarked on a program of cultivating the very social context that it required. The relationship runs two ways, which is to say that the connections between the history of story and the story of history are multiple and complex.

To make sense of those connections is to make more story, to advance *this* story instead of *that* story. Yet I hope that I have avoided, in the following chapters, what E. P. Thompson has described as the "condescension of posterity."[35] In as much detail as I thought my forbearing reader would endure, I attempt to explore early American novels as agents and products of social change. Throughout this volume I make many historiographic assumptions (one always does). For example, I see in the early national period a unique instance of cultural formation and transformation. Not only was America attempting to define itself in the aftermath of its Revolution, it was also attempting to constitute itself (literally, in the 1780s, with the framing of the Constitution) against revolution abroad and dissent at home. Just as important, at least for early American book production and print culture, were the substantial changes in the modes of production and the commercialization of culture then beginning throughout the Western world.

Prompted by their own recent political revolution and the changing economics of an unfolding Industrial Revolution, Americans of the early national period continued to realign their attitudes toward established social authorities, a process, as Perry Miller noted, that began almost as soon as the Pilgrims set foot upon American soil, but one greatly accelerated by the end of the eighteenth century.[36] The church more and more lost its traditional powers. Although religion remained a potent force in many individual lives, the structure of religious authority changed demonstrably with revivalism; with the emergence of new denominations, sects, and even religious cults; and with the locus of religious education and religious authority within the home being transferred from the father to the mother. Newspapers, increasingly virulent in their partisan affiliations in the early national period, also attest to a crisis of authority, a crisis most strikingly emblemized by the passage of the Alien and Sedition Acts in John Adams's administration. Pedagogy, too, had become, for the first of many times in American history, a focus of social and political crisis. Nearly every American leader saw the nation at risk unless the majority could be educated to the "right" principles, but how was that worthy end to be accomplished, given the rudimentary system of schooling of the time? In short, the fears of those in authority—expressed in the Alien and Sedition Acts, the attention to mass education, *and* the censure of fiction—serve as eloquent tribute to the turbulence of the era in which the first American novelists plied their trade and produced their art.[37]

In many ways, the novel was the perfect form for this imperfect time. As Mikhail M. Bakhtin argues, prose fiction has been perceived as a *subversive* literary form in every Western society into which it was introduced: subversive of certain class notions of who should and should not be literate; subversive of notions of what is or is not a suitable literary subject matter and form and style; subversive of the term *literature* itself.[38] The novel did not rhyme or scan. It required no knowledge of Latin or Greek, no intermediation or interpretation by cleric or academic. It required, in fact—from reader and writer—virtually no traditional education or classical erudition since, by definition, the novel was new, novel. Furthermore, the novel was, formalistically, voracious. It fed upon and devoured more familiar literary forms such as travel, captivity, and military narratives; political and religious tracts; advice books, chapbooks, penny histories, and almanacs. It appropriated drama (in its dialogic moments) and even (in its epigraphs and endings) poetry. It also appropriated nonliterary forms such as letters (almost one third of the novels written in America before 1820 were epistolary) or diaries as well as traditionally oral forms of culture such as local gossip, rumor, hearsay, folktales. It was a dangerously inchoate form appropriate for and correlative to a country first attempting to formulate itself.

Psychologically, the early novel embraced a new relationship between art and audience, writer and reader, a relationship that replaced the authority of the sermon or Bible with the enthusiasms of sentiment, horror, or adventure, all of which relocate authority in the individual response of the reading self. Speaking directly to that self, the early American novel ideologically represented and encouraged the aspirations of its new readers—aspirations in conflict, at many points, with ideas preached from the pulpit or taught in the common schools. Yet the early novel was not anti-intellectual. On the contrary, in novel after novel we see learning encouraged and find that reading and writing well were valued aspects of heroes and heroines. I argue in the chapters to follow that the novel inspired education by stressing the sentimental and social value of literacy—as seen in group discussions of reading depicted within the plots of novels and in the formation of similar reading groups in every section of America.

In these pages, I will discuss novels on two quite different, yet interrelated, levels. As Lewis Hyde has shown in his remarkable book *The Gift* (subtitled *Imagination and the Erotic Life of Property*), every work of art operates both within a market economy and a gift economy. When the *New England Primer* (ca. 1687) instructs its young readers, "My book and heart shall never part," it speaks to the gift nature of literature.[39] As Hyde notes, "that art that matters to us—which moves the soul, or delights the senses, or offers courage for living, however we choose to describe the experience—that work is received by us as a gift is received."[40] In what ways, then, were the first American fictions gifts to their first readers? Whether a given work is "good" or "bad" literature (especially by contemporary standards) seems to me a less significant matter than the question of what kind of response it engendered and how subtle or persuasive its message and meaning might have been for the reader.[41] At the same time, however, art always has to find some way to exist within a specific economy, and the persistent economic failure of every early American novelist who attempted to support herself or himself by writing fiction attests to the inescapably harsh facts of the market economy of the time. Considering the economics of the early American book trade, how did the novel commence and how did it survive? Why did a small number of American writers continue to produce novels with such little hope of financial remuneration? What was the cash value of the new art and how best could it be sold? These are elemental but crucial questions, and it is to such questions that this study of American fiction now turns.

2 The Book in the New Republic

The book is not an ideal object . . . it is a fabrication made of paper upon which thought symbols are printed. It does not contain thoughts; these must arise in the mind of the comprehending reader. It is a commodity produced for hard cash.
—An eighteenth-century German bookseller

Without him tyrants and humbugs in all countries would have their own way. He is a friend of intelligence and thought, a friend of liberty, of freedom, of law, indeed, the friend of every man who is a friend of order. Of all inventions, of all discoveries in science and art, of all the great results in the wonderful progress of mechanical energy and skill, the Printer is the only product of civilization necessary to the existence of free men.
—Charles Dickens (1850)

What is a book? Is it a commodity, like toothpaste, to be consumed by anyone who can be persuaded (the function of advertising) to buy one particular product instead of another? Or is a book a unique sign-system in which the reader necessarily participates as a producer of meanings, the locus of which is that one particular text? These two books—the book as manufactured artifact and the book as conveyor of meaning—are not the same, and during the course of this study I will discuss each in terms of the other. But I wish to begin more simply: with one book, the book as material fact and economic entity.

Privileging—or at least giving precedence—to that first book should not suggest that socioeconomic factors essentially determine the forms of literature. The process is more complex than that. The first American novelists, for example, were not totally discouraged by the fact that the economics of the early book trade distinctly discouraged American fiction. Furthermore, and as William Charvat some time ago observed, the model for the American book industry is not so much the diadic relationship of, in traditional capitalistic terms, the producer and the consumer, as a triadic interrelationship among the writer, the printer/publisher, and the reader. As Charvat argues: "The book trade is acted upon by both writer and reader, and in receiving their influence the book trade interprets and therefore transmutes it. Correspondingly, the writer and reader dictate to and are dictated to by the book trade."[1]

This complex intermediation of reader, writer, and printer/publisher/bookseller (the tradesmen of the profession) constituted, then as now, the American book industry. The Revolution, fostered by a native press perpetrating the ideology of independence, had encouraged New World printers to expand their trade.[2] Moreover, the suspension of trade with England during the war greatly encouraged local industry—both native printing and the manufacturing of paper, presses, ink, and type. With the resumption of peace and imports, a relatively large class of artisans, craftsmen, and entrepreneurs was already well established in the book trade and anxious both to protect and to extend what had been a recently flourishing business. Trade associations such as the Asylum Company of Journeymen Printers (1800) were formed, partly as professional organizations designed to assure the continuance of the apprentice system, but mostly to pressure Congress to enact protective tariffs for the American book trade.[3] In one form or another, that trade was pursued until nearly every city, town, or village in the new Republic came into contact with the printer or his art—either through a local publisher (usually of a newspaper), a bookseller (who was often part of a larger book-distribution network), a general store (that carried staples of the book trade such as Bibles or almanacs), a literary agent (who annually or semiannually made his way through town), or at the very least an itinerant peddler (who hawked books along with other goods as he made his rural rounds).

By today's standards, however, the book business in the early national period was strikingly small and localized, a situation that changed dramatically during the second quarter of the nineteenth century with the invention of mechanized printing, a technological advance in some ways as impressive and far-reaching as the invention of movable type in the fifteenth century.[4] New methods of transporting books (better roads, shipping routes, and eventually the railway) also vastly altered the print industry during the later nineteenth century, as did increased urbanization. Largely centralized, this new printing industry produced massive quantities of inexpensive books that could be expeditiously distributed to a wide audience. But if the printers of the early national period looked forward to this brave new world of mass publishing, they were still partly grounded in a very different Colonial print world. The supplies of the trade (and especially type) had to be obtained from England; most books in America were imported rather than published at home; and only a limited number of books (chapbooks, almanacs, Bibles, and a few other steady sellers) were readily available to the populace at large. Although the Revolution had officially ended that world, almost half a century would elapse before American publishing would be consolidated into large dynastic houses and cheap books would become big business.

The American novel first appeared during the time when the domestic publishing industry enjoyed a new sense of vigor, nationalism, and professional pride (but not much capital) and when every printer faced the renewed (and debilitating) competition from foreign imports, especially British imports. So the novelist, like the printer of the early period, operated within a transitional book market. An earlier, essentially aristocratic, system (primarily European) had supported through patronage or subscription the works of a relatively limited group of writers. The rising middle class, with its increasingly voracious appetite for books, especially novels, portended a new mass patronage of books based not on a work's appeal to the gentry but on its general popularity. The steadily increasing demand for books by the middle class prompted many writers to try to earn a living by their pen. But, as Martha Woodmansee has noted, in both late eighteenth-century Europe and America, none of "the requisite legal, economic, and political arrangements and institutions were yet in place to support the large number of writers who came forward."[5] The struggles of the book industry during the early national period and the struggles by native American novelists to establish their own genre mirror each other. In both cases, the spirit was willing, even if the economy was not.

The "average" printer of the early national period (surely a historical construct) who brought forth a novel, especially one by an unknown American writer, hoped that the volume might sell several hundred copies, enough to reimburse production costs and perhaps pay something over.[6] But the author only rarely profited by these literary transactions. Although an author such as Noah Webster supported himself handsomely by writing in nonfictional forms, not until the 1820s did America produce a financially successful novelist. James Fenimore Cooper, after publishing *The Spy* in 1821, went on to become, during the course of that decade, the "American Sir Walter Scott" (a comparison he found odious), to sell as many as forty thousand volumes a year and to achieve an average income of some $6,500 annually from his fiction.[7] Susanna Haswell Rowson and Hannah Webster Foster had published extensively before him, but neither of these bestselling novelists realized anything remotely resembling Cooper's financial success, and both supported themselves throughout their lives in ways other than by writing fiction. For a variety of legal and social reasons, their sales did not translate into a commensurate income. Cooper, in contrast, was fortunate enough to begin his career right at the time when the book industry was undergoing the dramatic alternations that made his success possible and even, to a degree, predictable.[8]

Although Susanna Rowson's *Charlotte: A Tale of Truth* (1791)—later known as *Charlotte Temple*—had sold nearly forty thousand copies by the first decade of the nineteenth century, many of the copies were from pirated editions that brought no recompense to either the author or her American publisher. That publisher's first edition, it might also be noted, ran to only one thousand copies.[9] One of the country's most prosperous and sagacious early printers, Mathew Carey simply had no basis for predicting the popularity of Rowson's book. In fact, a first printing of a late eighteenth century American novel typically ran somewhere between three hundred and fifteen hundred copies, so Carey's edition of *Charlotte* was relatively large by the standards of the time. In contrast, by 1825 a press run of ten thousand copies for an American novel was not unheard of; by 1830 the paperback novels or "story papers" that were distributed as "newspapers" through the U.S. postal system were regularly run in editions of thirty thousand copies.[10] Mass publishing had become possible—and profitable—in ways that Carey could only dream of. New copyright laws (to be discussed further in this chapter) also aided later writers. Thus Charles Brockden Brown could complain of pirated English books being sold at a fraction of the price of native products and swamping the American market; on the other hand, Cooper complained of his books being pirated by British companies and being sold in England, often in poorly printed, condensed, and retitled versions designed to appeal to the British reader.[11] In a real sense, the rapid development of American publishing, with the concomitant flourishing of the American novel, after the first quarter of the nineteenth century highlights the obstacles that confronted the earlier publishers and authors—cumbersome printing techniques and inefficient methods for distribution, no national or international copyright laws whereby an author's or publisher's rights could be protected, and a flood of competing European imprints on the American market.

Looking now in more detail at the methods of book production and distribution during the early national period, I would first emphasize that until well into the nineteenth century, printing, publishing, and marketing were usually three sides of the same business. An author was required to contact a printer and contract with him (rarely, her) to have a new book brought before the American public.[12] The author's official recompense would be whatever the printer agreed to pay for the rights to an edition of a certain number. Often the actual recompense was whatever the printer was finally able or willing to pay. The printer's recompense would come from the sale of those same volumes, so the printing shop that was also a publishing establishment was usually a bookstore, too. In this third establishment the printer also had to be his own entrepreneur. Through newspaper and magazine advertisements, through the vital exchange systems with booksellers in other areas, through literary agents, and through book subscriptions the printer sought to sell his product. Such industry was required. Since publishers were often small local businesses in a large land with a sparse and scattered population, it was difficult to gain a large audience for most books. But fiction especially was badly served by regional publication and limited availability. It is significant, in this regard, that until 1820 local printers (independent printers outside the major cities) still published over 50 percent of American fiction, even though fiction— unlike, say, newspapers or almanacs—was not really "local." By midcentury, however, when the novel business was flourishing, only 8 percent of American fiction was still published by local, regional printers.[13]

The early publisher had to make difficult decisions during a time of uncertain and rapidly changing literary tastes. Consistent with the sectarian or revivalist religions and the volatile partisan politics that divided society, reading was split into different camps, too. There was a demand for such literary entertainment as captivity narratives, travel books, the new personalized histories and biographies (all ostensibly nonfiction), and especially for novels. There was also a vogue in self-improvement books, ranging from reading-and-writing manuals (including dictionaries, primers, readers, and penmanship books) to books on etiquette, fashion, or even hairstyles.[14] Which works to publish and where to sell them? As publishers also knew, some old Colonial standbys, Bibles and other traditional religious works such as *Pilgrim's Progress*, as well as occasional political pamphlets and almanacs, were often extraordinarily popular. Thomas Paine's *Common Sense* reputedly sold one hundred fifty thousand copies and sparked a revolution.[15] Benjamin Franklin's *Poor Richard's Almanac* sold ten thousand copies per year; Nathaniel Ames's almanac sold sixty-five thousand copies annually. In one small town, Leominster, Massachusetts, for example, Elizabeth Carroll Reilly has determined that in 1772 Thomas Legate, a local storekeeper, purchased over twelve dozen almanacs—enough for three quarters of the town's families.[16] We might also note Noah Webster's 1803 boast that his *A Grammatical Institute of the English Language . . . Part I* (1783), later retitled *The American Spelling Book*, had sold 3 million copies.[17] Indeed, the Reverend Elijah R. Sabin, in the preface to his novel, *The Life and Reflections of Charles Observator* (1816), found it necessary "to obviate" the "common objection" that "there are already too many books in the world!"[18]

The problem for the printer, then, was not that there was no money to be made in books but in determining which books made money. The prodigious success of a few titles made the matter especially difficult. Why did Susanna Rowson's *Charlotte* and Hannah Webster Foster's *The Coquette* (1797) sell so well? Even more curious was the appeal of the anonymous *The History of Constantius and Pulchera* (1794), a book that was reprinted in both cheap and relatively expensive editions in Connecticut, New Hampshire, New York, and Maryland. How could a publisher gauge the demand (or lack of one) for a specific title? Would a book (especially a novel) offend censorious critics? Would it be lively enough for an increasingly secularized public? Those decisions were all the more crucial in that for most printers there was little margin for error. Isaiah Thomas or Mathew Carey skillfully plumbed and primed the market, but printing in the late eighteenth and early nineteenth century was not, in general, a remunerative profession. When Benjamin Franklin founded, for example, the Franklin Society in 1788, he did so in order to provide for aging, indigent printers or their orphaned progeny.[19] As both the purpose and the bylaws of this benevolent organization attest, printers often left their survivors nothing but debts. Few publishing establishments maintained a stable business over an extended period of time. Partners, locations, and printing shops were often changed, and such changes were often designed to skirt insolvency or bankruptcy. In fact (and a telling fact it is), out of all the hundreds of Colonial and late-eighteenth-century American publishers, only one establishment—that of Mathew Carey—survived until well into the nineteenth century.[20]

Operating with little capital and considerable overhead, these printers of the early national period knew that their business was precarious and that one major miscalculation could spell ruin. They consequently tended to be both hardheaded in committing themselves to some publishing venture and cautious in carrying it out. The market would be carefully assessed and so would the cost of the project, especially such negotiable terms as an author's payment (or expenses, for the author was sometimes required to bear part or all of the cost of the printing). Sometimes a publisher might advertise a book in advance of publication to stake (according to the unwritten laws of the trade) his claim to a title or to see how much interest a particular title elicited from prospective readers.[21] Many titles consequently exist today as ghost books, works that were never published at all.[22] Faced with the uncertain prospects of a new project, a publisher might decide that it would be wiser to publish another edition of a known work by a known writer (European or American) instead of taking a chance on an untested book and author. Printers were particularly cautious with the early American novel. Socially and morally suspect, the form was also new and untried in its American guise. To cut costs, most novels not only were published in small editions but were themselves small. Early American novels were rarely longer than three hundred pages and sometimes shorter than a hundred pages. It should also come as no surprise that most early printers, like most authors, brought forth only one American novel during the course of a whole career.

The early publisher who decided to print a particular volume generally did so in a cottage-industry fashion. His shop might have one or two indentured apprentices, often as young as six or seven years of age. The apprentices took care of such unpleasant chores as "treading out the pelts," literally stomping on sheep pelts that had soaked for several days in the slop pail, a first step in making the ink balls necessary to ink the type. Apprentices and the printer's children, too, would help with cleaning, would sort type, and when strong enough would actually operate the heavy presses. The work was hard. Several eighteenth-century accounts describe the usual build and gait of one who had long served at the press—an enormously developed right arm, a limp from having used the right foot on the "step" in order to make the "pull," and sometimes even distended or permanently dislocated shoulders.[23] The work was also general. To supplement the income from the press, the printer's wife might run the town post office out of the print shop; often she sold books (those imported or exchanged from different booksellers as well as those printed in the shop) and other goods—everything from household items and her own handicrafts to theater or lottery tickets, stationery, pens, ink, and fancy imported products. The printer was responsible for everything else: keeping track of supplies (before 1800, many of these were imported; after 1800, they were typically manufactured in the shop itself), setting type, seeing books through the entire publication process, and overseeing the sale of the published run.

The printer's main business, in short, was to turn the author's manuscript into a salable commodity and then to sell it. Conducting that business, he assumed functions that would be later delegated to the authors themselves or to specialized editors. To start with, what we might term the printer's artistic control usually began with his deciphering the original handwritten text, for rarely would he query the author about smudged, illegible words or problematic passages. The usual procedure was to insert any word or words that seemed to fit. In addition, the printer would silently "correct" (not always accurately) any mistakes in the author's punctuation, spelling, and usage.[24] Typically, the printer did the only proofreading, too, and did so as much from an artisan's concern for his own craft as from any commitment to the integrity of the author's text.[25] Even though printers often boasted of the accuracy of a text, it is clear, from surveying the hundreds of editions and "duplicate" copies of American novels published prior to 1820, that one area in which the individual printer fully exercised printerly prerogatives was in the physical layout of both the page and the book as a whole.[26] Especially important, in this context, was the selection of typefaces, since varying type sizes and different spacings between letters were regularly used for emphasis.[27] A fairly innocuous sentence could easily be given a more sensational cast by the strategic italicizing or capitalizing of words such as SEDUCTION or INCEST. Such printing devices naturally helped to sell books; such devices also testified that the book sold thereby was a product of *both* the writer's and the printer's art. Sometimes the advertisements for books even emphasized the printer's art more than the writer's, as in the ad of Isaiah Thomas, Jr., for Sukey Vickery's *Emily Hamilton* (1803): "The work will be neatly printed on good paper and a fair type, in a 12mo. volume, and will make about 300 pages. The price to Subscribers will be 75 cents, neatly bound and lettered."[28]

Intermediating between author and audience, the printer played a crucial role in shaping early American culture. Printers determined what possible volumes would become available, in what number, at what price, and where and how they would be sold. As Bernard Bailyn observes, printers were "at once the handicraftsmen, entrepreneurs, and cultural leaders" who were "second in importance only to the clergy as leaders of opinion and public educators."[29] The new American novel could not have been established had the printers of the time decided that Bibles, broadsides, and Fanny Burney or Robert Bage would sell better, and then devoted their efforts to that end. But the printers had their reasons, as businessmen and cultural leaders, for recognizing a possible market for a native literature, for fostering that market, for, in effect, attending as both midwife and godfather to the birth of a new American literary form.

A book's trials, however, were by no means over once some printer looked upon it favorably and was persuaded to bring forth an edition. The volumes of that edition then had to be sold, which was always a difficult task in a large and sparsely settled country that lacked any effective means of generally distributing goods. Many printers were located in smaller cities and towns, and even those in the larger cities did not have access to a concentrated population comparable to England's London. Whereas a million people lived in late eighteenth-century London, there were less than 45,000 in Philadelphia (then America's largest city) and some 20,000 lived in Boston. According to the first American census of 1790, the combined population of America's five largest cities was only 123,475, and the total population of the United States was 3,929,624.[30] It was not a demography that made for effective marketing. The population was widely scattered; the cities were relatively small; the local markets were quickly saturated. Matters were further complicated in that the one effective means of transporting large quantities of books was by sea, which meant that the coastal cities were readily supplied by volumes printed abroad. Besides, the mass of the growing population more and more lived beyond the older coastal cities and depended mostly on rudimentary roads, navigable waterways (including some early canals), and itinerant tradesmen for their commercial dealings with the larger world. In such circumscribed settings, many books circulated only locally, and writers in one area were often unaware of what their fellows in another were doing—if, indeed, they even knew of the existence of those fellows. Joseph Dennie, in a letter to Royall Tyler regarding the Walpole, New Hampshire, publication of Tyler's *The Algerine Captive*, aptly summarizes the too-common consequence of the combined problems of local printing and precarious distribution: "Your novel has been examined by the few and approved. It is however extremely difficult for the Bostonians to supply themselves with a book that slumbers in a stall at Walpole, supposed, by the latest and most accurate advertisements, to be situated 400 miles north of their meridian."[31]

Four hundred miles was a formidable distance. To travel by stagecoach from Boston to Walpole might take two weeks or longer. Nor was it an inexpensive trip. In 1800, a stagecoach journey could cost as much as $1 for ten miles.[32] Such fares were more than the early book trade could bear. Both booksellers and books, along with the whole budding manufacturing economy of the early Republic, required more expeditious, efficient, and inexpensive methods of transportation. Obviously mindful of this general problem, Isaiah Thomas purchased shares in several of the new turnpikes of the turn of the century—the Worcester and Stafford Turnpike, the Sixteenth Massachusetts Turnpike, and the Templeton and Fitzwilliam turnpikes.[33] These new roads—sometimes toll roads, sometimes supported by local subscription—were being built in Connecticut and Massachusetts, in New York, New Jersey, and parts of Pennsylvania. At the same time, too, a complex system of canals connecting rivers and towns in the Northeast was also begun. Such important early canals as those in Massachusetts on the Connecticut River at South Hadley or at Turner's Falls and, later, the Middlesex Canal at Lowell allowed goods to be moved in large quantities and at relatively low cost.

William Charvat has argued that Philadelphia and, later, New York began to replace Boston as the nation's publishing capital precisely because these cities had, through newly available waterways, relatively easy access to the ever-growing western regions of the country, which increasingly constituted a major market for American imprints.[34] Philadelphia's growing ascendancy dated, however, from the Revolutionary War era. Numerous printers had established themselves there during the war to print government pamphlets and tracts. Philadelphia was also the most important site for manufacturing presses, largely because one man, Adam Ramage, the new nation's finest press builder, had settled in that city in 1790 and had been followed by others who wanted to learn—and to improve upon—his trade. Furthermore, Pennsylvania was also a center for papermaking in America. There were over one hundred paper mills in the state by 1800 and just over two hundred by the time of the 1810 census.[35] Of course, problems of transportation applied as much to presses and paper as to the finished product, the printed book. And happily situated though he may have been—with the materials for his business close at hand, living in the largest city, and with easy access to an ever-larger market—the Philadelphia printer still had to sell his product to survive.

The imprint on the title page of the first edition of Charles Brockden Brown's *Arthur Mervyn* (1799–1800) indicates the way in which one Philadelphia printer sought to carry his books to the larger market: "Printed and published by H. Maxwell . . . and sold by Messrs. T. Dobson, R. Campbell, H. and P. Rice, A. Dickins, and the principal booksellers in the neighbouring states." Confronting a growing demand for books (both those published in America and those imported from abroad), printers established and elaborated an extensive network of booksellers. Volumes published by Mathew Carey in Philadelphia, for example, turned up in bookstores as far away as Boston and New Orleans, while Benjamin Franklin had contracted with such printers as Williams Parks and William Hunter to sell his books in the vast colony of Virginia.[36] Perhaps the most complex network in the new Republic was established by Isaiah Thomas. This marvel of makeshift practicality was comprised of loose trade agreements with scattered booksellers, agreements Thomas sustained when they seemed profitable but abandoned when they proved unprofitable or if a particular bookseller seemed unreliable or dishonest. These agreements did get books to the outlying markets, as is clear from an advertisement in the *Farmer's Weekly Museum* of Walpole, New Hampshire, an ad that ran almost weekly from July 24 to October 1, 1798: "The following Books, with many others, just received from Worcester and Boston, may be had of Thomas and Thomas at the Walpole Bookstore as cheap as either of those places." Included in the offer were three new American novels, *The Algerine Captive*, *The American Bee*, and *The Female Review* (all published the previous year) along with several popular British standbys—*Pamela*, *Robinson Crusoe*, and *The Vicar of Wakefield*—as well as schoolbooks, spelling books, dictionaries, and assorted supplies such as playing cards, ink, lead pencils, slate pencils, marbled paper, and blank books (bound unprinted books in which one could keep accounts or diaries). The advertisement concludes: "Orders from a distance, for books or newspapers, strictly adhered to. A liberal discount to country traders." The discount to the country trader was a common way in which the early American printer brought others into his distributing network. These country traders, whether itinerants or general storekeepers, served the most rural population. They often obtained books not from booksellers but from large dry-goods merchants in the major cities.[37] Their stock-in-trade was mostly established best-sellers, Bibles, hymnbooks, and almanacs. Thomas encouraged both groups to expand their literary offerings and to purchase their expanded stock directly from him.

What effect did the improved transportation systems and the expanding publisher's networks have on the shape of American fiction? Obviously, that is a difficult question to answer. But it is worth noting that nearly all of America's novels published prior to 1820 were first published in the North. There were exceptions, such as George Fowler's *A Flight to the Moon; or The Vision of Randalthus* (1813) and John Neal's *Keep Cool* (1817), both published in Baltimore; or (Adam Douglass's) *The Irish Emigrant* (1817) published in Winchester, Virginia; or (Jesse Lynch Holman's) *The Prisoners of Niagara; or, Errors of Education* (1810) published in Frankfort, Kentucky. But these volumes were all issued after 1809, with only marginal success, and none enjoyed a second edition. To put the matter in its most general terms, the new American novels tended to do best where they could best be distributed. As William J. Gilmore has argued, the vagaries of an imperfect distribution system governed both trade and society: "Economic growth and social differentiation of a township were, to a large extent, a function of geography and transportation networks. All levels of cultural participation . . . were partly dependent upon this same interrelationship of geography and transportation. All printed items traveled along the same roads and rivers as shoes and sheep, and were inhibited by the same mountains and mud." Gilmore even finds that levels of elementary literacy "vary directly with the level of involvement in the market economy" as well as with access to print culture.[38] It is interesting to speculate in this connection on how different the structure of American literature might be had the South had better roads or a more active publishing industry or been more accessible to the major Northern publishing centers in the years after the Revolution. The American Renaissance well might have had a Southern drawl instead of a distinctly Yankee twang.[39]

Hawkers also helped a cumbersome book distribution system to work. Essentially traveling salesmen, they supplied booksellers in little towns and villages or dealt directly with individual buyers who otherwise had no ready access to the book trade. In the tradition of chapmen—itinerants who had previously sold mostly chapbooks, penny histories, pamphlets, ballads, and inexpensive children's books—the turn-of-the-century peddlers carried the latest literary products of the cities out into the hinterland. The increasing need for this service was perhaps most marked by the changing reputation of the hawker. The profession by the end of the eighteenth century had lost some of the stigma of Puritan and Colonial days when laws had been passed forbidding hawkers from selling their wares in Massachusetts and even forbidding "taverners, alehouse keepers, common victuallers and retailers" from "receiv[ing] or giv[ing] any entertainment to any hawker, peddler or petty chapman."[40] These laws (primarily resulting from a suspicion of the printed word and a fear of the harm it might wreak upon the "unwary" rural population) were no longer enforced even before the Revolution, and the peddler with his horsedrawn wagon continued to ply his wares through rural postrevolutionary America, often selling the occasional novel along with his pots and pans, sometimes selling the occasional pot or pan along with his novels, Bibles, and other books. Occasionally, a charismatic peddler became almost a folk hero to the populace who awaited his arrival not only for books and goods, but also for news of events, fashions, and scandals in distant places. Correspondingly, the literary peddler became more sensitive to the book-buying needs and interests of the people.[41]

One obvious way to successful bookselling was taken by literary agents who concentrated on the larger and more accessible country towns and especially those such as Andover, Massachusetts, or Exeter, New Hampshire, that had some commitment to the values of education. But other agents were required to go beyond the main highways and byways. Long before Willy Loman, the outposts of New England tested many a salesman. In the farthest reaches of New England, in the territories of the Northwest ordinance, on the Eastern seaboard, and throughout the Deep South, selling books was difficult and often thankless work. John Tebbel discusses one agent whose meticulous accounts attest to an average sale of a book a day, the profit from which would barely cover the cost of the agent's meals on the road. Nor was this unusual. James Gilreath has argued that most literary agents were forced to pursue their profession only seasonally and supplemented their income from book peddling through other trades such as farming, blacksmithing, clockmaking, or cordwaining; many worked as literary agents only a short time before returning to more lucrative and less demanding occupations.[42] Nevertheless, some agents still rose to the challenge posed by this difficult profession.

The most successful, the most popular, and certainly the most colorful of the early book peddlers was undoubtedly Mason Locke Weems. Parson Weems (as he was affectionately known) traveled extensively throughout New York, New Jersey, Pennsylvania, Maryland, Virginia, the Carolinas, and Georgia, selling Mathew Carey's stock, including Weems's own *The Life of George Washington* (1808), a steady seller in the first part of the nineteenth century. Timing his appearances to coincide with country fairs, elections, market days, or other local events, Weems would enter onto the scene crying out "Seduction! Revolution! Murder!" A literary Friar Tuck, boisterous and charismatic, Weems was also a shrewd master of the literary marketplace. As he traveled around the country selling books, he also constantly sounded out booksellers and individual readers as to their literary preferences and then shaped his own impressionistic biographies accordingly, thereby anticipating the contemporary movie or television practice of polling the prospective audience and then creating the desired product. In addition, Weems advertised future projects at the same time that he sold his present stock, thus eliminating some of the vagaries of distribution by getting a sense of audience demand even as he also effectively fostered that demand.[43] Weems profited extensively from both his writing and his selling. His own highly fictionalized biographies were immensely popular, and once he demonstrated his success as an agent, he was able to negotiate with Carey for a 25 percent straight commission instead of the usual 5 percent for which he had first worked.[44]

Since Weems met the readers, talked with them, and knew their literary preferences as well as anyone in America, he regularly advised Carey on how best to conduct his business: "Let [the books] be of the gay and sprightly kind," he counseled his employer. "Novels, decent plays, elegant Histories, etc. Let the Moral & Religious be as highly dulcified as possible."[45] Weems especially advocated the publishing of fiction. Carey, of course, printed both European and American novels (including the best-selling *Charlotte*) and imported still other titles, so on this score there was no real difference between the two men. On a related topic, however, there was. In letter after letter, Weems argued that Carey's books—especially the entertainments the public craved—were too expensive for the average rural buyer. Here Weems's counsel was at odds with Carey's costs—and with Weems's, too, it might be added. The manufacturing and distribution expenses of the time simply did not allow for book prices that the public could generally afford—an impasse that would not be resolved for a few more decades. Later technological advances—such as horse- and steam-powered presses that replaced the old manually operated presses, the invention of rollers that accomplished in one motion the inking previously performed laboriously by hand, the invention of the Napier-Hoe cylinder press, and the production of machine-made paper—allowed the American publisher of the second quarter of the nineteenth century to print faster and cheaper than at any time previously in Western history and to produce thereby books that were genuinely affordable by the masses. But before that time, Weems had clearly sounded the direction in which publishing had to progress.

How much did turn-of-the-century books costs? The question is difficult to answer if we attempt to translate prices of the time into current figures. The whole structure of salaries and costs was different, and we cannot simply discount backward for two centuries of fluctuating inflation. A good estimate might be that a typical late eighteenth-century novel would have cost approximately three to four times more than an equivalent hardcover volume today (when measured against current wages and consumer indices).[46] But a more meaningful measure would be in terms of a late-eighteenth-century economy. In 1800, a carpenter in Massachusetts earned $1 per day, an unskilled laborer half that much. A pound of sugar cost $.13, a pair of leather shoes $.80, and cotton cloth $1 a yard.[47] A novel typically cost between $.75 and $1.50 (although one pirated edition of the popular *The History of Constantius and Pulchera*, paperbound and only 11 cm high, sold for only $.25).[48] A common day laborer in Massachusetts had to work two days to buy a copy of *Wieland* (1798). For the same amount, he could purchase a bushel of potatoes and a half bushel of corn. The cost of books was less clear for one class of people most likely to want to buy them—schoolteachers. Their wages fluctuated dramatically, depending on the wealth of the community as well as the qualifications, and sometimes the gender, of the teacher. For example, a "qualified woman teacher" in Connecticut could earn $.67 per week (board with local families being included in the salary), whereas "a man of culture and experience" might receive as much as $20 per month in addition to board in an affluent community.[49] Ethan Allen Greenwood, who would later become one of the prominent painters of his generation, earned $3 a month at his first teaching job in rural Massachusetts at the turn of the century, and then $14 a month at his second. From Greenwood's comprehensive accounts, we also know what many of his expenses were. For $.37 he might have dinner at a local tavern or lodging at an inn for one night, while $.20 would cover the cost of a week's washing. His firewood cost $2.75 a month (twice that much in severe weather), and a stagecoach ride in Connecticut from Suffield to Hartford cost $1.12. At the end of a typical month, there would be little left for luxuries such as a novel, and we know that Greenwood, an avid reader, mostly borrowed his books instead of buying them until well into his prosperous middle years.[50]

The cost of books was high for anyone in the new Republic, but it was almost prohibitively so for rural citizens. One of the main complaints of the twelve hundred farmers who participated in Shays's Rebellion of 1786–87 was that they simply did not have enough currency, a lack that plagued many rural citizens until well into the nineteenth century. The problem was sometimes partly alleviated by relying on "country pay," a barter system among families, local businesses, and itinerant peddlers whereby farm produce and products of home industry were exchanged for manufactured goods.[51] Sometimes books and other printed matter were part of this rural market-exchange system as is evident from an advertisement run in several issues of a struggling newspaper published in Springfield, Massachusetts: "Those gentlemen who engaged for their papers in grain are once more requested to make immediate payment, as the printers are in much want of that article."[52] But printers also needed paper and other supplies for which they could not always exchange the finished products of their art. Consider, in this context, another advertisement published on the end sheet of a turn-of-the-century novel: "PRINTING in all its GREAT VARIETY, performed on Reasonable Terms by I. Thomas, Jr. Worcester. Said Thomas keeps a large Variety of Books which he will sell very low *for Cash*."[53] Cash was the preferred medium of exchange for all printers, either at the time of purchase or as soon afterward as possible. Credit was, however, widely extended, especially to farmers and planters, who often received an annual payment for crops and then paid (or did not pay) their bills accordingly. The account books of Mathew Carey in Philadelphia, Isaiah Thomas in Worcester, Massachusetts, and William Hunter in Williamsburg, Virginia, all reveal that buying books on time was commonplace and accounted for as much as 70 percent of annual sales.[54]

Even if books could occasionally be purchased with chickens, salt pork, or a promissory note, they were not necessities, and, for many, late eighteenth-century America afforded few luxuries. As Samuel Griswold Goodrich ("Peter Parley"), a popular nineteenth-century writer, later recalled, writing of the small town in Connecticut in which he lived in 1790:

> Money was scarce, wages being about fifty cents a day, though these were generally paid in meat, vegetables, and other articles of use—seldom in money. . . . Books and newspapers—which are now diffused even among the country towns so as to be in the hands of all, young and old—were then scarce, and were read respectfully, as if they were grave matters, demanding thought and attention. . . . Even the young approached a book with reverence, and a newspaper with awe. How the world has changed![55]

Books were expensive; they were difficult to sell; yet the publisher's economic survival depended on sales. Sales in advance were the best sales of all in that they allowed for a more accurate calculation of possible profit. It is not surprising, then, that a subscription campaign sometimes arranged by a traveling agent such as Weems often preceded the sale (either by the printer or the agent) of the published volume and often determined whether that volume would be published. But subscription, too, had its drawbacks. Consumers were reluctant to pay in advance for a product that could not be examined in advance. Rural readers might well wonder if they would ever see the literary agent again after he had collected their deposits and departed, and they had little faith in the probity of printers they did not know. Would the publisher deliver what his agent had promised? Was his agent legitimate? What recourse had they if the purchased product was not produced or not delivered? Not even famous European authors could be assured of American subscription sales. Rousseau's *The Social Contract*, published in Albany, New York, in 1797, secured only 207 subscribers; Montesquieu's *The Spirit of Laws* (which would become a "classic" in its imported, European editions) simply could not raise the three hundred subscribers necessary to make a 1787 American imprint feasible, and so an American edition was delayed until 1802.[56]

When established authors such as Rousseau and Montesquieu could not attract subscribers for their major works, then why would an unknown American's as yet unpublished novel do better? The printer's aim was to cover, through subscription sales, the cost of issuing the volume, which for an edition of one thousand copies for a novel of the size of Charles Brockden Brown's *Arthur Mervyn; or, Memoirs of the Year 1793, First Part*, might run to some $500.[57] An American novel selling at, say, $1 per copy (the cost of the first volume of *Arthur Mervyn*) simply could not attract the necessary subscribers to repay its initial production costs. Isaiah Thomas, Jr., tried to raise subscriptions from the inhabitants of Worcester County, Massachusetts, for the first novel to be published in that area and promised to publish the names should three hundred people subscribe. The names were not printed with *Emily Hamilton*, presumably because the campaign was not successful, and the book was published on other terms. Moreover, when we do find subscription lists bound with early novels, there are always fewer than two hundred entries: in Rowson's *Trials of the Human Heart* (1795), some 140 names; in Herman Mann's *Female Review* (1797), just under 200 names; in Samuel Relf's *Infidelity, or the Victims of Sentiment* (1797), 146 entries; in the anonymous *Humanity in Algiers* (1801), approximately 150 names. The publisher could hardly expect a profit from any of these editions if the subscription list represented the likely market for his book. Again, there were strange vagaries in the early book trade, for some volumes did attract subscribers. A book by the feminist Judith Sargent Murray, *The Gleaner* (1798)—which includes the novella "Story of Margaretta"—drew 675 subscribers; Daniel Bryan's *The Mountain Muse: Comprising the Adventures of Daniel Boone* (1813), a verse narrative, had a phenomenal 1,350 subscribers from Connecticut, Kentucky, Louisiana, Maryland, New York, North Carolina, Ohio, Pennsylvania, South Carolina, and—the most by far— Virginia. Obviously, given the right subject, the right circumstances, and the right promotion, a book could do extraordinarily well. The problem was to get all of those particulars right.

As I have shown, buying novels in quantity (either by subscription or after publication) was well beyond the means of common people at the end of the eighteenth century. Yet there is evidence that those of modest to low income increasingly read many books. Ethan Allen Greenwood read nearly a volume a day even during his poorest student days. But he largely borrowed these books by joining three libraries—a fraternity library, a social library, and a circulating library—and literally thousands of other readers (especially novel readers) did essentially the same. Book borrowing was singularly intertwined with not just the rapid growth of reading and readerships but with an increasing demand for novels. In the succinct formulation of Robert B. Winans: "The increase in the number of circulating libraries was largely the result of the increasing demand for novels; the general growth of the reading public was caused primarily by the novel."[58]

The circulating libraries were the least expensive to join and were most directly linked to the popularity of fiction. In general, however, the development of a library system made books available to more readers than ever before, and, conversely, the upsurge in the number of libraries indicates the increasing avidity of early American readers as well as the changing demography of advanced literacy skills. Jesse H. Shera, for example, has calculated that between 1731 (the founding of the first library in New England) and 1800, a total of 376 social libraries were founded in America, 266 of which were founded in the decade from 1791 to 1800.[59] By the end of the century, most larger cities had several libraries catering to different classes and different tastes; even small towns generally boasted at least one library. The libraries, in short, helped to solve a major problem of distribution in the early national period in that they made books both accessible and affordable to a rapidly growing and largely new class of readers.

Many of the early American libraries were founded with the same rationale (and for the same unprivileged group of potential readers) as the first one of 1731. Realizing there were far more books that he wanted to read than he could afford, a young printer, Benjamin Franklin, drew up a plan for a "public subscription library" and set out to find prospective subscribers: "So few were the readers at that time in Philadelphia and the majority of us so poor that I was not able with great industry to find more than fifty persons, mostly young tradesmen, willing to pay down for this purpose forty shillings each and ten shillings per annum. With this little fund we began. . . . The library was open one day in the week for lending [books] to subscribers. . . . The institution soon manifested its utility, was imitated by other towns and in other provinces."[60] The demand for reading became more widespread, especially among women of all classes and workers of both sexes, and was soon reflected in the early fiction itself. In *The Factory Girl* (1814), the first novel of factory life in America, the heroine Mary Burham organizes the other workers to form a school and a library much on the Franklin model.[61] Or we might briefly note the bylaws of the Union Harwinton Library, which was begun by seventeen residents of a small Connecticut village fifteen miles west of Hartford. The Harwinton subscribers leveled such fines as $.01 "for each blot or blur in any book in any part where there is no reading and of the size of three common letters" or $.02 "for tearing a leaf through the margin"; and the library's treasurer carefully recorded each blot or tear in the group's small but precious stock of books.[62]

The social or subscription libraries were supplemented by two other kinds of public libraries, the institutional libraries and the circulating libraries. The differences between these three types frequently were blurred. In general, institutional libraries such as those at the men's colleges were not accessible to the mass population, whereas social libraries typically charged shareholders an annual membership fee and normally also required the purchasing of shares (sometimes for as much as $20 a share). These latter libraries, such as the New York Society Library, consequently tended to serve the more affluent segments of society and to select their holdings accordingly. In contrast, the circulating library was a commercial library (typically owned by a bookseller) that stocked the most popular books of the day and rented them at terms affordable even by common laborers. Libraries such as the H. Caritat Library in New York, the Philadelphia Circulating Library, and the Circulating Library of W. Pelham of Massachusetts charged only $6 a year and frequently allowed subscribers to pay their subscriptions by the year, half-year, quarter, or even month—a concession to those who might not have much ready cash on hand. For a relatively small fee, a borrower was allowed, at the Philadelphia Library, "three single volumes, or the whole set of any work, which are not to be charged oftener than once in each day."[63] The most intrepid reader on a modest income thus had access to an ample supply of books that could also be further circulated among friends and family members. There are numerous eighteenth-century accounts of the serving maid who read her mistress's novels as she carried them home from the library or of one woman reading a novel aloud to others as they quilted or spun. The circle of readers, in other words, extended well beyond the list of a library's subscribers.[64]

It should be clear that the burgeoning library system allowed many readers to read more books than ever before, and we also know, from the holdings and the records of these libraries, that more and more of the books read were novels. This tendency, however, was resisted in some quarters. For example, the Concord (Massachusetts) Charitable Library Society (1795–1800) explicitly excluded all novels except the Reverend Jeremy Belknap's *The Foresters* and Oliver Goldsmith's *The Vicar of Wakefield* from its holdings. So absolute was the proscription that when one woman patron brought her copy of *The Coquette* into the library, the librarian made a point of noting in the records that this book was privately owned and not part of the collection.[65] But such dedication to the antifiction cause was rare, and especially so with the circulating libraries that catered to the less affluent and had to anticipate the tastes of prospective borrowers in order to survive. Here fiction prevailed. Sometimes as much as 75 percent of a collection consisted of novels. The H. Caritat Library in New York, for example, offered approximately 1,450 titles under the heading "Romances, Novels, Adventures, & c."[66] Of this same library, John Davis, an Englishman traveling through the United States at the end of the eighteenth century, humorously observed:

> Its shelves could scarcely sustain the weight of *Female Frailty*, the *Posthumous Daughter*, and the *Cavern of Woe*; they required the aid of a carpenter to support the burden of the *Cottage-on-the-Moor*, the *House of Tynian*, and the *Castles of Athlin and Dunbayne*; or they groaned under the multiplied editions of the *Devil in Love*, *More Ghosts*, and *Rinaldo Rinaldini*. Novels were called for by the young and old; from the tender virgin of thirteen, whose little heart went pit-a-pat at the approach of a beau; to the experienced matron of three score, who could not read without spectacles.[67]

It might also be observed that the H. Caritat catalog of 1804 included a lengthy defense of both fiction *and* circulating libraries, clearly implying the connection between the two (although part of the defense itself is not so convincing): "The decrease of drunkenness in this country is, perhaps, owing to the introduction of circulating libraries, which may be considered as temples erected by literature to attract the votaries of Bacchus."[68]

As should be obvious, these early libraries were the single most important source of books (especially novels) for many new readers and thus served as a bridge between the restricted print world of the Colonial reader and the world of the mid-nineteenth-century reader for whom books were available virtually everywhere. Libraries cultivated the "fashion of reading," Franklin observed, and consequently created the audience—the consumers—who were necessary to support the expensive technology of mechanized printing in the next century.[69] In the process of doing so, they also supported the more elementary printing industry of their own time. First and most obviously, the libraries themselves, in effect, pooled the limited money that individual patrons could spend on books and served as a significant market for publishers. Isaiah Thomas provides one example of the common practice of catering to institutional buyers: "New Supply of Books," Thomas advertised in a newspaper circulated throughout Vermont and New Hampshire, "a Good Chance for Purchasers of Social and Private Libraries."[70] Second, and psychologically speaking, the libraries also encouraged patrons to spend money, personally and privately, on books. Like reading, book buying can also become fashionable, a habit, and readers often wish not just to read books but to possess them, to have them to turn to in times of crisis or moments of joy, to reread, to annotate, to mark as their own, and to display (as the symbol of their own ideas, feelings, and status). In short, the vogue of book borrowing fostered the vogue of book buying. Finally, many booksellers recognized the advantages of libraries and immediately opened their own. The necessity of maintaining a large stock-in-trade was thereby turned at once from a publisher's liability into a librarian's asset. Books could be advertised as being available for buying or borrowing, and the products not sold could be rented out as a source of continuing income.

My discussion of the book in the early Republic has so far considered the printer/publisher, the literary agent, the proprietor of the lending libraries, and the reader (who increasingly could borrow what she or he could not afford to buy). One other crucial participant in the book trade is obviously missing—the author. That absence is not an oversight. The early national era antedated the Romantic period's notions of the author as the prime creator of art and a concomitant critical privileging of the artist's intentions.[71] During the postrevolutionary period, a residual Puritan emphasis on relating "truth" or "history" still underscored the older notion that the writer merely formulated what everybody already knew. Such an appraisal did not encourage crediting the writer for any significant contribution to the business of publishing books. Consider, for example, this eighteenth-century definition of book:

> *Book*, either numerous sheets of white paper that have been stitched together in such a way that they can be filled with writing; or, a highly useful and convenient instrument constructed of printed sheets variously bound in cardboard, paper, vellum, leather, etc. for presenting the truth to another in such a way that it can be conveniently read and recognized. Many people work on this ware before it is complete and becomes an actual book in this sense. The scholar and the writer, the papermaker, the type founder, the typesetter and the printer, the proofreader, the publisher, the book binder, sometimes even the gilder and the brass-worker, etc. Thus many mouths are fed by this branch of manufacture.[72]

Or not fed. As is obvious from this definition, the author was still conceived as a minor participant in the process of literary manufacture and one whose cash expenditures were also minor. There was no compelling *economic* reason to support his or her labors, and, like it or not, for most authors during the early national period, writing still was, in Rollo Silver's phrase, a "vanity business."[73]

History has not been kind to the early American novelists. Relatively few manuscript collections exist of their works, and it is not always easy to determine what motivated them to write and against what obstacles. But what does survive confirms their subordinate place within the business of publishing. For example, the correspondence between Royall Tyler and his publisher, Joseph Nancrede, effectively illustrates these prejudices and practices at work. Despite the flattery that pervades Nancrede's letters to the author, it is clear that, in business terms, he views Tyler's contribution to the proposed project over which they contended as virtually negligible. Although he had promised to pay $250 for a "Cosmography" for children, as the publication date came closer, Nancrede informed Tyler that, instead, he would pay him only with two hundred copies of the book. Tyler responded that he would not accept less than a $200 *cash* payment, a demand Nancrede peremptorily refused in his letter of March 7, 1800: "You have a very exalted idea of the price of a manuscript, and a very diminutive one of the money of the Bookseller. If you expect that the labour—or, as you term it, the amusement of eight days—will yield you 'absolutely' two hundred dollars in cash, I ought to inform you that I cannot have anything to do with the undertaking." Nancrede also attempted in the same letter to smooth over the situation by comparing Judge Tyler favorably with Johnson, Pope, Swift, Voltaire, and Rousseau. But the fact remains, the "Cosmography" was never published. As Tyler insisted: "If writing for the public is attended with no more profit, I had rather file legal process in my attorney's office, and endeavor to explain unintelligible law to Green Mountain jurors; and when the *cacoethes scribendi* assails me, I will write sonnets to rustic loves, and tales for children; and look for my reward in the exhilarating smiles of partial friends round my own fireside."[74]

Fortune was not the anticipated end of literary endeavor. Neither, for many early American novelists, was fame. Of approximately sixty-five American novelists who published before 1820, less than a third were named on the title pages of their books; slightly over a third appeared either anonymously or pseudonymously but are known today (often because the veil of anonymity was only tenuously employed, with the author's actual name revealed in the advertisements for the specific book or in a subsequent publication by the same individual—as was the case for Brockden Brown, Susanna Rowson, and Royall Tyler). The remaining authors (and the largest single group) were and remain anonymous.[75] Sometimes a title page was simply that, a listing of the title. Sometimes a title page also bore a rubric such as "By a Lady," or "An American," or "A Lady of Massachusetts" as the only emblem of the author's hand. Whether this modesty was a vestigial holdover from the older genteel tradition of anonymous authorship, a gesture toward republicanism (the writer refusing to be identified as part of an intellectual elite), an act of self-protection (in view of the low status of fiction), or merely a matter of fashion is debatable. A unique letter, between Isaiah Thomas, Jr., and Sukey Vickery (whose identity as one of these early novelists was not revealed for nearly a century), indicates an intermingling of the motives for authorial anonymity with a clear (if genteelly underplayed) desire for copyright and profit. Thomas, who had already published Vickery's poetry (under the pseudonym Fidelia), wrote to her to express interest in her unpublished novel, the existence of which an intermediary, a Mr. Greenwood, had called to his attention. Since Vickery's response so tellingly expresses the ambivalence of early authorship, I quote it at length:

Sir,

Your very obliging letter entitles you to my sincere thanks. The flattering compliments you have bestowed on my trifling productions are greater, I am conscious, than they deserve. Had I known Mr. Greenwood would have mentioned my name as the authoress of the Novel I believe I never should have ventured to have had it thus exposed. It is, and ever has been, my wish to remain unknown. . . . On supposition the little work above alluded to ever should appear in print, I shall never consent to have my name or that of Fidelia appear to it. The novel is written in letters and founded principally on facts, some of which I have heard from persons with whom I am connected. I have been careful not to write any thing that could have a tendency to injure the mind of the young and inexperienced. I have written the whole of it at hours of leisure, and the greater part after the family had retired to rest. I am quite ignorant of the manner of disposing of copy rights, and a faint hope that I might possibly gain something by it induced me to mention it in confidence to Mr. Greenwood.

I will transcribe it as soon as possible for your perusal, should it be thought unfit for publication, I shall rest satisfied with the decision of your superior judgment, and repose sufficient confidence in your honor to believe my name will never be exposed as the occasion. . . .

Vickery's novel was published, as agreed upon, anonymously. One of the most thorough analyses of the double standard written during the early national period, *Emily Hamilton* did not sell particularly well, certainly not well enough to answer its author's "faint hope" to "gain something by it." Sukey Vickery married the same year, mothered nine children in rapid succession, and then died at the age of forty-one, without ever appearing in print again.[76]

A reluctance to be identified as an author does not enhance one's chances of succeeding as a writer. A name identifies and gives shape to a career; it aims readers at a writer's other works and encourages anticipation for more. The name could early even outweigh the work, as Cooper discovered when, in 1825, he tried—and failed—to sell *Lionel Lincoln* with complete anonymity. Yet the possible advantages of being known clearly did not counterbalance, for most writers, the known advantage of remaining anonymous. Furthermore, authorship, suspect for men, was even more so for women. The "lady" writer, especially, as Mrs. S.S.B.K. Wood asserts in her preface to *Julia, and the Illuminated Baron* (1800), had compelling reasons for desiring the anonymity that in this particular case could not be claimed:

> When the following pages were committed to the press it was the wish and expectation of the Author to remain in oblivion. A variety of causes have postponed its appearance; and conjecture ever busy, and curiosity ever prying, have lifted up the veil of conceal-ment, and many are acquainted with the name and situation which, shrouded in an happy mediocrity, it was hoped would have escaped the observation of the world. Baffled in this her favorite wish, she feels it a duty to apologize, with her very humble talents, for thus appearing in public. She very well knows, that writers of Romance are not highly estimated. She is likewise sensible that custom and nature, which have affixed the duties of women to very confined and very limited bounds, are by no means likely to patronize a female writer. She feels that her conduct needs excuse, and though the independence of her mind renders her unwilling to make one, yet necessity obliges her to it. She is so certain that so many will acknowledge the truth of her assertion, that she does not hesitate to declare, that not one social, or domestic duty, have ever been sacrificed or postponed by her pen.[77]

Madam Wood (as she was sometimes known) was one of the most socially conservative of the sentimental novelists, yet her apologia for her art was typical of her times. Female authorship had to be genteelly defined as an avocation, not a "manly occupation," as is clear in Wood's preface to *Ferdinand and Elmira* (1804), which pointedly opposes "the ordinary day-labor of the common English Novelist, who works for a living similar to a Mechanic, . . . [with the American]

Lady of refined sentiments and correct tastes, who writes for the amusement of herself, her Friends, and [last and presumably of least importance] the Public."[78]

We see, with Wood, the psychological pressures operating specifically upon the woman author. This daughter of a prominent judge apparently did not need the income from her novels to support her three children. But it is significant that she did not write during either of her marriages. Her four novels appeared well after the death of her first husband, her collection of tales after the death of her second. It would seem that female authorship was not fully consistent with matrimony, a conclusion supported by the numerous later nineteenth-century women authors who insisted that their real "profession" was dutiful wifehood and motherhood (note the ubiquitous Mrs. appended to many female names in the nineteenth-century popular fictional tradition) and that their writing (derogatorily referred to even by these writers as scribbling) was a mere avocation. Clearly this self-definition and public pose, along with the social conditions underlying it, does not encourage serious writing—even though many a nineteenth-century "amateur" scribbler outsold "professionals" such as Hawthorne or Melville by thousands and even tens of thousands of volumes.[79]

The prospects for authorship and especially female authorship in the early national period were bleak. But it is also important to recognize that some writers succeeded against the odds. Two examples—Hannah Adams and Jeremy Belknap—might serve to show the ways in which certain writers came to understand the impediments to authorship and found ways to overcome them. Perhaps the largest obstacle involved the distribution of the published work. Even those authors whose sales were guaranteed in advance by subscription were sometimes still paid in books. Thus Hannah Adams received fifty copies of her *Alphabetical Compendium of the Various Sects* (1784), only to discover that she could not sell those volumes locally since the publisher's well-advertised subscription drive had already preempted that market. To find purchasers for her book (and her books), Adams simply went farther afield than did her publisher. A shrewd woman, she learned from that first venture and, in 1791, when she put out a second expanded edition of her *Compendium*, she contracted for a larger run and for all the remaining copies of the book to be turned over to her once the publisher had sold enough to be reimbursed for his expenses. Since she had already discovered that she could advantageously market the work herself, she, in effect, hired the printer as a kind of subcontractor; once he was paid, all of the profit went not to him, the publisher, but to her, the author and entrepreneur.[80] Adams, incidentally, went on to become one of the most financially successful writers of the early national period. Yet even late in her life, the memory of various past injustices done her by different printers, publishers, and literary advisors still rankled, for she had learned, painfully, that "the penalties and discouragements attending authors in general fall upon women with double weight," a state of affairs to which Adams's *Memoir* gives ample testimony.[81]

The novelist Jeremy Belknap also profited from the lesson implicit in an early financial setback suffered when his allegorical novel *The Foresters* (1792) was first published. The contract gave all copyright privileges to his publisher, Thomas and Andrews of Boston, but also held Belknap responsible for part of their expenses. His final share of those expenses proved to be larger than the price he was originally promised for the novel. So for a later book, *American Biography* (1794–98), Belknap retained copyright privileges and carefully negotiated advantageous terms, as the second clause of his contract indicated: "The said Thomas and Andrews engages to print the said work at their own risque & expense and to find paper for the same; the paper & type to be to the satisfaction of the said Belknap."[82] Because the book proved popular (and it was its anticipated popularity that gave Belknap leverage in his negotiations with the publisher), the author's profit was assured. Thus did numerous women and men of letters learn—the hard way—the realities of the business of literature and thus did a few of them gain some recompense from that knowledge.

Others found other ways to profit from their work or at least to increase their chances of profiting. Parson Weems would regularly promote his next book while selling his present one (his books, incidentally, were often another author's work republished, slightly edited, under Weems's own well-known name). Noah Webster gained publicity by donating, with much public fanfare, numerous copies of *The American Spelling Book* to a town's local library, college, or boarding school. One commentator observes that sometimes Webster would hand out as many as three hundred volumes, an "equivalent in public credit to giving a million or so dollars today."[83] The publicity worked. States as far away as Georgia ruled that the Webster speller would be used in all of their "seminaries of learning."[84] Or Mrs. Rowson—an actress and singer as well as a novelist—frequently worked readings from *Charlotte* or subsequent novels into her public performances and after a stage performance would discuss her books with her audience.

Despite their best efforts, however, most authors of early fiction, including Charles Brockden Brown (often, erroneously, termed America's "first professional novelist"), fell somewhere in between the strained dilettantism of Madam Wood, on the one hand, and the diligent professionalism of Susanna Haswell Rowson, on the other. Neither did their uncertain place derive just from the economic vagaries of their public profession or the degree of private commitment to their art. The work (public and private) was, as noted, socially suspect. Like Brown, many writers appended only their initials to their texts although their full identities were generally soon known and, once known, were seldom denied. Many also vacillated between the older aristocratic notion of the gentleman author and the republican notion of the novelist as a professional wage earner (analogous to—although perhaps not as respectable as—a carpenter or a blacksmith). For authors who preferred both a place on the higher social levels and some payment for their labors, the matter of self-definition was definitely complicated.

The career of Joel Barlow especially illustrates that last conflict. Barlow, the son of a Connecticut farmer, was early recognized as brilliant by a local minister who helped him to acquire a Yale education; throughout his life, he was torn between the low status suggested by his origins and the higher aspirations encouraged by his training. Although a republican in his politics, especially in his later years, Barlow cultivated the image of himself as the gentleman-writer and justified the need for copyright laws essentially on elitist principles. He worked almost as hard as Webster to promote copyright laws and to recognize art as a commodity. The would-be literary aristocrat consequently stands uncomfortably in the would-be literary marketplace. Writing to Elias Boudinot, president of the Continental Congress, to urge him to support passage of copyright laws, Barlow maintains that until such laws are passed, nothing stops the "mercenary" printer from exploiting the "Gentleman" author in order to bring cheap editions of works before the "Vulgar" audience. The letter begins: "As we have few Gentlemen of fortune sufficient to enable them to spend a whole life in study, or enduce others to do it by their patronage, it is more necessary, in this country than in any other, that the rights of authors be secured by law." Barlow's best evidence for his argument is the case of John Trumbull, who, with an unauthorized reprinting of his *M'Fingal* (1775), "suffers in his reputation by having his work appear under the disadvantages of typographical errors, a bad paper, a mean letter & an uncouth page, all which were necessary to the printer to catch the Vulgar by a low price."[85] The matter to be redressed is not so much an economic offense as an aesthetic one. Laws are needed to protect "Gentlemen" and the country from all that is "Vulgar," "mean," "bad," and "uncouth" and that comes into being through the tradesman appropriating the gentleman's art. But despite his apparent unconcern with low economic considerations, Barlow's argument is very much about the *ownership* of art.

Until the passage of federal copyright laws, there could be no real profession of authorship. Publishing, too, required some protection. If a printer needed, say, to sell half of a first edition of a novel simply to recoup his costs, he could not afford to have another printer, impressed by the novel's sales, come forward with a competing—and perhaps cheaper—edition. Such a pirated edition deprived both the author and the publisher of the profits they would otherwise have received. Congress was initially reluctant to consider the book trade when it first passed laws regulating interstate and international commerce. Only through the combined efforts of writers, like Adams, Belknap, and Rowson, and the prodigious activities of Noah Webster (who traveled around the country selling his dictionary and simultaneously campaigning for passage of both state and federal copyright laws) were state governments prompted to enact legislation that protected the rights of individual authors and printers. By 1786, all the states had passed such laws, but they were of varying severity, vigor, and uncertain application. Finally, the Federal Copyright Act, enacted in 1790, granted authors copyright privileges over their own work for a fourteen-year period that could be extended by the author for a second fourteen years.[86]

The new law at first, however, had surprisingly little effect. Although authors could, after 1790, legally claim as their own their published work, a comparatively small number actually did.[87] Silver notes, for example, that in Massachusetts between 1800 and 1809 fewer than one tenth of all published books were copyrighted.[88] To claim legally the text was to claim socially the trade, and writers continued to be reluctant to advance that second claim. Perhaps because pretensions to aristocratic standards obviously died hard, as Charvat dryly concludes, the anachronistic late eighteenth-century demand for literary aristocrats led almost inevitably to a nineteenth-century model: the starving artist.[89] Perhaps, too, relatively few works were copyrighted because there was relatively little reason to do so. Why go to the trouble if one knows one will make nothing from a volume? Here, too, works of fiction were a partial exception to the general rule, for most of the first editions of early American novels include a copyright statement (typically filed by the publisher).

The passage of the 1790 copyright law was one important step toward giving the individual author legal control over his or her own work. Congress was more reluctant to foster an indigenous book industry by instituting special tariffs on cheap imports or by punishing American pirates of foreign editions, even though early American newspapers are filled with advertisements, editorials, and letters designed to promote such legislation.[90] Much of this persuasive material represented what might almost be called a concerted lobbying effort by those employed in the American printing industry. The Franklin Typographical Association of New York, for example, argued in one representative letter that "amongst the great mass of Books imported, many are found of a low and trifling nature, tending to corrupt the morals of our citizens. Congress, by laying the solicited Duty, would enable the Professors of Art to select and print such compositions only as would be really advantageous."[91] As in Barlow's letter advocating a copyright law, economic issues are entwined with aesthetic, nationalistic, and even moral considerations. It would be decades before such lobbying bore fruit. The tariff Act of 1789, in which Congress placed sliding taxes on various imported articles, did not even specifically mention books, which thereby became just another item of unspecified goods subject to an automatic 5 percent import tax. Alexander Hamilton's subsequent 1791 proposal to pass a special 10 percent protective tariff on foreign books failed in Congress; only with the Tariff Act of 1816 were foreign titles specifically taxed and then with a scant 5 percent duty. Not until 1830 did Congress finally pass international copyright laws that made pirating of foreign imprints illegal by extending copyright protection to foreign authors.[92]

It should be noted that the early American book trade's demand for tariff protection was itself deeply ambivalent. The same printers who decried the preponderance of foreign titles frequently printed pirated American versions of those same European titles. Prior to 1830, many of the same early American newspapers and magazines that carried editorials petitioning Congress to protect the native book industry also regularly ran ads promising British books at cheaper prices than the British editions. Thus Isaiah Thomas advertises in 1789 that subscribers for his forthcoming edition of Dr. William Cullen's *Practice of Physick* can buy the book, printed on good paper, of beautiful construction "page for page [from] the latest and best British edition, and at a savings of fifty percent."[93]

Whether or not they viewed themselves as laborers in the field of art, all the authors discussed in this study had to face the prospects of writing without any real remuneration. While some of the early American novelists could prefer to remain genteelly aloof from the mercantile aspects of the book trade and profit at least socially (if only in their own estimation) from the stand, no early American printer was allowed such luxury. The exigencies of economic survival brought these printers to publish pirated editions of English or Continental works that promised to sell well or to import them (if the book could be purchased more cheaply abroad than it could be printed at home, as was usually the case). In short, the early American printer faced obstacles enough and could little afford to support domestic authors as opposed to having foreign authors, especially British ones, support him. American writers were, consequently, almost priced out of the market even before they began to write.

The purely economic consideration of how much a specific title could make for its printer was not the only motivation for publishing a book. On the contrary, of all the various trade or mechanics' associations in the new republic, the printers' associations tended to be the most aware of what might be termed the nonmonetary value of their work. A projected volume might not offer any hope of profit but still be printed because it served social objectives that the printer considered worthy of supporting with his enterprise. Mathew Carey, for example, published several pamphlets on behalf of the striking shoemakers as well as the impoverished government seamstresses, and he did so to support his fellow laborers in their attempt to earn a living wage.[94] Or note the remarkable fact that even though libraries were, as I have shown, one important source of revenue for the early American printer, the Asylum Company of Journeymen Printers specifically exempted public libraries from the tariff duties they wished imposed upon all foreign books.[95] In short, the value of inculcating the habit of reading and an awareness of the value of new ideas—many of which must necessarily come from abroad—overrode any immediate material gain that might accrue by discouraging libraries from buying foreign volumes. Although there is an element of self-interest in that stand, there is also a clear concern for the public good.

Alfred F. Young has coined the term "citizen consciousness" to describe the blending of professionalism and patriotism fostered by many of the mechanics' organizations, a consciousness especially evident among the printers.[96] These early workers' associations were uniquely qualified to temper their pride in the new Republic with an acute awareness that unless the nation fulfilled its promise of equality and opportunity, a revolution had been fought and won in vain. Consider the punning diction of a toast given by the Baltimore Typographical Society on Independence Day of 1805: "Employers and employed, the two great parties of the world.—May a constant reciprocity of good *offices, bind* fast the chords of mutual friendship, each bearing in mind this solemn truth, that all power founded on injustice is *imposition.*" Even more pointed is the eulogy delivered in 1809 for Justus Brown, a printer who died in penury (it was yet another function of the Baltimore Typographical Society to bury impoverished printers who would have otherwise been consigned to a pauper's grave):

> His excellent qualities and amiable manners had secured to him the friendship & esteem of every person who knew him. A humble Christian, a zealous patriot and a worthy citizen, had his fortunes been as prosperous as his virtues were numerous, he would not have remained a striking example of the fact, that even in our favored country, rigid honesty, warm benevolence, and unremitted industry, some times go without merited reward.[97]

This theme, the relationship between virtue and economic reward *in a republic* (and that last phrase makes all the difference), also runs throughout many early American novels and is a plot device as commonplace as seduction. For many of those who wrote, published, sold, purchased, borrowed, or read the early American novel, the social, economic, racial, gender, and class inequities that remained within the Republic tarnished its potential glories. In an increasingly literate society, printers and writers had a unique means for helping to polish away that residual tarnish—or to attempt to forge the developing Republic into a better form.

The larger social concerns of the printers were of crucial importance to the genesis of the American novel. Through an alchemy of hope, patriotism, and professional pride, early American printers did publish some one hundred American novels before 1820, which, under the circumstances, constituted an impressive beginning for the new genre. In this beginning, we see a classic example of the ways in which art sometimes circumvents the economic facts that ostensibly determine it. In purely dollars-and-cents terms, there was no reason for anyone to write or, certainly, to publish a work of American fiction. Yet a patriot-printer, such as Isaiah Thomas, might have been only marginally concerned with financial considerations when he decided, in 1789, to publish and advertise the "First American Novel" just as George Washington was inaugurated as the first president of the American nation. Dedicated to the "Young Ladies of United Columbia," William Hill Brown's novel speaks all the more eloquently of and to the nonmaterial values of art precisely because its own material value was so minimal. Also, as I will show in the following chapters, there can be a considerable discrepancy between the weak financial grounding of an art (specifically, the novel) and the great social/psychological potency attributed to it—both negative and positive. Be that as it may, an awareness of the economic obstacles to book production in the new Republic attests that the American novel ultimately succeeded in spite of the very economy in which it began.

3 Ideology and Genre

I thank God, there are no free schools nor printing [in Virginia], and I hope we shall not have these [for a] hundred years; for learning has brought disobedience, and heresy, and sects into the world, and printing has divulged them, and libels against the best government. God keep us from both!
—William Berkeley, governor of Virginia (1671)

The opinion of the world in regard to works of fancy has of late years undergone a wonderful change. It is no longer considered an offense against either religion, morality, or prudence to peruse a book bearing the name of a novel. . . . To us it appears as if it were but yesterday, that the grave, the serious, the religious, and the prudent, considered novel reading as an employment utterly beneath the dignity of the human mind. . . . In those days, it was almost as disreputable to be detected reading a novel, as to be found betting at a cockfight, or a gaming table. Those who had sons would have supposed them forever incapacitated for any useful pursuit in life, if they exhibited an inclination for novel reading; and those who had daughters who exhibited such an inclination, would have considered them as totally unfitted for ever becoming good wives or mothers.
—James McHenry (1824)

Back in his native land "after an absence of seven years," Updike Underhill, the protagonist in Royall Tyler's *The Algerine Captive* (1797), observes a revolution in the reading habits of America:

When he left New England, books of biography, travels, novels, and modern romances were confined to our seaports; or, if known in the country, were read only in the families of clergymen, physicians, and lawyers: while certain funeral discourses, the last words and dying speeches of Bryan Shaheen, and Levi Ames, and some dreary somebody's *Day of Doom*, formed the most diverting part of the farmer's library. On his return from captivity, he found a surprising alteration in the public taste. In our inland towns of consequence, social libraries had been instituted, composed of books designed to amuse rather than to instruct; and country booksellers, fostering the new-born taste of the people, had filled the whole land with modern travels and novels almost as incredible.

This wandering son of the new Republic come home again is especially struck by the "extreme avidity with which books of mere amusement [are] purchased and perused by all ranks."[1] And Tyler's fictional comments are by no means the only observations on this remarkable new interest in fiction. As the editor of *New York Magazine* decisively proclaimed in 1797, "This is a novel-reading age."[2]

In chapter 2, I focused on the manufacture of fiction at the dawning of the Industrial Revolution and, correspondingly, on the economic origins of the American novel. I traced how the form first appeared in a transitional society, preindustrial in its modes of production yet protocapitalistic in its modes of consumption, and I surveyed how the new genre along with its early producers— individual authors and enterprising printers—survived financially in a post-colonial world that merely presaged mass book production and mass consumption. In this chapter, my focus is on the politics of genre and, more specifically, on the ideological position that the novel *as a genre* was perceived to take in the aftermath of the Revolutionary War—a vital and volatile time when the ideals of the nation had to be formulated and promulgated. I ask how the new form survived in a society that, on the highest levels, was intensely hostile to its appearance. What were the causes of that pervasive cultural censure? What were the consequences? How much were the arbiters of taste motivated by fears that they operated within a society that was becoming too diffuse, too individualistic, and too democratic?

According to former president John Adams, by 1805 America had entered an "Age of Folly, Vice, Frenzy, Brutality, Daemons, Buonaparte, Tom Paine, or the Age of the burning Brand from the bottomless Pit: or anything but the Age of Reason."[3] For other men of power and prestige, too, it was a chaotic new world, and the novel, more than any other literary genre, was seen as the sign of a time when their authority was being called into question.

MONUMENTAL SOCIAL changes seldom occur overnight, which means, as many historians have noted, that there is often little immediate correspondence between events—everything from civil wars to technological breakthroughs—and the *mentalités* of the people most influenced by events. The historian may supply a correlation (e.g., "The Revolutionary War caused a new individualism in America"), but it is not by any means clear that life changed drastically for the Connecticut farmer who before, during, and after the war still had to worry about tilling unyielding soil, milking cows, feeding a growing family—facts of life that remained, for most Americans, more present and more pressing than the political considerations and compromises whereby the Constitution was being forged somewhere in Philadelphia behind locked doors. As Rip Van Winkle discovered, the sign above the tavern may have metamorphosed from King George to President George, but the life of the village stayed largely the same.

When change does occur and the king elides into the president, those who would continue to hold power and position within a society must contrive documents or proclamations that articulate a carefully limited and defined concept of progress that does not contravene their status: a new deal, a great society, a light at the end of the tunnel. In a word, ideology persists and is both less and more than history. It is an attempt to *sell* history, to sell an interpretation of the time and place in which men and women live their lives to those same men and women. As Anthony Giddens has observed, ideology represents "the capability of dominant groups or classes to make their own sectional interests appear to others as universal."[4] Ideology, by this definition, succeeds when those to whom it is directed assume that it is normal, natural, definitive, and thus destined to endure.

Giddens's formulation is a useful refinement of Marx's well-known aphorism "The ideas of the ruling class are in every epoch the ruling ideas," in that it differentiates between "ruling ideas" and the perception (perhaps erroneous) that certain ideas are dominant, ruling.[5] This is a crucial distinction for this discussion. As noted earlier, the continuing censure of the early novel rivaled the novel's growing popularity, and that incongruity took a variety of unusual forms. Thus, before approximately 1790, many books sold in America that we would now unquestionably define as novels (e.g., *Tristram Shandy*) were advertised otherwise ("a sentimental history"). But, by the turn of the century, a whole range of nonfictional reading materials, including sketches, captivity narratives, and travel pieces, were advertised as novels. Publishers, booksellers, and lending libraries could all promote their business by indiscriminately applying the label *novel* to the commodity they dispensed. Yet the censure of the form, emanating from the pulpit and the press, remained potent enough so that, until well into the nineteenth century, virtually every American novel somewhere in its preface or its plot defended itself against the charge that it *was* a novel, either by defining itself differently ("Founded In *Truth*") or by redefining the genre tautologically as all those things it was presumed not to be—moral, truthful, educational, and so forth. Or newspapers and magazines would serialize works of fiction under a headnote defensively proclaiming the genre's moral advantages even as they also published, sometimes within the same issue, denunciations of the genre as a whole (denunciations that presumably applied to all works of fiction other than the particular specimen included in their publication).[6] The question, then, is how much potency did "ruling ideas" about the necessarily deleterious effects of the novel have?

Jürgen Habermas has argued that ideology is always implicitly or explicitly reactionary, a counterstance to some other force within a culture. An "ideology is always coeval with the critique of ideology."[7] The light at the end of the tunnel is proclaimed in response to a suspicion that one is stumbling through an unrelieved darkness. The pervasive censure of fiction eloquently attests to the force that fiction itself was perceived to have as an ideology (or as an agent of ideology). Had the novel not been deemed a potent proponent of certain threatening changes, there would have been little reason to attack it. Had the novel not been seen as a covert or even overt critique of the existing social order, there would have been no need to defend so rigorously what had not been called into question or to strive to persuade potential novel readers of the harm that they would do themselves should they foolishly indulge their appetite for fiction.

To the modern reader, the whole contretemps over fiction well may seem a tempest in a teapot, but it is important to remember that the early reviewers, by attacking fiction, were defending a vision of society that they viewed (the essential purpose of ideology—to assume, to presume, to subsume) as well ordered and manifestly worthy of defense. Their stand in striving to perpetuate this order reified the position from which they believed they spoke, the stance of a superior dismayed by another's reading habits but willing to warn the other of the grave consequences of his or her unfortunate literary tastes—novel reading today, licentious riot and senseless revolution tomorrow. Unwary readers might still be saved from that undesired end through the generous intermediation of the critic. Thus the *need* for the very social authority that the novels themselves presumed to question.

This need for the critic was the critics' need and it pervaded the higher reaches of the society. Timothy Dwight took time out from presiding over Yale, Jonathan Edwards from fomenting a religious revival, Benjamin Rush from attending to his medical and philosophical investigations, Noah Webster from writing dictionaries, and Thomas Jefferson and John Adams from presiding over a nation—all to condemn the novel.[8] But even that formulation devalues the seriousness of such attacks by differentiating the censure of fiction from the more public duties of these Founding Fathers. Denouncing the novel, they would have insisted, was ancillary to or coextensive with or even integral to the civic, religious, or educational duties of right-minded men. Culture, Raymond Williams has persuasively argued, was not defined as separate from the larger fabric of Anglo-American society until the middle of the nineteenth century. For the social spokespersons of the new Republic, an aberrant form of literary culture *equaled* an aberration in the very design of America.[9]

As Royall Tyler (in the passage quoted at the beginning of this chapter) humorously asserted, many people believed in a Gresham's law of texts or reading. Bad new works would supposedly drive out good old ones, so that a print world dominated by the Bible, *The Day of Doom*, sermons, tracts, and sundry other religious works well might be superseded by a new world of predominantly secular reading, of texts designed merely to amuse, not to instruct. This is not to say there were no amusing books before the novel. As noted in chapter 2, special laws were passed in Colonial America to eliminate chapmen with their chapbooks. This street literature (crime confessions, captivity narratives, picaresque tales, etc.) anticipated the early novel in form and even more in function. It was a literature about average people, even rogues—characters who often survived within or against the prevailing structures of authority—and it appealed to the authorities no more than the early American novel later did.

But the novel threatened not just to coexist with elite literature but to replace it, and its critics knew full well that changes in the primary reading of an increasingly greater number of people presaged far more than a faddish redeployment of leisure time (leisure being itself, as Williams reminds us, another nineteenth-century construct).[10] The crucial matter was not so much a question of how common citizens invested that time allowed for reading but the question of where the society vested the voice (or voices) of authority. While the novel was widely censured in Europe, the criticism in America may well have reached its particular level of vehemence because the novel was established here in the wake of the Revolution, at a time when disturbing questions (witness the Constitutional debates) about the limits of liberty and the role of authority in a republic were very much at issue. Might not the American novel by addressing those unprivileged in the emerging society persuade them that they had a voice in that society and thus serve as the literary equivalent of a Daniel Shays by leading its followers to riot and ruin? Many of America's best educated and most illustrious citizens thought so, and the genre provided a locus for their apprehensions about mobocracy on both the cultural and political level.

What I find most intriguing about this whole flyting with fiction is not its hysterical tone but its essential percipience.[11] The critics predicted the rise of the novel well in advance of its actual economic ascendancy and understood (for all their seeming paranoia) the cultural, social, and political implications of that ascendancy. With the historian's hindsight, we can appreciate just how validly their early warnings anticipated changes that, economically and technologically speaking, would not fully transpire until the mid–nineteenth century. If it now seems rather silly or overstated to blame one literary form for massive social ills, perhaps it is because the transition to a mass-market form of publication for a mass audience has been accomplished so thoroughly that the present world of print seems to us as fundamentally natural as their previous world seemed to them. No wonder the novel's early critics strove, through the power of the word, to stop a cultural revolution in the uses (in their view, abuses) of the word. That task was further complicated by their suspicion that in the new world of letters presaged by the novel they would have little to say. On a very elemental level, theirs was a fight for survival.

Sustained misgivings as to the social and moral effects of fiction represent, then, an attempt by an elite minority to retain a self-proclaimed role as the primary interpreters of American culture. It may well be that this group (and I define them only as they defined themselves through their critiques of fiction) never truly exerted an unquestioned moral authority in the local communities of the time. But they certainly sounded as if they did and regularly assumed a tone of inherited privilege, of moral and social rectitude. This ostensibly had its roots in the traditional Puritan religious paradigm (again, a model or ideal, not necessarily a fact) of the minister as the officially authorized translator of the text and as the literary critic of last resort interposing himself between the finally unfathomable authority of God and the all-too-human limitations of his audience. One of the most intriguing formulations of this model, for my purposes, and one which idealizes the role of the Protestant divine occurs in *The Power of Sympathy:* "[The Reverend Mr. Holmes] is assiduous in the duties of his profession, and in the love and admiration of his flock. He prescribes for the health of the body, as well as that of the soul, and settles all the little disputes of his parish. They are contented with his judgment, and he is at once their parson, their lawyer, and their physician."[12] In a theocracy, the minister's word is never limited to preaching the Word.

Just how much American communities really honored the pronouncements of men such as the Reverend Holmes is open to debate. But until well into the eighteenth and early nineteenth century, the local minister not only served as God's annointed spokesperson, he was typically the only citizen in a small town or village who had received a classical education at one of the prestige colleges. Wills and estate inventories regularly reveal that his library was the largest in his community. As expert witness to the world and the Word, the minister interpreted science, philosophy, and other forms of learning as well as religion for his congregation/audience. Although select members of that audience may have been versed on the particular subject of the preacher's discourse, for many the sermon would be the first word on the topic at hand and for most it was the final word.[13] As novels became increasingly available, increasingly affordable (either purchased or rented), and increasingly accessible to the public (both because of their own linguistic simplicity and their readers' improved literacy), they were increasingly perceived to be eroding the pulpit model of erudition and authority. Nor did the novels overlook that shift. It seems no coincidence, for example, that immediately after the description of the Reverend Mr. Holmes in *The Power of Sympathy*, the minister delivers a lengthy diatribe that is against novel reading and seduction and in favor of sermons, satire, and didactic essays. The only problem with his "metaphysical nicety" is that it is quite ignored. While he drones on, one of the members of his intended audience diverts herself "with the cuts in Gay's *Fables*" while another reads a copy of Sterne's *A Sentimental Journey*.[14]

Fiction was a particular threat to ministerial authority because the novel, by its nature, necessarily ruled out the very intermediation that the preacher was professionally prepared to provide. In the terminology of the linguist Dell Hymes, fiction entails a "dyadic sender-receiver form" of communication, a form in which there is a direct line of communication between the sender and the receiver. With this form, the *meaning* of the text is embedded in the experience of decoding the message and thus cannot be separated from the act of reading itself.[15] Although a scientific treatise may be paraphrased without any significant loss of validity or substance, a novel cannot, and to summarize the argument of the plot is not to convey the essence of the fiction. In a sense, the novel *is* its reading, and that reading must finally be private and personal.

For the critics of the novel, the power of fiction to preoccupy the reader was a double danger. On the public level, would not novels keep the poor from being good workers and women from being good wives? On the private level, was not the engrossed reading of the wrong text itself a kind of seduction or even a state of possession? "I have heard it said in favour of novels," a commentator wrote in the *Weekly Magazine* in 1798, "that there are many good sentiments dispersed in them. I maintain, that good sentiments being found scattered in loose novels, render them the more dangerous, since, when they are mixed with seducing arguments, it requires more discernment than is to be found in youth to separate the evil from the good . . . and when a young lady finds principles of religion and virtue inculcated in a book, she is naturally thrown off her guard by taking it for granted that such a work can contain no harm: and of course the evil steals imperceptibly into her heart."[16] Some exorcism consequently seemed called for, and the clergy (backed by educators and political leaders) strove to dispossess readers of the novel in order to repossess themselves of their "elect" status and role.

Writing in 1853, one anonymous reviewer for the Unitarian magazine *The Christian Examiner* assumed that the minister had already become a figure mostly of nostalgia, not a potent leader of his culture and the chief articulator of its ideals. Commenting specifically about the vogue for quaint historical novels about ministers, this reviewer noted that "as we read these records of ministerial life . . . the mind naturally reverts to olden times. . . . We see at a glance into what entirely new conditions society has fallen. Then the minister made himself felt; he was a man of power; he was far more erudite than those around him; the means of acquiring knowledge was far less than now. . . . The printing press had not achieved its present miracles of art, and public libraries were unknown."[17] Just as Governor William Berkeley of Virginia had predicted in 1671, there was, for this anonymous reviewer in 1853, an inextricable interrelationship between the rise of the popular press and the decline in public respect for religious and civil authority.

The change from a small and essentially elite readership of a few selected nonfictional (and often devotional) titles to a proto-mass audience for books, and primarily novels that did not require official exegesis, marked other changes, too. Fredric Jameson has argued in this context that the revolution in readership signaled a larger revolution in the whole social contract of the culture. "The older pre-capitalist genres were signs of something like an aesthetic 'contract' between a cultural producer and a certain homogeneous class or group public; they drew their vitality from the social and collective status . . . of the situation of aesthetic production and consumption, that is to say, from the fact that the relationship between artist and public was still in one way or another a social institution and a concrete social and interpersonal relationship with its own validation and specificity."[18] With the advent of the market-model of literary production, exemplified by the rise of the novel, we have not just a new form, new authors, and a new audience, we also have a new contract between the producers and consumers of print. With this redefinition of both author and audience, the established canon of literary forms and genres collapses and the whole *structure* of literary relationships is rearranged. With the advent of the novel, the indirect and secondary audience of much previous literary discourse became the direct, primary audience for much present literary discourse and the mediating middlemen, such as the expounding clergyman, were removed from the transaction.

Although my comments thus far have been directed to the American scene, a pervasive censure of fiction was by no means a purely American phenomenon. On the contrary, and as Mikhail Bakhtin has pointed out, the novel was officially opposed in virtually every European country into which it was introduced. Much of the censure of fiction in American periodicals was, in fact, based on European sources and was often directly appropriated from British publications, for fiction had already challenged British social institutions (an entrenched class system) in much the same manner that it would subsequently challenge different American social institutions (a residual puritanism and an emerging industrial-capitalism). As Bakhtin notes, the whole process of reading fiction empowers individual readers in ways innately inimical to social authority. "In a novel," this critic argues, "the individual acquires the ideological and linguistic initiative necessary to change the nature of his own image (there is a new and higher type of individualization of the image)." Within the novel, "there always remains an unrealized surplus of humanness"—a surplus that creates new needs, different desires, and that thus controverts the status quo. Moreover, the very temporality of the novel—its emphasis on the here and now rather than on a classical tradition of timeless forms, right readings, and proper responses—similarly aggravates desire in a way that extends far beyond the novel to compromise even the good work of those other forms: "The novelization of literature does not imply attaching to already completed genres a generic canon that is alien to them, not theirs. The novel, after all, has no canon of its own. It is, by its nature, not canonic. It is plasticity itself. It is a genre that is ever questing, ever examining itself and subjecting its established forms to review."[19] And it similarly subjects the forms of the society in which it is written and read (and the writings that support those forms) to review. No wonder the novel was derided by those who profited from the status quo and strove to perpetuate it.

It is not the purpose of this study to document the whole nexus of changing social ideology in postrevolutionary America, but I would observe that the rise of the novel (as well as the negative reaction to the novel) occurred simultane-

ously with other transformations within American society. By no means an isolated phenomenon, the emergence of the novel was part of a movement in the
late eighteenth century toward a reassessment of the role of the "average" American and a concomitant questioning of political, ministerial, legal, and even
medical authorities on the part of the citizens of the new nation who, having already accepted the egalitarian rhetoric of the Revolution, increasingly believed
that the Republic belonged as much to them as to the gentry. As Nathan O.
Hatch notes:

> From the debate over the Constitution to the election of Jefferson, a second and ex-
> plicitly democratic revolution united many who suspicioned power and many who were
> powerless in a common effort to pull down the cultural hegemony of a gentlemanly
> few. In a complex cultural process that historians have just begun to unravel, people
> on a number of fronts began to speak, write, and organize against the authority of
> mediating elites, of social distinctions, and of any human tie that did not spring from
> volitional allegiance.[20]

This process—in Gordon S. Wood's phrasing, the "democratization of
mind"—was happening across the nation.[21] Writing specifically of Virginia, for
example, Rhys Isaacs posits a remarkable transition in the aftermath of the Revolution from a gentrified society—where authoritarian figures served as interpreters of both a religious and legal tradition for a marginally educated but increasingly literate populace—to a society that put less confidence in its gentlemen
as infallible sources of information and opinion. Isaacs notes that one mark of
the change in social attitude was the increase in the number of newspapers,
religious tracts, and novels, all seemingly intended for a less educated audience,
but an audience increasingly sceptical about the authority vested in minister or
magistrate. As Isaacs summarizes:

> The Great Awakenings, and the popular dissent they promoted, effectively wrested the
> Bible and its interpretation from the custody of the learned; the republican principle
> of popular sovereignty subverted the conception of higher authority embodied in the
> wisdom of learned justices; newspapers and pamphlets (increasingly promulgating di-
> visive ideologies, and more and more frequently involving the vulgar in affairs formerly
> the preserve of the learned) combined with the newly invented book product of the
> 1750s, the sentimental novel, to turn the flow of print into a flood.[22]

In the North, too, the flood of print was perceived as threatening to an established
social order. Readers were increasingly eager to participate in the *creation* of
meaning, of public opinion, of culture—not just to serve as the consumers of
meanings articulated by others. And the novel, as Bakhtin insists, is par excellence
a genre that "authorizes" the reader as an interpreter and a participant in a
culture's fictions.

THE CENSURE OF THE novel in the late eighteenth century has been amply documented and there is no need to review the range of complaints. However, I do want to look in some depth at a few representative comments in order to examine the ideological assumptions underlying the critique and, conversely, the countering ideological position occupied by the novels themselves. Obviously, the main object of censure is the woman reader, who, not coincidentally, is also the implied reader of most of the fiction of the era. The primary issue, on several levels, is legitimacy—who is and who is not the legitimate audience of literature and, less theoretically, who are to be the legitimate heirs of the Republic.

"Of all the artillery" that can "soften hearts" and thus circumvent virtue, one "Leander" warned in 1791, "the most effectual is the modern novel."[23] Or, wrote another commentator, "novels . . . are the powerful engines with which the seducer attacks the female heart, and if we judge from every day experience, his plots are seldom laid in vain."[24] Still more explicit in its charges and histrionic in its tone is an 1802 jeremiad portentously titled "Novel Reading, a Cause of Female Depravity":

> Without the poison instilled [by novels] into the blood, females in ordinary life would never have been so much the slaves of vice. . . . It is no uncommon thing for a young lady who has attended her dearest friend to the altar, a few months after a marriage which, perhaps, but for *her,* had been a happy one, to fix her affections on her friend's husband, and by artful blandishments allure him to herself. Be not staggered, moral reader, at the recital! Such serpents are really in existence. . . . I have seen two poor disconsolate parents drop into premature graves, miserable victims to their daughter's dishonour, and the peace of several relative families wounded never to be healed again in this world.[25]

All this from reading novels! But hyperbolic as such charges might seem to the modern reader, they were taken seriously at the time—seriously enough that virtually every early American novel answered such criticism either prefatorially or in the plot: "These volumes," even the first American novel insists in its dedication, are intended "to represent the specious Causes, and to Expose the fatal Consequences of Seduction; to inspire the Female Mind With a Principle of Self Complacency, and to Promote the Economy of Human Life." In plain English, *The Power of Sympathy* promises to discourage licentiousness and to do what it can to prevent the Republic from being overrun with illegitimate children.[26]

That translation is not at all facetious. In the various critiques of the novel, female sexuality was regularly defined and the possible offenses of same were just as regularly considered not as a private matter but in the most public of terms. Note that the exemplum just quoted from "Novel Reading, a Cause of Female Depravity," is not limited to one particular young lady seduced by reading romances into seducing the husband of her "dearest friend" but also brings in the premature grave of "disconsolate parents" and the permanent grief of "several relative families." In short, female sexuality was not only fetishized but nationalized.[27] It became (at least for those who denounced novels from the privileged position of their elevated social class) a national resource. In both cases—engaging in sex or engaging in reading—what could be regarded as an ultimately private, personal experience has been publicized and politicized and is therefore (the main point) subject to censorship, restriction, and control. As the sociologlst Patricia Murphy Robinson argues in a different context: "Woman's strength as a sexual being is a constant threat. We have to face the biological fact that she is the sex that harbors and brings forth the very human beings the ruling class must have to create wealth. She is still the main sustaining force who cares for what she births. . . . Our sexuality in all its facets. . . . is interpenetrated by the reproduction of the species and through this the reproduction of the world. The control of our minds, as a sex, is an economic necessity."[28] To control female minds and feminine sexuality, the novel—its early critics would unanimously agree—had to be kept out of the wrong hands.

Whether or not one accepts this class analysis of sexism, it cannot be disputed that sexuality is always a historical construct that finds its expression—and its repression—within a specific social setting.[29] In regard to the critique of fiction, illicit sexuality was certainly at issue (as it was in most early American novels). But critical censure translated desire into a threat against the *institutions* of patriarchal marriage and the state upon which that system of marriage was based. "Novels not only pollute the imaginations of young women," wrote a commentator in the *Weekly Magazine* in 1798; novels also give women "false ideas of life, which too often make them act improperly."[30] The critic wishes to protect the susceptible young reader but, more important, wants to protect society from the unprivileged who are suddenly inspired with "unrealistic" ambitions.

The critic, telling the woman reader of her place, also tells the reader of his. The pronouncements against fiction assert (or reassert) a claim to social authority, as is made particularly clear in the extended commentary on novel reading by the Reverend Samuel Miller, a Presbyterian minister and a teacher at Princeton. With questionable concision, the Reverend Miller equates public and private lapses of virtue by moving from a Lockean argument based upon social good into, finally, a Benthamite argument on behalf of personal pleasure:

Every opportunity is taken [in novels] to attack some principle of morality under the title of a "prejudice;" to ridicule the duties of domestic life, as flowing from "contracted" and "slavish" views; to deny the sober pursuits of upright industry as "dull" and "spiritless;" and, in a word, to frame an apology for suicide, adultery, prostitution, and the indulgence of every propensity for which a corrupt heart can plead an inclination. . . . The author has no hesitation in saying, that, if it were possible, he would wholly prohibit the reading of novels. . . . For it may, with confidence, be pronounced that no one was ever an extensive and especially an habitual reader of novels, even supposing them to be all well selected, without suffering both intellectual and moral injury, and of course incurring a diminution of happiness.[31]

The elision of the novel's critique of accepted morality, gender roles, and class expectations (the role of workers) with suicide, adultery, and the indulgence of other such propensities is an effective (if underhanded) rhetorical maneuver. Even more so is the final assertion that happiness and novel reading are antithetical states. By this logic, it is in the individual's *interest* to give up such self-abuse.

The argument that novels unfitted one for one's position in life (always, of course, a subservient position) could even be advanced in novels themselves and thus—even if unintentionally—co-opted. I refer here to *Memoirs of the Blooms-grove Family* (1790) by the Reverend Enos Hitchcock (Yale graduate; Federalist; pastor of the Benevolent Congregational Church in Providence, Rhode Island; author; educator; and a novelist), whose novel sets forth, among other matters, a sustained critique of novels:

> The free access which many young people have to romances, novels, and plays has poisoned the mind and corrupted the morals of many a promising youth; and prevented others from improving their minds in useful knowledge. . . . Parents take care to feed their children with wholesome diet; and yet how unconcerned about the provision for the mind, whether they are furnished with salutary food, or with trash, chaff, or poison? How many thousands have, by a free use of such books, corrupted their principles, inflamed their imagination, and vitiated their taste, without balancing the account by any solid advantage?

Novels, this novelist notes, are "written in order to catch the imagination of the reader and beguile it into vice and error unawares."[32] But beginning with its dedication to Martha Washington (and a polite acknowledgment of the "high rank which [she] hold[s] in this rising Empire"), the *Memoirs of the Bloomsgrove Family* strives to beguile in a different direction and to inspire its readers toward self-improvement while carefully defining the direction of the desired improvement. For example, the book sharply criticizes any aspirations the reader might have toward a genteel education. The education that the Reverend Hitchcock advocates is in industry and good citizenship for men and in "economy and domestic employments" for women. Hitchcock especially insists that women's education and women's reading must be carefully prescribed so that women do not take into marriage "expectations" that are "above the drudgery of learning the necessary parts of domestic duties." Domestic drudgery, discouraged by novels, is necessary to the economic prosperity of the family and is equally necessary to the survival of the nation: "In a free country, under a republican form of government, industry is the only sure road to wealth; and economy the only sure

The FARMER's COTTAGE.

MORAL REFLECTIONS.

BEHOLD, where ſtands the cottage of the honeſt and induſtrious laborer. It is a neat habitation, ſituated where nature ſheds her beauties and her bleſſings with a liberal hand.

2. It is covered with a warm roof, and divided into convenient apartments. In the ſpring, ſummer and autumn the mother is ſeen ſpinning or ſewing at the door; the young children ſport before her on the green graſs.

3. They admire the warm rays of the ſun, which here and there dart through the thick ſhade. And they are delighted

FIGURE 2. "The Farmer's Cottage," from Herman Mann, *The Columbian Primer* (1802). Although the text indicates that "the mother is seen spinning or sewing at the door," she is here pictured as reading while her child plays and her husband ("the honest and industrious laborer") tills his field. *Courtesy of the American Antiquarian Society.*

means of preserving it. . . . [Thus] we see the necessity of educating females in a manner suited to the genius of the government."[33]

A Yale degree is fine for the gentry, but the populace needs more elemental stuff: no classics for the farmer, no art or musical training or other "female accomplishments" for the farmer's wife (or the merchant's wife, for that matter), and no novels, it might be added, for either. Yet Hitchcock writes a novel in order to read the novel out of the republic of letters. The best case one might make for such inconsistencies is that he was fighting fire with fire and addressed in the pages of his book those not likely to be found in the pews of his church. About his right to do so, he had no doubt, even though he deconstructs, in his own idiosyncratic fashion, both the message he imparts and the platform from which he delivers it.

IT HAS BEEN ARGUED, often enough, that early America was not a class society. Obviously, a hereditary ruling class was less entrenched in the former colony than it was in late eighteenth-century Britain.[34] Yet, in the critique of fiction, one sees how readily aspects of the British class system were transported to the New World and translated into terms consistent with the looser social structures of the young Republic. As has been well documented, the principal source of much of the critique of fiction was the Scottish Common Sense philosophers (men such as Henry Home, Lord Kames; Thomas Reid; James Beattie; and Vicissimus Knox), who, primarily in the 1740s and 1750s, criticized the novel immediately after its inception in England. Typically conservative in their social attitudes and especially so with regard to women, these men fulminated against the new genre in tracts and advice books that were imported to and reprinted in the New World. Even after this opposition to fiction had largely subsided in the Old World, it continued to flourish in the New. As Terence Martin and Emory Elliott have both noted, the writings of the Scottish Common Sense philosophers greatly influenced important teachers in American colleges, men such as William Smith at the College of Philadelphia, John Witherspoon at Princeton, and Thomas Clapp and Ezra Stiles at Yale.[35] These teachers passed on to their students an implicit suspicion of the undisciplined imagination, a conviction that literature must serve clear social needs, and a pervasive assumption that social need and social order were one and the same. Through these students—many of whom served as ministers—such ideas were readily disseminated throughout the populace.

I am not suggesting that all critics of the novel were progeny of the best families and products of the prestige colleges, whereas all readers and writers of the novel were not. Social/literary divisions are never so exactly drawn and do not give us perfect paradigms. Nevertheless, it is significant that most of the critics of fiction, who were often well born and well educated, voiced a particular concern for a different class of readers whom they *perceived* as being barely capable of reading fiction but eager to do so and, no doubt, highly susceptible to its dubious charms. Might not the unsophisticated reader, these critics worried, readily emulate unsavory portrayals of illicit sex, of dishonest dealings, of revolution and anarchy? Would not the farm boy and the servant girl become discontent with the station in life to which providence had consigned them and fulfill the duties of that station grudgingly or not at all? To use Timothy Dwight's term, all fiction was deemed potentially likely to destabilize "useful life"—a life "useful" to those who wished it to go on exactly as before.[36] Even though a few writers such as Hugh Henry Brackenridge and Royall Tyler graduated from men's colleges—the College of New Jersey (later known as Princeton) in the former case, Harvard in the latter—most did not. William Hill Brown, Charles Brockden Brown, and, of course, Susanna Rowson, Hannah Webster Foster, Tabitha Tenney, and the other women novelists immediately come to mind.[37] All of these writers operated in a rather different world from their critics—if only by virtue of the fiction they wrote—and in that world (and in their novels) they found some justification for what they were engaged in doing.

The novelists, in a number of different ways, responded to charges leveled against them. Most common was the method, already referred to in another context, employed in *The Power of Sympathy,* a novel explicitly dedicated "To The Young Ladies of United Columbia" and prefatorially committed to their moral instruction:

> Novels have ever met with a ready reception into the Libraries of the Ladies, but this species of writing hath not been received with universal approbation. . . . Of the Letters before us, it is necessary to remark, that . . . the dangerous Consequences of SEDUC-TION are exposed, and the Advantages of FEMALE EDUCATION set forth and recommended.[38]

As a novelist, William Hill Brown is well aware of the pervasive censure of fiction and basically accepts the standards by which novels have been generally judged but deflects those standards from his particular fiction through truth, teaching, and typography.

Other novels found other ways, sometimes even more strained and circuitous, to defuse or deny the ideological assumptions against which they had to contend. One of the more interesting of these defenses is found in the preface to *Monima, or the Beggar Girl: A Novel, in One Volume, Founded on Fact. By an American Lady* (1802). The author, Martha Meredith Read, dedicated her novel to Dr. Hugh Meredith—perhaps her father, perhaps her brother, perhaps an uncle. However close to the author the dedicatee might have been, her preface *assumes* the good doctor's opposition to fiction and then works around it by recourse to a new kind of argument in the novel's favor:

> To the man of deep erudition, [my novel] will, probably, appear insignificant, as it is
> impossible to connect other characters than low and illiteral ones with beggars; but to
> write merely for those who are already informed, argues much vanity and a defective
> judgment in the writer. To exhibit mankind in their true colours, to display characters
> *as they are,* to unfold the pernicious tendency of ignorance, prejudices and immorality,
> is the indisputed privilege of the Novel-writer; this, however, cannot be done but by a
> strict adherence to truth and nature; to deviate from this, the mind must become
> enveloped in mystery and darkness . . . To me, one tear of compunction shed by a
> disobedient child; one little emotion of remorse in the breast of the avaricious and
> contracted sons of fortune, would be far more dear, far more grateful than all the empty
> plaudits that can be bestowed upon well rounded periods or elegantly constructed sen-
> tences.[39]

Read first trivializes the "man of deep erudition" who seeks to trivialize her
audience. She is not writing merely for the educated—which would be sheer
vanity and arrogance. Rather, she is writing for those, like poor Monima, who
occupy another world, unsophisticated, uncelebrated, and often downright unsavory. Given that world, only realism (not aphorism, not dogma) might inculcate
moral lessons in those impervious to "well rounded periods or elegantly constructed sentences." In effect, the author subverts the criterion by which novels
like hers are commonly condemned by inverting them and her novel, too. She
will aim at moralism in an ostensibly immoral world but a world in which the
penniless Monima is again and again shown to be the most admirable character
in the novel, while the gentry (including hypocritical philanthropists) are portrayed as petty prigs—avaricious, lustful, dishonest, and deceitful: the world of
Hitchcock, Miller, and Dwight turned topsy-turvy.

The terms of Charles Brockden Brown's defense of fiction are also grounded
in both a calculated assessment of *who* the majority of his readers really are and
in a pragmatic appraisal of *how* to write for those particular readers:

> They who prate about the influence of novels to unfit us for solid and useful reading,
> are guilty of a double error: for in the first place, a just and powerful picture of human
> life in which the connection between vice and misery, and between facility and virtue
> is vividly portrayed, is the most solid and useful reading that a moral and social being
> (exclusive of particular cases and professional engagements) can read; and in the second
> place, the most trivial and trite of these performances are, to readers of certain ages
> and intellects, the only books which they will read. If they were not thus employed,
> they would be employed in a way still more trivial or pernicious.[40]

Brockden Brown parenthetically valorizes certain kinds of thoroughly pragmatic
reading in pursuit of professional improvement (i.e., class mobility) and then
asserts at length that his own fiction is the next best thing. He is also well aware
that many novel readers, many of those who read his novels, might not read

anything besides fiction and that reading is considerably preferable to what they might be doing in its place—a possible declension downward that never occurred to the critics of the novel. Or, in a somewhat different vein, Helena Wells similarly observes that the "studies" of most of her readers "go not beyond the page of the novelist" but rather than berate these readers for their ignorance, she insists that "it was a view [of] benefitting this class . . . which induced the writer to commit this trifle . . . to the tribunal" of criticism.[41]

Implicit in all of these defenses of fiction is a definition of realism at odds with the corresponding definition whereby they were condemned. Timothy Dwight's hypothetical novel reader, for example (and in his own terms), "must one day act in the real world. What can she expect, after having resided so long in novels, but that fortunes, and villas and Edens, will spring up every where in her progress through life, to promote her enjoyment. She has read herself into a heroine, and is fairly entitled to all the appendages of this character."[42] For Dwight, what is unrealistic is the teleology by which a poor girl might become, if only vicariously, a princess. To the novelists, however, it is quite *unrealistic* that no "low and illiteral" characters inhabit the pages of history, of biography, of classical literature, of all the works that comprise the education of men such as Timothy Dwight. And it is even more *unrealistic* for Dwight to expect average readers to prefer Milton, Locke, or Euclid (all writers alluded to in Dwight's discourse on novel reading) over *Monima, or the Beggar Girl*. Moreover, to read Locke or Milton or Euclid presupposes a familiarity with philosophical or poetic or mathematical discourse. One does not enter into these worlds without a suitable foundation. And where, one might ask, would Monima, the beggar girl, obtain that education? Certainly not at Yale. For Dwight, not *Charlotte Temple* but the Bible should be the reading of the "illiteral" masses. But in the changing world of the turn of the eighteenth century, many new readers wanted to read about characters like themselves, characters with whom they could identify and about whom they could fantasize. The Bible offered little opportunity for fantasies of *earthly* rewards or social empowerment, and Dwight on the Bible offered even less.

Although early novels advanced their own definition of realism, a number still ended as wish-fulfillment fantasies. Monima wins a fortune at the end of her novel; she does not die, derelict, in some Philadelphia back street. But not all of these fictions concluded so fortunately. Charlotte Temple and Eliza Wharton (the heroine of *The Coquette*) both die at the end of their best-selling stories. Even Monima focuses not just on fantasy's fulfillment but also on the injustices of poverty, on the *crime* of poverty. As E. P. Thompson has noted of the sanctity of property in late eighteenth-century law: "The greatest offense against property was to have none."[43] Monima's social status, as much as her sex, graphically attests to how far short of Jefferson's ringing dictum that "all men are created equal" a professed American democracy can actually fall.

Beyond and behind the fantasies intrinsic to individual novels (and this is a topic to be explored case by case when I consider specific early American novels) there is also a hard core of formal realism in the novel that was not acknowledged by the critics of the time. As Ian Watt has shown of earlier British novels, the realism operates on numerous levels: linguistic (characters sound as if they are talking to one another), situational (in Bakhtin's term, "chronotropic," or within the time/space of fiction), and personal (characters are viewed as individuals— not types—by the reader).[44] Benjamin Franklin (an avid novel reader and the publisher of the first American edition of a novel, *Pamela*) more simply defines the essential reality of early fiction: "Honest John [Bunyan] was the first that I know of who mixes narration and dialogue, a method of writing very engaging to the reader, who in the most interesting parts finds himself, as it were, admitted into the company and present at the conversation. Defoe has imitated him successfully in his *Robinson Crusoe*, in his *Moll Flanders*, and other pieces; and Richardson has done the same in his *Pamela*."[45] Franklin's formulation draws a crucial distinction between the novel and the other print forms such as biography and history typically recommended over fiction. While biography and history might be "true," they posit a wide gulf between the subject and the reader ("the great man" or the "great event" versus the ordinary reader and his or her uneventful life) and also between the author and the reader (the author proclaiming, the reader receiving wisdom and moral edification). The novel, in contrast, creates its *own* truth by involving the reader in the process of that creation. The distance between text and reader, author and reader is effaced: The reader is "present at the conversation" and becomes imaginatively part of the company. Whether an esteemed political leader or a lowly printer's apprentice, the reader is privileged in relationship to the text, is welcomed into the text, and, in a sense, *becomes* the text.

As earlier observed, the effacing of the distance between the events narrated in fiction and the reader's emotional response to the events alarmed many critics. The very act of reading fiction asserted the primacy of the individual as reader and the legitimacy of that reader's perceptions and responses. In an age increasingly concerned with the individual—whether from the philosophical perspective of thinkers such as Locke, who saw every mind as a blank page upon which experience wrote a "self," or from the political perspective of a new democracy that depended for its success, in some measure, upon the success of its individual citizens—the novel form validated individual identities and championed equality. In theory at least, it was bound to succeed and, happily, for its readers and authors, by the second quarter of the nineteenth century it had clearly done so.

Writing in 1824 for the *American Monthly Magazine*, James McHenry examined in some detail the connection I have suggested between the openly pervasive censure of fiction on the one hand and the covert importance of class difference (especially during the 1790s) on the other. Even though the contemporary reader may well suspect that McHenry overstates the case for the egalitarianism of his own time, his perspective on the previous era is persuasive:

> The liberal feelings, which seem to be, at present, more prevalent in society than at any previous period of the history of men with which we are acquainted, are undoubtedly the cause why many of the pursuits and entertainments of life that were formerly esteemed reproachful and humiliating are now viewed with complaisance, and followed without any sense of degradation. A taylor, a shoe-maker, or a weaver, who has thriven by his profession, is respected by the world, and admitted into society, if he can only pay his way, as freely as if he had never handled a single instrument of industry; nay, he is, nine times out of ten, received with more internal respect, than if he had been all his lifetime an idler. Yet many of us, who are not very old, may recollect the time when these industrious members of the community would have been kept at a distance from genteel company, with as much care as if their presence carried contamination with it.

McHenry also observes that now "the politician, the lawyer, the philosopher, and all who wish to see human affairs depicted on an extensive scale" praise novels, whereas these "were the kind of men that, in the days when novels were held in degradation, treated them with most contempt."[46]

In the course of a few generations, there was a revolution in the reading habits of Americans. In synergistic fashion, at the same time that more and more people became readers of novels, more novels became available as distribution improved and, even more, as the capital-intensive nature of publishing technology, achieved by the mid–nineteenth century, required that a system of mass production and mass consumption replace the older system of book production for essentially a small group of readers. In practical terms, the common American reader effectively replaced the socially prominent critic as the primary arbiter of nineteenth-century taste. This does not mean, of course, that common citizens had control over the means of production—for they did not—but it does mean that those who controlled the production of culture had to be attuned to the tastes and opinions of common citizens, the ways to cater to those tastes as well as the ways to manipulate them for greater profit.

The realignment of the economic base of American culture also necessitated a shift in the role and function of the critic. As Nina Baym has shown in her exhaustive study of the reception of the novel from 1840 to 1860, social authorities had to establish a new relationship to the novel and to the novel-reading public.[47] Instead of serving as the form's opponents and—much later and more hopelessly than the first critics—attempting to stem the tide, they chose, for the most part, to assent to the new cultural order. Ministers, as both Rhys Isaacs and David Reynolds have shown, increasingly borrowed from the novel genre that their predecessors had castigated. Many ministers even restructured the classic Puritan sermon into a quasi-novelistic story that presumed an audience familiar with fictional plots, characters, and technical devices.[48] Similarly, critics found themselves in the role of the handmaiden, not the harrier, of the novel. A certain critic might, on occasion, criticize the failings of a specific novel, but gone almost entirely was the dismissive rhetoric of the earlier reviewers who would have preferred—if they could have arranged it—that they (and all readers) never again darken their imagination or their morals with a novel.

The portentous changes in culture and authority that the early critics feared and predicted had already, in the wake of the novel, come to pass by the middle of the nineteenth century, and for the first time in history a mass audience was conceived of as the primary consumers of literature. In Baym's formulation, "not only was [the novel] a new form, it was a popular one; and it was an unprecedented cultural event for the masses to be determining the shape of culture. To follow the public instead of leading it, to surrender critical judgment to the extent of permitting a low literary mode to assume cultural significance, involved critics in new and difficult professional decisions."[49] Perhaps the issue is best described by another nineteenth-century reviewer, Allan Cunningham, who wrote retrospectively in 1833 about the advent, over a decade before, of Sir Walter Scott. When *Waverley* first appeared, "men beheld it with as much perplexity, as the out-break of a revolution; the more prudent held their peace, and waited to see what might come of it; the critics were in sad straits, having nothing wherewithal to measure it; . . . but the public, without asking their opinion, gave decisive judgment in its favor."[50]

Theirs was a judgment not just on *Waverley* but on the novel as a genre. As the first critics intuited, readers could claim the power to pass judgment for themselves on cultural forms "without asking the opinion" of those who, from the landing of the Mayflower onward, had been schooled in asserting judgment without waiting to be asked.

4 Literacy, Education, and the Reader

Is it not a little hard [as Swift asked] that not one gentleman's daughter in a thousand should be brought to read or understand her own natural tongue, or be judge of the easiest books that are written in it? . . . If there be any of your acquaintance to whom this passage is applicable, I hope you will recommend the study of Mr. *Webster*'s Grammatical Institute, as the best work in our language to facilitate the knowledge of Grammar. I cannot but think Mr. *Webster* intended his valuable book for the benefit of his countrywomen: For while he delivers his *rules* in a pure, precise, and elegant style, he *explains* his meaning by *examples* which are calculated to inspire the female mind with a thirst for emulation, and a desire of virtue.
—William Hill Brown, *The Power of Sympathy* (1789)

I have thought that many a complete letter writer has been produced from the school of the novelist . . . and hence, probably, it is, that females have acquired so palpable a superiority . . . in this elegant and useful art.
—Judith Sargent Murray, *The Gleaner* (1798)

This chapter, like the previous one, can appropriately begin with Updike Underhill's observation that a new American readership had emerged while he was away:

The worthy farmer no longer fatigued himself with Bunyan's Pilgrim up the "hill of difficulty" or through the "slough of despond" but quaffed wine with Brydone in the hermitage of Vesuvius, or sported with Bruce in the fairy land of Abyssinia, while Dolly, the dairy maid, and Jonathan, the hired man, threw aside the ballad of the cruel stepmother, over which they had so often wept in concert, and now amused themselves into so agreeable a terror, with the haunted houses and hobgobblins of Mrs. Radcliffe, that they were both afraid to sleep alone.[1]

From Bunyan and ballads to Brydone and Mrs. Radcliffe, the readers in the new Republic were obviously embarked on a pilgrimage of their own and, by the turn of the century, were already well on their way.

But could Dolly the dairymaid and Jonathan the hired man really read *The Mysteries of Udolpho* (1794)? That question is basic to the present discussion of early American culture. It was crucial then, too, as is attested to by John Adams's often quoted claim that America was the most literate nation on earth. "A native American who cannot read and write," Adams boasted, "is as rare as a comet or an earthquake."[2] Numerous travelers of the time, visiting from France or England, concurred with this appraisal, yet Lyle H. Wright estimates that in Adams's day only some 1.5 million individuals, or somewhat less than half of the population, were literate.[3] The discrepancy between the two claims is striking. Nor is it entirely explained away by Kenneth A. Lockridge's suggestion that Adams's "universal literacy" did exist but only in John Adams's America—an America that defined itself as New England, elite, urban, white, male.[4]

The question of literacy (and the concomitant question of the availability and efficacy of early American public education) has recently preoccupied numerous historians.[5] Despite sustained debate and detailed quantitative studies, no one has yet convincingly answered the basic question of just who could read and write in early America. Postulations range from what David D. Hall aptly terms the "storybook version of New England history" in which "everyone in Puritan times could read, the ministers wrote and spoke for a general audience, and the founding of a press at Cambridge in 1638 helped make books abundant" to a quite different picture, "argued most strenuously by Kenneth Lockridge, [of] illiteracy shackl[ing] half of the adult males and three-fourths of the women." Yet Hall also maintains that the "statistics" supporting this second version are as suspect as the older "storybook version."[6] Of course, both versions are stories—different stories (one positive, one negative) about the Puritans. We can applaud their early decision to tax the populace in order to institute mass schooling or we can emphasize that this schooling was provided only for male children. We can extol the Colonial schools for inculcating traditional values through textbooks such as the *New England Primer,* which instilled moral truths ("In Adams fall / We sinn'd all") along with basic literacy, or we can castigate the Puritan public schools for educating a select body of seventeenth- and eighteenth-century men to certain community assumptions about the divine status of class, racial, gender, regional, and social disparities ("Job feels the rod / Yet blesses God") and thus perpetuating a rigid body of religious and social dogma. In short, it is necessary to ask not only who could read but what they read; not only what they read but in what context.

The debate itself may be as interesting for the historiographic issues it raises as for the historical questions it seeks to answer. To start with, it is significant that even though some of the Founding Fathers—notably Franklin—argued that blacks needed to be educated in anticipation of the role they would play in the Republic after emancipation, few studies of the period address the question of black literacy.[7] It was, of course, illegal for slaves to learn to read or write and for whites to teach them. But the existence of such laws does not necessarily mean that they were universally obeyed, and we can note that the advertisements for runaway slaves in an eighteenth-century Boston newspaper suggest as many as one seventh of these fugitive slaves may have been able to read.[8] Yet studies of literacy in New England (where by far and away most of such work has been done, primarily because of the extensive records kept there) rarely mention the

African American population. Typically, blacks were poor and thus left behind very few of those records (deeds, wills, estate inventories, etc.) upon which quantitative studies of literacy are usually based—records that also exclude as much as 20 to 30 percent of the white population who owned no property.[9] One wonders, too, if blacks were not counted in many early records simply because, socially, they did not "count." Again ideology permeates even the most elementary record keeping.

Ideology and the corresponding accidents of the record enter into other questions of literacy, yet, despite differing statistics, some general conclusions can seemingly be derived from the competing quantitative studies of early American literacy. Virtually all recent studies have asserted a rise in literacy over the course of the eighteenth century. Christopher M. Jedrey, for example, in *The World of John Cleaveland*, has calculated signing rates for the inhabitants of Chebacco, Massachusetts, and concludes that in 1675 only about 25 percent of householders in the community could sign their names (the evidence for their wives is too fragmentary to offer any conclusions), whereas in 1771 among adult men elementary literacy was virtually universal and nearly 75 percent of adult women could sign (but again calculated for property owners of the village).[10] Studies by Linda Auwers, Ross W. Beales, Jr., Harvey Graff, and Lockridge confirm this striking advance in literacy, although their figures, too, necessarily exclude the poorest (non-property-owning) portion of the population.[11] Most historians also agree that education, predictably, suffered in the revolutionary years, with detrimental results to literacy, but that after the war there was renewed attention to education. Finally, the figures for the 1850 census indicate an impressive rate of literacy among whites: an almost identical rate for both white men and women of over 90 percent. Yet, writing in 1983 (and in an emphatically nonquantitative manner), Hall acknowledged that the literacy debate continued unabated and vowed to "cut the Gordian knot that literacy studies pose . . . by asserting that early and late, the great majority of Americans, men as well as women, could read."[12]

Hall's sweeping statement did not, unfortunately, sever the Gordian knot or otherwise resolve the controversy: A flow both of new articles that present figures for additional early communities and of review essays that point out the shortcomings of previous literacy studies still continues. This flow, however, attests not so much to a disagreement over the past but to disagreement in the present. The main issue here is historiographic. Specifically, what are the limitations of quantification as a methodology? How much—and by what principles—can we generalize from, say, a single town in one five-year period to a neighboring town a decade later?

The question is not simply methodological but addresses the underlying assumptions of quantificational history. Just as poststructuralist literary theory has in recent years challenged the premises of New Criticism, so too have the premises of history recently been under scrutiny, with theorists such as Hayden White insisting that all history is story-making akin to what the novelist does and that even seemingly objective, quantified findings can replicate the hegemonies within the society at large. But the metahistorical challenge is not the only one to quantification. In defensive reaction to current developments in the field, some historians have vociferously insisted upon a return to narrative history based on "traditional epistemology"—that is, a good, old-fashioned, un-self-reflexive, nineteenth-century-style positivism rooted in the conviction that "truth is absolute."[13] By the lights of this new positivism, metahistory is inimical to "real" history, and so, it must be added, is quantification.

In this historiographic context, quantification (posed between positivism and metahistory) becomes the discipline's New Criticism. By devaluing public pronouncements and by paying detailed attention to the records of a given town (court records, land transactions, etc.), the quantificational historian seeks to pass beyond broad generalizations about the "Puritan mind" or "main currents" of American thought, much as the New Critic eschews historical overview in favor of detailed readings of specific texts. Inevitably, quantifiers implicitly or explicitly use their findings to support larger generalizations about a period or a movement, but they do so through "careful scrutiny" of selected nonliterary documents. Birth and death records in Dedham, Massachusetts (1789–91), become the "well-wrought urn" of quantification. The shopkeeper's account book is not to be scanned and reduced to a historical footnote but must be fully and sensitively plumbed, analyzed, and interpreted by a "discerning reader/historian."

Much of the literacy debate, like controversies over levels of ambiguity in *Moby Dick,* comes from different ways of reading the record, as can be more clearly shown by focusing on one aspect of that debate—the matter of sign literacy (the frequency with which people signed their names on documents rather than marked with an X). Of what is sign literacy a measure (especially as it relates to women, for whom signing data is problematic)? Lockridge has found that in the early national period women's signing rate in New England was still only approximately half of what it was for men, and he extrapolates that the female rate of *literacy* was only half of that for men. Yet Margaret Spufford, in reviewing English documents of the seventeenth century, has found individuals who put a signature on one document and a mark on another. That difference raises some perturbing questions. Were there people who learned to sign only as adults? Or who forgot how to sign after schooling ceased? Or who could no longer sign (especially on wills) because of infirmity?[14] Do we count them, in any case, as literate or illiterate?

There may well have been psychosociological reasons why it was appropriate to sign in one instance (e.g., a husband present or absent) but not in another. Linda Auwers has suggested that such "switchers" may not have been able to either read or write but that, living in a society that prized literacy, they had learned to ape or fake a signature in order to *seem* literate.[15] Or consider how Linda K. Kerber, in examining twenty-eight divorce petitions filed between 1735 and 1745, discovered only four signed with marks instead of signatures (all four marked by women). But, looking more carefully, Kerber observed that numerous signatures were not those of the petitioners but had been provided by the clerk who drew up the petition. "Whether a transcribed signature means that the clerk was in haste," she cautions, "or that he did not think that the petitioner could write, or that the petitioner was illiterate, or, finally, that the petitioner was not present while the document was being transcribed, is difficult to know."[16] What we can suspect, however, is that some studies may have too readily assumed the meaning of evidence to be self-evident and with a semiotic, if not a historical, naiveness read in the sign (whether a signature or mark) proof positive of both the presence and the literateness of the individual whose name that sign signifies. All of these criticisms represent, for the quantificational historian, not so much a Gordian knot as a Pandora's box, since it is always "difficult to know" precisely the full context of any social act and the implicit rules governing even the simplest transactions.

This historiographic issue is an important one, but there are equally important ideological reasons why controversy persists over this particular topic. Literacy is not simply the ability to decode letters upon a page, the ability to sign a name instead of making a mark. Literacy is a *value*. In a democracy especially, literacy becomes almost a matter of principle, a test of the moral fiber of a nation. Revolutionary societies often proclaim their validity by boasting of improved literacy levels, and John Adams's insistence on universal literacy implicitly asserts a vision of a fair and equitable nation. In Benjamin Nelson's phrase, literacy is the "social basis of cultural belief and value systems."[17] It is not simply a "rate," a "measurement," but a vital aspect of a culture, inseparable from its educational systems and values, its larger goals and aspirations, its meaning and definition of itself. To say that women's literacy was only 50 percent or even 75 percent of that of men's is to say something about the principles upon which a new nation was based. Thus a number of recent studies have labored to explain away what seems to be a notable discrepancy in men's and women's signing rates and, in effect, to salvage Adams's boast. Women, these arguments generally run, quit school before they learned to write. Reading, they claim, was taught before writing in the "dame schools" and "summer schools" that most girls attended; consequently, the sign literacy rates argued by Lockridge and others fail to account for a possibly vast number of women who could read perfectly well but who could only make an *X* whenever a signature was called for. Women, after all, had no legal status, and so, since their signatures proved nothing, there was no real reason for them to learn to sign or, by extension, to write.[18]

As the tone of my summary might suggest, I have reservations about this argument on behalf of nonsigning readers (primarily white females, for the sign literacy rate of white men is generally acknowledged to be extraordinarily high). To start with, the argument does not differentiate between signing and writing. There may well have been readers who could not write, but who could sign. In any society that values literacy, there is a psychosociological need to learn at least to sign one's name and thereby elude the most obvious proof of illiteracy. Certainly, anyone today who has been around children has observed the three-year old's scribble upon the page and has heard the child's proud assertion that he or she has written "My Name." Although it is often dubious to argue backward from contemporary experience, it is significant in this regard that many editions of the *New England Primer* included a list of "some proper names for Men and Women to teach Children to spell their own."[19] In short, until more evidence is in, I would suggest that because nonsigning readers are mute—they left behind no historical record—at present they exist as a historiographic construct useful for questioning what data does survive (*Is* signing a reliable measure of literacy?) or for perpetuating the "storybook version of New England," but not particularly germane to the question of just who may actually have read the American novel. For even the most dedicated proponent of nonsigning readers, I would think, would have to admit to *levels* of literacy.[20] If someone, with the Bible opened to the proper passage, can make it through a well-known psalm, is that person really literate? Or must the person also be able to make it through, say, Cotton Mather's commentaries on the Bible as well? It seems highly unlikely that there were many American women of the early national period who could read Locke or Hume or even *Monima, or the Beggar Girl,* but who had to mark an X on public documents.

The postulation of nonsigning readers and other methods of "padding" the figures on behalf of women readers (or ignoring them for blacks) obscures basic social inequities. Once more, historiographic and ideological questions are intertwined. Since how many people in America were literate (men and women, blacks and whites) depends largely on the definition employed, the definition will always serve the interests of some larger argument. More to the point, what any statistics obscure is that literacy is a *process,* not a fixed point or a line of demarcation. "Literateness" is a more useful concept for my purposes since it suggests a continuum (and a continuing process of education and self-education) between, say, rudimentary reading and elementary ciphering on the one hand and the sophisticated use of literacy for one's material, intellectual, and political advantage on the other. Whether we set women's elementary literacy at 50 percent of men's or at 75 percent, it is indisputable that literateness (in the fullest sense of the term) was more valued, encouraged, and achieved in early America by men than by women. I argue this point at some length because, as I will show, the early American novel became one of the single most vociferous sources of encouragement for women in their striving for literateness. In this respect, the novel echoed the concern of significant numbers of Americans who perceived a disparity be-

P 6a Vol. 1.

Yon Cottager, who weaves at her own door;
Pillow and bobbins all her little store;
Content tho' mean _____

Sam.ˡ Hill sculp.

FIGURE 3. Illustration by Samuel Hill from William Cowper, *Poems* (Boston: Printed by
E. Lincoln for Manning and Loring and E. Lincoln, 1802). Group reading among the
common people. The woman works while a child learns to read (possibly her own child
or perhaps this is a "dame school"). *Courtesy of the American Antiquarian Society.*

tween the literateness of men and women in the new Republic and also a disparity in the educational *expectations* the new society had for its male and female members.

Ironically, while John Adams boasted of universal literacy in America, his wife frequently lamented her unliterateness to her daughters and her women friends.[21] She decried, for example, the hegemony of the nation's colleges and their male "puberty rite" (to use Walter J. Ong's term) of Greek and Latin as the "foundation of all the pretensions of the gentlemen to superiority over the ladies" and an obstacle to "liberty, equality and fraternity between the sexes." Similarly, she often expressed "regret" over the "trifling narrow contracted Education of the Females of my own country." "You need not be told," she wrote to John in 1778, "how much female Education is neglected, nor how fashionable it has been to ridicule Female learning."[22] She understood that the issue was not only inferior levels of learning but the way in which assumptions about gender (or class or race) precluded a better education.

There is a tremendous difference between Dolly the dairymaid who must sign an X on her marriage documents and Abigail Adams. On another level, Abigail and Dolly each suffered under a social apprehension that women's education was less important (on all social levels) than men's. Like literacy, education must be viewed as part of larger social and socializing functions. As Raymond Williams has argued, "there are clear and obvious connections between the quality of a culture and the quality of its system of education. . . . The way in which education is organized can be seen to express, consciously and unconsciously, the wider organization of a culture and a society. . . . What is thought of as 'an education' being in fact a particular selection, a particular set of emphases and omissions."[23] It should come as no surprise, then, that the historiography of early American education is as polarized as the literacy debate and along much the same ideological lines, even though the facts here are not themselves so much at issue. All scholars agree, for example, that education was important to Puritan America from its very beginnings. The Company of the Massachusetts Bay had made provision for the instruction of the young in America before leaving England. Even before the 1647 passage of the famous "ould deluder Satan" law in Massachusetts (a law requiring public support for education in every town of over fifty families), the more well-to-do inhabitants of the city of Boston had already banded together to fund a school. Throughout New England, other towns soon established schools, too, and, as Stanley K. Schultz notes, "followed essentially the same evolution of financial support from private subscription, tuition, rents, and grants of land to a more formal settlement of town rates."[24]

Yet what did this public support of education *mean*? One reading holds that the Puritan public schools, by insisting on provisions for educating even the children of the poor, facilitated egalitarianism in America. Bernard Bailyn and

Lawrence Cremin, to take two examples, have each eloquently argued that the seventeenth-century schools promoted a breakdown of elitism and residual British class barriers and that an American determination to counter the blankness of wilderness with the gifts of education, civilization, culture, optimism, and individualism led to a democratizing of American society. American democracy itself was thereby substantially grounded, according to this view, in the Puritan public school laws.[25] In contrast, Lockridge, Michael Zuckerman, and revisionist historians such as Samuel Bowles, Herbert Gintis, and Michael B. Katz have maintained that Puritan education preserved class and gender divisions, emphasized recitation and dogma rather than reasoning and knowledge, and thus prepared the way for mass public education, which, in the early national period, was largely motivated by the desire of elites to control an increasingly heterogeneous population and to incorporate the late arrivals on these shores into a submissive American workforce, ready to be even more firmly fixed in their place by the advent of wholesale industrialization.[26]

Questions of who was educated and to what end are complicated by the fact that no message is ever perceived divorced from the context in which it is received. A Protestant-based work ethic and a doctrine of Christian acceptance can have quite different social implications for the slaveholder as opposed to the slave, for the Pilgrim descendant as opposed to the recent immigrant, for the mill owner as opposed to the mill worker, for the husband as opposed to the wife. As Katz has observed, the same American educational system that for nearly two hundred years could be (in principle at least) free, universal, and compulsory could also be racist, sexist, and class biased.[27] Certainly, the Colonial New England schools did institutionalize the society's traditional hierarchies. As E. Jennifer Monaghan has shown, the Puritan public school laws were designed to teach "children to write and reade," but the word *children* in such laws almost always meant "boys."[28] When Walter H. Small surveyed nearly two hundred colonial towns, he found only seven that admitted girls into the schools.[29] Moreover, the primarily oral/aural mode of teaching these boys to read did nothing to challenge the status quo. On the contrary, as Edmund S. Morgan points out, the traditional rote method of instruction was well adapted to the "purposes of Puritan education. It was not designed to give play to the development of individual initiative, because individual initiative in religion usually meant heresy."[30]

The official educational program proposed for the new nation did nothing to revolutionize either the traditional Puritan pedagogy or the social hierarchies supported by that procedure. On the contrary, the Founding Fathers repeatedly stressed the need for an educational system that would reinforce political quiescence and social order. Women, of course, were a primary target of a conservative social message. They should be educated at public expense, the typical argument ran, but educated *to* a certain set of beliefs, primarily to the traditional belief in feminine subordination that, in the past century, had kept them out of the public schools in the first place. This thrust is obvious in Benjamin Rush's "Thoughts upon Female Education" (1787):

> The equal share that every citizen has in the liberty and the possible share he may have in the government of our country make it necessary that our ladies should be qualified to a certain degree, by a peculiar and suitable education, to concur in instructing their sons in principles of liberty and government.[31]

Rush's ringing insistence on an "equal share" to which "every citizen" is entitled somehow peters out into the "peculiar and suitable education" that he advocates for women. Yet as Nancy F. Cott observes, this was the typical position. In 1795, for example, the American Philosophical Society sponsored a contest on the topic of American educational improvements. Every submission to that essay contest included a proposal for universal free education—universal meaning, in this case, open to all white men and women.[32] Every proposal, however, justified female education as an education for potential mothers of men, for the caretakers of future voters and citizens, a position articulated by another eighteenth-century educator, Caleb Bingham, in 1791:

> While the sons of our citizens are cultivating their minds and preparing them for the arduous, important, and manly employment which America offers to the industrious, their daughters are gaining that knowledge, which will enable them to become amiable sisters, virtuous children, and, in the event, to assume characters [as mothers] more interesting to the public, and more endearing to themselves.[33]

Like Adams's boast of universal literacy, the call by men such as Rush or Bingham for female education suggests an androcentric ethos innocently unaware of its own prejudices. There was education and then there was female education—a different concept entirely.

The consequence of this educational theory in practice was a second-class education for girls, as Linda K. Kerber and Mary Beth Norton have both amply demonstrated.[34] Many girls continued to receive their education only at the dame schools or at the summer schools in which often itinerant teachers or local women taught subjects such as elementary reading and writing but advanced sewing and embroidery. And even though the Boston Act of 1789 stipulated that girls and boys be taught the same subjects in the public schools, girls were required to attend school for fewer hours per day and for fewer months per year.[35] Nor was the situation much better for the affluent who might be able and willing to purchase a private education for their daughters. Many of the finest academies excluded female pupils altogether. Others, such as the Leicester Academy in Worcester County, Massachusetts, boasted of their progressive commitment to equal education and taught boys and girls from the same texts. Yet even at Leicester Academy, female pupils studied the classics in translation while boys learned

Latin and Greek, and only boys could enter the Upper School, with its college-preparatory curriculum that stressed the classics, advanced mathematics, and philosophy.[36] The majority of schools for upper-class girls ignored academic subjects almost entirely in favor of oral recitation, embroidery, painting, piano, map drawing, and other skills suitable to the prospective wife of a successful man.

Many of the same men who recognized that female education could reinforce the status quo also insisted that mass education would be the answer to the widespread social unrest occurring throughout various elements in the population. Dr. Rush, in his widely publicized "Plan for the Establishment of Public Schools" (1786), insisted that mandatory mass education could "convert men into republican machines" that would "produce regularity and unison in government." General learning, he argued, "is favorable to liberty. A free government can only exist in an equal diffusion of literature. Without learning men become savages or barbarians."[37] Similarly, Noah Webster, perhaps the single most influential educator of the early national period, insisted that mass education was crucial to the survival of a republic. A Yale graduate himself, he frequently expressed his distrust of the unruly populace, especially those in the back country and the coastal cities, whom, he felt, indulged in licentiousness, drunkenness, and, worst of all, "secret corruption and brazen libertinism." A uniform curriculum in the public schools could instill the ideals of republican duty, patriotism, moderation, piety, and good sense and would thereby solve a range of social ills from private personal laziness to public political dissension. "Every class of people should *know* and *love* the laws," he insisted. "This knowledge should be diffused by means of schools and newspapers, and an attachment to the laws may be formed by early impressions upon the mind." Like Rush, Webster felt that in monarchies education is "partial and adapted to the rank of each class of citizens" while, in republican countries, even the poorest peasant's son had to be taught civility—proper manners, proper morals, and proper grammar.[38] Notably, each educator saw pubic schooling not just as a way of disseminating knowledge but also as a way of perpetuating the status quo and fostering loyalty to a federal government.[39] Perhaps only coincidentally, both Rush and Webster had a lifelong disdain of novels.

Inspired by this nationalistic educational philosophy, most of the new states mandated in their constitutions support for publicly funded education. The Massachusetts Constitution and Bill of Rights, for example, framed by John Adams, particularly stressed the connection between mass education and the principles of "public and private charity," "industry and frugality," and "honesty and punctuality." Adams, suspecting that social divisions were fixed in human nature, did not believe that public education would amalgamate the lower orders into the higher, but that education would bring the unprivileged into a more compliant attitude toward authority and would foster "the Virtues and Talents of the People" and even help quell the "affrays and Riots" that plagued Boston during the postrevolutionary era.[40] Schooling for the masses was also extended well beyond the already established New England cities, towns, and villages. The Land Ordinance of 1785 mandated that one lot in every new township be set aside for a town school, while the Northwest Ordinance of 1787 pushed westward the New England premise that "religion, morality, and knowledge, being necessary to good government and the happiness of mankind, schools and the means of education shall forever be encouraged."[41]

There was, however, a substantial discrepancy between the prescriptive statements on the importance of "universal" education and the actual performance of the institutions intended to achieve that goal. First, not all children attended school. According to Schultz, even after passage of the Boston education laws in 1789, only 12 percent of the school-age population (children from four to fifteen years of age) were educated at the public grammar and writing schools; only 7 percent at private institutions (usually wealthier children); and only 2.1 percent at the prestige Latin schools.[42] Similarly, Carl F. Kaestle and Maris A. Vinovskis have determined that there was an enrollment of only 24.7 percent of all children in New York City schools during 1795–96, although, as they also point out, that rate did rise to between 50 and 60 percent after 1830.[43] Furthermore, for those who regularly attended school, the quality of education varied widely from region to region, from school to school. Edward Everett Hale, in *A New England Boyhood*, contrasted his own education at the prestigious Boston Latin School with the educational opportunities otherwise available in the city: "There was no public school of any lower grade, to which my father would have sent me, any more than he would have sent me to a jail." Boston's other schools, for Hale at least, were characterized by the drudgery of rote memorization, by uninspired teaching, perpetual whippings, and "constant conflict with men of a very low type."[44] Mr. Hale would not have approved of the North Carolina schoolmaster William A. Chaffin, who, with a certain glee, listed forty-seven offenses in his "Rules of School," with punishments that ranged from one lashing for "every word you mis In your . . . Leson without Good Excuse" to ten lashes for "Playing at Cards at School" or "For Misbehaving to Girls."[45]

Nor did the public schools have much to recommend them when viewed from the other side of the desk. The diarists Ethan Allen Greenwood and Elizabeth Bancroft complained of having as many as sixty pupils in one schoolroom, and Tyler, in *The Algerine Captive*, gives us a more detailed, albeit fictional, portrait of just such a class:

> Excepting three or four overgrown boys of eighteen, the generality of [my students] were under the age of seven years. Perhaps a more ragged, ill bred, ignorant set never were collected for the punishment of a poor pedagogue. To study in school . . . was impossible. . . . What with the pouting of the small children, sent to school not to learn

but to keep them out of harm's way, and the gruff surly complaints of the larger ones, I was nearly distracted.[46]

If the foregoing portrait of education in the early Republic seems bleak as well as socially reactionary, it may well have been inevitably so. Formal education was one way—perhaps the best way—to educate the members of a postrevolutionary society to the values esteemed by that society's leaders and designed to perpetuate their society as they esteemed it. In other words, formal education almost necessarily institutionalizes social hierarchies, with the classroom itself serving as an apt metaphor for social authority and social control. Moreover, educational policy and praxis define who is to be literate within a society and to what degree, and thus they determine what tests for and uses of literacy are appropriate for different social groups. In a fundamental way, the educational program of a society attempts to constitute in advance its potential or projected readership.

But many Americans were not so ready to be simply constituted (in Philadelphia or in the schoolroom). Specifically, a number of Americans found other sources of education outside the established schools, sometimes even in direct contradiction to the methods and morals that were being taught in those schools. Simultaneously with the codification of mass education, there was a vital movement throughout the new nation toward self-education, often inspired by books that could be bought by adults as well as by children, books that were designed to amuse as well as to instruct.

In the last years of the century, with the war over, there was a sense of excitement for many in the new nation, and one emblem of that vitality could be read in the publishing trade. As suggested earlier, the market flourished with unprecedented numbers of books. Publishers were quick to meet a growing demand for self-help books and social guides, textbooks and teacher's manuals, histories and biographies, children's books, readers for adults, travelogues, captivity stories, crime narratives, and, of course, novels. Whatever its official or unofficial causes, there was at least a perception on the part of writers, educators, publishers, and booksellers that a new social class of readers wanted to increase their literary skills and to be able to turn those skills to their own amusement and advantage. Informal community reading groups, already prevalent before the war, sprang up in seemingly every county, partly in response to the widespread dicta that education was essential in a democracy—a dicta that takes on a different force entirely when enunciated by (not for) the unprivileged. Lending libraries, too, did an unprecedented business. Finally, books that promised to help readers become more literate were in particular demand. For example, Noah Webster's *The American Spelling Book*, popularly referred to as the "blue-back speller," sold millions of copies, by one estimate 70 million overall.[47] Perceiving a demand for more than a simple speller, Webster also compiled the third part of his *A Gram-*

matical Institute of the English Language . . . (1785), a collection of fictional or quasi-fictionalized accounts aimed primarily at older readers and drawn from history, Scripture, or the classics. Along with Caleb Bingham's *American Preceptor* (1794), *The Columbian Reader* (1798), and Lindley Murray's *English Reader* (1799), Webster's anthology went on to become a best-seller in the early national period.

The early American novel helped to generate and benefited from this educational excitement. Virtually *every* American novel written before 1820 (I can think of no exceptions) at some point includes either a discourse on the necessity of improved education (often with special attention to the need for better female education) or a description of then-current education (typically satirical, as in Tyler's portrait of the schoolroom) or, at the very least, a comment on the educational levels and reading habits of the hero and even more so the heroine. It might be noted, too, that most of the known novelists (including Jeremy Belknap, Hugh Henry Brackenridge, Charles Brockden Brown, William Hill Brown, Hannah Webster Foster, Charles Ingersoll, Herman Mann, Isaac Mitchell, Judith Sargent Murray, Susanna Haswell Rowson, Rebecca Rush, Sarah Savage, Benjamin Silliman, Tabitha Tenney, Royall Tyler, and Helena Wells) also wrote, separately, essays and often books on education. These writers' emphasis was not so much on public as on personal education, and they all encouraged individualistic striving toward self-improvement and self-education, typically on a rationalist model. Perhaps even more than the statements on public education by leaders such as Benjamin Rush and Noah Webster, the comments of these novelists reflect an important trend in American social thought in the new Republic and attest to the individual citizen's desire to achieve increased literateness, both within and without the existing system of schools.

Most of the novels countered the traditional concept of education as rote memorization and mechanical recitation by advocating, instead, "useful knowledge," learning through example, associational thinking, and, especially, the conjunction of instruction with amusement—in short, the implicit epistemological program of the genre, as well as the liberal social cause overtly championed by many novels. Learning should be both intellectually stimulating and *fun*, a radical revision of Puritan praxis. Implicitly and sometimes explicitly, novelists held up Franklin's experimental method as the model of learning or applauded Jefferson's concept of a hands-on utilitarian pedagogy. The novelist Sukey Vickery not only advocated a Lockean program in *Emily Hamilton* but, after marrying Samuel Watson, practiced what she preached in the education of their nine children. After they went to sleep at night, she studied mathematics in order that she might better teach ten-year-old Harriot "the *meaning* of simple Addition, why to carry the 10. . . . Wish her perfectly to understand the meaning of terms as she or the study will be found destitute of pleasure."[48]

The same educational philosophy pervaded a number of texts that set out

FIGURE 4. Illustration by Samuel Hill, "The Old Soldier," from the *Massachusetts Magazine, or Monthly Museum*, September 1791. Here group reading takes place across class, gender, and generational lines. The women are fashionably dressed while the old soldier wears homespun, is surrounded by simple implements (bowl, jug), and sits in front of a rude hut while the girl reads. *Courtesy of the American Antiquarian Society.*

deliberately to provide an alternative to Webster's speller, which explicitly stated that "the minds of children may well be employed in learning to spell and pronounce words, whose signification is not within the reach of their capacities."[49] Among the first of these was the novelist Susanna Rowson's *Spelling Dictionary* (1807), which advocated that children learn to "associate ideas" and that "cheerfulness" be a classroom ideal. Her method and pedagogical philosophy were based on "rational idea[s]," not tedious memory work.[50] The new century also saw some of the first teachers' manuals, manuals that acknowledged teaching as a *profession* and learning as a *process*. The *Juvenile Mirror, and Teacher's Manual, Comprising a Course of Rudimental Instruction* (1812), for example, begins by suggesting that children be taught reading and writing together, before the age of six, and that all instruction be based on rational principles. In contrast to the blue-back speller, this book advised that teachers "ask a child how he would spell [certain] phrases, if he were obliged to write them down, and we introduce the idea that he must learn to spell, before he can make his words and thoughts understood in writing." Students should also be encouraged to "write down words of their own selection every day" since "children learn to spell more by the eye than by the ear."[51] Or Francis Joseph Neef, an Owenite, in *The Method of Instructing Children Rationally in the Arts of Writing and Reading* (1813), argued for a Socratic method of instruction and an associational model of learning, which, he insisted, would enable children to acquire, rapidly and pleasantly, reading and writing skills and would also encourage the kind of probing, analytical thinking necessary for the improvement of society (a goal in keeping with Neef's socialist-utopian leanings).[52] Similarly, the social reformer Joshua Leavitt's *Easy Lessons in Reading for the Use of the Younger Classes in Common Schools*, published in 1823 and reprinted twenty-two times before 1849, actually parodied the time-honored system of rote memorization and "mechanical reading" to promote an alternative method of "thinking" and "vigorous habits of investigation."[53]

These educational reformers insisted not on the value of passively learning to spell and pronounce but on the need both for the *active* production of meaning in the free play of the mind that comes from reading imaginative literature and for the active production of meaning that arises from writing out one's own thoughts. Writing became the culmination of reading, and books served as models for the reader's own writings. The material and political advantages of good writing received special attention. Penmanship books, of course, had been around for a long time, but new ones appeared with remarkable frequency, and old standbys were pirated and reprinted in increasingly greater numbers. A fine hand, the writing masters all insisted, not only proclaimed a fine character but also improved one's prospects in life, as suggested by the epigram William Baker set his penmanship students to copy over and over again: "A Man's Manners Commonly Form His Fortune."[54] Similarly, the ponderous title of Daniel Hewett's book advertises its rationale: *Self-Taught Penman, in Thirty Lessons; A New System of Running Hand, in which the Art of Writing is displayed, and can be acquired without the Assistance of any Teacher. Calculated for those who cannot write at all; and also for those who wish to improve from a Bad Handwriting to a Good One, in the Shortest Time Possible* (2nd ed., 1818). Even John Jenkins, one of the most famous penmanship teachers, published in 1791 a self-help manual based on the principles he developed at his school. Writing, according to Jenkins, "is the key to arts and science, the register and recorder of them all; it is the life and soul of commerce and correspondence. It is the inheritance of posterity, whereby they receive whatsoever is left them in law, to live by—in letters, to learn—in evidence, to enjoy. It is the picture of time and the rule of futurity."[55]

Other self-improvement books went considerably beyond chirography. *The Complete Letter Writer* was reprinted (and often retitled and retooled) throughout the middle to late eighteenth century; it contained sample missives on a range of topics from poetry to politics. It also encouraged readers to make use of their new writing skills in such public forums as the newspapers, which stood ever ready to publish unsolicited letters and reviews. The *Short, Plain, and Cheap Directions for Reading Books to Profit* (sold at the J. Seymour Circulating Library, one of New York's chief purveyors of fiction) advised the reader to read with a "black-lead pencil lying by you," to mark significant passages and record their location on the blank leaf at the back of the book, to list any new words, and even to copy out particularly felicitous passages as a way of improving one's own style.[56] More immediately practical was *Every Man His Own Lawyer* (originally published in America by Benjamin Franklin), from which one could learn how to write receipts, leases, notices, and wills without incurring the expense of an attorney. Finally, on a lower level on the social and economic scale, an inexpensive pamphlet by the novelist Sarah Savage, titled *Advice to a Young Woman at Service* (1823), suggested that those same young women "reserve one hour a day for reading and writing." By writing to parents and siblings, a serving girl could daily make improvements in her "writing, and spelling, and the power of expressing [her] thoughts." If from the dollar she earned each week, the girl could save enough money to purchase one book a year, she "will in time," Savage advised, "get a pretty collection." But the servant girl is also cautioned to choose wisely, "for there are bad books in circulation, such as I should be sorry to have you even look at."[57]

The very proliferation of these self-improvement books attests to an emerging, broadly based interest in education that encompassed men and women, city and country citizens, and specifically addressed unprivileged readers. The manuals encouraged self-reliance, free thinking, inductive reasoning, and a questioning of principles and authority. Bare literacy and rote memorization can facilitate passive consumption of messages from on high. True literateness, however, ideally entails increased autonomy. With access to the world of books, the reader can choose among different authorities and take them according to the reader's evaluation of their worth. Whether this ideal is fully accomplished or not in a capitalistic system—where even bookish desire is manipulated to encourage commodity consumption—is an entirely different issue, and one that does not become crucial until the mid–nineteenth century. In the early Republic, the increase in the number of books was a new phenomenon partly necessitated by a new body of readers. For many of these readers, books were still unique and precious, not so much commodities as treasures.

"Being this day seventeen years old and feeling fully my own ignorance and the importance of time I am determined to avail myself of every opportunity of improving my mind and if possible not let a day pass without spending a few hours in reading and writing." Thus does Susan Heath, an affluent young lady of Boston in 1812, record her dedication to a relatively small world of literature but a world much larger than the tedious round of company and visiting and daily chores that otherwise occupy her. She records, too, her escape into novels or into quasi-novelistic devotional works such as *Temper* or *Practical Piety:*

> I sat down and read a little in Temper, as I begin to be apprehensive that I shall never finish it unless I make myself more time to read. . . . [Later] I stole upstairs under the pretense of going to bed—when I sat down and read an hour in Temper—at last I heard Mama coming and jumped under the coverlid with my clothes on and she thinking I was asleep took away my light.[58]

Books were precious in the new Republic. Careful readers, mindful of the fragility of books, carefully cut out and decorated thumb papers that protected a novel's pages, or pared the corners of textbooks and primers in order to preserve a text that often circulated among a wide community of readers. Sometimes as many as a dozen readers would inscribe a book over the course of a few generations, again suggesting that a book was not just a commodity but a special possession, an inheritance or a gift. Indeed, hundreds of inscriptions in early American readers directly and indirectly attest to how much the unique psychological experience of reading meant to early Americans and particularly to those just freed from proscriptions (or at least impediments) to literateness imposed by facts of gender, class, race, location, or the unavailability of books. As one, Elisabeth Haseltines, wrote in the front flyleaf of a religious narrative, "Those who to learning do incline / A golden treasure soon shall find."[59] And certainly Uri Decker's scribblings in her copy of Lindley Murray's *English Reader*, the most widely used reader of the early national period, indicate how much that one book meant to a young woman from a place designated only as Wolf Creek. Her handwriting is often uncertain; there are a few blots and some strokes scratched over; her name is repeated several times in the front flyleaves of the book, sometimes crudely in pencil and then more proficiently in pen. One entry, in pen and dated December 13, 1822, reads: "Uri Decker's Property. Steal Not this Book/ Fear of the Devil" (a slightly skewed rendition of a warning often found in early books). And on the rear flyleaf, in a notably improved hand, is a similar entry (this one drawn from the *New England Primer*): "Uri Decker's Book and Heart Shall Never Part." The date is now March 10, 1836. For at least fourteen years, Uri Decker has owned, written in, and read her book, apparently with no loss of interest or intensity.[60]

THE NOVEL IN THE NEW Republic was not culturally autonomous but, rather, was contiguous with other literary forms, was intertwined with the social and political concerns of the day, and was part of the activities of the reader's life. Virtually all early novels were published in a duodecimo format, typically 15 centimeters high, small enough to fit in the reticule carried by an eighteenth-century woman and easily taken along to a quilting bee or an afternoon of embroidery with one's friends (or, for that matter, easily concealed from censorious parents or neighbors). These volumes were small enough to be held in one hand—while the other rocked the cradle or stirred the pot. Toy books (tiny volumes designed primarily for children) could even be carried in a pocket (very much like the abundant tract literature of the nineteenth century that was designed to be carried out to the fields or into the factory).

For all the censure of fiction, the novel served as a major locus of republican education. As Royall Tyler wrote to his publisher when proposing a book for children: "*Sanford and Merton, Rural Walks, & C*, are found in the hands of almost all children whose parents wish to teach them something more than to dance, read and write." Tyler insisted that "a book which will amuse while it instructs children will sell in this country," and so did hundreds of books that could both amuse and instruct adults, and for much the same reasons.[61] First and foremost, many early novels (both imported and indigenous) operated at a relatively unsophisticated linguistic level. The vocabulary was often commonplace, the syntax simple, the story direct. Many popular novels, such as *Robinson Crusoe*, were also sold in shortened forms that were designed for children or for new readers.[62] The advertisements included in early American novels also indicate that they were often targeted specifically for children, women, or a new and relatively untutored readership, not for the intellectual elite.[63] Furthermore, the problems of being a new reader, particularly a woman reader, were partly solved in the novels themselves. We regularly encounter in the fiction of the time characters who lament their lack of an education and who strive to overcome that deficiency through study, reading, and literary and philosophical discussion groups incongruously situated among Gothic horrors in the center of sensational romance plots. Such characters serve as role models for marginally educated readers. Appealing to such readers, fiction reached out to a new, wide audience that might not peruse any other kind of books. The novel thus served, of necessity, as a source of education (this is a circular argument, but it was a circular

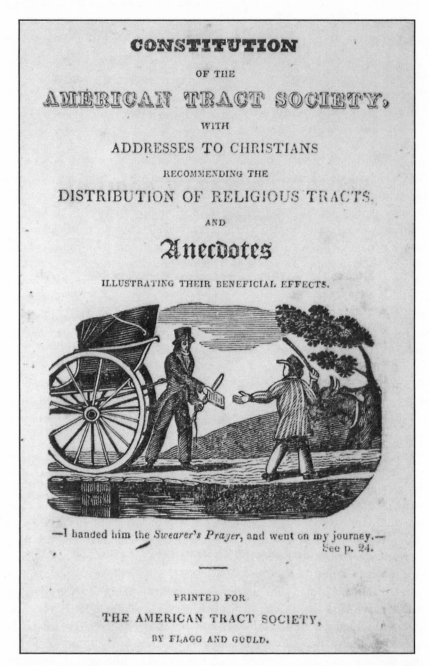

CONSTITUTION

OF THE

AMERICAN TRACT SOCIETY,

WITH

ADDRESSES TO CHRISTIANS

RECOMMENDING THE

DISTRIBUTION OF RELIGIOUS TRACTS,

AND

Anecdotes

ILLUSTRATING THEIR BENEFICIAL EFFECTS.

—I handed him the *Swearer's Prayer*, and went on my journey.—
See p. 24.

PRINTED FOR

THE AMERICAN TRACT SOCIETY,

BY FLAGG AND GOULD.

FIGURE 5. Cover illustration, *Constitution of the American Tract Society* (1824). Implicitly, the illustration suggests the material benefits of reading, as seen in the marked class difference between the gentleman offering the tract and the yeoman who receives it. *Courtesy of the American Antiquarian Society.*

process, too), presenting new subjects, new vocabulary, a new range of experiences, as well as information on topics as diverse as international diplomacy or comparative religion. As will become clear in the later portions of this study, early American novelists seldom passed up the chance to discourse on a variety of intellectual subjects.

Rolf Engelsing, one of the important practitioners of *l'histoire du livre*, has argued persuasively that by the end of the eighteenth century in Germany (and, by extension, throughout the Western world), reading was no longer largely limited to the Bible and other basic religious books for most people.[64] Not only was the number of books increasing apace with the increasing number of readers, but, in addition, more readers read more books in the course of a lifetime. Engelsing also argues that this change in quantity also effected a change in the quality and nature of reading. Instead of reading the Book "intensively" (reading the Bible over and over again), books were read "extensively," one book regularly replacing another, to result in a proto-mass consumption of print. Engelsing sees the novel as both a primary contributing factor to this change and its chief beneficiary. Engelsing's insight is crucial. The whole mentality of reading was changing by the end of the eighteenth century, at least in America, and, clearly, the Bible and Psalter no longer occupied the singular place they once had in the life of the community or of the individual reader. This is not to say that religion had lost its importance. Rather, other books rivaled the Bible for reading time in early America. Just as clearly, an increased demand for different kinds of books called the novel into being.

Engelsing by no means suggests that the year 1800 marks a crucial turning point and that the Bible was then put aside by most readers who henceforth merely raced through successive books. He is careful to qualify both his time line and his demography, since mass literacy spread at different rates, as did the technology of mass printing and mass distribution of printed matter. Yet Engelsing is much less careful in delineating the psychic costs of extensive reading. He suggests, for example, that extensive reading diluted the process of reading and thereby cheapened it. By his account, the extensive reader becomes a mere consumer of print, passively experiencing the text and finding in that experience mostly a motive for repeating it in a slightly different form.[65] But I would insist that, at least for the period and place here under study, it is condescending to assume that the people were reading more books but reading them less (less frequently, less carefully). Nor does reading more books necessarily betoken an increasingly passive form of consumption or comprehension. Socially, extensive reading can signify a new relationship of audience to authority (the reader may *choose* which books to cherish) and different possibilities for political action and social change; personally, it suggests an increased sense of autonomy and an education not necessarily grounded in theocracy but in democracy. Extensive reading—and I emphasize novel reading here—served for many early Americans as the bridge from elementary to advanced literateness, a transition in mentality the importance of which cannot be overstated. Similarly, to assume that the emergence of mass literature lessens the intensity of the reading experience is grossly inaccurate. What do we make, for example, of the dozens, perhaps hundreds, of young men who leapt off bridges or put a pistol to their foreheads with a copy of *Werther* in their breast pockets? Surely theirs was an intensive reading. Or of the young women who made a grave in New York City for poor Charlotte Temple; who, for two generations, left wreaths, locks of hair, and mementos of lost loves upon that grave; and who, when they discovered that Charlotte was not a "real" person but merely a fictional creation, felt utterly betrayed and enraged, for they had—they said—lost a friend.[66] In France, also during the late eighteenth century, the "Rousseauistic readers," in Robert Darnton's phrase, "fell in love, married, and raised children by steeping themselves in print."[67] In short, people then as now read themselves into their fictions and their fictions into their lives. Novel reading could thus provide as much of an emotional or spiritual experience (as well as a guide for living) as did the earlier intensive reading of the Bible.

Novels, then, were not merely light amusements, as we have come to think of them. As discussed in chapter 3, social authorities would not have feared the effects of merely escapist literature. Moreover, increasingly by the end of the eighteenth century, the dichotomy between amusement and instruction was being erased—largely through the instrument of the novel—so that the public craved books designed to "amuse while [they] instruct," in Royall Tyler's phrase. The novel, in addition, fostered reading skills (and with copying, writing skills) that might otherwise be forgotten with disuse. It expanded one's educational horizons well beyond the provinciality or even isolation of one's community and beyond the restrictions on mobility and self-expression placed on women in eighteenth-century society. Even the "extensive" reading of this fiction could be emotionally intense, psychically fulfilling, imaginatively active, socially liberalizing, and educationally progressive—quite the opposite of the merely consumptive, passive, repetitive act posited by the *Leserevolution* model.

The early American novel, as a genre, tended to proclaim a socially egalitarian message. It spoke for—often even in the title—orphans, beggar girls, factory girls, or other unfortunates, and it repeatedly advocated the general need for "female education." While exploiting a sentimental or Gothic plot, the novel also regularly provided a kind of education that could even parallel—admittedly, in a minor key—that which was provided by the men's colleges. Works of fiction, for example, often included Greek or Latin quotations (in translation or, in footnotes, conveniently translated for those unversed in classical tongues). The books also provided readers with clues for how to improve their vocabulary or writing skills, by using a variety of syntactic structures or sometimes even contextually defining an unusual word. Epistolary novels provided different patterns of discourse whereby the reader could shape her or his own correspondence. Perhaps more important, the female reader was also assured that writing—and writing well—was a virtue; that an unblemished prose style was as proper to a would-be heroine as a spotless reputation or a winsome smile. The characters in numerous early American novels comment, breathlessly, on the beauty of another's discourse; the fine form of a poem or letter; the grace and strength of a clear hand; the excellence of another's learning, intelligence, and expression. In contrast to the numerous contemporaneous attacks against intellectual women (witness some of John Trumbull's verse on the subject), fiction championed these women in a way that was apprehensible—and inspiring—to women whose own education (and educational opportunities) might be severely restricted. In such fashion, the novel effectively valorized the very education that it also allowed.

The education the novel allowed was often, I would insist, distinctly active and not a mere passive perusal of the work. "Copy well!" Hannah More admonished her readers in 1799. Elaborating upon this method of self-education, she observed: "Ladies, though they have never been taught a rule of syntax, yet, by a quick facility in profiting from the best books and the best company, hardly ever violate one; and . . . often exhibit an elegant and perspicuous arrangement of style, without having studied any of the laws of composition."[68] And in women's diaries from the time we see that poems, sections from favorite essays and novels, and even letters from friends are all recorded. Sometimes admired originals are copied in a second sense, too. Thus in her own copy of Murray's *English Reader*, Mary M. Ball wrote poems titled "Forget-Me-Nots" and "Bethlehem's Stars" modeled on a poem anthologized by Murray, "The Rose."[69] Or in a somewhat different vein, Margaret Smith writes to her younger sister, Susan, on June 6, 1797:

> Your affectionate letter . . . gave me pleasure not only from the tenderness of your expressions, but from the propriety and correctness of your style. Never again make any excuses about writing nor do not allow yourself the excuse of "want of practice," but deprive yourself of it by writing frequently: do not confine yourself to one correspondent, but enlarge your number and be attentive to all. Their [*sic*] is nothing which practice improves more than letter-writing; ease is its greatest beauty and how otherwise can it be acquiring [*sic*].
>
> You will not be able to correct yourself . . . in two or three letters, for the rules of grammar are too confining a particular to be always supplied; but it is by constantly reading elegant writing; whene [*sic*] our ear becomes accustomed, to well constructed and well divided sentences. I always find I write much better immediately after reading works of an elegant and correct style.[70]

We can note that the educational transaction recorded here takes place between the older sister and the younger one, through personal forms of communication such as the letter, and by the model of "elegant and correct" reading, which is thus quite outside the organized school system.

Or we might notice how, in her diary, Patty Rogers imitates the style of her favorite author, Laurence Sterne:

> Read in a sweet novel the D——r brought me.—It affected me so, I could hardly read it, and was often obliged to drop the book to suppress my grief!—Went to Bed, Lay, and thot of the Lovely Woodbridge—Shed a *torrent* of tears, at the *Recollection* of past i.nterviews with him! . . . He [Woodbridge] press'd me to his *Bosom* with a *fondness* I thought expressive of approbation, "*never never* P——y hesitate a *moment* to Let me know if 'tis in my power to make you *happy!* would you would you, no Sir! *said* I, at the same time kissing his Hand with *trembling* Lips!"[71]

Patty Rogers here models both her prose and her prospects upon the very fiction that inspires them—the "*trembling* lips" that, in recollection and italics, underscore the kiss bestowed, making it both more moving and more conventional, much as Parson Yorick partly ducked and indulged a similar excess of sentiment.

Patty Rogers's prose style tells something of what she read by showing how one particular author influenced at least her style. But how did other novel readers—the readers for whom the early novel was written—react to the individual books they individually read? Obviously, there is no possible way to resolve fully this problem, for we can hardly resurrect readers long dead to put to them questions that were not asked in their time. Short of direct testimony, indirect must do, and one reads hundreds of diaries or letters for even a chance reference to fiction. But we do not really obtain what we are after there either. Even then, letters and diaries verged toward what they are now, the public record; as such, they are more likely to indicate how readers thought they should read (also valuable information) than how they actually did. But still there are clues. By surveying the inscriptions, the marginalia, and even the physical condition of surviving copies of early American novels, I have gained at least a fleeting contact with the novel's first American readers, and I am convinced that, at least for some readers, a novel was a precious possession. In this sense, the full text of the early American novel does not end with its printed word but is extended into the scribblings and the lives of its earliest readers.

We might, for example, note how one reader (Betsey Sweet/Betsey Garbor) accurately sums up the tawdry physical object of the pirated 1802 edition of *Charlotte Temple* that she read and owned: "The Paper is Very Poor but No matter for that, it Will do Very Well to Scrabble Over when I have Nothing Else to be about." And scrabble she did. At the front of the book is an elaborate handmade and hand-colored bookplate, with the name "Betsey Sweet" carefully hand-lettered and all framed by blue, yellow, and red borders drawn with unusual care and skill. More elegant penned designs adorn the back cover, which includes the following legend: "If I this Book to you do Lend / and you the Same do Borrow / I Pray you Read it through / today and Send it home tomorrow." What is singular here, however, is that Betsey kept this notably cheap book (so carelessly manufactured that the title page designates the author as "Mrs. Rawson" [sic] for most of her life, carrying it with her into marriage, and reinscribing it with her married name (which strongly suggests that she reread it at various points in her life), and did not merely throw it away as one might, today, discard a cheap paperback.[72]

Other readers more obviously valued this same best-seller. "So true a tale," Sally B[owles?] wrote after the last sentence of her volume of *Charlotte Temple*. Another reader inscribed a brief poem on the endpapers of another volume: "The rose will fade / the truth withers / But a virtuous mind / will bloom forever." The verse echoes the "innocent flower" metaphors associated with Charlotte throughout the novel. This same reader also drew a portrait (really, a doodle) of a young girl in a long nineteenth-century dress, presumably a rendition of the heroine. Similarly moved to poetry by Charlotte's plight, still another reader wrote in still another volume and with more sincerity than clarity: "She was fair and sweet as the Lilly Inosentas [sic] / the young lamb folly misled / her love betrayed her misery / Cros'd the awful final ocean / in the twentieth year of her age—So ended the unfortunate Charlotte." Or W. M. Green in 1823 apparently saw clear connections between Charlotte's life and death and some sad event in his (women did not commonly sign with initials) or her own and, with a page-long poem, filled the back cover of the book with bitter admonitions about the "pang that rends in twain my heart" and friends who "have daggers cold & green" and who "know how to plunge them too." Most graphically of all, another reader wrote but two words in an otherwise pristine 1809 edition of *Charlotte Temple*: "My Treasure."[73]

A survey of the extant copies of one novel, *Charlotte Temple*, in the collection of one library, the American Antiquarian Society, reveals a surprising range of reader response and, more important, also begins to suggest the outlines of a contemporaneous interpretive community. We can ascertain, for example, that this novel was an appropriate present for a sister to make to her brother. One volume is inscribed on the front cover: "Denise Babcock her Book given to her brother Paul Babcock." The brother has written on the inside back cover, "Paul Babcock His Book, 1805," and he has also signed his name at intervals throughout the text. Another volume is inscribed, simply "James Mott—a present by his sister." Men, obviously, were not excluded from Rowson's community of readers, nor were they reluctant to claim membership in that community. Nor were parents necessarily worried about the effect of the book upon their children, as seen in a copy that Sarah Elizabeth Godwin received from her mother.[74]

What the comments and the gift inscriptions both most clearly suggest is that a personal copy of the novel constituted a prized possession. Writing in Pittsburgh on March 10, 1872, in a copy of *Charlotte Temple* published in 1824, William T. Dunn noted: "This book was presented to me by my grandmother Dunn, about the year 1830." The vestige of the boy-reader who received the novel from his

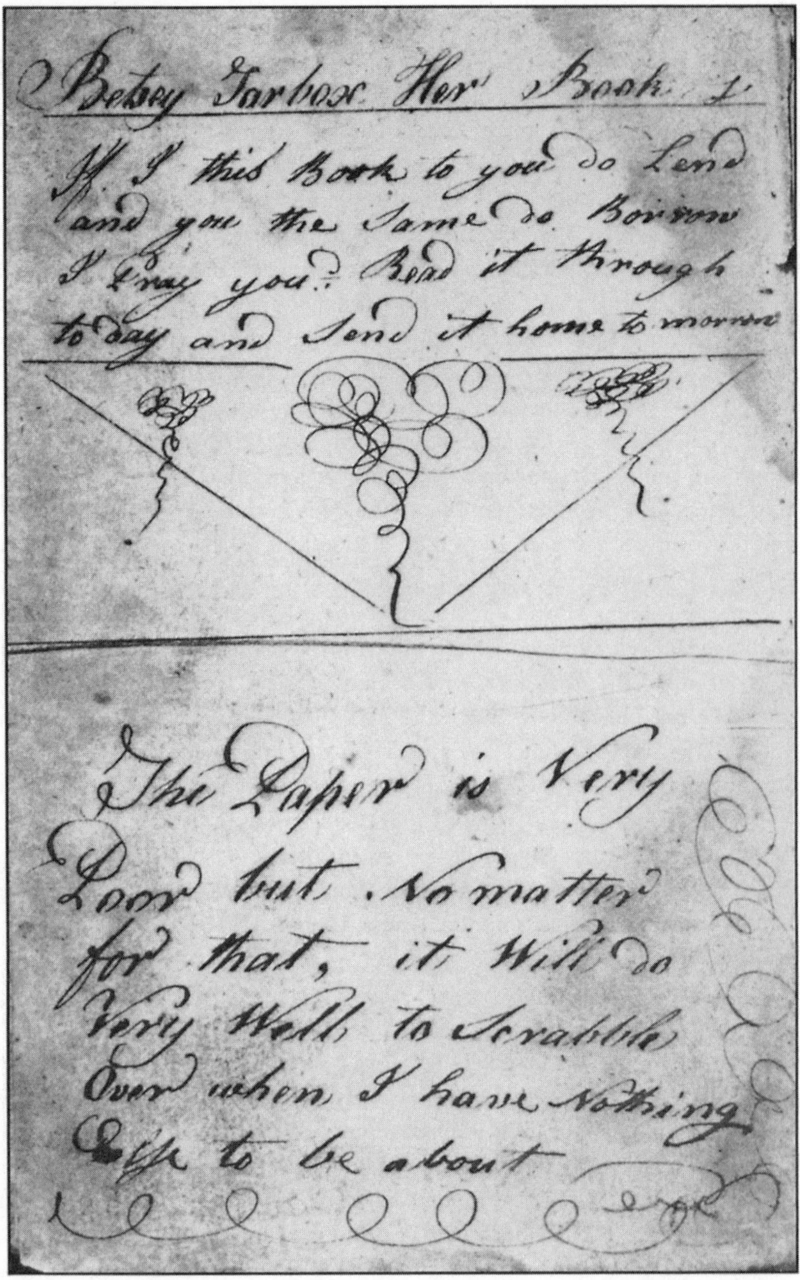

Betsey Tarbox Her Book

If I this Book to you do Lend
and you the Same do Borrow
I Pray you Read it through
to day and Send it home to morrow

The Paper is Very
Poor but No matter
for that, it Will do
Very Well to Scrabble
Over when I have Nothing
Else to be about

FIGURE 6. "Scrabblings" by Betsey Garbor on the rear flyleaf of her 1802 copy of Susanna Rowson's *Charlotte Temple. Courtesy of the American Antiquarian Society.*

grandmother forty years earlier is still there on the endpapers, where an unformed hand does math calculations and records distances between various Ohio towns.[75] Or sometimes a story is hidden in the inscriptions. Written on the inside front cover of one of the more intriguing copies I have found is "Susan Smith Property Bought October the 9 1806," but on the back we find, "William Smiths Book Bought October the 4 1806," along with two signatures of William Smith. Did she buy it from him (sister/brother? wife/husband?) so that it would be her book, or did he use the back inside cover to claim prior purchase and consequent ownership? We cannot answer that question, but in either case the significance is the same; the two dated declarations attest to the importance of the book as property. A more obvious battle over book ownership takes place within the covers of an 1833 edition of *Charlotte Temple:* "Mrs. Ewell" writes her name in a rather elegant hand on the inside front cover. On the back flyleaf, however, "Joseph Ewell His book" is countermanded by "Sarah Ewell *Her* Book." Furthermore, Joseph then signs his name twice, but Sarah three times, her fancy *S*'s covering the back pages. And she, subversively, also writes her name inside the book, at the blank spaces at the end of a few of the chapters. Or witness the family drama in another edition of that best-seller where Jane, Jacob, and Eileen Drake all proclaim ownership (Jane staking her claim twice)—a small community of readers in contention for possession of the text.[76]

Of course, not all readers were so positive about their books. One copy of Samuel Relf's *Infidelity, or the Victims of Sentiment* (1797), for example, is inscribed on the inside back cover: "A book more polluted with destruction and abominable sentiments cannot be put into the hands of anyone—shame to him who wrote it, to her who patronized it, and to the age and country that produced it." This offended reader signed himself or herself "a friend to the traduced sex" and also commented throughout the text on various passages of questionable morality ("Impious!"), on the plausibility of the plot ("Oh!"), and on the tragedy of the resolution ("Just vengeance!" as one of the heroes lies dying). This same reader apparently knows and annotates biographical references made in the book and, most damning of all, goes through the text with a malicious thoroughness correcting typographical mistakes, grammatical errors, and infelicitous sentences (even changing the occasional "who" to "whom" with all the officious glee of a freshman composition teacher). Although the book emphatically was not prized, nevertheless it elicited a strong reaction.[77]

Relatively few copies of early novels survive. Even fewer of these have responses as extensive, as telling, and as passionate as those just considered from *Charlotte Temple* or from one particular copy of Relf's *Infidelity*. Sometimes, however, even the way a writer writes a name in a book gives clues to the level of literateness of that reader. Often there is only one name, "E. D. Robinson," or one statement of ownership, "Harriet Wilkins Shaftsbury Her Book," sometimes in a fine, clear hand, sometimes in an unfinished one. Sometimes there is not a name but a name repeated; three or four times, six or seven times a reader, now forgotten, rewrote her or his name, usually at different times and with an evolving signature. With one name there might be an added flourish on the *W*, with another a crude little scroll under the family name. On a flyleaf of a sentimental novel, Harriet Shaftsbury aspired to be John Hancock, her declaration more modest but no less independent than his. What I am "reading" here—in the no longer blank spaces that frame these early novels—are the perhaps universal signs of pride that one takes in a literate society in signing one's name (as much a social identity as a simple skill) as well as in owning one's own book. E. D. Robinson, for example, writes his name four times, somewhat crudely, and writes "No. 1" after two of the signatures.[78]

In numerous copies of different books, one can, in fact, trace a signature over as many as ten or twenty years, often watching the signature become steadier and more elegant. In many extant textbooks, one also finds interlineations, inventive dialogues based on dialogues within the text, or even doodles and grafitti—all of which appear in Caroline W. Graves's copy of Susanna Rowson's *A Spelling Dictionary, Divided into Short Lessons, for the Easier Committing to Memory by Children and Young Persons; and Calculated to Assist Youth in Comprehending What They Read.* Or a first edition of Hannah Webster Foster's best-selling novel *The Coquette* could itself become at least in part a lesson book. The unknown reader who spent $1 to buy this copy of the novel underlined difficult vocabulary words throughout the text and recorded, in a notably shaky hand, a number of these words on the blank pages at the end. This reader not only vicariously participated in Eliza's cruel betrayal and inevitable death but also picked up the meaning of such words as "volubility," "satire," and "misanthrope" along the way. We see here, in short, a novel-reader aspiring after improved literateness— inspired, perhaps, by Foster's insistence, throughout the novel, on the unparalleled importance of education.[79]

Even such rudimentary scribblings should remind the sophisticated historian that these novels were written for the readers of the time and that they played a vital (if unquantifiable) role in those readers' lives. Indeed, the pertinent fact is the lost reading, not the surviving book. Nevertheless, by surveying hundreds of copies (especially so-called duplicate copies) of early American novels, we can determine that these texts were cherished; they were shared among friends and relatives, contended over by brother and sister, or bequeathed across generations—rather like a family Bible. Broken boards, turned-down pages, and abounding marginalia do not make for a place of honor in an early Americana book collection, but they do reveal patterns of reading, patterns of use, the surviving traces of an interpretive community long since gone. But through those traces, some of the early readers remain surprisingly vivid even after nearly two centuries. One of my favorite of these readers never even left her name. Intuitively,

I would posit that she was a woman, probably a young woman. She read one of the pirated versions of *The History of Constantius and Pulchera*, an edition issued in paper covers by Edward Gray of Suffield, Connecticut, in 1801. It is hard to imagine a less impressive volume. Some of the pages are printed on blue paper, some on white. Possibly there were two separate printings and the book was made up of signatures from each printing, possibly the printer merely ran out of one cheap paper and substituted another (the blue paper typically used for inexpensive book covers). Typos abound. Yet what is most striking about this book is the contrast between the artifact as published by the printer and the artifact as embellished by the reader. The book has been covered in decorated paper stamped with a geometric design, perhaps a small piece of wallpaper. Inside the back cover is a beautiful little drawing, meticulously rendered, of delicate buds in different stages of blossoming, colored in with black and pale brown (which may have been, originally, sepia) inks. In a few places in the book, the reader has been moved to poetry, some copied, some original. This poetic commentary on tragic events of the plot is rendered in a neat round hand. "So quick the pangs of misery return, we joy by minutes & by years we mourn," occurs on a page detailing one of the various stormy ocean voyages that separate the book's lovers. "Hope is the comfort / & the bliss of life, / tis joy in sorrows, / & tis peace in strife," she writes near the climax of this tale of life's and love's vicissitudes. The novel itself—a story of lovers imprisoned, shanghaied, shipwrecked, abandoned, and finally reunited—might move the contemporary reader only to a condescending smile, but it moved one early reader to poetry and art.

"To the Young Ladies of Columbia, This volume, intended to inspire the mind with fortitude under the most unparalleled Misfortunes; and to Represent the happy consequences of Virtue and Fidelity, is Inscribed, with Esteem and Sincerity, By their Friends and Humble Servants, The Publishers." So reads the dedication of this cheap (it sold for only $.25) and pirated edition of an early best-seller. It may well have been written to exploit an audience of marginally educated readers and republished by Edward Gray to exploit a readership also financially marginal. But it is both patronizing and ahistorical to conclude that our present assessment of the commercializing of literature fully comprehends the place of *The History of Constantius and Pulchera* in the lives of its actual readers. It was a commodity, of course, but it was also valued and read as something more.[80]

That "something more," I would emphasize, shows that the first novels did not simply expend themselves through their strained stories as consumable plots, as prepackaged entertainment and escape. On the contrary, these books, even the most unlikely (especially the most unlikely), played a vital role in the early education of readers previously largely excluded from elite literature and culture. Their provocative plots encouraged reading. Differing from (and yet deferring to, through calculated partial imitation and revision) more traditional literary forms such as the biography, the history, the religious or the social or political manifesto, the early novel spoke to those not included in the established power structures of the early Republic and welcomed into the republic of letters citizens who had previously been invited, implicitly and explicitly, to stay out.

Part Two

5 Commodity and Communication: The First American Novel

"Oh, why did Willie do such a thing," she asked, "when we were such good friends?"

"The names are fictitious," Mrs. Brown assured her.

"But everyone knows whom he means," Mrs. Apthorp lamented.

—Purported conversation over the publication of *The Power of Sympathy*

Selling the First American Novel

In the opening chapter of his unfinished history of the triadic relationships between the reader, the author, and the publisher, William Charvat summarizes the crucial importance of the 1790 Copyright Act:

That the country had got along without a copyright law for over 150 years does not mean that it had not had a literature worth protecting, but rather . . . that a small and scattered reading public and poor transportation depressed the commercial value of all books. Time would take care of population and transportation, but no literary profession was possible until law had given products of the mind the status of *property*.[1]

That italicized last word, *property,* accords to "products of the mind" a rather different status than that which criticism generally acknowledges and allows. Mind, post-Romantic thinkers like to believe, is free, and its expression even more so. Discounting a few exceptional cases such as Edward Taylor or Emily Dickinson, which by their very rarity prove the larger rule, literature is written to communicate and the means of communications is publication. The goal of writing, then, is not just meaning but, in Robert Escarpit's telling phrase, "the multiplication of meaning," the whole process by which meaning is transmitted to a multitude of readers.[2] Although the entity of the published book is a necessary part of that grand process, it is by no means its end. Once the product of the author's mind passes from idea to artifact and takes its form in the printed page, it necessarily becomes somebody's property and, as such, is subject to the same kinds of market conditions that govern the distribution of hogs or hog shares, patent medicines or blue-chip stocks, or any other commodity.

It is as commodity that I will first consider *The Power of Sympathy*, and appropriately so, for, thanks to its designation as "the first American novel," this particular text has long been commodified and institutionalized by the very processes of literary scholarship that presumably celebrate literature as "art." Moveover, criticism, in this case, merely continues what history began. Written one year previous to the passage of the federal copyright law, the novel from the beginning existed as property at least as much as it existed as art. Its original value was as much in timing as in text. Isaiah Thomas publicized this "first American novel" in a series of advertisements printed to coincide with the preparations for the inauguration of the first American president and in a language designed to invoke any active or even latent nationalistic fervor.

Before addressing *The Power of Sympathy*'s first claims to firstness, I wish to consider the whole larger debate—lasting now for over a century—as to just which novel was first. This debate suggests that the "origins," "causes," and "firsts" we find depend largely on what we are looking for, and thus the whole historiography of early American fiction becomes both circular and story. It is circular in that the first novel is always first by definition—not the definition of "first" but of "novel." The definition leads us finally to one particular text, and then that text becomes the Ur-novel from which other later texts at least figuratively descend, certified as novels by their genealogy and proudly wearing the family name. It is story in that the circle of limiting definition and validating text has to be filled out, the contained history explained and expounded upon.

When, for example, a few generations ago the "fathers" of the American novel were "officially" Hawthorne and Melville, the clear proof that an older text counted as a novel was its artistic excellence. The unlikely story set forth was a tale of fiction's full flowering in the New World. We learned (and even more so with New Criticism) to savor these select progenitors, and the descendant sons could take pride in the typically American, self-engendered grand trunk of their family tree. Or James Fenimore Cooper can provide a different beginning for the American novel. As noted earlier, Cooper was the first to earn a living as a novelist. It is a significant "first," surely, so long as we are clear that we are recounting a *business* history of the novel (and where do Hawthorne or Melville fit into that history?). But still more recently, the credit for being first has increasingly gone to Charles Brockden Brown, which, as Bernard Rosenthal has noted, is "puzzling" in that Brockden Brown was neither literally first nor the first to support himself by his pen.[3] Nor do claims of Brockden Brown's quality take us any further (except back in time) than similar claims advanced on behalf of Hawthorne or Melville.[4] Nevertheless, Brockden Brown has been accorded a de facto status as "first major novelist" by virtue of the amount of criticism devoted to his work, by his institutionalization within the academy (on course syllabi, doctoral reading lists), and by the implicit imprimatur of having his complete works appear under the rubric "Center for Editions of American Authors / An Approved Text / Modern Language Association"—the earliest American novelist to be accorded this distinction. (And who could be more "approved" than that?)

Other less canonical authors have also been put forth—sometimes by "interested" descendants, sometimes by "disinterested" scholars—as the one true source and origin of the American novel. Charlotte Ramsay Lennox's *The Life of Harriot Stuart* (1751), Hugh Henry Brackenridge and Philip Freneau's *Father Bombo's Pilgrimage to Mecca* (1770; first published 1975), Francis Hopkinson's *A Pretty Story: Written in the Year of Our Lord 2774* (1774), Thomas Atwood Digges's *The Adventures of Alonso: Containing Some Striking Anecdotes of the Present Prime Minister of Portugal* (1775), the anonymous *The Golden Age; or, Future Glory of North America Discovered by an Angel to Celadon, in Several Entertaining Visions* (1785), and Peter Markoe's *The Algerine Spy in Pennsylvania* (1787) have all been seriously proposed as the first American novel and have all been deposed on different grounds—too short *(A Pretty Story, The Golden Age)*, too unavailable *(Father Bombo)*, too nonnovelistic *(The Algerine Spy)*, or too British *(Life of Harriot Stuart, Adventures of Alonso)* either in subject matter or by virtue of the author's or the book's place of origin or by any combination of the three.[5] However, and as William C. Spengemann has cogently argued, criteria for "Americanness" are most inconsistently applied. As Spengemann points out in "The Earliest American Novel: Aphra Behn's *Oroonoko*": "To be sure, *Oroonoko* was not written in America, but then neither were most of Franklin's *Memoirs*, or *The Prairie*, or *The Marble Faun*, and *The American*."[6] And who would exclude any of those last titles from an American literature syllabus? For Spengemann, and as his title avers, *Oroonoko* is the first American novel simply because it is set in a section of the New World once part of "America" (specifically, Surinam).[7]

Clearly, different fictions can be put first for different reasons and to different effects. But by a convergence of various criteria—written in America, by an author born in America, published first in America, set in America, concerned with issues that are specifically grounded in the new country and not simply transplanted from England—more and more *The Power of Sympathy* has been generally accepted as the first American novel. That reading of the history of the novel also has its own revealing history. Joseph Tinker Buckingham was apparently the first person to posit *The Power of Sympathy* as the "first American novel," and he did so in 1850 in a book entitled *Specimens of Newspaper Literature*. As his title suggests, Buckingham was not particularly concerned with definitively claiming precedence for some particular work, nor was he much interested in investigating the provenance of the novel that he casually described as first. Thus he attributes the anonymously published *Power of Sympathy* to Sarah Wentworth Morton. It was an easy mistake to make given the source of Buckingham's study. The newspapers of the late 1780s were filled with the accounts of the Apthorp/ Morton scandal; the newspaper advertisements for *The Power of Sympathy* stressed the connection between the novel and the scandal; and, finally, Sarah Wentworth Morton was vaguely remembered, even in 1850, as one of the most celebrated poets of her generation. Why could she not have been a novelist too?

Francis S. Drake, in his *The Town of Roxbury* (1878), subsequently repeated the attribution, again in passing, and never stopped to wonder if the woman who was the wife of Perez Morton (the prototype for the novel's infamous seducer) and who was also the sister of Fanny Apthorp (whose seduction and suicide are recounted in the novel) would want to publicize that family scandal.[8] And neither did such considerations keep Arthur W. Brayley, the editor of the *Bostonian*, from suggesting the same attribution when in October 1894 he began serially publishing *The Power of Sympathy* with considerable fanfare and specifically to celebrate the first American novel. Brayley attributed the work to one Philenia, the name under which Morton wrote much of her poetry.[9] A reader of the *Bostonian*, Rebecca Valentine Thompson, came forward to assert that her uncle, William Hill Brown, and not Morton, had been the work's author. Her attribution was reported in the December 1894 issue of the *Bostonian*. Since then, a host of scholars have unearthed letters, presentation copies, and still other evidence all attesting that William Hill Brown was, indeed, the novel's author.[10]

The great search for the first American novel flourished, not surprisingly, in the last decades of the nineteenth century. As Herbert Ross Brown has shown, it was a time when nearly every American magazine was calling for the "great American novel," and surely one cannot have a great one without first having a first one.[11] A nation just coming into being as a major power in the Western world required an imperial literature, and an imperial literature required a pedigree. *The Power of Sympathy*—whether penned by Morton or Brown—was well suited for a high place in that pedigree because of its national purity. And it also served simply by providing a locus for critical endeavor. There have now been two nineteenth-century editions of the book (one ascribed to Brown, one to Morton), a twentieth-century Facsimile Text Society scholarly edition, a scholarly university press edition (with variorum), and also a paperback edition of the novel (bound with the first indigenous best-selling novel, *The Coquette*) complete with a critical introduction suitable for the college classroom. Leading journals in the field—*American Literature, Early American Literature, New England Quarterly*— have published articles on the novel and its author, and there is also a published collection of William Hill Brown's poetry and verse fables.[12] Very few early American novelists have sustained so much scholarly attention. All of that concern surely proves something, and, if this seems a circular argument, as of course it is, so, too, is all of literary history. As Foucault insists, "history" becomes tautological the very moment we attempt to establish its limits.[13] No Native American would see the landing of the *Mayflower* as the beginning of anything except, perhaps, the end. The fragmenting of knowledge into periods—firsts—is humanly necessary, but the fragments are by no means intrinsically inevitable or experientially real. Yet once made, these fragments also become commodities— as attested to even by the scholarly institutionalizing of the "first American novel."

THE INSTITUTIONALIZING of the first American novel goes, however, a long way back. Isaiah Thomas early recognized the cultural cachet of publishing just such a volume. Thomas, as noted earlier, was one of the most prosperous printers in eighteenth-century America, an exception to the rule that publishing was not generally a lucrative profession. Running seven presses, a bindery, and a paper mill, he employed as many as 150 people and operated on a scale that allowed him the relative luxury of publishing an occasional unprofitable American product.[14] He had been particularly active as a patriotic printer during the Revolution, was determined after the Revolution to promote an emerging American culture, and, happily, could afford to do so. Ironically, his success as a pirater and reprinter of British titles underwrote his different success as a collector and publisher of American titles. His large legacy to America, besides a number of early American imprints, is the American Antiquarian Society (AAS), which he founded and which he endowed with his collection of books and manuscripts as well as the land and a building for the library. His legacy also includes *The History of Printing in America,* a detailed compendium of early American publishing practices and the definitive book on the subject until well into the twentieth century. Although other histories have now superseded it, Thomas's volume is still a valuable source of information about the early American book trade.[15]

That Thomas was the publisher of the first American novel is appropriate for still another reason. As suggested earlier, the novel as a genre was curiously self-made in America and struggled to succeed in the face of considerable social opposition. Thomas, too, overcame substantial obstacles to become an important publisher. His story is reminiscent of that of Benjamin Franklin, another self-made printer and one of Thomas's friends. A descendant of Evan Thomas who came to Boston from Wales in 1640, Isaiah Thomas endured poverty as a child. His education was minimal and probably amounted to only a few weeks of official schooling. At the age of six he was sent off to work in a printing office and was in his seventh year apprenticed to a rather harsh master, Zechariah Fowle, a printer in Boston. When he was fourteen, Thomas was in charge of Fowle's entire printing shop. He was already more capable at the craft than was his master, yet he still received the minimal wages and endured the miserable conditions that were typically the apprentice's lot in the eighteenth century. At seventeen Thomas ran away, intending to book passage to London where he could further improve his skills as a printer. That venture failed, but Thomas did secure a release from his apprenticeship to Fowle. Despite their differences in the past, Thomas at twenty-one became Fowle's partner in the publication of the *Massachusetts Spy* and then bought out Fowle to be the full owner of the newspaper that became one of the most vociferous proponents of the American Revolution as well as a successful newspaper that continued to be published into the twentieth century.[16]

We know that Thomas was an ardent patriot, and there is even a persistent story that he rode with Paul Revere warning the countryside that the British were coming. With the occupation of Boston, he moved his press to Worcester and continued to print patriotic (or, from the British point of view, seditious) broadsides and pamphlets throughout the war. After the war, he remained in Worcester and continued his printing business. Perceiving that distribution would be a key factor in his success, he soon set up different branches of his bookshop—principally in Massachusetts, but also in Maine, Maryland, New Hampshire, New York, and Vermont—and also devised an elaborate sales itinerary for the agents who traveled between these shops and the main shop in Boston. The branches were co-owned by Thomas and various partners who had often begun as printers in Thomas's shop. As early versions of limited partnerships, these arrangements protected Thomas from complete loss should any branch fail. As early versions of franchise branches, they encouraged the local partners to work diligently for their own profit and for Thomas's too. Thomas also established less formal connections with booksellers in at least a dozen other cities and towns in New England, the Middle States, and the South. But primarily because of the haphazard way in which business agreements were recorded, preserved, and abided by, no one has yet been able to compile a comprehensive history of Thomas's diverse, far-flung, and generally successful business dealings.[17]

Those dealings can occupy us briefly but appropriately in a chapter on *The Power of Sympathy* because the novel results perhaps as much from the publisher's intentions as from the author's, and it is finally Thomas's enterprise, not William Hill Brown's, that gives the book its official status as book, as a fact and artifact in the history of the book in America. To start with, Thomas himself was an innovative publisher. New and different projects appealed to him. Most notable in this regard is his famous "Standing Bible." Thomas purchased enough extra type to set an entire Bible. He had the pages set in England (because of a lack of skilled compositors in New England) and then shipped to his shop. He would print a small edition as needed and, once that edition sold out, simply print another from the ever-ready plates. This was a case of perfectly and profitably adjusting supply to demand, but a case made possible by the fact that Thomas could afford the investment of the stored type and did not have to break down the standing type for the next publishing venture at hand.

We know that Thomas applauded the republican commitment to self-improvement. Perhaps his own humble origins and remarkable self-education emphasized for him the ways in which the written word could help others to rise in both the world and their own estimation. He intended that his newspaper, the *Massachusetts Spy* ("common sense in common language") be open to readers of the lower classes, not just the higher, and that it have a special appeal to mechanics. He published in 1785 his *New American Spelling Book*, designed to compete with Noah Webster's best-selling lexicon; he also brought out in the same year an improved speller by a professor at the University of Edinburgh, William Perry, in some editions cleverly retitled *The Only Sure Guide to the American Tongue* (1785). Perry's speller went through fourteen editions and had a total sale of some three hundred thousand copies. Perhaps mindful of Thomas's success with this competing text, and deciding it was better to join him than to try to beat him, Webster even allowed Thomas to publish an edition of *The American Spelling Book* in 1789. Thomas issued, too, several of the informational almanacs popular during his time, and we might also note that his *Massachusetts Magazine, or Monthly Museum*, was editorially intended to "improve the taste, the language and the manners of the age."[18]

As the singular success of Perry's speller indicates, Thomas could aptly gauge the demands of his audience. He also cultivated the demand that he was ready to meet. One amusing example of such self-promotion can be seen in Thomas's cheap ($.04), brief (thirty-one pages), toy-book version of *Robinson Crusoe*, which included a specific address to the child reader: "If you learn this Book well, and are good, you can buy a larger and more complete History of Mr. Crusoe, at your friend the Bookseller's, in Worcester, near the Court House." On the title page, beneath the publisher's imprint, Thomas also added, "Where May be had a Variety of Little Books for Children."[19]

A variety of books for adults could also be had at the same shop. Thomas's edition of George Minot's *The History of the Insurrections in Massachusetts in 1786* (1788) was, during the period of Shays's Rebellion, a local best-seller. Although he himself was a moderate Federalist, Thomas published socially conservative writers such as Webster and Jedidiah Morse and also published Paine's *The Age of Reason*, the most revolutionary tract of its day, as well as the feminist writings of Judith Sargent Murray and Mary Wollstonecraft. He also printed other works that the social authorities of the time would have found, but for different reasons, as offensive as Paine or Wollstonecraft. Examples are crude crime narratives such as *The Lives and Dying Confessions of Richard Barrick and John Sullivan, High-Way Robbers, Together with the Last Words of Alexander White, Murderer and Pirate* (1786) and, even more salacious, such European volumes as *Amours and Adventures of Two English Gentlemen in Italy* (1795) or *Aristotle's Complete Master Piece, in Three Parts; Displaying the Secrets of Nature in the Generation of Man* (1795), a work that was, as one of the printer's biographers notes, "the standard hayloft reading for curious boys in that generation."[20]

There is even some evidence to suggest that Thomas was the first American publisher of John Cleland's *Fanny Hill, or the Memoirs of a Woman of Pleasure* (1749). But more interesting than the possibility itself is the way in which the very tenuousness of the evidence suggests something of the nature of eighteenth-century publishing. We do know that Thomas wrote to his English bookseller, Thomas Evans, for a copy of the novel and received in answer a short, shocked reply: "The Memoirs of a W. of P. which if you must have, must beg you will apply to some of the Captains coming here, as it is an article I do not send to my Customers if I can possibly avoid it." We do not know whether or not Thomas found an obliging captain, but more than a century after the printer's death, when some marbling wore off a newspaper that had been bound in Thomas's shop, it was observed that the stock Thomas had marbled over included two title-page sheets from an edition of *Fanny Hill* that bore a fictitious London publisher's imprint. We also know that in 1819 Peter Holmes was fined $300 in the Worcester Court of Common Pleas for selling a copy of the novel, and, the following year, Stillman Howe was sentenced to six months hard labor for the same offense. Residents of Worcester did not have ready access to sea captains with contraband to sell. Were these men passing on copies of the novel reprinted and purchased clandestinely in Thomas's Worcester shop? The evidence is hardly conclusive, but the two sentences do suggest that if Thomas had published *Fanny Hill*, he would have gone to considerable lengths to hide that fact.[21]

The Power of Sympathy presented no such problems and would have appealed to Thomas as a prospective publishing project for several reasons. The book would be the "first" American novel and thus had a definite nationalistic potential; its particular attention to female virtue and female education argued its social morality; its effective exploitation of a current and rather lurid scandal gave it the potential for turning a profit. But it should also be noted that at least one consideration probably weighed heavily against it. The available evidence indicates that Thomas himself was suspicious of fiction. We know, for example, that he published relatively few novels, either American or imported, during his prolific career. Furthermore and more explicitly, in his personal copy of *Emily Hamilton* (a novel published by his son), he recorded his misgivings about fiction in general. In his own unmistakable, unfinished hand (he had very little formal education), Thomas maintains that "the perusal of Novels generally tend[s] to *enlighten* than to *distract* the mind." Nevertheless, he continues, "if in the opinion of Some, there is a Novel in which there is [even] a line to excuse a vice, then it behooves those (I mean the heads of families, Such as Father, Mother, or Guardian) to expel Such Books from their Homes."[22] This from the publisher of *Aristotle's Complete Master Piece!* That Thomas's practices as a printer were not fully consistent with his apprehensions as a concerned parent and a proponent of public morality should occasion no great surprise. A certain disjunction between one's actual policy and one's affirmed ideals is often simply part of the cost of doing business. And *The Power of Sympathy*, of course, is hardly *Aristotle's Complete Master Piece*.

Nevertheless, the very enterprise of publishing *The Power of Sympathy* occasioned much the same ambivalence that pervades the text itself, as is obvious even in the advertisements in the *Herald of Freedom* announcing that the novel is forthcoming:

An American Novel

We learn that there is now in the Press in this town a Novel, dedicated to the young ladies, which is intended to enforce attention to female education, and to represent the fatal consequences of Seduction. We are informed that one of the incidents upon which the Novel is founded, is drawn from a late unhappy suicide. We shall probably soon be enabled to lay before our readers some account of so truly Novel a work, upon such interesting subjects.

Subsequent advertisements running simultaneously in the *Massachusetts Spy, or Worcester Gazette* and the *Massachusetts Centinel* similarly announced the immediate publication of the "FIRST AMERICAN NOVEL" and similarly play off one type of interest (patriotic and moral) against another (a covert promise of at last hearing the whole scandalous story).[23] Thus in the "An *American* Novel" ad, the "late unhappy suicide" as the signifier and the "fatal consequences of Seduction" as the signified are conjoined only in "Novel" discourse and even there admit the possibility of other "interesting" subjects to be found in the coming book.

The same dichotomy in the advertisements carries over to the book itself and particularly to the prefatory material, which was typically provided by the printer. To explore more fully the partly pietistic, partly prurient split in the book, let us imagine an early reader holding the recently published novel in her hands, ready to read it, and opening the cover to look first at the title page and the frontispiece. The former bears a guarantee, "FOUNDED IN *TRUTH*," as well as a pietistic poem:

Fain would he strew Life's thorny Way with Flowers,
And open in your View Elysian Bowers;
Catch the warm Passions of the tender Youth,
And win the Mind to Sentiment and Truth.[24]

As a reading directive for a new and as yet unsophisticated audience, all this represents a complex and comprehensive authorial program indeed. We have, in the promise, the text as truth and, in the poem, the text as flower, as vision, as vicarious pleasure, and as, at best, a way to truth. The deconstructionist will notice that we end up led to Truth but also ostensibly began with truth, so these two truths are hardly synonymous, and each well might serve to call the other into question.

Matters become still more complicated, however, when the reader's eye falls on the left-hand page, the frontispiece, for here we have a clear sign of the truth in which the novel originates. Thomas hired Samuel Hill, one of America's foremost engravers, to provide the frontispiece, entitled "The STORY of *OPHELIA*." This exceptionally realistic and detailed engraving is clearly another story, a portrayal of the tragic resolution of a recent and well-known scandal. We view a vial of poison on the table, a goblet tipped on the floor. A young woman lies dying, her head thrown back and her mouth open. An older woman, in maternal dress and bonnet, holds the younger one's hand while an elderly man stands in the half-open doorway, his mouth agape and his own hands clasped in alarm. The contemporary reference is unmistakable. Fanny Apthorp had fatally poisoned herself, partly to escape further exposure that would necessarily have followed from her father's determination to make a public accusation against Morton, her sister's husband. It is a story that will be retold (Letters 21 to 23) in the novel with only minor changes in details: Morton, for example, becomes Martin. This frontispiece attests that the prefatory promise intended to placate literal-minded critics ("FOUNDED IN *TRUTH*") is, indeed, true. But it was, no doubt, true in quite the wrong way, for airing the whole scandal was not the kind of truth that those social authorities generally critical of fiction had in mind, especially since Perez Morton came from their own social level. In short, the first American novel eschews "lying" for exposé; it promises to provide the truth and it does so with a vengeance.

The title page and frontispiece are themselves followed by a dedication, which when set in modern typeface seems innocuous enough. It is appropriate for both the young female reader for whom the book is ostensibly intended and the moralistic critic who would weigh the book's intentions:

> To the young ladies, of United Columbia, these volumes intended to represent the specious causes, and to expose the fatal consequences, of seduction; to inspire the female mind with a principle of self complacency, and to promote the economy of human life, are inscribed, with esteem and sincerity, by their friend and humble servant, the author.

But even a casual glance at Thomas's typography (see figure 9) registers the prominent placement of the word "SEDUCTION." This key word is centered in the middle of the page; occupies an entire line; and is written in the darkest, clearest, boldest type on the page. Even the spacing between each letter gives further prominence to the word. What we have here is another graphic illustration (literally and figuratively) of the role of the printer in the creation of the American novel and in the "seduction" of the American reading public. Such matters as punctuation, spelling, capitalization, and layout were typically the province of the printer, not the author. So the author's dedication (stressing the seemliness of the book's intention) is the printer's advertisement (stressing the steamy subject matter). In such duplicity begins America's first novel and American fiction. The frontmatter of the first American novel almost paradigmatically sets forth tensions implicit in the form itself. As I have shown, those tensions themselves derive largely from the different and even contradictory demands placed on fiction by the professional readers and critics who, on the one hand, thought they knew what the public needed, and, on the other, by the printers, the booksellers, and the nonprofessional readers who gradually and sporadically worked out what the public actually wanted.

Reader Reception of the First American Novel

The public of the time did not particularly want *The Power of Sympathy*. Despite Thomas's best efforts to promote his product, the book quickly sank into an oblivion from which it did not emerge until antiquarians, in the middle of the next century, resurrected it as a "first" in American culture. Puzzled by the early obscurity of such an important novel, a few of these nineteenth-century scholars accounted for the virtual disappearance of *The Power of Sympathy* by claiming that the book had been "banned in Boston," which would definitely be another first in American fiction. This claim continued to be advanced until recent times, and there is some contemporaneous evidence that Perez Morton wanted to suppress *The Power of Sympathy*, for the scandal on which it was based had started to die down at the time of the novel's first publication. Apparently, however, Morton was persuaded to drop his scheme, or, equally plausible, Thomas would not permit his author to be censored and Morton decided it was not worth it to buy up the extant copies of the books himself. In any case, as Richard Walser has demonstrated, any scheme to suppress the novel failed almost as dismally as the work itself failed in its own right.[25] The novel, we know, was still available, listed in John West's 1797 catalogue at a price of $.83⅓ a decade after its publication.[26]

We also know that Thomas tried to generate interest in the book after its publication by reprinting eleven excerpts in the first volume of his *Massachusetts Magazine, or Monthly Museum* (1789). These samples were ostensibly submitted by one Calista, who wished to share portions of the "first American novel" with the new magazine's readers. Printed under the headline "Beauties of 'The Power of Sympathy,' " they had titles such as "Seduction," "Suicide," or "Female Study." This ploy elicited little more attention than did the novel itself. Except for a few brief reviews, the book's publication had not been celebrated in the other magazines and newspapers of the time. For whatever reason, it simply failed to establish an audience. In this case at least, Isaiah Thomas had rather misjudged the public. Or perhaps he had merely misjudged the virtues of novelty, of being the first with an American novel. If so, it was not a substantial miscalculation. Soon another seduction novel set in America, *Charlotte Temple*, written by a woman only marginally American and published first in England, would capture the attention of the American reading public and prove conclusively that American fiction was a marketable commodity.

There is no way to resurrect any of those late-eighteenth-century readers and to interview them in detail as to how and why they liked (or disliked) *The Power of Sympathy*. Some few signs of their reactions, however, still remain in the

FIGURE 7. Frontispiece, *The Power of Sympathy. Courtesy of the American Antiquarian Society.*

POWER of SYMPATHY:

THE

TRIUMPH of NATURE.

FOUNDED in *TRUTH.*

IN *TWO* VOLUMES.

VOL. I.

FAIN would he ftrew Life's thorny Way with Flowers,
And open to your View Elyfian Bowers ;
Catch the warm Paffions of the tender Youth,
And win the Mind to Sentiment and Truth.

PRINTED at *BOSTON,*
by ISAIAH THOMAS and COMPANY.
Sold at their Bookftore, No. 45, NEWBURY STREET.
And at faid THOMAS's Bookftore in WORCESTER.
MDCCLXXXIX.

FIGURE 8. Title page, *The Power of Sympathy, Courtesy of the American Antiquarian Society.*

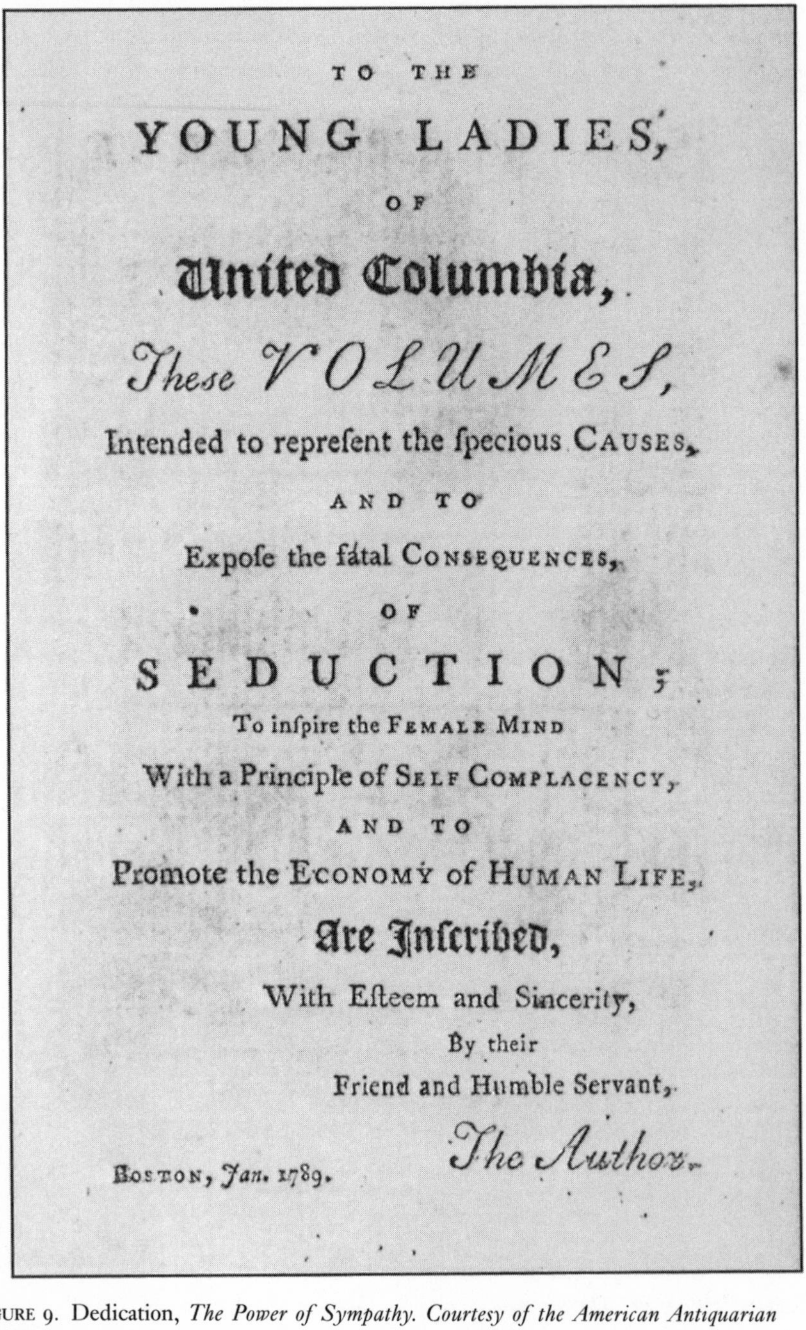

TO THE

YOUNG LADIES,

OF

United Columbia,

These VOLUMES,

Intended to reprefent the fpecious CAUSES,

AND TO

Expofe the fátal CONSEQUENCES,

OF

SEDUCTION;

To infpire the FEMALE MIND

With a Principle of SELF COMPLACENCY,

AND TO

Promote the ECONOMY of HUMAN LIFE,

Are Infcribed,

With Efteem and Sincerity,

By their

Friend and Humble Servant,

The Author.

BOSTON, *Jan.* 1789.

FIGURE 9. Dedication, *The Power of Sympathy. Courtesy of the American Antiquarian Society.*

surviving books themselves. For example, Isaiah Thomas's own copy of the novel has been preserved in the AAS. Specially bound in a deep tan, richly grained calf, a red leather label on the spine embossed with gilt lettering and with end-papers beautifully marbled in the Old Dutch style, the book suggests that Thomas took pride in *The Power of Sympathy* once he decided to publish it. But one other surviving copy of the novel bears more obvious signs of readers' reactions and from a more unbiased source. This copy (now in the Library of Congress) bears two signatures, Rebecca Thomas and Geo. H. Child, and is underlined throughout. Consistently, the passages marked center on loss, and certain phrasings (such as "Adieu my friend—Little Happiness is left for me in this World") are underlined two and three times and are even accompanied by marginal comments like "How pathetick." Or one of Harrington's last letters to Worthy (Letter 53) is underlined, but Harrington's observation on "how unfortunate is the man who trusts his happiness to the precarious friendship of the world" is marginally denied with the protest "It is not true." One reader, at least, was moved enough to respond to the book and also knew enough of the novel's source to pencil "Morton" beside Brown's barely circumspect alteration of the name to "Martin."[27]

A much more explicit, extended, and intriguing record of how and how differently the novel could be read survives in opposing reviews published in the *Massachusetts Centinel* and the *Herald of Freedom* and printed in February 1789, a few weeks after the novel itself first appeared. Written pseudonymously (as was typical of the time), the interchange between Civil Spy and Antonia also reveals something of the social context in which reading took place and hints at the ways in which gender expectations, then as now, underlie literary theory.

The contretemps began when, in his review, Civil Spy expressed "disappointment" that the novel failed to fulfill its prefatory promise to expose the Apthorp/ Morton scandal. This reviewer indignantly observes that "the frontispiece, designated from the Story of Ophelia, naturally leadeth to a conclusion, that the author considered the circumstances in that story, as greatly contributory to the promotion of the design of his undertaking." But promotion and design, design and performance, do not fully accord: "It is not until we arrive near the end of the work, that we find any thing to authorize the title."[28] Obviously, for this reader at least, the frontmatter of the book and particularly the engraving constituted a kind of covenant between the reader and the text, but one that the text only minimally honored—a breach of the spirit of the contract if not the letter.

Civil Spy's insistence on a literally adhered to reading contract is even more obvious in his strictures on the novel's disarming claim of being "founded in truth": "The story of *Ophelia*, however recent and local the particulars related in it, referreth to Rhode Island for its origin. Perhaps the Rhode Islanders may be so far acquainted with it, as to be profitably entertained by reading it in the author's dress; but I am strongly inclined to believe that the story would be less familiar in Rhode Island, than in Boston." Boston is not Rhode Island; Martin is not Morton; truth is not fiction. But still worse is the story of Harriot, Harrington, and the elder Harrington that was, in the novel at least, set in Boston. For this reviewer, that story simply has no fictional standing because it has no factual grounding. Civil Spy "had never heard of any thing similar to it in this part of the world," and, "in a country so lately inhabited by civilized people, as Massachusetts—in so young a town as Boston, and so small, as that the most trivial circumstances, and terminating with such dire events, as related, could not have been completely kept from public cognizance, until printed by Isaiah Thomas and Company." The confidence with which this last claim is advanced attests that in the little world of late-eighteenth-century Boston, any scandal must be known by all. But the force of the whole argument gives us a figurative circle of censure and apology in which the new form was caught precisely because of the different demands of fiction and of fact. When the novel's primary sin, for critics such as Civil Spy, is its novel-ty, the emerging form can be expected to protect itself by promising truth in fiction, and, when it makes that promise, it can expect to be taken literally and to be condemned if the promise is not fulfilled.

Fortunately for the novel's future, not all readers of the time were so insistent on getting the truth, the whole truth, and nothing but the truth, nor were they all so certain that they already knew just what the whole truth was. In response to Civil Spy, Antonia (possibly Catherine Byles, Brown's confidante and relative) offered a quite different response to the novel:

> Having paid my tribute to tears to this chaste and moral performance and having experienced pride in that the first American Essay (in this stile) might vie with the most sentimental and unexceptionable British, or Hibernian Story, I cannot omit expressing my suprize, that the only "observations" on this ingenious work, which have yet appeared, should be those published in the last Centinel. Whether they were "made" by an old snarling misanthrope or a young cynical Fop, is to me indifferent, but I venture to determine, they never arose in the mind of a friend to either women or virtue!

The book is now praised for its patriotic import and its moral message: Truth again, but now writ large. In response to Civil Spy's complaint that Brown altered the names and the setting of the Morton/Apthorp scandal and omitted some of the details, Antonia insists that the author circumspectly protected the principals in the "truly tragical catastrophes." But most of all, for Antonia, the "Author merits the most grateful acknowledgments from *our sex*," because of the "respect and tenderness" he has shown to "youthful females." He is a "champion of feminine innocence, a promoter of religion and chastity, and a pleasing monitor of inexperienced minds." This, she insists, is far more important than gossip-mongering, and Civil Spy (whom she subsequently dismisses as a "pupil of Chesterfield") dubiously prefers the whole salacious story that is not in the text to Moral Truth, which is.

Antonia's charge, naturally, elicited Civil Spy's countercharge, a countercharge couched in a pervasive sarcasm that speaks this critic's certainty of his privileged position in the discourse simply by virtue of his being a man as much as his first comments admit no quibbling as to what is truth. A sample of his response will suffice to give the tone of the whole piece: "Mr. Civil Spy finds himself much affected by having brought on himself the resentment and contempt of the Lady Antonia. He was altogether insensible of the stupidity and pitifulness of his observations upon a late novel, until Madam Antonia so graciously undertook for his good—and the good of the publick—to exhibit the unjustness and futility of his remarks in a proper light—which she performed in a manner so modest—so learned—and so *mistressly* as could not have been expected—even from 'a masterly pen.' " The origin of the "truth" herein expressed is obvious. Since the mistress lacks the master's pen, it is beneath the dignity of the master to debate seriously any comments made by such a wanting person. It is beneath his dignity to be offended, too, by the charges that have been leveled against him, so the offense is translated into jest: "Thrice blessed, reputed author of The Power of Sympathy!—admired—pathetick—delicate—elegant work! Alpha and Omega of Novelty—'in this style'—in lieu of being a 'misanthrope'—a cynic—'an enemy to women and virtue'—why might not Civil Spy have been, an 'amiable youth'— a 'reputed author'—a 'pleasing monitor'—or an anything, worthy of the honour and esteem of Madam Antonia." Here again, it requires no Freud to translate his humor back to its source. Poison in jest? No offense in the world.

We can hardly call this critical disagreement a debate or a dialogue because no real discussion takes place. Civil Spy's strategy is simply to label Antonia's position feminine and thus, by extension, inconsequential, an occasion for veiled contempt and not reasoned response, a contempt that also extends to the novel Lady Antonia champions. The very fact of her defense of the book is his best proof that his original strictures were justified, which, perhaps, is the real point to be garnered from this nonexchange. All the difficulties that early fiction faced were doubly faced by novels such as *The Power of Sympathy* or subsequent fuller versions of the sentimental or seduction novel that especially addressed women's situation in the society and women as readers. The adjudicators of what constituted art or suitable subjects for art were not women and simply could not take seriously writers or readers who were.

We might also briefly notice how much this nonexchange anticipates issues recently and more explicitly examined by feminist criticism. For example, Mary Jacobus, in "Is There a Woman in This Text?" has suggested that the main question of women's literature is not the "sexuality of the text" (whether a text is written by, for, or about women) but the "textuality of sex" (an assumed a priori or normative standard that insists that any text that is defined as "feminine" is intrinsically lacking).[29] Civil Spy is already a past master of that latter ploy. Thus his satirical aspersions on Brown's style in his second response to Antonia implicitly posit an absolute and universal "masculine" standard of taste that must necessarily overrule Antonia's biased and idiosyncratic "feminine" standard.

At this point we might do well to ask if Civil Spy and Antonia really addressed the same novel. I would suggest that they did not, that one read a promised story of an ostensibly true scandal involving seduction, incest, and suicide and was somehow disappointed when the scandal in part (the Martin subplot) fell short of the known facts and in part (the Harrington/Harriot subplot) outrageously exceeded them. The other read a didactic novel that promised to edify the female reader and was delighted when it did so. Differently reading the duplicitous prefatory material, these two *could not* read the same novel.

The possibility of such deep gender division in reading the text and responding to it has large implications for the early novel. Essentially (and admittedly simplifying a complex matter), I would suggest that women of the time read *against* a tradition that derided "learned women" (to use the common and almost always derogatory eighteenth-century term that Civil Spy employs in his response). But they also read *in* a new, republican tradition that rewarded feminine virtue. Thus women often justified their reading by claims to "self-improvement" (moral or otherwise), and prefaces could promote books on those same grounds but not overtly champion increased women's rights and thus threaten to destabilize the status quo. Nevertheless, and as is implicit in Civil Spy's attack, reading for feminine edification was often condemned as a waste of time and a source of irresponsible ideas. Even modest, moral fiction intended for women was still suspect. The woman reader was thus caught in the middle, with no socially sanctioned rationale for her novel reading, while the male novel-reader must have felt somewhat defensive about enjoying a form often implicitly and explicitly feminine. Furthermore, and to emphasize again a point I have made before, all the material evidence available—extant lending-library rosters, subscription lists published in novels, and inscriptions found in extant copies of novels—attests that men as well as women read even the most sentimental novels such as *Charlotte Temple*. What kinds of refractions occurred within the man who was reading a form identified with women, about women, in a society where men were not supposed to be concerned with the intellect or lives of women? And how did this genderization of a genre affect the would-be male— or female—author? These are rhetorical questions, obviously, but they are posed by Civil Spy's reactionary response—as if he had forgotten that he wasn't supposed to comment on novels, to take them seriously, until Antonia reminded him that women read them.

A Novel Divided against Itself

Even on the level of plot summary, there are obvious incongruities and disjunctions in *The Power of Sympathy*. Essentially, the book begins as a seduction novel. Harrington, the main male character, initially writes to his friend Worthy about his plan to conquer Harriot. Worthy counsels virtue, not seduction, and Harriot further convinces Harrington that matrimony, not sex, is the proper resolution for his passion. At this point the novel is all that it moralistically claims to be, a didactic story denouncing vice and particularly the "vicious" sin of seduction. But that project lapses when Harriot and Harrington, virtually on the eve of their planned marriage, learn that they are brother and sister. Subplots and digressions embedded within the main Harriot/Harrington plot further demonstrate how the novel departs from the simple statement of purpose contained in the prefatory promise that "the dangerous consequences of seduction [will be] exposed and the advantages of female education set forth and recommended" (p. 5). Far from adhering to this worthy program, the subplots center on subjects ranging from rape to slavery and become progressively more morally complicated or morally obscure. Furthermore, the original didactic intentions of the book are both regularly reasserted and regularly undermined as the novel progresses. Worthy, for example, increasingly becomes the spokesperson for the text's morality within the text, and he also increasingly becomes a sententious prig whose very limitations serve the plot and resolution of the fiction.

This division in the novel runs so deep that at times it almost seems as if we have two distinct and even contradictory discourses, a didactic essay and a novel, shuffled together and bound as one book. The moral essay is embodied in the long letters of Worthy, Mrs. Holmes, and the reported speeches of the Reverend Mr. Holmes. Little in this material is novelistic. The letters especially are, to modify one of Bakhtin's terms, nonsituational. Neither replies to other letters nor responses to the unfolding action of the plot, they are little set pieces, didactic lessons that could be addressed to virtually anyone and delivered upon virtually any occasion. The real model for this portion of the novel is not the already established epistolary novel but the even more established format of the collected sermons of some respected divine. These letters read as if they were delivered from a pulpit to a suspect audience requiring moral edification. Consequently, the reader does not identify with Mrs. Holmes or Worthy, but is cast as a subordinate in need of the counsel these morally privileged personages dispense. The young female reader especially is told to listen attentively, to sit a little straighter in her chair. I would also here note that the comments in the novel against novel reading are delivered in the epistolary sermons.

Side by side with the didactic epistles, however, are quite different letters that, taken together, give us a salacious, sexually charged novel. Harrington feels real lust, then real love, then real anguish as he progresses from prospective seducer to fiancé to brother and, finally, to suicide, while Harriot's distress at not being able to sublimate her love for Harrington into a safe sibling affection is great enough to cause her death too. Now *that*'s a novel! Nor is its novelty explained away by the characters expostulating on the moral significance and meaning of all that befalls them. Worthy and Mrs. Holmes can do that, thank you. And these moral spokespersons regularly interpose themselves between the action and the audience to offer their interpretations of the text. Yet their surplus of concern is called into question by its very excess as well as by its ineffectuality. Thus Mrs. Holmes's letters finally speak mostly of their own long-winded emptiness in contrast to the force of Harrington's missives and Harriot's, which derive substantially from the fact that, try as they might, they cannot put into adequate words all that prompts them to write. Furthermore, when the moral advice that overflows in the novel serves so little the protagonists to whom it was ostensibly directed, how can the reader hope to be aided by it? Such considerations lead to a large question. Just as Civil Spy and Antonia read two different books, did not Isaiah Thomas publish and William Hill Brown write two different books that only masqueraded as one?

The early reviews, the frontmatter, the disjunctive format of the novel itself all suggest that William Hill Brown had neither a precise authorial program nor a clearly conceived audience in mind. To borrow Ross Chambers's recent paradigm for interpreting fiction, this novel is not only *about* a seduction, in narrative method it enacts one, too.[30] The reader is calculatingly led from one moral lesson to the next by the interspersing episodes of a more enticing story. At the end of the text the reader has perused all the lessons but possesses the story and perhaps has even been possessed by it. Perhaps the first partner and victim in any such seduction by the text is the author himself. It is suggestive that the unfolding novel is substantially shaped by the authorial equivalent of what a psychologist could well term displacement and denial.

First and most obvious, we can consider the odd distribution of novel time. Far more of the text is given over to the didactic than to the dramatic, especially in the first sections. The moralists have the preponderance of the letters and seemingly the largest claim on the reader's time and attention, while the lovers have the story. Differently put, the text's primary residence is with one discourse while its primary concern is with the other. This disjunction rather resembles the conjunction of a tired marriage and a fresh affair. The straying partner's various gestures of affirming "my real union is here"—fresh flowers for the deceived wife, special meals for the cuckolded husband—seldom settle things for either party, and, similarly, Brown's regular protestations of his moral intentions are finally too much to be taken at face value.

Admittedly, the book does have, with its emphasis on education, a certain unity. The catalogue of female misfortunes can be refracted through the lectures on morality that dominate the text to emphasize effectively the primary need for real female education in a society that generally denied that need and, consequently, the attendant need for reshaping society into forms more suitable for men *and women*. But here, too, we encounter problems. The program just sketched out is premised on a young female reader, ill educated and hardly prepared to cope with questions of seduction (or of much else, for that matter), learning from the novel. The novel, however, assumes the very education this reader lacks. Unlike novels such as *Charlotte* or *The Coquette, The Power of Sympathy* is rampant with erudition. Syntax and vocabulary are both often inordinately complex. There is, throughout, an almost desperate display of the author's learning as seen in the frequent and frequently obscure literary allusions to dozens of writers ranging from Cicero to Goethe to La Rochefoucauld to Chesterfield to Barlow, Dwight, and Webster. This parade of references would not reassure the average young woman of the time that she was welcome into the novel and that the novel spoke particularly to her but serves rather to emphasize the educational accomplishments of the writer, his competence, his intelligence, his expertise. And also his ambivalence; fiction is not all fluff and fancy, the author seems to proclaim, but is learned, respectable, didactic—hardly even a novel at all.

William Hill Brown seems to be painfully aware of the implications and isolations of being the first American novelist and tries to compensate by writing virtually a nonnovel, which partly explains the eclectic format of the novel itself. The epistolary method, borrowed from Richardson, also imitates the popular journal and letter mode of writers such as John Dickinson or British writers such as Dr. John Gregory and Lord Chesterfield. The numerous discourses on topics ranging from metaphysics to educational philosophy approximate the ubiquitous moral tracts of the time, and moral spokespersons such as Mrs. Holmes or the Reverend Holmes give advice in a popular advice-tract format. There are also political asides that resemble broadsides, irrelevant encyclopedic details in the almanac mode, descriptions of physical settings reminiscent of travel narratives, and—as already noted—various sermons, which do come close to constituting a standard collection of same.

I began this section by considering the text as divided between moral discourse and novel discourse. I end with a whole host of other types or models of discourse sounding in the background. Along the way the opening disharmonious duet has picked up a whole cacophonous chorus. No wonder no one clear note or melodic line sounds in the novel. Yet the odd mixture of duplicity, diversity, excess, and inconsistency that we encounter in this first novel does have a characteristically American tone that will be deployed to better advantage in nineteenth-century works like *Moby Dick* or *Uncle Tom's Cabin*. In short, even with the first American novel we already have, firmly established, the author as *bricoleur*, and soon she/ he will be better at that trade.

Reading *The Power of Sympathy*

> We are happy to be able to announce to the public, that the accusations brought against a fellow Citizen, in consequence of a late unhappy event, and which has been the cause of so much domestic calamity, and public speculation, have, at the mutual desire of the parties, been submitted to and fully inquired into, by their Excellencies JAMES BOWDOIN and JOHN ADAMS, Esq., and that the result of their inquiry is, that the said accusations "have not been *in any degree* supported, and that therefore there is just ground for the restoration of peace and harmony between them."—And in consequence thereof they have recommended to the parties, with the spirit of candor, and mutual condescension, again to embrace in friendship and affection.
>
> We would add, that were it not for the verdict of the Jury of Inquest to the contrary (for Verdicts must always be respected) it would have been the wish of many, that the extraordinary conduct of the deceased, had been early attributed to the only accountable cause, an insane state of mind.[31]

Appearing in the *Herald of Freedom* on October 9, 1788, some four months prior to the publication of *The Power of Sympathy*, this announcement demonstrates how easily history can be fictionalized without the intermediation of novelists. Only the names of the uninvolved authority figures—a former governor of Massachusetts, a future president of the United States—are given. To protect the innocent? To protect the guilty? The name most missing, of course, is that of Perez Morton, a wealthy Harvard-educated patriot who would go on to become Speaker of the Massachusetts House of Representatives and the state's attorney general, and who was also, not coincidentally, a personal friend of both Adams and Bowdoin. Nor need the scandal be named. All who lived in Boston in 1788 would know the fate of Fanny Apthorp, who had just killed herself. Many would also know more; would know that she killed herself rather than accuse and publicly confront the brother-in-law who had fathered her child, as was being demanded by her father. Against such knowledge, validated by a jury's deliberations and a coroner's verdict, John Adams and James Bowdoin set their discreet defense of Morton and their more explicit insinuation that everything (seduction? suicide? story?) could best be charged to the disordered mind of the now deceased woman. Against that calculated accounting the twenty-three-year-old William Hill Brown, a close neighbor of the Mortons and only a year older than the beautiful Fanny, set his novel.

On this level, then, the first American novel serves not to fictionalize a local scandal but to "factualize" (and "factionalize") it. More specifically, Brown refuses to allow the voice of public authority to consign all the blame to the woman while the man remained, at least in Adam's and Bowdoin's rendering, unnamed and innocent. Given his material—most of which was published in the local newspapers—Brown could have chosen to support either story, the official one (that few common citizens, judging by the newspaper reports, really believed) or its alternative. He chose the alternative. He made few changes in the details, disguising only the setting, the names of the characters, and the sex of Fanny's child (changed from a daughter to a son, probably to provide some variation from the main plot, which must, because of the power politics of seduction, focus on an illegitimate daughter). But in every essential, Brown's story is an indictment of Morton and an exoneration of Fanny Apthorp—and by extension a verdict against the judgment of Adams and Bowdoin.

Consider, for example, how Brown's pseudonyms operate on quite different metonymic levels. James Apthorp is both thickly disguised as Shepherd and also given the function designated by the name. In this character we see the father as a shepherd who comes to the defense of his lamb too late and too vehemently and who thereby inadvertently occasions its slaughter. Fanny becomes the highly allegorical Ophelia, a young woman perfectly sane, if weak willed, until the verdicts and public accusations go against her. Perez Morton, however, as Martin, is a different matter. Such a minor change in name leaves him exposed, identified, condemned by and in the novel: "By a series of the most artful attentions, suggested by a diabolical appetite, he insinuated himself into her affection—he prevailed upon the heart of the unsuspicious *Ophelia* and triumphed over her innocence and virtue" (p. 60).

We might notice also how Brown begins with this verdict on the affair and not with the affair itself or the preliminaries to it. Even before he presents the seduction, he has cast Ophelia as, essentially, the villain's innocent victim. But can an innocent young woman be involved with her own sister's husband and in her own sister's home? The author encourages us not to ask that question by excluding as much as possible all sisterly considerations from the plot. Thanks to Mrs. Martin/Sarah Wentworth Morton, the husband and the sister can inhabit the same house, and that useful service rendered, the wife largely disappears from the text. Harriot and Mrs. Francis, explicitly the guests of *Mrs.* Martin, do early note that their hostess puts on a "face of vivacity" seemingly at odds with "the feelings of her heart," but once the story of Ophelia begins to unfold, any story of Sarah is not even hinted at until after Ophelia's suicide.[32] Only then does the sister have a place—a place that, ironically, partly redeems the very suicide that belatedly acknowledges the sister's place. Ophelia, in the note that she leaves, apologizes more for betraying her married sister than for bearing an illegitimate child. She acknowledges that she "had been doing an injury to her sister who was all kindness to her; she prayed for her sister's forgiveness . . . she was always sensible to her obligation to that sister. . . . She intreated [*sic*] her sisters to think of her with pity" (p. 67). Who could condemn further a woman who has so thoroughly condemned herself? Certainly not the injured sister, nor the collective "sisters" who are the implied readers of her story.

For Martin, however, there are, in Brown's rendering, no extenuating circumstances. This wealthy and esteemed gentleman betrays his wedding vows, Ophelia's virtue, and also his implicit obligations to his community. After Ophelia returns from Europe to visit her sister, Martin is soon offering to set her up in "an elegant apartment at his house in town" (p. 60). As the affair begins, he is promising to divorce his wife in order to marry her. But once Ophelia has borne his child, "the affection of *Martin* now changed to the vilest hatred," and, hypocritical in the extreme, he is the "first to brand her with the disgraceful epithets, of undutiful and unchaste" (p. 61). Ophelia retires to the country and anonymity to bear and raise her child, but her father chafes at the injustice of seeing his daughter suffer while Martin still occupies an eminent social position, seemingly untouched by his deeds. When Ophelia kills herself to avoid the public exposure her father intends to make, Martin is quick to shift all of the blame for the girl's death onto the father: "He reminded Shepherd of his obstinacy in *persisting* in an explanatory meeting, and refusing to grant Ophelia's request in suffering the affair to subside." Martin says imperiously to Shepherd, "You cannot accuse me as the *immediate* cause of *Ophelia's* death; the facts are as I have stated them—and thus was a straying, but penitent child, driven to despair and suicide by a severe use of paternal power" (pp. 69–70).[33] Martin/Morton's lawyerly training obviously serves him well; but Brown, just as capably, builds a more convincing case by juxtaposing this seducer's shallow, self-serving words with his even shabbier deeds.

Although Martin is not explicitly punished in *The Power of Sympathy*, another story in the novel, that of the elder Harrington, shows how one's sins can come back to haunt one. When the young Harrington gives up his first program to seduce the "orphaned" Harriot and decides, instead, to marry her, the stage is set for the traumatic revelation that "HARRIOT IS YOUR SISTER!" (p. 106). And so was Fanny, by eighteenth-century law and custom, Morton's sister. The numerous parallels between the two stories (sister, secret sin, seducing lawyer, public exposure) suggest that we conjoin them to read the end of Martin's story, which is not given in the text, through the end of the Harrington/Harriot story, which is. The Honorable Mr. Harrington, sixteen years after his interlude with Maria, is revealed publicly as a seducer. He must watch in anguish as both his legitimate and his illegitimate children die tortured deaths. He himself endures a Dantesque nightmare, a vision of hell in which men like himself and Martin occupy the innermost circle. Within eighteenth-century Boston, Perez Morton may seem to have escaped the consequences of his actions. Within the moral universe of the novel, Martin's punishment—in this life and in the life to come— waits in time and is not to be denied.

In the present social universe of the novel, however, Martin's apparent immunity as opposed to Ophelia's suicide tokens the partiality and imperfections of human institutions and the moral bankruptcy of those who argue the justice of the very status quo that privileges them as its spokespersons. In short, a careful reading of the novel is also a critical reading of the society in which it is set.

Adams and Bowdoin hardly refute that subversive reading. If anything, they inadvertently affirm it. Better men than Perez Morton, they are still willing to equivocate, perhaps even to prevaricate (were those charges against Morton really not "*in any degree* supported"?), and to set aside justice ("the verdict of the Jury of Inquest") in the name of justice by blaming all the "extraordinary conduct of the deceased" on the deceased woman's "insane state of mind," as if the pregnancy and delivery too had been mere figments of her imagination. That rough paraphrase of what the two proclaim should serve to indicate how tenuously they argue to protect one of their own and, by extension, to preserve the myth of a gentleman's moral primacy.

The myth of moral primacy as voiced by the socially prominent is regularly exposed in the novel.[34] The Honorable Mr. Harrington, for example, first seduces the indigent Maria and then further profits from her now lowered state. Pregnant and penniless, who is she to accuse *him*? The Reverend Holmes, although given to long-winded pedanticism on such subjects as how "we are blinded by pride and self love, and will not observe our own imperfections" (p. 40), at first seems a somewhat admirable (if self-satisfied) man. He did, after all, shelter the abandoned Maria. But when Maria dies the Reverend denies the daughter her birthright by sending her away to be raised, anonymously, by the peevish Mrs. Francis, and he deceives the world as to the continuing virtue of his friend, Judge Harrington. That deception proves devastating when the legitimate son of this "good" man meets his illegitimate daughter, a meeting that explodes the Honorable Mr. Harrington's pretentions to honor and the Reverend Mr. Holmes's pretensions to ministerial wisdom.

But Worthy, both the moral spokesperson of the novel and the main recipient of its satire, especially illustrates how effectively Brown can conjoin those two functions in one character. Worthy first priggishly patronizes just about everyone in the novel. "I have seen many juvenile heroes during my pilgrimage of two and twenty years," he can intone in an admonitory letter to Harrington, certain that the experience of those years renders him an expert observer of the human scene. He goes on to advise his friend not to be "easily inflamed with new objects— agitated and hurried away by the impetuosity of new desires" (p. 10). Worthy will never be so hurried, not even when the happiness of his fiancée or the life of his friend hang in the balance. Thus, when Myra, Harriot's friend and Worthy's fiancée, requires his comfort and his counsel, Worthy remains distant, uncommunicative, physically and emotionally removed. Residing peaceably in the rational little world of Belleview, the rural retreat he then shared with the Reverend Holmes and his widowed daughter-in-law, Mrs. Eliza Holmes, he apparently prefers not to be disturbed by his fiancée's sorrow over her suffering friend, and he is moved only slightly more when his friend hints of impending suicide. One imagines the three of them, Worthy and the Holmeses, ensconced within their bogus "Temple of Apollo," discoursing on incest, seduction, scandal, suicide, and novel reading, while first Harriot languishes, then Myra mourns, and finally Harrington dies.

"My dear friend," Harrington writes Worthy, typically, to no avail, "I have a great desire to see you—I wish you could come home speedily. . . . When life becomes insupportable and we find no blessing in it—have we not a right to resign it?" (Letter 48, p. 142). Harrington, receiving no answer, writes again soon after: "Why must I wait the lingering hand of the grisly messenger to summon me to the world above?" (Letter 54, p. 161). The first intimation of suicide Worthy receives is in Letter 48; he does not even bother to respond to this and other disturbed missives until Letter 58, which begins, "Let your mind be employed, and time will wear out these gloomy ideas" (p. 165). Or even worse, after Harrington's suicide threats become even more overt, Worthy writes: "I thank you for your letters, but I wish you had something better for the subject of them" (Letter 61, p. 168). He does make one late promise to "be with you soon," but, before he can see his friend, Harrington has blown out his brains with a pistol in imitation of another epistolary novel, *The Sorrows of Young Werther*. This book, with him at his death, is as much a guide and a friend as was the most misnamed Worthy.

Only too late do these moral characters see the error of their ways, and then they are as ineffectual in their reformation as they were in their original course. The litany of apology of Worthy, the Honorable Mr. Harrington, or Mr. Shepherd is countered by a roster of the personal tragedies their carelessness occasions and stands in muddling contrast to the grim and realistic determination of Fanny Apthorp whose diary/suicide note was published in most of the Boston newspapers after her death: "I have felt from the first that this matter would go against me, but I have resolved never to live after it has," or to the poignant last letter written by Elizabeth Whitman to the unnamed father of her child (and quoted in *The Power of Sympathy*), "I know that you will come, but you will come too late" (p. 35).[35]

The self-dramatized apologia of men like the Honorable Mr. Harrington who grieve over past failures is juxtaposed with the melodrama of young men and women deranged by grief. We have the whole paraphernalia of sentimental fiction—women who die in childbirth, stillborn infants, abandoned orphans raised in anonymity and penury, broken health, self-inflicted or merely self-willed death, insanity. This is the focus of the fiction, and it is also precisely what was happening around the corner at one of the best addresses in Boston. That countergrounding in "truth" makes all the difference. It should make any reader—especially the modern one conditioned by the so-called sexual revolution—question the usual condescending tone with which critics typically deal with seduction novels. *The Power of Sympathy* is not a tale of seduction telling the women that they should have been more careful. It is more a condemnation of men like Martin/Morton and the Honorable Mr. Harrington and also of those such as Mrs. Holmes or the Reverend Holmes who supported the authority of a Martin or a Mr. Harrington and defended their acts—the low-level Adamses and Bowdoins of the novel.

Brown persistently questions claims to special position or preeminence. He has Harrington, for example, describe in Letter 17 how a "party was overthrown by a strange piece of folly." A beautiful, intelligent, accomplished young woman, Miss P——, attending the "little" gathering, overhears a derisive comment between a "lady and gentleman" who "scornfully" dismiss her as "a mechanick's daughter."[36] Upset, the young woman flees the festivities, whereupon "disorder and confusion immediately took place, and the amusement was put an end to for the evening" (pp. 52–53). Nor is that the end of the matter. Harrington delivers a diatribe against elitism, insisting that class considerations can never be just grounds for judging character. "Inequality among mankind is a foe to our happiness," he proclaims, and is out of place in a "democratical" government. "Were I a *Lycurgus* no distinction of rank should be found in my commonwealth." The "nature of the constitution" should triumph; all men should be "free and equal." Yet the incident with Miss P—— (as well as an earlier incident in which Mrs. Holmes savagely satirizes the ill manners of the noveau riche Mrs. Bourne and her gawky fourteen-year-old daughter) suggests that Harrington's friends do not all share his egalitarianism. Nor does Harrington always abide by his best principles. Upon first being attracted to Harriot, an orphan of dubious birth and no social prospects, he decides that she might suitably serve only as a kept mistress. "I am not so much of a republican," he early confides to Worthy, "as formally to wed any person of this class. How laughable would my conduct appear were I . . . to be heard openly acknowledging for my bosom companion, any daughter of the democratick empire of virtue" (Letter 3, p. 12).

Love presently prompts a different estimation of the lady's worth. But even though Harrington's love—which occasions the end of his misogyny and elitism—is applauded in the novel, that love still leads to disaster for the young couple. The children's disaster, however, is really grounded in their father, who was *not* swayed by love from his original design to seduce the hapless Maria nor prevented by love from abandoning her when it proved convenient to do so. In both cases, law and custom are at odds with love, and in both cases law and custom carry the day. Yet the two cases are hardly parallel. To consort with one's social inferior is not the same as to consort with one's sister. More accurately, three "sins" are dubiously conjoined—offenses against established (though ostensibly questioned) social mores (misalliances), offenses against established and ostensibly unquestioned sexual mores (seductions), and offenses against the incest taboo. That odd conjoining serves to force the reader to gauge the real weight of each offense.

For many conservative social authorities of the time, any such weighing no doubt constituted the seduction of the reader, too. Indeed, the sustained subtext of the sentimental novel was a covert questioning of the very rules textually affirmed by the tragic fall of some too-weak woman who does not properly resist the seducer's blandishments. Although seduction is ever the focal point of these novels, their illumination did not always fall precisely where the conventional moralists would have cast it.

What we might term the socioeconomics of seduction, central to *The Power of Sympathy* and to almost all other early American sentimental novels, can here be briefly reviewed. Essentially, what the modern reader must almost of necessity view as a melodramatic plot device would be, for the late eighteenth-century reader, no such thing. Seduction spun so many of these sentimental plots precisely because seduction set forth and summed up crucial aspects of the society—the author's, the characters', the contemporary readers' (especially if they were women)—that did not have to be delineated beyond the bare facts of the seduction itself. Seduction thereby becomes a metonymic reduction of the whole world in which women operated and were operated upon.

The same story of seduction was told over and over again, within the fictions and without them. For example, Sarah Connell Ayer noted in her diary entry of March 13, 1810, the sad case of an unnamed "young Woman who lives with us" who was seduced by a "gay young man." Since Connecticut law demanded that the father of illegitimate children pay $200 per child for their support, the gentleman married the woman but then, the very next day, left the state. "There is a certain class of Men," Ayer continues, "well skill'd in the arts of seduction, who when they find a young girl in such state, consider her as directly in their power, and how many have fallen victims to the baseness of those who call themselves the lords of creation."[37] Both the information and the import of Ayer's narration would be right at home in *The Power of Sympathy* as another entry in the novel's catalogue of seduction. Or note a similar collapsing of custom and misogyny in the events that make up the historical basis of Mrs. P. D. Manvill's *Lucinda; or, the Mountain Mourner. Being Recent Facts, in a Series of Letters* (1807), a novel that went through six editions in the first part of the nineteenth century. Lucinda, after being raped by the devious Mr. Brown, returns to live with her father and stepmother who, although poor (he is an impoverished schoolteacher, she a seamstress), are loving and forgiving and happy to care for their daughter. But the magistrates of the community, upon learning that Lucinda is pregnant, try to incarcerate her or force her to leave their community, a vestige of the old Puritan custom of "warning out" (exiling pregnant woman from the community and thereby sparing it the expense of supporting an illegitimate child). Lucinda's health fails soon thereafter, and the magistrates, ashamed of their verdict, rescind it. In subsequent editions of the novel, the magistrates (real or fictitious) even append to the novel their own defense of their actions—actions that by the early nineteenth century were beginning to require some defense.[38]

As these narrations by Ayer and Manvill indicate, law in the new Republic did not protect the seduced (or raped) woman and, in some cases, worked against her. In Connecticut in 1810, a law that tacitly acknowledged a man's superior earning power and his prime role as provider by requiring that he contribute to the support of an illegitimate child could be circumvented with the two-step procedure of first rendering the birth legitimate by marrying the mother and then abandoning both wife and baby. As the episode behind *Lucinda* suggests, the legal and economic procedures whereby the community could imprison or expel an unwed mother contrasts sharply to the sentimental novel's verdict that the community, not the young woman, was most in error.

Equally relevant to *The Power of Sympathy* and to the development of the early American sentimental novel is the fact that, all over America, laws concerning fornication were being reevaluated in the 1790s. The Connecticut law, for example, seems progressive, indeed, when compared with the procedures in Massachusetts a generation earlier. In some two hundred cases of fornication tried before the Middlesex County, Massachusetts, Superior and General Sessions Courts between 1760 and 1774, always the offending woman—never the guilty man—was subject to punishment and public humiliation. Even in cases where fornication was proved by the arrival of a baby too soon after a hasty marriage, the sin was only the woman's, and that same sin was regularly prosecuted. But in 1786, three years prior to the publication of *The Power of Sympathy*, the Massachusetts Fornication Act somewhat liberalized matters by "permitting a woman guilty of the crime to confess her guilt before a justice of the peace, pay an appropriate fine, and thereby avoid [public] prosecution." After 1791, women in Middlesex County stopped confessing their guilt at all, apparently aware that "though they did not confess, they would not be indicted." With this change in law and custom, as the legal historian William E. Nelson notes, a woman for the first time could attempt to sue the putative father of the child for paternity without herself incurring a criminal charge. A woman did precisely this in Middlesex in 1790, eliciting considerable public discussion in the local newspapers. In other states, too, matters of sexual morality were being debated, particular laws were changing, and the more basic question of the role of the law in society was being examined. Was it the function of law to prosecute "sin" (however sin was defined) as it had been in Puritan times? Or was it the function of law in an enlightened republic to protect property (however property was defined— daughters? wives?), to protect rights (even of the illegitimate), and to keep order?

Increasingly, the consensus of society leaned toward the latter alternative but not without the strenuous objections of social spokespersons such as Timothy Dwight or Chief Justice William Cushing, who saw this tendency as suspiciously "French" and as further evidence of the breakdown of social authority and the "declension in morals."[39] The decriminalization of civil sin, they feared, would lead to libertinism and atheism. Civil sin, in sexual matters, had also, of course, been female sexual sin. So the "declension in morals" that these men feared may have had some relationship to the fact that the old ostensibly higher morality also gave men a freer hand.

The Power of Sympathy especially speaks to that last artful dodging and does so not just by exposing a comparable dodging in Martin and the elder Harrington and intimating something of its consequences. The novel is also a surprisingly subtle anatomy of seduction and insists upon the relevance of seduction to the whole moral fiber of the new American nation. More particularly, *The Power of Sympathy* attests that the very mechanism of seduction signifies a grossly inequal distribution of social power and social worth, imbalances that should be corrected in a country purporting to be a republic. One main implication is that seduction is a social disease that will not be fully cured until men such as the elder Harrington and Martin are forced to surrender much of their inauthentic status or are shamed into exercising it more responsibly. Another is that women can learn to take preventative measures, be taught to appreciate the high price that must be paid for seduction given the time and place within which they live.[40] As Mrs. Holmes at one point observes, a well-educated woman who understands the "real charms of economy and simplicity" cannot be victimized ("enslaved") by even the smoothest of deceivers (Letter 40). Better to promote awareness than to perpetuate ignorance, especially when ignorance foredooms one to the status of victim in both the private and the public realm. Like almost all early American novels, *The Power of Sympathy* advocates improved female education and condemns any who would condemn women for aspiring above their place. Improved education should allow a woman self-confidence (so she need no longer depend upon a man for her knowledge of the world); social status and mobility (thus obviating the need to trade her body for a higher position in the world); moral values (discovered for herself and not provided by another for that other's advantage); and, above all, a realistic (so says William Hill Brown) suspicion of men.[41]

THE SOCIOLOGICAL dimensions of seduction and the communal responsibility of and for individual vice preoccupy the early American sentimental novel and are intrinsic to the social assumptions underlying the first American novel. In my discussion of *The Power of Sympathy* I have focused on seduction—how it was socialized, legalized, and fictionalized and how it might be forestalled by severer punishment of the seducer and by superior education for women. Certainly, this is a major, if not the major, concern of the book as well as the connecting link between its sensational story and its moral lesson plan. But it must also be emphasized that seduction in this novel is a metaphor not just of women's status in the Republic but of a range of problems, all of which might be reduced to the same structure or seduction plot—that is, a range of problems that arise when moral value and social responsibility are outweighed by the particular desires, no matter how basely self-serving, of privileged individuals or classes. The door is thereby thrown open to any sins that choose to walk in—lust, avarice, oppression—and the open door, the worst of a society's sins, is the instituted inequality of the society itself. In the main and subsidiary seduction stories in *The Power of Sympathy*, seduction depends upon the superior social status, education, and economic prospects of the man as well as upon a legal substructure that, essentially, makes the seduction a female not a male crime. The novel underscores the double jeopardy into which women are placed by misogyny in both its individual and its cultural manifestations.

In passing or at some length, William Hill Brown addresses numerous other social issues by noting the disjunctions between sanctioned behavior and professed ideals. These issues range from such relatively innocuous considerations as the continuing and antirepublican popularity of British tastes (especially in books) or manners to far more heinous matters such as slavery. Three times Brown halts his seduction tale to comment pointedly on the evil paradox of a nation founded on the premise of human equality still practicing slavery. He promotes a social judgment of this sin by stressing that those who own slaves are "haughtier, more tenacious of honour, and indeed possess more of an aristocratick temper" (p. 53); are, in short, un-American and threaten the peace and unity of America (pp. 53–54). He promotes a sentimental judgment by the eloquent and sustained digression telling of a slave woman who courageously accepts the "mark of the whip" (p. 103) that otherwise would have fallen upon her child who accidentally broke a glass tumbler, a slip any child could have committed. Harrington conjoins this narration with the main plot of the novel and his own misfortunes by invoking Laurence Sterne and the "power of sympathy" that necessarily binds one human being to another—regardless of gender, class, or race—within the human community and that, in a republic, makes no person free until all are free. Like seduction, slavery cannot be tolerated in a society where "all men are declared free and equal, and their tempers are open, generous and communicative" (p. 54).

But while Brown takes pains to connect private and public vice, the individual and the larger society, and all through the agency of sympathy, it would be grossly misleading to suggest that the novel finally and fully coheres in that one program. For the same power of sympathy that holds together the fabric of Brown's fictionalized republic also has a menacing underside that is nowhere reasoned or moralized away in the novel. That sinister sympathy, of course, centers in incest, the irresistible and ultimately tragic attraction between Harriot and Harrington that does not cease even with these characters' demise.[42] Harrington seizes upon Harriot's death as a chance to take his own life. He might then join her in some afterlife in which the deity will forgive their love, their death, and in which the now necessarily spiritual passion of brother and sister will not be tainted by social censure.

The final words of the novel (presented, as was conventional, in an epitaph) constitute an admonition: "May we never love as these have lov'd." These words, like Harrington's hopes, anticipate a better future, but they also assert the darker powers of sympathy that nothing in the novel can dispel. The concluding epitaph, like the opening epigraph, duplicitously signals a moralistic novel that ultimately affirms an amoral universe—a novel that both believes *and* rests content in its disbelief.

6 Privileging the *Feme Covert*: The Sociology of Sentimental Fiction

In the new Code of laws which I suppose it will be necessary for you to make I desire you would Remember the Ladies, and be more generous and favorable to them than your ancestors. Do not put such unlimited power into the hands of the Husbands. Remember all Men would be tyrants if they could. If particuliar care and attention is not paid to the Ladies we are determined to foment a Rebellion, and will not hold ourselves bound by any Laws in which we have no voice, or Representation.
—Abigail Adams to John Adams (March 31, 1776)

As to your extraordinary Code of laws, I cannot but laugh. We have been told that our Struggle has loosened the bands of Government every where. That children and Apprentices were disobedient—that schools and Colledges were grown turbulent—that Indians slighted their Guardians and Negroes grew insolent to their masters. But your letter was the first Intimation that another Tribe more numerous and powerful than all the rest were grown discontented. . . . Depend upon it, We know better than to repeal our masculine systems.
—John Adams to Abigail Adams (April 14, 1776).

The Sociology of the Female Reader

In centering his fictive universe on both seduction and female education, William Hill Brown dramatized one of the chief issues of his time and place—the status of women in the Republic. Seduction, of course, served as both metaphor and metonymy in summing up the society's contradictory views of women. The huge social interest vested in women's sexuality, which was fetishized into a necessary moral as well as a social and biological commodity, meant that women themselves had little voice in the matter. Female education was, then, in a number of the first sentimental novels, an education in the value of playing the proper sexual roles available to women who were thereby seduced by the sentimental plot as well as in it. Wife or mistress, woman's function was to be socially possessed or dispossessed. Taken either way, she constituted mostly one more proof of male prerogatives and privilege. In other words, it is no surprise that *The Power of Sympathy* posits the very premise, the essential powerlessness of the female, that any real problematics of seduction might be expected to question.

Even on the level of narration, the first American novel confirms female victimization in that women are seduced in the novel not by their own uncontrollable desire but by the verbal chicanery of men. This masculine narrative superiority is part and parcel of the narrative method of *The Power of Sympathy*. Harrington can abandon his plan to "triumph over" Harriot, but he still dominates in all discourse between them. In the course of the novel, Harrington writes his friend Worthy twenty-six times; he writes Harriot only twice. Harrington's letters occupy almost half the entire narrative; Harriot's take up less than one tenth of the novel. Harrington's voice counts and is counted; it is *his* story he is telling, and that unequal distribution of story time tends to seduce the reader as well as the female protagonist whose tale has already been subsumed into Harrington's mastering narration. Who, after all, would want to identify with Harriot, who has no surplus of identity to lend to another?

The social and narrative problems that Hannah Webster Foster addresses are both similar to Brown's and a universe removed. While also concerned with the interrelationship between seduction and female education, Foster has significantly altered the plot structure of the sentimental novel by allowing her heroine some status and by relating the novel primarily from the female point of view. She thereby casts *The Coquette* as more a woman's story than a man's. Whereas Harrington relates his choice not to seduce Harriot but to marry her, Eliza Wharton must choose for herself between matrimony and coquetry, between one set of constraints and another. Still more to the point, by validating the capability of the finally fallen heroine, Foster affirms both the need to educate women and the uselessness of any such education in a society that has no place for educated women.

Eliza is a capable woman, yet she ultimately fails as miserably as any of the hapless victims in Brown's novel. I would suggest that this narrative bad end is not only crucial to *The Coquette* but is pointedly relevant to the whole debate on women's status carried on in diaries, letters, newspapers, magazines, and advice books of the time and, of course, in the early sentimental novel as well. The horns of women's impossible dilemma can be summed up in two opposing questions: If a woman is inferior (susceptible to flattery, easily cajoled, prone to seduction), is she really educable, and, more to the point, does she in any way deserve a voice and a vote in the Republic? On the other hand, if some women are as capable as any man (Abigail Adams, Mercy Otis Warren, and other exemplary women), then why all the fuss about needing better schools, better education, and what is all this Wollstonecraftism about? It is an impasse that every woman's movement has had to face. If women are inferior, they can hardly expect to be treated as equals; if women are equal, then why the clamor for special privileges?

The Coquette, countering received ideas on women's circumscribed power and authority, was an important voice in the debate on women's role in the Republic. But unless the sociology of the early reader is kept in mind, the novel is deprived of its chief narrative thrust. The book gives us, essentially, a portrait of the life, loves, and death of a well-known woman of the new Republic sympathetically portrayed for this protagonist's unknown contemporaries. Elizabeth Whitman, Eliza Wharton's prototype, was much criticized and scorned in contemporaneous newspaper accounts. In the novel, however, she takes on a surprising dignity. And in the disjunctions between Eliza Wharton and "Elizabeth Whitman" (also a fiction in the sense that her scandalous life was thoroughly allegorized in dozens of sermons and editorials), we may catch some glimpses of an implied reader of early American fiction and read something of the dilemmas confronting her, too, in her society. Reading this reader, I would even maintain, is a necessary prerequisite to reading the novels she read.

The first step in that preliminary reading is to reconstruct the conditions under which she read.[1] We cannot simply reconstruct her, for she is no more a monolith than is "the female reader" today. However, her society tended to define her monolithically, as societies tend to define most members of low-prestige groups. Although the educated woman may well have enjoyed a more privileged life than her serving sister, by law vast differences in wealth, educational level, capability, class, or race were outweighed by one common feature. Both were "women," a social construct as much as a biological entity.

How was woman "written" in the society at large, and how did the early novel both contribute to and countermand that social text? To answer the first part of this contextual question, I will necessarily conduct various forays into the history of emerging America. In answering the second part, I will chart the ways in which numerous sentimental novels entered into the public debates on women and incorporated different arguments on women's status into their very structures. Only then will I return to *The Coquette* to examine how cogently and capably Foster gave voice to the "hidden woman" and dramatized her demise both as a personal tragedy and a social failure. Just as *The Power of Sympathy* can be seen as a counter-text to the Bowdoin/Adams proclamations, so can *The Coquette*, as I shall subsequently argue, be seen as a counter-text to the Elizabeth Whitman allegory of the fall of an intellectual woman.

WHO WERE THE IMPLIED readers of the early American sentimental novel? The novels themselves suggest a ready answer in that many of them are addressed, either prefatorially or in the text, to the "daughters of United Columbia," who are, implicitly or explicitly, young, white, of good New England stock, and for the most part unmarried. Their class, however, is rarely specified, and different novels give us female characters drawn from various social levels, ranging from the working poor to the relatively well-to-do. The very rich rarely appear in early novels except, occasionally, as seducer/villains or as wealthy women typically victimized by fortune hunters, which suggests that the wealthy were not paramount consumers of fiction. Similarly, although black women are sometimes included in subplots (typically to demonstrate the inhumanity of slavery), they are never the focus of sentimental intrigue, nor is it likely that they read sentimental novels in any number. Finally, few of the novels focus significant attention on mature women, matrons. Sentiment seems to have been mostly a province of the young.

Young people constituted a ready audience. Because of the high mortality rate during the Revolutionary War and the population explosion in its aftermath, by the first decades of the nineteenth century, a full two-thirds of the white population of America was under the age of twenty-four.[2] Furthermore, because of the increasing attention to childhood education in the later part of the eighteenth century, young people, especially women, tended to be more literate than old people. The early American writer capitalized on this market of potential readers by featuring young people prominently in the plots of the majority of early American novels of all genres. In fact, the mean age of the hero and heroine in novels written in America before 1820 is under twenty-five, as was the national mean. Most of the plots of early American novels also center around issues of importance to young readers. In sentimental fiction, particularly, far more emphasis is placed on a young woman deciding whom to marry than on an older wife determining how best to raise her family.

An emphasis on marital decisions also reflects other demographic considerations. The average marriage age of the republican woman was between twenty-two and twenty-three years of age, and her average life expectancy in 1800 was only forty-two years of age.[3] Since no college in America admitted women until 1837, when Oberlin first opened its doors to women, and since female secondary education was rare, a significant portion of a woman's life (perhaps as much as one-fifth) passed in what might be called a premarital state—beyond childhood but not yet, to use the eighteenth-century term, "settled."[4] While virtually all young women, even the wealthiest, were occupied either inside or outside the home in some kind of labor (sometimes remunerated, sometimes not), a woman's chief social goal during these years was to find a suitable husband, either independently or with the aid of her friends and family. Diaries of young women describe how part of virtually every day was spent visiting with one's friends and otherwise circulating, very much as do the characters in numerous sentimental novels.[5] Assessing one's male companions or studying men in company or sounding out one's acquaintances about a certain man's reputation are all recorded again and again and with good reason. Because of eighteenth-century laws of coverture, a woman had to be particularly careful in her choice of a mate, for, after marriage, she became, for all practical purposes, totally dependent upon her husband. Her rights would be "covered" by his, and it was his legal and social prerogative to define what those rights would be.

For the large available audience of unmarried young women, sentimental novels fulfilled the social function of testing some of the possibilities of romance and courtship—testing better conducted in the world of fiction than in the world of fact. Both Susanna Rowson and Hannah Foster demonstrated, for example, that a reformed rake did not make the best husband after all and that a womanizer was likely to also be a woman-hater. But by portraying dashing roués, sentimental novelists still allowed women to vicariously participate in a range of relationships with diverse suitors and to imagine what the aftermath of marriage to different men might be like. Most of these novels, however, did portray, at least on one level of discourse, the dangers of unsuitable relationships and, as I have shown with *The Power of Sympathy*, graphically described the heavy portion of blame and suffering that would necessarily fall on the shoulders of the sexually transgressing woman.

The concomitant unstated premise of sentimental fiction is that the woman must take greater control of her life and must make shrewd judgments of the men who come into her life. Implicitly and explicitly, the novels acknowledge that married life can be bitterly unhappy and encourage women to circumvent disaster by weighing any prospective suitors in the balance of good sense—society's and her own. A novel such as Sukey Vickery's *Emily Hamilton*, to cite but one example, considers little more than questions of matrimony. Women who choose wisely are briefly described, catalogued, and ranged against a contrasting catalogue of women who do not. The most pathetic of the latter, a Mrs. Henderson who is brought to the verge of death by a violent, alcoholic, profligate, and emotionally abusive husband, was based on the sad life of one Mrs. Anderson, a neighbor of Vickery (who was herself an unmarried young woman when she penned her first and only novel).[6]

Mary Beth Norton has suggested that young women in early America, particularly those in the higher classes, may well have enjoyed more leisure during their premarital years than at any other time. The daughters of well-to-do families were often free of some of the household tasks that occupied their mothers such as overseeing the ever-fluctuating household help or raising children.[7] But these young women were by no means perpetually idle and looking about for a good read. On the contrary, one of the chief arguments against novel reading in the eighteenth century held that such idle employment kept young women from contributing to the family economy. Linda K. Kerber has noted, in this regard, that household manufacture occupied a large percentage of even upper- and middle-class women's time in both cities and the country until well into the middle of the nineteenth century and that unmarried daughters participated in virtually all aspects of household production, including working the loom and the spinning wheel.[8]

During their premarital years young women even of the middle classes often worked outside the home, especially as teachers, while those lower on the social scale could seek work as domestics or, increasingly, in the new factories or mills. Or young women might engage in various given-out industries and thereby earn a minimal income while working in the home (typically making straw bonnets or stitching boots or shoes).[9] Although officially "unsettled," women in their premarital years were very much a part of the domestic economy and even contributed to the beginnings of the industrial economy in early America.

Yet they still made time for novel reading, either as a respite from other work or often as an accompaniment to it. For example, young Julia Cowles of Connecticut squeezed in a full syllabus of novel reading (*The Unfortunate Lovers, Adventures of Innocence, The Boarding School, Sir Charles Grandison, Amelia, Memoirs of the Bloomsgrove Family*) amidst her round of household duties—washing, cleaning, quilting, spinning, ironing, sewing: "Been so much engaged in read[ing] 'Grandison,' " she apologized to her diary, "that other things have been neglected, especially my journal." Or in Pennsylvania Molly Drinker read aloud from *The Mysteries of Udolpho* while her mother, Elizabeth, plied her needle— much the way Miss Granby reads aloud to Eliza Wharton and her mother in *The Coquette*. On another day, Mrs. Drinker herself read *The Haunted Priory* but then concluded her diary entry with a long list of the various household chores she had also accomplished "to shew that I have not spent the day reading."[10]

Women often met together to engage jointly in such tasks as sewing or quilting; while the others worked, one member of the group would read aloud—typically from a sentimental novel. Such group reading was often followed by discussions on topics ranging from national politics to local gossip. Not only was the novel thus made a part of the daily life of republican women, but the discourse of fiction was itself made contiguous with or incorporated into their discourse. In effect, then, just as a local scandal was easily fictionalized (a common source for sentimental novels), so, too, might the fiction be readily "scandalized" (that is, transformed by oral discourse and circulated as story). And through the grammar of these simple transformations, the news of the day—fictional, factual—could make its rounds.

Important social matters are reflected in sentimental plots, including the preoccupation with extramarital sex and the social and biological consequences of sexual transgressions. That preoccupation no doubt did not cause, as the critics of the early novel regularly asserted, a sharp rise in illegitimacy. But it is correlated with it. During the revolutionary and postrevolutionary era as many as 30 percent of all first births occurred less than nine months after marriage; the percentage of conceptions prior to or without benefit of matrimony was not equaled again until the present permissive era.[11] Many social authorities were alarmed by that new laxity, and the emerging novel provided them with a convenient scapegoat. I would suggest, however, that the novelist, as much as the professed moralist, simply perceived and addressed an issue of the time. The main difference was that the novelist's critique of illicit sexual behavior often had a feminist import and emphasized the unfortunate consequences of seduction for

See page 22.

Amelia: or the faithless Briton.

FIGURE 10. Frontispiece, *Amelia: or the Faithless Briton. An Original American Novel* (Boston: W. Spotswood and C. P. Wayne, 1798). Amelia, abandoned by the British soldier who seduced her and fathered her child, is prevented from killing herself by a forgiving father. *Courtesy of the American Antiquarian Society.*

the individual woman, not the social mores (although these were in the novel, too) against which she had offended.

The sentimental novel also portrayed, frequently in graphic terms, the deaths of many characters in childbirth. Although, then as now, the overall life expectancy for women was higher than for men, every young woman facing marriage also faced the prospect of death in childbirth, which did increase women's mortality rate above men's during prime childbearing years.[12] Julia Cowles was not too busy with her novels and her spinning to note that in 1802, in her small community of Farmington, Connecticut, four women between the ages of twenty and twenty-four had died, and she could not help but identify with them: "Shall I, who am now 17 years of age, live to see that time and leave, as 3 of them did, families? Ah! methinks I shall . . . be cut of[f] in the bloom of my life. . . . And time shall be no longer."[13] Cowles's diction and description come straight from the sentimental novels we retrospectively criticize for their lack of realism.

The lurid portrayal of death in childbirth allegorized what every early American woman already knew. Intercourse begot children, and having to bear a child was a mixed blessing. In postrevolutionary America, birth control was still considered immoral, so even though earlier sanctions against premarital sex had waned to a certain extent, the biological realities of pregnancy, then as now, burdened only the newly "liberated" woman and not the long-liberated man, a fact virtually every sentimental novel emphasized (without ever mentioning birth control).[14] And, of course, death in childbirth could come to married and unmarried women alike.

Demographic studies indicate that the *average* number of children born to an American woman in 1800 was an extraordinary 7.04, a number which does not include pregnancies that ended in miscarriage or stillbirth.[15] A typical American woman could thus count on spending virtually all of her mature years bearing and raising children. Fertility was higher in America than in most European countries at the same time, and many a European visitor noted the remarkable change in New World women after marriage. As Alexis de Tocqueville observed, "in America the independence of women is irrecoverably lost in the bonds of marriage."[16] But it did not take de Tocqueville to tell them so. Norton has documented how some of these women described their own condition. One Molly Tilghman wrote of her sister, Henny, in 1788: "She is decidedly *gone* [pregnant] to my great grief, and to her own too." Or Abigail Adams employed another apt metaphor when she noted of a young woman in her family, "it is a sad slavery to have children as fast as she has."[17]

The high fertility rate of the postrevolutionary period is striking, but what is even more striking is the precipitous fall in the rate during the next century. The fertility rate declined by 23 percent before 1850, by 50 percent before 1900.[18] Since no new technologies for preventing births (such as the recent birth control pill) were widely distributed in those years and since prophylactics were certainly known in late-eighteenth-century America (and used widely in other countries, notably France), this striking decline in the birthrate reveals a massive change in American social attitudes even within a generation or two. Equally interesting is the fact that relatively few written documents survive to chart the changing social attitude except, perhaps, novels in which a small, intimate family of only three or four children is more and more often posited as an ideal. It seems, then, that there was a dramatic shift from an abhorrence of contraception to a widespread but discreet and private reliance on methods of reducing family size. Carl N. Degler further argues that women were primarily responsible for this shift in attitude and that their increasingly asserted control over family size paved the way for greater reform movements at the end of the century. But whatever the causes and consequences, the unprecedented, rapid decline in fertility rates in the nineteenth century was one of the chief indices of women's changing role in family and society.[19]

Another index was the rising literacy and education levels of women. Nor does it seem merely coincidental that fertility rates fell almost 25 percent during the same period in which women's sign literacy rate (according to Kenneth A. Lockridge's data) more than doubled. Demographers chart a surprising correlation between the levels of education and fertility. Better-educated parents (the mother's education level being especially pertinent) tend to have fewer children.[20] The high correlation between increased female literacy and decreased fertility suggests that education brought with it a sense of control over one's body, over one's role in the reproductive process, and even some control over one's husband. I am not being entirely facetious, therefore, when I suggest that, with its double focus on improving female literacy and controlling sexuality, the sentimental novel may well have been the most effective means of birth control of the time.

By its emphasis on improved female education and its sensationalizing of the dangers of childbearing, the sentimental novel seems intimately linked—as mirror or catalyst or both—to larger social forces at work in the lives of women readers. But what was woman's status in the early years of the Republic, from 1789 to 1820? In almost all the sentimental novels, we see women dominated by larger social and economic forces, controlled by selfish parents, sadistic husbands, or strong-willed seducers. Viewing the typical sentimental novel as a reflection of the society, one must conclude that women were powerless and that the primary relationship between men and women entailed domination, exploitation, appropriation, and abandonment on the one hand and submission, appeasement, and other such defensive strategies on the other. Yet just how accurately did these novels reflect the lives of women readers and their relationships to the men in their lives?

As Perry Miller noted, the Revolution gave American legal thinkers a unique opportunity to invent new systems of law and new standards of justice.[21] For the most part, however, the new Republic modestly revised British principles and procedures and did so essentially to maintain the existing power structures of class, race, and gender in America. Marylynn Salmon has shown that most of the legal changes that occurred in America between 1775 and 1800, especially those bearing on women's rights, were "gradual, conservative, and frequently based upon English developments."[22] As the American jurist St. George Tucker indicated in his 1803 annotations of *Blackstone's Commentaries,* a cornerstone of English law, American judicial practices preserved the inequities between men and women, particularly the idea that a married women is a *feme covert* [*sic*], a hidden woman, whose rights are both absorbed by her husband and subject to her husband's will. Tucker also observed that American women were, de facto and de jure, victims of "taxation without representation; for they pay taxes without having the liberty of voting for representatives." As his very phrasing emphasizes, the Revolution freed America from an oppressive Colonial status, but it had not freed American women from their subservient status. As Tucker summed up the matter, "I fear that there is little reason for a compliment to our laws for their respect and favour to the female sex."[23]

Although the situation varied from state to state and sometimes from case to case, one can make a few generalizations about women's legal status in the new Republic. Before marriage, a young woman was typically considered the property of her father. Sometimes, as Kerber has pointed out, this concept of property could take grotesque forms. For example, in the Connecticut court case of *Samuel Mott v. Calvin Goddard* (September 1792), a father was able to sue his daughter's rapist for damages on the grounds that "the plaintiff's daughter and servant," by being made pregnant, had been rendered "unfit for service."[24] Kerber also notes that St. George Tucker was particularly offended by the terms of the proceedings whereby the rapist could be prosecuted only through the legal fiction that the victim's father's property had been irreparably damaged—a holdover from British law and a clear testimony to the woman's primary status as property not as person. In sentimental fiction, too, the unmarried young woman was, for all practical purposes, the property of her father. The common *Clarissa* theme of the avaricious parents who essentially sell their daughter into an economically advantageous marriage was not just an extravagant borrowing from earlier British fiction but was also an apt metaphor for the legal status of the postrevolutionary American girl.

It was an apt metaphor for the legal status of republican wives as well. Marriage, for the women involved, was mostly a change in masters. The new bride, admittedly, was to be protected by her husband, and she was protected, so far as the law was concerned, because her rights were subsumed in his. Yet as many legal historians have shown, a wife's status as *feme covert* effectively rendered her legally invisible. With some notable exceptions, the married woman typically lost her property upon marriage. She lost her legal right to make a will or to inherit property beyond the one-third widow's rights that, by common law, fell to her upon her husband's death. For the most part, in 1800, by law and by legal precedent, a married woman's signature had no weight on legal documents and she had no individual legal identity.[25]

As with many key historical issues, there is substantial debate over just how much coverture "actually" limited women's lives. The pioneering women's legal historian Mary Beard disputed nineteenth-century feminist reformers who described marriage, in Harriet Martineau's memorable phrase, as the "political non-existence of women."[26] Beard argued that both the equity courts and common law gave married women far more legal rights than those allowed by Blackstone or codified into the statutes of the different states. Relatively speaking, Beard was right in stressing that equity and common law tended to extend to women some measure of power and control. But one can easily romanticize the degree of equality granted here, and recent studies of equity rulings by Salmon and Norma Basch suggest that Beard may well have been too optimistic in her estimates.[27] For the most part, the nineteenth-century reformers accurately perceived the injustices of coverture. In Basch's summation, "the law created an equation in which one plus one equaled one by erasing the female one." The married women's property acts passed in New York in the mid–nineteenth century (and the result of considerable reformist activity) not only improved women's prospects but provided the locus of further feminist protest by emphasizing that the traditional concept of coverture was a "source of crippling sexual discrimination." The antebellum feminists, Basch continues, were "neither naive nor misguided" in focusing their attack on coverture, for that focus "was essential to an exploration of the conflict between motherhood and citizenship [and] the critical first stage in bridging the world of domesticity and the world of politics."[28]

Various commentators of the time emphasized women's legal powerlessness. One of the most eloquent assessments is that of Judge Hertell of New York, who in 1837 argued on behalf of a married woman's rights to retain her own property. Hertell noted that the current marriage laws gave a husband "uncontrolled, indefinite, irresponsible and arbitrary power" over every aspect of his wife's life and subjected her to an "abject state of surveillance to the will, commands, caprices, ill humours, angry passions, and mercenary, avaricious and selfish disposition, conduct and views of her husband." For Judge Hertell, a wife's situation, at least metaphorically and often literally, was comparable to slavery or imprisonment.[29] Cott, Norton, and Kerber have all found repeated statements in private papers of late-eighteenth-century women about the privations of marriage; women such as Abigail Adams, the diarist Eliza Southgate, Judith Sargent Murray, Susanna Rowson, Mercy Otis Warren, and others all noted that women suffered in life proportionate to the rights they surrendered by law.[30] Even Abigail Adams's request that her husband "Remember the Ladies" in the new Constitution was primarily addressed to the legal and social inequities of married women (rather than a more direct plea for political rights). "Do not put such unlimited power into the hands of the Husbands," she wrote, because "all Men would be tyrants if they could." She counseled her husband to "put it out of the power of the vicious and the Lawless to use us with cruelty and indignity with impunity."[31] Abigail Adams's prediction is starkly substantiated by a private complaint in verse by Grace Growden Galloway, the wife of the politician Joseph Galloway:

> . . . I am Dead
> Dead to each pleasing thought each Joy of Life
> Turn'd to that heavy lifeless lump a wife.[32]

The flat despair of that declaration of dependence and defeat anticipates writers such as Sylvia Plath or Anne Sexton and emphasizes the debilitating potentialities inherent in the system of coverture.

Mrs. Galloway's private complaint remained private in her lifetime. It is now more acceptable for a woman to speak the woe that is marriage, especially her own, but it is now also more acceptable for a woman to remove herself from that same marriage. In the late-eighteenth-century colonies, however, and also in the new Republic, divorce, for most women, was simply not an option. As a result of a British ruling, Colonial divorce bills were effectively rescinded in the decade preceding the Revolution. Pennsylvania and New York, for example, granted no divorces during the prerevolutionary era. Not until 1785 in Pennsylvania and 1787 in New York could any foundering marriage be officially dissolved. Maryland granted its first absolute divorce in 1790. There was, furthermore, a good deal of variation from state to state. In South Carolina, absolute divorces were not allowed until 1949 (although legal separations could be granted there by Courts of Chancery).[33] What was universal, however, was a declared, public, official abhorrence for divorce, and both social pressures and legal practice insisted on the sanctity of marriage. For example, until well into the next century, women were granted divorces only if they could prove extreme physical abuse and their own total innocence. Consequently, a "guilty" woman, whether confirmed adulteress or occasional shrew, was often denied a court hearing. The impasse was early dramatized in Gilbert Imlay's sentimental novel *The Emigrants* (1793), which was apparently written with some help from his lover, Mary Wollstonecraft, and is essentially a fictionalized tract in favor of divorce. As Imlay notes in his preface, "I have no doubt but the main misfortunes which daily happen in domestic life, and which too often precipitate women of the most virtuous inclinations into the gulf of ruin, proceed from the great difficulty there is . . . of obtaining a divorce."[34]

Women's restricted status within marriage (and the corresponding restrictions on divorce) presumed a patriarchal domestic order often breached during the Revolutionary War years when many American women were suddenly forced to survive without the economic assistance or legal protection of a husband. As numerous historians have demonstrated, the war ambiguously emphasized to women both their private capability and their public powerlessness. Thousands of women during the war suddenly became responsible for running a family business or for continuing the operations of a family farm. Those women, of course, were still also responsible for the array of household manufacture essential for survival in the rural market economy. Extant letters indicate that sometimes a conscientious husband might write home giving his wife advice on how to manage complex business or agricultural operations, but there was little he could actually do while he was away fighting, and there was always the possibility of his death. Women managed, as they have managed during all wars, to keep the economy going, surreptitiously circumventing their lack of legal rights, often to their financial detriment. Many learned firsthand the shackles law placed upon them, as wives and also as widows. In most states, women could not legally inherit property or businesses. The assumption that they could not manage, at odds with the fact that they did, was rendered even more ridiculous when destitution at home followed the husband's death in the war. Only through extralegal maneuverings by widowed women and their male kin could the law's clear intent— property was to be controlled by men—sometimes be subverted.[35]

Having demonstrated their capability in the face of a national emergency, many women in the postwar years felt that they had fully earned those new rights and responsibilities that they had exercised, de facto, already. The new Constitution, however, did nothing to acknowledge women's contribution to the war effort. In only one state, New Jersey, and only briefly, were propertied women (black and white) granted the vote. That enfranchisement was unusual enough that newspapers as far away as Boston reported on women voting in local New Jersey elections.[36] Equal pay was not even an issue; it was assumed that women would earn less. Technically, a woman factory worker could not even collect her earnings without a man's signature (although this restriction may not have been widely enforced). Not until the end of the nineteenth century could a woman serve on a jury or, concomitantly, be tried by a jury at least partly of her peers. Married or single, she had virtually no rights within society and no visibility within the political operations of government, except as a symbol of that government— Columbia or Minerva or Liberty.

As one immediate consequence of the Revolution, the family and, more particularly, woman's role in the family became a matter of considerable social concern. There is almost a natural tendency, after any war, to seek within domesticity some release from what might be termed a postmarital letdown. The comfort and safety of hearth and home are welcomed, by women as well as men, after the dangers of battle, the chaos of war. There is something comforting in seeing that much of the old order has survived. Consequently, Sally the Shopkeeper, like her latter-day daughter Rosie the Riveter, soon found her new occupation gone and was obliged to return to her old one—tending house and husband and raising children to repeople the Republic.

Typically, too, after the War of Independence, some women were reluctant to relinquish the freedoms that they had gained while men were occupied elsewhere and otherwise. As a poem published in the *Massachusetts Magazine, or Monthly Museum,* in 1794 proclaims:

No ties shall perplex me, no fetters shall bind,
That innocent freedom that dwells in my mind.
At liberty's spring such draughts I've imbib'd,
That I hate all the doctrines of wedlock prescrib'd.[37]

Or as another anonymous poem published the following year in the *Philadelphia Minerva* declares:

Man boasts the noble cause
Nor yields supine to laws
Tyrants ordain;
Let Woman have a share
Nor yield to slavish fear,
Her equal rights declare,
And Well Maintain[38]

The diction has gone from post-Freneau to pre-Emerson, but the sentiments remain the same. A spirit of "woman's rights" was felt throughout postrevolutionary America, celebrated by some, derided by others.

Certain demographies of the time contributed to this strain of female independence. Studies of Massachusetts and Pennsylvania suggest that the number of unmarried and never-married women increased, as would be expected, in the postwar era. Many men had died in the war, leaving widows behind. Records show that a number of these widows (perhaps at least partly to circumvent legal problems arising from not being able to inherit their husband's land or business) quickly remarried, sometimes to relatives of the deceased husband, sometimes to men considerably younger than themselves, thus further depleting the pool of men available to a young woman reaching marriageable age.[39] But despite the surplus of unmarried women in the late eighteenth century, spinsterhood hardly embodied a respectable option in the society of the time. On the contrary, the spinster was an object of pervasive cultural ridicule. As we see in the plots of numerous sentimental novels, the specter of spinsterhood drove more than one sentimental heroine into the arms of a seducer. Eliza Wharton is merely one case in point, a case that I will subsequently consider in some detail. For the present, suffice to say that when, at the age of thirty-seven, she finally yielded to her seducer's blandishments, she knew exactly what she was doing, and so did many readers of the time who obviously sympathized with her plight.

The sentimental novel as a form mediated between (and fluctuated between) the hopes of a young woman who knew that her future would be largely determined by her marriage and her all-too-well-founded fears as to what her new status might entail—the legal liabilities of the *feme covert*, the threat of abandonment, the physical realities of repetitive pregnancy, and the danger of an early death during childbirth. Many republican women expressed deep reservations about marriage. "I keep my name still," Betsey Mayhew wrote to her good friend Pamela Dwight Sedgwick in 1782, "I think it is a good one and am determined not to change it without a prospect of some great advantage." Somewhat less hard-headed but no less ambivalent was Sarah Hanschurst: "I often Run over in my mind, the many Disadvantages that Accrue to our Sex from an Alliance with the other," she wrote to her friend Sally Forbes, but "the thought of being Do[o]med to live alone I cant yet Reconcile . . . [T]he Appeallation of old Made . . . I don't believe one our Sex would voluntarily Bare."[40] Or in the literature of the time, Mrs. Carter, in Charles Brockden Brown's *Alcuin*, can paraphrase Mary Wollstonecraft and insist that marriage is a vital institution "founded on free and mutual consent" and one that "cannot exist without friendship" or "without personal fidelity." For her, "as soon as the union ceases to be spontaneous it ceases to be just." Yet that idealistic portrait must be set against her own earlier description not of marriage as it should be but marriage as it too often was in America. The married woman "will be most applauded when she smiles with the most perseverance on her oppressor, and when, with the undistinguishing attachment of a dog, no caprice or cruelty shall be able to estrange her affection." Carter's final pronouncement on the role of women in marriage anticipates that of Judge Hertell: "Females are slaves."[41]

As any number of public and private documents attest, marriage was a crucial matter for women of the time. Just as they knew and differently adumbrated the central question in their lives, so, too, did the authors of the fictions they read, fictions that were primarily sentimental. That last literary adjective carries, in contemporary discourse, a heavy load of negative connotations and suggests self-indulgent fantasies bearing little relationship to real life. Yet the private and nonfictional commentaries of the time suggest a contiguity between the sociology of the early American family and the plots of the sentimental novel that is easily overlooked by the contemporary reader. Indeed, the seemingly melodramatic death with which so many of the sentimental novels end both fictionalizes and thematicizes the seriousness of the women's questions raised in the plot. Given the political and legal realities of the time, the lack of birth control, the high fertility rate, and the substantial chances of death at an early age, many of the readers fared no better than did their most unfortunate fictional sisters.

The sentimental novel spoke far more directly to the fears and expectations of its original readers than our retrospective readings generally acknowledge. Conveniently divorcing the novel from the social milieu in which it was originally written and read, recent critics easily condemn as clichéd and overdone the plight of the assailed, sentimental heroine hovering momentously between what seems a mechanical fall (seduction) on the one hand and an automatic salvation (marriage) on the other. Yet for her and her reader the choice was desperate. Moreover, if the right decision would not necessarily assure her happiness, the wrong one would guarantee suffering in abundance. So the contemporary critic literalizes and thereby trivializes what the contemporaneous reader took symbolically and thus seriously.

Style, too, has changed since the late eighteenth century, and the language of sentiment interposes itself between the modern reader and the eighteenth-century text. In our lean and antirhetorical time, the very excesses of the novel's sentimental "effusions" (a term derogatory in our vocabulary, not theirs) call the sentiments thereby expressed into question. Yet other discourse of the time employs much the same language as does the early American novel. Consider, for example, the courtship correspondence of John and Abigail Adams as represented by the following excerpt from a 1764 letter from John (signing himself Lysander) to Abigail (Diana):

> You who have always softened and warmed my Heart, shall restore my Benevolence as well as my Health and Tranquility of mind. You shall polish and refine my sentiments of Life and manners, banish all the unsocial and ill-natured particles in my Composition, and form me to that happy Temper, that can reconcile a quick Discernment with a perfect Candour.[42]

Harrington himself could not have said it more sentimentally. As Jane Tompkins has recently reminded us, contemporary tastes and values applied indiscriminately to older literature may illuminate contemporary tastes and values but say little about the literature itself.[43]

Addressed to young female readers, the first novels performed vital functions within their society and did so more than parallel vehicles such as sermons or advice books. The most important of these functions in my view was the reappropriating of choice. "Seduction," at first glance, implies female powerlessness; nevertheless, by reading about a female character's good or bad decisions in sexual and marital matters, the early American woman could vicariously enact her own courtship and marriage fantasies. She could, at least in those fantasies, view her life as largely the consequence of her own choices and not merely as the product of the power of others in her life—the father's authority, the suitor's (honorable or dishonorable) guile, the husband's control. Thematicizing, then, the necessity of informed choice, these fictions championed the cause of female education that they typically proclaimed in their prefaces. Weighed in that balance, many of the novels of the time are not the frothy fictions that we commonly take them to be but evince, instead, a solid social realism that also constitutes a critique (even if sometimes covert) of the patriarchal structure of that society. Thus, if many early novels end unhappily, it may be because they acknowledge the sad reality of marriage for many women. As Catherine Maria Sedgwick wryly notes in her story "Old Maids" (1835), it is best to conclude a story with the wedding if one wants to end on a happy day, for "it is not probable another will succeed it."[44]

Other forms of literature in the new Republic also specifically addressed the woman reader, most notably a wealth of advice literature often penned by clergymen. But this literature usually referred women more to the kitchen and the nursery than to the study or the library. Only in fiction would the average early woman reader encounter a version of her world existing for her sake, and, more important, only in the sentimental novel would her reading about this world be itself validated. As an added bonus, in not a few of these novels, women readers encountered women characters whose opinions mattered. Numerous sentimental novels, beginning with the first one, took time out from the main seduction plot to show women discussing politics, law, philosophy, and history—those same arenas of discourse from which the woman reader was often excluded. As Rachael Rachel M. Brownstein has recently observed, such reading, for women, serves crucial functions:

> Recognizing the problems and the conventions of a woman-centered novel, the reader feels part of a community and tradition of women who talk well about their lives and link them, by language, to larger subjects. Looking up from a novel about a girl's settling on a husband and a destiny so as to assert higher moral and aesthetic laws and her own alliance with them, the reader can feel the weight of her woman's life as serious, can see her own self as shapely and significant.[45]

A *feme covert*, a hidden woman, the early American reader had even greater motivation than the contemporary woman reader to find books that rendered her life, in fiction if not in fact, significant.

Sentimental Fiction as Social Commentary

Given a married woman's status as *feme covert*, many late-eighteenth-century readers (particularly women readers) were, understandably, vitally concerned with marriage and strove to educate or otherwise prepare themselves to make a good choice in marriage. Questions of the importance and nature of the family and woman's role within the family were widely debated. As recent historians such as Degler, Kerber, and Norton as well as Jay Fliegelman, Philip Greven, and Michael Zuckerman have pointed out, with considerable differences in emphasis or interpretation, there was in the eighteenth century at least a theoretical concern with reforming patriarchal structures. It has also been argued that some substantial changes did occur in the daily family life of Americans in the new Republic. Amorphous psychosociological shifts such as an emerging ideal of affectional marriage (rather than patriarchal authority and wifely subordination), a relaxing of parental control over one's offspring (especially in the matter of choosing marriage partners), an increased substitution of affection for authority in the

LA LECTURE.

FIGURE 11. This lithograph, *La Lecture* (Boston: c. 1830), was probably copied from a French print. Note the rapt attention of the female reader as she reads her book (which is the size of a typical early American novel). By the nineteenth century, a book became a symbol of status, especially among fashionable young women such as the one portrayed here. *Courtesy of the American Antiquarian Society.*

dealings between parents and children, and a new emphasis on the mother's responsibility for imparting to her children both knowledge and principles of virtue have all been traced to the last part of the eighteenth century. All such changes, it has been further argued, became still more institutionalized in the next century through industrialization and the increasing gender specialization within the family. With the father cast as the primary wage earner and more and more often employed away from the home, the mother, even if she also worked for wages, was deemed responsible for childrearing and household management.[46]

The extent and nature as well as the consequent implications of large changes in the family raise issues that simply do not admit definitive historical assessments. Did women, despite few advancements in political and legal rights, achieve a new domestic status that testified to an egalitarian impulse in the society as a whole, or was that new domestic status intended to tell a wife that she had none elsewhere and that her place was in the home? The very terms with which the question is posed invite a reading of the historian's personal predilections as much as of the historical record. Nor did the commentators of the time, unhindered or unhelped by any historical perspective, deal any more conclusively with the same question. Yet we can observe that the impetus for change was both proved and problematized by a wealth of advice literature that debated questions of domesticity, questions, not coincidentally, much debated in the early novel.

The sentimental novel, in particular, was generically suited to addressing, in detail, the range of ideological assessments of the family and the implications *for women* of different visions of what the family should be. Furthermore, since the sentimental novel focused almost exclusively on young women standing virtually on the doorstep of definitive marriage choices, it necessarily dramatized the grounds on which the final crucial step was taken. What qualities, in her, would promote a happy match? In him? How should she best be schooled to cultivate the former and to perceive the latter? Would a purely domestic course of training or formal schooling best foster her husband's future happiness? And hers as well? More specifically, and this was a major question of the day, did education enhance or impede a woman's chance of making a suitable match and, correspondingly, did education alter her expectations of what a good marriage should be? Was she to be the submissive helpmeet or the equal partner? Was she to be motivated mostly by duty or desire? What other questions should she be asking? To whom could she best turn for advice—suitors, friends, or parents? All such questions were extensively discussed in the didactic advice literature of the time, but they were worked out in far more detail and by example in the sentimental novels.

The didactic literature on the role of women tended to be divided into two highly polarized camps. The more prevalent of these, the conservative or traditional position, relied especially on the biblical story of Eve's ordained subservient status to argue the justice of God and man's established ways with women. The opposing view, "equalitarian feminism" to use Cott's phrase, or the "group consciousness" movement, which took place between 1770 and 1800, admitted women's "shared weakness relative to men" but questioned "whether this weakness was natural or artificial, biological or cultural."[47] And if women's supposed "natural inferiority" were really imposed by custom and culture, then, the argument implicitly and often explicitly ran, it could largely be remedied through an equal or at least improved education. As I will show, specific sentimental novels took up one or the other side of this debate, but at either pole, the need to portray with some recognizable validity the social conditions of the young women who might read a particular novel subtly altered its reading of their actual and ideal case.

Three writers—Jean-Jacques Rousseau, James Fordyce, and John Gregory—best represent the conservative or traditional view of the role of women. Although not American, they were each exceptionally popular in America. Both Rousseau's *Emile* and Gregory's *A Father's Legacy to His Daughters* (1774) were American best-sellers in 1775, and both, along with Fordyce's *Sermons to Young Women* (1765), were widely published and read in America in the postrevolutionary era.[48] In these three books, to summarize briefly, woman were portrayed as naturally subservient within the family, and each author also argued that education made a woman less submissive and thus less appealing. In *Emile*, for example, the great French republican philosopher heaps contempt upon any woman who might believe that the new radicalism and egalitarianism somehow includes her. For Rousseau, any social contract between man and woman must be premised on her natural inferiority. Thus her necessary subordination in all matters, domestic and social.[49] Before marriage, maidens were to be chaste and retiring, rarely seen and seldom heard. After marriage, wives were to efface themselves in perpetual attendance on their husbands' needs and desires. Such service, moreover, should come naturally, and education, Rousseau argued, destroyed a woman's natural charm and equable disposition, thereby rendering her unfit to fulfill her chief function of happily bringing happiness to others. The Reverend James Fordyce and Dr. John Gregory popularized similar views. In *Sermons to Young Women*, Fordyce maintained that a woman's most important function was to serve and please her man, while Dr. Gregory asserted that such traits as vitality and spirit were unfeminine, unfashionable, and unattractive. He insisted that only a languishing, pallid passivity would attract a potential husband and repeatedly lays the blame for any domestic disharmony on woman's natural selfishness and vanities along with any unnatural and necessarily unrealistic education.

Books by Rousseau, Fordyce, Gregory, and other similar social theorists were widely read and discussed in postrevolutionary America; their ideas were paraphrased and promulgated in dozens of essays that appeared in newspapers and magazines. One representative sample of this social theory in the popular culture–

advice column mode is "From a Mother to Her Daughter, Just on the Point of Marriage," from the *Boston Weekly Magazine* of 1804. The bride-to-be is counseled:

> You have a father, whose mild and beneficient exercise of authority must have taught you to wish, that your husband may possess all the prerogatives, which all laws, divine and human, have given him in the headship of his own house, and to remove far from you, every desire of degrading, much more of endeavoring to make him contemptible by any efforts to usurp his place yourself.

The young lady should have no problem; all her life has been a study in her subservient status. But even more conservative, or perhaps merely more explicit, is another piece, "Woman; An Apologue," from a different 1804 issue of the same paper:

> Women were created to be the companions of man, to please him, to solace him in his miseries, to console him in his sorrows, and not to partake with him the fatigue of war, of the sciences, and of government. Warlike women, learned women, and women who are politicians, equally abandon the circle which nature and institutions have traced round their sex; they convert themselves into men. . . . And, besides, where is the feeling and amiable women who would exchange the ineffable happiness of being loved for the unsubstantial pleasure of fame?[50]

Fame, for a woman, is by definition (gender definition) unfeminine, infamous.

A few writers of sentimental novels championed this conservative view of woman's proper place and function. In Helena Well's *Constantia Neville; or, The West Indian* (1800), for example, Mrs. Hayman patiently endures all the abuses heaped upon her by a cruel and loutish husband.[51] The more she suffers from the accepted status quo, the more she affirms it. Even while engaged in such tasks as raising her husband's illegitimate offspring (there are apparently several), Mrs. Hayman lectures the readers on the joys of being a dutiful wife. But when it comes to marital bliss there are singularly few objective correlatives in this novel. The protagonist can claim that she is content, but contemporary readers (in the unlikely event that the book might reach them—it was never reprinted) would doubtless reach a different verdict. Similarly, in S.S.B.K. Wood's *Amelia; or, The Influence of Virtue* (1802), the protagonist struggles to provide a "useful lesson" in submissive wifehood. Obeying the deathbed request of her adopted mother, Amelia marries Sir William Stanly, only to learn that Sir William still loves another. Too sentimental a heroine to grant him a divorce, Amelia must accommodate herself to her husband's extended affair with the other woman. Through all, Amelia endures—virtuous, innocent, patient, perfect, and quite un-appreciated. Like Mrs. Hayman, she even takes on the task of raising her hus-band's illegitimate child. As Wood assures us, Amelia "was not a disciple or pupil of Mary Woolstonecraft [*sic*]. . . . She was an old fashioned wife and she meant to obey her husband: she meant to do her duty in the strictest sense of the word. To perform it cheerfully would perhaps be painful, but . . . it would most assuredly be best."[52]

This passage humorously epitomizes the contradictions that underlie the conservative sentimental novels. Both Mrs. Hayman and Amelia submit to all that is required of them. But given women's official status of the time, they really had little alternative. The fiction, in short, attempted to valorize a choice where, according to that same fiction, there was none. The very form of the medium, too, worked against the message it was assigned to convey. Whereas a tract might extoll the virtues of submission in the face of all trials, a novel must *create* trials to which a dedicated heroine then virtuously submits. But those trials fully visualized give us not an inspiring icon of feminine virtue but a perturbing portrait of the young wife as perpetual victim. The tract can lecture in the abstract, but the conservative novel, portraying through concrete example, evokes (quite inappropriately for its own rhetorical purposes) the legal, social, and political status of the average female reader, and that reader is not apt to applaud the tortured image of her own condition. I would also suggest that fictions such as *Amelia* and *Constantia Neville* set forth the sad truths of many women's lives in the late eighteenth century more tellingly than did the overtly reformist novels. As heroines, Amelia and Mrs. Hayman are, ultimately, inescapably, failures—even if they do eventually receive some compensatory reward (i.e., heaven, authorial approval, etc.). They are failures because their stories deny any cult of ideal domesticity far more convincingly than their commentary affirms it. Indeed, and on an elementary level, the infidelities of the husbands suggest a breakdown of the family, a breakdown the wives are powerless to prevent. The heroines' suffering may be chaste, but it is also banal, even ignominious, and suggests that both wives would have done better if they (or their parents) had chosen more wisely. The novels end up inadvertently advocating the need for better female education and for greater female self-sufficiency, which is precisely what they set out to deny.

The sentimental plot simply would not serve the objectives that the conservative writers had drafted it to advance. Women, of course, could be portrayed as innately inferior to men; weak in body, mind, and spirit; needing guidance, counsel, a controlling hand. Marriage could be cast as the one proper refuge, after the father's home, from the dangers of the wide, wide world. Yet if the wife was protected by a caring husband, her wants essentially the same as his and his the same as hers, where then was woman's subservient status? Somehow her haven also had to be at least in part or in potentiality her hell—or who was marriage for? That contradiction could neither be resolved nor glossed over but served instead to indict—to deconstruct—the very theory of domesticity that regularly led the conservative sentimental novel to this impasse. So Helena Wells, in *The Step-Mother; a Domestic Tale, from Real Life* (1799), for example, can urge her readers "to think of *man* as a *lord* and *master*, from whose *will* there is no appeal."[53] Thinking of not thinking; willed will-lessness; the appeal of the un-appealing: The duplicity of the advice highlights the tyranny it would explain away, invokes the very appeal that it would deny, and since that appeal cannot be carried to a higher court (lord and master), God's ways to women are pointedly called into question. Simply put, this counsel for total defeat necessarily carries its own cry for radical revolution.

Interestingly enough, the most consistently conservative of the sentimental writers, S.S.B.K. Wood, seems to have practiced in her own life a more liberated philosophy than she promulgated in her fiction. There is, first, the obvious fact of her writing career. There is also the curious matter of Wood's tribute in the dedication to *Julia, and the Illuminated Baron* (1800), to "Constantia," who is none other than Judith Sargent Murray, the most vocal proponent of the equal-itarian feminist position in early America.[54] That reference makes one wonder if the contradiction the modern reader discovers in Wood's portrayal of the sub-missive helpmeet is perhaps grounded partly in the ambivalence of the author and not just in the recalcitrance of the form.

JUDITH SARGENT MURRAY, MORE than any other single American writer, rep-resents the equalitarian position. Her *Gleaner* essays were published serially, re-published in a collected edition that attracted nearly seven hundred subscribers, and were pirated (in whole or part) dozens of times in the 1790s.[55] Through their subject matter alone, these essays, dealing with such disparate topics as military strategy, the new Constitution, political philosophy, or legal reform, attest to at least one woman's wide-ranging intelligence and her readiness to address cogently issues ostensibly beyond woman's ken. The most persistent topic of the *Gleaner* pieces, however, is closer to home but no less radical in its import and implica-tions. Murray regularly advocated the need for better female education and ar-gued the relationship between such education and greater independence. She also stressed the importance of female education for fulfilling the traditional role of wife and mother but noted, too, that "marriage should not be presented as a sumum bonum [*sic*]." For Murray, education would serve a woman in whatever state she happened to find herself. "The term *helpless widow*," for example, "might be rendered as unfrequent and inapplicable as that of *helpless widower*."[56] In one important essay, "On the Equality of the Sexes," Murray argued that if women lacked the same power of reason and judgment exhibited by men, it was only because they also lacked the proper training in those skills. Following Locke, she maintained that "we can only reason from what we know and if an oppor-tunity for acquiring knowledge hath been denied us, the inferiority of our sex cannot fairly be deduced from thence."[57] Certain that education would bring advancement, Murray even predicted, "I expect to see our young women forming a new era in female history."[58]

Best known as an essayist, Murray was also an author of sentimental fiction. Most notable for my purposes is her novella, *Story of Margaretta* (1798), in which she reformulated the role of the sentimental heroine by revising that heroine's educational preparation for the role. In her essays, Murray had advocated that natural philosophy, astronomy, mathematics, geography, and history be taught along with such traditionally feminine subjects as painting, needlepoint, French, and piano playing. This is the curriculum set for the protagonist in *Story of Margaretta*, a work instructive, as Murray intended, in several different senses.

Margaretta Melworth begins her career as a sentimental heroine somewhat unthinking in her actions and apparently destined for disaster. Fortunately, however, she encounters a sagacious woman who teaches her that education is necessary for any woman who would answer sensibly the one question posed to almost all sentimental heroines: Whom shall I marry? This emphasis on education, often promised in the prefatory statements, is rarely so carefully executed as it is in Murray's plot. Because she gains some education, Margaretta escapes the standard sentimental role of the helpless victim of fate, fate typically taking the form of a designing man whose machinations the innocent heroine simply cannot decipher. Schooled to weigh the worth of various propositions and proposals, Margaretta has no problem disposing of those who are found wanting, especially an ominously named suitor (and would-be seducer), Sinisterus Courtland, who is, she later discovers, already married and the father of three children. With equal good judgment she chooses Edward Hamilton, and everything in the novel suggests that their union will be one of "mutual affection." That promised reward for female perspicacity is a powerful argument in favor of just such capability and also a not-so-covert suggestion that, in the schoolroom and the home, many women were being sadly short-changed.

Judith Sargent Murray was herself apparently inspired by the ideas and examples of other female philosophers, including Aphra Behn (1640–89), Mary Astell (1666–1731), Lady Mary Wortley Montagu (1689–1762), and, most specifically, Catharine Macaulay (1731–91), one of the finest historians and social philosophers of the late eighteenth century and the author of the feminist *Letters on Education* (1790), a work advocating views on education similar to Murray's. Macaulay, incidentally, was widely known in the New World. As Dale Spender notes, she visited America in order to see and judge for herself the promise of the new country, and she maintained an active correspondence with George Washington throughout the revolutionary period. Macaulay's inspiration can also be seen in the work of a number of other American feminists such as Abigail Adams, the diarist Eliza Southgate, and the anonymous "Female Advocate," all of whom linked feminist reform with the promise implicit in the new republican form of government.[59]

For the earlier writers, however, and for Murray, too, feminist reform could best begin in the family. Women's greater domestic equality could then pave the way to larger forms of equality as well. As we see in *Story of Margaretta*, education allows for a rational choice of a good husband who believes in affection and not in wifely deference. Because Margaretta has proven herself to be both virtuous and wise, she *deserves* a larger role in the home and in society, and, conversely, because America is young and virtuous, it *needs* women like Margaretta. The implicit assumption here is that virtuous women will be rewarded; the governing term *virtue* has simply been redefined and the scope of the expected reward expanded to include not just a good marriage but greater legal and political power, too. In short, Murray does not share Mary Wollstonecraft's suspicion that oppressive systems are systematically and designedly so. She believes that the goodwill latent in the existing order might become the lever whereby that same order could be moved to be more just and fair.

If Wollstonecraft seems to have been the more perceptive of the two, Murray was still on firmer ground than were such advocates of social radicalism as Thomas Paine, Montesquieu, and Condorcet, all of whom expressed far less concern with women's continuing domestic subservience than with her coming political emancipation as part of a revolutionary reordering of society at large.[60] Somehow, these men seemed to assume, we could achieve the latter without altering the former. In contrast to that self-serving contradiction, we see a dilemma of the sentimental reformers, all of whom were going to alter the former without affecting the latter. The changes proposed by the reforming novelists turn out to be largely grounded in the old order, and what is advocated is a readjustment of the marriage contract rather than a second revolution led by "the Ladies."

Only a few novels significantly questioned received ideas as to woman's place. Fewer still disputed the sanctity of the sexual double standard, and even those did so with a measure of ambivalence. In James Butler's *Fortune's Foot-ball: or, The Adventures of Mercutio* (1797), one woman character rails against the "tyrannical custom" that forbids women to make advances toward the men they might like. "How peculiarly hard that woman's situation, who possessing the most unadulterated passion . . . must, in obedience to an arbitrary custom, linger out her days in the most excruciating torture."[61] But after eight months of an illicit and apparently guilt-free relationship, the young woman dies at sea while her lover escapes to other adventures and liaisons. Conversely, but not altogether differently, Laura, in Leonora Sansay's 1809 novel of the same name, lives with Belfield without benefit of matrimony, but then, after his death, her harrowing illness, and a bout of insanity, she meets a man with whom (so the novel portends) she might enjoy an egalitarian (and, this time, legal) match. And the double sexual standard is pointedly and overtly challenged by Gilbert Imlay, who argues in *The Emigrants* that men and women should be allowed the same sexual rights, including the right to divorce.[62] But Imlay does not envision female freedoms beyond sexual freedom, and his female characters are often Rousseauisticly passive helpmeets.

A few other novels also call into question the social program of the double standard. The title character of Sukey Vickery's *Emily Hamilton* observes "that the world has been too rigid, much too rigid, as respects the female sex," and at one point ironically argues that if we must accept the "assertion" (derived, she notes, from *Pamela*) that "reformed rakes make the best husbands," then "might it not be said with equal justice, that if a certain description of females were reformed, they would make the best wives?"[63] Or in the anonymous *Adventures of Jonathan Corncob, Loyal American Refugee* (1787) and in William Hill Brown's *Ira and Isabella,* minor women characters enjoy sexual freedom, but it is difficult to determine if these "loose women" serve as vehicles for or objects of an indiscriminate satire. For the most part, those who noted that the traditional double standard was unfair still had, when it came to sexual affairs, nothing else to put in its place.

No early American novelist went as far as Mary Wollstonecraft in reevaluating the political and sexual roles of women. Her *A Vindication of the Rights of Woman* (1792) was the single most important theoretical contribution to the equalitarian cause. Printed in America in 1792 and reprinted in 1794, the book persuasively advocated the justice of women's equality in matters social, political, and sexual.[64] Quantitative studies of the period indicate that Wollstonecraft's feminist tract was available from some 30 percent of the libraries in America (based on a controlled sample of libraries whose records still exist) during its first years in print, and the fact that it had its own American printing and reprinting similarly attests to its popularity.[65] Moreover, the *Vindication* appears in advertisements bound in the back of early American novels more often than any other philosophical tract (suggesting that publishers perceived that readers of novels might be predisposed to purchase this feminist book).

Like Montesquieu and Condorcet, Wollstonecraft argued that no society can call itself free unless it grants equality to both sexes. But more than either of the male social theorists, Mary Wollstonecraft focused on the usual workings of the matrimonial bond, on the biased nature of the social contract between the sexes, and on the freedoms women lost in order for men to be still more free. She did not reject marriage. On the contrary, she praised domestic union as humanity's highest state, but only if redefined as a partnership of equals, based on mutual affection and respect. Furthermore, unlike Murray and other American reformers, Wollstonecraft knew full well that marriage could not be restructured unless the society, too, was restructured. In the *Vindication,* she pointedly and systematically refutes the social vision promulgated by Rousseau, Fordyce, and Gregory, and she proposes an alternative organization in which men and women would have the same social and political privileges and would be allowed the same legal freedoms as well as freedom of movement, freedom of personal expression, and freedom of sexual expression.

Many Americans were intrigued by the promise implicit in Wollstonecraft's radicalism, but many others found her vision extremely threatening and labored to countermand it. For example, an article entitled "Rights to Woman" in the *New England Palladium* of 1802 portrayed a "Mary Wolstoncraft [*sic*] Godwin" sitting on a throne-like chair surrounded by a host of adoring women and a few quisling men. Arrogant, silly, and ugly, this parodic Wollstonecraft lectures her assembled audience on nature versus nurture and is especially convinced that, given the right physical conditioning, women can even be as strong as men. Her diatribe concludes when "the lady herself says, women are entitled to all the rights of men, and are capable of assuming the character of *manly women*."[66] This was a common refutation of Wollstonecraftism—it would make women manly, with bulging muscles and hair sprouting in inappropriate places, a metamorphosis to be avoided at all cost.

Wollstonecraft's ideas were all the more suspect when viewed in the lurid light that her life seemed to cast on her feminist philosophy. After she died of septicemia following the birth of her and William Godwin's daughter, a child conceived out of wedlock, Godwin published *Memoirs of the Author of "A Vindication of The Rights of Woman"* (1798). Intended to celebrate the strength and independence of Wollstonecraft's life and philosophy (which, Godwin insisted, changed much of his own thinking), the published memoirs, to say the least, fell far short of that objective. Not that the book failed to gain notice; it was translated almost immediately into French and German and was published in America in 1799 and again in 1804. Everywhere the reaction to the work was immediately and violently negative. Reviewers did not praise Wollstonecraft's unconventional thought but condemned her unconventional life. Her different affairs and her suicide attempts were read as a total refutation of her philosphy, so much so that Godwin attempted, in a second edition, to play down the damning evidence of Wollstonecraft's illicit relationships with other men. But it was too late. Once the *Memoirs* was published, Wollstonecraft was no longer a heroic "female Werter [*sic*]" (his term) or a challenging social thinker; she became, instead, an object lesson on the dangers of feminist ideas and ideals—as if a woman could not live in the world she advocated but had no problems in the one she opposed. Thus the *European Magazine* prophesied that the *Memoirs* would be read "with disgust by every female who has any pretensions to delicacy; with detestation by every one attached to the interests of religion and morality; and with indignation by any one who might feel any regard for the unhappy woman, whose frailties should have been buried in oblivion." Or the *Anti-Jacobin Review* not only railed against the impropriety of her life but, in its index, listed under the heading "Prostitution" the cross reference "See Mary Wollstonecraft." The *Memoirs* were thereby translated into a compelling argument for the status quo, and Wollstonecraftism (a word originally used to designate the equalitarian feminist movement) became a damning label for the loose feminine morals in which libertarian principles, ostensibly, necessarily ended.[67]

The life and death of Mary Wollstonecraft, thus interpreted, demonstrated how radical life imitated conservative art and thereby validated the social vision of the most reactionary of early American sentimental tales with their plots of aberrant female crime and consequent female punishment. Transformed from a feminist social theorist and philosopher into a fallen sentimental heroine, a woman who had loved badly and necessarily lost, Wollstonecraft, like many other female protagonists, provided merely another admonitory example of the downward path to sexual disgrace and dishonorable death. The parallels between this reading of her life and standard plots are obvious. Essentially, had she never asserted her own freedom, the whole tragedy could have been avoided. Here, especially, was a woman too capable for her own good, one who desperately required a father's, a husband's constraining hand. There are even the requisite hints of the happiness that might have been hers when, after a few preliminary and necessarily abortive affairs that drove her to attempted suicide, she meets the man she can truly love and finds him as ready to love her. But even here a fatal weakness undoes her. She dies bearing the baby conceived out of wedlock, leaving him to mourn for some forty years his loss—and hers—before death claims him, too. Even better, a subsequent generation could read in the fate of Wollstonecraft's first daughter further proof of the mother's folly. In 1816, when Fanny Imlay, the illegitimate daughter of Wollstonecraft and Gilbert Imlay, discovered belatedly the sad facts of her own beginning, she took her life, leaving only a note to the world in which she described herself as "one whose birth was unfortunate," as sentimental an epilogue to a sentimental tale as anything a Mrs. Wood or a Mrs. Wells could ever conceive.

If even one of the most brilliant and independent women of the era could be so subject to the various ills that seduced female flesh was heir to—abandonment, temporary insanity, attempted suicide, death in childbirth, enduring infamy, and the suicide of an illegitimate daughter—how could the average American woman reader hope for a different outcome if she should venture the same perilous journey? Considering the referential powers attributed to texts in the late eighteenth century, it was tempting to "read" the *Memoirs* as the punishment meted out for the ideas promulgated in the *Vindication*. Justice had been done, and the very questions that Wollstonecraft was determined to pose had been, so far as her society was concerned, definitively answered. The *Memoirs* was further compromised by its timing, published during the violence of the French Revolution, which was viewed as a case study on the largest public level for all that was wrong with Wollstonecraftism or other such radical thinking, just as the author's life was viewed as her own refutation on a private and personal level. After 1799, virtually every portrait of Wollstonecraft in America was a negative one. To put oneself forward as a proponent of Wollstonecraftism was to advocate private licentiousness and public corruption. As America entered the nineteenth century, any new "rights" for women were simply the traditional ones reentrenched—a right to marriage, to children, to domesticity.

Writing in 1808, the Reverend Samuel Miller could heave a sigh of relief that the Wollstonecraftism of a few years earlier had thoroughly passed away. He, happily, even has to remind his readers what some of the unlikely tenets of that erstwhile radical feminism had actually been:

> Whatever opinion may be formed on this subject, I take for granted, we shall all agree, that Women ought not to be considered as destined to the same employments with Men; and, of course, that there is a species of education, and a sphere of action, which more particularly belong to them. There was a time indeed, when a very different doctrine had many advocates, and appeared to be growing popular:—viz. that in conducting education, and in selecting employments, all distinctions of sex ought to be forgotten and confounded; and that females are as well fitted to fill the Academic Chair, to shine in the Senate, to adorn the Bench of Justice, and even to lead the train of War, as the more hardy sex. This delusion, however, is now generally discarded. It begins to be perceived, that the God of nature has raised everlasting barriers against such wild and mischievous speculations; and that to urge them, is to renounce reason, to contradict experience, to trample on the divine authority, and to degrade the usefulness, the honor, and the real enjoyments of the female sex.[68]

Perhaps because the novel as a genre was already associated with corruption and libertinism, after the publication of the *Memoirs* American sentimental writers were quick to deny that they might be guilty of borrowing from Wollstonecraft.[69] The contretemps over the *Memoirs* also effectively silenced many of the advocates of women's rights in America. Even though the Wollstonecraft scandal, grotesquely magnified by the Reign of Terror in France, did not necessarily *precipitate* a reactionary retrenchment, it certainly served as a potent sign of the dangers inherent in radical action and a symbol of the negative consequences, for women, of unconventional lifestyles.

It is not within the scope of this study to document and analyze what changes in the prescriptive literature occurred in the nineteenth century, but I wish to conclude, briefly, by suggesting that, over the course of the next generation, both the conservative side of the debate on the role of women and the reformist position gradually changed in tone and focus so that they were no longer dialectical opposites but rather simply different approaches to a similar view of woman as par excellence the republican mother.[70] A nineteenth-century rhetoric of "true womanhood" or a "cult of domesticity" extolled women as specially gifted for the crucial task of rearing children. As Ruth H. Bloch has observed, a new focus on motherhood effectively reversed an older Puritan emphasis on the paramount importance of the father in the intellectual, moral, and social molding of children.[71] And at least on the level of rhetoric, this hyperbolic language of republican motherhood also seemed to offer women new social status, as was argued in 1802 by the Reverend William Lyman:

> Mothers do, in a sense, hold the reigns of government and sway the ensigns of national prosperity and glory. Yea, they give direction to the moral sentiment of our rising hopes and contribute to form their moral state. To them therefore our eyes are turned in this demoralizing age, and of them we ask, that they would appreciate their worth and dignity, and exert all their influence to drive discord, infidelity, and licentiousness from our land.[72]

The question of political power—central to Wollstonecraftism and important to American reformers as well—was rendered irrelevant by this co-opting ideology that mothers were indirectly responsible for *everything* that was crucial in the society. In the words of one advocate of omnipotent motherhood, "compared with maternal influence, the combined authority of laws and armies and public sentiment are little things."[73]

With the cult of domesticity, there was also a shift in women's fiction. Earlier novels, as noted, had focused on women's life preparatory to marriage and posited a good marriage as virtue's reward. Portraying the lives of girls and unmarried young women, these novels necessarily described how such women proceeded within and around the restrictions placed upon them by their society, a plot structure that can be observed in progressive novels such as *The Coquette* and also more conservative books such as Wood's *Amelia* or *Julia*. To generalize, the plots of most sentimental novels of the early national period concentrate on a young woman's freedoms prior to wedlock, often epitomized (and tested) through the seduction plot or an equivalent subplot. But as Helen Waite Papashvily observes, after approximately 1818, the seduction plot virtually disappears from sentimental fiction, and, with the graphic exception of *The Scarlet Letter,* the "fallen woman" does not figure prominently in the design of nineteenth-century American fiction.[74] At the same time, the sentimental heroine grows up. Numerous nineteenth-century novels centered on older women working out their lives within their domestic sphere, whether as matron or "old maid."[75]

Writing in 1804 in the *Literary Magazine*, in an essay entitled "Female Learning," Charles Brockden Brown early identified the contradictions in the contemporary ideology of women, the presumed opposition between female intellect and domesticity. "A woman who hates reading," he countered, "is not necessarily a wise and prudent economist." But he also understood, with remarkable sensitivity, that polar categorizations of women—maternal paragon *or* learned woman, wife *or* author—necessarily diminished both the woman writer and the woman reader, who could always be condemned for being too much or not enough of one or the other. "Of that numerous class of females, who have cultivated their minds with science and literature, without publishing their labours, and who consequently are unknown to general inquirers; how many have preserved the balance immoveable between the opposite demands of the kitchen, the drawing room, the nursery, and the library? We may safely answer from our own experience, not one."[76] From the personal evidence Brown had at hand, women simply could not maintain rich intellectual lives while bearing the full burden of *perfect* domesticity. Despite the rhetoric, or perhaps because of it, during the first decades of the nineteenth century, a cult of "true womanhood" all but smothered the cry for female equality, a cry faintly but subversively heard in those sentimental novels such as *Charlotte Temple* and *The Coquette* that remained steady sellers into the last half of the nineteenth century and the dawnings of America's first full-fledged feminist movement.

Disjunctions in the Sentimental Structure

Just as women could ambivalently embrace the promise of marriage along with its promised restrictions, and just as neither the reactionary nor the reformist novel could univocally assert its politics of marriage, so, too, do we regularly encounter in the very structure of the sentimental novel tensions and unresolved contradictions. There is often a glaring gap between the public morality officially espoused and the private behavior of the characters who voice or supposedly validate that morality. What is promised in the preface is not always proven in the plot. As earlier noted, much early sentimental fiction was forced into a difficult balancing act—not always successfully executed—between readerly demands (especially from the professional readers) for moralistic restraint and writerly demands for artistic license. But that wavering and uncertain balance can be read not just in the sociology of the production of these texts but in the texts themselves and even in the first readers of these texts. Indeed, I would suggest that these texts find one of their chief loci in the difference between the reader's private reservations about her own limited legal and social standing as opposed to her public acceptance of ostensibly unquestioned social values and established good order. Such private discourse mirrors a larger discourse between the reader and the sentimental novel in its different versions and between the novel in all its versions and the critics who saw it rightly as raising issues that they would have preferred to remain repressed.

Consider, for example, Samuel Relf's *Infidelity, or the Victims of Sentiment*, a novel to which I have previously referred as one of the few that survives with its original subscription list bound in the volume. Almost one-half of the book's original subscribers who can be identified by gender are women; two of the men who subscribed, James A. Neal and John Poor, were not only preceptor and principal, respectively, of young ladies' academies, but they advertised themselves as such in the subscription list itself (which, after all, is a *public* declaration of one's reading habits), suggesting that they approved of the "lesson" of the book for their charges. But what lesson did young women readers learn from Caroline Courntey, the heroine of the novel and an obvious ancestress of Hester Prynne? Like many a sentimental heroine, Caroline submits to her parents' judgment and weds, much against her own wishes, the elderly Mr. Franks. This dutiful daughter is thereby rewarded with an unhappy marriage. Neglected by her cruel husband, she finds solace in the concern of a younger, more sympathetic man. That infatuation, apparently unconsummated, is nevertheless the "infidelity" of the title and brings death to both participants and disaster to their friends and families. Yet the epigraph to the novel reads, "——'Tis not a sin to love." To which the reader can only reply that it was and it wasn't. Marriage is vindicated by the fatal consequences of its failure. The probably nonadulterous lovers are vindicated by their sinless love. "Persecuted innocence" (to use the novel's own diction) has been sacrificed in order that compromised propriety might be saved.[77]

Other characters took other ways to much the same sentimental impasse. Thus, the thoroughly virtuous Mrs. Morley in Wood's *Dorval* does not even flirt with the possibility of seduction. Unfortunately for that formerly wealthy former widow, her new husband turns out to be, in order, a fortune hunter, a bigamist, and a murderer. Feminine virtue, the rock on which the sentimental novel was founded, was, in this case, clearly no match for masculine vice. Or, in a somewhat different fashion, moral spokespersons could practice considerably less than they preached. The jejune and platitudinous Worthy in *The Power of Sympathy* is germane here, as is, in Susanna Rowson's *Mentoria; or, The Young Lady's Friend* (1791), the equally inappropriately named Prudelia, whose ever-ready sententia serve mostly as a moral smoke screen behind which she busily pries into the possible sins of her neighbors instead of cultivating any virtues of her own.

The sentimental form was also modified and its meaning compounded when main characters were rendered novelistically, not morally; when they were brought down from the heights of spiritual grandeur to be portrayed as flawed and, consequently, as believable human beings. When Harrington, for example, ignores Worthy's long-winded advice and seeks refuge, instead, in suicide, his end is not a heroic vindication of high ideals but a recognition that his tragic dilemma lies beyond the reach and scope of any available code of conduct. The power of sympathy, in this text, runs head first into its own powerlessness in the face of overpowering incestuous desire. Conversely, moral issues are complicated when the villain of the piece is recast as more than just another advocate of illegitimate affairs. Belfield in Sansay's *Laura*, Count Hubert in Isaac Mitchell's *The Asylum; or, Alonzo and Melissa* (1811), and, most obviously, Carwin in Charles Brockden Brown's *Wieland, or the Transformation* (1798) are all examples of such humanized antagonists—the seducer who is himself seduced by delusions, misconceptions, and his own naive egotism. These characters suggest dangers other than and embody the consequences of falls more subtle than mere physical seduction.

Charles Brockden Brown's Carwin is perhaps the most complex and certainly the most discussed villain in early American fiction. But Montraville, in Rowson's *Charlotte Temple*, provides a less analyzed example of how problematic villains spin problematic plots.[78] Charlotte Temple, it will be remembered, elopes with this seducer partly because she has been misled by the dubious logic of Mademoiselle La Rue but primarily because she loves Montraville and fully expects that he will immediately marry her. The seducer in this best-seller sins primarily because he, too, sees himself as an honorable suitor anticipating wedlock. Charlotte, however, is no heiress, and marrying her would preclude the affluent life to which Montraville aspires. He partly evades that first dilemma by procrastinating marriage, which presently leads to his second dilemma when he chances to meet another woman who is virtuous, beautiful, kind, and even rich. Should he remain with Charlotte, his now pregnant mistress, or should he eschew vice, in favor of the virtue of a clearly rewarding marriage?

Partly to exonerate Montraville, Rowson provides a second male character, Belcour, who conventionally counsels that sin should not be sanctioned, that a mistress must be renounced. Belcour, a parallel and parody of the stock moral adviser, is determined to see "morality" prevail and even contrives to be found "sleeping" beside Charlotte, who really is asleep and quite unaware of the plot against her. The discovery of a "betrayal" that never took place persuades Montraville to abandon the young woman. The two former lovers are then further victimized by Belcour. As a proponent of the sentimental credo that a "perfidious girl" such as the pregnant Miss Temple deserves whatever fate befalls her, he keeps for himself the money provided by Montraville to take care of Charlotte.[79] So Montraville, the concerned seducer, is not the true villain of the piece, and a standard moral dictum is compromised by the way Belcour employs it to serve his vicious purpose.

Or perhaps Montraville is the real villain in that his villainy is so sanctioned by his society that it can pass as virtue. Rowson's larger point here well might be that a standard double standard of sexual conduct allows even a relatively decent young man to become, indirectly and second hand, a murderer. Montraville thus interpreted serves as a symptom of a much larger social phenomenon, just as Charlotte's fate also attests to the social context in which it is realized. She is a victim not so much of her wayward desires but of a shoddy education, of evil advisers (including one schoolteacher), of her legal and social inferiority. Many of the first commentators on the novel also read the book in this way—as a work of "truth" and "realism" in which Charlotte was rightly pitied and wrongly sentenced. Most notably, the assessment in the London *Critical Review* (1791) powerfully argued for both the truth of the work as a whole and the

Charlotte Temple

FIGURE 12. This stipple engraving of a sweet, innocent-looking Charlotte, from Mathew Carey's 1809 edition of Susanna Rowson's novel, has been carefully hand-colored by an anonymous reader. *Courtesy of the American Antiquarian Society.*

innocence of its title character. This review was tipped into early American and British editions of the book and was later reprinted opposite the preface in all eighteenth-century and many nineteenth-century American editions. As that review concludes:

> Charlotte dies a martyr to the inconstancy of her lover, and the treachery of his friend.—The situations are artless and affecting—the descriptions natural and pathetic; we should feel for Charlotte, if such a person ever existed, who, for one error, scarcely, perhaps, deserved so severe a punishment. If it is a fiction, poetic justice is not, we think, properly distributed.[80]

Rowson, I suspect, felt so, too. In a fiction grounded in sexual crime and feminine punishment, she problematizes the official justice ostensibly implicit in her conventional plot.

Other early novels also realigned what Herbert Ross Brown has called the "sentimental formula" ("a simple equation resting upon a belief in the spontaneous goodness and benevolence of man's original instincts").[81] For example, instead of positing clear-cut moral choices between virtue, on the one hand, and vice, on the other, a number of early novels present heroines with more complicated and, consequently, more believable moral dilemmas. She must choose, say, between loveless respectability and unrespectable love, not simply between marriage and illicit sex. Thus, in the anonymous *Margaretta; or, The Intricacies of the Heart* (1807), the female protagonist prefers passion to propriety and rejects the dependable Captain Waller, who proposes matrimony, for the dashing Will de Burling, who plans to marry an heiress but will keep Margaretta as his mistress. As Margaretta declares, "I think I was not destined by nature for an humble cottage."[82] Numerous abductions and other trials and tribulations later, she finds that she must again choose between the good Waller and the handsome de Burling. Now herself possessed of both a title and a fortune, she once more bypasses social respectability, although settling this time for marriage—but marriage to the penniless de Burling.

Or a husband could subvert the social authority implicit in his role by too much insisting on that role and authority. In Wells's *The Step-Mother*, Caroline Williams, the put-upon heroine, repeatedly advocates that a woman do whatever her husband requires, but the reader sympathizes more with Mrs. Malcolm, an emotionally and perhaps physically abused wife, who escapes a loveless marriage to form an illicit love relationship with a young man of egalitarian views. Both women must balance the quite different questions of to obey or not to obey the husband, to resist or not to resist the tyrant. Or the parents' claims to control the daughter could similarly be called into question by the very tyrannical overtones of their assertion. A protagonist must frequently choose between a father she loves and a lover her father, often for no valid reason, opposes. Almost half of the sentimental novels written in America before 1820 employ this cruel parent motif. One example is *The History of Constantius and Pulchera*, in which Pulchera's father forces her to break off her engagement to Constantius so that she can marry Le Monte, whom she does not love and who, even worse, is French. Only after a mind-boggling series of misadventures on the high seas, in Europe, and in Canada are the true lovers reunited. All the calamities could have been avoided through a little parental reasonableness, but perhaps that is the point of the book. Or notice how *The Unfortunate Lovers, and Cruel Parents* (1797) advertises its plot in its title. And in both Charles Brockden Brown's *Clara Howard* (1801) and Margaret Botsford's *Adelaide* (1816), we see young men and women marry because of parental pressure, not from love, and suffer from that decision into the next generation.

The sentimental plot could also be complicated by posing, for the central heroine, the dubious charms of a restrictive domesticity, on the one hand, against the freedom from stultifying convention promised by a socially unsuitable but passionate suitor, on the other. In a few of these novels, virtue is presented as no less demeaning an alternative for an intelligent young woman than vice. Not infrequently, a capable heroine clearly foresees the protracted unhappiness that would be hers if she married the respectable male character whom society views as her proper mate. Just such a dilemma faces Deborah Sampson in *The Female Review*, which makes it easier for her to opt for transvestism and the army, a revolutionary choice for which she is not punished in the novel. Similarly, Martinette de Beauvais, in Charles Brockden Brown's *Ormond* (1799), disguises herself as "Martin" and enlists in freedom's cause, thereby acquiring an appropriate metaphoric platform from which to question the propriety of society in general and of woman's assigned roles in particular. These are extreme cases, but they reinforce choices made in other novels where a heroine sees the constrictions implicit in her proposed marriage. Moralists say that virtue should be rewarded. But is marriage to a stodgy moralist truly a reward for a sensitive, capable heroine? In the best of these novels, the issues raised by the plot often go considerably beyond the prefatory promise of safe social truth in fictional packaging.

Even the early sentimental novel cannot be reduced, then, to the simple formula that contemporary readers and critics commonly ascribe to it. The recipe was more complicated than we assume as, from the very beginning, one key ingredient was to experiment with the recipe. Instead of positing simple answers about the powers of pious procreation, many of the novels question the efficacy of the prevailing legal, political, and social values, even if the questioning is done by innuendo rather than by actual assertion of a contrary view. What else can we make of fallen women who are more the victims of circumstance than the embodiments of sin and who scarcely deserve the punishments that are heaped upon them? Of seducers who are not villains? Of villains, like Belcour, who ascribe to the standard morality? Furthermore, the seducer, proud of his conquests but contemptuous of the women he seduces, often inversely mirrors the values of the moralist. The one, to prove his reputation, would despoil what the other, to prove his, would preserve. For each, the heroine is almost incidental. For the heroine, both are equally unappealing. She is caught in a double bind, and, in the best sentimental novels, her predicament demonstrates that the postulated dichotomy of the clearly virtuous and the clearly vicious central to this fiction is itself a fiction.

Virtue (writ large) does not always save the heroine. Bombarded with pompous precepts, on the one hand, and assailed by promising temptations, on the other, the perceptive female protagonist merits the reader's attention and sympathy. Prefatory assurances to the contrary, hers is no easy choice. Chaste, she is rewarded by a limiting marriage, often to a limited man. Should she fall, her death is hardly triumphant proof that the social norms are just, that vice has been rightly punished. Anticipating the later Romantic tradition, these protagonists seek to establish their own destinies.[83] Given the mores of late-eighteenth-century American society and the biological reality of pregnancy, they cannot succeed. But often we wish they could.

Reading *The Coquette*

William Godwin's 1798 publication of the *Memoirs* of Mary Wollstonecraft had the unexpected effect of immediately translating her life into an allegory of feminine crime and punishment, and American public opinion was quick to draw the reactionary moral. When a thirty-seven-year-old woman came to the Bell Tavern in Danvers (now Peabody), Massachusetts, to give birth to a stillborn child, and then followed that child to her own death on July 25, 1788, a similar fictionalizing was at once set in motion, as can be seen in even the first published account of the event, which appeared in the *Salem Mercury* for July 29, 1788. Purportedly written by one Captain Goodhue, the landlord of the Bell Tavern, this first notice effectively balances asserted propriety (she was waiting for her husband) and suggested scandal (did she really have one?):

> Last Friday, a female stranger died at the Bell Tavern, in Danvers; and on Sunday her remains were decently interred. The circumstances relative to this woman are such as excite curiosity, and interest our feelings. She was brought to the Bell in a chaise . . . by a young man whom she had engaged for that purpose. . . . She remained at this inn till her death, in expectation of the arrival of her husband, whom she expected to come for her, and appeared anxious at his delay. She was averse to being interrogated concerning herself or connexions; and kept much retired to her chamber, employed in needlework, writing, etc. . . . Her conversation, her writings and her manners, bespoke the advantage of a respectable family and good education. Her person was agreeable; her deportment, amiable and engaging; and, though in a state of anxiety and suspense,

she preserved a cheerfulness which seemed to be not the effect of insensibility, but of a firm and patient temper.[84]

Within days the account was picked up and reprinted by the *Massachusetts Centinel* and then in dozens of other newspapers throughout New England. It was the stuff of good rumor, of gossip, of sentimental novels.

What led to the Elizabeth Whitman mystery? Surely many other woman had borne a child out of wedlock and died of puerperal fever. But, as even the foregoing report suggests, the essential appeal of this story was its contradictory nature. To start with, what was a nice woman like Elizabeth Whitman doing in a tavern like that and in that condition? Miss Whitman was the daughter of a highly respected minister, the Reverend Elnathan Whitman. On her mother's side, she was descended from the Stanley family, which had governed Connecticut almost from its Colonial beginnings. She was also related to the Edwards family, to Aaron Burr, and to the poet John Trumbull. Two of her suitors had been Yale preceptors. She had corresponded regularly with Joel Barlow. Hartford's highest society knew and respected her for her wit, her intelligence, and her charm. Yet she died in a tavern, seduced and abandoned, a fate right out of the novels that vociferously warned against just that fate. Nor were the novels the only texts bearing on the matter of her demise. Once Whitman's identity was revealed, ministers, journalists, and free-lance moralists industriously made *meaning*—their meaning—of her otherwise incomprehensible life. In the redaction of an anonymous essayist in the *Boston Independent Chronicle* of September 11, 1788, for example, Elizabeth Whitman's life and death becomes, simply, "a good moral lecture to young ladies."[85]

Readers in the early Republic were well versed in the process whereby the complexities of a disordered life could be reduced to a simply ordered moral allegory. Virtually every condemned crook, con man, or other criminal recorded the outlines of his or her life before ascending to the gallows. Published in inexpensive chapbook form, republished in newspaper columns throughout America, these confessions straddled the line between truth and fiction as much as did the Elizabeth Whitman allegories that were reprinted all over New England. Most readers of *The Coquette* would have already known the outlines of Whitman's life either from the newspapers or from sermons of ministers who regularly mined gossip for material. These readers would also have known the lacunae in Whitman's story that have continued to intrigue biographers down to the present day. Although Whitman left a cache of poems and letters at her death, none refers to her lover by name—and the ironic pseudonym she used to refer to him, Fidelio, provides no clue to his identity either. Pierrepont Edwards, by the middle of the nineteenth century, was generally assumed to be the model for Major Peter Sanford, but other candidates for the honor have also been proposed: Aaron Burr, the New York state senator James Watson, Joel Barlow, and an unnamed French nobleman whose parents objected to his secret marriage to a Protestant minister's daughter from Connecticut. The secret marriage theme, incidentally, at one point had considerable currency. Caroline W. Dall (in 1875) and Charles Knowles Bolton (in 1912) both tried, a century after the events, to salvage the reputation of the lady by proposing a secret wedding.[86] In different ages, the historical record differently fabricates the story of Elizabeth Whitman—seduced woman or suffering wife, smirched or sacrificed or sanctified—mostly to confirm its story of itself. But in Victorian hagiography or eighteenth-century moral tracts, the histories of Elizabeth Whitman all share the governing assumption that lost virginity signifies, for a woman, lost worth; that the sexual fall proves the social one, so much so that in this case the signifier and its significance are one and the same.

The earliest accounts of Whitman's decline and fall served the dual purpose of criticizing any intellectual pretensions that a woman might possess and of condemning the novel as a new form that fostered such pretensions. Whitman became, in effect, a case study, a woman first misled by her education into a taste for novels and then corrupted through indulging that unwholesome appetite. The first American novel argues, ironically, against novels by promulgating just this interpretation of this character's fate: "She was a great reader of novels and romances and having imbibed her ideas of *the characters of men*, from those fallacious sources, became vain and coquetish [*sic*], and rejected several offers of marriage, in expectation of receiving one more agreeable to her fanciful idea." It was the official view. In fact, William Hill Brown practically plagiarizes the verdict delivered in the *Massachusetts Centinel* on September 20, 1788: "She was *a great reader of romances*, and having formed her notions of happiness from that corrupt source, became vain and coquetish."[87] Thus was one of the most learned American women of her generation translated into a poor, pathetic victim of fiction whose dishonor and death could be partly redeemed only by serving to save others from a similar end.

To turn that well-known scandal and accepted story into one of the most reprinted early American novels, Hannah Webster Foster had to reread this protagonist and her plight, had to deconstruct the entrenched interpretation so that a novel one might be advanced. One of the more striking changes in Foster's different account is the deletion of the charge of an addiction to fiction. *The Power of Sympathy*, it will be recalled, did not even refer to itself as a novel on its title page, whereas in 1797, when *Charlotte Temple* was well on its way to becoming a steady seller, Ebenezer Larkin published a book that he hoped might be similarly successful under the title *The Coquette; or, The History of Eliza Wharton: A NOVEL*.[88] In the intervening decade, the novel had come of age in America and no longer needed the protective coloration provided by an occasional sermon against novel reading. In *The Coquette*, fiction is valorized. When Eliza is at her most rejected and depressed, her friends and moral advisors send her novels to read. More pointedly, Eliza's seducer, Major Sanford, numbers among his manifest faults a singular unfamiliarity with fiction, especially with the works of Richardson.[89]

Other alterations in the Whitman story were more subtle. Several historical characters, for example, underwent name changes while retaining the same initials, which suggests an intentional blurring of the division between fiction and fact and an invitation to the reader to enjoy that same blurring. Eliza Wharton both is and is not Elizabeth Whitman. Similarly, two of Whitman's historical suitors, the Reverend Joseph Howe (whom her parents originally chose for their daughter but who died before the marriage could take place) and the Reverend Joseph Buckminster (who subsequently sought her hand) are lightly fictionalized into the reverends Haly and Boyer. Historical personages have also been advanced as the originals for the protagonist's women friends as well. But Peter Sanford (by initials or occupation) does not figure forth a historical personage but remains a literary one. A "second Lovelace," Elizabeth/Eliza's seducer becomes allegorized in Foster's novel very much as Whitman had been allegorized in the newspaper accounts. Conversely, the heroine gained in fiction the complexity of which she had been deprived in the early allegories of her life and death.

None of the early accounts of Whitman's life, for example, credit her with a rational weighing of a prospective husband's qualifications, despite the fact that her second suitor, the Reverend Buckminster, was well known in his day as a man subject to prolonged fits of depression and outbursts of uncontrolled temper. "She refused two as good offers of marriage as she deserved," avers the *Boston Independent Chronicle*, "because she aspired higher than to be a clergyman's wife; and having coquetted till past her prime, fell into criminal indulgences."[90] Foster, however, transforms this reductionist account. Elizabeth's anticlericalism and social climbing become Eliza's determination that her marriage must be an egalitarian match based on mutual affection. A clergyman's wife herself, Foster well knew just what that employment entailed (as is shown even more clearly in her second novel, *The Boarding School*), and, more to the point, her fictional Eliza, the daughter of a minister's wife, also knows the prerequisites for the position and knows, too, that she does not fit the bill. As she admits to her mother, "My disposition is not calculated for that sphere. There are duties arising from the station which I fear I should not be able to fulfill, cares and restraints to which I could not submit" (p. 162). Having narrowly escaped one loveless marriage— through the fortuitous death of the fiancé—imposed upon her by the "shackles" of "parental authority" (p. 140), she is determined to marry in the future only if reason and fancy, her mind and her heart, are both engaged.

Socially conservative readers may well have intimated the seeds of Eliza's downfall in this daughter's belated declaration of independence and her egalitarian concept of marriage. Foster, however, takes considerable pains to affirm her protagonist's ideals. When, early in the novel, she leaves her mother's home, in which she was immured with her dying clergyman fiancé, she goes to visit her friends, the Richmans, whose marriage exemplifies the Wollstonecraftian ideal of a partnership of equals. That relationship is Eliza's ideal too. Her "heart approved and applauded" (p. 181) this couple's happiness. Her tragedy is not that she set her sights too high but that she encounters no equivalent of a General Richman. What she is offered, instead, is a difficult choice between unsatisfactory alternatives, a common quandary in early American sentimental novels and a dilemma, no doubt, faced by many American young women.

The Coquette, then, is not simply an allegory of seduction. The generic shift from sermon to novel in the Whitman/Wharton narrative entails a concomitant transformation of focus and philosophy. Set within a specific context of limiting marriage laws and restrictive social mores, the novel is less a story of the wages of sin than a study of the wages of marriage. In the realistic world of this fictional account, virtue and virtuous women are not always rewarded. Sanford's lawfully wedded wife, for example, a woman shown to be intelligent, kind, honest, and attractive, fares almost as disastrously as Eliza. She is ruined financially by her marriage to Sanford, and her child, too, is still-born. Furthermore, even Mrs. Richman, the epitome of republican motherhood in the novel, cannot be permanently happy within her familial sphere. "I grudge every moment that calls me from the pleasing scenes of domestic life" (p. 210), she writes, soon after the birth of her daughter—who soon afterward dies, a realistic tempering of the proclaimed joys of domesticity.

By fictionalizing the lives of the women who surround Eliza, Foster provided her early readers with an opportunity to see, privileged in print, women very much like themselves. As the community of women within the novel exchange views and ideas on such crucial subjects as friendship, marriage, and economic security, their letters constitute a dialogical discourse in which the reader was also invited to participate, if only vicariously. For its first audience particularly, *The Coquette* set forth a remarkably detailed assessment of the marital possibilities facing late-eighteenth-century women of the middle or upper-middle classes. Crucial questions for just such women are asked and dramatized in the text. What were her choices? What kinds of behavior would promote or prevent certain matches? How do men view the whole matter of courtship and marriage? On that last score, the twelve letters that Sanford sends his friend, Charles Deighton, provide a telling example of male discourse in contrast to female discourse, and Sanford effectively voices the self-justifying evasions, the hypocrisy, and the overt misogyny of the seducer. Similarly, the nine letters exchanged between the Reverend Boyer and his friend Selby attest to how much respectable men assume the subordinate status of women and thereby validate Eliza's apprehensions about the restricted life that would be hers if she were to marry Boyer and become a clergyman's wife.

The bulk of the novel is "woman-talk": women confiding, advising, chiding, warning, disagreeing, deceiving, and then confronting each other. A full two-thirds of the seventy-five letters that constitute *The Coquette* are written by women to women, and not always about the men in their lives. Eliza, especially, exhibits in her discourse the ideas and aspirations of a *feme sole*—the independent, unmarried woman. In contrast to that state is the status of Eliza's close friend and most regular correspondent, Lucy Freeman, who, in the course of the novel, marries to become Mrs. Sumner. As a married woman, she can no longer be so free as she formerly was with her time or attention. To quote Eliza: "Marriage is the tomb of friendship. It appears to me a very selfish state. Why do people in general, as soon as they are married, center all their cares, their concerns, and pleasures in their own families? Former acquaintances are neglected or forgotten; the tenderest ties between friends are weakened or dissolved; benevolence itself moves in a very limited sphere" (p. 150). "Women's sphere" is here aptly portrayed as "a very limited sphere"—a closed and enclosing concern for a husband's well-being—which gives us one of the earliest fictional critiques of the "cult of domesticity."

The Coquette, however, does not openly challenge the basic structure of patriarchal culture but, instead, exposes its fundamental injustices through the details and disasters of the plot. Consider, for example, how, after the Reverend Haly's death, Eliza's mother, along with the young woman's female friends, worries constantly about her marital prospects, for she does not have an inheritance of her own. They do not advise (much less prepare) her to earn a wage; they only urge her to obtain a husband who does. Yet her manifest talents—her beauty, her charm, her intelligence—constitute no negotiable capital in any matrimonial transaction. "Forgive my plainness," Eliza's friend, Lucy Freeman, writes of the Reverend Boyer. "His situation in life is, perhaps, as elevated as you have a right to claim" (p. 152). Neither does a fortune of one's own substantially alter one's case, as the example of Nancy Sanford amply attests. The wealthy woman, as much as the poor, is still dependent upon a husband's good sense and good will. All women are thus potential paupers and married women especially so. But without a husband to provide for her and lacking the skills to earn her own living, a woman's situation can be as desperate as was the historical Elizabeth Whitman's at the Bell Tavern. Dying, the abandoned woman left "2 ginneys, 1 crown, 2–4 pistoreens dollars," and a few other paltry possessions (six silver spoons, a few rings, a couple of dresses, handkerchiefs, ribbons, and caps; an "ink case with Sealing wax, wafers, etc."; and "Sundry Babe cloths").[91] That sad inventory, in actual and symbolic measure, movingly sums up the unmarried woman's social worth and her final estate.

Other features of the society are also summed up in the novel. As Eliza fully realizes, when a woman marries a man, she must marry not only into his class but into his occupation too. She anticipates being "completely miserable" (p. 153) as a minister's wife, and Sanford effectively reiterates those all-too-well-founded fears: "You are aware, I suppose, when you form a connection with that man, you must content yourself with a confinement to the tedious round of domestic duties, the pedantic conversation of scholars, and the invidious criticisms of the whole town" (p. 171). Boyer is a pompous, self-satisfied clergyman who attempts (the choice of words here is most appropriate) to "seduce [Eliza] into matrimony" (p. 184) by soberly expatiating on the advantages of being joined to such an admirable man as himself. "He is," Eliza writes, "very eloquent upon the subject; and his manners are so solemn that I am strongly tempted . . . to laugh" (p. 184). And so is the reader. But Major Sanford is hardly an alternative. Witty and charming as he may be, he is also a thoroughgoing misogynist, and a thoroughly dishonest one at that. His letters to Deighton are filled with stupid and shallow remarks about the stupidity and shallowness of women. He insists, for example, that he can be "severe upon the sex" because he has "found so many frail ones among them" (p. 234)—as if he were a latter-day Diogenes searching for an honest woman. He also insists that if he seduces Eliza, the fault will be entirely hers. "She knows my character and has no reason to wonder if I act consistently with it" (p. 176). Yet he has just implored her to "let the kind and lenient hand of friendship assist in directing my future steps" (p. 160), which is hardly the open avowal of his intentions that he subsequently and quite hypocritically pretends he has made.

What seemed to Eliza to be choices, alternative men and alternative lifestyles, do not constitute, then, a dialectic that will yield a final synthesis such as the egalitarian marriage of the Richmans. We have, instead, oppositions that cancel one another out to emphasize that the choices Boyer and Sanford embodied were not ultimately so different after all. For each, she was mostly a prize and a proof of his own prowess. In each case, more could be proved by discarding the prize than by claiming it. As will be remembered, Eliza does decide to marry the minister but "was entangled by a promise" (p. 208) to tell Sanford first. When Boyer discovers his prospective bride in conversation with that rival, he storms from the scene. He will not hear Eliza's explanation, for his dashed hopes (he thinks) and offended vanity (we see) provide all the explanation he needs. Soon he is writing to renounce his love and to catalogue her various faults and failings and all from pure "benevolence." Sanford, delighted by his success in destroying Eliza's chances with Boyer, also soon leaves town. He goes away "on business" promising to return in a few months, but a year later he is still gone, and in that whole time he has not once written to the woman he claimed to love. Eliza, faced not with a freedom of choice but an absence of suitors, begins to realize that she has been played for a fool, a truth brought home even more forcefully when Boyer announces his engagement to a suitably appreciative, suitably proper woman and when Sanford finally returns, having acquired, while away, both a wife and that wife's fortune. Eliza naively sought to exercise her freedom only to learn that she had none.[92]

The course of that learning is crucial to the novel and must be examined in some detail, for the genesis of Eliza's fall lies at least as much in the virtues of Boyer as in the vices of Sanford. When that clergyman first goes off in his terminal huff, Eliza well can wonder "whether [she] had sustained a real loss in Mr. Boyer's departure?" (p. 207). But Sanford's subsequent departure, along with the continuing absence of any other official suitors, soon casts a different light on her first loss, from which the second has followed. She must remain in the fishbowl of Hartford, scorned by those who knew all along that her flirtations— her decision to "sow all my wild oats" (p. 186) (very tame wild oats) before settling into the restricted role of the clergyman's wife—could only lead to disaster. Publicly humiliated by the way in which the town so obviously relishes and affirms her discomfiture, she is brought, partly through her failing spirits and partly through Mrs. Richman's counsel, to reevaluate the Reverend's dubious charms. Her letter to him is all humility and self-abnegation, but perhaps the most poignant detail in this pathetic missive is her hope that even if his "affections are entirely alienated or otherwise engaged," he still might consent to consider himself her friend. That last hope is as vain as all her others. Again Boyer writes to shower her with accusations before announcing his betrothal to "the virtuous, the amiable, the accomplished Maria Selby" and finally counseling Eliza to "adhere with undeviating exactness to the paths of rectitude and innocence" (p. 216).

"O my friend, I am undone" (p. 217), Eliza writes upon receiving Boyer's letter, using the precise word that in seduction novels typically signals a woman's fall. "His conduct," she continues with an even more loaded term, assures her "ruin." "By confessing my faults and by avowing my partiality to him, I have given him the power of triumphing in my distress; of returning to my tortured heart all the pangs of slighted love. And what have I now to console me?" (pp. 217–18). Three times Eliza voices the plaintive cry of the seduced woman. Soon thereafter, she falls more conventionally into the affair with Sanford and, concomitant with that fall, into physical infirmity, mental instability, and narrative invisibility. Increasingly, others must recount the story that was once her own but that in the very mode of its telling has been taken from her.

This negation of the female self—her freedoms, her possibilities—forms the basis of the sentimental plot, just as it informed the lives of a vast majority of the sentimental novel's readers. One effective method Foster employs to convey this demeaning of her central character is to have her literally render herself as she has been symbolically rendered by her society. At crucial junctures in the novel, Eliza *chooses* silence, but that narrative silence, a depotentizing in the novel as a whole, provides the subtext from which we can best read the protagonist's fall. How, Foster in effect asks, can a woman denied voice and will be seduced? Simply put, she has no say in the matter. Succumbing to Sanford merely confirms and symbolizes what rejection by Boyer has already proved. We have sex as an only half-sublimated suicide and as a decline into a figurative death (a horrific rendition of "the little death") that will soon slide into the real thing.

"How to write a novel about a person to whom nothing happens? A person to whom nothing but a love story is *supposed* to happen? A person inhabiting a world in which the only reality is frustration or endurance—or these plus an unbearably mystifying confusion?" These questions, rhetorical and very real, raised by Joanna Russ in her classic essay "What Can a Heroine Do? Or Why Women Can't Write," perfectly epitomize the narrative problems Foster faces in rewriting Elizabeth Whitman's story.[93] The same general problem is inherent in the entire sentimental subgenre. How does one privilege the voice of a woman who, given the society in which the novel is written and read, enjoys neither voice nor privilege?

More specifically, how can the life and death of Elizabeth Whitman emphasize meanings other than those already overencoded in the society and overexpounded in innumerable sermons, newspaper accounts, and didactic essays of the time? Russ suggests that one form women have evolved for writing the essentially unwritable is, in her term, the "lyric mode"—that is, a fiction that organizes "discrete elements (images, events, scenes, passages, words, what-have-you) *around an unspoken thematic or emotional center*." In circling around that unspoken, invisible center, the lyric novel necessarily repeats itself (which is also a quintessential feature of the epistolary form). That circling is the meaning; the novel is *about* this silent center because "there is no action possible to the central character and no series of events which will embody in clear, unequivocal, immediately graspable terms what the artist means" since the society precludes all the symbols and "myths of male culture" (like lighting out for the territories or signing on for a whaling voyage) that could serve to express—or to elude—the woman's situation for the woman reader. "There is nothing the female character can *do*— except exist, except think, except feel."[94] Eliza Wharton's long protracted fall and the silence that surrounds it constitute the invisible center around which this sentimental novel turns.

The Coquette and other sentimental novels in the new Republic are ultimately about silence, subservience, stasis (the accepted attributes of women as traditionally defined) in contradistinction to conflicting impulses toward independence, action, and self-expression (the ideals of the new American nation). But what is the resolution of that central conflict? If the sentimental novel, as I am suggesting, entered fully into the current debates on the status of women, then what do we make of a novel, such as *The Coquette*, that jumbles all the terms? Mrs. Richman, like Judith Sargent Murray, argues that women must join men in articulating the political concerns of the nation—lest the emerging consensus be ludicrously one-sided—a position antithetical to that enunciated by writers from Rousseau to Chesterfield to Gregory. Yet Mrs. Richman advocates Eliza's marriage to Boyer.

Is marriage to a Boyer the best that an intelligent, well-educated woman can do, particularly when the alternative, Major Sanford, is no alternative at all? "What a pity," Eliza confides to her friend Lucy, "that the graces and virtues are not oftener united! They must, however, meet in the man of my choice; and till I find such a one, I shall continue to subscribe my name Eliza Wharton" (p. 148). She does, of course, precisely that. As Eliza Wharton she departs initially from her mother's house, and as Eliza Wharton still she departs finally and through death from the text of the novel, from the tragedy of her life, which hardly constitutes a vindication of the rights of women.

Eliza Wharton sins and dies. Her death can convey the conservative moral that many critics of the time demanded. Yet the circumstances of that death seem designed to tease the reader into thought. It is in precisely these interstices—the disjunctions between the conventional and the radical readings of the plot—that the early American sentimental novel flourishes. It is in the irresolution of Eliza Wharton's dilemma that the novel, as a genre, differentiates itself from the tract stories of Elizabeth Whitman in which the novel is grounded and which it ultimately transcends. Tracts readily prescribe how a young woman should lead her life and make her marriage. But in the fullness of *The Coquette*, we see just how the governing equation that innocence and virtue are to be rewarded must break down in a society in which women have no power to procure their own rewards but depend, in marriages or affairs, on the luck of the draw. Thus the novel's surplus of socially unsanctioned significance calls the more conventionally grounded stories of Elizabeth Whitman into question. It is easy, of course, to avoid too much novel reading. It is also easy to avoid social climbing and an anticlerical cast of mind. But how does one escape the social parameters of female powerlessness and female constraint?

That rhetorical question is left pointedly unanswered in the novel by the juxtaposition of the independent Miss Wharton, *feme sole*, and Mrs. Wharton, the quintessential *feme covert*, who, as a virtuous widow, has been ironically deprived of her covering. If virtue is to be rewarded, then surely Mrs. Wharton's life should be rich, an example to both her daughter and the reader. Yet the mother is exactly what the daughter does not want to be, and the novel validates the daughter's judgment. Observing the older woman in conversation with Boyer, Eliza wryly recognizes that her mother would "make him a [better] wife than I" (p. 186). And Eliza is right. The mother is precisely the kind of woman whom Boyer should marry. Desiring little or nothing for herself, she is a cipher in search of an integer, an empty sign seeking for another's (a husband's) excess of significance to provide her own meaning. Quite characteristically, her endeavors to dispel her daughter's doubts about matrimony never address the substance of those doubts but slide into an extended encomium on the clergyman himself, his worth to the community, his friends, the rewards that will accrue from selfless devotion to such an unselfish man. For Mrs. Wharton, the worth of his wife, of any wife, is immaterial; her duties go without saying. As even that advice suggests, for this conventional woman, female being, by her own definition and her culture's definition, is nothingness.

As that advice also suggests, Mrs. Wharton's philosophy of wifehood considerably compromises her performance as a mother. The nullity at the core of the older woman's existence renders her utterly ineffectual as a moral guide, as a concerned advisor, and even as a sympathetic confidante of her daughter. Four times in the novel Eliza, on the verge of a mental breakdown, writes to a friend about how she must feign happiness so as not to perturb her poor mother. Her mother, in turn, confides to a friend that she suspects something might be bothering her daughter, but she lacks the will to inquire what it might be. Instead, she stands silently by, a mute witness to her daughter's progressive physical and mental debilitation. Even more obvious, Eliza yields herself to Sanford virtually before her mother's eyes—first in her mother's garden and then, after the weather turns cold and Eliza's health deteriorates, in her mother's parlor. It is a harrowing denouement: Eliza, physically emaciated and mentally deranged, allowing herself to be repeatedly "seduced" in her mother's house; Sanford triumphing over both women; Eliza presently dying; Mrs. Wharton wringing her hands but living on as a continuing testimony to her daughter's tragic death and her own ineffectual life.

The full tragedy of the novel, however, is that ultimately there was no tragedy at all—only the banal predictability of a fall that was precisely what the most conservative proponents of the status quo labored to prevent. Or perhaps the tragedy is that it can readily be reduced to this formulation and is thus reduced even in the telling. Consider how Eliza's desire for freedom devolves into sexual acquiescence, accomplished with an appalling lack of desire. Eliza Wharton, vividly rendered in Foster's fiction, still cannot be separated from her story, which is necessarily conjoined with Elizabeth Whitman's different but finally unknowable story, so much so that the historical personage and the fictional person shared a common tombstone. It is as if the tragic and the trivial, the real character's puzzling death and the fictional character's problematic one, had all been interred together, leaving the survivors—within the text and without—to puzzle out the meaning of it all.

The female mourners at the end of the novel articulate their sense of having lost through Eliza's death not only a friend and a relative but also a part of themselves and their own desires. I would also suggest that many readers of the time, turning over a story they already knew and did not know at all, must have felt a similar shock of recognition, which might partly explain the great popularity of the novel. Writing a preface to the 1855 edition of *The Coquette*, Jane E. Locke referred to the extraordinary appeal of Foster's Eliza Wharton, who had become, by that time, virtually a cult heroine in both her novelistic form and as dramatized in a popular 1802 play based on the novel, *The New England Coquette.*[95] Readers, according to Locke, read Eliza's story as their own and cherished her story, their story, the story of an "actual" American woman who had loved badly and lost. Here was a New England Clarissa who had lived in Hartford, who had attended the theater in Boston, who had died and was buried in Danvers—real places, places that one could visit. And the readers did, like pilgrims to a sacred shrine. Some nineteenth-century editions of *The Coquette* included engravings of the Bell Tavern in Danvers. Even after The Bell was torn down, its doorstep, upon which, according to legend, Whitman had written her initials as a signal to Fidelio, was removed to the Peabody Historical Society, where, into the twentieth century, lovers would come to look upon it and to touch it. Whitman's gravestone, in the Main Street Burial Ground and bearing essentially the same inscription reported in the novel, became a favorite trysting place for nineteenth-century sentimental lovers, who during the century carried away portions of the gravestone to keep as talismans—like pieces of the One True Cross. By the twentieth century, the whole engraved name had been chipped away from the stone, its absence a tribute to Eliza's continuing cultural presence.

Mostly, however, Eliza/Elizabeth was honored by those who bought or borrowed *The Coquette* and read and reread it virtually into oblivion. Like such popular books as the *New England Primer*, of which very few early copies remain today, less than a dozen copies of the first edition of this novel survive and equally few of the second edition of 1802. Yet editions of the book remained steadily in print until 1874. It enjoyed its greatest popularity between 1824 and 1828, when it was reissued eight times. And in 1866, it was still important enough to be added to the Peterson and Brothers "Dollar Series" of popular fiction—"The best, the largest, the handsomest, and the cheapest books in the world," according to the Peterson advertisements.[96] But most noteworthy for my purposes is the popularity of this text to late-eighteenth-century readers. At a time when American novels were not plentiful (nor, for that matter, other books), *The Coquette* occupied a special place. As Locke notes:

> It is not surprising that it thus took precedence in interest . . . of all American novels, at least throughout New England, and was found, in every cottage within its borders, beside the family Bible, and, though pitifully, yet almost as carefully treasured.[97]

Our retrospective reading, I have argued throughout this chapter, must somehow recover and make sense of that sense of treasuring lost.

7 The Picaresque and the Margins of Political Discourse

But the great security against a gradual concentration of the several powers in the same department, consists in giving to those who administer each department, the necessary constitutional means, and personal motives, to resist encroachment of the others. . . . Ambition must be made to counteract ambition. The interest of the man, must be connected with the constitutional rights of the place. . . . If men were angels, no government would be necessary. . . . In framing a government which is to be administered by men over men, the great difficulty lies in this: you must first enable the government to control the governed; and in the next place oblige it to control itself. A dependence on the people is, no doubt, the primary control on the government; but experience has taught mankind the necessity of auxiliary precautions.
—James Madison, *The Federalist*, No. 51 (1788)

He that is not for us, is against us.
—Motto of the Federalist *Gazette of the United States* (1798)

The Rhetoric of Republican Dissensus

A number of novelists of the early national period turned the essentially conservative subgenre of the sentimental novel (with its fetishization of female virginity) to a subversive purpose by valorizing precisely those women whom the society had either overtly condemned (the fallen woman) or implicitly rendered invisible (woman as *feme covert*). Yet even the most progressive sentimental novels still focused primarily on women's restricted familial role. Within the confines of the novel and the society, women only sporadically and peripherally entered into the political discourse of the era, either as objects of the debate or participants in it. Certainly a number of sentimental novels (such as *The Coquette* and *The Power of Sympathy*) include scenes in which female characters discuss political issues, but given the Constitutional silencing of women, this fictive act is just that—a fiction. Lacking any legal standing, women's political opinions could be dismissed as easily as John Adams dismissed his wife's plea. "Every man, by the Constitution, is born with an equal right to be elected to the highest office," the Reverend John Cosens Ogden of Portsmouth, New Hampshire, declaimed in 1793. "And every woman, is born with an equal right to be the wife of the most eminent man."[1] No wonder sentimental fiction remained closeted, circumscribed by home and hearth. No fictive young woman could ask, existentially, "To be or not to be?" for all versions of that question were preempted by the patriarchy's more controlling consideration, "Is she or isn't she?"

In the picaresque novels with which I am concerned in this chapter, politics is the central issue, and, not surprisingly, women mostly enter the picaresque world in passing. Except for one subgroup of novels that I term the *female picaresque* (discussed in detail later in this chapter), the picaresque virtually excludes women precisely because women *were* excluded from the politics of the new Republic and also from the more perfect, imagined polis formulated by most of early America's political visionaries. In custom, law, theory, and literature, the political world of the new Republic was predominately a world of men.

But what was that world of men? If it was ostensibly centered in the Founding Fathers and the revolutionary emergence of a new political order, it, nevertheless, necessarily took shape tangentially to that center—not in Independence Hall but in the city itself, in the shanties that dotted its margins; in the shacks around its malodorous, fever-infested swamps; and in the surrounding countryside where cash was scarce and where a revolution had not brought the prosperity for which so many had hoped. Political discourse centered, too, not in the promised equality of all men but in a different practice that allowed some men to be more equal than others (slaves, the poor, not to mention the women). How, a number of writers asked, could the novel portray the nation's complex and contradictory political realities? The picaresque seemed to many to be the perfect form to address the divisive political discourse of the era. The loosest of narrative forms, the picaresque conveniently allows a central character (or characters) to wander the margins of an emerging American landscape, to survey it in all its incipient diversity, to sound out its different constituents from the most lowly, uneducated yeoman to those of high birth and great learning (or at least with pretensions to same, as in Hugh Henry Brackenridge's send-up of the American Philosophical Society).

Just as *The Coquette* and *Charlotte Temple* provided the reader with strategies for valorizing women degraded and demeaned according to the social mores of the time, so, too, did the picaresque, by its very insistence upon diversity and indeterminacy, emphasize the complexity of the political world of the postrevolutionary era, the many variations on the definition of what constituted an American, and the myriad applications of that often repeated term *republicanism*. A narrative strategy of circumlocution worked for picaresque novelists for two different but related reasons. First, the increasing displacement of the gentry as the foremost representatives of America's government after the Revolution diffused language, made the official language of government not just balanced Enlightenment prose but also the direct, colloquial, impassioned panegyric of the kind heard (too often, many averred) in the state houses as well as in the town square. To men thoroughly versed in a tradition of classical rhetoric, much of the fractious political debate of the early national period sounded like glossolalia. To many novelists, however, the cacophonous discourse sounded like the stuff of fiction, and picaresque novels often replicated those discordant sounds through dialect, deliberate violations of standard English prose, and other linguistic idiosyncracies, including slang and arcane professional jargon. Second, the decade of the 1790s saw an increasingly repressive political agenda designed to stem the tide of republicanism and Republicanism. A movement to enact measures that would curb the most radical elements in the society (and, for many, the Constitution seemed part of this restrictive movement) and protect the privilege of an educated elite culminated in the passage of the Alien and Sedition Acts in 1798. As I will show, the picaresque, with its tireless circumambulations around the locus of debate, countered this official attempt to homogenize the polis with a rambunctious heterogeneity. It did so with impunity because the very form of the fiction made it impossible to pin down the political agenda of the author. Just as the sentimental novel hid its message for hidden women, so, too, did the picaresque novel use the smoke screen of its own irrepressible rhetoric to evade the era's repressions.

Later in this chapter, I will assess both the picaresque's projection of its own fictive America and the cosmology created in that image. I will also look at the lives of a number of picaresque novelists who did not fall any more clearly or neatly into the narrow classifications of the party politics of the time than did their exuberantly ambiguous novels. But before entering the picaresque world of the novels or of the authors, I would like to focus, briefly, on the discourse of the time and place in which picaresque fiction was written and read. The picaresque novel is indubitably part of the "wordy battles" and "paper wars" (in Washington Irving's phrase) of the era, but while the official rhetoric of dissent and "dissensus" seems, at first glance, absolute (either/or, us/them), the picaresque continually blurs oppositions into ambiguities. It is even tempting to argue that the confusing (and often confused) cosmology of the picaresque more nearly represented the mentality of many late-eighteenth-century Americans than did the eloquent delineations of republican ideology argued by the Founding Fathers and their most vociferous opponents.

IN 1783, WHEN Thomas Paine learned that the treaty of peace had been signed with Britain, he immediately ceased publication of *The Crisis*, for, in his words, "the times that tried men's souls are over."[2] Would that he had been right. For many, from Founding Fathers to impoverished farmers, they were just beginning, and the next two decades would prove far more trying than the previous one. "The pressure of an external enemy hooped us together," Thomas Jefferson wrote of the War of Independence, fully aware that, without the immediate and overt crisis of a war fought on their own soil, Americans had to confront an equally pervasive but more nebulous war within the Republic—between the haves and have-nots, between competing visions of what America was and was to be.[3]

The rational Enlightenment document of the Constitution—with its rhetoric of fairness and freedom and its cautious regulating of the former and restricting of the latter—disguises the acrimonious debate that preceded its passage and obscures the carnivalization of republican principles enacted in the numerous public displays of the postrevolutionary era—everything from rallies and parades to strikes and insurrections.[4] As the whole process of confederation emphasized, Americans had fought and died for very different revolutions, some for a relatively simple bid for American autonomy from England, others for an entire restructuring of America's political and social system. While many members of an educated class or gentry conceived of a republic governed by and for gentlemen, many middle- and lower-class Americans stood ready to elect legislators like themselves who pledged to serve their interests as opposed to what they saw as the narrow and special interests of the nation's aristocrats (with that last term itself becoming increasingly pejorative in the new republic).[5] Split by factions and by subfactions within these factions, the nation seemed, to many Americans, on the verge of another revolution.

The dichotomizing of postrevolutionary politics is reflected even in the names of two of its major parties—the Federalists and the Anti-Federalists. The antipathy embodied in those names underscores a perception of difference, at least among each party's most outspoken proponents. For example, Anti-Federalist rhetoric was often grounded in class awareness and class resentment. Whereas most of the Colonial-appointed counselors of prerevolutionary America had been wealthy citizens, often from prominent old families, in postrevolutionary America, many Anti-Federalists insisted that "men of family, wealth and of eminence and grandeur" were also the most likely to be "men of ambition and to form parties to promote their views." America had not fought tyranny abroad to replace it with tyranny at home, they argued. "Precisely," men like Alexander Hamilton agreed, pointing a finger in the opposite direction, to what they saw as the growing tyranny of mobocracy. Advocating rule by "the wise and good and rich," Hamilton predicted that the union would collapse because of "the influence of many inconsiderable men in possession of considerable offices." Inconsiderable men, Hamilton believed, would, as state legislators, combine forces to block the Federal Constitution that, among other things, was designed at least partly to curtail the power of local government. And many Anti-Federalists viewed Hamilton's polemics in favor of central control as King George come again. Each party denounced the other as the enemy, the threat, the negation of every truth each held to be self-evident and sanctified by the sacrifices *they* had made during the war. As Ronald P. Formisano has noted, although actual party organization and even voter participation remained weak during the 1790s, the acrimony of partisan rhetoric spread throughout American society. Both sides "tried to stigmatize their opponents as illegitimate. Federalists denounced Jacobins, the French party, anti-federalists, conspirators, demagogues, democrats, antis, disorganizers, a faction, and the evil-minded. Republicans cried out against monarchists, the junto, the Essex Junto, a faction, aristocrats, the order, dictators, high partisans, the arrogant, conspirators, and the tyrannical." Each rhetoric, if taken seriously, simply canceled the other out.[6]

Hugh Henry Brackenridge perfectly captures the contradictions of republican discourse—both Federalist and Republican—in an early scene in *Modern Chivalry*. Captain Farrago enters a town on an election day and observes a "man of education" running for the legislature against an illiterate weaver. The gentleman convincingly expounds, for the benefit of his unlearned opponent and any other interested parties, that "when you go to the senate house, the application to you will not be to warp a web; but to make laws for the commonwealth." Knowing some low trade does not prepare one to run a government; knowing Thucydides does. Brackenridge's satire, capturing the tone of this learned and certain man, runs both ways. It mocks an illiterate running for public office, and it equally mocks another's assumption that an aristocratic and dilettante education in and of itself qualifies one to rule. Note, for example, Captain Farrago's assent to this position, which Brackenridge (a Republican) renders in tones replete with Federalist preferences: "A free government is a noble possession of the people; and this freedom consists in an equal right to have the benefit of the laws when made. Though doubtless, in such a government, the lowest citizen may become chief magistrate; yet it is sufficient to possess the right; not absolutely necessary to exercise it."[7] This is Federalist theory in a nutshell: All (white) men are created equal, and so long as we all acknowledge that equality, we need not practice it. Naturally, after the voters have listened attentively to the learned man, they proceed to elect the weaver.

Many common people found it easy to resent a gentry who proclaimed liberty and submission in the same breath. As a Rhode Island Republican noted in a bit of doggerel during the Confederation period:

> These men I hate 'cause they despised me
> > With deep contempt—and 'cause they advis'd me,
> To hold my tongue when th'was debate
> > And not betray my want of wit.[8]

That resentment alarmed its recipients, who read therein something of their own declining authority within the Republic. Men such as Hamilton, John Adams, and even George Washington were dismayed by what they saw happening in the nation they thought they had created. They anticipated a violent outcome of the American experiment and questioned the foresight of their former idealism. In 1786, Washington, for example, could "predict . . . the worst consequences from a half-starved, limping government, always moving upon crutches and tottering at every step." Or, referring specifically to Shays's Rebellion in Massachusetts, he wrote: "But for God's sake who will tell me what is the cause of all these commotions? . . . I am mortified beyond expression that in the moment of our acknowledged independence we should by our conduct verify the predictions of our transatlantic foe, and render ourselves ridiculous and contemptible in the eyes of all Europe."[9] He was worried about more than what the neighbors might think. "We are fast verging to anarchy and confusion!" Washington insisted, by which he meant that illiterate weavers, so to speak, seemed to be winning elections everywhere.[10] And Hamilton spoke more directly for many of America's Founding Fathers when he noted, sadly, "This American world was not made for me."[11]

The alarm of the privileged is eloquently recorded in history. Because they had the most to lose from any redistribution of power, they wrote persuasively of what horrors might await any (and especially the middle class) who caved into the forces of anarchy abroad in the land. But their story was only one-half of the story of the early national period, and, as is suggested by even the brief passage I have quoted from *Modern Chivalry*, many early American novels told the other half as well. In the Anti-Federalist or the Republican fable of new injustices for old, the nation in the Confederation years endured not only one of the worst recessions in the memory of its citizens but a recession disproportionately suffered by the poorer and middling classes. In New York City, for example, in the first years of the Republic, some 4 percent of the population owned over half of the city's noncorporate wealth.[12] Ballooning unemployment meant that even many in the artisan class owned no taxable property, and destitution often also meant disenfranchisement. Could not the virtuous poor also be good citizens? Debtors' prisons overflowed with honest workingmen who had no means to pay their bills or support their families, and many predicted that the urban poor would be permanently locked into their poverty by a political system that rewarded the rich at the expense of the poor.[13]

For rural Americans the situation, if anything, was worse. Farm prices were so low that farmers could barely recoup the relatively low costs of preindustrial cultivation. Did the new government even *care* about the nation's farmers, the agrarian Anti-Federalists asked? In their view, the men who formulated the nation's first laws had callously ignored the welfare of its most industrious and essential citizens.[14] For most farmers, subsistence living was a norm, and the government seemed content to leave it at that. One consequence was a collapsed market. For the most part, there was no cash for those commodities that could not be produced among the local population, anything from sugar to *Charlotte Temple*. Nor was there money to pay off mortgages. Farm foreclosures and imprisonments of yeomen for debts reached an all-time high, as did also executions, crime being one occupation ever open to the desperate. In such conditions, it is no surprise that thousands of farmers, inspired by Daniel Shays's exhortations, should march upon the Massachusetts legislature to protest the excess tax burden placed upon the property of the farmer (who had no taxable income but did have taxable land) and to urge the printing of more paper money with which farmers might pay their debts and mortgages and have access to some of the commodities that streamed into the port cities but not into the cash-deprived countryside.[15]

The debate over the ratification of the Constitution typified the fragmentation of the early American public, with Republicans or Anti-Federalists fearful of a powerful central government controlled, in the words of Mercy Otis Warren, by "aristocrats" who practiced "chicanery, intrigue, and false coloring" and who "plume themselves, more on their education and abilities, than their political, patriotic, or private virtues." In contrast, Adams, in his *Defense of the Constitutions of the United States of America,* insisted that "democracy never has been and never can be so desirable as aristocracy, or monarchy," but he also fully realized that, short of oligarchy or enlightened monarchy, America's future depended on the ratification of the Constitution, which through its Madisonian system of checks and balances, and the separation of powers, could cushion some of the force of the elected legislatures and even create a de facto oligarchy, particularly in the executive and legislative branches. A tripartite government, with each branch partly checked by the other two, minimized the spreading mood of populism that men like Adams feared in the new nation.[16]

The procedures by which the Constitution was finally framed have been recounted many times and do not need to be recapitulated here except to emphasize that the document that has been the keystone of American government for two hundred years was designed by fifty-five uncommon men from twelve colonies (Rhode Island was at no time represented). When the Constitutional Convention was originally convened in Philadelphia on May 14, 1787, so few delegates attended that the Convention had to be postponed for over a week until more delegates could be rounded up. Fear of protests and insurrections by the populace mandated that the Constitutional deliberations be conducted in secret (the full proceedings were not published until 1840), and the Constitution was presented to the nation as a completed document, a product not a process, and one that could only be ratified in toto or rejected, amended but not itself changed. It was signed by only thirty-nine of the delegates, twenty-nine of whom were graduates of the colleges and more than half of whom were lawyers. Yet even this similarity of background did not assure consensus for, as Robert Ferguson has pointed out, throughout the Convention, the delegates were in such radical disagreement over what a Constitution should do and say that a final text was achieved only when the points of contention were linguistically—not necessarily ideologically—resolved through calculatingly ambiguous wording of the Constitution itself. Motivated largely by their shared fears of a factious nation, the delegates agreed on the final day of the Convention that they should disguise their differences and present a pretense of "apparent unanimity" to the world at large: for, of course, if a handful of elite men could not agree over the text that would provide the foundation of new nation, then how could the society at large be brought to consensus?[17]

The fact is that the society could *not* be brought to total agreement, and the issues that were glossed over by a mystifying ambiguity at the Convention re-mained—and remain—pressing issues once the Constitution was ratified. As many commentators have noted, the same problems that persisted before ratifi-cation persisted after, even if the effects of political fragmentation were more limited by its institution. Alfred F. Young has shown, for example, that the Con-stitution may have more clearly pointed up the class divisions in American society and especially those within the Federalist party. Before ratification, many artisans favored a Constitution that, through protective tariffs as well as domestic mea-sures, purported to facilitate American commerce and seemed to promise better economic conditions, particularly for the urban worker. With time, however, and no appreciable improvement of living conditions, workingmen grew increasingly disaffected from the Federalist party with its ruling conviction that wealthy mer-chants or landed gentry were innately suited to be the leaders of men and that sensible artisans and mechanics would happily acquiesce to a subordinate rank within the party and the Republic.[18]

They did not. The Democratic-Republicans in New York, for example, soon gained the support of the city's mechanics (and not just those at the lowest end of the wage scales). A significant proportion of professionals—lawyers, teachers, doctors, ministers—also joined the Anti-Federalist ranks, which still included many farmers who had long and vociferously opposed Federalist politics. Citi-zenship remained the clarion call of this new and potentially disruptive coalition: "After thy creator, love thy country above all things," proclaimed one Republican slogan. But perhaps most striking, this patriotism did not, for its proponents, contradict their keen interest in the revolutionary happenings in France. Inter-preting in radical terms the inherent indeterminancy of the Constitution, many citizens invoked that document as the justification for their political zeal. Former opponents of a Constitution now supported it to the letter—or, more accurately, to their radical reading of its letter. And here we see political history subsumed into literary criticism, as just what that "letter" meant became a subject of endless dispute and contradictory interpretation even within the earliest years of the text's existence. According to the new reading of many Republicans, the Constitution guaranteed libertarian rights, the kind of rights that made America "an asylum to the oppressed" of the rest of the world. It was a *revolutionary* document as they saw it, not the moderating or even reactionary document conceived by men such as Adams.

The same text, as an appropriate stand-in for the ambiguous and multivalent nation, thus engendered different contradictory and self-consuming readings of itself. The Constitution could be upheld by those, like Adams, who defended a curtailment of civil liberties in the face of the frightful possibilities of Jacobinism but could also justify, for others, that same Jacobinism. George Clinton, the governor of New York, for example, could hail New York state's "free and happy Constitution" in 1777, could ten years later still praise "our excellent constitution," and could, with no sense of contradiction, in 1797 address his infant grandson as "Citizen George Clinton Genêt" and assure him that "your drum . . . is at Granny's braced for you to beat to arms against Tories and aristocrats if necessary." In short, the *existence* of the Constitution proved as little in 1795 as it did in 1855 or 1985; its *interpretation* meant everything. Constitutional fundamentalists could argue about its meaning and application then as now, and Federalists interpreted the Constitution to defend moderation and even reaction with the same degree of certitude that Jacobins felt when they invoked it in a call to reform or even further revolution.[19]

What I am suggesting is that "America" has existed as a self-contradictory and self-perpetuating symbolic construct right from its formative years, and American novelists, like other citizens of the new Republic, early debated, but did not resolve, the meaning of the "legacy America" (to borrow Thomas Pynchon's phrase)—what it was, what it *meant*.[20] No matter that recent quantitative studies have documented the wide range of class and economic affiliations of the Republicans. Most Federalists, then, would have simply agreed with William Cobbett (in his reactionary Philadelphia phase) that the Republicans were "butchers, tinkers, broken hucksters, and trans-Atlantic traitors"—and complicated charts and tables would not have altered the picture.[21] For men like Cobbett, the Republicans were not simply members of a different party to be analyzed and politically outmaneuvered, they were devilish, dangerous, selfish, unruly, treacherous—in a word, *un-American*. They were, differently put, as un-American as men like Cobbett seemed when viewed through Republican eyes.

TO DECIDE HOW MUCH the rhetoric of, on the one hand, a Washington or a Cobbett and, on the other, a Mercy Otis Warren or a George Clinton reflected "actual" social conditions is as dubious now as it was then. Suffice to say that differing versions of America informed much early American fiction, and many novels pitted one version against another in a continuing dialogue (if not, more formalistically, a dialectic) on the shape of republicanism and its potentialities and pitfalls. Rarely did these opposing versions of America correspond to the specific political dogma of one party or another, but, more often, they suggested the ramifications of power politics in a nation yet establishing its own political structures and the rules whereby it would operate. Sometimes, in fact, the novels fantasize power without politics—a wish-fulfillment version of entitlement as enticing as *Cinderella* but fraught with the same contradictions and affirmations of the status quo that pervade all cultural fairy tales. No pain, no gain. But what is particularly intriguing about the political discourse of the early national period is that, in many ways, it is every bit as fantastic, contradictory, and self-conflicted as any discourse in the most rambling and ambivalent picaresque novel—*Modern Chivalry*, Royall Tyler's *The Algerine Captive*, Tabitha Tenney's *Female Quixotism*, or a host of other picaresque novels to be discussed later in this chapter. With amazing grace, picaresque novelists could leap from one construction of reality to its inverse, yet the rhetorical alacrity of the creative writers never exceeded the verbal gymnastics of America's most respected (and often stodgiest) public citizens.

Writing to the Chevalier de la Luzerne, George Washington enthused over the same America he, more privately and locally, decried: "In short . . . the foundation of a great empire is laid, and I please myself with a persuasion, that Providence will not leave its work imperfect." And Franklin, writing also in 1786, to M. Le Veillard, noted that "America never was in higher prosperity," although he well knew that commodity prices had plummeted (a full 30 percent during the 1780s) and that farm wages had fallen to practically nothing. Similarly, while even Jefferson doubted the stability of the Constitution, he assured his friends in France that, far from approaching bankruptcy, America flourished and "the Confederation is a wonderfully perfect instrument."[22] The raison d'être for these extravagantly optimistic statements was the general audience to which they were addressed. The Founding Fathers spoke in quite a different voice among themselves, castigating the American mob and fearing that they ruled, tenuously at best, a nation on the verge of financial ruin or political chaos. But America was all affluence, egalitarianism, and rising glory when these same men sought to justify to Europeans the Revolution they had recently supported. They also employed a similar optimism and similar clichés of progress when they attempted to ingratiate themselves with the lower electorate, with the "mob," that some of them, such as Washington, despised, and that even the most magnanimous, such as Jefferson, distrusted.

What is significant for my present purposes, however, is not the schisms in the society, the inequalities in earnings and property, the divisiveness of party politics, and the reevaluation of the role to be played by the gentry within American society but the way in which both Federalist and Anti-Federalist could call upon the same republican rhetoric to justify contradictory actions, assumptions, and visions of the Republic. The invoked mythic "America" had little to do with depressions, inflations, poverty, greed, insurrections, disenchantment, and political disaffection—the whole range of disturbances in the new Republic—but had everything to do with postrevolutionary ideals and an attempt, through language, at least, to realize those right ideals and to hold in check the misguided if not malicious programs of others lest the nation perish. Even in the bitter election of 1800, both Adams and Jefferson could each invoke the same words (*commonwealth, virtue, independence, citizenship, equality*) to argue opposing visions of a nation.[23] By the same divided logic, Americans could hear identical language and understand different intentions. And even more to the point, this awareness of the multivalence of rhetoric, when both emitted and received, strikes me as crucial to our understanding of how early Americans read texts and could, to use but one example, make a best-seller of *The History of Constantius and Pulchera*, a work so diffuse, episodic, and self-contradictory as to be virtually unreadable today.

Gordon S. Wood, partly attempting to explain the myriad contradictory statements on the new Republic issued in different contexts (private versus public, local versus international) by its leading citizens, has argued that the quintessential feature of late-eighteenth-century discourse was its contextuality. Schooled in classical rhetoric at the colleges, the gentry understood rhetoric not as the communication of definitive truth but as situational discourse aimed at persuading a clearly defined implied reader or auditor of the present worth of a present proposition for that particular audience (not to mention the speaker). Washington's contradictory verdicts on the Republic, depending upon whether he addressed an American friend in a personal letter or a Continental statesman in some quasi-official capacity, may strike the modern reader as duplicitous at best or even downright hypocritical. But Washington might have said, simply, that he was a gentleman, and he wrote as one. Amateur politicians and writers, the Founding Fathers prized elegance, erudition, and classical balance (note the differences in implied audience, for example, suggested by even the title of Paine's common *Common Sense* as opposed to Adams's pedantic *Defense of the Constitutions*). As a matter of course, these gentlemen weighed the worth of an audience and tailored their address accordingly.

Consider in this context the first and second parts of Franklin's autobiography. In one, written for an illegitimate son, all the "errata" stand out and Franklin is revealed as a self-made and self-serving man. In the other, solicited by an admirer for the express purpose of edifying America, Franklin emerges as a pious moralist, almost a prig. The discrepancy between the two "Franklins" has generated sundry literary assessments of the author's duplicity. But if we ask for the real Ben Franklin in these differing portraits, the figure that emerges is a late-eighteenth-century man in full possession of the rhetorical strategies characteristic of the class into which he was not born but to which he aspired. As Wood notes, "the art of persuasion . . . was regarded as a necessary mark of a gentleman and an indispensable skill for a statesman, especially for a statesman in a republic. Language, whether spoken or written, was to be deliberately and adroitly used for effect, and since that effect depended on the intellectual leader's conception of his audience, any perceived change in that audience could alter drastically the style and content of what was said or written."[24] No wonder James Madison observed among his peers at the Convention that "no Constitution would ever have been adopted by the convention if the debates had been public." Nor did Madison see any contradiction between defending the extraordinary measures the

Convention used to ensure the absolute secrecy of its proceedings on the one hand and proclaiming in the newspapers his preference for open government on the other. As Madison argued in an article in the *National Gazette* in 1791, liberty and republican virtues could only be promoted where there was a "general intercourse of sentiments" facilitated by public and frequent elections, free trade and open commerce, more and better roads, and "particularly a circulation of newspapers through the entire body of the people."[25]

Madison's occasional advocacy of a free press is especially interesting because newspapers, like novels, were perceived by many social authorities to be agents of social dissension. They gave voice to the wrong elements, and then they compounded the crime by speaking badly, by abandoning the proper art of rhetoric in favor of a rougher, more direct, and, the gentry would argue, more incendiary brand of persuasion. *Anybody* could read a newspaper, so, by the best genteel rules of discourse, one had to be especially careful about what one said there. The newspapers, moreover, stridently advocated their political positions, often in the most alarmist and revolutionary terms, and, equally sinister, more and more people were reading this particularly ungenteel form of discourse. By 1810, in fact, some 22 million readers were being served by 376 newspapers that covered the full political spectrum.[26] Neither did American newspapers properly censor the contents of their pages. As the extensive coverage of both the Apthorp/ Morton scandal and the Elizabeth Whitman story should indicate, early American newspapers delighted in the sensational, especially in scandals among the high born. Furthermore, most newspapers opened their columns to any citizen, and, within this new public forum, the private citizen often spoke with a directness and forthrightness rarely seen before in print in America.

Expanding upon Wood's argument, I would suggest that the passage of the infamous Alien and Sedition Acts during the Adams administration may well have arisen partly because those in power did not know how to interpret the rhetoric they read in the newspapers and did not understand the new rules of the inflammatory vernacular discourse that suddenly seemed ubiquitous in the nation. If Adams, for example, was conscious of the distance between his own public words and his private sentiments, he may well have deemed other writers to be speaking in the same manner. That possibility would be appalling if beneath the virulent rhetoric of the Republican newspapers a far worse brew of barely restrained anarchic impulses seethed. After all, the one previous time when such native rhetoric had flourished there had been a revolution against Britain—a revolution Adams had advocated. What was to prevent it from happening again?

The Alien and Sedition Acts of 1798, in answering that last question, refined and legalized the profound misgivings of those in authority regarding the unruly discourse of those who had not been educated into a hierarchical system of values and the values of a hierarchical system. Again interpretation (not simply discourse) is at issue, for the Alien and Sedition Acts were vague enough to be effective against the rhetoric of those who challenged the status quo yet need not apply to the equally virulent rhetoric of those who challenged the challengers. Thus one "Burleigh" could write in the *New York Commercial Advertiser* in 1800 a not untypical bit of anti-Jefferson propoganda: "Do you believe in the strangest of all paradoxes—that a spendthrift, a libertine, or an atheist is qualified to make your laws and govern you and your prosperity?" Because it was directed at Jefferson, this was not considered seditious. The Acts were designed to suppress only disturbing or dangerous rhetoric, and thus blatant censorship was justified for the proponents of the Alien and Sedition Acts by their conviction (a *convenient* conviction) that the disturbing was dangerous.[27]

Inspired partly by the virulence of party politics in the 1790s, partly by fear of what was happening in France, and partly by the apparent connection between France's revolutionary government and the American Republican party (dramatized by the XYZ Affair), the Alien and Sedition Acts mandated the prosecution of anyone suspected of opposing "any measure or measures of the government of the United States." The law against seditious libel states:

> If any person or persons, . . . shall counsel, advise, or attempt to procure any insurrection, riot, unlawful assembly, or combination, whether such conspiracy, threatening, counsel, advice, or attempt shall have the proposed effect or not, he or they shall be deemed guilty of a high misdemeanor, and on conviction, before any court of the United States having jurisdiction thereof, shall be punished by a fine not exceeding five thousand dollars, and by imprisonment during a term not less than six months nor exceeding five years. . . . *And be it further enacted*, That if any person shall write, print, utter or publish, or shall cause or procure to be written, printed, uttered or published, or shall knowingly and willingly assist or aid in writing, printing, uttering or publishing any false, scandalous and malicious writing or writings against the government of the United States, or either house of the Congress of the United States, or the President of the United States, with intent to defame the said government, or either house of the said Congress, or the said President, or to bring them, or either of them, into contempt or disrepute; or to excite against them, or either or any of them, the hatred of the good people of the United States . . . then such person, being thereof convicted before any court of the United States having jurisdiction thereof, shall be punished by a fine not exceeding two thousand dollars, and by imprisonment not exceeding two years.[28]

The full effect of these statutes (as well as the persecutions which both preceded and followed their actual passage) upon the whole range of discourse—from newspaper columns to novels—is incalculable, but no wonder that many early American novels (especially those novels that criticized aspects of American society) chose to transpose their criticism to a foreign setting.

The Federalists in power employed the gentlemanly art of persuasion to maintain, against the laws' detractors, that the Alien and Sedition Acts need have no effect whatsoever on the shape of American discourse. These laws, their proponents asserted, did not enforce censorship or even self-censorship, for that, of course, would violate the new Constitution—the very Constitution the Acts were designed to protect. The Acts merely forbad libel, incendiarism, and other evils. They were designed to promote "Truth," to protect the very foundation of the new nation. And who, the Federalists wondered, would want to speak in favor of lies?

Thomas Jefferson, for one, did. He argued before Congress that even "false, scandalous, and malicious" opinions ought to be allowed to "stand undisturbed as monuments of the safety with which errors of opinion may be tolerated where reason is left free to combat it."[29] Jefferson opposed the Alien and Sedition Acts precisely because they inhibited the free expression of public opinion that, for him, allowed the consensus upon which the new nation had been and had to be based.

Jefferson's worst fears about the effect of the Alien and Sedition Acts were borne out immediately after their passage, and the end of the century brought a crisis in political discourse. The Federalist *Gazette of the United States* (Philadelphia), in 1798, coined its revealing (and symptomatic) motto: "He that is not for us, is against us." And as the Acts attested, he who is against us probably should be prosecuted. In 1798, the leading Republican newspaper in New England, the *Independent Chronicle*, was symbolically burned at a Fourth of July Federalist rally in Newburyport, Massachusetts, in a ceremony accompanied by appropriately incendiary rhetoric. Federalist editors all over New England decried the treason of their Republican competitors and called for censorship and suitable punishment. The *Boston Centinel* stated "whatever American is a friend of the present administration of the American government is undoubtedly a true republican, a true Patriot. . . . Whatever American opposes the Administration is an Anarchist, a Jacobin and a Traitor"—accusations rendered serious by a law that required the imprisonment of anarchists, Jacobins, and traitors.

As is common during times of cultural confusion and repressive political legislation, the denouncing of others' treachery became increasingly a matter of rhetorical demagoguery. Even silence, the *Connecticut Courant* argued, could be a sign of the traitor, for when Jacobins were silent, it was "ominous of evil. The murderer listens to see if all is quiet, then he begins. So it is with the Jacobins." The *Courant* was also quite willing to point out which newspapers were silently Jacobin, potentially murderous. At much the same level of hysteria, the *New York Gazette* invited vigilante groups to scour the countryside, looking for writers of seditious libel, for Republican editors, and other similarly suspect citizens, for "your country was never more in jeopardy than at the present moment." France and Satan had equally conspired, this paper maintained, to get at least a few traitors elected to Congress.[30]

A deeply polarized society in which the political issues of the time are passionately debated is one thing. A ruling party that enacts laws to punish anyone who advocates policies other than its own is quite another. The secretary of state, Timothy Pickering, regularly read the Republican newspapers, searching for sedition. He recruited like-minded volunteers to carry out this same good work in the far places of the Republic and had them report their findings back to him so that the culprits might be punished. Even the private correspondence of noted Republicans, such as the congressman John Clopton, was scrutinized. Adams, apparently, never initiated any of these legal proceedings, but he personally approved of the trials against his more outspoken political opponents and countenanced the suppression of any political discussion or debate that did not fully accord with his particular vision of the Republic. "Most High God," President Adams intoned on March 6, 1799, in his National Proclamation of Day of Fasting, "withhold us from unreasonable discontent, from disunion, faction, sedition, and insurrection." The pompous prose and pose of the prayer are emphasized by the political foresight that prompted it. Soon, during the course of the 1799 presidential campaign, in which Jefferson ran against the incumbent Adams, many editors and writers of the opposing press were imprisoned for their seditious opinions, and others were silenced by the threat of that same punishment. As James Morton Smith has shown, of the major newspapers prosecuted for sedition, only the *Bennington, Vermont Gazette* continued to publish its pro-Jeffersonian views, undeterred by the fact that its editor languished in a federal prison.

Smith's *Freedom's Fetters*, published in 1956, remains the definitive study of the Alien and Sedition Acts. Its persuasive eloquence is no doubt grounded in the politics of its own time, and even though no overt mention of Senator Joe McCarthy or the Cold War concern for un-American activities intrudes into the text of this meticulous study, nevertheless, the story of America's first attempt to suppress dissent certainly sets forth a pertinent allegory for those who, in the twentieth century, would labor at the same task. John Adams, Smith reminds the reader, was soundly defeated by Jefferson, who referred to the election of 1800 as a "contest of opinion" decided by the "voice of the nation." Jefferson affirmed the right of the people "to think freely and to speak and to write what they think." In a polemical conclusion written very much for the reader of 1956 (and by no means irrelevant to the reader of subsequent times) Smith insisted:

> The American experiment in self-government, which was conceived in liberty, was dedicated to the proposition that public discussion is a political duty; that men may disagree on public issues; that the opportunity to speak their minds on supposed grievances affords the best means of deciding on proper remedies; that in the marketplace, or on the battleground, of opinions, the people will be able to distinguish truth from error; and that the sounder principles and measures will prevail. Without free speech and a free press, representative government is not truly representative. Without them, popular government cannot function.[31]

Smith's conclusion repeats Jefferson's and reminds us that the debate on what margins of freedom should be allowed in political discourse has been a central issue in America for some two hundred years. How appropriate, then, that the first attempt to force a resolution of this debate, the Alien and Sedition Acts, became not the envisioned solution to the problem but the single most potent example of what Leon Howard has called America's "age of contradictions," a postrevolutionary time when the rhetoric of freedom and republicanism vied with an equally persistent rhetoric of fear and repression.[32]

Rhetorical and Narrative Strategies in the Picaresque

Because of its loose structure and formalistic latitude, the picaresque could readily address a range of social issues within the new Republic and, more important, could effectively exploit the diverging rhetorics of the early national period, sometimes for a serious purpose but often for comic effect. Even when ostensibly founded on such seemingly apolitical topics as the nature of Providence or of female virtue, the picaresque still explored the diffuseness of the era, often by comically undercutting or otherwise challenging the very basis for any practical or philosophical debate. At other times, and as I briefly noted in regard to *Modern Chivalry*, early American picaresque novels directly confronted political controversy, sometimes supporting one side, sometimes another, and sometimes undermining or parodying both.

By its very structure—or, more accurately, by its structurelessness—the picaresque allowed the early American novelist numerous fictive possibilities. To begin with, the writer could explore a full range of contradictory impulses within the new nation as well as a whole spectrum of different philosophical premises on topics as diverse as religion or legislative procedures. The picaresque also appealed because it did not require an author to take a "position" on any of the various issues adumbrated within the text. Animadversions, not pronouncements from on high, are basic to the picaresque modus operandi. Furthermore, the picaresque can always disguise any social stand it does take by hiding behind its own comic business. In effect, it can evade both censure and censorship through its indeterminacy, for just what or who is the butt of the joke or the actual object of serious discussion is not fully certain. Another advantage is the very way in which the form necessarily conjoins issues or ideas with the different people who embody them—rich and poor, rural and urban, Northern and Southern, Eastern and Western, male and female, gentleman and pauper, black and white. The novel as tract necessarily verges into the novel as travelogue and vice versa. Finally, the picaresque form in America borrowed from its Spanish antecedents a preoccupation with marginality, with extremes, with the most contradictory aspects of the society. Typically, the picaresque hero (much less frequently, heroine) is an outsider by virtue of special social circumstances (which themselves partly serve to define the society) or because of personal predilections (such as succumbing to the very curiosity and wanderlust that spin the picaresque plot).

The picaresque's marginality, central to the form since its inception, is crucial to its development in early America. Specifically, the picaresque, like a margin, delimits what is included as well as what is excluded, who is in and who is out. Opposition, moreover, always defines, simultaneously, both the self and the other—the grounds of agreement and contention. But I would also argue that the picaresque novel in early America is also marginal in the sense that it over-flows its own ostensible boundaries, brimming with unreconciled contradictions, with simultaneous pictures of different Americas imposed one upon the other, and even with different constructs of the cosmos all concurrently entertained. Its whole is both more and less than the sum of its parts. Indeed, the picaresque always contains a surplus of its own measure, and that excess is its margin of safety.

The picaresque constructs its own politics or polis, a crazy quilt of American attitudes and practices. The loosest subgenre of all, it hovers ever on the edge of a formalistic collapse under the burden of its own inclusiveness. Its tendency is to get as much into the discourse as possible, often concatenating character upon character, scene upon scene, adventure upon adventure, and all in a manner often bewildering to the modern reader. What kind of novel is this anyway? What kind of America is this anyway? What fictive principles unite the various com-peting versions of the new Republic in the picaresque plot? What stitches it all together is usually no more than a certain satirical thread or tone, a comic energy or movement—but not an Ariadne's thread that, if carefully followed, can lead the reader out of the picaresque's fictive labyrinth. On the contrary, it leads the reader in. And the reader who would try too hard to unravel the loose ends will probably end up with only some random scraps and pieces (rather like a new nation without a Constitution, as James Madison might say).

The Madisonian model of rhetorical checks and balances presumes counter-vailing forces and interests that ultimately lead to a prevailing (if sometimes precarious) stability. The picaresque novel also mobilizes disharmonious ideolo-gies, sometimes by treading some fine line between them, sometimes by carefully weighing each against the other, but most often by careening wildly between extremes, exploring the inherent danger of one polarity only to be propelled into the pitfalls of the other. The end product of this rhetorical and narrative seesaw is not some fictional utopia—the ideal America—but a raw (if energetic) republic, a diverse and divided society in which the inherent contradictions of republican discourse have not been totalized. Again, the picaresque novel is engaged in exploring the margins of society and not in trodding some middle way.

Narrative irresolution, furthermore, is another characteristic traceable to the Spanish origins of the form. As Walter L. Reed has observed in his illuminating study of the evolution of picaresque fiction, the structure of these novels typically entails a series of self-refutations. In Cervantes, for example, one character often unequivocally condemns empty moralizing immediately before launching into a "long moralizing digression of his own."[33] Thus the picaresque continually repeats and repeals itself, so that replication and refutation ultimately become not thesis and antithesis but merely two sides of the same picaresque coin, the tossing of which constitutes the plot. The result is that the picaresque plot typically has no center—rhetorically, logistically, or morally. The action proceeds sequentially with each episode bearing little relation to contiguous episodes except perhaps as comic negation. Even at the novel's end, the picaro's ritual homecoming, like Odysseus's, is not necessarily final, as if the hero's wanderlust has only temporarily abated. Sooner or later, we suspect, he will be heading out again for the territories with musket, spear, or winnowing fan.

The form's morality, like its end, is often provisional. When a lesson comes at all, it comes typically at the end, almost tacked on, but since an appended apothegm has usually been compromised or refuted in earlier sequences, there is no good reason to assume that its having last place has any final significance. After all, the book had to conclude somewhere, but its action can usually be extended beyond its end. In the moral universe of the picaresque, the process of exploration continues indefinitely, and morality is usually left just where we found it, sliding along the outreaches of the outrageous.

Examining a specific early American picaresque novel might help to clarify the ways in which self-contradictions are central to the form. James Butler's *Fortune's Foot-ball; or, The Adventures of Mercutio* (1797), one of the simplest, if not silliest, specimens of the subgenre, vacillates between mutually exclusive possibilities, beginning with the pun in the title. Is Mercutio the sport of fate or finances? Ambiguous fortune motivates many picaresque episodes as an initial quest for cash is obscured by a series of bizarre adventures and subplots that complicate the meaning of a capitalistic allegory of success against odds. Mercutio, for example, begins rich, is deprived of both property and privilege, and then, finally, after being suitably successful at his plebeian adventures, is returned to his original estate. The implication is that one needs capital to be able to exert control over one's own destiny. Yet only through misfortune (and missed fortune) does Mercutio see the world and star in the plot.

Even more contradictory than the different social visions of *Fortune's Foot-ball* are the two theological universes that it inhabits. One is a pietistic, Christocentric cosmos ("Miracles! Miracles all! . . . all bounteous Providence!" a character proclaims near the tale's conclusion); the other is a world ruled by chance, by contingency ("But alas! Fortune, that fickle Goddess, had raised her foot with a design to give him another kick"). There is, admittedly, a certain order to that dichotomy. God gets the credit for anything good, while Fortune is blamed for all unhappy events. But since the division is about equal, it becomes virtually impossible to say just who or what really rules in the world of the text or in the text of the world. Butler's preface, incidentally, differently raises much the same question. "In penning the following memoirs, I had no other object in view than my own amusement," the author stridently proclaims at the outset. But then he stages a strategic withdrawal to conventional moralism and assures the "critics" that his novel will "propagate sentiments of virtue" and "stimulate youth to a humble resignation to the dispensations of providence."[34] Do we here have amoral hedonism enlisted in the cause of pious instruction or deferring to it?

It is difficult to answer that last question, just as it is difficult finally to determine what force drives Mercutio (a.k.a. Fortune's Foot-ball) from London to Venice to Marseilles to San Marino to Constantinople to Moscow and finally back to London again. Nor is there any logic to the manifold misfortunes that befall Mercutio during the course of his wanderings. He either witnesses or endures war, murder, slavery, pirate attacks, storms on both land and sea, and numerous other mishaps natural or man-made. But what is the underlying logic of the more or less senseless sequence of crimes, follies, and disasters that constitute the novel? Is it a commentary on European decadence? Or possibly a critique of American foibles safely translated to a European setting? Or perhaps Butler simply intended an escapist fantasy? But why then the ubiquitous digressions on fortune and Providence? Neither can the novel be read as a kind of *bildungsroman*. Mercutio apparently learns nothing from his trials, and we as readers learn little about him. Nor is the ending any clearer than the beginning (or the middle either, for that matter). A few characters are married off in the final paragraphs. But these unions seem pro forma and the quickest way to terminate the action, for the weddings neither arise from the intrinsic logic of the plot (it has not any) nor resolve the chaos at the heart of the novel. The narrative simply exhausts itself—and the reader—without ever answering any of the central issues (about humans, about Providence) that it asks.

The connection between the rhetorical structure of even a simple picaresque novel such as *Fortune's Foot-ball* and the language of republicanism should be obvious at this point. In each case, the discourse offers a surfeit of signs but a dearth of signification. We are left wondering what all the rhetoric—and all the action—might mean. What is permitted or even encouraged by the counterbalancing but self-negating structures of fictive or nationalistic rhetorics that might be disallowed by a more direct, explicit, or univocal rhetorical strategy? In *The Rise of the Novel*, Ian Watt, with what seems to me an essential insight, connects rhetorical indefiniteness, cosmological dislocation, and picaresque wanderlust to the heated debates over the respective role of individuals and the State in eighteenth-century England and, concomitantly, the beginnings of commodity capitalism (which, of course, paralleled similar economic and ideological developments in the new Republic and undergirded much of the rhetoric of republicanism). Noting the uses to which religion is put in Defoe's *Robinson Crusoe*, Watt observes that Crusoe is an "occasional conformist with a vengeance" who assumes or discards his religious professions as "it is economically expedient to do so." Religion in *Robinson Crusoe* thereby becomes a social form that fulfills an economic function—for it is economics, after all, that serves as the prime mover of Defoe's plot and motivates *all* the activities of the novel's hero. As Watt notes, "leaving home, improving on the lot one was born to, is a vital feature of the individualist pattern of life" and part of the "dynamic tendency of capitalism itself, whose aim is never merely to maintain the *status quo* but to transform it incessantly."[35]

Change, difference, possibility, mobility, and restlessness or flux are crucial in that the status quo, of course, cannot in and of itself generate commodity consumption. Republican virtues such as commonwealth and citizenship may make for a harmonious society, but they also make for a sluggish economy and a dull plot. The picaresque form, like the Republic's joint attention to individual profit and social order, spurs the desire for new experiences, new objects, new symbols of status and success. More than any other form, the picaresque embodies this driving yearning for something more endemic to the capitalist spirit. The frenetic attention to fashion (as opposed to culture) means that the market continually renders its own products obsolete, or, to quote Georg Lukács, "every organic development vanishes and in its place steps a directionless hither-thither, an empty but loud dilettantism."[36]

And *Fortune's Foot-ball* does bounce merrily along with a "directionless hither-thither" perfectly predicted by its title. Thus the novel can switch from ersatz feminism (Leonora lamenting that "arbitrary custom" restricts her freedom even as she invites Mercutio to join her for the night) to deferred sex in the Sternean typographical mode ("She requested that he would accompany her into the house—he complied—what man could have refused?—Their love became reciprocal—mutual caresses succeeded the most unequivocal protestations of eternal fidelity, and***************************") to postcoital Puritan musings ("Like all the descendants of Adam, [Mercutio] had a spark of that frailty, which, in those recesses of reason when the soul is left unguarded, and open to the hostile attacks of misfortune, expels both religion and philosophy") and all in the same passage.[37]

At the end of his lust (the breaks in the text) and wanderlust (the substance of it), Mercutio returns to England to settle into virtuous married life with one Isabella. The third object of his amorous desires (and the only one to survive the various catastrophes that constitute the plot), Isabella is not really distinguishable from her predecessors, Lucinda, whom Mercutio wooed against the opposition of her aristocratic parents, or Leonora, who wooed Mercutio without the consent of *her* aristocratic parents. But then again, as Watt also notes (and borrowing here from Max Weber), romance (whether lust or love) poses a serious threat "to an individual's rational pursuit of economic ends, and it has therefore . . . been placed under particularly strong controls in the ideology of industrial capitalism."[38] Mercutio's three equivalent ladies reduce love to an exchange value, to a consumable picaresque commodity, whereas only one burning passion might have elevated love to the end and driving purpose of the novel. Mercutio's reinstatement into a life of married "ease and affluence" marks, then, not the triumph of passion or even the claims of propriety but only the cessation (and perhaps only temporarily) of his picaresque adventures. It is not even clear whether the ending can better be read as *Paradise Regained* or *Paradise Lost*.

Yet it should now be clearer why Providence (like sexuality) has only a sporadic role to play in this picaresque plot and why Mercutio's travels can never be a *Pilgrim's Progress*, The Christian ideal implicit in that last title too overtly challenges a different paradigm of progress: Young man makes good. Material good, it must be emphasized. In terms of republican iconography, the picaresque gives us Benjamin Franklin turning his two loaves of bread into a small fortune and then turning that success into narrative, into a celebrated and celebrating autobiography. It is a parable of personal and capital gain within a new republic. Like Franklin, Butler brings in Providence only when the adventures threaten to become too unseemly, while the credit for all that is seemly can be (directly) the protagonist's and (indirectly) God's.

The picaro's journey is quintessentially an earthly journey, and, in the American form, one firmly rooted in earthly values. Yet those stark values are disguised by the discursive form of the novel just as they were modified in the society by its jingoistic rhetorics. Gaining a fortune is rarely the *explicit* goal of the picaresque novel, any more than the telling phrase "life, liberty, and the pursuit of property" could be left in the final version of the Declaration of Independence. In both the novel and the society, the ultimate conflicts of class and wealth are translated into self-enhancing searches for independence, adventure, opportunity, and individualism. Commodity capitalism is hidden beneath a rhetoric of national expansion and prosperity for all. Just as the sentimental novel's obsession with virtue (for which read virginity) cloaks deeper corollaries such as the legal and economic subjugation of women, so too does the picaresque disguise its material imperatives behind tempering tales of no-account and highly idiosyncratic adventurers.

Watt and Lukács tend to view the picaresque as mostly a literary analogue to the pathological condition of capitalistic alienation. In both the literary and the social form, they suggest, a dominant acquisitiveness perverts natural relationships and subordinates possible happiness to necessarily unsatisfiable desire. Yet that critique (a twentieth-century retrospective diagnosis of the high cost of rampant capitalism) curiously mirrors the rhetoric of the aristocratic Federalists, who—at the other end of the nineteenth century's plunge into industrial capitalism and from the point of view of the socially reactionary, not the socially radical—scorned the bourgeois preoccupation with property and denounced the novel as the source and symbol for the disruptive materialistic desires of the lower orders. As suggested earlier, there was something dubiously self-serving in a privileged class denouncing the acquisitive aspirations of the unprivileged. The self-interest inherent in an eighteenth-century elite's protests against commodity consumption makes more contemporary denunciations of the bourgeoisie vaguely unsettling too. In any case, the picaresque novel, whether it sensed this dilemma or not, still managed to have things, characteristically, both ways: The objective of rising in the world ambivalently presented as capitalistic restlessness becomes both the pattern of the protagonist's success and the point of the novel's cultural critique.

Even the *Adventures of Jonathan Corncob, Loyal American Refugee*, one of the few early American picaresque novels to follow the earlier Spanish model and present the picaro as a rogue, remains calculatingly uncommitted to the justice of what Jonathan wants or of what he gets. Published anonymously in London in 1787, the novel was purportedly written by a Loyalist American who, after the Revolution, set up permanent residence in England. The novelist, however, well may have been an enterprising Englishman attempting to capitalize on interest in the New World by pretending to be both a refugee and a Loyalist. But the larger point, as one critic has noted, is not the nationality of Jonathan's creator but the locus of Jonathan's own allegiance. His loyalty "is to himself rather than to any country or institution."[39] After bundling with a nice Presbyterian girl improbably named Desire Slawbunk, Jonathan presently embarks on a life of picaresque adventures to avoid acknowledging paternity and entering marriage. Like Mercutio, this character then endures a series of trials ranging from encounters with pirates to bouts with venereal disease (the aftermath of what he thought was the seduction of another "innocent" young woman). In general and as the disease attests, Jonathan is mostly the victim of his own dubious and unexamined desires, so while he comments cynically on the folly of Americans, the reader is left to wonder if the folly in the novel is not mostly the narrator's own:

> Obliged to fly my country for the first little mistake I ever made in bundling; flogged by the first captain of the Navy I ever saw; and p-xed by the first woman I ever intended to make my wife: surely, said I, no man was ever so ill-treated by his evil genius as I am. I have been beat at Barbados; almost choked with the reed end of a clarinet; blown naked out of bed in a hurricane; p-ssed upon by the guard of a prisonship; and to crown all, here I am with my legs and wings pinned down like a trussed pullet's.[40]

Trussed—and yet writing still! Can this narrator be trusted at all? The matter is as much in doubt at the novel's end as it was at its beginning.

Jonathan's misadventures evince another aspect of the early American picaresque, its global episodism. Not content to wander New England, the republican picaros regularly take themselves and their text "elsewhere"—as if America were too homely and too new to accommodate adventure. S.S.B.K. Wood's *Ferdinand*

and Elmira: A Russian Story (1804) moves from Russia to Poland to Siberia to England with various side journeys in between. *Adventures of Alonso* (1775), by Thomas Atwood Digges, traverses the Western world, from Lisbon to Algeria to Rio to the Isthmus of Panama. Even those few picaresque novels set in America usually manage to work in an ocean voyage or two. The best-selling *The History of Constantius and Pulchera*, while ostensibly occurring during the Revolutionary War, incorporates numerous transatlantic crossings, during one of which Pulchera (disguised as Lieutenant Valorus) is shipwrecked on a deserted island and is saved from becoming dinner for her fellow survivors only by the timely arrival of a bear. Or in *The Algerine Captive*, Royall Tyler far more dexterously interweaves Updike Underhill's picaresque adventures in America with his captivity in northern Africa to have each setting provide a mirror for the other. And although *Modern Chivalry* remains mostly homebound, Teague O'Regan still makes a brief excursion to France.

Situating the fiction on foreign ground was, as noted, safer for the author than keeping it rigorously at home. But that displacement could have artistic advantages as well. Umberto Eco has argued that a judicious blending of the foreign and the familiar may well be a necessary feature of any highly exotic fiction. Referring specifically to Ian Fleming and the James Bond stories, Eco notes that one reason for the reader's engagement with all the preposterous, sensationalized, and melodramatic events of such highly stylized and implausible plots is that *something* in the novel is always portrayed as very real. Using "the technique of the aimless glance," Fleming will occasionally describe in detail not some wild or grotesque event but an utterly commonplace character or object.[41] And this note of borrowed realism then casts its aura over the rest of the text. In just that same fashion, the author (the painter William Williams) of *Mr. Penrose: The Journal of Penrose, Seaman* (published in 1815) takes pains to describe in minute detail the flora and fauna of Nicaragua, where Llewellyn Penrose is shipwrecked, before setting forth the standard picaresque sequence of life-threatening adventures such as one character hunting killer whales in a bark canoe and with only a small harpoon for a weapon.[42]

Like the sentimental novel, which allowed a woman to vicariously survey her marital options within the "comfort of her own home" (as the advertisements used to say), the picaresque did provide a glimpse into a world inaccessible to the typical early American reader. A good citizen of Hatboro, Pennsylvania, for example, who borrowed *The History of Constantius and Pulchera* from the local lending library in 1799, not only read one of the best-sellers of the generation, not only read about the Revolutionary War now almost a generation in the past, not only read of the brave Pulchera disguised as a still braver young soldier to fight in the war, *but also* gained all sorts of esoteric information about life in Europe, about life aboard ship, about life at every level of American society. Sometimes given only cursory attention but sometimes described in lavish and loving detail, exotic events were "realized" for the early American reader. No wonder that many picaresque novels were popular in the new Republic. They represented a unique chance for average Americans, citizens in a country still marginal to the world of Western civilization, to encounter, at least imaginatively, that larger world.

The episodic structure of the picaresque particularly facilitated instruction, for it encouraged a novel to be *encyclopedic,* to provide a virtual catalogue of strange costumes and customs that the reader would not be likely to encounter firsthand. As Janice A. Radway has noted, a middle-class or lower-middle-class woman today, whose life (outside of the books she reads) may be largely regulated by repetitive routines of house and child care, well might appreciate being taken, imaginatively, into a larger would.[43] But what Emily Dickinson called the "frigate" possibilities of imaginative literature would have been far greater for earlier readers simply because there was, in 1790, no mass media that could shrink the vast world to the small dimensions of a television screen and render it all one global village. As ludicrous and implausible as picaresque plots seem to modern readers, these plots still performed an important educative function for their first readers while providing a certain psychological release. Escapism is not necessarily evil when one's life is confined, by economics or gender, to some provincial hamlet or to the even more restrictive world of home and hearth—worlds from which most elite readers who deride escapist literature have already escaped.

In this respect, the picaresque novel was closely related to the nonfictional travel narrative, one of the most popular literary forms in the late eighteenth and early nineteenth century. Typically written by Americans exploring the nation's backcountry or, more often, by Europeans surveying an exotic new land, these travels-through-America books were widely read in both America and Europe. But the early American picaresque novel turned the tables in a sense and often showed Americans surviving against innumerable difficulties posed by strange European customs such as a rigorous class system (villains in American picaresque novels are often European noblemen) or pirates or other nonindigenous varieties of treachery. Whether nationalistic allegories of the pitfalls of Europe's "higher" civilization or simply encyclopedic accounts of life in distant places (places from which many American families had recently emigrated), the picaresque was a kind of travel book that allowed the reader to experience, at least vicariously, places far away. The publishers, incidentally, saw it in that light, too. In two separate editions of *The History of Constantius and Pulchera* (one published in 1796 and one in 1797) bookseller's advertisements (printed at the back of each book) included titles such as Saunder's *Journal, Travels, and Sufferings* and Jedidiah Morse's textbook *Elements of Geography.*[44] In short, travel writing extended from the picaresque and the "travel liars" (Percy G. Adams's term for the most fantastic of the travel books) to geography textbooks, and those two poles are, appropriately, both in opposition to one another and conjoined by that opposition.[45]

There is another important connection between the picaresque and ostensibly nonfictional forms of travel writing. The former borrows from the latter a crucial structuring device—the one device that gives some unity or cohesion to the otherwise diffuse picaresque form. Constraining the fictive anarchy of the picaresque is the picaresque hero, who is both the object of the various vicissitudes that make up the plot and the subject through whom that plot is recorded. In that second role, the protagonist necessarily imposes his own unique language, his own interpretive design, upon all he sees and sets down. Even when the events are filtered through an omniscient and aloof narrator, the locus of the events remains the central character, whose point of view still shapes those events. For example, in Charles Sargent's *The Life of Alexander Smith* (1819), the story of the mutiny on the *Bounty* is told by one of the mutineers, who assumes the role of "captain" on the Island of Pitcairn. Clearly, we would have a different story had the narrative centered on Captain Bligh. Or in a novel as diffuse as *Ferdinand and Elmira*, all that supplies any sense at all to the bewildering plot is the much simpler tale of thwarted love embodied in and acted out by the eponymous lovers, and around that one misadventure all the others are (however loosely) clustered.

Yet some picaresque novels exploit an inherent contradiction in travel narratives by emphasizing how the traveler/hero must be both part of and apart from what he surveys. He is both witness and judge, and each role compromises the other. The judge necessarily reveals his own personal and social prejudices, which, grounded in his own culture, usually make him an unsatisfactory interpreter of strange and foreign ways. We often sense that he would have done better by them and by himself had he remained safely at home. The witness, in contrast, seems mostly a compiler of exotica, a victim of his own motiveless curiosity and driven to no particular end. When these two roles are effectively combined—as in *The Algerine Captive, Modern Chivalry, Mr. Penrose*, and, to a lesser extent, Elkanah Watson's *A Tour of Holland* (1790), or *Adventures of Jonathan Corncob*, the result can be a narrative duality that gives depth (and ambivalence) to the novel's vision.[46]

Politically, narrative dualism also prevents these picaresque novels from being hopelessly provincial. Thus Mr. Penrose is far less the bourgeois burger adrift in the wilderness than is his counterpart, Robinson Crusoe, mostly because Penrose comes to appreciate and even emulate the Indians and the blacks he encounters. For all his lamentations about wishing to see his native country before he dies, Penrose regularly betrays his English imperialistic propensities by siding with the Native Americans. He marries an Indian who dies bearing his child; then he remarries another Native American. The dynamic in these relationships is very different from Crusoe's managing his native manservant, Friday, as is also suggested by the name Penrose gives his daughter. "America," a mixture of New World and Old, Native American and Englishman, is a different symbol of the polis from the maternal Columbia with her classical toga and impeccably Caucasian ancestry. In other ways, too, Penrose increasingly overcomes the distance between observer and observed, as is evident in an exchange he has, late in the novel, with Quammino, a brutalized slave who has escaped to the Moskito Coast where he finds safety with Penrose and his friends. In one of their frequent conversations, Penrose asks the old man if he has been converted to Christianity:

> "What good would that have done to me?" said he. "Would it have made White men love me better? No! No! Dont they Curse and Dam each other, fight, cheat and kill one the other? Black men cannot do any thing Worse than what White men do. . . . How can they expect Blacks to be good and No Christians when they who say they are Christians Are worse than we who know not the books of God as they do?"

The "savage's" discomfiting weighing of the best that civilization has to offer is not disputed in the book. "All this time I sat silently puffing," Penrose responds, "for I had Little to answer in behalf of my own colour, but told him that I believed him a much better man than many Thousands who call'd themselves Christians."[47]

As *Mr. Penrose* illustrates, in the best picaresque novels, the hero undergoes some change from the experiences he recounts. Yet even that formulation asserts too much of an opposition between the perceiver and the perceived, the teller and the tale. For ultimately these picaresque novels are *about* interpretation— about how experience is transformed into narrative. Nor can that experience be judged by standards exterior to it. We have no other world than the one the picaro (or the narrator of the picaresque tale) traverses and relates. There is no other America, for example, to juxtapose against the America of Captain Farrago and his manservant, Teague O'Regan. The "facts" of the picaresque world, contradictory as they usually are, still constitute that world, and the picaro ultimately *is* the picaresque world he describes. In this way, the protagonist of the early American picaresque becomes both a representative man and a commentator on the most diverse, contradictory, obscure, and idiosyncratic elements in the Republic.

In reading the text of different marginal lives, the picaresque hero also reads himself. That process is then carried one step further by the reader, who is encouraged, paradoxically, to judge and identify with the picaro and the various characters and events the picaro encounters and describes. Both readings, moreover, can ran both ways. While some early American picaresque novels perpetuate—sometimes in an extreme form—the restlessness and alienation of commodity capitalism, or, more locally, the aspirations of a new Republic based on free enterprise, others seem to offer a critique of the very aimlessness they describe. It is as if the text both sanctions the society in which it is grounded and opposes it. As I will show, in *The Algerine Captive*, Underhill's captivity in Algeria makes him realize that, despite America's manifest faults (and these have been fully explored in volume 1 of the novel), "there's no place like home." But the novel does not end with a finally realized affirmation of the status quo, and the patriot, in several senses, come home again. On the contrary, the political and social problems encountered in the first half of the novel remain for the returning captive. Even more to the point, the very condition of his captivity has made Underhill understand far more trenchantly the appalling nature of slavery, the manner in which it threatens to destroy America, and the determination with which it must be opposed. For Underhill, a Constitution that condones slavery constitutes the nation against itself; owner against enslaved; slaveholder against abolitionist; the institution of slavery opposed to the cherished principles of liberty in what should be "the freest country in the universe."[48] The Constitutional compromise on slavery was itself un-American and must be undone. "By uniting we stand, by dividing we fall," and unless the impossible contradiction of slaves in a free society can be resolved peacefully, the war out of which the nation was forged remains to be fought again. The novel that seemed to promise escapist adventures in foreign climes has itself escaped from those limitations and even more than its protagonist has come home again, and it comes home with a vengeance, largely through the double perspective with which the alien/traveler/ex-patriot/patriot reflects back upon America itself.

Lucien Goldman, in *Towards a Sociology of the Novel*, disputes the idea that the novel is predominantly a socially conservative literary genre. Although best-sellers (indeed, the novel itself) are basically a product of bourgeois culture, certain writers have still used the form to oppose the dominant culture. As Goldman argues: "A number of individuals who are essentially *problematic* in so far as their thinking and behavior remain dominated by qualitative values" have survived in society, "even though they are unable to extract themselves entirely from the existence of the degrading mediation whose action permeates the whole of the social structure. These individuals include, above all, the creators, writers, artists, philosophers, theologians, men of action, etc., whose thought and behavior are governed by the quality of their work even though they cannot escape entirely from the action of the market and from the welcome extended them by the reified society."[49] As noted in chapter 2, none of the market conditions of advanced capitalism had been fully worked out in the new Republic, but, as also noted, after the Revolution, Americans increasingly concerned themselves with materialistic considerations (partly, it must be added, because a promised prosperity eluded so many). And if the duplicitous picaresque form was particularly fitted to that divided social context in that it could both condemn the materialistic propensities of the bourgeoisie while deriding the older aristocratic version of that same material compulsion, it also allowed its practitioners to play precisely

Goldman's "problematic" role and to trouble the mainstreams (either Federalist or Republican) with different, discordant, marginal thought. Although admittedly no novelist before 1820 wrote with Thomas Paine's vehemence, the rights of man—particularly the solitary wandering man—were not foreign to their consideration.

Perhaps no novel better exemplifies the double perspective of the picaresque and its reliance on contradictory rhetorical strategies than does Brackenridge's *Modern Chivalry*. Published sporadically over nearly a quarter of a century, from 1792 to 1815, the book is a sprawling, disconnected, and almost endless work. The narrative, too, is disjunctive, divided, split so evenly between Captain Farrago and his not-so-trusty servant Teague O'Regan that much critical debate has centered precisely on the question of just who is the real protagonist. Farrago embodies the ostensible moral center of the book or is at least most given to making moral pronouncements, but O'Regan provides most of the adventures which keep the novel going. Between the two of them they just about constitute one duplicitous picaresque character conjoining high life and low, the ego and the id, the different agendas abroad in the land through which they jointly wander. This joint venture in divided interests and conjoined duplicity has its ancestry partly in another elemental pair, and that debt is both acknowledged and compounded in the novel itself:

> You may have my bog-trotter. . . . I am pretty well tired of bothering myself with him. . . . I have had as much trouble on my hands with him as Don Quixotte [*sic*] had with Sancho Panza; and I cannot but acknowledge as some say, that I have resembled Don Quixotte myself, at least in having such a bog-trotter after me. . . . But I hope I shall not be considered as resembling that Spaniard in taking a windmill for a giant; a common stone for a magnet that can attract, or transmute metals. It is you that are the Don Quixottes in this respect, madcaps, and some of you from the madcap settlement . . . tossing up your caps at every turn, for a new constitution; not considering that when a thing gets in the way of changing, it will never stop until it gets to the end of liberty, and reaches despotism, which is the bourne from whence no traveller returns. (P. 783)

Characteristically, the Captain slides from one form of address to another, and a self-reflexive observation on his own literary analogues and ancestry soon gives way to his chief political program of opposing all change. Thus, he fancies, is the role of Don Quixote transformed from his own noble endeavor, and transmuted to his madcap auditors, a fancy worthy of the Don at his maddest. They are no more prepared than Teague, no more than he, to mend their ways.

The pairing of two slippery polarized protagonists is also grounded in the very nature and history of the picaresque. In the earliest forms, the picaro is poor, frequently a servant, often a foundling, always a sharper. He swindles and con-nives in order to survive in a society that is itself corrupt and corrupting. The reader is encouraged to sympathize with the prankster protagonist. We admire him and his amoral ingenuity as opposed to his privileged antagonists and the immoral legalities whereby they hope to keep him in his place. In short, the picaresque is radically populist by design. It was suited to a nation that at least preached democratic principles and, in theory, sympathized with the aspirations of its Teague O'Regans. But while the picaresque formalistically favors the underprivileged, it also attests that the uneducated can be gulled and the unwary abused. It demonstrates that the underdog is often underhanded. What is condemned in one manner of speaking is required in another. As the previous quotation amply illustrates, the novel, in the guise of Captain Farrago, is ever ready to warn the unruly and unreasoning mob of the danger into which it is about to rush. *Modern Chivalry*, thus viewed, is a sustained critique of some of the most anarchic propensities in American democracy.

The novel is also a sustained critique of the persistent critiquer. In the passage just quoted, the Captain goes on to predict for at least a few of his listeners "the guillotine, before a fortnight. . . . This happened in the French revolution, and it will happen with you if you give way to your reveries" (p. 784). His reference to the French Revolution, the bugaboo that immediately silenced most early American political reformers, is his real argument. Opposing reform, the captain regularly proffers a different solution to the political questions of the day. His advice is always simple: accept, be quiet, let those wiser wisely rule. Again and again, he denounces what he perceives he has encountered—backwoods ignorance, pretentious American pseudointellectualism, the hypocrisy of religion, the pitfalls of sentimentality—and again and again his words label him as no better than (indeed, as hardly distinguishable from) the subjects of his discourse.

His most common subject and auditor is his servant, O'Regan, who, to run the equation backward, is himself no better than the Captain. O'Regan is a *reductio ad absurdum* of the American dream and of the democratic ideal that any man—even an illiterate immigrant—can succeed in the New World. O'Regan is unscrupulous but ambitious, uneducated but convinced that his lack of education does not handicap him in the pursuit of success. More to the point, those whom Farrago and O'Regan meet during the course of their wanderings almost always share the servant's point of view and are ready to help him rise in the world. O'Regan is nearly elected to the legislature, is almost inaugurated into the American Philosophical Society, is just about ordained a Presbyterian minister, and even comes close to being named chief of the Kickapoo. He is prevented from achieving these distinctions only by the timely intervention of Farrago, who, as a proponent of order and rationality, regards the sundry honors showered on his servant as so many gross miscarriages of justice that a man of honor must set right. But Brackenridge also hints that Farrago may be motivated by unacknowledged jealousy as well as by the pragmatic desire to retain the services of O'Regan. The Captain's aristocratic convictions conveniently serve his mundane needs.

With such unresolved ambiguities Brackenridge's plot thickens and his meaning expands. O'Regan fails too frequently to be the traditional picaro who calls into question the structure of his society. Mostly, the program of Captain Farrago prevails, and the book has often been read as authenticating the elitist standards to which he and his class adhere. That reading, however, simplifies all that is subtle in *Modern Chivalry*. Briefly, although Captain Farrago is often partly right, he is also frequently sententious, generally priggish, and invariably dull. At fifty-three, a bachelor with little experience in life, he has set out to discover the world. But his new education merely confirms his old prejudices. In fact, for eight hundred pages, he views his fellow citizens with a mechanical misanthropy and never considers the possibility that an illiterate man might be wise or a poor man prudent. His attitude toward others is unremittingly patronizing. Lawmakers in Philadelphia, he would insist, have only the best interests of the populace at heart, even though that populace consists mostly of "uppity" provincials who do not even merit their betters' concern. His views are too simplistic, too "reactionary" to be taken seriously.

Furthermore, as Robert Hemenway and Emory Elliott have each differently demonstrated, Farrago's practice continually compromises his theory.[50] The reason and justice whereby he thinks he lives should, he claims, rule all men. Yet his reason and justice never carry the day, never even carry him to triumph in his minor disputes with O'Regan. Again and again we see Farrago expounding to citizens and servant, who remain unswayed by his rational pronouncements. Then, to achieve his ends, the Captain must play the confidence man himself in order to prevent his man from conning the public. We see him resorting to ad hominem arguments, hysterical rhetoric, appeals to fear, vanity, and small-mindedness. Or, as when O'Regan is about to be sent to Congress, Farrago takes him aside to twist the real issues through an exercise in dubious logic that perfectly exemplifies the Captain's self-serving agenda:

> When a man becomes a member of a public body, he is like a raccoon, or other beast that climbs up the fork of a tree; the boys pushing at him with pitch-forks, or throwing stones, or shooting at him with an arrow, the dogs barking in the mean time. . . . They will have you in the newspapers, and ridicule you as a perfect beast. There is what they call the caricature; that is, representing you with a dog's head, or a cat's claw. . . . I would not for a thousand guineas, though I have not the half of it to spare, that the breed of O'Regans should come to this; bringing on them a worse stain than stealing sheep; to which they are addicted. You have nothing but your character, Teague, in a new country to depend upon. Let it never be said, that you quitted an honest livelihood,

the taking care of my horse, to follow the new fangled whims of the time, and to be a statesman. (P. 17)

It works. The servant will keep his place, so the master can also retain *his*. But the master achieves his ends through the traditional means of the picaro, of the powerless, by using his wits. Here, as elsewhere, a specious argument does the trick; irrationality prevails, even in the name of reason.

As Claude M. Newlin demonstrated in his pioneering 1932 critical biography of Brackenridge (still the best discussion of that author's political vision), the novelist's own sentiments were deeply divided, and his novel, not surprisingly, dramatized the divisions in his political thinking as well as the political divisions in western Pennsylvania during the 1790s that culminated in the infamous 1794 Whiskey Rebellion.[51] I would somewhat extend that observation and argue that the relationship between the political life, the nonfiction political histories, and the political fiction of Hugh Henry Brackenridge effectively capsulizes the various tensions I have discussed in this chapter and gives us a more complicated version of history as a contradictory discourse than does even the novel.

Brackenridge himself, a curious combination of elitist and plebeian, of Princeton-educated classicist and backwoods lawyer, cut quite an unlikely figure in the new Republic. While he was writing a detailed study of Blackstone's commentaries applicable to American jurisprudence, he frequently appeared in court rumpled and dirty, his hair unkempt, without socks, and, more than once, without shoes. On one occasion, fearing to get his only suit wet in a rainstorm, he rode naked through the countryside, for "the storm, you know, would spoil the clothes, but it couldn't spoil me."[52] His political positions evolved along the fissiparous pattern of divisive party politics described in the first part of this chapter. More specifically, as a young legislator in Pennsylvania, he championed Federalism or at least the adoption of the new Constitution. Yet he later vehemently broke away from the Federalists and opposed many of the economic measures undertaken by Alexander Hamilton as Washington's head of the Treasury, particularly Hamilton's land taxes, his excise tax on whiskey, and his willingness to have the government exchange bonds on land at their face value—a practice that encouraged speculators to purchase land at rock-bottom prices from poverty-stricken farmers on the frontier and then to sell it back to the government for its original value. Some of the most cutting satirical denunciations in *Modern Chivalry* are reserved for rich land speculators who, Brackenridge believed, exploited the penury of others and profited at the expense of the whole nation.

A Federalist during the Confederation period, a Jeffersonian and Anti-Federalist in the subsequent time, a sympathizer with the French, and then, after 1797 (and what he saw as the failure of republicanism in France), an enemy of the ongoing French Revolution, Brackenridge never felt bound by any party loyalty to maintain one position. More important, he understood politics not as principle or belief in action but as rhetoric in action, and in action mostly as speech. Throughout his career he was known—to his admirers and his enemies—as a great orator and, like both Farrago and O'Regan, delighted in the power of verbal persuasion, in his ability to talk himself into and out of almost any situation.

That power was fully tested during the Whiskey Rebellion, in which Brackenridge played a major role not as insurgent or counterinsurgent but merely as available spokesperson. His voice was at the service of both sides, and consequently both sides had considerable suspicions about where that voice came from. To explain his role in the rebellion and to exonerate himself, Brackenridge published, in 1795, *Incidents of the Insurrection in the Western Parts of Pennsylvania, in the Year 1794*. It is a work of some 350 pages in which Brackenridge both recounts his own role at the center of the rebellion but also disclaims any real role in that same rebellion. This curious book raises at least as many questions as it answers. To whom does Brackenridge wish to exonerate himself, the populace or the government? That matter remains as unresolved at the end as at the beginning. But what does emerge is a wily and slippery narrator, an author whose history of the Whiskey Rebellion is as much a fiction as his fictionalized version of the same rebellion in volume 4 of *Modern Chivalry*. Like Farrago in the novel, Brackenridge in the history attempts to counsel moderation to each side primarily by trying to persuade each camp that he is their friend and spokesperson while also convincing them that a pitched battle against the other side would result in unacceptable loss and bloodshed. An example from his account reveals the retrospective historian as participant-narrator and masterful rhetorician. In this scene (and Brackenridge's method in the history as in *Modern Chivalry* is always scenic, dramatic), the insurgents are determined to attack Pittsburgh, and Brackenridge's design is to dissuade them from their plan:

> INSURGENT: "Are we to take the garrison?"
> BRACKENRIDGE: "We are."
> INSURGENT: "Can we take it?"
> BRACKENRIDGE: "No doubt of it."
> INSURGENT: "At a great loss?"
> BRACKENRIDGE: "Not at all; not above a thousand killed and five hundred mortally wounded."

As he intended, the insurgents decided to march through Pittsburgh as an orderly army instead of attempting to sack the city.[53]

Or on another occasion Brackenridge attempted to quell threatened revolutionary violence by enacting a little satire at the expense of Washington and Hamilton and the federal government. His impromptu dialogue between General

Knox and Cornplanter, however, did not amuse the crowd, so Brackenridge returned to the federal representatives to attempt to persuade them not to attack the rebels as he had, immediately before, attempted to dissuade the rebels from attacking the government officials. It was a slippery business and one that almost ended in Brackenridge's conviction for treason. Hamilton became convinced that Brackenridge had been the chief fomenter of the Whiskey Rebellion, and his dramatization of Cornplanter as well as President Washington was taken as proof of his revolutionary propensities. Whereupon Brackenridge persuaded Hamilton that the satire had had an entirely different purpose and that Cornplanter, not the Father of the Nation, had been the butt of all the jokes. "Mr. Brackenridge," Hamilton apologized, "your conduct has been horribly misrepresented." That exoneration prompted General Neville, one of the author's political enemies, to proclaim Brackenridge "the most artfull fellow that ever was on God Almighty's earth; he has put his finger in Bradford's eye, in Yates' eye, and now he has put his finger in Hamilton's eye too."[54]

Even after the failure of the rebellion and despite concerted Federalist opposition, Brackenridge continued his Republicanism, still attempting to organize the farmers and mechanics against the Federalist leadership. But his aristocratic education, his ambiguous role in the earlier insurrection, and the people's general reading of the man himself rendered his motives suspect. The unprivileged distrusted the Princeton graduate's advocacy of their cause, and in a letter to the *Pittsburgh Gazette* on October 5, 1799, one who signed himself "A Real Farmer" even suggested that "old Hugh himself" had been up to his old tricks again, pretending to be different yeomen or mechanics and writing letters to local newspapers in support of himself under various plebeian pseudonyms, actively putting himself forward as a candidate for the Assembly while neglecting, in these specious pronouncements on his own behalf, to inform the public that, during his earlier term as a legislator, he had voted against precisely the egalitarian legislation that he had "promised . . . to effect."[55]

The position of the man is hard to pin down in his account of the *Incidents of the Insurrection*—a purportedly nonfictional account and ostensibly aimed at his own exoneration—and is equally ambiguous in his political career, but the author of *Modern Chivalry* vanishes almost entirely behind a smoke screen of various contradictory asserted intentions and shifting narrative perspectives. By James Kelleher's count, "the author-narrator's descriptions of the reasons for writing the book recur like a motif fifty-three times. On twenty-two of these occasions he confesses a serious moral intention. Significantly less often he denies in a mock-serious tone that the book is a satire (five times); calls it an exercise in style only (seven times), a burlesque (once), an adventure narrative (four times), pure nonsense (five times), playful satire (once) and history-memoir-biography (eight times)."[56] In effect, the narrative, like the hero, is a farrago, a hodgepodge, an adventure in discourse on a whole range of political opinions regarding the operations of democracy and the failures and the triumphs of the new Republic, and all bound up in one continuous, shape-shifting saga.[57]

Yet the shifting shapes of the fiction and the narrative slipperiness that facilitates those slides do, finally, have a certain political logic:

> Why should I undervalue democracy; or be thought to cast a slur upon it; I that am a democrat myself. . . . *Nor is it democracy, that I have meant to expose; or reprehend, in any thing that I have said; but the errors of it: those excesses which lead to its overthrow.* These excesses have shown themselves in all democratic governments; whence it is that a *simple* democracy has never been able to exist long. An experiment is now made in a new world, and upon better principles; that of *representation and a more perfect separation, and near equipoise of the legislative, judicial, and executive powers.* But the balance of the powers, is not easily preserved. *The natural tendency is to one scale.* The demagogue is the first great destroyer of the constitution by deceiving the people. He is no democrat that deceives the people. He is an aristocrat. (P. 507; italics in the original)

If these words of Captain Farrago sound remarkably like Madison, it is by no means purely coincidental. Brackenridge and Madison were schoolmates at Princeton, were close friends, and were two of the leaders of Princeton's Whig Club. What this passage from *Modern Chivalry* points up is the contradictory views of human nature implicit in both the picaresque novel and in the republican paradigm. Humans are innately good and therefore deserve to govern themselves; humans are innately stupid, petty, corruptible, and thus require a system of checks and balances lest democracy run toward anarchy at the one extreme or tyranny at the other. Checking the balances and straddling the oppositions, the picaresque, and *Modern Chivalry* in particular, charts out the margins of political discourse in the new nation.[58]

The Female Picaresque

> A woman on horseback, presents her form to advantage; but much more at the spinning wheel.
> —*Modern Chivalry*

As I have shown, the circumscription of the female character within the domestic sphere constitutes a defining feature of sentimental fiction. In contrast, the picaresque novel defines itself by its own mobilities—formalistic and on the level of plot and characters, too. The picaresque hero can comment upon slavery, class disturbances, party politics, and different immigrant groups precisely because his travels carry him into encounters with diverse segments of the population and across those dividing lines that mark out the contours of the society. His journey is also the reader's journey and his freedom the reader's freedom. Whenever a particular episode might become too constraining and threatens to fix the action in, say, prison or matrimony, the logic of the plot still requires that the novel move on, and freedom (the protagonist's and the reader's) is regularly retained through evasive action. Furthermore, such exercises in independence, unlike comparable ventures on the part of female characters in the sentimental novel, are sanctioned in the plot. So if the picaresque explicitly celebrates an essentially male freedom, then just where do women come in—as characters, authors, and readers? Can *Modern Chivalry*, for example, prefatorially addressed explicitly to the male reader ("If you are about to chuse a wife, and expect beauty, you must give up family and fortune; or if you attain these, you must at least want good temper, health, or some other advantage" [p. 31]), even be read by women, and, if not, then what kind of chivalry is it? One might claim that just as the sentimental novel examines women's issues, why could not the picaresque form fairly be written only for men? But I would argue that, in a patriarchical society in which resources (income, books, status, freedom, and the rest) are inequably divided, what is sauce for the gander rarely serves the goose as well.

As the quotation from *Modern Chivalry* with which this section began illustrates, merely reversing the terms of an argument by no means reverses its underlying assumptions. The woman on horseback is still subordinated to her more typical position behind a spinning wheel. Both postures, moreover, are appropriated as service to a proper master. Why ride a horse? To get from hither to yon or to show one's form to advantage? In short, Brackenridge's surveyed woman is precisely the antithesis of his surveying hero. When she is not invisible in the text or entirely omitted from the narration, she exists adjunctive to his good, his ends. Therefore, to create a female picaresque novel in which a woman on horseback traverses, assesses, and describes town and countryside almost necessarily, given the culture in which it is read, devolves into self-parody. The female simply does not have the same freedoms—to journey, to judge, to have her judgments heeded—as does the male, and that is a fact of picaresque fiction almost as much as it is a fact of sentimental fiction.

Not surprisingly, in those novels in which a woman comes closest to enacting the role of the standard male picaro, she does so only in male dress. Both the Martinette-goes-to-war sequence in *Ormond* and the whole of Herman Mann's *The Female Review* allow a woman male freedom: first, because all of her companions think of her as him; second, because that deception itself serves a larger redeeming cause, patriotism, the good of her country. A feminized picaresque fiction, consequently, requires both justification and narrative deception. While the reader is in on the ruse, the characters the picara meets are not, and most of the interest of the book derives from a continual but covert textual dialectic of knowledge and ignorance, of male and female, of power and powerlessness. For once the picara's true (i.e., female) identity is revealed, her power no longer exists. In short, her very role in the fiction is specious and surreptitious, is con-

DEBORAH SAMPSON.

Published by H. Mann. 1797.

FIGURE 13. This frontispiece of *The Female Review* (1797) emphasizes both Deborah Sampson's patriotism and her femininity, in marked contrast to her masculine exploits in the novel itself. *Courtesy of the American Antiquarian Society.*

ditional upon its being asserted in ways that challenge neither the status quo nor the double standard. Personal power without political power can provide a momentary fantasy but is no solution to the larger dilemma of female disenfranchisement within the polis.

Since the cross-dressed picara retains her power only as long as its inauthentic basis is not revealed either literally or figuratively, the novels often flirt, almost pornographically, with the threat of exposure.[59] For example, in *The Female Review* (and, remember, most of the subscribers to the novel were men of substance) Deborah Sampson at one point suffers not only a head wound but also a wound to her right thigh, just (we are specifically told) below her groin. To reveal the second injury would reveal her sex, so much so that the wound can be seen as an obvious stand-in for the hidden sex. She allows a doctor to remove the one bullet, but she herself secretly extracts the other one with a penknife (and, it might also be added, with obvious Freudian implications). Her sex, however, does not go entirely undiscovered. Later, as she lies unconscious with yellow fever, a doctor feels for her heartbeat to find if she is still alive and finds also something else. Breasts prove the woman, but a woman's wiles soon bring the doctor to promise silence, and Deborah is off again, this time westward, to travels on the frontier, encounters with Indians, and to still more narrow escapes from women who find this "blooming soldier" irresistible. A curious amalgam of stereotypically masculine and feminine attributes, the young soldier, as a kind of Revolutionary Michael Jackson, enchants most of the females s/he meets. What do women want? Deborah Sampson knows. But it is not so clear that Herman Mann, the author, does. Although the novel recounts several incidents of her exemplary courage (and courage in the exploitative masculine model: She must kill an Indian in self-defense before she is truly "manly"), Sampson's chief occupation is to keep men from uncovering her hidden femininity while simultaneously preventing women from falling in love with her covering masculinity. The title page, too, hints equally of patriotism ("she performed the duties of every department, into which she was called, with punctual exactness, fidelity and honor") and prurience (she "preserved her chastity inviolate, by the most artful concealment of her sex").

Yet the doctors, colonels, merchants, majors, and captains (as well as Miss Hannah Wright, Miss Alice Leavens, Miss Hannah Orne, and the other misses whose names were included in the volume) apparently saw themselves as supporting through their subscriptions a purely pious tale. In contrast to the lists bound with all other early American novels, the one found in *The Female Review* is unusual in that it contains no pseudonyms such as "A Friend to the Publication" or "A Young Lady of Massachusetts," phrasings obviously intended to hide the patron's true identity.[60] But consistent with its tranvestite plot, *The Female Review* cross-dresses generically too. Nowhere announcing itself as a novel, this fiction masks its own fictionality by passing itself off as a proper history of the Revolution.

Another novel of cross-dressing, also set during the Revolution, further underscores the inherent contradictions between female, on the one hand, and picaresque, on the other. *The History of Constantius and Pulchera; or, Constancy Rewarded: An American Novel* was one of the best-selling novels of the early national period. Originally published in brief installments from June 1789 to January 1790 in the American monthly periodical *Gentleman and Ladies Town and Country Magazine*, the novel also went through eight editions in English between 1794 (its original date of book publication) and 1802, was translated into German for the Pennsylvania market, was reprinted again in 1821 and 1831, and was then published in a plagiarized edition, under the title *History of Lorenzo and Virginia; or, Virtue Rewarded*, by one T. H. Cauldwell, D.D., in 1834. It was available in a pirated paperbound edition that sold for a quarter and in a handsome, calfbound duodecimo that sold for over a dollar. Despite its popularity, however (or perhaps because of it), the book has baffled contemporary critics. It is surprisingly brief (some copies are only twenty-five or so pages long) and extremely episodic (as if with each installment, the author had mostly forgotten what he or she had written last month). A number of critics have even insisted that the book is so discontinuous, its plot so ludicrous, its rhetoric so preposterous, and its moral so muddled that it must surely have been originally intended as a *parody* of the sentimental or picaresque forms, for "it is impossible to take [it] . . . seriously."[61]

Yet apparently the original readers of *The History of Constantius and Pulchera* did just that. Nothing in the twenty-one copies of the novel that I have inspected suggests that they were read any differently from, say, romantic novels such as *The Coquette* or *Charlotte*. Most are signed in the usual fashion and using the usual formula, "Elizabeth Smith, her Book." Others, however, are signed several times, sometimes by members of the same family, sometimes (judging by the dates and inscriptions) by different generations of the same family, sometimes shared among friends or relatives with different family names. Most striking for my purposes, however, in one copy of the cheap, poorly printed edition pirated by Edward Gray in 1801, there is clear evidence of a reader who not only saw nothing funny in the work but who obviously valued it and drew connections between it and her own view of the world. As noted in chapter 4, she embellished the book itself with fine handmade covers and a delicate drawing of flower buds and, at crucial points in the text, supplied her own poetic and philosophical gloss on the events of the nebulous plot.

Why, we must ask, is the book virtually unreadable today or readable only as a parody of itself? Robert Darnton addresses essentially the same question when he sorts through Jean-Jacques Rousseau's mailbag and finds dozens of fan letters addressed to "l'Ami Jean-Jacques" from readers enraptured by *Julie, ou la nouvelle Héloïse*—"six volumes of sentiment unrelieved by any episodes of violence, explicit sex, or anything much in the way of plot"; in short, by today's standards, an unreadable book. Yet this unreadable book, with its overinflated prose and its overheated didacticism, went through a minimum of seventy editions before 1800, as many editions as any other novel in any country by that date.[62] Perhaps we read differently today from the way we did in 1800.

In 1800, many Americans—and there is no way of knowing just how many— read *The History of Constantius and Pulchera*, and what they read, starting with the frontispiece with its evocation of Romeo and Juliet, was a sentimental story of star-crossed lovers conjoined with a female picaresque adventure tale. At first the sentimental predominates. The first appearance of the heroine is standard romance: "In the suburbs of the city of Philadelphia, in the soft season of the year, about one o'clock, on a moon shining morning, on the terrace of a high building, forty feet from the ground, appeared a most beautiful lady of the age of sixteen—she was clad in a long white vest, her hair of a beautiful chestnut colour, hanging carelessly over her shoulders, every mark of greatness was visible in her countenance, which was overcast with a solemn gloom, and now and then, the unwilling tear unnoticed, rolled down her cheek."[63] Yet in the novel's preface, explicitly addressed to the "Daughters of Columbia," prospective readers are promised "novelty" that will be "like a new Planet in the solar System" of "the Ladies' Libraries." They are also assured that the novel will not arouse "party spirit" and the "many emotions" of the divided "political world" but, rather, will focus on women's concerns and is designed for the "Amusement of the Fair Sex." That statement, in itself, is, of course, a political statement, one that recognizes women's exclusion from or indifference to official party politics. The book opposes the world of men's politics to the world of the lady's library— different planets in the same (or, perhaps, not the same at all) universe.

Although, to say the least, much shorter than *La Nouvelle Héloïse*, *The History of Constantius and Pulchera* mimics the strained language of feeling that Rousseau deploys throughout his six-volume novel: "O transcendently propitious heaven! thrice bountiful, inexhaustible, magnificent Providence! inexpressible, benevolent, and superlatively beneficent fates! The most exalted language is more than infinitely too inexpressive to give an idea of the grateful sensations which occupy my breast" (p. 94). Just as recent authors run up against the limitations of language in one way, early novelists did so in another way. Pulchera, still disguised as Lieutenant Valorus, has just tested her lover's constancy, and his exclamations follow upon her revealing her true identity. No words—not even *these* words— can capture his joy. But notice that his effusive language would normally be her language. Pulchera is in control. She contrives the meeting, the test, the revelation. Constantius's role is essentially passive, responsive, in a word, "feminine." The novel focuses on Pulchera's prowess and adventures, and Constantius, consistent with the passive connotations of his name, is finally reduced, rhetorically, to the role traditionally occupied by a woman, that of the grateful heroine over-

Constantius! once more your
Pulchera beholds you.

FIGURE 14. The frontispiece of this edition of *The History of Constantius and Pulchera* (New York: John Tiebout, 1801) gives little indication that Pulchera—here passively receiving the attentions of Constantius—is actually the main character in the novel and the novel's chief adventurer. *Courtesy of the American Antiquarian Society.*

whelmed by good fortune and the capable attentions of another. One almost expects the fellow to swoon.

The narrative transvestism or emotional role reversal, however, does not overtly challenge the status quo, and that consideration may well explain the "secret" to the novel's success. The heroine rushes from harrowing adventure to even more harrowing adventure, but she does so "innocently" because, ostensibly, she proceeds in opposition to her own more proper desires. The novel essentially grafts the typical picaresque adventure story (such as *Fortune's Foot-ball*) onto a sentimental novel through the ingenious device of captivity (a device to be explored at greater length in a subsequent section on the female Gothic novel). Because Pulchera is repeatedly abducted and thus, by definition, deprived of volition in the matter, she cannot really be held responsible for breaking virtually every imaginable restriction placed upon the eighteenth-century American woman. She is, happily, *forced* into her different unlikely roles as picara, world traveler, cross-dressing soldier, prize master on a brigantine captured by pirates, and sole woman stranded with a group of men on a remote desert island. In her assumed role as Valorus, she is constantly thrown into the company of disreputable men, and, just as constantly, she overpowers or outwits or otherwise triumphs over them all. She is transformed, onomastically and metaphorically, from Pulchera—suggesting a typically feminine beauty, pulchritude—to Valorus, a hero. As Lillie Deming Loshe has noted, there is a certain "cheerfulness" in the way the narration lurches from one unlikely and outlandish adventure to another, with Pulchera/Valorus thoroughly enjoying her successes in situations no eighteenth-century woman had any business even fantasizing.[64] And then her exhilarating trials all end in the domesticity she would have entered on page 1 except for the intervention of her parents (who, of course, had wanted to marry her to a designing French aristocrat). She has her adventures and her Constantius, too. He is, indeed, a final triumph and also an appropriate reward (playing the role of the traditional heroine again) for all of her other earlier triumphs.

It is, in short, a wonderful fantasy. Pulchera/Valorus violates all of the restrictions placed upon eighteenth-century women but still ends up, thanks to her unflagging ingenuity and overall capability, safe at home again and at last in possession of her constant American lover. No wonder the novel was a best-seller! This American heroine saw the world, proved her mastery of it by triumphing over a whole host of designing men, and then returned home to an America that had won its independence (her own story of independence, like Deborah Sampson's, is set during the Revolutionary War) to enter into a marriage that, mercifully, is left undescribed at the novel's end. Like all good escapist literature, *The History of Constantius and Pulchera* allows the reader a temporary reprieve from her own situation but never requires her to question its governing assumptions. Catharsis arises precisely from the novel's lack of realism—signaled by its exuberant rhetoric—which allows the reader freely to imagine freedom without in any way having to pay the personal or public price that any effort to realize that freedom necessarily entails.

Another factor probably contributed to the popularity of this curious little tale. It is among the shortest, sparest, and simplest of early American novels. Even when the vocabulary is at its most florid ("transcendently . . . propitious . . . bountiful . . . inexhaustible . . . benevolent . . . superlatively"), the "words of three, four, and five syllables" are those that are found in Dilworth's, Perry's, and Webster's spelling books. In effect, rote vocabulary lessons have become enlivened into plot, and words have gained significance by being incorporated into story. What to us seems like a highly erratic, episodic, and undeveloped plot may, therefore, have seemed almost like magic to an inexperienced reader making her way from her speller to a novel in which those long lists of words memorized in the schoolroom suddenly transported a girl very much like herself about the globe and through a whole series of adventures while Constantius waited mostly at home. The novel is simple in its disjunctive vocabulary, and it is simple, too, in its disjunctive story, calling upon the reader's ready imagination to fill in the lacunae in the notably undelineated plot. In what is almost a child's ordering ("this happened and then this happened and then this happened . . ."), impetus and excitement derive not from the narrative skills of the author but from the reader being able to re-create a tale of utter implausibility and to participate thereby in the global derring-do of a sixteen-year-old girl from the suburbs of Philadelphia.

Only in cross-dressing or captivity do a few women characters find something of the same full freedom that the picaresque regularly grants to its male protagonists. Moreover, that freedom, it must be emphasized, is conditional and temporary, and definitely not for domestic consumption. Clearly, "Mrs. Constantius" (née Pulchera), back in "the suburbs of Philadelphia," may wistfully recall her life as Valorus, ship's mate and soldier, but she will not swashbuckle through the marketplace. As Arabella, the satirized heroine in British novelist Charlotte Lennox's *The Female Quixote* (1752), aptly observes, when a woman "at last condescends to reward [a man] with her Hand . . . all her Adventures are at an End for the Future."[65] Returned to female dress and mien again, Deborah and Pulchera presumably live happily ever after. But such an ending does not elicit the imagination of the author, and both the "happiness" and the "after" can be appropriately left to the readers, who will all have their own experiences on that same score.

Tabitha Gilman Tenney, in *Female Quixotism: Exhibited in the Romantic Opinions and Extravagant Adventures of Dorcasina Sheldon* (1801), portrays a protagonist whose adventures are hardly as extravagant as those of Pulchera or Deborah Sampson. Perhaps Dorcasina's wildest act is to dress up her previous name, which was the more mundane Dorcas. In this novel the picara never strays more than thirty miles from her place of nativity. Her adventures are mostly in reading and are all emphatically and stereotypically female. A devotee of romances, she reads to imagine herself the object of male adoration. Theoretically, she need imagine no further than that essentially passive state. Love should conquer all, which means she need conquer nothing—not enemy soldiers, not pirates, not even the more difficult nonfictional books in her father's library. Tenney's genius is to tie the form that most emphasizes freedom from society back to limitation (read: female limitation) and society (read: patriarchal society). The protagonist's "romantic opinions" and "extravagant [albeit mental] adventures" only circumscribe the fixity of her place.

An intelligent woman, an heiress of a thousand pounds a year (rightly designated in the novel as "a great fortune"), Dorcasina renders herself pathetic not just by her novel reading but by her willingness to believe in the whole fantasy of love perpetuated in the novels she reads. She takes "happy ever after" at face value and sets out to discover the man who will render her so. She is consequently victimized by both her own delusions and by men who calculatingly exploit those delusions and see in her only a windfall profit to be easily won by passionately declaiming a few romantic phrases plagiarized from those same novels in which her delusions are grounded. She reads too trustingly, both the books and the men she meets. Just as *The History of Constantius and Pulchera* was a kind of elementary how-to-read-a-novel novel, *Female Quixotism* is a more subtle hownot-to-read-a-novel novel. Tenney allegorizes the reading process and turns it upon itself; one must be a resisting reader, a critical reader, a reader able to read other readings of the fiction, able to read the context in which the text is read.

Dorcasina emblemizes the passive consumer who presents no critical opposition to the texts she reads. She reads her life the same way—postulating a gentleman behind an uncouth, illiterate servant (she has just finished *Roderick Random*), seeing true love in the faces of false men whose dissembling is motivated by the materialistic consideration of her fortune. She is saved from the most calculating of these men only by his fortuitous arrest for outstanding debts. Mr. Seymore, a dubious schoolmaster of uncertain past, intends to rise in the world through a fortunate match despite the fact that he is already married. His plan was to wed Dorcasina and then to have the middle-aged woman incarcerated in an insane asylum so that he could enjoy her cash unencumbered by her company. Bilked of the real prize at the last moment, his revenge is to tell his ostensible prize just where she stands in his regard: "Ridiculous vanity, at your age, with those grey locks, to set out to make conquests! I . . . assure you that any man would be distracted to think of marrying you except for your money."[66] The veil is lifted, and Dorcasina sadly recognizes the delusions under which she has long labored. Even sadder, she realizes that it did not have to end that way: "Had my education been properly directed . . . I believe I might have made acquirements, which would have enabled me to bear a part, perhaps to shine, when thrown among people of general information" (2:212).

An emphasis on female education begins even with the novel's epigraph: "Felix Quem Faciunt Aliena Pericula Cautum. In plain English—Learn to be wise by others harm, / and you shall do full well." As in many early works, the Latin quotation is translated into "plain English" for those who do not have the benefit of a classical education—for, more specifically, the "Columbian Young Ladies, who Read Novels and Romances" and to whom the volume is dedicated. This epigraph, along with the novel's preface, reiterates the eighteenth-century assumption that narrative directly addresses questions on the conduct of life. By reading of Dorcasina's delusions and consequent suffering, the reader should "learn to be wise" and "do full well" in her own personal existence. The key, then, is not for women to stop reading—but for women to read the right kinds of books, the right kinds of novels even, not the novels Dorcasina reads but the novel in which she reads them. It is all a matter of choice, and Tenney, moreover, makes clear the grounds of her protagonist's unfortunate propensity to mislead her fancy with bad fiction. Had Dorcasina's mother lived, we are told, the daughter's education would have been well regulated, sensible. Instead, her father has indulged his own appetite for bad novels and nourished his daughter's. In the process, the widower has also ensured that his only child will remain at his side, a devoted daughter who is also his housekeeper and companion.

The importance of female reading, Tenney insists, is all the greater given the intellectual climate of the time in which *any* female reading was seen as suspect. After Dorcasina rejects her first suitor because he does not, in his speech or letters, sound like Werther or Harrington, no more male attention disturbs her novelistic retreat for many years. "Notwithstanding the temptation of her money, and her agreeable person," most men who knew of Dorcasina's love of novels avoided her, "wisely forseeing the inconveniences which would result from having a wife whose mind was fraught with ideas of life and manners so widely different from what they appear on trial." The author seems to endorse such prudent reservations but not the baser doubts of men put off simply by Dorcasina's love of books: "Others there were, who understood only that she spent much time in books, without any knowledge of the kind which pleased her. It was sufficient to keep them at a distance, to know that she read at all. Those enemies to female improvement, thought a woman had no business with any book but the bible, or perhaps the art of cookery; believing that everything beyond these served only to disqualify her for the duties of domestic life" (1:17). This double-edged focus makes *Female Quixotism* more than a satire of one silly woman who reads too many equally silly books. The novel is also a larger different satire on a whole society in which a deficient educational system and dubious sexual politics render women devoid of judgment by deeming judgment, in a woman, a superfluous quality.

One early incident in the novel effectively epitomizes the dual focus of its pervasive satire. When the father attempts to marry his daughter to the only son of his best friend, Dorcasina anticipates "a sensible pain at quitting my dear and affectionate father, and this delightful spot where I have passed all my life, and to which I feel the strongest attachment. But what gives me the greatest pain," she continues, "is that I shall be obliged to live in Virginia, be served by slaves, and be supported by the sweat, toil and blood of that unfortunate and miserable part of mankind" (1:9–10). Her condemnation of slavery continues for another page and a half. She is articulate, moral, intelligent; she denounces slavery in all of its forms and goes considerably beyond her father's reservations on the matter, for while he believes slavery is evil, he also insists it is an "inherited" evil now so entrenched as to be, perhaps, beyond cure. That prognosis is not good enough for Dorcasina. She refuses to accept "inheritance" as any adequate justification for perpetuating an immoral system, and the author obviously concurs with her judgment. But note the impossibly romantic solution Dorcasina devises for what she rightly sees as America's most serious problem. She will marry the Virginian (whom she styles Lysander) with the express purpose of convincing him, through his ardent love for her, that he has no choice—no wish—but to free his slaves. Love, she fondly imagines, should conquer all, even social injustice, and even on the largest social level: "Wrapt in the glow of enthusiasm," she envisions "his neighbors imitating his example, and others imitating them, till the spirit of justice and humanity should extend to the utmost limits of the United States, and all the blacks be emancipated from bondage, from New-Hampshire even to Georgia" (1:11). With such effusions from her protagonist, Tenney brilliantly captures the excesses of sentimental rhetoric. Yet the excess of romantic posturing that renders this solution ridiculous is surely no less suspect than the excess of social hypocrisy and injustice that requires it. Dorcasina, however, is not so naive as not to know that the first decisive action toward her envisioned emancipation of the slaves must be taken by her husband. She might be his prime mover, but his will still be the prime move. In short, Dorcasina grotesquely mirrors the status quo even as she questions it. But by subjugating all of her opinions to a notion of romanticism and domestic love, she would be, at one and the same time, both a secret revolutionary and a standard *feme covert*. Yet, one well might ask, what other alternatives has she? The only political solution Dorcasina can envision is a hopelessly romantic one—perhaps because hopeless romanticism decently obscures the fact that the very position from which she plans to act, the subservient domestic helpmeet, is itself a form of slavery.

The picaro adventures on the margins of social possibility; the picara either ends up ensconced in domesticity or, like Dorcasina, never really leaves it, which makes the female picaresque a fictional form fundamentally divided against itself. We have, on the one hand, extravagant escapist fantasies typically dependent upon a woman's cross-dressing (the male picaresque in drag) and, on the other, a woman's picaresque adventures as a mostly imagined escape that both counterbalances and weighs the public and private constraints under which her fantasy labors. Dorcasina is no Don Quixote, for the simple reason that even if he challenges only windmills, he still traverses the landscape he misreads and validates that misreading by his various misadventures. The carnivalesque elements in *Don Quixote*, borrowed largely from Rabelais, thus serve to question the official cultural and political hierarchies, in some ways to reverse them completely—which is precisely what also happens in *Modern Chivalry* or *Mr. Penrose, Seaman* when convention is turned topsy-turvy.[67] But in *Female Quixotism*, Dorcasina's excursions in her quixotic mental world do not trouble the status quo. Only after she awakens to see the "real" world does she begin to question such fundamental matters as the nature of matrimony or the nature of men. "I begin to think all men are alike," Dorcasina confides to her faithful womanservant, Betty, after she has been released from her romantic notions of life, "false, perfidious, and deceitful; and there is no confidence to be put in any of them" (2:201).

When Dorcasina finally sees how the rest of the world views her and how, using that view, Seymore intended also to use her and her money, she seeks refuge with her friend Harriot Stanly, now married to the same Captain Barry who earlier pretended to woo Dorcasina out of some twisted desire to show her what the "real" world was like. Coming to this domestic refuge, however, Dorcasina is surprised to encounter not the wedded bliss she had expected (and that she feared might contrast too painfully to her own lonely state) but sadness and disharmony. Dreams and delusions still. As the protagonist confesses to her now married friend, she had formerly thought that "in a happy union, all was transport, joy, and felicity; but in you I find a demonstration that the most agreeable connection is not unattended with cares and anxieties." The new Mrs. Barry must concur in that evaluation: "I have been married a twelvemonth, to the man whom of all the world I should have chosen. He is everything I wish him to be; and in the connection I have enjoyed great felicity. Yet, strange to tell, I have suffered more than I ever did before, in the whole course of my life" (2:207). As Dorcasina notes, the once "sprightly Harriot Stanly" has been "metamorphosed, by one year's matrimony, into a serious moralizer" (2:207) and a diminished version of her former self. This second realization parallels the first as a liberation from fantasy. "The spell is now broken," Dorcasina can proclaim, referring equally to the fictions of her novels and the fictions of her society, which were not, after all, that different from one another.

Almost triumphantly, Dorcasina takes control of her life and of the final words of the text. Only the end of the novel is in the first person. Her concluding letter to Harriot announces that she will spend the rest of her days in assisting others less fortunate than herself, in sewing, and in reading novels. She also informs Harriot, who has never read even one novel, that "I [still] read them with the same relish, the same enthusiasm as ever; but, instead of expecting to realize scenes and situations so charmingly portrayed, I only regret that such unallayed felicity is, in this life, unattainable" (2:212). Her life has allegorized her reading, just as the lives of those who do not read novels allegorizes the bleakness of a life without any imaginative escape (i.e., romantic fantasy or picaresque adventures). Given those alternatives, Dorcasina chooses fiction.

In a perceptive analysis of the romance as a genre and, more specifically, of Charlotte Lennox's *The Female Quixote*, Laurie Langbauer has recently argued that Lennox's book "associates the dangers of romance with sins of women, and through this association clinches its derision of the form. Romance's faults—lack of restraint, irrationality, and silliness—are also women's faults." As Langbauer also notes, this same connection was early drawn by Henry Fielding, who, in a review of Lennox's novel, observed that he preferred *The Female Quixote* to *Don Quixote* precisely because it was more plausible that a woman, not a man, would be ruled by romances:

> As we are to grant in both Performances, that the Head of a very sensible Person is entirely subverted by reading Romances, this Concession seems to me more easy to be granted in the Case of a young Lady than of an old Gentleman. . . . To say Truth, I make no Doubt but that most young Women . . . in the same Situation, and with the same Studies, would be able to make a large progress in the same Follies.[68]

Fielding's logic is as circular as it is androcentric. Women read silly books because women *are* silly or vice versa (it really does not matter). Cervantes missed the point in his classic; no man, surely, would really succumb to fiction's influence as "most young Women" are wont to do. In contrast, Tenney denies Dorcasina Everywoman status. Every woman who reads *Female Quixotism* is encouraged to see herself as different from what Dorcasina was, and, indeed, Dorcasina becomes different too. Furthermore, Tenney refuses to hang both the satire and the blame, as Fielding conveniently does, on the ostensible folly of women. Why, she wants to know, are women so susceptible to the fantasies of romance they encounter in novels? Maybe it is because the world outside of novels holds so little else for a capable, intelligent woman.

Female Quixotism runs counter to the male picaresque, to the sentimental romances affirming a patriarchal status quo, and also to another trend already under way in 1801 and one that became increasingly popular throughout the first half of the nineteenth century despite (or, perhaps, concomitant with) the highly restrictive legal and social conditions of women. I refer to the fad for female adventures starring women in their plots and almost always in their titles—*The Female Fishers, The Female Marine, The Female Robinson Crusoe, The Female Spy. A Domestic Tale, The Female Wanderer, The Female Spy; or, The Child of the Brigade*—even *The Female Land Pirate*. In contrast to these female picaresque fantasies, Tabitha Tenney's book provides a hard core of realism—and it does not paint a very pretty picture of women's lives. Dorcasina retreats to fiction at the end of her life because, first, her education has been so elementary that she simply cannot read anything more challenging than popular fiction and, second, because fiction itself is finally far more satisfactory than anything she has found in the world at large. She prefers, not unreasonably, a happy fantasy life to an unhappy actual one.

I WOULD HERE ADD a brief epilogue—an appropriately marginal allegory on the marginality of women's lives—to this discussion of the politics of the female picaresque. Although a best-selling novelist (and one of the best early American novelists), Tabitha Tenney remains virtually unknown as an individual. In the *History of Exeter*, her husband, Dr. Samuel Tenney, is accorded almost two pages of fulsome comment: "He was a man of fine presence, and of much dignity. His domestic and social relations were of the happiest character. He was universally esteemed and respected, and in his death, his townsmen felt that they had met with no ordinary loss." The novelist, in contrast, receives four lines: "Dr. Tenney's wife was Tabitha, daughter of Samuel Gilman, a highly accomplished lady. She was the author of two or more published works, the chief of which was *Female Quixotism* which had much popularity in its time, and went through several editions." The Tenney family history contains the same prescription—"wife of," "daughter of," "a highly accomplished lady"—and, ironically, so, too, does the history of the Gilman family. There are letters reproduced in the Gilman volume from Dr. Samuel Tenney to Tabitha's father, but they do not mention the daughter. In contrast, I know of only one letter by Tabitha, but it, too, is about Samuel Tenney. On October 25, 1823, she wrote the Honorable William Plumer, who was seeking information for his proposed biography of Dr. Tenney. "It would certainly be most gratifying," the wife observes, "to see some account of my late husband appear in the way which you propose." The letter reveals virtually nothing of Tabitha's own life or thoughts, but, then again, Mr. Plumer was not interested in those. The historical record here affirms the vision of women that Tenney criticized. Woman's place is as daughter or wife or mother; she passes unnoticed in the written record, except, of course, in novels.[69]

In only two sources have I found any record of Tabitha Gilman Tenney that goes beyond the usual and formulaic "highly accomplished lady" encountered in practically all dictionary entries on the author. One account is an amusingly idiosyncratic personal memoir, *A Few Reminiscences of My Exeter Life*, by Elizabeth Dow Leonard. Writing in 1878, Leonard particularly remembers the earlier "authoress" because novelists then "did not grow as now, plenty [*sic*] as blackberries, but were as hard to find as a real phoenix or one-horned unicorn." Novelty, however, did not assure esteem or even notice. As Leonard confesses: "I blush to say, with all my pride in the rich achievements of my native village, I never read [*Female Quixotism*]. . . . Those who did read it pronounced it superlatively silly, and [Tabitha Tenney] tried in after years to recall it without success." I have not uncovered elsewhere any evidence to corroborate this report of authorial regret, but, valid or not, Leonard's account constitutes a sad post-script to the long neglect of one of America's first best-selling novelists.[70]

The only other information on Tenney appears in the private record, not the public. I refer to a diary by Patty Rogers, which has never been published, a marvelously detailed account of the reading and romances of an eighteenth-century American young woman. The diarist, an expansive young woman who was apparently well known in the town of Exeter for both her volubility and her love of fiction, was one of Tabitha Gilman's contemporaries. The two, however, apparently, did not much care for one another. Patty found Tabby too reserved, but then, as Patty directly and indirectly records, others, including her beau (the preceptor William Woodbridge), found Patty too excitable. This opinion may also have been shared by Patty's second suitor (or would-be seducer: the issue is unclear), a former doctor in the Revolutionary army, the thirty-seven-year-old Samuel Tenney, who had apparently returned to Exeter with the dual intentions of marrying and entering politics.

The diary records in intimate detail Patty Roger's love for novels, how her various suitors "seduce" her with fiction, the way Woodbridge (she styles him Portius in her diary) eventually forsakes her for a girl of more sense and less "sensibility" ("He said some persons had too much sensibility!"). She also de-scribes how Dr. Tenney, her father's friend, begins to ply her with billets, poetry, and, above all, novels. On one occasion, he gallants both her and Tabby Gilman home. At another time (she has now renamed him Philamon) he takes "liberties" with her in a carriage, and later he takes "liberties" (the same ones? different?) on her doorstep ("You treated me ill," she reprimands him, "as if you thot me a bad girl—Nobody else treats me so ill"). And all the while he also publicly courts Tabitha Gilman, a sober, serious, quiet young woman, a year younger than Patty, and, the latter records, "a person peculiarly disagreeable to me—not from any injury she ever did me, but there is a Certain something, in her manner, with which I am ever difficulted." The older doctor, a former soldier in the Revolutionary War, denies that he favors Tabby and regularly flirts with Patty, who just as regularly sets down their exchanges in her diary, interweaving the sentimental plot of her small life with the plots of the various novels she reads (*History of the Human Heart, Ganganelli, A Sentimental Journey*, etc.). Of course, the ambitious doctor presently marries the more sensible Tabby, and, since Patty's diary ends here, we learn no more from her of her rival.[71]

With the arrival of the husband on the scene, the official record takes over. He was elected to Congress for three terms, and the couple lived, during his term of office, in Washington, D.C. They had no children. In 1801, a year after moving to Washington, Tabitha wrote *Female Quixotism*, a novel in which there is little mention of the world of masculine politics but that does feature Dorcasina Sheldon, a young woman who in personality, in voice and style, and in her passion for novels remarkably resembles Patty Rogers. In 1816, after Samuel's death, Mrs.

Tenney returned to Exeter, where Patty Rogers, yet unwed and now renowned for her sewing, her piety, and her charitable works, still resided. In her later years, Tabitha Tenney stopped writing, took up sewing, and was esteemed as well for the originality and intricacy of her needlework. There is no more to tell, and even this inconclusive account exists only in fragments, suggesting other stories that operate equally on levels of history and fiction: Is *Female Quixotism* a satire against the writer's old rival? Or did the author, married, thirty-nine years old, and childless when she published her novel, recognize a bond between herself and Patty that she may not have been willing to acknowledge in 1785, when Dr. Tenney played each woman's virtues off against the other's shortcomings? For even though Patty does seem to provide the inspiration for Dorcasina in *Female Quixotism*, we should also remember that the biblical name Dorcas is simply the Greek version of the Aramaic Tabitha (as we are specifically told in Acts 9:36), and, moreover, that biblical reference to the good, charitable Dorcas/Tabitha of Joppa whom Peter raised from the dead applies equally to the older character and the older author.[72]

The politics implicit in this possible conjoining of writer and rival transcends the fractious and almost exclusively masculine debate on what shape the new nation should take. It is the same politics that can be observed in the life, letters, and literary legacy of Tabitha and Patty. One imagines the two old women— Tabitha died in 1837 at the age of seventy-five and Patty in 1840 at seventy-nine—living on in Exeter, both esteemed by the community, each engaged in charitable works and spinning tales of her youth in the early years of the Republic while she also plied her needle. It is a world of women's lives as far removed from the world of *Modern Chivalry* or *The Algerine Captive* as from *The Female Review* or *The Female Land Pirate* but not that different from the final days of one Dorcasina Sheldon, who emerges, when viewed from the end of both her original and her author, as a most representative female picaresque hero.

Reading *The Algerine Captive*

The contrast between the scholarly attention devoted to Royall Tyler, as opposed to the pervasive neglect of Tabitha Gilman Tenney, could hardly be more marked. In an exemplary critical biography, G. Thomas Tanselle has meticulously examined Tyler's life and literary career. Tanselle has also resurrected and published in the *Harvard Library Bulletin* correspondence between Tyler and his publisher, Joseph Nancrede. There is also a more general assessment of Tyler in the widely available Twayne series. Moreover, primary materials for further study are available in the extensive Royall Tyler Collection at the Vermont Historical Society. The enterprising scholar can peruse correspondence between Tyler and other writers as well as publishers, relatives, and friends; can study typescripts (and some manuscripts) of Tyler's poems, plays, essays, and fiction. The diary and autobiography of the author's wife, Mary Palmer Tyler (which include invaluable insights into Tyler's working methods, his schedules, his opinions, and his literary and personal habits), can be studied, as can another memoir by Tyler's son. The social historian can trace Tyler's role in Shays's Rebellion as well as his various legal decisions as a Vermont Supreme Court judge in extant court records and state archives. In addition, Marius B. Péladeau has collected and edited, in one thick volume, *The Prose of Royall Tyler* (1972) and, in a somewhat smaller volume, *The Verse of Royall Tyler* (1968). The unfinished autobiographical novel *The Bay Boy* has recently been published; *The Contrast*, reprinted or excerpted in various anthologies of American literature of the early national period and in numerous general surveys of American literature, is widely available; and four of his lesser plays are currently in print. Finally, although *Female Quixotism* is available only on microfilm as part of the Early American Imprints (Evans) series, *The Algerine Captive; or, The Life and Adventures of Doctor Updike Underhill, Six Years a Prisoner Among the Algerines* (1797) can be read in both a facsimile reprint of the London edition of 1802 and also in a paperback "edited for the modern reader."[73]

Because the archive is so extensive, intentionality in Tyler's work can be assessed more easily than in most early American texts. Tyler's own reports on his life, juxtaposed with the reports of those who knew him, allow us to envision what he envisioned as the shape and purpose of his life—his own story of himself. To move from these different but not inconsistent portraits of the author to the fiction requires, obviously, a critical leap, but it is a leap that provides valuable glimpses into an early American writer's assumptions about the powers of narrative, about the role of fiction in the polis, and, finally, about the interrelationships between picaresque and political structures.

Even without this kind of background, however, one can make a number of judgments about Tyler's work. *The Algerine Captive*, for example, employs a different set of fictive rules and structuring principles from those of such picaresque fantasy tales as *Fortune's Foot-ball* or *The History of Constantius and Publchera*. Nor does it satirize such fantasies in the manner of *Female Quixotism*, nor is it a shape-shifting and ultimately unfinished political allegory like *Modern Chivalry*. On the contrary, Tyler's novel is, by the standards of the early American picaresque, remarkably cohesive. Even its narrative indefiniteness and inherent contradictions are largely resolved through the way in which the whole tale is rendered in the first person and by a narrator fumbling his way through America and stumbling toward his own meaning of America. Whereas *Modern Chivalry* embodies an inconsistent narrative voice double-talking its competing modes toward a nonconclusion in which plot and perspective remain determinedly indeterminate, *The Algerine Captive* ends by resolving the narrator's irresolution, which has all along been the main subject of the text. For Updike Underhill's fitful voyage in search of the "real" America is also, like all classical quests, a voyage of self-discovery.

As even his name suggests, Updike Underhill is a seriocomic figure in a comically serious work. The comedy in volume 1 results largely from the high seriousness with which the protagonist views himself. It is a view unsustained by any attendant action. Yet Updike grows in the course of the novel precisely because he flees from virtually every challenge he encounters. Instead of heroically facing adversaries or resolving crises, his characteristic modus operandi is first to try to talk his way out of any immediate impasse and then to beat a rapid retreat to safer ground—a different locale, a different occupation, a different persona—to whatever seems safely distant from the former threat. Like the ruling Federalists, he assumes that one can resolve conflict by evading it or suppressing its public articulation. But such solutions—on the psychological, the sociological, and the political level—necessarily portend further and fuller disasters.

For Underhill, that deferred disaster finally comes when he naively accepts a position as a doctor on a slave ship (as if he can maintain his abolitionist sentiments while serving slavery's masters). Serving slavery soon leads to his own six-year enslavement among the Algerines. Yet his captivity, paradoxically but in keeping with the ironic reversals of the book, sets him free. He is at last freed from his own earlier elitist assumptions about the "barbaric" Americans; from his own inability to change either his life or his society (escape, after all, is not social action); and, ultimately, from his picaresque restlessness. The burden of this freedom is that he must now devote himself to *improving* the American society that he earlier saw as meriting only condemnation, derision, and evasion. While volume 1 of the novel provides a consistent critique of the excesses of American society—and especially the masses, the mob—volume 2 shows that even the charlatanism, gullibility, avarice, cupidity, and stupidity that Underhill encounters in volume 1 are preferable to the despotism of Algiers and the hateful institution of slavery upon which that too-well-ordered society is based. Democracy has its drawbacks, certainly. But the alternatives—oligarchy, suppression of dissent, and slavery—are far worse evils than (on the most specific level) unruly schoolchildren, than (on the most general level) a populace willing to be duped by quacks and hypocrites or too prone to criticize the president.

BEFORE EXAMINING THE novel in any detail, however, I will first briefly assess Tyler's political and literary career. The former is particularly interesting, for, like another early picaresque novelist, Tyler was not only a lawyer and a judge but also played a key role in one of America's postrevolutionary insurrections. Like Hugh Henry Brackenridge during the Whiskey Rebellion in western Pennsylvania, Tyler served as a mediator during Shay's Rebellion in rural Massachusetts. Also, as even a few of the stories that Tyler himself endlessly repeated to all auditors throughout his long life should make clear, for both men the divisively polarized party factions of the 1790s did not always accord with their particular viewpoints on what political program might best serve the emerging polis or what form that polis should assume. Confronting armed revolutionaries, both writers, one a Federalist and one a Republican, argued for a discourse less desperate than rebellion. Each also attempted to resolve apparently irreconcilable dissent by resorting to obviously novelistic devices. Both assumed duplicitous personae, acknowledged the appeal of antagonistic and seemingly antithetical political positions, and played out safer versions of the inimical conflict that they sought to forestall. Both, in brief, sought to alter the history of their time by calculatingly fictionalizing both history and the time.

Tyler's retrospective version of the role he played in putting down Shays's Rebellion—calming a band of rebels with the wit and wisdom of his own oratory—left out (as all narratives leave out) some of the more interesting aspects of his story. More specifically, Tyler himself was in flight when he became involved in Shay's Rebellion. All of Boston, it seemed, was talking about "Nabby" Adams (daughter of John and Abigail) turning down, largely at her father's instigation, a rather wild, young, Harvard-educated lawyer and accepting instead a proposal from her father's private secretary, Colonel William Stephens Smith. Writing many years later, Mary Tyler noted that this romantic disappointment, coupled with the debts Royall had incurred while trying to build up his farm, sent him into a deep depression, during which time he also let his legal practice slide and neglected his other business ventures (a pattern that continued, intermittently, to the end of his life).[74] But as if wars were made to solve the problems of the young, in January 1787 Daniel Shays gathered forces to attack the federal arsenal at Springfield, Massachusetts; General Benjamin Lincoln put out a call for men willing to defend the arsenal; and the twenty-nine-year-old Tyler, eager to leave Boston and try adventure, joined Lincoln's forces as a major and an aide-de-camp.[75]

Tyler, as an old man increasingly suffering the effects of illness and poverty, especially enjoyed recounting how he had helped put down Shays's Rebellion. "You all remember with what zest he used to relate his adventures during that expedition when he took a meetinghouse full of Shays's men," Mary Tyler recalled in the autobiography she addressed to her children and grandchildren. She also tells how he took particular pride not in his martial but in his verbal prowess:

> He found their arms stacked outside the door, while they were within, probably listening to some Yankee Cromwell, who excited them to resist oppression and unjust rulers. Your father walked in followed by a file of soldiers, and ascending the pulpit steps with his wonted elegance spoke so forcibly on the other side that they finally agreed to lay down their arms and return home, soon after which Shays was apprehended and the rebellion quelled. How much good his speech did I know not, but I do know that,

whatever his theme, he very seldom spoke in vain, sometimes perhaps "making the worse appear the better reason"; but few were the audience who could resist his eloquence.[76]

"Grandmother Tyler" here elides several events to imply a causal relationship between her late husband's power of positive speaking and the cessation of political dissent in Massachusetts. But according to the son's redaction of his father's legend, Tyler's eloquence did not end with the men in the meetinghouse persuaded to surrender their arms and to pay obeisance to federal law and order. In this longer version, Shays himself managed to slip across the border into Vermont, a territory not yet part of the Union, and adverse to any dictates of authority, especially those emanating from the notoriously autocratic Governor Bowdoin of Massachusetts. There, surely, the rebellious Daniel Shays could find sanctuary. It was a crisis that again called for Royall Tyler, who, armed only with his notable verbal skills, finely honed at Harvard, called upon Governor Chittenden of Vermont, dined with him, discoursed, and, by daybreak, had convinced him that official political asylum should not be granted to the rebels or their leader.[77] Shays, however, still escaped, probably abetted by Chittenden's own men. Nevertheless, General Lincoln wrote Tyler praising him for his role in the affair: "You have done a great deal; we cannot command success; to deserve it has the same merit." But perhaps equally important for the career of a future novelist, Tyler's travels took him to new places, encounters with new people, and he seemed unusually sensitive to both, as is clear even in the official report (with its barely concealed admonition) delivered before the Massachusetts legislature. "Proclamations," he insisted, "can never Coerce the General Sentiment of the People," especially since "the Bulk of the People in Vermont are for affording protection to the Rebels."[78] One cannot stifle the passions of dissent and discontent by proclamations or official decrees.

"My good Friends," Tyler wrote the Palmers (Mary's parents, with whom he had previously boarded) on February 17, 1787, at the height of the rebellion, "how I wish you could look in upon me, and see your old friend the center, the mainspring of movements, that he once thought would have crazed his brain— this minute, haranguing the governor and Council, and House of Representatives; the next, driving 40 miles into the State of New York, at the head of a party to apprehend Shays: back again in 20 hours: now, closing the passes to Canada: next, writing order to the frontiers."[79] Tyler was also soon writing more than orders to the frontier. In April 1787, *The Contrast*, which he claimed he had completed in only three weeks, was produced professionally at the John Street Theatre in New York City. Tyler's escapades in America's backwoods were transformed into comedy. The various New England yeomen he encountered were conjoined into a fictional Yankee, Jonathan, one of the most popular figures to come out of early American literature and the prototype for hundreds of subsequent stage and fictional Yankees. The play was immensely successful. When it was published in 1790, George Washington's name headed the list of its subscribers. On a more homely level, Mary Tyler wrote of her uncle who "had not taste for reading; his heart was all in his business." Although he had read nothing except the newspapers until the appearance of *The Contrast*, "he found the Yankee character, Jonathan, [the play's] great charm," and thereafter, "in the evenings . . . he seldom sat down with us, without bringing out *The Contrast*, of which he had a printed copy, reading it aloud, till his wife would almost scold, saying she should know it all by heart."[80]

Much of the work's popularity may also have derived from the way in which it disposed of insurrections, and especially Shays's Rebellion. Jonathan early vows, "I did think the sturgeons [insurgents] were right," but is persuaded by his master, the Colonel Manly, to embrace a more moderate position:

> Colonel said that it was a burning shame for the true blue Bunker Hill sons of liberty who had fought Governor Hutchinson, Lord North, and the Devil, to have any hand in kicking up a cursed dust against a government which we had, every mother's son of us, a hand in making.

Again the word is mightier than the weapon or is at least given that potency in the world of words that comprises Tyler's drama. Manly's patriotic argument can convert Jonathan to safe, sane political opinions and presumably might serve just as well for any radicals who happened to take in the play (although, it must be admitted, there were probably few Shaysites among the well-to-do New Yorkers who could afford $.75 or $1 for a night at the theater).[81] Politics is here again conceived as discourse and discourse as power. As Tyler would demonstrate again and even more conclusively in *The Algerine Captive*, a political agenda can entail considerably more than a speaker's election and can include matters that weigh heavily on the individual lives of those who do not pay enough attention to the words with which they have been wooed.

It is important to emphasize that Tyler's Federalism was temperate and that he did not, in doctrinaire fashion, attribute major human faults and foibles only to members of the other political party. For example, Tyler, along with Joseph Dennie, contributed for ten years the popular Colon and Spondee columns to various New England newspapers, and these popular columns were certainly known for their Federalism. In a letter to Tyler, Dennie observed that he was welcomed on his travels for his pro–Federalist sentiments: "The Aristocracy were pleased that the satire of Colon & Spondee was levelled against the foes of Federalism. Such is the state of parties here that this apparently [*sic*] trivial circumstance has procured me a host of friends, not lip service friends but such as will render me pecuniary."[82] Yet the Colon and Spondee columns (Tyler, apparently, wrote as Spondee) could be surprisingly apolitical, as the first advertisement for the series, in the *Eagle* of July 1794, makes abundantly clear:

Salutatory and Valedictory Orations, Syllogistic and Forensic Disputations and Dialogues among the living and the dead—Theses and Masters' Questions, Latin, Greek,
Hebrew, Syriac, Arabic and the ancient Coptic, neatly modified into Dialogues, Orations
& c. on the shortest notice . . . Dead Languages for Living Drones . . . Anagrams,
Acrostics, Anacreontics; Chronograms, Epigrams, Hudibrastics, & Panegyrics; Rebuses,
Charades, Puns and Conundrums, by the *gross*, or *single dozen.* . . . Adventures, Paragraphs, Letters from Correspondents, Country Seats for Rural Members of Congress,
provided for Editors of newspapers—with Accidental Deaths, Battles, Bloody Murders,
Premature News, Tempests, Thunder and Lightning, and Hail-Stones, of all dimensions, adapted to the Season. . . . Serious Cautions against Whoredom, Drunkenness, &
c. and other coarse Wrapping-Paper, *gratis*, to those who buy the smallest article.[83]

The columns, among the most popular in early America, were beloved as much
for their wit as for their Federalism.

Tyler himself had few of the aristocratic aspirations that often characterized
what we might term the "high Federalists." The son of a wealthy politician and
businessman, he had managed to spend his own inheritance at an early age. He
had to support himself, knew the meaning of a day's work, and knew, too, at
various times in his life, penury. Although far better educated than most of his
associates in Vermont, he prided himself on his lack of pretension. "Those around
us," Royall purportedly told Mary, "will like you all the better for not appearing
in any way above them, and I need not tell you that it is love and not mere
outward circumstances that will constitute happiness."[84] It was advice not really
needed; Mary Palmer Tyler also suffered little from aristocratic pretensions. She,
too, was born into a wealthy family, but her father had lost virtually all of the
family money while she was still a young girl. As the daughter of one of Boston's
first families, all "cultured and gentle," she had, in a matter of weeks, become
subject to a "thousand mortifications." The women of the family had to "wean
themselves of the idea that they must be ladies." Mary's schooling ceased immediately; an older brother, at age fourteen, left a private academy for the harsher
education of the sea (to slightly alter Melville, a merchant ship became his Yale
and his Harvard); her parents sought to take in boarders and to find teaching
jobs, which was all that their genteel upbringing had prepared them to do.[85]

Tyler and his wife apparently lived quite happily in Guilford, Vermont (even
though it was well known as a bastion of Republican, even insurrectionist sentiment), and then, later, in Brattleboro, Vermont, both of which were isolated in
those early days when not even a stagecoach penetrated the Green Mountains.
By all reports, even when a state supreme court justice, Tyler lived modestly, no
differently from his neighbors. It was, early and late, a married life far removed
from his own youth as the son of a wealthy Boston merchant or as a somewhat
wild (he used the word "dissipated") scholar at Harvard in 1772, when students
were still ranked according to the social status and wealth of their families rather

than (as would subsequently be the case) by a more egalitarian alphabetical order.[86]

It is also clear that despite the declamations against aristocrats filling the Republican press during the 1790s, the Tylers were highly regarded, even loved, by their Republican neighbors. They were particularly appreciated for the education and culture (Mary, too, was an author) they brought to a far corner of New England. As the editor for the *Brattleboro Chronicler* fulsomely wrote about their arrival: "Their first coming to the high hill overlooking the whole town seems to us as the morning dawn of intellectual life in this region or the beginning of an Elizabethan age in Brattleboro."[87] Even though he was a Federalist at the time of the bitter 1800 and 1801 national and state elections, during which opposing party affiliations sometimes severed friendships and divided families, Tyler was still appointed to the state supreme court by a Republican legislature. On the court, he became close friends with the Republican chief justice, Jonathan Robinson, a friendship that would last a lifetime. Tyler himself was subsequently appointed chief justice after the 1807 elections in which the Republicans totally dominated the state. Ironically, in 1813, when the Federalists gained control of the legislature, they removed all the justices, including Tyler, replacing them with Federalists more committed to the party's hard-line political vision. But then Tyler had always boasted that he made "just" decisions, not necessarily "politically correct" ones.

Both as a lawyer and, later, a judge, Tyler traveled all over the Vermont backcountry, especially when he served on the state supreme court, which was required by law to sit for one term every year in each of the state's fourteen counties.[88] Traveling extensively and regularly, staying in local homes and inns, Tyler increasingly came to appreciate the virtues of the yeomen he had satirized (albeit affectionately) in his early play. That appreciation was itself more than repaid. After his removal from the state supreme court, with his own law practice defunct, his finances in total disarray, himself in the depths of one of his severe depressions and suffering from a debilitating and disfiguring face cancer that was also slowly rendering him blind and that required him to be heavily drugged with laudanum, the judge and his wife were kept from starvation mainly through the aid of the common citizens of Vermont. (The only other family income derived from what Mrs. Tyler could eke out by her needle.) The townspeople still appreciated the coming of the Tylers to such a remote region and expressed that appreciation with sustaining gifts, which Mary Tyler movingly recorded in her diary: "Madam Boot sent us a fine goose & turkey—more providential supplies"; or "Mrs. Fessenden by her kind and sympathetic conduct drew tears from my full heart—May God bless her here & hereafter—this evening she sent me coffee—sugar & butter & rice."[89]

Near the end of his life, in pain and poverty, Tyler returned to *The Algerine Captive*, revising it ostensibly for re-publication but also to divert his mind from his suffering. In those same final years, he also began an autobiographical novel, *The Bay Boy*, which repeats large portions of *The Algerine Captive*. His wife would often read to him from the earlier novel, and he would work on revising it or would rework portions of it into his evolving autobiographical piece, writing slowly on a slate because he could no longer hold a pen or see his marks upon a page. Then, while her husband slept, often in the daze of opium that mercifully relieved his pain, his wife would transcribe what he had written. Perhaps he hoped that the revised novel might reap the financial reward never produced by the original edition, the kind of remuneration other American fiction writers were beginning to enjoy by the 1820s. As Mary Tyler wrote to her daughter, Amelia, a year and a half before her husband's death: "This writing occupies my time so intensely that it cuts off the little resource I had in my needle—but I have strong hope if we can rub along and get something finished for the press it may be of greater advantage than anything I could earn in any other way." But Mary Tyler did not imagine that publication would bring an end to all their poverty, as is indicated by her realistic appraisal of a publisher's plan to issue most profitably the revised edition of *The Algerine Captive*. She writes to her daughter:

> [He] said there was now such a rage especially in [Europe?] for American literature, that his intention was when the first volume was finished to send it to his correspondents in London—and have an Edition printed there at the Same time it was printing in New York—and to secure the Copy right in both countrys and he had no doubt of a rapid sale—as for terms—he says there were three ways of proceeding—one was for the author to print at his own expense—another to let some responsible bookseller print at certain Shares of profit. . . . and the other, for the author to sell the copy right for fourteen years for Such Sum as he could get—this last is the only way we could do—as you know the Destruction of the poor is their poverty—but it is most probable even this way it will command a few hundred dollars—which will be a blessing.[90]

Tyler died the following year, leaving unpublished three new plays as well as the unfinished revisions on *The Algerine Captive* and the unfinished *The Bay Boy*. His epitaph noted only his career as a Vermont judge and said nothing at all of the literary works that had provided early fame but no relief from final poverty.

Ironically, even as Tyler lay dying, James Fenimore Cooper, the author who most capitalized on the "rage for American literature," could, in 1822, praise his predecessor's fiction. Yet the terms of Cooper's praise virtually prophesied that anything Tyler might finally produce would be no Cooperesque best-seller. Much had changed between 1797, when Tyler wrote his novel, and 1822, when Cooper sought to retrieve it from obscurity with precisely those props of praise ("a forgotten masterpiece," "a strangely neglected work") required by texts that can no longer stand quite on their own. Cooper praises "Mr. Tyler's forgotten, and we fear, lost narrative of the Algerine Captive . . . which relate[s] to times long past. Any future collector of our national tales, would do well to snatch [it] from oblivion, and to give [it] that place among the memorials of other days, which is due to the early and authentic historians of a country."[91] As Cooper's tribute implies, Tyler had become a relic, a cultural monument to literature past (and passed), without ever having been a professional writer. As noted in an earlier chapter, even at his most vigorous and famous, Tyler could not support himself by his pen; in his final days, he could only pathetically pretend to be a professional author. His life and death starkly image the plight of the novelist in the early Republic.

Tyler outlived his books, but he also lived long enough to see that many of the crucial ideological disputes of the 1790s were simply rendered irrelevant by another generation's different concerns or at best remembered almost with nostalgia as that new generation faced its own problems—modernization, industrialization, sectionalism, and even the dawnings of American imperialism. The author died in the summer of 1826, a summer that saw hundreds of celebrations all over America to commemorate the fiftieth anniversary of the signing of the Declaration of Independence. It was also a summer during which two of America's most respected Founding Fathers passed away, mourned by the populace. Thomas Jefferson and John Adams, two old friends, turned bitter rivals, turned friends again in old age. "You and I," Adams had written to Jefferson in 1813, "ought not to die, before we have explained ourselves to each other." And they died, many letters later, each on the same portentous day: July 4, 1826.[92]

Writing at a time of divisive national politics, when political tempers boiled, the novelist somehow remained remarkably aloof from partisan bickering. It would be difficult, reading *The Algerine Captive*, to discern its author's Federalist affiliation from the text itself—as difficult, perhaps, as it is to perceive Brackenridge's Republicanism in *Modern Chivalry*. Each novel eschews narrow party politics to address larger and more general political issues. Slavery, for example, the principal political target of *The Algerine Captive*, had champions, or at least apologists, on both sides of the official party line. Furthermore, personal pettiness, avarice, prejudice, and ignorance infected the ranks of Republican and Federalist alike, rich man and poor, Northerner and Southerner. Or Updike Underhill, the narrator of *The Algerine Captive*, often sounds, as he berates American provincialism, very much like Washington or Hamilton or Adams at their most vituperative and most elitist. Yet Underhill, too, with all his aristocratic pretensions and plebeian origins, is also a subject of the novel's satire. Finally, the real brunt of Tyler's satire is not the wrong party but tyranny itself. The novel fictionally opposes the tyranny of history, the tyranny of religion, the tyranny of law, the tyranny of ignorance and cupidity and affectation; and, most of all and as becomes increasingly clear in volume 2, the tyranny of slavery, upon which the economies of Algeria and the United States *both* were based.

IN PRAISING TYLER, JAMES Fenimore Cooper not only defined him as a historian but defined the term as well:

> We say the historians—we do not mean to rank the writers of [fictional] tales, among the recorders of statutes, and battles, and party chronicles; but among those true historians which Dr. Moore says, are wanting, to give us just notions of what manner of men the ancient Greeks were, in their domestic affections, and retired deportment; and with whom Fielding classes himself, nearly in these words: "Those dignified authors who produce what are called true histories, are indeed writers of fictions, while I am a true historian, a describer of society as it exists, and of men as they are."[93]

Cooper, following Fielding, reverses the usual prescriptions for fiction and history. History is a fiction and the novelist is the true historian. In *The Algerine Captive*, Tyler confuses the issues further by claiming his fiction is factual and by pretending that he writes, valiantly, against the mass popularity of fiction. Fiction masquerading as fact and railing against fiction: it is a complicated narrative game Tyler here plays but one that he sustains throughout the first portion of his novel and that, I would suggest, is a key to the large political purpose of his picaresque tale.[94]

The novel begins with a genealogy that, by the very act of placing the narrator in history, effectively displaces much of the history that the tale occupies. As Don L. Cook observes, Updike's account of his origins conveniently disregards likely detail or careful chronology—and all for the sake of a good story.[95] The "honored ancestor," Captain Underhill, acting as a go-between whereby Queen Elizabeth and the earl of Leicester seek to advance different affairs of the heart and of the state, gives us a version of history as Harlequin romance. The text, moreover, admits as much. The crucial scene, the private interview between the Captain and the Queen that conduces to the premature "decease of the Earl of Leicester," has "never yet received the sober sanction of the historian," and only a "traditional family anecdote" vouches for the truth of the account. On the American side, too, the commonly accepted historical record is undermined when Updike Underhill tells the story of how his Puritan forebear was accused of "adultery of the heart" and banished from Boston. The ostensible sin of the pharmakos victim compromises the ostensible sanctity of those who find him guilty.

The descendant Underhill amasses impressive documentation to clear the name of his impuned ancestor. But disputing one suspicion highlights another, which is to say that the enterprise of the character mirrors a larger enterprise of the author. The novelist and the narrator both suspect that the historical record, the archive, lies—or, rather, serves mostly its own view of itself. Note, for example, how the narrator's account calls the very sequences of history into question by calculated anachronistic juxtapositions:

The writers of those times differ as to the particular offense for which he was punished. Some say that it was for holding the antinomian tenets of the celebrated Ann [*sic*] Hutchinson; others say that the charge against him was for saying, *That the government at Boston were as zealous as the scribes and pharisees, and as Paul before his conversion.* The best account I have been able to collect is that at the time when the zeal of our worthy forefathers burned hottest against heretics and sectaries, when good Roger Williams, who settled Providence, the pious Wheelwright, and others were banished, he, with about sixty other imprudent persons who did not believe in the then popular arguments of fines, imprisonment, disfranchisement, confiscation, banishments, and halters for the conversion of infidels, supposed that the Christian faith, which had spread so wonderfully in its infancy when the sword of civil power was drawn against it, in that age, surrounded by numerous proselites, needed not the same sword unsheathed in its favor. These mistaken people signed a remonstrance against the violent proceedings which were the order of that day. . . . Some of the remonstrants recanted, some were fined, some were disfranchised, and others, among whom was Captain Underhill, were banished. (P. 34)

It is hard to miss the parallels between the repressive politics of the times in which Captain Underhill lived and the equally constrained contemporary world of 1797, in which Tyler's readers first perused *The Algerine Captive*. Congress was already framing the Alien and Sedition Acts, the newspapers were filled, pro and con, with talk of new ways to require "fines, imprisonment, disfranchisement, confiscation, banishments" and other punishments for those who protested too vociferously against authority. But if the magistrates could be wrong in Captain Underhill's case, Tyler implicitly suggests, then cannot magistrates be wrong again? What is the morality of legislating extreme morality? Notice, in this context, the supreme silliness, from the point of view of the reader of 1797, of the offense for which the captain was banished from his community:

At a certain lecture in Boston, instead of noting the referred texts in his Bible, according to the profitable custom of the times, this gallant soldier had fixed his eyes steadfastly, and perhaps inordinately, upon one Mistress Miriam Wilbore; who it seems was, at that very time, herself in the breach of the spirit of an existing law which forbade women to appear in public with uncovered arms and necks, by appearing at the same lecture with a pair of wanton open-worked gloves, slit at the thumbs and fingers for the conveniency of taking snuff. (P. 36)

The incident—its causes, its persecution, its history—becomes a *reductio ad absurdum* of the whole process of enforcing proper behavior so much at issue in 1797.

The ancestral account of the injustices Captain John Updike endured goes on (with a continuing relevance for the "now" of 1797) to undermine the authority not just of Underhill's accusers but of those who have kept the official record.

"It is said by some authors that he was charged with the heinous crime of adultery," the narrator observes. John Winthrop, Cotton Mather, and Jeremy Belknap are all implicated in perpetrating the "error." Deliberately? Does historiography compound the abuses and offenses of history? The "unwary reader" is warned that official history, like official dictates, is mostly an expression of the scotomas and stigmatisms of the official vision of the time. "The rigid discipline of our fathers of that era often construed actions, expressions, and sometimes thoughts into crimes" (p. 35). In compensation, the text proliferates with competing versions of the text—public and signed accusations, testimonies, and "Brother Underhill's" own account, "indorsed" and fortuitously preserved, "pasted on the back of an old Indian deed." The narrator, "according to the beneficial mode of modern historians," decides to "transcribe literally" this document for the reader, and thus the fiction itself enacts the process whereby any account, however fictional, can be incorporated into the official record. Equally to the point, Captain Underhill concludes his epistle: "I came from England because I did not like the lords bishops, but I have yet to praye to be delivered from the lords bretherenne" (pp. 39–40). From lords bishops to lords bretherenne to lord president?

The descendant Underhill, after quoting his ancestor's justifying epistle, coyly observes: "It is with great reluctance I am induced to publish this letter which appears to reflect upon the justice of the proceedings of our forefathers. I would rather, like the sons of Noah, go backwards and cast a garment over our fathers' nakedness; but the impartiality of a historian, and the natural solicitude to wipe the stains from the memory of my honored ancestor, will excuse me to the candid" (p. 40). So, which will it be, disinterested history or apologetic genealogy? Or is there, finally, any discernable difference between the two? The fictionalizing of history in this novel postulates the fictionality of history and suggests that ostensibly definitive judgments—"adultery of the heart" or "Jacobinism"—are simply the strained conventions of certain readings that valorize only those readings. The conventions of history are, moreover, the conventions of morality. History, in the novel, gives us the devolution of moral edict to ridiculous charge and harsh sentence (banishment for being taken in by the fenestrations of a glove). Tyler thus early establishes the picaresque's characteristic self-refuting moral vision and also something more. *All* moral vision, the text seems to suggest, can be self-serving and self-refuting; perspective constantly changes; prejudice is next to humanness. The danger lies in attempting to elevate prejudice into law, desired morality into enduring edict, and history into a self-confirming typology of only the revealed truths that the proponents of that history would themselves ask all others to contemplate.[96]

Clearly, the same novel could not be narrated by the fictional grandson of, say, Cotton Mather, as opposed to the putative descendant of a Puritan miscreant (miscreant, of course, only according to the official history). The picaresque as a form requires a protagonist whose place, whose genealogy, is marginal and at least partly in question. Updike Underhill is just such a character. Like his ancestor, he is no paragon of virtue. Something of a ne'er-do-well, something of an overeducated bumpkin, and something of a snob with little basis for his defensive pretensions to superiority, Underhill serves as a kind of low-status Everyman, an Everyman particularly recognizable in late-eighteenth-century America. His story—the ambiguous background, the fitful beginnings, the small hypocrisies of his convictions, the moral blind spots but also his essential good will and energy—allegorizes his country's unofficial present, just as Captain Underhill's story allegorizes certain aspects of its unofficial past.

Yet very little of Tyler's tale is clear, and that, I would suggest, is part and parcel of his allegory. Where is truth in the story of Captain Underhill? Where is truth in the story of Updike? If there is truth at all, it is "truth" with a small *t*—contextual, multivalent, never fixed and final, and not at all prepared to support a superstructure of received history or manifest destiny. Consider, for example, the odd auguries that attend the protagonist's birth on the otherwise insignificant day of July 16, 1762. His mother dreams that her son will be "beset by Indians," who will play football with his head. The dream is interpreted to mean that the youngster is "born to be the sport of fortune and that he would one day suffer among savages" (p. 43). Both premonitions, of course, come true, which serves to raise certain ontological questions. "The learned reader will smile contemptuously, perhaps, upon my mentioning dreams in this enlightened age" (p. 44). The smiling "learned reader" is here quite wrong and might do well to question the questioning prompted by learning. Updike, too, will find that a little learning is a dangerous thing. As the narrator suggests, "It was the error of the times of monkish ignorance, to believe everything. It may possibly be the error of the present day, to credit nothing" (p. 44). An earlier scepticism about history does not preclude a different scepticism about scepticism.

The status of truth—revealed truth, dreams, history, learning—becomes a major preoccupation of *The Algerine Captive* and supplies one connecting thread in a novel otherwise rambling, episodic, and, in a word, picaresque. Underhill, as the retrospective narrator of his life and his six years' captivity in Algiers, must somehow wrestle with the whole notion of what truths he has to tell. More specifically, just what is his story, and how can he best present it? Yet the whole first section of the novel, from the preface through to chapter 5, is mostly about how *not* to make story. The fiction examines such questions as what should be discounted in any story and what might be included despite its seeming irrationality. The result is, to use a term coined by Linda Hutcheon, "historiographic metafiction," fiction that self-consciously explores the whole process of making any historical fiction.[97] Not until chapter 5 do we encounter the kind of narrative beginning normally expected in the first pages of an autobiographical account: "In my childhood I was sent, as is customary, to a woman's school in the summer and to a man's in the winter season, and made great progress in such learning as my preceptors dealt in" (p. 45). The fact that the novel, for some five chapters, has been questioning history, truth, and learning adds further weight to the satirical implications of the phrase "such learning as my preceptors dealt in."

We soon learn that his preceptors dealt very little in learning at all. Reading, as did virtually all schoolchildren of the early Republic, from Dilworth's spelling book, young Updike learned mostly to recite "as loud as I could speak, without regard to emphasis or stops" (p. 45). But Tyler's satire is not limited to the pedagogical shortcomings of early American education. The local minister, a Harvard graduate who "prided himself on the strength of his own lungs," makes an annual inspection visit to the district school and is impressed by the boy's bellowing forth his lessons, impressed enough to convince Updike's father to "put Updike to learning." By waiting at table or otherwise serving the more well-to-do students, Updike might be able to earn his way through Harvard, just as his minister did before him: "I rubbed through and am now what I am," the minister avers, while the reader wonders precisely what he is.

The first minister is countered but not canceled out by a second one. A Boston clergyman who happens to be traveling through New Hampshire encounters Updike's father and informs him that all a boy learns at college is Greek, a subject "entirely useless." This minister insists that "learning . . . has its fashions, and, like other fashions of this world, they pass away" (p. 48), an assessment with which the narrator will later agree: "The little advantage this deceased language has since been to me has often caused me sorely to regret the misspense of time in acquiring it" (p. 50). Neither does Updike's classical learning profit his family. At one point the young scholar decides to imitate a passage from the *Georgics* and kills "a fat heifer of my father's, upon which the family depended for their winter's beef, covered it with green boughs, and laid it in the shade to putrify, in order to raise a swarm of bees, after the manner of Virgil" (p. 50). Seeing in this failed attempt at beekeeping that learning has unfitted his son for a farmer's life, the father accedes to the mother's request that the boy continue his "career of learning"—anything, one imagines, to get rid of him.

A classical education, the distinguishing mark of America's gentry, hardly distinguishes young Mr. Underhill, who, for that matter, was not much distinguished before he obtained his education either. As in the incident with the heifer, regularly Tyler's satire runs both ways, condemning, evenhandedly, both the affectations of the high and the limitations of the low.[98] Having parodied, for example, a pedantic minister and his deleterious influence on an untutored common man, Tyler immediately turns his satirical gaze upon other such "average Americans" to show their shortcomings as well. But especially in the protagonist the flaws of both the high and the low conjoin. Consider here how Updike, unsuited for farming by learning, contracts to serve as a preceptor in a neighboring village. He naively envisions himself as a godlike guardian of the minds of youth, a living monument to education with "my scholars seated in awful silence around me, my arm chair, and my birchen sceptre of authority" (p. 51). It hardly works out that way. When the young master first enters his new school, he is met with some sixty students, ranging from small toddlers to hulking lads of eighteen, each at a different level of learning, and all clamoring at once for "master's" attention. His training for Harvard hardly trained him for that chaotic scene.

The protagonist's misadventures as a schoolteacher soon bring his career to an end but do so in a fashion that validates the premises about the fictionality of history with which the novel began. One day an overgrown and surly student seats himself in the master's chair before the fire and refuses to move when Underhill arrives on the scene. "Father finds wood, and not you," the churlish boy observes, whereupon Underhill immediately revises his previously asserted philosophical opposition to corporal punishment and smacks the youth with a ruler. Soon after the student's father appears at the schoolhouse bearing a whip and threatening to thrash the teacher should he ever lay hands on his poor innocent boy again. "The next day, it was reported all over town what a cruel man the master was. 'Poor Jotham came into school half frozen and near fainting; master had been sitting a whole hour by the warm fire; when he begged him to let him warm himself a little, the master rose in a rage and cut open his head with the tongs, and his life was despaired of' " (p. 53). When a short time later the boys burn down the schoolhouse, Updike again is blamed, but this time for "want of proper government." Now he is much too lax as a disciplinarian. "The beating of Jotham was forgotten and a thousand stories of my want of proper spirit circulated" (pp. 54–55). The now missing building constitutes the best proof of those stories. Underhill is judged officially, albeit unfairly, a failure and must seek his fortune in other endeavors. But his immediate change in prospects does not, to say the least, perturb him: "I am sometimes led to believe that my emancipation from real slavery in Algiers did not afford me sincerer joy than I experienced at that moment" (p. 55).

This early episode (along with the protagonist's final reaction) is paradigmatic. The plot progresses by escape as Underhill regularly retreats from one scene of failure to another and just as regularly learns little along the way. Admittedly, the school was impossible, but so was the ludicrous master. Although we are never shown Underhill in the act of teaching (perhaps because none ever took place), his method of pedagogical address is amply indicated by his discourse in such unlikely establishments as the local tavern. There he enters into a conversation about racehorses by offering up his own "descant upon Xanthus, the immortal courser of Achilles" (p. 53), to the befuddlement of his audience. Or at a quilting bee with the ladies, he discovers "a happy opportunity to introduce Andromache, the wife of the great Hector, at her loom, and Penelope, the faithful wife of Ulysses, weaving her seven years web" (p. 53). His classical allusions elicit only "a stupid stare until I mentioned the long time the queen of Ulysses was weaving." Then "a smart young woman observed that she supposed Miss Penelope's yarn was rotted in whitening, that made her so long; and then she told a tedious story of a piece of cotton and linen she had herself woven under the same circumstances" (p. 53). But the prize for tediousness is immediately claimed by the smart young man, who caps the woman's story by declaiming "forty lines of Greek, from the Odessey," and then passing on, with no stop or mercy, to "a dissertation on the *caesura*" (p. 53).

Tyler's pattern here—satirizing with the same incident the learned ignorance of his protagonist and the untutored ignorance of the populace—continues throughout volume 1. Updike and the people he encounters are not so different after all, but only the older retrospective narrator, not the young untested man, recognizes that fact. For just as the yeomen he encounters brandish their willful ignorance as if it were some badge of honor, so, too, does Underhill brandish his spurious learning, and he also is unwilling to change. Throughout volume 1, he seems singularly incapable of learning the lessons his own experience teaches and so retreats from failure to failure. For example, after abandoning his career as a pedagogue, at least partly because of his own inability to speak the same language as those whom he ostensibly serves, Updike turns to medicine and apprentices himself to one of the most celebrated physicians in early America. From the wise and "celebrated Dr. Moyes," he learns something of the doctor's science but nothing of his humanity and "could not help being astonished that a man of [Dr. Moyes's] acknowledged learning should not sometimes quote Greek" (p. 65). When subsequently he goes to study with the esteemed Dr. Kittredge, he is equally surprised to find that "excepting when he was with his pupils or men of science, I never heard him use a technical term." He possessed "all the essence, without the parade of learning" (p. 76), and what fun was that? Incidentally, Underhill himself fails when he attempts to put into practice the method for which these famed doctors are esteemed, for his patients judge him precisely as he first judged Dr. Moyes. Only after he spatters his practice with snippets of Tully, Virgil, and Lily (the one occasion on which his classical learning serves him) is he deemed "the most learned because the most unintelligible" (p. 85). Patients now come in greater number, but all Underhill amasses is promises of payments (empty recompense for empty words), so he decides to go south to warmer climes and, surely, fuller purses. That last expectation soon proves to be merely another of the delusions that can promote his wandering but not his rise.

Penniless in the South, as unsuccessful at doctoring there as he had been in New England, Underhill contemplates teaching again but soon decides that he would prefer "laboring with the slaves on their plantation [to] sustaining the slavery and contempt of a school" (p. 97). His overblown rhetoric marks more his opposition to schoolmastering than to slavery, and he resolves his present impasse by hiring on as a surgeon on a slave ship. The irony of his administering to slaves (so that they can be sold profitably back in America) despite his professed hatred of the institution and the further irony of slavery being practiced in a country ostensibly founded on a declaration of all men's equality are both underlined by the names of the ships on which Underhill and his countrymen practice their trade. In a real sense, aboard, first, the incongruously named *Freedom* and then on the equally misnamed *Sympathy*, Underhill leaves America to come home to it, and what at first promised to be an excursion into the wider world of Europe and Africa, crossing seas and encountering other peoples and other ways, soon proves to be anything but that liberating experience.

Just as *The Algerine Captive* seems about ready to take off in the direction of such picaresque fantasy novels as *Fortune's Foot-ball* or *The History of Constantius and Pulchera*, it switches to a second form that is structurally and ideologically inimical to the picaresque. As Tanselle has aptly noted, Tyler produces an oddly hybrid novel when he grafts a captivity tale onto a picaresque trunk.[99] But it is a captivity tale with a powerful political message, not simply a sensationalized account of a white adventurer living among exotic captors. Instead of adventure on the high seas, we have a gruesomely detailed rendering of the barbarities of a slave ship, the details borrowed largely from slave narratives and most obviously from the account by Olaudah Equiano, first published in London in 1789 and reprinted in New York in 1791.[100] Aboard the *Sympathy*, Underhill witnesses from the perspective of one of the captors the deprivations that Equiano documented from the perspective of one of the captured. "I execrated myself for even the involuntary part [Involuntary? Who has enslaved *him?*] I bore in this execrable traffic. I thought of my native land and blushed" (p. 109). Underhill's previous and persistent metaphorising of his own service as slavery now rings false indeed. The horrors of the voyage seem finally to penetrate the erstwhile invulnerable obtuseness of this picaro, and, for the first time, he can empathize with someone totally unlike himself. He imagines "the peaceful husbandman dragged from his native farm; the fond husband torn from the embraces of his beloved wife; the mother, from her babes; the tender child, from the arms of its parent; and all the tender, endearing ties of natural and social affection rended by the hand of avaricious violence" (pp. 108–9). When the captain inquires how many slaves Underhill would like to purchase, he "rejected [his] privilege with horror, and declared [he] would sooner suffer servitude than purchase a slave" (p. 109).

This is the second time in the novel he has made such an offer, and this time the fates take him at his word. His ship is attacked by an Algerian ship, the *Rover*, that in name mocks the previous pattern of Underhill's life and, in effect, ends it. Seized himself "by the hand of avaricious violence," the innocent picaro ends his wanderings to experience firsthand just what slavery is all about. Furthermore, his forced servitude follows appropriately from his own involvement in the slave trade. Recognizing the poetic justice of his punishment, he finally begins to take some responsibility for his past actions and to realize that, in a republic, one's tolerance of injustice in its most extreme form, slavery, is synonymous with one's complicity. Both expiation and reform (private and public) are in order:

I have deplored my conduct with tears of anguish; and I pray to a merciful God, the common parent of the great family of the universe, who hath made of one flesh and one blood all nations of the earth, that the miseries, the insults, and cruel woundings I afterwards received when a slave myself may expiate for the inhumanity I was necessitated to exercise towards these, MY BRETHREN OF THE HUMAN RACE. (P. 110)

At the end of volume 1, Tyler foregrounds the political import of this picaresque tale. As the volume concludes, Underhill, captured by Algerians, makes a promise which he will later keep by writing his own story:

Grant me . . . once more to taste the freedom of my native country, and every moment of my life shall be dedicated to preaching against this detestable commerce. I will fly to our fellow citizens in the southern states; I will, on my knees, conjure them, in the name of humanity, to abolish a traffic which causes it to bleed in every pore. If they are deaf to the pleadings of nature, I will conjure them, for the sake of consistency, to cease to deprive their fellow creatures of that freedom which their writers, their orators, representatives, senators, and even their constitutions of government have declared to be the unalienable birthright of man. (P. 118)

Again, *The Algerine Captive* seems broken-backed in its odd conjoining of apparently inconsistent parts. The picaresque novel that verges into a captivity tale does so to register the full horror of slavery. To that end the travelogue of the protagonist's disconnected life can gradually carry him to a confluence with a different traveling, the forced voyage of the captured Africans being conducted to the slave markets in the land of the free. And then a different ship can carry him back to, literally, where they came from, and, figuratively, where they were going to. With that captivity accomplished, however, the novel proceeds to lapse into a travelogue again, a travelogue that seems far more conventional than was the account of Underhill's early excursions through America, perhaps because Tyler himself had never seen Algiers and had, in effect, plagiarized his captivity tale from several popular Algerine captivity narratives of the day. Obviously, he hoped to exploit the then-current national preoccupation with the outrages perpetrated on Americans by Barbary pirates to expose worse outrages perpetrated by Americans on Africans. It is a worthy objective but, as almost every contemporaneous reviewer and contemporary critic has noted, volume 2 is "much inferior" to volume 1.[101] volume 2 mostly reprises, without much plot or perspective, the strange ways and religion of the Algerines.[102]

Yet one cannot simply dismiss the rambling and often repetitious second half of the narrative, for it is here that the political implications of the whole novel coalesce, and, more to the point, Tyler here shows how much one's perception of any country—America or Algiers—depends mostly upon the perspective from which one views. In volume 1, the callow Underhill had no problem distinguishing his own superiority from the patent and manifest inferiority of the mob. But once he joins the ranks of the unprivileged, he radically revaluates the hierarchies that he earlier upheld:

> The higher his rank in society, the further is man removed from nature. Grandeur draws a circle round the great and often excludes from them the finer feelings of the heart. The wretched are all of one family and ever regard each other as brethren. Among the slaves of my new master, I was received with pity and treated with a tenderness bordering upon fraternal affection. They could not indeed speak my language, and I was ignorant of theirs; but, by dividing the scanty meal, composing my couch of straw, and alleviating my more rugged labors, they spoke that universal language of benevolence which needs no linguist to interpret. (P. 126)

The same man who despised his fellow Americans because they did not speak Greek can now comprehend the "universal language of benevolence." Among his fellow captives he finds not a single "man of any rank, family, or fortune" (p. 127)—none of the noble enslaved who populate typical narratives of romantic captivity—yet he finds men and women of dignity and merit, of honesty and integrity, of courage and charity. Under the harshest of conditions, he meets the oppressed of different races, nations, and religions, and, a captive himself, he discovers, for the first time in his life, a sense of community and finally learns the one language he really needs to know.

Underhill's transformation initially occurs on an emotional level, one that has nothing to do with learning or status. But his captivity also forces him to reexamine his intellectual assumptions as well. Certainly the most interesting (and controversial) of Underhill's revelations in volume 2 occurs when the captive engages in a philosophical and theological argument with his captor. Attempting to convert Underhill, the Mollah challenges him to a debate on the relative worth of Christianity and Islam. "A wise man," the Mollah insists, sounding more like Locke than a Mahometan priest, "adheres not to his religion merely because it was that of his ancestors. He will examine the creeds of other nations, compare them with his own, and hold fast that which is right" (p. 139). When Underhill consents to subject his own Christianity to this rationalist comparative test, the Mollah's arguments are not easily answered:

> My friend, you surely have . . . read the writings of your own historians. The history of the Christian church is a detail of bloody massacre: from the institution of the Christian thundering legion, under Constantine the Great, to the expulsion of the Moors out of Spain by the ferocious inquisition, or the dragooning of the Huguenots from France, under Louis the Great. The Mussulmen never yet forced a man to adopt their faith. . . . We read in the book of Zuni that the souls of true believers are bound up in one fragrant bundle of eternal love. We leave it to the Christians of the West Indies, and Christians of your southern plantations, to baptize the unfortunate African into your faith, and then use your brother Christians as brutes of the desert. (P. 142)

Once more Underhill is "abashed" for his country. He cannot at all answer the Mollah, and, after five days of such failure, he "resumed [his] slave's attire and sought safety in [his] former servitude" (p. 143).

The diction here—safety in servitude—is potent. In the manner of other early American picaresque novels, *The Algerine Captive* seems singularly ambivalent about its own Christian principles, and Tyler's contemporaries were quick to note this wavering. "Read 'Algerine Captive,' " the painter and critic William Dunlap noted in his diary. "The authors zeal has made him scurrilous in respect to Thos Paine, and yet in the statement he makes of Mahometanism, he appears rather to favour the Musselman." More publicly, a writer for London's *Monthly Review* noted that "in the dialogue with the Mollah, the author too feebly defends that religion which he professes to revere," and the reviewer for the *Monthly Anthology and Boston Review* similarly expressed "apprehension" over the "conversation between Updike and the Mollah," since "the author has so decidedly given the Mollah the best of the argument, that the adherence of Updike to Christianity seems the effect rather of obstinacy than of conviction. We enter our solemn protest against this cowardly mode of attacking revelation."[103] Ironically, Tyler was criticized for showing an open-minded attitude toward religion in a novel that begins by condemning those who criticized Captain John Underhill's open-minded attitudes.

Although Tyler retrospectively defended himself and his novel against those charges by insisting that his novel advocated neither "infidelity or even scepticism" but aimed, simply, at dispelling the "vulgar prejudices against Islamism," I would suggest that his first reviewers correctly surmised the subversiveness of his plot.[104] There are more similarities between Tyler's Algiers and America than most Americans in the 1790s would have cared to admit. The class, religious, political, and racial hierarchies in Algiers simply extend and exaggerate the same hierarchies dividing the American political and social scene. In each country, Underhill finds greed, deceit, quackery, and superstition. And most obviously, Algerians abducting Americans and forcing them to serve as slaves merely reverses the usual direction of the trade. The institution is the same, the heinousness of the activity is the same, only the peoples and the continents are switched. But with one proviso: The "barbarians" of the Barbary Coast are more civilized in their practice. As the Mollah points out, the Algerines do not convert their captives and then keep them enslaved, as is regularly done in the "land of the free." Algiers thus becomes a distorted mirror version of America. Or, more accurately, it becomes the mirror version that especially shows up American distortions.

For Underhill, to travel is to see different things, but, more important, to sojourn for six years in Algiers is to see things differently. The protagonist learns much from his captivity, and what he finally knows juxtaposed against what he previously did not know serves to produce the singularly complex and surprisingly humane satiric vision through which the novel is narrated. One angle of that vision can note and denounce the various frauds and failures whom Updike early encounters, such as the hard-swearing, slave-beating Southern clergyman or the Northern minister who opposes all "human learning as carnal and devilish" (p. 54). But another angle sees that a failed, pompous young pedant is hardly the measure of all that he thinks he perceives. The example of others such as "the celebrated Doctor Moyes, who, though blind, delivered a lecture upon optics and delineated the properties of light and shade to the Bostonians" (p. 63), contrasts unfavorably to young Updike's abilities as both propounder and perceiver.

Happily, the Updike Underhill who returns home is not the same man who earlier sailed away. He is older, wiser, more able to accept pluralism in society and even in religion. He is ready to be more settled, as indicated by his promise to become a "useful physician" (as opposed to his previous doctoring both on the slave ship and before it), and to become also a "good father, and a worthy FEDERAL citizen."

The "federalism" here recommended is open-minded, pluralistic, democratic, and utterly opposed to oligarchy or autocracy, to one people's dominating over another. The young protagonist revels in his picaresque adventures, even though they mostly proceed from or to failure. The somewhat more mature protagonist, while captive in Algiers, tends to romanticize the America in which he can then no longer live. The older narrator's vision—expanded by his captivity and oppression—infuses the entire novel with a classic eighteenth-century form of humanitarianism; in Raymond Williams's phrase, a "passionate insistence on care and sympathy, based on an implied standard of plain, virtuous and responsible living."[105]

Tyler's final solution to the problems of American democracy, which he satirized in volume 1 and then unequivocally condemned in volume 2, is ultimately not political in any systemic sense but returns us—individual readers—back to the republican values of individual responsibility, individual conscience, and individual action within and for the good of the commonwealth. Like the sentimental novel, which provided the nation's single most telling critique of patriarchy without offering specific agendas for eliminating institutionalized sexual discrimination, the picaresque novel pointed out what was rotten in the American polis but stopped short of outlining a project of political change. The early American novel carved out its literary territory in the here-and-now of the contemporary American social and political scene and commented upon and criticized that scene, but left the solution of these problems up to the individual reader— the indeterminacy of the solution as basic to the form as the incisiveness of its critique. In this respect, The Algerine Captive is thoroughly representative. The text, written essentially to keep an earlier promise—"every moment of my life shall be dedicated to preaching against this detestable commerce" of slavery—is both product and proof of Underhill's awakened consciousness and conscience and is intended to effect the same process in the reader. But it is up to the reader to implement the political message implicit in that development and made explicit by the end of volume 2: "For to no nation besides the United States can that ancient saying be more emphatically applied; BY UNITING WE STAND, BY DIVIDING WE FALL" (p. 224). The pedant and the untutored; the Northerner and the Southerner; the Federalist and the Republican; the urbanite and the country yeoman; the rich and the poor; most specifically, the master and the slave, black and white; even, perhaps, men and women—all must be included, for, without unity, without equality, then the Mollah, after all, was right.

ALTHOUGH I HAVE EXAMINED seven copies of the first (1797) edition of *The Algerine Captive* (a substantial portion of the surviving volumes from the original edition of one thousand copies), none offers up any significant evidence as to how the book was actually read by early American readers or just who its readers were. But one anecdote, related to her children by Mary Palmer Tyler, provides a fitting epilogue to this chapter and gives us a delightful account of a real writer and reader corroborating on the production of an early American novel. This anecdote is all the more appealing in that it is the only one I know that intimates, in telling detail, the various assumptions in the new Republic about the appropriate audience of fiction, the role of the reader, and the status value of fictional "truth":

> Your father finished "The Algerine Captive" and, by way of trying, like Moliere, the worth of the work, he was in the habit of reading it, as he finished the chapters, to an old woman who lived with us as maid of all work; she was a woman who had seen better days and was quite intelligent. She had imbibed the common prejudices against the "horrid Algerines" and felt greatly interested about Dr. Updike Underhill; had heard of people of that name in Rhode Island, and wondered if he ever got home, and understanding from your father's answer that he had, "And he has got your honor to write his life and adventures?" Upon receiving what she took to be an affirmative, "Well! I do hope he will come here while I stay; do you think he will?" "It is quite doubtful," said your father. "Oh, I do hope he will; but you will let me hear you read what you write, I know." "Certainly." And, of course, every evening after her work was done, she would put on a clean white apron and her best cap, and come to see if he had any ready to read to her, and was greatly disappointed if he had not. She evidently believed it all true, and years afterwards I saw her . . . [and] she asked us seriously if Dr. Underhill ever came to visit us.[106]

There is a curious relationship here of master and maid, author and reader. Who, it might well be asked, is serving whom? Dressed in her clean apron and best cap, the maid is the ideal reader—ever ready, once her work is done, to enter into the fiction. The author refuses to clarify the status of the text, its fictionality, while, all the time, measuring the success of his fiction by his maid/reader's honest reaction to the false truth of what he reads to her. Mrs. Tyler, writing retrospectively to preserve the anecdote for posterity, further confuses the differences between fact and fiction, story and the story of that story. We have here more than just a metaphor of authority—the author beguiling the reader through the medium of text. For Tyler's role as employer whose household is managed in part by the labor of the maid who is also his first, primary, and most immediate audience and, as well, the consumer and ultimately the purchaser/employer of *his* artistic labors emphasizes the interdependence of author and reader, writing and reading, text and performance. The maid might well be a stand-in for Tyler's ideal, implied reader—just as the author himself is a stand-in for Updike Underhill, the guest who never comes to dinner.

8 Early American Gothic: The Limits of Individualism

> From the time when the predatory spirit, which led the northern Barbarians to ravage the south of Europe, had subsided, and given place to its natural offspring, in the establishment of feudal monarchy, the history of this quarter of the world begins to assume a consistent shape; and it offers itself to our contemplation, as relative to the spirit of nations under three successive aspects. These are the spirit of Hierarchy, the spirit of Chivalry, and the spirit of Commerce. Out of these different materials the genius of the government has forged instruments of oppression almost equally destructive. It has never failed to cloud the minds of the nation with some kind of superstition, conformable to the temper of the times. In one age it is the superstition of religion, in another the superstition of honour, in another the superstition of public credit.
> —Joel Barlow, *Advice to the Privileged Orders* (1792–94)

> When it shall be said in any country in the world, my poor are happy; neither ignorance nor distress is to be found among them; my jails are empty of prisoners, my streets of beggars; the aged are not in want, the taxes are not oppressive; the rational world is my friend, because I am the friend of its happiness: when these things can be said, then may that country boast of its constitution and its government.
> —Thomas Paine, *The Rights of Man* (1791–92)

Class Consciousness in a "Classless" Society

The humor and the title of Royall Tyler's popular play *The Contrast* both derive from the sustained juxtaposition of innocent American values with urbane but corrupt European ones. That contrast is, in effect, an early American variation of what Raymond Williams has schematized in English literature as *The Country and the City*. In Tyler's play Colonel Henry Manly (consistent with his name) is early portrayed as a representative American man—honest, direct, and forthright. He is compared to the more dubiously named Billy Dimple, who has been to Europe, where he has squandered his inheritance in the pursuit of fashion and European sophistication. This second character quotes Chesterfield and copies the forms of gentility but has little concern for the substance of morality. That same opposition is also played out in a minor key. Manly's country servant, Jonathan, is, at first, tempted by luxury, but he remains essentially a good, earnest, solid, and stolid Yankee, while Billy's servant, Jessamy, who is foppish and irresponsible, is a more openly materialistic and misogynistic parody of his master, Dimple. The unfolding play then complicates these contrasts, showing that Dimple is hardly the sophisticate he pretends to be and that Manly, more ambiguously, might not be all that he first seems either. He is, after all, a prig; his American patriotism is a self-parody; his speech, like the campaign slogans of the era, is too full of itself. "His conversation," his sister Charlotte aptly notes, "is like a rich, old-fashioned brocade,—it will stand alone."

Tyler can safely compromise the opposition between honest (but priggish) Manly and corrupt (but harmless) Dimple on which the play first turns. *The Contrast*, after all, is drawing room comedy, a form that typically proves its urbanity (like a *New Yorker* cartoon) by gently mocking even the social norms that underlie its comedy. But Tyler does little with the other opposition that supports these two players in their contrasts, the master/servant relationship also basic to the play. Both Manly and Dimple depend upon the labor of their servants, and, at the same time, each labors to instruct his servant in his own prejudices and predilections. The country versus the city, the American versus the European dichotomies come under scrutiny in the plot, but the master/servant relationship is a given, unquestioned and unquestionable.

Gender assumptions, as much as class assumptions, are also posited as natural in this play. Maria Van Rough is the traditional heroine who serves as both the plot's catalyst and prize. The locus for the contrast between Dimple and Manly, she is, in compliance with her father's materialistic wishes, betrothed to the former, but she is in love with the latter. She does not approve of Dimple's recently acquired European pretensions; her father is displeased by Manly's more limited prospects: "Money makes the mare go; keep your eye upon the main chance, Mary."[1] Only near the end of the play, with the revelation that Dimple intends to marry the homely, but rich, Letitia while making Manly's beautiful sister, Charlotte, his mistress, does Van Rough relent and allow his daughter to marry the man of her choice. This reversal, however, only confirms the play's superstructure of values. Old Van Rough finally discovers that Dimple has lost his fortune, so the daughter still weds the more well-to-do of the two men, the one who, happily, has been her choice all along. Her virtue is rewarded by a proper match; his status by a proper mate. The outcome of the play—and its implicit connections between gender and class—would be quite different had Maria, say, contracted a passion for the lowly Jonathan. Now *that* would be a contrast.

That resolution simply would not happen, except, perhaps, as part of some convoluted comic plot device that would itself have to be set right by the end of the play (as in *A Midsummer Night's Dream*, with its temporary aberrations that are possible only under the cloak of magic and nightfall). *The Contrast* affirms a class structure, rich and poor, master and man, and, concomitantly, demarcates the limits and extent of class through the "circulation of women," Claude Lévi-

Strauss's famous phrase for the universal (he insisted) social "exchange" of women that expresses and solidifies the infrastructure of a given society.[2]

The Contrast can be seen as a critique of capitalistically inspired mercantile marriage, yet one can readily detect in this play the same type of limited social criticism that Williams documents in that large body of English literature that seemingly opposes the values of the city to those of the country:

> If what was seen in the town could not be approved, because it made evident and repellent the decisive relations in which men actually lived, the remedy was never a visitor's morality of plain living and high thinking, or a babble of green fields. It was a change of social relationships and of essential morality. And it was precisely at this point that the "town and country" fiction served: to promote superficial comparisons and to prevent real ones.[3]

In much that same fashion, the preoccupation with the Manly/Jonathan versus Dimple/Jessamy contrast conveniently obscures the fundamental contrast operating on either side of the conjoining (but potentially destabilizing) slash. As Williams shows at length in *The Country and the City*, the whole dichotomy needs careful scrutiny. It is simply too easy to posit, in *The Contrast*, a division between "good old people" (i.e., traditional Americans, stalwart and virtuous) and "bad new people" (those perverted by a current materialism, licentiousness, and aristocratic affectation) and to imply thereby that only the present is plagued by these vices and is plagued only by its fall from the principles of a purer past.

Williams in his first chapter, an "escalator" through pastoral literature, brilliantly demonstrates that virtually every generation has posited a previous Golden Age, a time of "simpler" values, pure and uncorrupted, when noble leaders ("true gentlemen"/Founding Fathers) did not concern themselves with pomp and circumstance but benevolently dispensed their own power in the form of wisdom. This idyll of the perfect pastoral past serves to highlight the evils of the far-from-perfect present—materialism, greed, vain desire. But Williams insists that there is something pernicious behind this simplistic division of the world into country and city, past and present, traditional and modern, a social dichotomy and a longing nostalgia that can be traced at least as far back as Hesiod. The danger of such contrast is that it short-circuits any systemic critique of one's *own* society ("We may be corrupt now, but our heritage and our founding principles are pure") while also obscuring the privations experienced by the unprivileged of the past. Depoliticizing the past in turn depoliticizes the present. "We have heard this sad song for many centuries," Williams laments, "a seductive song turning protest into retrospect, until we die of time."[4]

From this point of view, it should come as no surprise that the early theatrical success of *The Contrast* derived not from Manly but from Jonathan, the comic country Yankee who went on to become a stock figure in American literature and folk culture. One of the most famous actors of the early Republic, Thomas Wignell, played the Jonathan role, and, in 1790 when the play was published in book form, it was Thomas Wignell's name—not Royall Tyler's—that appeared on the title page. The actor stands in for the author; the servant stands in for the man. Yet these are no egalitarian gestures. The original frontispiece affirms the play's status as drawing room comedy. The engraving by Peter Rushton Maverick depicts the postures, clothing, wigs, and interior design of the Anglo-American gentry.[5] For this gentry (illustrated in the text and present in the audience), Jonathan is a figure shrouded in nostalgia—the simple yeoman, impressionable but ultimately harmless. He is a higher class's wish-fulfillment version of the underling. We laugh with Jonathan—but only because we know that he is powerless to do very much should we decide that we are really laughing at him. The play that takes his part does not privilege his role.

The Contrast was the most popular play in early America. It satirized the bourgeoisie's pretensions to aristocratic manners without seriously challenging the class structure of American society. As I have shown, Tyler's critique of his society extends considerably farther in *The Algerine Captive*, and that, it seems to me, is the point. The same author writes differently for two different genres. The two genres differently address different audiences. The theater, more than any other form, was associated with America's upper classes. "Ladies and gentlemen are requested to desire their servants, to take up and set down, with their horses [*sic*] heads toward the East-river, to avoid confusion," ran an advertisement in the *New York Packet* published at the same time as *The Contrast*. "Also, as soon as they are seated, to order their servants out of the boxes."[6] In contrast, the early novel's growing audience included especially those marginally middle-class Americans most eagerly clamoring for prosperity, independence, and the commodities that could not be produced down on the farm (aspirations for which Dimple, for all his ersatz Europeanism, serves as a *reductio ad absurdum*). Novels were more affordable than plays and could be shared. They could even be read aloud to an audience that did not have to pay for the entertainment.

PARTICULARLY IN THE Gothic novels to be discussed in this chapter, previously unprivileged heroes and heroines compete, even for their survival, against a whole host of designing aristocrats. The admittedly ludicrous settings (castles in Connecticut) of some of these novels still effectively mark their contrast between an old enforced and artificial order on the one hand and an emerging individualism on the other. However, this genre's social reference is not limited to abuses and hierarchies of the past. As I will subsequently show in more detail, the Gothic can subtly challenge the status quo of so-called traditional or premodern society while also criticizing the inherent problems of so-called modern society, especially progressive philosophical or economic theories (liberalism, deism, rationalism) based on a notion of human perfectability. The struggling individual has, in the

Gothic world, a remarkable potential for good but an equally powerful motivation (and opportunity) for corruption. Mind is infinitely susceptible to benevolence and fellow feeling and simultaneously prey to superstition, delusion, or its own deviousness. Moreover, class privilege only extends the abuses of individuals by giving them the authority to assert their will over others. The Gothic, in short, focuses on the systemic possibilities and problems of postrevolutionary American society and of the postrevolutionary self in action in that society. The comic tone that characterized most picaresque novels yields to melodrama and sensationalism, and the sentimental novel's challenge to the social structure begins to take on philosophical and even metaphysical dimensions.

Any consideration of class in the literature of the early Republic is complicated, it might here be noted, by the well-established tradition of denying even the existence of the phenomenon. In a recent, laudatory review of Sean Wilentz's *Chants Democratic*, a landmark study of class consciousness in early America, Charles G. Steffen (himself a notable contributor to our knowledge of class in the new Republic) wryly observes: "For Americans, historians included, 'class' is a fighting word."[7] Other historians (literary, social, economic, and labor) have also "battered away" at the adage that, in a nutshell, "there is no class in America."[8] Yet the received notion of America's past still predominately posits a stable, egalitarian, consensual, and essentially classless early American society. Even in highly sophisticated historical analyses, as Joyce Appleby has shown in her survey of recent historiographic trends, there is often an implicit, unexamined nostalgia for premodern *communitas* and a corollary notion that changes wrought in the structure of society, governance, and economics toward the end of the eighteenth century forever destroyed a previously stable (or at least quiescent) state. Nostalgic accounts suggest that the postrevolutionary years were characterized by divisiveness (as if no one in the new Republic was exhilarated by the prospect for change, openness) and that this debilitating turmoil stemmed largely from the forces of modernization, industrialization, and capitalism creating social stratification and class conflict (as if none of these differences existed before the war).[9]

Gary B. Nash, one of the best analysts of early American class structures, has argued that the persistent myth of a classless prerevolutionary American society has been abstracted primarily from the literature of the time and that many studies based upon literature have tended to recapitulate a sentimentalized, idealistic vision of a vanished, egalitarian America.[10] As one case in point, Nash cites the oft-reprinted "What is an American?" chapter of Michel-Guillaume-Jean de Crèvecoeur's *Letters from an American Farmer* (1782), which, in particularly fulsome terms, insists:

[When an] enlightened Englishman . . . first lands on this continent, he must greatly rejoice that he lived at a time to see this fair country discovered and settled; he must necessarily feel a share of national pride, when he views the chain of settlements which embellishes these extended shores. When he says to himself, this is the work of my countrymen, who, when convulsed by factions, afflicted by a variety of miseries and want, restless and impatient, took refuge here. . . . Here he beholds fair cities, substantial villages, extensive fields, an immense country filled with decent houses, good roads, orchards, meadows, and bridges, where an hundred years ago all was wild, woody, and uncultivated! . . . He is arrived on a new continent; a modern society offers itself to his contemplation, different from what he had hitherto seen. It is not composed, as in Europe, of great lords who possess every thing, and of a herd of people who have nothing. Here are no aristocratical families, no courts, no kings, no bishops, no ecclesiastical dominion, no invisible power giving to a few a very visible one, no great manufacturers employing thousands, no great refinements of luxury. The rich and the poor are not so far removed from each other as they are in Europe.[11]

Who would not want to believe Crèvecoeur's vision of America? Nor is that simply a rhetorical question, since, as I have shown in previous chapters, there were many Americans (women, blacks, various immigrant and religious groups, the indigent and the reformers who championed their cause) who *could* not believe it. For many, however, the nostalgic myth of a once idyllic nation served as the countering image to the bleak portrait of America featured in much of the literature of disenchantment of the 1790s, such as the "Influence of the American Revolution" (1789) in which Dr. Benjamin Rush diagnosed the "contagion" of rebellion spreading through a decidedly postlapsarian America. Note the tone of privileged authority with which Rush writes of that which is destroying or perhaps has already fatally destroyed a far better American past:

The termination of the war by the peace in 1783, did not terminate the American Revolution. The minds of the citizens of the United States were wholly unprepared for their new situation. The excess of the passion for liberty, inflamed by the successful issue of the war, produced, in many people, opinions and conduct which could not be removed by reason nor restrained by government. . . . The extensive influence which these opinions had upon the understandings, passions and morals of the citizens of the United States, constituted a species of insanity, which I shall take the liberty of distinguishing by the name *Anarchia*.

Dr. Rush described the prevalence of "anarchia" as a kind of collective "insanity" and traced out the etiology of that social disease. In his view, an "ardor in trade and speculation," along with the new government's issuing of a "fallacious . . . amount of the paper money," had "unhinged the judgment, deposed the moral faculty, and filled the imagination, in many people, with airy and impracticable schemes of wealth."[12]

Dr. Rush's denunciation of the greedy minions of commodity capitalism and materialism strangely mirrors some modern Marxist idealizations of premodern society (an idealization that Raymond Williams pointedly questions). It is, as Rush's example illustrates, a rhetoric that can too easily lend itself, even when employed by Marxist historians, to an essentially conservative historiography. Following Rush or Crèvecoeur, modern historians regularly criticize the ennui of postrevolutionary America by contrast with a mythological classless prerevolutionary society characterized by social stability, harmony, traditional values, and community. As Appleby sardonically observes of this enterprise:

> The normative quality given continuity and persistence then leads to an interpretation of change as the promoter of tensions, fear, anxiety, and guilt. Indeed, the whole range of pathological terms that figure in our histories comes from investing traditional society with a set of warm and wonderful features perpetually at risk. Twenty-three actions for the recovery of debt in a ten-year period, if twice that of an earlier decade, become poignant testimony to the disintegration of social solidarity or reflections of the unbearable tensions rending a once organic community.[13]

I have briefly considered the implicit "country versus city" assumptions of some recent historiography because I find many of the same concerns in the early American novel. That is, the novels are often subversive in the sense that they frequently pit a struggling, poor, or middle-class hero or heroine against a far more powerful adversary, one who often claims a traditional authoritarian role in the society at large and over the protagonist's life. Throwing off the shackles of authority, in this scenario, takes on many of the features of classical liberalism of the Adam Smith variety. The desired goal is personal freedom, economic independence, and a substantial measure of self-determination. These are underdog dramas replete with graphic imagery designed to invest the individual's physical and emotional struggle with metaphysical dimensions. Yet, at the same time, liberalism, in many of these early novels, is the bugaboo (just as it is in much current historiography). The liberal ideology of individualism and the Smithian ideal of personal freedom lead not to the liberal end of a more perfect society but to perversions of the self and corruption of the society. For the villain, too, sees himself as a proponent of individualism and a champion of personal freedom—*his* freedom. Even when ostensibly espousing radical causes (as a number of villains do), he seeks mostly to justify his own avarice and thirst for power. The problem, then, is not that the modern world radically deviates from the traditional but that it reflects, like a funhouse mirror, many of its basic assumptions in grotesque new ways. Liberalism, far from mandating a revolutionary restructuring of society, merely opens the way for a different social hegemony with its own possibilities for oppression and exploitation. The villain, whether aristocrat or self-made man, succeeds only because, on some level, his society privileges his place through its laws and, as Paine insisted, its constitution. Democracy may permit new groups of people to reach the top, but there still *is* a top—and a bottom. Even if all men are created equal, they do not long remain so.

The class conflict as well as the conflicting visions of America as a class society found in the early Gothic novels attest, I would suggest, to the complexity of the social moment in which these fictions were written, as well as to the fact that the writers were attuned to subtle changes, changes that we, employing the perspicacious vision of hindsight, have not yet fully gauged. With remarkable acuity many of the early novelists *sensed* both the promise and the problems inherent in the ideology of individualism and even anticipated the devolution of individual self-interest and the emerging contradictions of bourgeois ideology schematized by Georg Lukács:

> As a necessary result of capitalism's anarchy of production, the bourgeois class, when struggling for power and when first in power, could have but one ideology: that of individual freedom. The crisis of capitalist culture must appear the moment this ideology is in contradiction with the bourgeois social order. As long as the advancing bourgeois class—in the eighteenth century, for example—directed this ideology against the constraints of feudal estate society, it was an adequate expression of the given state of class struggle. Thus the bourgeoisie in this period was actually able to have a genuine culture. But as the bourgeoisie came to power (beginning with the French Revolution), it could no longer seriously carry through its own ideology; it could not apply the idea of individual freedom to the whole society without the self-negation of the social order that brought this ideology into being in the first place. Briefly: it was impossible for the bourgeois class to apply its own idea of freedom to the proletariat. The unsurpassable dualism of this situation is the following: the bourgeoisie must either deny this ideology or employ it as a veil covering those actions which contradict it.[14]

The veil Lukács would here lift is essentially the same one behind which a number of early American novelists sought to peer. As I have emphasized throughout this study, because the novel as a form was marginalized by social authorities, because novelists could neither support themselves by their trade nor claim a respectable position within society because of it, the early American novel, generically and within its unique cultural moment, was ideally positioned to evaluate American society and to provide a critique of what was sorely missing in the exuberant postrevolutionary rhetoric of republicanism and, conversely but simultaneously, what was most dubious about an elite's jeremiads against an increasingly heterogeneous social order. Just as those two dialectical ideologies—of promise and of peril—existed in roughly equal proportions in the early national period, so too did the novel analyze the limitations of each vision of the future and revision of the past. In short, the American novel caught its society precisely at the moment Lukács documents, as the bourgeoisie was coming into power, and trained its sights upon that process of nascent empowerment. In plot and characterization, the early American novel was less concerned with dialectical extremes than with the ramifications of polarized ideologies within the workaday world.

The Gothic exhibited a particular genius (even in those novels that fall far short of aesthetic genius) for supplying the metaphors with which to explore a transitional culture. Without, in any way, offering a full-scale critique of bourgeois ideology, the early American Gothic often provided a perturbing vision of self-made men maintaining their newfound power by resorting to the same kinds of treachery that evil aristocrats of both European and early American Gothics used to assert their own perverting authority. The traditional Gothic constellation of grotesque images and symbols and the hyperbolic language of emotional torture or mental anguish are, in the American novels, appropriated to expose the weakness and potential for evil within the new Republic. Whether in the interconnected stories that constitute Isaac Mitchell's *The Asylum* (1811), in which Old World aristocratic values are transported to the Republic, or in Charles Brockden Brown's *Arthur Mervyn* (1799–1800), in which the spirit of materialism, like the contagion of yellow fever, sweeps the nation's capital, the Gothic created its own symbolic space where the hierarchies of a traditional society and the excesses of individualism could both be called into question.

Castles in the New Republic

Two of the first commentators on the phenomenon of the Gothic novel, William Wordsworth and the Marquis de Sade, each saw the emerging form as a comment on the history of the time. For Wordsworth, the Gothic novelists superseded and opposed their sentimental predecessors by brutally fronting the brutality of the modern world—its industrialization, its decay. For the Marquis de Sade, the Gothic was the fitting expression of the "Iron Age," his term for a world wracked by revolution, oppression, and crime. Certainly, it was a time of widespread social unrest. In both France and America, there was a revolutionary restructuring of society. In Geneva (1782), Holland (1794), Poland (1794), Ireland (1798), and Naples (1799) there were attempts to do so.[15] To fictionalize such a tumultuous time, such a *depraved* time, de Sade insisted, Gothic novelists found it "necessary to call hell to the rescue."[16]

But to interpret the late eighteenth century as simply an era of revolution is to homogenize a most disparate period in history. The age was also characterized by its reactionary zeal. In the United States, as I have shown, the late 1790s saw the passage of the Alien and Sedition Acts, arguably the most extensive legislative abrogation of civil liberties in American history, and, in England, the same decade witnessed the State Trials of 1793 and 1794, the prosecution of *The Rights of Man*, and the "Twin Acts" against "treasonable practices" and "seditious meetings," all of which had their effects on the literary enterprise of the era. The conviction and imprisonment of Joseph Gerrald for sedition in 1794, to cite one specific case, so alarmed William Godwin that he immediately wrote a toned-down ending of *Things as They Are; or, The Adventures of Caleb Williams* (1794). "In compliance with the alarms of booksellers," he also suppressed the original preface ("It is now known to philosophers that the spirit and character of the government intrudes itself into every rank of society") to the first edition of his novel. In 1795, however, Godwin decided to publish his original preface with the second edition of *Things as They Are*, and also to explain the reason for its earlier suppression. "Terror was the order of the day," he retrospectively observed, "and it was feared that even the humble novelist might be shown to be constructively a traitor."[17] Notice how Godwin here uses the code word "terror," synonymous with revolution run amok in France, to impugn the repressive tactics of his own government.

The trials in England received almost as much attention in the American press as did the revolutionary happenings in France or the various American trials for sedition. All of these contradictory social events were watched closely by American writers, most notably by the members of the New York Friendly Club, who included among them the young Godwinian Charles Brockden Brown. In the aftermath of their own Revolution, in a time of political dissent and countering oppression both within the land and abroad, American novelists, too, summoned hell to their fictive aid and found in the Gothic mode an apt formulation for their own disquietude.

Sometimes early American Gothic novels appropriate and re-create for an American audience almost intact the various external trappings of the Gothic as first envisioned in dreams (he claimed) and then set down in text by Horace Walpole. What Walpole dreamt soon became a veritable fictional industry in the capable hands of Ann Radcliffe, the best-selling English writer of the eighteenth century.[18] Evil aristocrats, castles, ghosts, unnatural figures who appear and vanish in the murky gloom proliferate in these novels, which also typically feature an ordinary heroine (less often, a hero) who ultimately prevails against all the dark trappings of the plot. The heroes (these protagonists are always male) in other early American Gothic novels, however, not only confront external villainy but also come to face the terrifying potentialities for villainy that they discover within themselves.

As I will later show in some detail, there were widely different versions of the Gothic. Nevertheless, the diverse early American novels that we have come, historically, to label Gothic are unified by a concern (not always the *same* concern) with both individual psychology and the psychology of social relationships, with the inherent limitations of individual consciousness and the consequent need for some control of individual freedom, with the equally inherent weaknesses of existing systems, and with the need for social reform. None of the early American novels offers a simple solution to the multiple and multifaceted problems of the individual within society, nor do we expect them to. Sometimes, in fact, the analysis is ineffectively ambivalent or downright muddled, as in S.S.B.K. Wood's *Julia, and the Illuminated Baron* (1800). This particular Gothic account of villainy perpetrated by *l'ancien régime* against the unprivileged is strangely transformed into an allegory of the evils of social dissent and upheaval. The villainous Count de Launa—a French aristocrat who resorts to any treachery, even murder, to augment his power and wealth and who abducts, with lascivious intent, the virtuous orphan Julia—is also revealed to be a member of the Illuminati, a secret society largely responsible for the French Revolution. That last social event hardly served the best interests of French aristocrats. The Count would not seem to know which side his croissant was buttered on, and Wood's allegory of middle-class virtue triumphing in the struggle against corrupt aristocratic values (read: vice) stumbles itself into a struggle with its own inconsistent conservative social convictions.

Wood's metaphors may be more mixed and her skill more limited than some other early American Gothicists, but her novel nevertheless emphasizes and exaggerates one feature of the English Gothic adopted by many American writers, that is, the simultaneous critique of both the upper class and the lower, of *l'ancienne noblesse* and the *ignobile vulgus*. As Ronald Paulson has noted, the mob, in Matthew Gregory Lewis's *The Monk* (1795), recapitulates the hypocrisy and corruption of the tyrannical monastery it overthrows, and thus a reaction against religious and class oppression soon leads to a carnivalesque indulgence in ruthless destruction and murder that culminates in the fiery roof of the building crashing down upon the rebel/revelers. The end of the old order (the monastery) is the end of the new one (the mob), too.[19] Lewis deploys his symbols more capably than does Wood, but the same simultaneous social critique of the high and the low, the individual and the mob, occurs again and again in early American Gothics. Besides permitting the author to explore both group psychology and the workings of one aberrant mind, the double focus also proves a perfect base from which to evaluate the advantages *and* limitations of republican ideals of self-improvement and self-determination. The same quality necessary for the elevation of the hero—ultimately, an unshakable self-confidence in one's reading of oneself and the world—also provides the villain with his rationale and raison d'être. In short, the way up can also be, in ways Dante did not anticipate, the way down, since the recipe for great social success is also the recipe for megalomania, for both individual and social evil of the highest order.

Whether specializing in subtle psychological analysis or sensational physical effects (in the "Costume Gothic" mode), early American Gothics nearly always feature an important female character—as victim, victor, or villainess. But in none of these roles does the Gothic woman challenge the excesses of individualism, for the simple reason that there was no construct of the "self-made woman" within the early Republic. The critique of individualism in American Gothic fiction is therefore limited primarily to novels in which a young man measures his powers against society, sometimes in extreme form (as with *Wie-land*'s Carwin) and sometimes more prosaically (as with Arthur Mervyn) by working his way up the social ladder. Often this tested protagonist is an employee of a man who is rich, powerful, and corrupt. Novels such as *Edgar Huntly* or *Arthur Mervyn* examine the problematics of individualism but, and this is a crucial distinction, not from the point of view of the authority figures who have most to lose from an acquisitive middle class but from the point of view of those who, materially, have much to gain and who also have, the novelists warn, much, humanly, to lose. As Huntly observes (echoing sentiments of his author): "Our countrymen are prone to enterprize, and are scattered over every sea and every land in pursuit of that wealth which will not screen them from disease and infirmity, which is missed much oftener than found, and which, when gained, by no means compensates them for the hardships and vicissitudes endured in the pursuit."[20]

THE RESILIENCE OF THE Gothic form in American fiction is remarkable and seems due less to its specific social critique than to the richness of the symbols the Gothic uses to signify its meaning. Gothic allegories of the corrupted self persist throughout the nineteenth century and well into the twentieth. Some of the best-known heroes of the American Renaissance or of the Southern—Roderick Usher, Roger Chillingworth, Ahab, Thomas Sutpen, to name only a few—have a distinct Gothic ancestry. Furthermore, the Costume Gothic novel has proved to be an equally persistent subgenre, and its basic plot structures and devices have persisted with surprisingly little variation from the last decades of the eighteenth century right down to the present. Books with "covers featuring" (in Margaret Atwood's description) "gloomy, foreboding castles and apprehensive maidens in modified nightgowns" can be found in almost any drugstore or supermarket—an essential commodity like cornflakes or aspirin.[21] Clearly, Americans still have an affinity for castles in literature, particularly if those castles loom ominously over a young, beautiful, vulnerable heroine.[22]

The pictorial label on today's mass-produced Costume Gothics signifies the same relationship between individuals and institutions, between women and men, that we find at the heart of even the earliest of America's Costume Gothics. Foreboding castle and apprehensive maiden are the two essential ingredients. The castle, in ruin or at least disrepair, symbolizes crumbling authority, the hierarchies of the past literally deteriorating yet still very much present in the form of the castle itself.[23] The empty castle also speaks to the enduring absence of the humans who upheld an old social order, families dwindling or departed and a whole earlier age lost. Nor is there nostalgia inherent in that remembrance of time past. On the contrary, the heralded past, symbolically as well as psychologically and particularly for the captive heroine, betokens repression and oppression, torture and incarceration, social tyranny and political corruption, and (here, again, the castle's state of dissolution signifies) private decadence and the enforced debauchery of others. Analogous to some ancient appalling deity implacably demanding a surfeit of innocent flesh, the Gothic castle is a nightmare presence in the twilight of its own existence, but a relic striving to prove its own continuing vitality by triumphing over a living creature. And the best triumph of all is over a young virginal woman, for in that victory the castle would perpetuate its commitment to sin and death at the cost of her possibilities for fostering love and life.

The castle, more than a symbol, has a life of its own. In novel after novel, the *agency* of evil is (or seems to be) the castle it/himself, and that individuation marks the potentizing of this inert dwelling within Gothic fiction. The evil count or baron typically absents himself from the action, leaving the castle to exercise an authority no longer vested in his person alone. He may pruriently watch over the tortures inflicted upon his captive within his chamber of horrors; he may even direct the action, but, like a pornographer, he knows that proving power, not enjoying sex, is the name of the game, and he all-too-clearly intuits that, without the agency of the dank dungeon, without the assistance of fearful apparitions, his relationship with the heroine is far too equal to be stimulating. The two of them at last alone together is just the old battle of the sexes again, a battle he is not sure he can win. Thus, he allows the castle to stand in for himself and to embody the potency that he only contingently possesses. Yet the castle, as his power displaced and deferred, calls that power into question even as it asserts it in ostensibly the most unquestionable terms. It is hard to say no to a dungeon, but what kind of man needs a dungeon to speak in his place?

The substitution operates on other levels as well. By pitting the maiden primarily against the agency of the decaying castle, Costume Gothics provide her with an adversary both more and less than human. The meaning of her *agon* can consequently go well beyond the social and political implications of the action. The Gothic is by no means simply a seduction novel in monumental dress. In the sentimental novel, the heroine was bound by home and hearth; her plight officially centered almost exclusively in her physical self, in the preservation of her virginity. The Gothic, however, transforms home into castle, and that is a different iconography entirely. The castle is not *her* home, nor is it her dream of home. It is a nightmare domesticity, a house with doors locked shut from the outside to enclose a perverted sexuality within. It is a would-be whore/horror house in an empty social setting. The Gothic heroine has no surrounding community to support her or to tell her just what she ought and ought not do.

The typical early American sentimental heroine severs her bonds with community once she fails her test; but in early American Gothic novels, those bonds are severed long before the test begins. In Isaac Mitchell's *The Asylum; or, Alonzo and Melissa* (1811), for example, Alonzo has joint billing in the title but plays only a minor part in the Gothic plot. After Melissa has survived a host of horrors,

Alonzo happens upon her accidentally when he decides to take refuge from a thundershower in a conveniently located castle. He then seems singularly incapable of penetrating the web of preternatural or superhuman constraints that hold her there. He even leaves her behind to go seeking help, only to discover, on his return, that she, predictably, has vanished once more. Typically, the Gothic heroine has no one to save her and thus must save herself. Against a host of human and supernatural adversaries, she proceeds alone.

Or not completely, for the reader vicariously accompanies the heroine throughout her various trials. This relationship between reader and text marks another departure from the sentimental form. As Fielding early observed and as numerous subsequent critics have pointed out, the sentimental novel, especially in its seduction format, necessarily flirts with prurience and readily beds down with pornography. The reader is sidelined by the conventionally sentimental, is cast as a voyeuristic observer of the protagonist's private affairs. For example, in *The Coquette*, we read over Deighton's shoulder his letters from Major Sanford, which reveal a misogyny that the Major is careful to conceal from Miss Eliza Wharton. *We* anticipate what she will find out the hard way about the dangers with which she flirts—dangers that we know all too well and dangers that give point to the crucial question "Will she or won't she?" In a sense, the reader plays Pandarus to the plot, investing his or her erotic impulses in another's action, and the heroine's seduction, the consummation of her enterprise and ours, finally conjoins character and reader in a community of judgment that can sadly come only after the fall. By contrast, the Gothic reader and the Gothic protagonist all along occupy much the same position. Both are mostly in the dark, and the reader, as much as the protagonist, can fear those things that go bump in the night. No overview perspective is provided. On the contrary, the text wisely remains determinedly indefinite at precisely those points where clarity could dispel the murky ambiguity on which it turns. We may finally sympathize with the sentimental heroine, but we pity the Gothic heroine all along, and since her fear is our fear, we do not anticipate her fall but depend upon her instincts for survival.

For all the sustained mystery of the Gothic, however, there is also a countering (and often terrifying) explicitness that again marks a departure from sentimental form. Conventions of decorum or censorship required that any seduction should occur offstage, and all attendant details such as precipitating desire or consequent pregnancy were decently veiled in a language of circumspection and circumlocution. Characters, too, were often similarly abstract. Only in the very best sentimental novels were different women protagonists presented as individuals rather than as types or exempla. In Gothic fiction, however, the most lurid actions occur center stage and are recounted in lush, lavish language and with a high degree of specificity. Psychology, not morality, is at issue, and psychology must be personalized, individualized. Women could be defined by their character, their capabilities, and not, as in the sentimental, by the state of their maiden-head or their marital status. The Gothic also enlarged the arena in which the heroine could realize her nature. Gothic heroines such as Clara Wieland or Constantia Dudley in *Ormond* (1799) face threats other than possible seduction or *mésalliance*, perform actions more positive than passive sexual resistance. The Gothic thereby extended the arena of eighteenth-century fictive concerns; for women especially, the circle of action expanded from the narrow confines of the drawing room to the great house, to the bare expanse of wilderness, and, most important, to regions of the mind quite unplumbed in the usual sentimental test.

Narratively, the Gothic prepared the way for romance and other nineteenth-century variations on earlier fictional formulae.[24] By its intermingling of high and low mimetic modes, especially by lending the aura of realism to the fantastic, it opened new fictive possibilities beyond either the bedroom or the drawing room, seduction fiction or comedies of manners. Retrospectively, we can also see the Gothic as combining the sentimental novel's introspection and anatomizing of the nuances of human emotions (especially in the epistolary mode) with the picaresque's fascination with the different, the exotic, the bizarre. But the Gothic goes considerably beyond this fruitful concatenation of seemingly antithetical fictional forms. By testing the definition of "reality" and putting to a critical test the assumptions of realism, Gothic novels raise rational, human questions about the possible nature of the irrational and the suprahuman. They ask (often without waiting for an answer) precisely what line separates the darker impulses of the imagination from the external manifestations of the bizarre.[25] By so doing, the Gothic challenges the primacy of the individual mind and the claims of reason. The very postulation of that challenge demarcates the inherent limitations of the tabula rasa as a model of mind and calls into question the Enlightenment's persistent concern to define itself, to count itself into unquestionable existence. The sleep of Reason, as Goya noted, begets monsters.

One of the more interesting manifestations of this new challenge to individual consciousness in Gothic fiction is its utilization of the uncanny (a term from Freud but more recently given currency by Christine Brooke-Rose, Hélène Cixous, and Tzvetan Todorov). By *uncanny* I refer to a frightful interpenetration of the known and even monotonously knowable (the Gothic's tendency to relentless repetition) by the utterly inexplicable—the waking nightmare of the ghost suddenly appearing in the doorway, the encounter with the severed hand or head.[26] The esoteric unknown (one focus of the picaresque) provides little real basis for terror, since the reader has no way to conjoin the encountered danger with his or her own quotidian life. But when the horror occurs in appallingly familiar circumstances, there is nowhere (literally or figuratively) for reader or protagonist to hide. It *can* happen here! Clara Wieland's death-defying encounter with Theodore in her bedroom not only recalls, as numerous critics have noted, the seduction novel but also anticipates Alfred Hitchcock's cinematic device of making individuals most susceptible to evil in the middle of familiar surroundings and while engaged in habitual actions—being slashed to death, for example, while taking a shower, not on a dark, deserted street.

The uncanny's intrusion into the natural processes of life asserts a norm (a basic status quo) from which things have been diverted and to which they should more or less return. But that is hardly a reassuring proposition for the individual who now must be on guard in even the most mundane circumstances. For once reader and character have experienced the Gothic's unpredictable disorder, any reestablished order is no longer certain. Clara Wieland's obsessed narrative may be retrospective from a critic's taxonomical perspective, but for the narrator and the reader, the events are now, here. The retelling itself is a monument to compelling Gothic experiences that are over but by no means finished. Even in the Radcliffean explanatory mode—and almost all American Gothics adopt Radcliffe's compulsion to explain—mystery is not solved but merely transferred from the external world to the internal, from nature out of joint to perception, at least for a time, out of focus.[27] And where, these novels continue to demand, does the one end and the other begin—and how can one ever tell for sure? If fooled once (the ghost *looked* real, the blood *felt* sticky and warm), cannot the reader or the character be fooled again? Moreover, at some level, villainy requires a villain. And which, one might ask, is worse, a cosmology of malignant spirits or a community populated by ruthless people who will stop at nothing to satisfy their deviant desires? Rationality resolves none of these questions; explanation merely translates the locus of evil from the supernatural, the abstract, and the remote to the human, the personal, and the present.

The propinquity of the appalling is underscored by the opening scene of numerous early American Gothic novels. Typically, we have a peaceful, bucolic set piece describing the American landscape. Thus, the "whipperwhill's sprightly song echoed along the adjacent groves" as Alonzo and Melissa, seated within a fertile glen, discoursed on the beauties of nature. With alarming ease, however, that pastoral setting is unsettled, suggesting that the supernatural and the subhuman inhere in the natural and the human. Whether the heroine, like Melissa, is abducted from her bower to be imprisoned in the decrepit castle or whether some twisted individual like Carwin moves into the neighborhood, it is soon clear that nothing will ever be the same again.

The interpenetration of the uncanny and the quotidian creates a constant narrative tension and dis-ease. The reader may hope that the ending of the novel has put to rest those unruly elements arising seemingly from nowhere, but the clear implication is that disorder and villainy are only more or less temporarily forestalled. Thus, the House of Usher falls into the tarn; the black-veiled minister dies; the monster turns his back on civilization and returns to lagoon, ocean, wilderness—someplace other than the world of humankind. Yet the tarn endures, the monster is not dead, the minister dies, but the veil that rendered him frightful still remains. The horrors raised by the narrative are temporarily quelled, but they are not, in the larger universe of which the Gothic is but a symptom, totally abrogated. It is in this sense that the Gothic works a final trick upon the reader. Far more subtly than those picaresque novels (such as *Modern Chivalry*) that simply clowned their way to a nonconclusion, the Gothic resists ending even as it assumes the cloak of conventional sentimental closure. But a solemn distribution of rewards and punishments scarcely brings to life again the innocent dead, nor does an appended Radcliffean explanation of the misestimated dangers undo the real fears that the reader and protagonist previously endured. In this sense, the Gothic novel is, in its conclusion, typically neither open nor closed— but slightly ajar.

ISAAC MITCHELL'S *The Asylum; or, Alonzo and Melissa* was the single most popular Gothic novel in early America and the best of the Costume Gothics. First serialized in the *Poughkeepsie Political Barometer* in 1804, then expanded and published in book form by Mitchell, a Poughkeepsie newspaper editor, in 1811, it was also soon sold in a pirated, uncopyrighted version plagiarized almost verbatim from the newspaper serialization and published by one "Daniel Jackson, Jun." as *A Short Account of the Courtship of Alonzo and Melissa; Setting Forth Their Hardships and Difficulties, Caused by the Barbarity of an Unfeeling Father* (1811). This pirated version was reprinted at least twenty-five times throughout the nineteenth century, generally with Jackson's name on the title page.[28] The book continued to be a steady seller up to the twentieth century. Writing in 1907, Lillie Deming Loshe noted that the novel "is probably known to-day to many who have never read *The Mysteries of Udolpho*."[29] Mark Twain had a copy of the book in his library in 1869 and in *Life on the Mississippi* lists it among the books still widely read in America; a less illustrious reader, George Maynard, notes on April 18, 1905, in his copy of the book, that he had first read it "with great interest" when he "was a boy . . . nearly fifty years ago."[30]

Like virtually all nineteenth-century readers of the book—widely known, simply, as *Alonzo and Melissa*—Twain and Maynard read only the second volume of Mitchell's novel. The unusual publishing history of the book makes it particularly interesting for my purposes. As suggested by the frontispiece to the Poughkeepsie edition (a scene of soulful sentiment in a shadowy graveyard), the first full *Asylum* grafts a Gothic tale onto a sentimental one. After a brief introduction of Melissa Bloomfield—who will be the main character of the second, Gothic volume—the novel spends some 250 pages retelling a sentimental story set in Europe. Related by and about one Selina du Ruyter Bergher, the sentimental first half of the novel is a standard account of parental interference in a young couple's love and the couple's consequent flight from patriarchal authority. That flight brings them to America, to Selina's retrospective recounting of her story, and to Melissa's reenacting of it in a Gothic mode, which also finally accounts for the high praise given to both Mrs. Radcliffe and Brockden Brown in Mitchell's preface. The long-deferred Gothic novel anticipated in the preface is more original in execution and has more interesting implications than its sentimental antecedent and frame. The Gothic volume also grants its heroine far more latitude than does the sentimental half. Unlike Selina, who acts mostly through a well-timed series of swoons, Melissa shows a dash and a verve that carry her successfully through a remarkable sequence of adventures. It is *her* forthright story, not Selina's fainting one, that was originally published in the *Barometer*, that was plagiarized by Jackson, and that became the nineteenth-century best-seller.

The Gothic half is by far the better read, but something is lost when only it is read. What was long missing was not so much the sentimental story itself but the political import underlying the Gothic story yet emphasized by the sentimental one. Since most of the first volume is a flashback (admittedly a very slow one) set in Europe, Mitchell can overtly conjoin the abuses perpetrated by aristocratic Old World villainy with the abuses perpetrated by Colonel Bloomfield, an American gentleman who has retained too many of the Gothic features of a European class system that a good American should have left behind. Indeed, the first page of the novel introduces this Americanized aristocrat as a homegrown Gothic villain. Bloomfield, we are told, is a landowner of British extraction descended from an ancient family; he is a man who "prided himself with all that distinguished haughtiness so characteristic of national prejudice and manners" (1:30). Mitchell portrays Bloomfield's financial dealings and his class bias in damning detail. We are told that he has augmented the "patrimony he inherited from his father" largely by buying up cheap land that he has then "advantageously rented." Because he is one of the few people in western Connecticut with ready cash, he hires poor workers at reduced wages instead of paying, as was more typical, in goods or room and board, and then, apparently, he supplements those low wages with loans at substantial interest rates. The results are debts that must be discharged; or, in effect (and very European this), a peasantry required to work for virtually nothing. Moreover, along with the worst features of the old European gentry, Bloomfield exhibits some of the more dubious features of the emerging American one. Boasting of his own bloodlines and referring to America's wealthiest citizens as "a kind of nobility," he can also quite inconsistently insist that anyone in America who is smart enough and diligent enough can be rich. Armed with this liberal justification for his own position, he need have no qualms about how he disposes his wealth. American equality as much as European privilege can define the poor as "inferior kind[s] of beings" (1:30) who deserve whatever happens to them. All that is required is a few concessions to appearance. Like Franklin in Philadelphia, Bloomfield maintains a plain, puritanical mien and obviously expects moral credit for this affectation of modesty. But in all his actions, he is really governed by a cold and calculating assessment of his own immediate self-interest. Thus he brags that he married late and "chose

He took her miniature from his bosom, he held it up, and earnestly viewed it by the moon's pale ray.

FIGURE 15. This frontispiece from Isaac Mitchell's *The Asylum; or, Alonzo and Melissa* (Poughkeepsie: Joseph Nelson, 1811) perfectly captures the mixture of sentiment and Gothicism that pervades Mitchell's novel. *Courtesy of the American Antiquarian Society.*

his wife as he would have done a farm, not so much for beauty as for convenience" (1:30). He has few enemies, we are told, and fewer friends.

This portrait of the American farmer is very different from that found in Crèvecoeur's panegyric to the classless society. Bloomfield is also a different corrupt aristocrat from those seen in early American Gothics such as Susanna Rowson's *Reuben and Rachel* (1798) or Wood's *Amelia; or, The Influence of Virtue* (1802), which were set in Europe mostly, it seems, because the authors could not accommodate the requisite high-born villain to an American setting. Mitchell, with some sophistication, combines his European and American tales through the agency of Melissa Bloomfield, the colonel's daughter, the auditor of Selina's tale of sentimental adventure and the protagonist of her own Gothic one. Riding about the bucolic American countryside, Melissa happens upon the emigrant Selina, who tells of how her unscrupulous, mercenary father sought to force her to wed the wealthy Count Hubert, a boorish man many years her senior. Instead, she secretly marries the man of her choice, Colonel Bergher, who presently, in self-defense, must shoot the count and then has to escape with his young wife, hotly pursued by the minions of the offended aristocracy. Since the count was related to the ruling families of practically every European country, the nobility of a whole continent, it seems, is intent on capturing the offending lovers. The young couple flee first to England, then to America, where, in New London, beyond the reach of Europe's rulers or their spies, they are at last living happily together and learning to support themselves by farming.

Volume 1 concludes with Melissa, after hearing Selina's tale, drawing a double moral—"She perceived to what misfortunes an opposition to parental authority must lead, and also the dreadful effects of parental authority" (1:206)—and then voicing a final foreshadowing lament: "O my God! preserve me from trials similar to these" (1:206). Melissa's life, to this point, has seemed idyllic and provides an American contrast to Selina's tale of European tribulations. But early in volume 2, Melissa learns that the man to whom she is betrothed, Alonzo, has just lost his family fortune. In one of the first actions of the Revolutionary War, the British have confiscated his father's fleet. And worse, fellow American tradesmen take advantage of the father's suddenly compromised financial position to refuse to pay him the debts they owe. Consequently and quite characteristically, Colonel Bloomfield immediately breaks off his daughter's engagement to the no longer suitable Alonzo and insists she marry a man of her father's choosing. Melissa refuses. In order to frighten her into compliance, Bloomfield confines her in a Connecticut castle of "real Gothic architecture" (2:59).

The Gothic villain Americanized leads to a sentimental novel Gothicized, and Mitchell transplants, virtually intact, a European castle from Radcliffe's fiction to the wilds of Connecticut. This old, abandoned, decaying, pseudomedieval fortress comes replete with moat, battlements, heavy gates, darkly empty rooms, and even exotic herbs and flowers in an ominously overgrown garden. Kept captive within the castle by a sanctimonious spinster aunt who is also convinced of the rectitude of this action, Melissa maintains her integrity and independence and virtually orders the aunt from their joint captivity. With a reluctant captive residing within its walls, the castle thereupon begins to act as Gothic castles are wont to do, and Melissa is subjected to a whole round of unnatural visitations. After a "deathlike stillness," she hears noises, including the whispers of several unseen men in the courtyard. While she is supposedly alone in her own room, a cold hand grasps her arm, yet, when she gathers her wits and lights a taper, she sees nothing but the empty dark. She bravely proceeds down the stairs to see that the doors are all locked and again hears whispers, "AWAY! AWAY!" Like Carwin's "Hold, Hold!" the command is both a warning and a threat. More like Clara in *Wieland* than the swooning Selina of the sentimental half of *The Asylum*, Melissa does not succumb to debilitating fear but resolutely confronts the threats, assuming them to be more cruel attempts by her father to bring her to submit to his will. Whereupon the preternatural occurrences come all the faster; the next morning she is treated to the sound of falling bodies, a rolling ball of fire, a black-clothed figure on the stairway, and another figure, this one bleeding and carrying a bloody dagger, who approaches and then falls down seemingly to die at her feet while a second voice counsels her, in almost comically understated terms, to "Begone! Begone from this house!" By the clear light of the following day, Melissa "endeavored to reason cooly on the events of the past night but reason could not elucidate them" (2:86).

The unraveling of the plot is too complex to summarize here. Suffice to say, chance predictably intervenes both to unite with some regularity the lovers and almost as often to separate them. Nevertheless, Melissa not only weathers her Gothic test alone, she also converts it into a test for both her father and her lover. When a cousin of the same name conveniently dies, Melissa and a well-disposed uncle scheme to conflate the two identities so that her own family and her lover mourn for her. Only when Alonzo proves his enduring constancy, despite her death, by resisting another maiden (really Melissa in disguise), and only after her father has been brought to confess his own wrongdoing through another masquerade arranged by Melissa, does she finally marry her beloved.

Only retrospectively, too, do we learn the real "cause" of the supernatural events Melissa witnessed in the castle. It was not her father, the self-made American gentleman so proud of his American "nobility" and British lineage, who inflicted on his daughter the machinations in (and of) the castle. Her tormentors were a band of lowly criminals who apparently used the site of her imprisonment as a clandestine base of operations from which to sell contraband merchandise, apparently to other disloyal Americans and to the advancing British as well. Hoping to remove Melissa from the building without harming her physically or alerting her to their illegal doings, they sought to frighten her into compliance with their intentions through the agency of such devices as grotesque masks, fake blood, pasteboard figures, and the secret passageways that must abound in any self-respecting castle, even an American model. The more Melissa resisted, the harder they tried, and vice versa, but with her will ultimately outweighing theirs just as it also outweighed, and in exactly the same circumstances, her father's.

At the end of the novel, with the criminals apprehended, the inexplicable supernatural dangers prove to be quite comprehensible ones—private and public crimes, cowardice, greed, and particularly an underhanded pursuit only of one's own coldly calculated advantage. This conclusion emphasizes the similarities between the British-American self-made aristocrat and the Loyalist lower orders. In their willingness to substitute materialism for principles (love of family, love of country) and to use perverted means—Gothic means—to achieve their dubious ends, each mirrors the other's aspirations. Each, ironically, is foiled by Melissa, whose life was endangered by the same men threatening her nation as well as by her own father, who, like the Loyalist thieves within and the British without, too much posited aristocratic privilege over more human values. *The Asylum* ends, then, as an allegory of the Revolution but one that emphasizes internal, not external, sources of oppression and division. And what is internal abides.

In another sense, too, the novel's conclusion is characteristically ajar. Alonzo and Melissa, finally wed, anticipate settling into a "happy, secluded Asylum." That end and that language both evoke the rhetoric of Jeffersonian agrarianism with its idealization of rural retreat. By the time the novel was published, however, the word *asylum* had taken on a second, euphemistic association. It also named a retreat for the criminally insane, as exemplified in the huge and appropriately Gothic fortress of Newgate Prison or, even more, in the new walled institution built in York, England, and described in pastoral, even Jeffersonian, terms by Samuel Tuke in *Description of the Retreat, an Institution Near York for Insane Persons of the Society of Friends* (1813). This new kind of asylum, justified by a belief in the salutary benefits of the country and of removal from the hubbub of modern, urban social life, also signaled a new attitude toward Otherness, an Enlightened age's solution to the problems of evil and madness. This benign institutionalization of the insane, as Foucault suggests in *Madness and Civilization*, was a way of controlling and objectifying the irrational Other by appointing select members of the society (the doctor as priest) to "certify" the existence, the treatment, and the cure of the Other in order that the society at large need not be disturbed by its presence.[31] But Mitchell's ending, with its encircling series of revelations and its rewriting of Revolutionary history, suggests that no civilization can totally evade the signs of its own madness and that no asylum (in either sense of the word) can exist divorced from its society, or even, in any real sense, distanced from it, for isolation itself necessarily turns the asylum as pastoral retreat into the asylum as prison.

There is still another disjunction in the various conjunctions that tie together the novel at its end. The final reconciliations bring together not just the lovers and the parent and child but also warring nations and thus mark the end of the Revolutionary War with its attendant horrors. An Englishman who had saved Alonzo and whom Alonzo, later, was able to save, departs for home, where he plans to open a pub called "The Grateful American." But Mitchell's narrative is, after all, retrospective. At the same time that the novel was serialized in the *Barometer,* the newspaper already rightly predicted another war with England, and, by 1811, when the novel was published, war seemed inevitable. Even as the author was writing of the promise of the past, that promise was being forgotten. So the novel's Gothic images, signifying division in the present and division from the past, could continue to inform the American consciousness during the after-math of the Revolutionary War, the War of 1812, the Civil War, the Spanish-American War, and even up to the verge of World War I. As Fredric Jameson has argued of the social potency of literary symbols, "fantasy or protonarrative structure" is, merely and ultimately, "the vehicle for our experience of the real."[32] Mitchell's novel—plagiarized, pirated, bowdlerized—exerted its peculiar sym-bolic force as division and violence ruled again. And again. Even fallen, his Gothic castle continued to signify.

The Gothic Within

What happens to the early American Gothic once the castle has fallen into the tarn? Can the paradigms for private villainy and perverted authority be grounded in America? Can a Philadelphia, not a Paris or a London, be the city of brotherly corruption? In other words, does the Gothic *require* the castle or is the ruined castle an external sign of a deeper decay within? Can one challenge hierarchy, authority, patriarchy, and traditional values without recourse to Europe with its potent symbols and synecdoches for other forms of oppression—the Inquisition or the Directory? Does America have enough of a history to sustain the Gothic's generic challenge to history, its rewriting and unwriting of history?

Such questions occupied a second group of Gothic writers in the new Repub-lic. Their models were not so much the Costume Gothics of Walpole, Radcliffe, and Lewis but the reformist novels—called by their detractors Jacobin novels—of Robert Bage, Mary Hays, Thomas Holcroft, Elizabeth Inchbald, Charlotte Smith, Mary Wollstonecraft, and, most of all, William Godwin. To speak of models, however, is to obscure the crucial point that any novel of reform necessarily addresses its own specific social situation. Reform, like revolution, comes from inside a system, and the political writer must focus on the perceived inequities and injustices of the political present in which she or he writes. The castle thus becomes simply irrelevant for reform-minded American Gothicists. In eighteenth- or early-nineteenth-century Connecticut, it was anachronistic and strikingly out of place, at best an eccentric Yankee's Disneyland trivialization of a European past or an attempt to beat Mark Twain to King Arthur's court. As a central symbol and setting, it was therefore simply jettisoned by the new Republic's own Jacobins—"Adelio" (author of *A Journey to Philadelphia*, 1804), the anonymous author of *St. Herbert* (1813), Rebecca Rush, Caroline Matilda Warren, George Watterston, and, most of all, Charles Brockden Brown.

Two novels that indicate how some of these problems were solved in the homespun versions of the reformist novels also both prominently employ the cruel-parent motif and so provide revealing contrasts with *The Asylum*. Neither *St. Herbert, a Tale* (originally serialized in the New York *Weekly Magazine* in 1796 and then published in book form in 1813) nor *Kelroy, a Novel* (1812) was ever reprinted. Each appeared anonymously—the first "By an American Lady" (whose identity remains unknown) and the second "By a Lady of Pennsylvania," actually Rebecca Rush, the daughter of the Philadelphia jurist Jacob Rush and the niece of Benjamin Rush. Each addresses important narrative problems, and *Kelroy* does so with a remarkable facility, deftly interweaving comic and tragic scenes to ground a convincing Gothic disaster in an astutely observed novel of manners. Furthermore, Rush had a good ear for language and remarkable powers of characterization. Her Mrs. Hammond is a striking creation; Harrison T. Meserole has deemed her "the most memorable female villain in American literature."[33] All in all, Rush's novel is one of the best written in America before 1820. Yet posterity has not dealt generously with her. There is still no modern reprint of this eminently readable work, and only a dozen or so copies of the original edition survive. Her own time did not deal particularly generously with her either. The author earned only $100 from her novel, received little critical notice after its publication, and never wrote another—a significant loss to American literary history.[34]

Let us look first, however, at *St. Herbert*, an anonymous novel in which the European castle is modestly but successfully domesticated and that conjoins, as does *The Asylum*, a sentimental love story with a Gothic thriller. As in *The Asylum*, true love is continually thwarted, for three generations, in fact. In *St. Herbert*, however, there is a conjunctive relationship between the human world and the preternatural, which is now symbolized not by some incongruous castle but by a fully believable old manse still surrounded by a dark forest. No moats, turrets, or battlements are necessary. This old American house, with its creaking doors (or was it a moan?) and its drafty corridors (a supernatural sigh? the chilling presence of the undead?) itself sets forth the ambiguity of the preternatural in an appropriately American mode. Nor is that mode fixed; the character of the house seemingly changes with the mood of its inhabitants. Originally used by the evil, aristocratic Maurisson to imprison in fearful isolation the woman whose love he could not buy, it later serves as a happy refuge for St. Herbert and Louisa Howard, the daughter of the woman Maurisson could hold captive but could not possess. But Maurisson presently spoils this match, causing the second Louisa to die of grief after bearing a daughter, also named Louisa, a daughter who apparently inherits, too, a family penchant for both misfortune and the abandoned manse. This third-generation Louisa as a young woman decides that her marital prospects are hopelessly blighted and seeks temporary refuge in the haunted house, where she is, for a time, seemingly comforted by the mournful associations it embodies. Yet she still declines and dies, whereupon her tardy lover returns from trying to seek the fortune that would have made him a suitable husband, discovers Louisa is no more, and, in despair, commits suicide upon her grave, leaving only the aging manse as a still-abiding monument to love misclaimed, misestimated, misdirected, or otherwise gone awry. Only St. Herbert endures to tell the sad tale of three unhappy generations and to testify to the powers for corruption in the new Republic. Significantly, he finds solace not in religion (the usual panacea) but in the wise counsel of an Indian, who inspires him with a model of endurance in the face of tragedy.[35]

Stoicism is the only consolation at the end of *St. Herbert*, but the ending of Rebecca Rush's *Kelroy* offers even less than that. Indeed, the grim conclusion of each novel well might explain its early unpopularity and virtual disappearance from the literary scene. The nineteenth-century reader generally preferred to have a reformist social message sweetened by a happy ending, and such an ending is precisely what the "American Lady" and the "Lady of Philadelphia," adhering to the logic of their plots, chose not to provide.

Kelroy does not require a haunted house, much less a castle, for its effects. The Gothic here lies partly within the avaricious soul of Mrs. Hammond and partly within the immediate source of that soul's defects, the rigid class requirements of Philadelphia in the first quarter of the nineteenth century. For a "classless" society, America certainly has received its share of social criticism from novelists. Rush, for example, grounds the villainous Mrs. Hammond in emerging New World ideas as to just what constituted the good life and in the darker aspirations of an American would-be aristocracy not backed by the historic claims and trappings of their European equivalents. This same grounding also gives us the Richardsonian cruel-parent motif. Put the two together, they spell mother as the evil agent of the plot, as the Gothic antagonist in the most deceptive dress of dust cap and apron. All that mitigates the villainy of Mrs. Hammond is her naivete, and here, too, Rush displays a keen understanding of her society and particularly of its patriarchal power beyond the reach and machinations of Mrs. Hammond. Certainly, that lady is *less* sinned against than sinning, but she is not entirely without pathos. Merchants and realtors regularly take advantage of her inexperience in financial matters. More to the point, she is fully aware of her own inability, as a woman, to earn her own way in the world. Mrs. Hammond must seek some mode, consistent with accepted female roles, of providing for herself and her daughters. Widowed at thirty, with two young children to raise, she realistically calculates that her chances for making another good marriage are not very high. She has been left enough for her and her daughters to live modestly, but modest living is not her forte. Rightly estimating that her best assets are her daughters as they might be desired by men of means, she sets out to marry them to best advantage—their advantage and hers.

Her concern was perhaps initially more for her daughters than for herself. However (and this is the etiology of villainy in the female mode), she increasingly employs a proclaimed solicitude only for her daughters' welfare to justify her own self-indulgence, her own preference for high living. Ruthless maternalism more and more verges into megalomania, as ostensibly unquestionable ends (what mother would not promote her children's happiness?) occasion most questionable means. Mrs. Hammond resorts to deception, prevarication, and forgery. Most damning of all, she finally exhibits an utter disregard for the feelings of her youngest daughter, Emily, who is characterized, above all, by her delicate feelings, and that maternal disregard gives, of course, the lie to all of Mrs. Hammond's motherly rationalizations.

The mother is capable in her conniving fashion. After her husband's death, while her two daughters are growing to marriageable age, she cuts herself off from society to be a good widow mourning the death of her husband and solaced by the daughters who occupy her care (but actually to conserve the family's limited financial resources until they can do the most good). When Lucy, the older of the two, turns sixteen, the whole family "comes out": "Nobody's parties were half so crouded, or so fashionable as Mrs. Hammond's; nobody was half so elegant, or so fashionable as her daughters; and by some well timed innuendoes . . . she circulated a belief that their fortunes would be as immense, as their claims to admiration were indisputable."[36] Mrs. Hammond understands that affluence (not female virtue) is what is rewarded in America. She displays her daughters in the most expensive European fashions of the day, wagering, in effect, her limited legacy on the chance that a suitably wealthy man can be brought to marry the girl, to support her in an appropriate fashion, and to contribute something to his mother-in-law's support, too. At first it seems as if it all well might work. Mrs. Hammond, more than Lucy, lands the visiting Lord Walsingham. The new husband is a man of impeccable social standing, considerable wealth, and exemplary kindness (which Mrs. Hammond foolishly misinterprets as malleable weakness).

With one daughter down and one to go, Mrs. Hammond next concentrates her efforts on the seventeen-year-old Emily. Unfortunately, Emily's aspirations do not coincide with her mother's, whereas Lucy's unfortunately did. The younger daughter soon encounters Walsingham's friend, the Wertherian Kelroy, clothed all in black and enveloped in an aura of Romantic sensibility, and falls hopelessly in love with him even though he has not a penny to his name. He, hearing this beautiful young lady play soulfully upon the piano, is presently equally smitten, while, naturally, Mrs. Hammond is enraged. As her assets dwindle, as her debts mount, and as her son-in-law proves far less accommodating than she had hoped, she decides that the second half of her plan must succeed better than the already faltering first half and does everything in her power to direct her second daughter to that end. When Kelroy goes off to India to make his fortune, and perhaps to gain thereby the mother's approval, she intercepts the lovers' letters and forges substitutes in which each informs the other of diminished love and divided attentions. Only then does Emily, in despair and (she thinks) on the rebound, reluctantly agree to marry Dunlevy, a nice enough and (for the mother) rich enough suitor.

What I find particularly intriguing in this novel is the way in which Rush, a year after the publication of Jane Austen's *Sense and Sensibility* (1811) and before *Pride and Prejudice* (1813) and *Emma* (1816), already Gothicizes the novel of social manners by turning the Austenesque plot of arranging suitable marriages for the suitable into a grim matrimonial poker game. Metaphors of hazard and chance (particularly references to cards and lottery) pervade *Kelroy*. And appropriately so; for women, the gamble of marriage was the only game in town. If Mrs. Hammond can make her daughters appear rich, they can marry well; if she fails, they will marry poorly and live poor, for they have no income nor earning ability of their own. Personal worth counts for little in a materialistic world in which women get anted up before society and auctioned off to the highest bidder or (the game is played from the other side, too) the best bluffer. Rush acutely perceives the Gothic underside to this "circulation of women," and her early story of pride and prejudice reveals the tawdry underpinnings of the social edifice that Austen depicts with irony, subtlety, but also with a certain genteel obfuscation. As I regularly ask my students, would it be the same happy ending if Darcy lost his fortune and Pemberley, too, the day before the wedding? Of course not. And Rebecca Rush, more than Jane Austen, emphasizes the mercantile basis of bourgeois "love."

The hypocrisy at the heart of an only theoretically classless society and particularly the low social status of women as mostly objects of social exchange along with their incommensurately high responsibility (responsibility without concomitant privilege) as perpetuators of etiquette, manners, even sense and sensibility, stands fully exposed at the end of *Kelroy*. The prospects for any woman, particularly a discerning one, are not bright. As Walsingham tells Emily:

> Experience will teach you the real characters of the beings who chiefly compose your species. You will find them a set of harpies, absurd, treacherous, and deceitful—regardless of strong obligations, and mindful of slight injuries—and when your integrity has been shocked, and every just, and native feeling severely tried, the sensibility which you now so liberally bestow on others, will then be absorbed in lamenting its own cruel disappointments, and inefficacious tenderness; and you will gladly consult the dictates of your understanding, to prevent being preyed on by continual depravity. (P. 129)

Nothing in the novel dispels this gloomy prognosis, not even the conclusion in which Mrs. Hammond, at least, finally gets her just desserts. Rush effectively contrives a most suitable end for the avaricious mother, but it is an end so utterly pathetic that we can neither sympathize with her plight (for she has earned it) nor celebrate her demise. It is a defeat, moreover, forged out of what first seems to be this dubious character's total victory. With both her daughters wed (although not as much to her advantage as she anticipated), the mother finds that her own well-being really does not depend on theirs. She wins $50,000 in a lottery. She does not, however, long enjoy this first substantial wealth, as opposed to the simulacrum of the real thing. At the very apex of her new good fortune, Mrs. Hammond, no longer as young as she pretends to be, suffers a debilitating stroke. Bedridden, paralyzed, fully aware that she is going to die, she summons Emily to her bed. Newly wed, Emily has by no means recovered from what she thinks has been Kelroy's defection. The daughter holds her mother's limp hand while the mother frantically tries to tell her something but simply cannot articulate whatever it is that she wants to say.[37] Neither Emily nor the reader ever knows if Mrs. Hammond intended a deathbed confession, a plea for forgiveness, or merely another of her capable rationalizations.

Mrs. Hammond dies with her last unspoken words constricted in her throat, to be followed soon after by her victim daughter. Emily finds in the dead woman's desk proof of her mother's deviousness and proof, too, of Kelroy's abiding love. The daughter is devastated to discover a stack of letters that the designing mother had intercepted, Kelroy's letters to her and hers to Kelroy, along with damning copies of the forged "dear John" letters from each to the other. But despite Emily's death, followed soon after by Kelroy's as well, the image of the end that predominates in the book is of Mrs. Hammond, choking upon her last incomprehensible utterance, a grim reaping for this republican mother. Her final fate, being reduced to a most ironic rich silence, resoundingly refutes her governing assumption that human value is synonymous with net worth.

I WILL PASS OVER briefly a number of reformist Gothicists who borrow all too obviously from the work of Charles Brockden Brown. Carnell, for example, in "Adelio's" *A Journey to Philadelphia; or, Memoirs of Charles Coleman Saunders*, combines the worst features of Carwin, Clithero (from *Edgar Huntly*), and Colden (from *Jane Talbot*) without exhibiting the psychological complexity of any of these hero-villains. Or in *The Gamesters; or, Ruins of Innocence* (1805), Caroline Matilda Warren pairs Leander Anderson with Edward Somerton to explore the symbiosis of evil in much the same manner as does Godwin with Caleb Williams-Falkland or Brown with Arthur Mervyn-Welbeck and Edgar Huntly-Clithero. Warren's protagonist for a time resists the villainous assaults of Somerton but is finally seduced by this high roller and ends, miserably, having destroyed everyone he loved and everything he once possessed through his uncontrollable aleatory passions and his attempts at high living. Brown's characters are copied and so are his characteristic plot devices. In the two novels of George Watterston, *Glencarn; or, The Disappointment of Youth* (1810) and *The Lawyer, or Man as He Ought Not to Be* (1808), Brownian ploys proliferate, especially the endless repetition of mistaken identities, the deployment of psychological and physical doubles, a reliance on ventriloquism, and the larger narrative strategy of the confession that substantially indicts the narrator who would thereby exonerate himself.[38]

More than an obvious homage to Charles Brockden Brown conjoins these novelists and their novels. They are all concerned with the very way in which evil can be rooted in the concept of individualism. Characters in these novels flagrantly demarcate the self from the other, the individual from society, to pit themselves against the enemy that stands in their way, which, collectivized, constitutes the actual community. In short, these characters lack any sense of social responsibility that might act as a check upon individual desire; they simply cannot balance the abstract claims of a community to which they belong (for they do not see themselves as belonging to one) against their individual and mostly materialistic tendencies. In each novel, a character seeks to distinguish himself (never herself) from his peers. The personal or social weaknesses of others provide means to do so—are, indeed, the very rungs of the ladder to success. Metaphors of self-improvement or self-realization thereby become diabolical as they set the aspiring self *against* the rest of the world in a battle of wills. The resultant contest of survival predates Social Darwinism but also somehow exceeds it by requiring no ostensibly neutral construct such as fitness or progress to justify in theory its tyranny in practice.

Not coincidentally, the legal profession in particular is attacked in these Jacobin novels; here again, the Brownian legacy is apparent. Brown's antipathy for the law, incurred during his own early legal apprenticeship, is well known: "[I] was perpetually encumbered with the rubbish of law, and waded with laborious steps through its endless tautologies, its impertinent circuities, its lying assertions and hateful artifices." But more than that, the business of law was mostly business. Its enterprise attested that American society was more vitally concerned with property rights than with human rights (indeed, slaves *were* property, and, arguably, wives were too), was more interested in protecting the advantage of individual men than in promoting justice in the nation. Moreover, as these reformist novels endlessly attest, the law lived not by its letter nor even its spirit but by its misuse, by pettifoggery, demagoguery, and sophistry. Issues were decided by the abilities of slippery-tongued barristers to talk away the facts, to twist words into justifications of the unjustifiable. All the villains of the Jacobin novels have mastered these requisite skills and can, like Morcell of *The Lawyer*, profit from them both professionally and personally. For as Watterston or Brown knew full well, the most capable lawyer typically serves the highest bidder and not the person with the best or the most socially beneficial cause: "Intellectual ore is of no value [to the lawyer] but as it is capable of being turned into gold, and learning and eloquence are desirable only as the means of more expeditiously filling our coffers."[39] In another sense, too, law is of the marketplace, and seeking justice translates out as hiring the best legal counsel that money can buy. In Watterston's novel that counsel is Morcell or his mentor, the equally sleazy barrister Dorsey. Of course villainy prevails! It is ardently sought by those in a position to avail themselves of its services and to reward it accordingly.

The same novels that provide a salient, systemic critique of America's early maladies do not, however, abound with suggested remedies, although the villain's final discomfiture may inoculate the reader against following his course. Thus a Carnell or a Leander Anderson dies a violent or even self-inflicted death, in isolation and finally aware of his own corruption; a Morcell or a Somerton belatedly recognizes his previous evil ways and devotes his remaining days to benevolence and philanthropy, totally subjugating his individual desires to the good of the society he earlier discounted. But it must be noted that either of these solutions is itself an essentially personal and individualistic reaction to what has been exposed as a systemic problem, and a problem of individualism at that. The antagonist, in short, exhibits even in reform the faults and fault lines of his society; consequently, the new philanthropist, at last weaned from his previous evil ways, hardly refutes the world of getting and spending that he so recently, profitably, and selfishly inhabited.

Rereading *Arthur Mervyn*

The very decision to write a novel in the new Republic, especially a Gothic novel, constituted an ideological choice almost as definite as the decision to write a Federalist manifesto. Nor do I find it merely coincidental that Brockden Brown, in 1803, publicly rejected *both* the novel form and his earlier Godwinism. This is not to argue a causal connection between genre and narrow party politics: Republicans and Federalists both wrote novels, and even a construct such as Federalist dubiously categorizes and conventionalizes a writer such as Royall Tyler. However, and as Brown knew full well, writing a novel in 1800 meant writing for an audience that included unprivileged readers. It meant, in many cases, alienating men of education and social probity who had little patience for tales of mystery, for parables of perverted power and passion. Moreover, the Gothic in particular questioned the rules of rationalism that, for those in power, conveniently ordered their interest and their status. "The man of Truth, Charles! the pupil of Reason," his friend Dr. Elihu Hubbard Smith wrote to Brockden Brown in 1796, "has no mysteries. . . . The man of poesy, Charles, is not often that of Philosophy & Truth."[40]

It must be remembered that the term *Gothic* was originally pejorative and connoted the barbaric, the archaic, the unspeakable. As David Punter, a Marxist theorist of the Gothic, has noted, even in its form—deliberately "fragmentary, inconsistent, jagged"—the Gothic challenged the Age of Reason's ruling premises about the purposes of discourse, the status of knowledge, and the limits of both realism and rationality and thus consistently undermined the cherished complacencies of emerging bourgeois culture.[41] If humans cannot decide for themselves what is good and what is evil, or, worse, if they cannot master their propensities for the latter, then what is the basis of human society? That question, of course, has particular pertinence in a democracy that officially ascribes to liberalism (i.e., laissez-faire capitalism) and the Protestant ethic (both of which are implicitly grounded in the same rationalist faith in the perfectability of human nature). But what if the most successful person is the most selfish, the most conniving, in short, the most evil? What if rationality is measured by what one can get away with, by the ability to fool most of the people most of the time? A prime function of bourgeois ideology is to avoid those very considerations by making a mythology of success and casting any rags-to-riches scenario as proof positive of equal opportunity for all. The Gothic, however, especially as handled by writers such as Rebecca Rush or George Watterston or Charles Brockden Brown, asked precisely those questions that bourgeois ideology labored to suppress. It was all so *easy*, Welbeck insists in *Arthur Mervyn*. If you are rich enough, you can get away, literally, with murder.

Brockden Brown, however, does not particularly concern himself with this Liverpudlian emigrant proficient at duping Americans. Welbeck is too easy a target. He wears his villainy as obviously as he wears the ill-gotten gains it allows him to flaunt, the (rented) Philadelphia mansion that displays his high status to the world. Welbeck is all palpitating lust, deceit, avarice, and duplicity. He sins; he dies. It is a story we have read before. What is intriguing about Brown's adaptation of the Gothic form (and here he goes further even than Godwin) is the way in which he shifts the expected anatomy of evil from the prime villain to the villain's possible apprentice, the eponymous Arthur Mervyn. Moreover, by making Mervyn's life at least outwardly conform to accepted bourgeois patterns, to America's own idealizations of its own principles (the country versus the city, the Protestant ethic), Brown raises perturbing questions about how much the Gothic might be rooted in the very essentials of American democracy. Welbeck's evil proves little. Any social program will occasionally misfire and throw out not a proper citizen but a villain whose evil grotesquely caricatures the society's own values (in Welbeck's case, a burning desire for both material possessions and social respectability). And Welbeck *is* a caricature. But if Arthur Mervyn, all-American boy, is also evil, then we must delve far deeper to grapple with the problem.

There are no Connecticut castles in Brown's fiction, no clanking chains, but Brown fully indulged a Gothic fascination for the least acceptable aspects of the human psyche. He was obsessed with evil: its various forms, both private and public; its social etiology and consequences; and particularly with the ways in which rationalization, prevarication, and hypocrisy (in short, subverted narratology) provided the Age of Reason with its perverse mirror image. In a world wracked by disease—the metaphor of the yellow fever—story itself is cast as one of the prime carriers. Thus Welbeck's ensnaring narrative implicates the archetypal youth from the country, Arthur, more and more in a web of complex evil. As Welbeck's accomplice and confidante, Arthur gains his first real education in the ways of the world. How are we going to keep him down on the farm . . . ? Becoming a man of his world, Arthur, in turn, soon has his tales to tell to the benevolent, archetypally middle-class Dr. Stevens, who is increasingly implicated in the Gothic happenings of that unfolding narrative. And the narration of these different narrations itself unfolds in Philadelphia in the plague year of 1793, which provides, far more than any castle, the perfect Gothic setting for the machinations of Brown and Welbeck and Mervyn's interconnected plots.

CHARLES BROCKDEN BROWN occupies a distinct place in this history of the origins of American fiction, partly because of the reception his work received in his own time and continues to receive in ours. Unlike most of the early novelists, Brown survives in the historical archive in a way that makes both him and his work uniquely accessible to the modern reader. We have fragments of his diaries and over 150 of his letters, some manuscripts of his works, various unpublished ephemera, and a remarkable range of articulate early responses to his work. In *Charles Brockden Brown: A Reference Guide*, Patricia L. Parker records forty-three published assessments of Brown written between 1798 (the publication date of his first novel, *Wieland*) and 1820. He liked to think of himself as the best American novelist of his generation, and on that score his peers agreed. His *Ormond* (1799) was the first American novel to be published in England. Almost immediately after Brown's death in 1810, his friends and fellow writers began promoting a complete edition of his novels, and in 1827 that demand was fulfilled to become another American first. At this same time, still one more first was in the works. In 1824, John Neal turned Brown's life into a type of the "plight of the American writer," praised abroad, neglected at home. By 1830, Charles Brockden Brown became the first American novelist to be cast, in the best Romantic tradition, as the moody iconoclast, appreciated by the "intelligent, the cultivated, and the reflecting classes of society" but, of course, spurned by the philistine masses. He was, well before Melville, Hawthorne, or Poe, the starving "man of genius," the writer consigned finally to silence for want of a suitably appreciative audience.[42] That very iconography of the neglected great author serves to encourage contemporary readers not to make the same mistake.

As a neglected early writer, however, Brown rather resembles his fellow fictionalists, for none of them, not even Rowson or Foster, could support themselves with their novels. Brown, in fact, did better than most, managing for much of his life to earn a living through his fiction, his editing, and his political writings. Certainly he was frustrated by the difficulties of being a writer in the early Republic, but, unlike the indomitable Parson Weems, he did not feel called upon to sell his books door-to-door along the nation's highways and byways. Nor did he take to the stage or the schoolroom, like Rowson or Foster, to support and promote his literary habit. Unlike most of his colleagues, he enjoyed public esteem: "The flattering reception that has been given, by the public, to *Arthur Mervyn*, has prompted the writer to solicit a continuance of the same favour, and to offer to the world a new performance."[43] Although only one of his novels, *Edgar Huntly*, was reprinted in America during his lifetime, it must be noted that a second edition was the exception for American novels before 1820, not the rule. Less than five years after Brown's death, Paul Allen's full-length biography of the writer was in press, whereas, as I have shown for most early American novelists, only fragments of information survive to the present, and for many virtually nothing remains but a book—not even the name of the author who wrote it. Brown, in contrast, could anticipate that he would survive in the archive, for his admirers were educated and important enough to write reviews for the kinds of magazines that were being assiduously collected by the historical societies springing up in the years after the Revolution. Furthermore, most of the extant copies of the first editions of his novels that I have handled do not evidence the kind of hard use that characterizes first edition specimens of other early novels, and they seem to have been obtained by these same libraries (dedicated, as the libraries were, to preserving the heritage of a new nation) soon after their initial publication, often in pristine form. Brown's books had become collector's items without being widely read.

The evidence suggests that even though Brown never achieved financial success with his fiction, he did attain one goal he set for himself, the cultivation of an elite audience. Brown, as earlier noted, understood who most of America's novel readers were, and he also, like all early novelists, understood the opprobrium under which any American novelist wrote. He articulated his ambition to adapt the novel to moralistic purposes, as did practically all of his peers, and, more exceptional, he also articulated a desire to cultivate for the novel an audience of educated readers. In his prefaces and in his literary criticism, Brown strove to educate the educated to the intellectual benefits of novel reading. At the same time, he also wanted to retain the novel's primary unprivileged readership—the "class of readers" who read few books besides novels. "To gain [the] homage" of those "who study and reflect," he insisted in the advertisement for the unpublished (and now lost) *Sky Walk*, it was not necessary "to forego the approbation of those whose circumstances have hindered them from making . . . progress" in the world, for "a contexture of facts capable of suspending the faculties of every soul in curiosity, may be joined with depth of views into human nature and all the subtleties of reasoning."[44] It is some measure of Brown's success, perhaps, that Samuel Miller, who was otherwise intolerant of novels and novel reading, could begrudgingly praise Brown's "respectable specimen[s] of fictitious history" in his *A Brief Retrospect of the Eighteenth Century* (1803).[45] But then again, Miller was a personal friend, and Miller, no doubt, sighed with relief when Brown, during the same year in which Miller's history appeared, publicly renounced his previous writings and, presumably, those "idle and thoughtless" readers who favored novels over literary criticism or political tracts, both of which constituted the literary program Brown set himself for his "late" (he was only thirty-two) years.[46]

My concern here, however, is not with Brown's psychobiography or with his motivations for abandoning fiction after 1801 but with his readers and the various ways in which readers, then as now, have attempted to make sense of *Arthur Mervyn*. No other novelist of the early national period has been accorded such an extensive body of response, and this abundant record of reaction would at first seem to be a luxury for a critic who has had to re-create responses to early fiction from scrabblings and other fragmentary sources. With Brockden Brown, there is a different theoretical issue posed precisely by this plethora. Brown is the only canonical writer discussed in this study, the only writer to be regularly taught in the college classroom or to have commanded a body of critical response. The history of *Arthur Mervyn* is not, then, simply a matter of its publication dates and a record of, for the most part, subsequent public neglect but is a history of how the novel has been interpreted. It carries its readings with it. One cannot now read Brown "innocently," the way early readers read *The Asylum*, say, or *The History of Constantius and Pulchera*, the way contemporary readers read *The Exorcist* or *Airport IV*. All modern editions of Brown's novels come packaged with a critical introduction that also alerts the reader to the canonical stature of the book. Moreover the range of opinion on *Arthur Mervyn* is so varied that one must read *against* this body of interpretation; thus every reading of the novel becomes essentially a rereading or even an unreading of other readings.

The critical reception of *Arthur Mervyn* is as labyrinthine and contradictory as anything in a Gothic novel (even, for that matter, in one of Brown's own Gothic novels). Most of the debate centers on the character of Arthur Mervyn. He is a "hero whose virtue . . . stands in need of no riches." He is an inconstant scoundrel who betrays the love of a good woman for the lucre of a wealthy widow. He is a model of "enlightened self-interest" and "rigid morality" but also a "young American on the make" and a "meddlesome, self-righteous bungler who comes close to destroying himself and everyone in his path." He is a man of "constancy" and "virtuous impulses" or a "modern bourgeois teenage Tartuffe," a "chameleon of convenient virtue"—and a "chameleon of convenient vice." He is an "innocent," "an American Adam," who has, however, a "tendency toward casuistry and rather indiscreet curiosity." He is "a mama's boy, pampered and spoiled," an "imp of the perverse." Or: "Neither a hero nor a villain," Mervyn "lacks the force of will to be either." He is, symbolically and structurally, Maravegli, the self-sacrificing gentleman and the type of saintly benevolence. He is, figuratively and even literally, Clavering, the consummate con man posing as a country bumpkin for his own nefarious purposes. "Pierce Arthur Mervyn," yet another critic writes, "and all you find is Arthur Mervyn."[47]

Will the real Arthur Mervyn please stand up? Mervyn at one point asks, "Who and what was Welbeck?" but readers of the novel have far more insistently asked, "Who is Mervyn?"[48] This is, indeed, the central question of the novel. It supplies the structuring narrative device of the book and serves as both its modus operandi and raison d'être. The narrative configures as a trial. Mervyn stands accused of being Mervyn by the prosecutor, Wortley; he pleads a different Mervyn (two of them, in fact) before the judge, Dr. Stevens. The reader, as jury, must render his or her own verdict on the whole proceedings.

The ersatz trial effectively literalizes a most important element of the Gothic, its challenge to rationality, by making inquiry both the subject and the form of the text. Neither Stevens nor the reader is ever granted any definitive grounds for final judgment. In fact, the extended metaphoric trial becomes possible only because a more literal one is subverted in the novel and subverted partly through the suppression of evidence by our metaphoric judge and moral guide, Dr. Stevens. Wortley, who is Stevens's "dearest friend" and who, Stevens assures us, is "venerable for his discernment and integrity" (p. 12), views Mervyn as a dissembler, a criminal. Mervyn, Wortley is convinced, aided Welbeck in defrauding creditors (Wortley among them) and is, moreover, implicated in who knows what other heinous crimes perpetrated by the villainous Welbeck. At the beginning of volume 2, Wortley informs Stevens with some satisfaction that an actual warrant for Mervyn's arrest has been issued. Stevens is deeply perturbed because he wants to believe in Mervyn's innocence but also knows that much of Mervyn's defense would be inadmissible in a court of law. For Mervyn defends himself, like some republican Scheherazade, by telling stories—complex, encircling narratives (at one point he narrates a tale within a tale within a tale) that often turn on little more than hearsay and conjecture, neither of which have any standing in a standard court of inquiry.

Mervyn's innocence, however, is not all that is here on trial. The larger legal system is also under scrutiny. The law, in a very real sense, is not the solution to a dilemma but is part of the problem, and Dr. Stevens, as the metaphoric judge, also becomes, by volume 2, almost a coconspirator in the case. Furthermore, everything we see of the legal system in the novel calls its justice into question. Honest men, like Stevens's friend Carlton, rot away in debtors' prison, placed there by vindictive creditors who do not need the cash that holds another captive. Lawyers scalp their clients. One wishes to charge Mervyn a 50 percent commission to help him sue to obtain a reward he has already rightly earned. Or the law enables wicked men to flourish. On the highest social level, there is the elder Thetford—a usurer who charges an interest of 5 percent per month—who thrives on the side of the law; and there are equally wicked men lower on the social scale, like Philip Hadwin, who legally cheats his penniless niece of the inheritance that rightly should be hers.

It is by no means clear that Stevens's evasive procedure is above reproach either. In both a literal and figurative sense, the doctor takes the law into his own hands and prefers to decide Mervyn's case on a personal, individualistic basis—as if personal bias can better weigh the guilt or innocence of an individual than can the more formalized proceedings of the legal system. Stevens's decision to judge Mervyn for himself makes him, moreover, an accomplice in Mervyn's life, much as Mervyn became increasingly implicated in Welbeck's dealings after accepting Welbeck's story.

We might notice, too, how the promise of confidence that Welbeck extracts from Mervyn and that Mervyn, in turn, elicits from Stevens only problematizes the burden of each discourse. What is the responsibility of the listener to the teller, the judge/interpreter/critic to the text? Can Stevens possibly be objective (Can Mervyn? Can we?) once he has heard of extenuating circumstances, good intentions, noble motives? Even if we demand the facts, and nothing but the facts, those facts themselves are shown to be open to different interpretations and to alter as they pass from narrator to narrator.

One particularly telling example of the indeterminacy of the data is provided by the body buried in the basement. For Welbeck, an undesired duel with his former benefactor ended quite differently than intended. To paraphrase his account: I aimed to miss him, he to kill me, he missed his aim, I missed mine, and you (Arthur) heard only one shot because we fired simultaneously, and now, unfortunately, we have a body to dispose of, but these things happen, and fortunately the basement is handy. Welbeck's rationalist account for Arthur then becomes Arthur's Gothic tale told to Stevens. Mervyn describes the burial in gruesome detail and even confesses that by the light of a flickering taper he thought he saw Watson's eyes open and then close. Too frightened for his own safety to consider the possibility that Watson may be still alive, Mervyn first, like a man bereft of reason, runs through the dark labyrinthine corridors of the tomb-like basement, collides with a wall, bloodies himself, and then, even more horrified, returns to help Welbeck complete the task. Stevens, moved by that story but recognizing that it might not be convincing in court, decides not to inform the authorities. Which gives us yet another version of the story. Sounding very much like the defendant, the judge explains, "I did not perceive any immediate advantage to flow from imparting the knowledge I had lately gained to others" (p. 225). It is a rationalist account again and one almost as dubious (what of Captain Watson's relatives?) and as self-serving as Welbeck's.

By this point in the narrative, Dr. Stevens, for better or worse, has essentially cast his lot with Mervyn. For him, the innocence of the young, handsome, fever-wracked stranger whom he took into his home has become almost an article of faith. He helped Arthur knowing full well that he risked the life of his wife and child, and his own life, too, on which many of the city's sick depend for what little aid can be offered to them. Indeed, in the face of the monstrous disorder threatening the City of Brotherly Love and giving the lie to its name, Stevens still asserts a personal benevolence and cares for his fellow citizens without seeking to profit from their distress. But he also premised his kindness to Arthur on the innocence that he perceived in the young man's face: "Had I heard Mervyn's story from another, or read it in a book, I might, perhaps, have found it possible to suspect the truth; but, as long as the impression, made by his tones, gestures and looks, remained in my memory, this suspicion was impossible. . . . The face of Mervyn is the index of an honest mind" (pp. 229–30). Confidence men, the good Dr. Stevens's reading has already warned him, can look honest and helpless when it suits their needs. He thus confronts two contradictory texts, the story he reads in Arthur's face and Arthur's story as he would read it were it not authorized by that author's face. No wonder Wortley's accusations perturb the doctor's reading of his reading. Is he being particularly perceptive or particularly gullible? Arthur's question is transposed into Stevens's question, and that way moral chaos lies: "If Mervyn has deceived me, there is an end to my confidence in human nature. All limits to dissimulation, and all distinctions between vice and virtue will be effaced. No man's word, no force of collateral evidence shall weigh with me an hair" (pp. 248–49).

There is in the doctor's dilemma both a touching humanitarianism and a frightening absolutism. Why, we well might ask, does he stake so much on a young man he has known so briefly? It is partly, I would suggest, because he views Arthur less as a man than as an embodiment of the culture's self-sanctifying myths, which is precisely how Arthur labors to be seen. Mervyn, as he describes himself in his narrative, is a poor, unschooled country boy (a "perfect example of indigence" [p. 46]) whose determination and intelligence have already more than effaced the fact of his humble origins. At one point, he tells how he employed his self-taught knowledge of Latin to translate an Italian manuscript. Or he will dispose of some complex point of jurisprudence (corporate, international, or maritime law; indemnity procedures; civil liberties; whatever) and thereby attest to his mastery of law, which is an all-the-more-remarkable accomplishment considering he has not been trained to that or any other profession. For Mervyn, as a kind of latter-day Franklin, is exactly the pattern of American success in which Stevens believes. As William Hedges aptly observes, "Mervyn has a mission not only to do good but to make good," and nothing in Stevens's ethos or experience prepares him to deem that Protestant ethic in action to be a crime.[49]

It is his own dream of radical innocence in a fallen world come to meet him with a smiling face. Small wonder he believes.

Arthur also believes in Arthur as an American Adam and is as intent upon proving his innocence to Stevens as Stevens is on accepting his proof. The young man's whole narrative is, in fact, specifically intended to refute Wortley's charges. Volume 1 is a cagey self-defense cast in the form of a moral autobiography. Arthur tells of how he was forced to leave home by a widowed and unwise father who was himself victimized by a lascivious dairymaid who schemed her way into marriage with the father and then turned him against the son; of how, after being robbed by unscrupulous innkeepers, he arrived, penniless, in the city to be further victimized, through his very innocence, first by Wallace and then by the calculating Welbeck; of how he freed himself from that bondage and also triumphed over numerous other temptations only to be felled by the dread yellow fever and left, for all his acts of kindness, dependent on the kindness of another. Autobiography verges toward hagiography (Arthur and Stevens's) as *Arthur Mervyn, First Part* ends with Arthur's summation of his case before his reluctant judge and his sympathetic jury who, both embodied in Stevens, also stand with the prisoner at the bar:

> In consequence of your care, I have been restored to life and to health. Your conduct was not influenced by the prospect of pecuniary recompence, of service, or of gratitude. It is only in one way that I am able to heighten the gratification which must flow from reflection on your conduct—by shewing that the being whose life you have prolonged, though uneducated, ignorant, and poor, is not profligate and worthless, and will not dedicate that life which your bounty has given, to mischievous or contemptible purposes. (Pp. 214–15)

Over a year later, and with the publication of volume 2, Dr. Stevens can early assure the reader that he has fully accepted "the truth of the tale" (p. 219). But as the very fact of volume 2 amply attests, the tale is not yet all told, nor is the trial over. Wortley reappears with a more damning bill of particulars and with witnesses to support him. This second brief for the prosecution is presented while Mervyn is away, by his own testimony, doing good deeds in the country. When Arthur reappears not only is he again charged for his role in the Welbeck/Wortley fraud, he also faces the further charge that his whole previous defense was a fraud. The life he postulated has been countered by an opposing portrait of the young man as rogue and reprobate. This different Mervyn allegedly seduced his stepmother and then stole his father's money and best horse to make his getaway. It is hardly the stuff out of which an American Adam is officially made.

The ongoing trial, as the organizing narrative device of the novel, allows Brockden Brown to investigate rules of psychological and social discourse and to show

how the individual self, the social setting, and any story in which each gets told
are all a matter of selection. It is not surprising, then, that the Franklin homol-
ogies of this novel are often remarked, for Franklin presides over both the story
of the central character and the story of the making of that story. Brown, of
course, need not have had his fellow Philadelphian specifically in mind when he
wrote *Arthur Mervyn,* but it may be of more than passing significance that by
1793 (the year in which the action of *Arthur Mervyn* takes place) three biographies
of Franklin had appeared, each based on portions of Franklin's own *Memoirs,*
each purporting to be true, and each presenting a rather different man—Franklin
as the wise and virtuous American patriot, Franklin as unprincipled opportunist
and even traitor, Franklin as conniver and lecher. That the "venerable Ben"
emerges from what purported to be an English translation—*The Private Life of
the Late Benjamin Franklin* (1793)—of the scurrilous French *Mémoires de la vie
privée de Benjamin Franklin* (1791) only emphasizes what a little judicious selection could do.[50] It might also be remembered that Brown's first published work
(1789) was a eulogy for Franklin (who would not die for another year) and that
an editor, apparently deciding it was too good for its subject, published it as a
eulogy for Washington (who would not die for another decade).[51] Before he wrote
his novel in the form of pretended problematic biography, Brown already knew
how duplicitous and self-serving (various selves) the real thing could be.

Shaping his narrative to meet the charges against him, Mervyn tries to make
his tale unquestionably true by making it preeminently mythic, and the paradigms
for that myth were already part and parcel of American popular culture and the
larger ideology of individualism—poor boy from the country, the dangers of the
city and the sharper, the shield of perfect innocence, the road to riches. The
problem, however, is that the material out of which he makes his story is not
quite the same as his story as he would make it, and Arthur, as unintentional
deconstructionist, regularly stumbles into the interstices between the two. We
notice, for example, how frequently he acknowledges, for the reader and Stevens,
that he had not quite, in some particular instance, told the whole truth. Something was omitted because it would have served "no useful purpose" (useful to
whom?), or he had promised confidentiality, or he had, simply, forgotten. In
retrospect, he reports, these omissions almost inevitably have had disastrous consequences, and "sincerity" and openness, he has learned, "is the best policy." But
he keeps having to relearn that same lesson as he once more must retell of still
another incident in part 2 that had been fudged in part 1, now explaining the
hitherto suppressed parts of his previous story the better to prove his past good
intentions and his present honesty.

His defense is his story of his life, but it is even more his and Stevens's and
the time's belief that a "full, circumstantial and explicit story" can "remove every
doubt" (p. 385). That is Arthur's narrative and moral credo. As Norman Grabo
has observed, volume 2, especially, is virtually an orgy of self-revelation, with

Mervyn rushing about telling complete strangers (such as Watson's family in Baltimore) the story of his life.[52] As he becomes more and more confident with each narrative "conquest," he intrudes into other people's business or enters (with escalating frequency) their houses without so much as knocking. The power of compelled belief informs his tale. He utterly convinces Stevens of his innocence, and even Wortley withdraws his accusations. Words prevail; Mervyn triumphs; his best con, perhaps (the issue is not conclusively resolved in the novel), is his resolute insistence that he has never conned anyone.

One measure of Arthur's success is that he finally takes control of his own story. Only near the end of the novel (2:chap. 22) do we learn how the text itself has been transmitted. As nearly all critics admit, it is an awkward device, but it is an important one that both records Stevens's motivations for preserving this story and also calls those motivations (Stevens's and Arthur's) into question:

> Mrs. Wentworth has put me [Arthur] upon a strange task—not disagreeable, however, but such as I should, perhaps, have declined had not the absence of my Bess, and her mamma, made the time hang somewhat heavy. I have, oftener than once, and far more circumstantially than now, told her my adventures, but she is not satisfied. She wants a written narrative, for some purpose which she tells me she will disclose to me hereafter.
>
> Luckily, my friend Stevens has saved me more than half the trouble. He has done me the favor to compile much of my history with his own hand. I cannot imagine what could prompt him to so wearisome an undertaking; but he says that adventures and a destiny so singular as mine, ought not to be abandoned to forgetfulness like any vulgar and *everyday* existence. Besides, when he wrote it, he suspected that it might be necessary to the safety of my reputation and my life, from the consequences of my connection with Welbeck. (P. 412)

Mervyn's is an exemplary life that should be preserved for posterity; it is a suspect life that must be preserved from punishment. Artful Arthur, who so often earlier told his tale, here artlessly wonders why anyone might want it to be written down but obligingly becomes Mrs. Wentworth's scribe, just as he had earlier been Welbeck's or Stevens had been his. This deferring of the authority for authorship invites a complicity in the act of reading, a symbiosis of confessor and confessee, of text and reader. Or differently put, the whole narrative process is textualized and contextualized. As I have shown, when Stevens rewrites Arthur's story, he writes/rights Arthur and thus himself and then is himself rewritten, or at least edited, by the subject and object of his own discourse. As Arthur writes, "To bed, my friend, it is late . . . but let me take these sheets along with me. I will read them, that I am determined, before I sleep, and watch if you have told the whole truth" (p. 412). Mervyn's story becomes Stevens's becomes Mervyn's. . . .

Neither is Arthur, ostensibly in the scribal service of Mrs. Wentworth, necessarily any more dependable or subservient than he was in the narrative service of Stevens. On the contrary, considerable evidence indicates that once he begins writing his own story, he also begins more efficiently to direct the course of his life. For example, no longer promoting the pretense that he yearns only "to plough, to sow, and to reap" (p. 11), he casts his lot with the city and agrees to become Stevens's apprentice and work toward a medical career. Even more obviously, no longer enamored of sweet, country "Bess" (Eliza Hadwin), he proposes to his "mamma," a wealthy widow, Achsa Fielding (with whom, naturally, he has exchanged life stories), and in the last line of the novel, Arthur relinquishes his pen in favor of marriage (Freudian critics like this) and prepares to become "the happiest of men" (p. 446). Marriage, the conventional happy ending of sentimental fiction, resolves the machinations of the plot. And there the case, the protagonist, and the novel all rest.

HE WON THE GIRL, didn't he? Is not that proof positive of the conventional hero and thus the appropriate end of Arthur's narrative enterprise? Except perhaps "mamma" was the wrong girl. That ending has perturbed readers from Brown's day to ours. Even more to the point, by Arthur's own account, *only* a "full disclosure" of all that he had done could be adequate grounds for judging his case and recognizing his innocence. Yet readers from the first publication of the novel to the present have found Arthur's final, definitive account to be both unfinished and indefinite. Virtually all of Brown's first reviewers demurred over basic points in the plot, while the textual openings left by Arthur's telling—and retelling—of his tale and by Stevens's conscientious further retelling in the set-down narrative itself have left ample room for contemporary critics to construct their own—and very different—stories of Arthur Mervyn.

Typically, nineteenth-century readers laid the blame for inconsistencies at the author's feet, not at Arthur's. Early reviewers complained of the novel's repetitions and doublings of identities—Mervyn's resemblance to both Clavering and Lodi, for example—and a number of contemporaneous commentators—most notably, Percy Bysshe Shelley as well as Brown's biographer, William Dunlap—expressed "disgust" that, after fully describing Arthur's love for the orphaned, indigent, innocent Eliza Hadwin, Brown then had his hero precipitously drop this fifteen-year-old maiden for a wealthy widow who was all of twenty-six years of age. Could a man who had all along aggressively brandished his benevolence finally act in that callous fashion, they wondered. These first critics did not concern themselves with the psychological inconsistencies or the structural indeterminacies of the plot, but they virtually all agreed that the work was "flawed" in that it set forth too many "trivial occurrences" and was, finally, "unfinished." Dunlap even felt compelled to address these charges in his *Life of Charles Brockden Brown* (1815) and did so by explaining that "the faults which deform this

interesting and eloquent narrative, are altogether owing to haste, both in com-
posing and in publishing. The work was sent to the printer before the writer had
fully determined its plot."[53]

The early responses to Brown's fiction do not provide an univocal interpretation of *Arthur Mervyn* but emphasize its "gaps," those areas where the reader
is exasperated by contrivance or baffled by seeming deflections from the "lessons
of justice and humanity" (p. 3) promised by the book's preface. Nor do Brown's
own statements on his novel help us to "read" his most problematic character.
Modern critics who favor a "Mervyn the Virtuous" reading regularly cite the
letter Brockden Brown wrote his brother, James, on February 15, 1799, in which
we find one of the clearest examples of an extrinsic "statement of intention"
penned by an early American novelist. To be sure, the letter explicitly indicates
that Mervyn is designed to be a good man: "Arthur is intended as an hero whose
virtue, in order to be productive of benefit to others, and felicity to himself,
stands in no need of riches." Yet Brown's letter was not, of course, intended for
contemporary critics still debating Arthur's morality. It was addressed to the
brother who, despite his general distrust of the whole literary vocation, had agreed
to oversee *Arthur Mervyn* through the press while Charles tripped off to New
York. The opening portions of the letter suggest that James had objected to the
final incidents of part 1 of the novel, the scene in which Welbeck convinces
Mervyn that the $20,000 that Mervyn wishes to will to Clemenza Lodi (and that
originally belonged to her brother) are actually the product of Welbeck's coun-
terfeiting skills, whereupon Mervyn, in righteous horror, at once burns the bills,
only to discover later that they were valid after all. After first apologizing for
allowing his brother's "last letter to remain so long unanswered," the author
defends this awkward plot device on moral grounds, the unfolding of which are
all to be revealed when the second volume of the novel is published. In that
volume, Brown promises, Mervyn, though penniless, will come to the aid of the
Hadwins and will be rewarded for his efforts by "marriage with the youngest;
the death of the elder by a consumption and grief, leaves him in possession of
competence, and the rewards of virtue. This scheme, as you see, required the
destruction of the bills."[54]

This letter—and the critical uses to which it has been put—embodies itself
another allegory of problematic reading. To start, nearly all early American novelists claimed that their books served to inculcate virtue, but that claim, as I have
shown, was often only pro forma, and it is difficult to take any statement of moral
intentions as definitive. Furthermore, there is a tendency among historians (literary or otherwise) to privilege the written record, to trust those documents that
do survive to convey an unvarnished rendering of the truth, as if no diarists two
hundred years ago ever engaged in dubious self-dramatization or no correspondents craftily shaped their letters to their own private and particular purposes.
Might not the artist be mostly attempting to assert the "higher purposes" of his

calling to his more affluent brother or defending his "artistic integrity" against another's critique of a weakness in his plot? The "condescension of posterity" also shows itself when we take seriously and absolutely the kinds of statements that we would view more sceptically if uttered by our peers. Nor can we read the letter as a definitive statement of the author's intentions with respect to his character. The same missive that promises a virtuous hero also promises that this hero will marry Eliza. He doesn't. Does that mean he isn't?[55]

While the early critics typically blamed the writer for the inconsistencies or excesses in the plot, most twentieth-century commentators have preferred to exonerate Brown and to indict Arthur Mervyn. Any divergences from an implicitly or explicitly promised line of development or other similar "flaws" become further evidence of Arthur's naivete and of the errors youth is prone to (the more forgiving appraisal) or of his devious nature and dishonest ways (the more censorious one). This essentially New Critical argument assumes that the text itself is flawless. "Seeming" faults are only seeming, are craftily concealed reading directions, are, in short, there to be explained away by the discerning critic. The critic, in essence, is not the reader of the text but its editor, smoothing away its apparent flaws. Such explication, typically expended on authors already canonized (indeed, the sign of canonization), may well be one effect of what Foucault has called the "birth of the author" during the nineteenth century. Conversely, the Romantic glorification of the supremacy of the artist in the intellectual pantheon is itself reified by twentieth-century critics finding just the author they went looking for.[56]

No wonder, then, that modern criticism has had a field day with *Arthur Mervyn*. First, the novel's trial-like structure inherently favors a psychological investigation of the repressions and omissions in the official record, which is thereby rendered still more official through the critic's Freudian authority. Even more important, the very indeterminacies in the text that demand critical enterprise also leave ample room for that same enterprise. Thus, James Russo, to consider an extreme example, can, in effect, reinvent the entire plot, eliding different characters into one in order to rid the novel of ambiguities and excesses. In Russo's reading, Mervyn *actually* is Clavering in disguise and Clavering/Mervyn is also Lodi and Colvil too. Welbeck becomes a relatively harmless old codger ruined by this composite villain, who assumes, as convenience demands, the name and identity of "Arthur Mervyn." Yet some loose ends still remain. What was the horrific sight that Mervyn witnessed through the opening in the attic at the end of volume 1? He promises to tell and never mentions it again. Russo proposes that Brown intended to write a third volume of the novel that would take care of all such problems, which is not so different from Dunlap's explanation of the "faults which deform this interesting and eloquent narrative" after all.[57]

Although few would go as far as Russo, most modern critics follow the example of Stevens in the text and seek a totalizing reading that largely resolves ambiguities and inconsistencies through explanation, judicious evasion, or, more often, by recourse to some overriding ideology that "makes sense" of difference. Leslie Fiedler relies on Freudian analysis to give us the real character of Mervyn behind his confused testimony. Or other critics have proposed to place *Arthur Mervyn* in its "historical context" and have thereby both fully condemned and fully exonerated its protagonist.[58] Yet no contemporary reading dispels those problems that the early reviewers rightly recognized. Gaps do remain. Clavering tells his pathetic story to the admiring Arthur—his double? his avatar?—but Mrs. Wentworth subsequently relates a different and altogether less flattering story of the same character. Brown never accounts for this discrepancy; Arthur never acknowledges it; yet much of our appreciation for Arthur rests on his explanations about Clavering to his disbelieving aunt, Mrs. Wentworth. More damning still is the problem of the body in the basement. Was the captain really dead? Did his one "glance, languid but wild" (p. 110) attest to Arthur's wild imagination (quite understandable under the circumstances), or did it prove a murder not in the past but in progress and a murder in which Arthur plays a crucial part? Not, perhaps, coincidentally, much the same scene is later reenacted with Arthur cast as the victim about to be "buried alive" by the ghoulish "hearse men" in plague-wracked Philadelphia. When Arthur "opened [his] eyes," a stranger "assisted [him] to regain [his] feet" (p. 149). In vivid contrast, Arthur did not try to aid a man perhaps still alive but, instead and for all practical purposes, shoveled all the faster.

Or we might notice how regularly seemingly significant characters simply vanish from the narrative. There is Wallace, who gets volume 2 going and then is himself gone; Miss Carlton, who at first seems a possible love interest for Arthur, except she cannot afford him; Miss Fanny Maurice, another possibility, except her mother will never give up any of her cash. But the most important disappearing act (and the one that many of the early critics resented) is Eliza's. She drops from the novel just before what should be the climax of the subsidiary love story in which she supposedly stars. Achsa invites Eliza to live with her; Arthur goes out to the country to get the girl and delivers her to "mamma." Afterward, Eliza is seen only once, briefly, when she confirms Arthur's bout of somnambulism. Is she pining away in grief for her beloved, whose heart more and more belongs to "mamma"? Or is she relieved to be so easily rid of one so obviously inconstant? Arthur proclaims that "there is nothing upon earth more dear to me than my *Bess*" (p. 404) and then never even notices dear Bess's response when Achsa proves dearer.

The inconsistencies in the narration finally center most of all in the protagonist himself and do so most obviously when Mrs. Althorpe insists that Arthur was not the boy he claimed to be. Dr. Stevens has summoned his friend so that she might be a more "objective" witness than Wortley. Mrs. Althorpe, who has long known the Mervyn family, tells of a lazy youth who refused to plough but passed his time in moody walks, who shunned the schoolroom for a life of pampered leisure, who mocked his father and held himself aloof from his neighbors. She also repeats the accusation—held by "all the neighbors"—that Mervyn had "made a prostitute" of his future stepmother and then, after her marriage to the father, had publicly derided both of them before making off with all of his father's cash and his best horse too. The doctor decides that this "narrative . . . ill accorded with the tale" told by Arthur.

Arthur apparently thinks so, too, and in volume 2 dramatically revises his earlier idyll of the country versus the city to switch, in effect, stories in midstream. The protagonist's proclaimed love of the country ran like a leitmotif through volume 1. He regularly forswore the evils of city life and promised a salutary return to the countryside: "I saw that the city was no place for *me*. . . . My ancient occupations rose to my view enhanced by a thousand imaginary charms" (p. 46); or "I wondered at the contrariety that exists between the scenes of the city and the country; and fostered with more zeal than ever, the resolution to avoid those seats of depravity and danger" (p. 154). With approximately the same frequency that Welbeck verbally commits himself to death before dishonor and with as little effect, Arthur vows to return to the simple life of the ploughman and the day laborer.[59] Only after Stevens reveals Mrs. Althorpe's different version of his country life does Arthur sheepishly admit that he never really liked the farmer's life at all, that he spent as little time behind a horse as he possibly could manage, and that he did, indeed, pass most of his youth dreamily wandering among his father's hundred acres. "It is true," he says in answer to Mrs. Althorpe's charges, "I took up the spade and the hoe as rarely, and for as short a time, as possible" (p. 341).

The poor boy from the country who makes good in the city was already a feature of the American pantheon. But making good through thrift, ability, hard work, and a saving innocence teaches one social lesson, whereas making good through pose and prevarication, through cunning and conning, teaches quite another. Both Arthur and Stevens would shun that second lesson, and do so through another story. Arthur at once comes up with a version of his past that subsumes the two versions already presented by claiming a justifying motive for the deceptions of his previous account and a higher nobility implicit in and redeeming the actions that Mrs. Althorpe found so dubious. He now admits that he hesitated to tell Stevens of his *real* childhood because the truth was too painful to repeat. The new story he then provides is as conventionally believable as the old one and considerably more interesting. Sawny Mervyn was a drunken, ignorant, sadistic father (a penny-pinching Scotsman, a shiftless peasant, an overbearing patriarch) who brutalized his poor wife (the martyred, helpless female). Of course (this plot is easy to fill in), Arthur (though frail of body, he was bold of spirit) always interceded on his mother's behalf. He *could* not take up the plough, for he was too busy protecting his "darling mamma." Besides, she had already lost her other children to a genetic malady that cut their lives short before their nineteenth birthdays (Arthur is eighteen as he speaks) and weakened him. Mrs. Mervyn *begged* her last, living son not to labor in the fields. How could he refuse her? His life depended on acceding to her request, and her life depended on him. All of this—suffering, self-sacrificing, surviving against awesome odds— is most moving. Arthur is either an even better man than Stevens previously suspected or an even more accomplished storyteller.

Arthur was the first to try to render a totalizing reading of his life, and he, too, has loose ends that he must somehow tie up. More specifically, his focus on his virtuous concern for his mother does not quite address Mrs. Althorpe's charges regarding his stepmother. Admittedly, Arthur, like Mrs. Althorpe, cannot be too explicit on this subject. Sexuality, in these early novels, always had to be presented in euphemistic terms, and Arthur only hints of an attempted seduction, not his of her but hers of him. The lascivious servant, Betty Lawrence, apparently threw herself regularly and "voluptuously" (one of his favorite words) into the virtuous youth's path. And on one such occasion (presumably Betty was *sans-culotte*), a neighbor spied the two of them and concluded the obvious. "It was useless to attempt to rectify his mistake," Arthur laments, "by explaining ap-pearances, in a manner consistent with my innocence. This mode of explication implied a *continence* in me which he denied to be possible. . . . A temptation which this judge of human nature knew *he* was unable to resist, he sagely concluded to be irresistible by any other man, and quickly established the belief among my neighbors, that the woman who had married the father had been prostituted to the son" (pp. 346–47). Brutal father, victim mother, seducing servant who con-nives herself into the role of wicked stepmother: again, it all fits together and is conventional enough to bear the stamp of truth.

Arthur produces no evidence to confirm his second story, just as he produced none to confirm the first. Late in the novel, Brown does lead us to expect some final resolution in an imminent deathbed meeting between Arthur and his father, now dying of alcoholism and in debtors' prison, presumably robbed blind by Betty (but possibly robbed by his son). The tone of that last encounter—"Arthur, my son, forgive me; I knew not what I did" or "Ungrateful wretch! Do not come now to triumph over my total defeat!"—could resolve the nature of the past relationship between the two and solve the ambiguity at the heart of the plot and protagonist, even as it also allowed the author another of the deathbed scenes he liked so well. Instead, Arthur makes his way to the jail to find his father already dead. The only note of certainty added to the tale is the definitive silence of death, which somehow casts a darker hue over the very question that a few final words might have answered.

Stevens and the trusting reader must accept Arthur's story mostly on faith. For Stevens, faith in the character is also faith in the land whose story Arthur's story at its best sets forth—the land of opportunity, the country of the free. Yet

America, in the novel, is also a society wracked by greed and lust, is the country ravaged by yellow fever. The new nation's capital, Philadelphia, the City of Brotherly Love, has become a hellish nightmare-scape, with death endemic, the signs (visible, audible, and olfactory) of disease everywhere, and corpses rotting in the street. Nor does Brown spare us the appropriately Gothic details. The decorous castle in the quiet countryside of Connecticut is succeeded by a far more fearful and believable symbol of human order gone awry. The elaborate Bush-hill mansion has become Bush-hill hospital has become a plague house, a hideous asylum from which there is no escape and in which the dying elicit only the laughter of the attendants who do not tend them: "You will scarcely believe that, in this scene of horrors, the sound of laughter should be overheard. While the upper rooms of this building are filled with the sick and the dying, the lower apartments are the scene of carrousals and mirth." With such death's head "debauchery and riot" (p. 173), the social implications of the plague are fully drawn:

> The city . . . was involved in confusion and panick, for a pestilential disease had begun its destructive progress. Magistrates and citizens were flying to the country. The numbers of the sick multiplied beyond all example; even in the pest affected cities of the Levant. The malady was malignant, and unsparing.
>
> The usual occupations and amusements of life were at an end. Terror had exterminated all the sentiments of nature. Wives were deserted by husbands, and children by parents. Some had shut themselves in their houses, and debarred themselves from all communication with the rest of mankind. . . . Men were seized by this disease in the streets; passengers fled from them; entrance into their own dwellings was denied to them; they perished in the public ways. (Pp. 128–29)

Stevens has jeopardized his life to help his fellow Americans, to deny that yellow fever can represent his countrymen, his nation. He is, in effect, poised between the public manifestations of the plague, with its story of debauchery, deceit, division, and death, and Arthur's story of innocence, benevolence, and virtue rewarded, with its personification of the liberal credo and its proof of the validity of the ideological basis for the American experiment in democracy. Given those alternative visions, his choice of Arthur is both self-evidently understandable and plagued with damning doubts. For what if Mervyn proves to be just another con man? That fear must be measured against the backdrop of the other metaphors for disorder Stevens sees all around him. The urgency with which he believes Mervyn underscores the very desperateness of the considerations that underlie that belief. He does not want to be (metaphorically speaking) the victim in a Gothic story. He does not want to discover America as the Haunted Castle, Rush's fictive land, Anarchia, where dissension and dissimulation reign. Stevens's belief in Arthur thus provides his own, positive answer to Crèvecoeur's question "What is an American?"

But what *is* Stevens's America? The novel provides no ready answer. We see incipient urban corruption graphically metaphored in the plague and more pervasively present in the generally corrupt business dealings that undergird much of the business of the novel, and the temptation is to cast the country as the natural and saving alternative to the death and decay rampant in the city. Yet the "traditional" world of the countryside is hardly the seat of pastoral virtue and bucolic bliss that Mervyn describes in his early eclogues. Country people, too, can be contentious, petty, narrow-minded, and self-serving. Philip Hadwin, to cite one example, is a drunkard who abuses his wife and children and cheats his niece out of her property. Nor is the pestilential Philadelphia, the thriving mercantile capital of America, only a Gothic cityscape. As Jane Tompkins has shown, for every act of metropolitan deceit and corruption, Brown provides a countering example of urban benevolence.[60] Take your pick: America the corrupt or America the beautiful. There is ample evidence for either reading.

The ending of the novel especially invites different readings and does so, first, by inverting much of the previous novel. As Emory Elliott observes, Arthur finally plays Stevens to Achsa's Arthur and has as great a need to believe her improbable story as Stevens had for believing Arthur's.[61] Arthur meets the woman who will become his bride in the unpropitious setting of a house of prostitution. He, of course, quickly explains his presence there (he valiantly sought to rescue Clemenza Lodi from captivity and iniquity), and she, in turn, tells him an equally implausible tale designed to prove her incontestable innocence. She also tells him (and he accepts as true) a more suspect story of how a daughter of a rich Portuguese Jew of the merchant class was able to marry into the British aristocracy; of how her new husband presently ran off with an older woman and then, subsequently, bigamously, married yet another woman, this one a French aristocrat; of how he participated in the Revolution but was, nonetheless, killed by Robespierre's henchmen; of how that death has set her free. The political message here is appropriately mixed. The violation of traditional British class structure leads to unhappiness; France is wracked by the Terror; both facts seem to affirm a conservative political message. Yet the timely intervention of Robespierre makes possible the marriage that gives us the requisite happy ending of the whole novel, which hardly validates traditional values. The Terror makes a space for a highly unconventional but seemingly passionate love.

In accepting Achsa's story, Arthur also accepts Achsa as his wife—his *rich* wife, and here we are not too far removed from that "contrast" that I postulated at the beginning of this chapter: rude Jonathan wedding Maria Van Rough. Women were allowed to dream of marrying above their class. That is a fantasy ending promoted by a number of eighteenth-century novels for women. But Achsa tried it once and didn't like it. She therefore subsequently sets her sights on a nubile, innocent, country youth, who is often described by his physical beauty, whereas Achsa is consistently defined as beautiful of mind but emphatically not of body. The sexual role reversals implicit in that relationship portend a tantalizing Wollstonecraftian egalitarianism and remind the reader that Brown was, after all, the author of *Alcuin*, one of the most important feminist tracts of the 1790s. Finally, Achsa's ancestry, if not her religious practice, is Jewish, and that religious and ethnic difference serves only to enhance her cosmopolitan desirability in Arthur's provincial estimation.

If Arthur is a hero and this marriage is the reward for his virtue, it is a singularly appropriate reward. Thanks to the love story that has displaced the Gothic story with which the novel began, cultural diversity, feminism, and class mobility are all incorporated into the society imaged by this union. The ending also vindicates Arthur's previous account of himself and thus Stevens's faith in that account, which was really his faith in his country. America works—not as some stable, traditional, premodern community (that idyll of the American past is absent from *Arthur Mervyn*) but as a vital, dynamic society that flourishes in heterogeneity and originality.

But if Arthur is as much the dupe of Achsa's tale as Stevens may have been of Arthur's, then the con man, pretending to love her but really after her wealth, is still up to his old tricks and has himself perhaps been conned into marriage with a woman of dubious, if not ill, repute. In this reading, the final marriage need not portend the dawning of a new and more open society but can signal a reign of deceit and disorder more insidious than either a duplicitous Arthur or a duplicitous Achsa (he marrying her only for her money, she leading him on without any) imagined. The ending holds out the promise of individuality and energy yet does not entirely exclude the possibility of egomania and alienation—oppositions that, as the plot of the entire novel suggests, can be flip sides of the same republican coin.

Two radically different stories, each with its concomitant America, are shadowed forth. As the history of the novel's reception attests, both stories are latent within the text and both are possible within the nation that the text evokes. One reads the ending and makes one's choice. And the choice must be, finally, the reader's, for there is no way of knowing for sure Brown's own intentions concerning his ambiguous and indeterminate narrative. What we do know is that his friends frequently lamented the writer's inability to stick to the straight-and-narrow path of rational (by which they often meant nonfictional) discourse. "He starts an idea," Dr. Elihu Hubbard Smith complained in his diary, "pursues it a little way; new ones spring up; he runs a short distance after each; meantime the original one is likely to escape entirely."[62] Brown himself, in an early novel that he, appropriately, never finished, remarked philosophically on the complexity and indeterminacy of mind:

> The vicissitudes to which the human character and opinions are liable cannot be considered without astonishment. No one more widely differs in his sentiments and dispositions from others than at different periods from himself, and those intellectual

revolutions always correspond with external circumstances. We vary according to the variations of the scene and hour, and it is not less difficult to tell what our views and opinions will be twelve months hence than to foresee the particular circumstances in which we shall then be placed.[63]

Brown posits an intriguingly modern concept of personality, an awareness of fragmentation—the mutable, indeterminate, changeling self—without the anxiety that pervades the censorious remarks made by his friend, Dr. Smith. Indeed, Brown's theory of personality short-circuits dogmatic notions of intentionality (one cannot even know one's *own* intentions) or historicity (context continually changes) and thus undermines critical attempts to arrive at a definitive reading of Arthur Mervyn the character; of *Arthur Mervyn* the novel; of Charles Brockden Brown the writer; or, for that matter, of the reading self.

It did not, in short, take the twentieth century to invent Derrida or Bakhtin. *Arthur Mervyn*, I would finally suggest, might best be seen as an early American version of Bakhtin's "dialogical" text, a carnivalesque performance in which the author resolutely refuses to delimit his intentions while also allowing his characters their own ambiguities and even a spirit of "revolt" against any constraining proprieties the text might threaten to impose. In Bakhtin's view, the dialogical text is particularly subversive since it challenges complacency, forces the reader's active participation in the text, and resolutely refuses to assuage uncertainty with comforting, final solutions. As noted in an earlier chapter, Bakhtin found the freedom of the individual to make an interpretive choice innately subversive and applauded the tendencies of a novel such as *Arthur Mervyn* (the example is mine, not his; he preferred Rabelais) to challenge, frustrate, and finally deny the interpretive propensities and ideological premises of the individual, especially of the individual committed to a rationalist model of mind, a rigid ideal of a static hierarchical social order, and a concept of fiction as some mechanical rehearsal of the pieties of the time.[64] *Arthur Mervyn* can, of course, accommodate the pieties of its time or ours, but only through a provisional and partial reading that is both asserted and questioned within the text. In contemporary parlance, then, Brown, soon after the inception of the novel in America, wrote metafiction, fiction about the making of fictions—the writer's, the character's, the reader's, and the nation's.

9 Afterword: Texts as Histories

Fiction is a lie that tells the truth.
—Jean Cocteau

Friedrich von Schiller, one of the most eminent historians of the late eighteenth century, was carried into the lecture hall in Jena upon the shoulders of enthusiastic admirers who deposited him at the podium where he would answer, once and for all, a question he had raised before: "What Is Universal History and Why Do We Study It?" Universal History, Schiller explained, discovered in the past a vast network of causal relationships that, with relentless logic, produced the present. It was the task of the Universal Historian to chart out those causalities in order that the reader might see the coherent whole that was modern Europe, might understand how previous events had produced a stable Continental society that enjoyed an enduring peace and that promised (history portended as much) to last forever. Schiller's speech on that May day in 1789 was constantly interrupted by cheers from the crowd, who could not foresee, any more than the Universal Historian, that in less than two months another crowd would storm the Bastille and launch Europe into its most revolutionary epoch.[1]

This anecdote is also an admonition, for any attempt to make a Universal History *assumes* an interpretation of the present and then discovers or even creates a past that validates that interpretation. Perhaps even more dangerously, it also projects the past-present into the future, as if the status quo, as defined by the historian, were expressly designed for eternity. A revolution looks different, too, depending on which side of the ocean or Bastille one views it from, all of which would seem to be an obvious enough assertion. Yet it is unsettling in that the alternative to Schiller's Universal History or to the positivism of nineteenth-century history seems to be cultural relativism, a valueless history with its own attendant political and theoretical nightmares.

Obviously, I have not suggested a relativistic reading of the early American novel, nor do I propose, in this brief afterword, a Universal History of the American novel. In fundamental ways, both relativistic account and totalizing history assume the objectivity of the historian, the ability of the historian to catalogue what *is*, even though the end and interpretation of that descriptive categorization are quite different in each case. Less obviously but no less thoroughly than Universal History, cultural relativism is, finally, a myth in that no historian ever fully avoids value judgment. The simplest fact that one *is* a historian choosing to examine a particular period in history and a particular problem already encompasses a complex hierarchy of values, ranging from assumptions about periodization (why define the Revolutionary War as a beginning, not an ending—or a middle, for that matter?) to categorization (are these facts, and do they bear on the question at hand?) to authority (what institutional or other hegemonies allow any scholar the *leisure* to pursue this search?).

Oppositional or dialogical history challenges conventional literary history by questioning both the relative value of what is examined and the implicit values of the examiner.[2] It sees the very processes and ambitions of historiography as products of much larger forces, and it seeks to understand the relationships between those present forces and the hierarchical imperatives of the past. History can be crudely but compositely defined as an assemblage of texts (the labor of historians) addressing a different assemblage of texts (the archive). The historian, first, attempts to engage in an exchange with the past through the mixed and amorphous record of what does survive and through the particular interests and agenda of the individual historian—what she or he is looking for and to what end. Second, that exchange is inevitably filtered through the medium of competing histories and other interpretations. In essence, every history—borrowing here, disputing there, consciously or unconsciously filling in omissions left in different accounts or reshaping the territory that another historian has already mapped—reembodies its predecessors even as it labors to suppress them. As Paine noted, "when once any object has been seen . . . it is impossible to put the mind back to the same condition it was before it saw it. . . . It has never yet been discovered, how to make man *unknow* his knowledge, or *unthink* his thoughts."[3] A dialogical history pretends neither to unknow nor to know absolutely. Quite the contrary, it focuses its attention on those areas where the case seems the most obvious and gets to work where there is consensus. If we already have the answer, we well may have been asking the wrong question.

Some of the pitfalls of a monological literary history are appropriately illustrated by the contemporary critical reception of *Arthur Mervyn*. Most commentators who read Charles Brockden Brown approach him backward through the standard nineteenth-century fictional syllabus of Melville, Hawthorne, and Poe. The governing but unexamined assumption underlying this retrospective genealogy is that a few selected writers somehow constitute a unique "American pantheon" and are, simply (and perniciously), the representative authors deserving of special attention. Criticism has already rendered its crucial verdicts, and its remaining business is mostly to buttress further its case. Criticism thus becomes a kind of house committee on un-American fictional activities, with consequences pedagogical (what works are taught), economic (what are reprinted), political (who is privileged, who is invisible), and, finally, interpretive (what becomes the grid whereby we assess other works). Read through this American tradition in order to be placed at the head of it, *Arthur Mervyn* almost inevitably becomes father to the powers of darkness, not brother to *The Power of Sympathy*. The title character, Arthur himself, can be seen as an early unreliable narrator cunningly misdirecting his own story. The gaps in the text exist to be explained away by the enterprising critic who comprehends far more what is at issue than do the other characters in the fiction. Indeed, Maravegli, Estwick, Mr. Hadwin, Curling, Lodi, the Carltons, the Watsons, Fanny Maurice, and, most of all, Stevens all become so many fools serving simply to be gulled by the likes of Welbeck or Arthur. They become the blank faces on the social mask through which the author covertly strikes, to be followed only by the most discerning readers, and the novel becomes a kind of *Moby Mervyn, Confidence Man*, the predictable, if implausible, product of a predetermined canon.

Read within the context of his contemporaries, however, Mervyn seems rather less dark and diabolical than much recent criticism suggests. He need not be an Ahab, a Chillingworth, or even an Usher; he might be mostly a Reverend Boyer or a Major Sanford or even an odd and inconclusive amalgam of the two. And the novel, too, looks different as a cheap two-volume duodecimo ready for the local lending library than as a Center for Editions of American Authors "Approved Text" replete with a "Historical Essay," "Textual Essay," "Textual Notes," "List of Emendations," "Historical List of Substantive Variants," and "Record of Collations and Copies Consulted."[4] The doubles in the novel can seem less Freudian aberrations and portentous symbols and can be seen as plot devices that were conventional and even commonplace in the novels of the time.[5] Various gaps in the text are no longer clear evidence of sinister repressions that the "careful reader" must discern but might be merely the failures of a hasty writer (or an ambivalent man) to tie up his story's loose ends, loose ends of the type that plague (from a modernist perspective) many early American novels. A common feature in these works is the scramble, in the penultimate chapter, to dispose of various subsidiary characters and events in order that the final chapter can focus on the protagonists and their ending. In short, *Arthur Mervyn* as a work of fiction and as a fictional character looks different depending on the historical context in which we place it/him. Our problem as readers is a version of Dr. Stevens's, and our solution can be no more final than his. Or, to return to the theoretical issue of canon that I have raised before in this study, *what* we read shapes *how* we read—a reversal of the usual critical presupposition.

We have a choice of Mervyns. Dialogical history gives us a choice of pasts, too. But that very choice or pluralism is subversive since it implies that a literary tradition is not simply inherited but constructed, and constructed according to the critical categories we devise. For example, as Annette Kolodny has demonstrated, when Moses Coit Tyler set out in 1878 to discover the origins of American literature, he found beginnings that affirmed what he was looking for: a "common national accent" in the American literary past; a tradition "single in its commanding ideas and in its national destinies"; an American literature char-

acterized by "uniformity," like the nation itself.[6] Yet, as critics as diverse as Kolodny and Harold Bloom have argued, an imperative toward canonization, toward
the creation of a univocal history (literary, social, political—the three are always
intertwined) requires the exclusion of what does not fit into the a priori definition
of precisely what is to be defined.[7] Moreover, a uniform American literature
defines a uniform American and, by extension and implication, excludes those
who do not fit the definition by reasons of gender, race, ethnicity, religion, class,
education, wealth, region, place of origin (as with immigrants or, conversely,
Native Americans), or language.

Nor are the consequences of a reductive theory of American identity purely
literary. If high school and college textbooks, standardized tests (typically the
most conservative measure of an educational system), doctoral reading lists, or
scholarly monographs regularly present a homogeneous America, then the literary
or pedagogical image of a nation is at odds with (or simply irrelevant to) the
increasingly heterogeneous American population receiving this message. If, after
a brief period of educational revisionism, there is again a call for the "basics,"
then once more pedagogy narrowly defines what is and what is not essential or
basic to America. The spirit and educational philosophy of Noah Webster prevail,
and the humanities classroom takes on the rather dubious role of perpetuating
the status quo by providing a restrictive, exclusionary answer to the question
posed earlier by Crèvecoeur: "What is an American?"[8] It is an answer maintained
through a rigorous (if unconscious) process of selection that perpetuates itself
generation after generation, as new instructors teach what they were taught, as
publishers reprint (with new introductions) what is still being taught, and as
scholars analyze the same old works according to whatever current critical interests prevail, the whole cycle spinning merrily on.[9]

With notable (but relatively few) exceptions, literary history is a history of the
most available texts. The conditioning of our perceptions of what literary history
is operates on even the most elementary level. An example might be useful here.
A number of times in this study I have referred to the "What is an American?"
section of Crèvecoeur's *Letters from an American Farmer*. Scholars of American
literature certainly know that Crèvecoeur did not conclude his farmer's letters
with the same unqualified sense of American egalitarianism he early exhibited,
nor did the author himself retain his original opinion of the land to which he
had immigrated but which he later left.[10] When, near the end of the volume,
Crèvecoeur's narrator/double witnesses the punishment inflicted upon slaves in
South Carolina, we have a very different vision of America than that with which
he began—and a very different answer to the question "What is an American?"
From the earlier paean, *Letters from an American Farmer* devolves to disillusionment with a system that seemed to promise so much and, at least implicitly,
requires the reader to think about reform, about improving a nation that does
not fully live up to its promise and its possibilities. Predictably, however, the later

sections of Crèvecoeur's classic are anthologized far less often than the exultant (if unrealistic) letter 3. For most readers of Crèvecoeur (who typically encounter his work in anthologies, if at all), the important analysis of American racism set forth in the latter portions of the book simply does not exist. It is not part of our literary inheritance.

The issue here is not that literature provides an inaccurate reflection of history but that no documents (from Crèvecoeur's *Letters* to signing evidence on marriage records) can simply be "read" as if they were objective, scientific data produced or preserved as some pure product of a people and the abiding record of their times. The record always suppresses more than it tells. Why, we must ask, are certain records kept in the first place? Why are they saved? The whole process of historiography, the archive itself, must be subjected to rigorous analysis. Who is keeping the records and for what purpose? Who is writing, to whom, and why?

Another example from the early national period can again illuminate the politics of literary history. The Connecticut Rising Glory Poets are often described as representative of the time and place in which they wrote. But what do they represent? The glory of American society or the views of a somewhat hypocritical gentry determined that the Revolution should proceed no further than their own self-interest required; a reasoned opposition to the "irrational" (such as the Shaysites) or a calculated attempt to keep "unruly" peasants in their proper, lowly station? As Kenneth Silverman points out, when Joel Barlow, John Trumbull, David Humphreys, Lemuel Shaw, and other poets began, in late 1786, their "counter-mobocracy" literary campaign in the form of "The Anarchiad," this series of satires, speeches, and poems (first published in the *New-Haven Gazette* and then reprinted throughout the East) spoke to fears in much of the populace, for the series sold out so fast that "Humphreys was unable to find extra copies to send to Washington."[11] "The Anarchiad" stressed the need for a strong, centralized government, praised the wise authority of that government, and celebrated a pastoral ideal quite contrary to the realities of country life as perceived by Shays's outraged agrarians. Inverting an earlier language of Whig sentimentalism, the Rising Glory Poets ominously equated Shays's "anarchists" (i.e., anti-Americans) with evil seducers out to despoil the serene dignity of Columbia. In short, the poets attempted to counter incipient social unrest by extolling the vision of an abiding, enduring Federalist Republic grounded in the enlightened interest of entitled men. When accepted as representative Americans, their bias becomes the given, the glory of the early Republic, while the Shaysites are encoded in literature as the would-be destroyers of a nascent democracy.

Yet, if we are going to rely on literature to present us with the data of social history, with a portrait of the American self, we cannot look only at the literature written for privileged readers, which advocated the interests of those readers. By looking at a different genre, the novel, a genre derided by authority figures even while it was increasingly read by the lower orders (as well as by some of those official spokespersons who more publicly condemned it), one almost inevitably encounters a *different* representative view of America. Although the American novel would soon become respectable (and perhaps lose some of its oppositional edge with age and respectability), its original, lowly status virtually assured that it would early speak for those also marginalized by American society as a whole. Many of America's first novels, as I have shown, emphasized the class, gender, and racial inequities in the new land and even explicitly advocated an end to these inequities. In a novel such as Martha Meredith Read's *Monima, or the Beggar Girl*, for example, we have a strikingly different version of America than the one provided by the Connecticut poets, yet *Monima* was widely read too— first published in 1802, reprinted in both New York and Philadelphia editions the following year, and pirated, plagiarized, and paraphrased, in condensed forms, in various American magazines and newspapers until the middle of the nineteenth century.

Read's representative American was not some established member of the gentry nor even a poor boy in the process of making good but a most disenfranchised member of society, a "beggar girl":

> Every day during the week, the almost heart-broken Monima was compelled to beg; it would be an endless task to recount the insolence, repeated insults, the cold contempt, the mortifying strictures on idleness, the affected pity of the *seemingly feeling*, and the ostentatious charity of the naturally contracted and cringing hypocrites, with their bitter effects on her tender heart. Another week of such excruciating harassment, would have made her an inmate for the grave.

Yes, the diction is sentimental. But Read's portrait of America is far *less* sentimental than that presented by the Rising Glory Poets or in Crèvecoeur's letter 3. Read's novelistic vision of America gives us a New World as corrupt as the Old. The Revolution did not perform its office for all Americans equally; wealthy Americans as convinced of their own privilege as any European aristocrats rob Monima of her money in order to force her first into financial dependence and then into sexual submission, graphic metaphors for oppressions by class and gender.

Nor does Martha Read limit her critique to a ruling class. The assistance provided to Monima by the bourgeoisie is equally debilitating. They offer her demeaning employment at starvation wages: "Four months elapsed thus with a degree of comparative happiness; but tho' Monima was indefatigable in her industry, still she could not earn a cent more than merely enough to provide necessary diet and fuel." An early indictment of commodity capitalism, this sentimental novel shows the way in which middle-class Americans carefully calculate how much they must pay the worker to keep her alive (and thus able to work) without giving her the means to rise above her social class—a cycle of economic enslavement. The novel also includes a stinging critique of well-to-do philanthropists who validate their own achievements through pious precepts about America as a "land of opportunity," precepts singularly inapplicable to Monima's distress. Even the proletariat mostly jeer the poor girl when, assaulted and robbed of her "small store of cash" by the villainous De Noix, she shouts, "Murder! Murder!"—fully aware that this calamitous theft could well spell the death of herself and her infirm father: "A mob quickly gathered about her. Some judged her to be intoxicated, whilst others were for examining her throat to see if it were cut. A considerable time the unfortunate girl was the jest, and butt of the hardened unfeeling populace. Her wailing, her lamentation, her tears were of no avail, they rather increased the sport and derision of the mob."[12]

If Monima's plight strikes the contemporary reader as ludicrous or overdone, whereas "The Anarchiad" represents the "real" America, perhaps it is because scholarship has long had a vested interest in documenting one genealogy and not the other.[13] The problem lies not in using literature as a source for social history but in thinking that literature, any more than history, exists except as humans compile, preserve, and canonize it; or in forgetting the ideological purposes served by the study of literature and history within a society. Moreover, what is officially saved exists not merely in its own right but according to the formulations whereby it is preserved. Thus, if we analyze, in scholarly publications and classroom lectures, the earlier Godwinian novels of Charles Brockden Brown primarily in terms of the same author's purported conversion to a middle-aged conservatism, we in effect perpetuate a parable of impetuous, improvident revolutionary youth maturing to sober, sensible, right-minded adulthood (and, one must add, to the end of art also). Or, conversely, with Barlow we reverse the procedure and teach early Federalist works such as "The Anarchiad" or *The Vision of Columbus* (1787) but decently cover up his decline by ignoring later radical texts such as *Advice to the Privileged Orders* (1792–94). In short, we carefully select our authors, we select *from* those authors, we select our genres and our readers—all to confirm the history our literature "proves."

Ideology, of course, is present in *any* version of American literary history (and certainly the present study is no exception), but the predominant ideology postulated to date has been much more the ideology of the Rising Glory Poets than of Martha Read. Like history, literature selects its data, its canon, in order to confirm not the past but the present, as Raymond Williams movingly notes in his personal account of how his father, a rural laborer, set to memorizing a work of literature, Herrick's patronizing paean to the rural poor, *A Thanksgiving* (1647):

> As it happens, I first read this poem as a child, under a roof and porch probably lower than Herrick's, and I could then neither get the lines out of my mind nor feel other than angry about them. My father had brought it home, in a book called *Hours with English Authors*, which was a set-book for an evening class he was attending in the village. He had been asked (it is how values are taught) to learn it by heart; he asked

me to see if he could. I remember looking and wondering who the poor were, and . . . if the poet's condition was indeed so low. I understand that better now.[14]

Literature is one way in which values are taught in a society, and canonization is the mechanism for that larger enterprise. By focusing on fiction, I have attempted to *re-place* the standard literary syllabus of the new Republic by adding another voice to the history of America's postrevolutionary epoch. But making history is only one reason to read early novels, and, borrowing here from New Criticism, I hasten to emphasize that fiction is *not* history and that literature can never be simply "reduced" to history. We cannot turn the early American novel into some Procrustean bed exactly accommodating the complex history of an era, nor, conversely, can we insist that postrevolutionary history is a bed in which the early American novel comfortably lies. To subject novels to a reductive content analysis in order to extract their historical "meaning" misses the meaning of the genre and deprives a major form of republican discourse of its power and effect. For the early American novel entered fully into its own culture not simply as a commentator on the times but as an active participant in the *interpretation* of events—which is to say, as a *creator* of events. The historian who would return to these novels for some Universal History of the age necessarily meets with frustration, in that novels are not only susceptible to varying interpretations but require them, not only resist rational reduction to an ostensible message but are inimical to the whole prioritizing of the rational over the "wisdom of the human heart."

Novels are *not* history. "Literature becomes redundant," as Dominick La Capra warns, "when it tells us what can be gleaned from other documentary sources."[15] That caveat is crucial. If we read literature simply for its historical content, for its data, we are throwing out the fruit and settling simply for the chaff—chaff, moreover, that can better be gleaned from less contradictory and less ambiguous sources. More to the point, such historicizing of literature renders each a kind of puppet parody of the other. In a process of dizzying circularity, the meaning of history is reduced to the meaning of a text whose meaning is proven by its historical context. Neither history nor fiction speaks in a unitary voice, or with enough authority to drown out the other. As Jorge Luis Borges has insisted in a somewhat different context, "the concept of a definitive text," or, he might have added, a definitive reading, "belongs to religion or fatigue."[16]

The early American novel happened at those places in its society where issues were unresolved, at the interstices between public rhetoric and private expression. The very formlessness of the new form made it resistant to univocal readings and served as a catalyst to enveloping explications, tentative trials, and forays into alternative possibilities of meaning where readers might not willingly venture on their own. The new novel genre welcomed the participation of its readers—even those marginally educated new readers who had no place, except a passive and subservient one, in the classical rhetorical tradition.

CHARLOTTE TEMPLE.

FIGURE 16. Although published in an 1811 edition of *Charlotte Temple*, this frontispiece suggests that readers already associated Charlotte with pathetic death and dying, all of which became almost a cult by the mid–nineteenth century. *Courtesy of the American Antiquarian Society.*

In the intensely personal, secluded world of the imagination, even the most commodified best-seller can assume a special, even intimate, possibly subversive shape. The "mass privacy" of the novel both is and is not the "real" world and may be—depending on the interaction between an individual reader and an individual text—either more or less powerful than other events occurring outside that interaction.[17] A novel never simply mirrors reality. It *is* its own artificially framed world, an organized structure with its own rules and interpretations. At the same time, it is part of a larger structure (or a different one) and is determined by those economic, institutional, and ideological forces that govern its composition, its publication, its circulation, its reading, and the end—canonization or obscurity—to which it is read.

A novelist, it must also be remembered, *chooses* to write fiction precisely for what the form allows and for what it disallows. In America during the early national period that choice necessarily meant doing something suspect. For all the protestations of being "FOUNDED IN TRUTH," a novel was still a novel, and at least part of what made it interesting was that it was written in defiance of an established social and literary tradition and for readers not recognized by many other literary forms or acknowledged only as minor participants in the whole process of making literature. As I have suggested earlier, the novel, in certain fundamental ways, *is* its readings and its readers. And those readers selected novels over tracts or histories precisely because novels were *not* tracts or histories. You could empathize with the characters in novels in ways you could not with the generals and kings of the history books. You could believe in them in ways in which you did not believe in the generals and kings. They spoke your language, and a language, as novelist Margaret Atwood has observed, is everything you do, even the grammar of a seduction and the declaration made by a subsequent death.[18]

I have been arguing, unfashionably, for the mimetic properties of the novel because the reader of the early national period read mimetically, so much so that for many readers fiction came to have a paramount reality of its own. The grave of Charlotte Temple over which so many lovers wept provides an apt symbol of the relationship between early American readers and their books, and it is with that multivalent and symbolic scene of pilgrimage to a fictional character's real tomb that I wish to conclude this study. For, unlike a Universal History, which totalizes the past and presumes to predict the future, novels such as *Charlotte Temple*, *The Coquette*, or *Arthur Mervyn* are very much rooted in a perpetual present, the interactions between a text and a reader—any reader—which gives enduring life to the artifact of a book and enlivens words printed on a page into a novel, a finally magical creation whose origins, inspirations, and aspirations no historian or critic can presume to master.

Notes

N.B.: A bracketed author's name, in the text or in the endnotes, indicates that I have not been able to authenticate the identity of the author. Also, since orthography, punctuation, and even wording can change with the publisher, I have tried to retain the idiosyncratic features of the individual edition from which I quote. However, this has proven to be difficult in cases where the type is unclear and where the range of typefaces is too various to be reproduced here (see page 79). Even on a textual level, interpretation—not simple transcription—is sometimes required.

Introduction to the Expanded Edition

1. At least since Lillie Deming Loshe's *The Early American Novel, 1789–1830* (1907; repr., New York: Frederick Ungar, 1966), scholars have written about early American fiction. *Revolution and the Word* pays homage to its many important predecessors, including Herbert Ross Brown, *The Sentimental Novel in America, 1789–1860* (New York: Pageant, 1940); Helen Papashvily, *All the Happy Endings; A Study of the Domestic Novel in America, the Women Who Wrote It, the Women Who Read It in the Nineteenth Century* (New York: Harper, 1956); and Henri Petter, *The Early American Novel* (Columbus: Ohio State Univ. Press, 1971). However, it was not until *Revolution and the Word* and the Early American Women Writers series at Oxford University Press that early fiction became "canonical." Since their appearance in paperback classroom editions, Susanna Rowson's *Charlotte Temple* and Hannah Webster Foster's *The Coquette* have almost become "best-sellers" once again. Several subsequent new editions of both novels have been reprinted by academic and commercial presses.

2. Two influential discussions of the interrelationships of cultural power, value, and standards of judgment are Pierre Bourdieu, *Distinction* (Cambridge: Harvard Univ. Press, 1984), and Barbara Herrnstein Smith, *Contingencies of Value* (Cambridge: Harvard Univ. Press, 1988).

3. Bernard Bailyn, *To Begin the World Anew: The Genius and Ambiguities of the American Founders* (New York: Knopf, 2003), pp. 7–8.

4. For a fascinating discussion of plagiarism in early America (including the accusations leveled against Thomas Jefferson), see Jay Fliegelman, *Declaring Independence: Jefferson, National Language, and the Culture of Performance* (Stanford: Stanford Univ. Press, 1993).

5. Grant Farred, *What's My Name? Black Vernacular Intellectuals* (Minneapolis: Univ. of Minnesota Press, 2003).

6. Jan Lewis has recently found evidence that women were brought (briefly) into the discussion of the Constitution during the heated debates on slavery. See Lewis,

" 'of every age sex & condition' ": The Representation of Women in the Constitution," *Journal of the Early Republic*, 15 (1995), 359–97. See also Linda K. Kerber, *No Constitutional Right to Be Ladies: Women and the Obligations of Citizenship* (New York: Hill & Wang, 1998).

7. In 1843, more than fifty years later, and after the death of all those who participated in the Constitutional Convention, Congress voted to publish Madison's notes. Robert A. Ferguson, *Law and Letters in American Culture* (Cambridge: Harvard Univ. Press, 1984).

8. Leonard L. Richards, *Shays's Rebellion: The American Revolution's Final Battle* (Philadelphia: Univ. of Pennsylvania Press, 2002), p. 4. For a fascinating discussion of the kinds of arguments made against independence on the ground that it would encourage rule of the mob, see Woody Holton, *Forced Founders: Indians, Debtors, Slaves, and the Making of the American Revolution in Virginia* (Chapel Hill: Univ. of North Carolina Press, 1999).

9. A fine collection of essays on this subject is Seyla Benhabib, ed., *Democracy and Difference: Contesting the Boundaries of the Political* (Princeton: Princeton Univ. Press, 1996).

10. Robert Ferguson has called the American Revolution "the greatest literary achievement of eighteenth-century America," in "Finding the Revolution," *The Cambridge History of American Literature*, vol. 1, *1590–1820*, Sacvan Bercovitch, general ed. (Cambridge: Cambridge Univ. Press, 1994), p. 347.

11. The classic text in the social history of the period is Gordon S. Wood's magisterial *The Creation of the American Republic, 1776–1787* (New York: Norton, 1969). While I am entirely convinced by Wood's evidence of widespread dissension in this period, I disagree with Wood on the value of "unity" as a necessary (and even inevitable) reconfiguration of postrevolutionary energies.

12. Dana D. Nelson, "Conster/Nation," in *The Futures of American Studies*, ed. Donald E. Pease and Robyn Wiegman (Durham: Duke Univ. Press, 2002), p. 575. For an incisive analysis of unity as an antidemocratic norm, see also Nelson, *National Manhood: Capitalist Citizenship and the Imagined Fraternity of White Men* (Durham: Duke Univ. Press, 1998).

13. Sheldon S. Wolin, *The Presence of the Past: Essays on the State and the Constitution* (Baltimore: Johns Hopkins Univ. Press, 1989).

14. *Blues, Ideology, and Afro-American Literature* (Chicago: Univ. of Chicago Press, 1984), p. 65.

15. William Hill Brown, *The Power of Sympathy*, ed. William S. Kable (Columbus: Ohio State Univ. Press, 1969), p. 4.

16. Grantland S. Rice, in *The Transformation of Authorship in America* (Chicago: Univ. of Chicago Press, 1997), pp. 147–72, provides an astute reading of the novel as a kind of "coquette" that whispers promises but delivers only flirtation itself. He also surveys critics of early American fiction—including Michael Gilmore, Michael Warner, Carroll Smith-Rosenberg, and Steven Watts—who differently define or defend republicanism or liberalism (pp. 153–56).

17. For a productive account of class that raises methodological challenges to traditional labor history, see Nicholas K. Bromell, *By the Sweat of the Brow: Literature*

and Labor in Antebellum America (Chicago: Univ. of Chicago Press, 1993). For a discussion of labor history in relation to cultural history and historical materialism, see Lenard R. Berlanstein, ed., *Rethinking Labor History: Essays on Discourse and Class Analysis* (Urbana: Univ. of Illinois Press, 1993). See also Joan W. Scott, "On Language, Gender, and Working-Class History," *International Labor and Working-Class History*, 31 (1986), 1–13; and Christine Stansell, "A Response to Joan Scott," *International Labor and Working-Class History*, 31 (1987), 24–29.

18. One of the finest articles to address the issue of affect is Lauren Berlant's "Poor Eliza," first published in *American Literature*, 70 (September 1998), 635–68. See also Elizabeth Barnes, *States of Sympathy: Seduction and Democracy in the American Novel* (New York: Columbia Univ. Press, 1997); Wendy Brown, *States of Injury: Power and Freedom in Late Modernity* (Princeton: Princeton Univ. Press, 1995); Peter Coviello, "Agonizing Affection: Affect and Nation in Early America," *Early American Literature*, 37 (2002), 439–68; and Glenn Hendler, *Public Sentiments: Structures of Feeling in Nineteenth-Century American Literature* (Chapel Hill: Univ. of North Carolina Press, 2001).

19. Gayatri Chakravorty Spivak, "The Problem of Cultural Self-Representation," in *The Post-Colonial Critic: Interviews, Strategies, Dialogues*, ed. Sarah Harasym (New York: Routledge, 1990), pp. 50–55. See also Perry Anderson, *In the Tracks of Historical Materialism* (London: Verso, 1983).

20. Benedict Anderson raises similar issues in *Imagined Communities: Reflections on the Origin and Spread of Nationalism* (London: Verso, 1983; rev. ed. 1991).

21. Elizabeth McHenry, *Forgotten Readers: Recovering the Lost History of African American Literary Societies* (Durham: Duke Univ. Press, 2002). See also Carla Peterson, *Doers of the Word: African-American Women Speakers and Writers in the North (1830–1880)* (New York: Oxford Univ. Press, 1995).

22. Jürgen Habermas, *The Theory of Communicative Action*, trans. Thomas McCarthy (Boston: Beacon, 1984), and *The Structural Transformation of the Public Sphere*, trans. Thomas Burger (Cambridge: MIT Press, 1991), and Michael Warner, *The Republic of Letters* (Cambridge: Harvard Univ. Press, 1990).

23. Antonio Negri, *Insurgencies: Constituent Power and the Modern State*, trans. Maurizia Boscagli (Minneapolis: Univ. of Minnesota Press, 1999). Much light can be shed upon the U.S. Constitution by comparing it to other constitutions by new republics. See Martin Van Gelderen and Quentin Skinner, eds., *Republicanism: A Shared European Heritage* (Cambridge: Cambridge Univ. Press, 2002), vols. 1 and 2; H. Jefferson Powell, *The Moral Tradition of American Constitutionalism* (Durham: Duke Univ. Press, 1993); and Cass R. Sunstein, *Designing Democracy: What Constitutions Do* (New York: Oxford Univ. Press, 2001). See also Vine DeLoria, Jr., and David E. Wilkins, *Tribes, Treaties, and Constitutional Tribulations* (Austin: Univ. of Texas Press, 1999).

24. There is a rich literature on the social history of the early American crowd. Among recent examples is David Waldstreicher, *In the Midst of Perpetual Fetes: The Making of American Nationalism, 1776–1820* (Chapel Hill: Univ. of North Carolina Press, 1997). Sandra M. Gustafson, in *Eloquence Is Power: Oratory and Performance in Early America* (Chapel Hill: Univ. of North Carolina Press, 2000), makes a similar

argument to the one I am making about the novel in discussing the continuum of speech in early America, including discussions of not only the pulpit but of women's speech, Native American speech, revolutionary speech, and postrevolutionary "representative" speech.

25. Lawrence Buell, "American Literary Emergence as a Postcolonial Phenomenon," *American Literary History*, 4 (Autumn 1992), 411, 412.

26. *The Cultures of U.S. Imperialism* (Durham: Duke Univ. Press, 1993); *Journal of American History*, 88 (2001), 829–65. A pivotal moment in the study of colonialism in regard to American history was Gary Nash's presidential address to the Organization of American Historians in 1995, "The Hidden History of Mestizo America."

27. Patrick Wolfe, *Settler Colonialism and the Transformation of Anthropology: The Politics and Poetics of an Ethnographic Event* (New York: Cassell, 1999). See also Michael Warner, "What's Colonial about Colonial America?" in *Possible Pasts: Becoming Colonial in Early America*, ed. Robert Blair St. George (Ithaca: Cornell Univ. Press, 2000).

28. Todorov, *The Conquest of America: The Question of the Other*, trans. Richard Howard (New York: Harper Torchbooks, 1987); Spivak, *In Other Worlds: Essays in Cultural Politics* (London: Methuen, 1987), and "Can the Subaltern Speak?" in *Marxism and the Interpretation of Culture*, ed. Cary Nelson and Lawrence Grossberg (Chicago: Univ. of Illinois Press, 1988), 271–313.

29. Nelson, in *American Literary History*, 15 (Summer 2003), 367–94. Another excellent assessment of work on this topic is Ania Loomba, *Colonialism/Postcolonialism* (New York: Routledge, 1998). See also Ralph Bauer, "Creole Identities in Colonial Space: The Narratives of Mary White Rowlandson and Francisco Núñez de Pineda y Bascuñán," *American Literature*, 69 (1997), 665–95; Jorge Canizares-Esguerra, *How to Write the History of the New World: History, Epistemologies, and Identities in the Eighteenth-Century Atlantic World* (Stanford: Stanford Univ. Press, 2001); Michael Denning, "Globalization in Cultural Studies: Process and Epoch," *European Journal of Cultural Studies*, 4 (2001), 351–64; John Docker, *1492: The Poetics of Diaspora* (New York: Continuum, 2001); Roland Greene, *Unrequited Conquests: Love and Empire in the Colonial Americas* (Chicago: Univ. of Chicago Press, 1999); Annette Kolodny, "Letting Go Our Grand Obsessions: Notes toward a New Literary History of the American Frontiers," *American Literature*, 64 (1992), 1–18; Rob Kroes, *Them and Us: Questions of Citizenship in a Globalizing World* (Urbana: Univ. of Illinois Press, 2000); Mary N. Layoun, *Wedded to the Land? Gender, Boundaries, and Nationalism in Crisis* (Durham: Duke Univ. Press, 2001); George Lipsitz, *American Studies in a Moment of Danger* (Minneapolis: Univ. of Minnesota Press, 2001); Jose Rabasa, *Writing Violence on the Northern Frontier: The Historiography of Sixteenth-Century New Mexico and Florida and the Legacy of Conquest* (Durham: Duke Univ. Press, 2000); Daniel K. Richter, *Facing East from Indian Country: A Native History of Early America* (Cambridge: Harvard Univ. Press, 2002); John Carlos Rowe, ed., *Post-Nationalist American Studies* (Berkeley: Univ. of California Press, 2000); Patricia Seed, *American Pentimento: The Invention of Indians and the Pursuit of Riches* (Minneapolis: Univ. of Minnesota Press, 2001); William C. Spengemann, "What Is American Literature?" *Centennial Review*, 22 (1978), 119–38.

30. See Immanuel Wallerstein, *Capitalist World Economy* (Cambridge: Cambridge Univ. Press, 1979); Gayatri Spivak, *The Spivak Reader*, ed. Gayatri Spivak, Donna Landry, and Gerald MacLean (New York: Routledge, 1995), and *A Critique of Post-colonial Reason: Toward a History of the Vanishing Present* (Cambridge: Harvard Univ. Press, 1999); Homi K. Bhabha, *The Location of Culture* (New York: Routledge, 1994); Dipesh Chakrabarty, *Provincializing Europe: Postcolonial Thought and Historical Difference* (Princeton: Princeton Univ. Press, 2001), and *Habitations of Modernity: Essays in the Wake of Subaltern Studies* (Chicago: Univ. of Chicago Press, 2002); Arjun Appadurai, *Modernity at Large: Cultural Dimensions of Globalization* (Minneapolis: Univ. of Minnesota Press, 1996); Walter Mignolo, "The Many Faces of Cosmo-polis: Border Thinking and Critical Cosmopolitanism," *Public Culture*, 12 (Fall 2000), 721–48; Lisa Lowe, *Immigrant Acts: On Asian American Cultural Politics* (Durham: Duke Univ. Press, 1996).

31. This address was published as "Loose Change," *American Quarterly*, 46 (1994), 123–38. For examples of "inter-American" studies, see Maria de Guzman, "Consolidating Anglo-American Imperial Identity around the Spanish-American War (1898)," in *Race and the Invention of Modern American Nationalism* (New York: Garland, 1999), and David Kazanjian, "Charles Brockden Brown's Biloquil Nation: National Culture and White Settler Colonialism in *Memoirs of Carwin the Biloquist*," *American Literature*, 73 (2001), 459–96.

32. A number of recent works address early American imperialism: Greene, *Unrequited Conquests*; Nabil Matar, *Turks, Moors, and Englishmen in the Age of Discovery* (New York: Columbia Univ. Press, 1999); John Carlos Rowe, in *Literary Culture and U.S. Imperialism: From the Revolution to World War II* (New York: Oxford Univ. Press, 2000). See also the superb collection edited by Martin Daunton and Rick Halpern, *Empire and Others: British Encounters with Indigenous Peoples, 1600–1850* (Philadelphia: Univ. of Pennsylvania Press, 1999). See also Vicente L. Rafael, *Contracting Colonialism: Translation and Christian Conversion in Tagalog Society under Early Spanish Rule* (Durham: Duke Univ. Press, 1993), and Priscilla Wald, *Constituting Americans: Cultural Anxiety and Narrative Form* (Durham: Duke Univ. Press, 1995).

33. Leonard Levy, *Legacy of Suppression: Freedom of Speech and Press in Early American History* (Cambridge: Belknap, 1960); David McCullough, *John Adams* (New York: Simon and Schuster, 2001); John Chester Miller, *Crisis in Freedom: The Alien and Sedition Acts* (Boston: Little, Brown, 1951; repr. 1964); James Morton Smith, *Freedom's Fetters: The Alien and Sedition Laws and American Civil Liberties* (Ithaca: Cornell Univ. Press, 1956).

34. Perry Miller, *The New England Mind: From Colony to Province* (Cambridge: Harvard Univ. Press, 1956); Sacvan Bercovitch, *The Puritan Origins of the American Self* (New Haven: Yale Univ. Press, 1975), *The American Jeremiad* (Madison: Univ. of Wisconsin Press, 1978), and *The Rites of Assent: Transformations in the Symbolic Construction of America* (New York: Routledge, 1993).

35. Christopher Newfield, *The Emerson Effect: Individualism and Submission in America* (Chicago: Univ. of Chicago Press, 1996). I fully concur with Newfield's argument about compromise and moderation, but would argue that Emerson articulates impulses in American culture that go back to its founding moments.

36. For a range of studies on democracy and disagreement, see James Bohman and William Rehg, eds., *Deliberative Democracy: Essays on Reason and Politics* (Cambridge: MIT Press, 1997); Amy Gutmann, ed., *Democracy and Disagreement* (Cambridge: Harvard Univ. Press, 1996); Stephen MacEdo, *Deliberative Politics: Essays on Democracy and Disagreement* (New York: Oxford Univ. Press, 1999); and Iris Marion Young, *Inclusion and Democracy* (New York: Oxford Univ. Press, 2000).

37. Jacques Rancière, *Dis-agreement: Politics and Philosophy*, trans. Julie Rose (Minneapolis: Univ. of Minnesota Press, 1999), pp. 115–16.

38. Homi K. Bhabha, ed., *Nation and Narration* (New York: Routledge, 1990), and *The Location of Culture* (New York: Routledge, 1994).

39. The eminent Constitutional legal historian Robert Alan Dahl has recently argued that the Constitution fails as a truly democratic instrument. He also corrects the exaggerated notion that it has been widely admired and emulated by those in other democracies. See *How Democratic Is the American Constitution?* (New Haven: Yale Univ. Press, 2002).

40. Roberto Gonzalez Echevarria, *Myth and Archive: A Theory of Latin American Narrative* (New York: Cambridge Univ. Press, 1990).

41. Jean Franco, *An Introduction to Spanish-American Literature* (Cambridge: Cambridge Univ. Press, 1969), pp. 34–36.

42. Hugh Henry Brackenridge, *Modern Chivalry*, ed. Claude M. Newlin (New York: American Book Co., 1937), p. 507; italics in the original.

43. Doris Sommer, *Foundational Fictions: The National Romances of Latin America* (Berkeley: Univ. of California Press, 1993).

44. For an interesting discussion of Sampson, see Mechal Sobel, *Teach Me Dreams: The Search for Self in the Revolutionary Era* (Princeton: Princeton Univ. Press, 2000). See also Alfred F. Young, "The Women of Boston: 'Persons of Consequence' in the Making of the American Revolution, 1765–1776," in *Women and Politics in the Age of the Democratic Revolution* (Ann Arbor: Univ. of Michigan Press, 1993).

45. For a survey of the rich variety of approaches to inter-American studies, see *The Futures of American Studies*.

46. Quoted in McCullough, *John Adams*, p. 67.

47. For a variety of arguments and approaches to postcolonial literary studies, especially as a corrective to the Eurocentric traditions of "comparative literature," see the January 2003 issue (vol. 118) of *PMLA*, "America: The Idea, the Literature," coordinated by Djelal Kadir. See also Srinivas Aravamudan, *Tropicopolitans: Colonialism and Agency, 1688–1804* (Durham: Duke Univ. Press, 1999).

48. For a penetrating early critique of the function of the ideological underpinnings of New Historicism, see Marguerite Walker, "Academic Tootsie: The Denial of Difference and the Difference It Makes," *Diacritics*, 17 (Spring 1987), 2–20. A collection sympathetic to New Historicism from the same era is H. Aram Veeser, *The New Historicism* (New York: Routledge, 1989).

49. For an interesting comparison to the U.S. situation, see Joan B. Landes, *Women and the Public Sphere in the Age of the French Revolution* (Ithaca: Cornell Univ. Press, 1988).

50. See Elizabeth Barnes, *States of Sympathy: Seduction and Democracy in the American Novel* (New York: Columbia Univ. Press, 1997); Gillian Brown, *Domestic Individualism: Imagining Self in Nineteenth-Century America* (Berkeley: Univ. of California Press, 1990), and *The Consent of the Governed: The Lockean Legacy in Early American Culture* (Cambridge: Harvard Univ. Press, 2001); and Julia Stern, *The Plight of Feeling: Sympathy and Dissent in the Early American Novel* (Chicago: Univ. of Chicago Press, 1997). For a thoughtful review essay, see Wai-Chee Dimock, "Feminism, New Historicism, and the Reader," *American Literature*, 63 (December 1991), 601–22. Dimock is one of the few theorists who differentiates the approaches of feminist literary scholars of the 1980s and 1990s. See also Nancy Armstrong, *Desire and Domestic Fiction* (New York: Oxford Univ. Press, 1987), which focuses primarily on British fiction.

51. Winfried Fluck elaborates upon the so-called Davidson school in "From Aesthetics to Political Criticism: Theories of the Early American Novel," in *Early America Re-Explored: New Readings in Colonial, Early National, and Antebellum Culture*, ed. Klaus H. Schmidt and Fritz Fleischmann (New York: P. Lang, 2000), pp. 225–68.

52. Michel Foucault, *The Archaeology of Knowledge*, trans. A. M. Sheridan Smith (New York: Pantheon, 1972); Michel Foucault, *Power/Knowledge: Selected Interviews and Other Writings, 1972–1977* (New York: Pantheon, 1980).

53. Lora Romero, *Home Fronts: Domesticity and Its Critics in the Antebellum United States* (Durham: Duke Univ. Press, 1997), pp. 4–5.

54. For a wide range of essays embracing the position of "participant critic," see Henry Jenkins, Tara McPherson, and Jane Shattuc, eds., *Hop on Pop: The Politics and Pleasures of Popular Culture* (Durham: Duke Univ. Press, 2002).

55. Eve Kosofsky Sedgwick, "Paranoid Reading, Reparative Reading," in *Touching Feeling: Affect, Pedagogy, Performativity* (Durham: Duke Univ. Press, 2003), pp. 123–51. An earlier version of this essay was part of the introduction to Sedgwick's *Novel Gazing: Queer Readings in Fiction* (Durham: Duke Univ. Press, 1997).

56. Walter Benn Michaels, *Our America: Nativism, Modernism, and Pluralism* (Durham: Duke Univ. Press, 1995).

57. These comments on the affective logic of opposition were arrived at in dialogue with two readers of this introduction, Alice Kaplan and Monique Allewaert.

58. For an overtly "alternative" history of America, see Howard Zinn, *A People's History of the United States, 1492–Present* (New York: HarperCollins, 1999, new ed.).

59. For an excellent summary of Shays's rebellion, see www.calliope.org/shays. The site offers teachers of American history lively audio-visual formats for studying at key historical events. See also Davd P. Szatmary, *The Making of An Agrarian Insurrection* (Amherst: Univ. of Massachusetts Press, 1980), and Richards, *Shays's Rebellion*.

60. Richards, *Shays's Rebellion*, p. 164.

61. These issues are addressed forcefully in Linda K. Kerber, "Separate Spheres, Female Worlds, Woman's Place: The Rhetoric of Women's History," first published in *Journal of American History*, 75 (June 1988), 9–39, and reprinted in *No More Separate Spheres! A Next Wave American Studies Reader*, ed. Cathy N. Davidson and

Jessamyn Hatcher (Durham: Duke Univ. Press, 2002). See also my earlier special issue of *American Literature*, 70 (September 1998), with the same title, "No More Separate Spheres!" For another collection that builds on this work, see Monika Elbert, ed., *Separate Spheres No More: Gender Convergence in American Literature, 1830–1930* (Tuscaloosa: Univ. of Alabama Press, 2000).

62. For other texts that complicate the notion of the separate spheres, see Julie Ellison, *Cato's Tears and the Making of Anglo-American Emotion* (Chicago: Univ. of Chicago Press, 1999); Ruth Frankenberg, *White Women, Race Matters* (Minneapolis: Univ. of Minnesota Press, 1993); Kathleen Anne McHugh, *American Domesticity: From How-to Manual to Hollywood Melodrama* (New York: Oxford Univ. Press, 1999); Dana D. Nelson, " 'No Cold or Empty Heart': Polygenesis, Scientific Professionalization, and the Unfinished Business of Male Sentimentalism," *differences*, 11 (1999), 29–56; Shirley Samuels, *Romances of the Republic: Women, the Family, and Violence in the Literature of the Early American Nation* (New York: Oxford Univ. Press, 1996), and the essays in Samuels's collection *The Culture of Sentiment: Race, Gender, and Sentimentality in Nineteenth-Century America* (New York: Oxford Univ. Press, 1992).

63. This is discussed at length in chapter 6.

64. Ranjana Khanna, *Dark Continents: Psychoanalysis and Colonialism* (Durham: Duke Univ. Press, 2003).

65. Special thanks to Eden Osucha for helping me assemble this genealogy of identity politics. For a brilliant exegesis of these issues, see Lowe, *Immigrant Acts*. How multiple conditions of identity apply can be seen in the fact that while one was defined as a slave if one's *mother* was a slave, the 1790 immigration act states that "the right of citizenship shall not descend to persons whose *fathers* have never been resident in the United States" (pp. 6–22).

66. Kaplan, "Manifest Domesticity," pp. 183–208; and You-Me Park and Gayle Wald, "Native Daughters in the Promised Land: Gender, Race, and the Question of Separate Spheres," pp. 263–90, both in *No More Separate Spheres!*

67. Blair St. George, *Possible Pasts*, p. 10.

68. Christopher Castiglia, *Bound and Determined: Captivity, Culture-Crossing, and White Womanhood from Mary Rowlandson to Patty Hearst* (Chicago: Univ. of Chicago Press), 1996. See also Michelle Burnham, *Captivity and Sentiment: Cultural Exchange in American Literature, 1682–1861* (Hanover: Univ. Press of New England, 1997); Gary L. Ebersole, *Captured by Texts: Puritan to Post-Modern Images of Indian Captivity* (Charlottesville: Univ. Press of Virginia, 1995); and Michael Moon, "A Long Foreground: Re-Materializing the History of Native American Relations to Mass Culture," in *Materializing Democracy*, ed. Russ Castronovo and Dana Nelson (Durham: Duke Univ. Press, 2002), pp. 267–93.

69. Diana Fuss, *Identification Papers* (New York: Routledge, 1995), and *Essentially Speaking* (New York: Routledge, 1989). The oft-cited, if historically problematic, article on this topic is Carroll Smith-Rosenberg, "Female World of Love and Ritual," *Signs*, 1 (1975), later included in *Disorderly Conduct: Visions of Gender in Victorian America* (New York: Knopf, 1985).

70. Judith Halberstam, *Female Masculinity* (Durham: Duke Univ. Press, 1998). See

also Alfred F. Young, *Masquerade: The Life and Times of Deborah Sampson, Continental Soldier* (New York: Knopf, 2004).

71. Judith Butler, preface (1990) to *Gender Trouble: Feminism and the Subversion of Identity* (New York: Routledge, 1999), xxxii. See also Butler's *Bodies That Matter: On the Discursive Limits of "Sex"* (New York: Routledge, 1993), and *Excitable Speech: A Politics of the Performative* (New York: Routledge, 1997). For an excellent historicization of sexuality, see also Carla Freccero and Louise Fradenburg, eds., *Premodern Sexualities* (New York: Routledge, 1996), and Jonathan Goldberg, *Queering the Renaissance* (Durham: Duke Univ. Press, 1994). For a transnational account of sexuality, see George Chancey and Beth Povenelli's special issue of *GLQ*, 5 (1999) "Thinking Sexuality Transnationally." And, of course, the monumental theorization of sexuality is Michel Foucault, *History of Sexuality*, vol. 1, trans. Robert Hurley (New York: Vintage, 1990).

72. See, for example, Bruce Burgett, *Sentimental Bodies: Sex, Gender, and Citizenship in the Early Republic* (Princeton: Princeton Univ. Press, 1998), and Burgett's "Between Speculation and Population: The Problem of 'Sex' in Our Long Eighteenth Century," *Early American Literature*, 36 (2002), 119–53; and Caleb Crain, *American Sympathy: Men, Friendship, and Literature in the New Nation* (New Haven: Yale Univ. Press, 2001). See also Lisa Duggan, "Queering the State," *Social Text*, 39 (Summer 1994), 1–14; George Haggerty, *Men in Love: Masculinity and Sexuality in the Eighteenth Century* (New York: Columbia Univ. Press, 1999); David Halperin, *One Hundred Years of Homosexuality* (New York: Routledge, 1990); Michael Warner, "Irving's Posterity," *ELH*, 67 (2000), 773–99, and *The Trouble with Normal: Sex, Politics, and the Ethics of Queer Life* (New York: Free Press, 1999). See also the essays in Mary Chapman and Glenn Hendler, *Sentimental Men: Masculinity and the Politics of Affect in American Culture* (Berkeley: Univ. of California Press, 1999). For two recent historical assessments of early American masculinity in more traditional terms, see Joseph J. Ellis, *Founding Brothers: The Revolutionary Generation* (New York: Knopf, 2001), and Joanne B. Freeman, *Affairs of Honor: National Politics in the New Republic* (New Haven: Yale Univ. Press, 2001).

73. Eve Kosofsky Sedgwick, *Between Men* (New York: Columbia Univ. Press, 1985), theorizes the role of men and the role of women in homosocial situations of bonding.

74. Henry Louis Gates, Jr., *Figures in Black: Words, Signs, and the "Racial" Self* (New York: Oxford Univ. Press, 1987), and *The Signifying Monkey: A Theory of African-American Literary Criticism* (New York: Oxford Univ. Press, 1989); Houston A. Baker, Jr., *The Journey Back* (Chicago: Univ. of Chicago Press, 1984).

75. Hazel V. Carby, *Reconstructing Womanhood: The Emergence of the Afro-American Woman Novelist* (New York: Oxford Univ. Press, 1987); Patricia Hill Collins, *Black Feminist Thought: Knowledge, Consciousness, and the Politics of Empowerment* (New York: Routledge, 1991); bell hooks, *Feminist Theory: Thinking Feminist, Thinking Black* (Boston: South End, 1989); Gloria T. Hull, Patricia Bell Scott, and Barbara Smith, *All the Women Are White, All the Blacks Are Men, but Some of Us Are Brave* (Old Westbury: Feminist Press, 1982); Deborah E. McDowell and Arnold Rampersad,

Slavery and the Literary Imagination, Selected Papers from the English Institute, 1987 (Baltimore: Johns Hopkins Univ. Press, 1989).

76. For an overview, see William L. Andrews, *To Tell a Free Story: The First Century of Afro-American Autobiography, 1760–1865* (Urbana: Univ. of Illinois Press, 1986); Vincent Carretta and Philip Gould, eds., *Genius in Bondage: Literature of the Early Black Atlantic* (Lexington: Univ. Press of Kentucky, 2001); Frank Shuffleton, *A Mixed Race: Ethnicity in Early America* (New York: Oxford Univ. Press, 1993); Eric J. Sundquist, *To Wake the Nations: Race in the Making of American Literature* (Cambridge: Harvard Univ. Press, 1993); Ronald Takaki, *Iron Cages: Race and Culture in Nineteenth-Century America* (New York: Knopf, 1979); and Robert S. Levine, *Martin Delany, Frederick Douglass, and the Politics of Representative Identity* (Chapel Hill: Univ. of North Carolina Press, 1997). See also Vincent Carretta, ed., *Unchained Voices: An Anthology of Black Authors in the English-Speaking World of the Eighteenth Century* (Lexington: Univ. Press of Kentucky, 1996).

77. Paul Gilroy, *The Black Atlantic: Modernity and Double Consciousness* (Cambridge: Harvard Univ. Press, 1993); Wahneema Lubiano, ed., *The House That Race Built: Black Americans, U.S. Terrain* (New York: Pantheon, 1997); and Robin D. G. Kelley, *Race Rebels: Culture, Politics, and the Black Working Class* (New York: Free Press, 1996), and *Freedom Dreams: The Black Radical Imagination* (Boston: Beacon, 2002).

78. See Jean Neinkamp and Andrea Collins, introduction to Tabitha Gilman Tenney, *Female Quixotism* (New York: Oxford Univ. Press, 1992), for a discussion of race and racism in the novel.

79. For fascinating discussions of how and why Native Americans "haunt" the American landscape, see Rénee Bergland, *The National Uncanny: Indian Ghosts and American Subjects* (Hanover: Univ. Press of New England, 2000), and Jill Lepore, *The Name of War: King Phillip's War and the Origins of American Identity* (New York: Random House, 1999). See also Alan Gallay, *The Indian Slave Trade: The Rise of the English Empire in the American South, 1680–1717* (New Haven: Yale Univ. Press, 2002); Hilary E. Wyss, *Writing Indians: Literacy, Christianity, and Native Community in Early America* (Amherst: Univ. of Massachusetts Press, 2000); and Cheryl Walker, *Indian Nation: Native American Literature and Nineteenth-Century Nationalisms* (Durham: Duke Univ. Press, 1999).

80. Anibal Quijano and Immanuel Wallerstein, "Americanicity as a Concept, or the Americas in the Modern World-System," *International Social Science Journal*, 134 (November 1992), 551. See also Barnor Hesse, "Forgotten Like a Bad Dream: Atlantic Slavery and the Ethics of Postcolonial Memory," in *Relocating Postcolonialism*, ed. David Theo Goldberg and Ato Quayson (Malden, Mass.: Blackwell, 2000), pp. 143–73. For two important texts on the relationship between colonialism and slavery, see also Srinivas Aravamudan, *Tropicopolitans: Colonialism and Agency, 1688–1804* (Durham: Duke Univ. Press, 1999); Joan Dayan, *Haiti, History, and the Gods* (Berkeley: Univ. of California Press, 1998). For an excellent historical survey, see Michael L. Conniff and Thomas J. Davis, *Africans in the Americas: A History of the Black Diaspora* (New York: St. Martin's, 1994).

81. Different analyses of racism and imperialism are discussed by Ann Stoler in

"Tense and Tender Ties: Intimacies of Empire in North American History and (Post) Colonial Studies," *Journal of American History*, 88 (2001), 829–65. See also Russ Castronovo, *Fathering the Nation: American Genealogies of Slavery and Freedom* (Berkeley: Univ. of California Press, 1995); Eric Cheyfitz, *The Poetics of Imperialism: Translation and Colonialization from the Tempest to Tarzan* (Philadelphia: Univ. of Pennsylvania Press, 1997), Saidiya Hartman, *Scenes of Subjection: Terror, Slavery, and Self-Making in Nineteenth-Century America* (New York: Oxford Univ. Press, 1998); and Amy Kaplan, *The Anarchy of Empire in the Making of U.S. Culture* (Cambridge: Harvard Univ. Press, 2002). For a survey of historical writing, see Ian Tyrrell, "Making Nations/Making States: Historians in the Context of Empire," *Journal of American History*, 86 (December 1999), 1015–44.

82. An excellent compendium of whiteness studies is Mike Hill, ed., *Whiteness: A Critical Reader* (New York: New York Univ. Press, 1997). See Eric Lott, *Love and Theft: Blackface Minstrelsy and the American Working Class* (New York: Oxford Univ. Press, 1995); David Roediger, *The Wages of Whiteness: Race and the Making of the American Working Class* (New York: Verso, 1999); and Robyn Wiegman, *American Anatomies: Theorizing Race and Gender* (Durham: Duke Univ. Press, 1995).

83. For a survey of approaches, see Carolyn Sorisio, *Fleshing out America: Race, Gender, and the Politics of the Body in American Literature, 1833–1879* (Athens: Univ. of Georgia Press, 2002), and Jared Gardner, *Master Plots: Race and the Founding of an American Literature, 1787–1845* (Baltimore: Johns Hopkins Univ. Press, 1998).

84. Lee D. Baker, *From Savage to Negro: Anthropology and the Construction of Race, 1896–1954* (Berkeley: Univ. of California Press, 1998); and Roxann Wheeler, *The Complexion of Race: Categories of Difference in Eighteenth-Century British Culture* (Philadelphia: Univ. of Pennsylvania Press, 2000).

85. See Catherine La Courreye Blecki and Karin A. Wulf, *Milcah Martha Moore's Book: A Common Place Book from Revolutionary America* (University Park: Pennsylvania State Univ. Press, 1997). See also Kevin J. Hayes, *A Colonial Woman's Bookshelf* (Knoxville: Univ. of Tennessee Press, 1996); Carla Mulford, *"Only for the Eye of a Friend": The Poems of Annis Stockton Boudinot* (Charlottesville: Univ. Press of Virginia, 1995); David S. Shields, "British-American Belles Lettres," in *The Cambridge History of American Literature*, ed. Sacvan Bercovitch (Cambridge: Cambridge Univ. Press, 1994), 1:307–43; and Shields, *Civil Tongues and Polite Letters in British America* (Chapel Hill: Univ. of North Carolina Press, 1997).

86. That experience became the basis for a monograph, originally delivered as the 1986 James Russell Wiggins Lecture in the History of the Book in American Culture at AAS, *Ideology and Genre: The Rise of the Novel in America* (Worcester, Mass.: American Antiquarian Society, 1987), and is reprinted in *Reading in America: Literature and Social History*, ed. Cathy N. Davidson (Baltimore: Johns Hopkins Univ. Press, 1989).

87. A series of review essays in *Journal of Modern History (JMH)* recapitulate the ferment in European book history of the late 1980s. See Roger Chartier, "Text, Symbol, and Frenchness," *JMH*, 57 (December 1985), 682–95; Robert Darnton, "The Symbolic Element in History," *JMH*, 58 (March 1986), 218–34; Domick LaCapra, "Chartier, Darnton, and the Great Symbol Massacre," *JMH*, 60 (March 1988), 95–

112; and James Fernandez, "Historians Tell Tales: Of Cartesian Cats and Gallic Cock-fights," *JMH*, 60 (March 1988), 113–27.

88. Hugh Amory and David D. Hall, eds., *A History of the Book in America*, vol. 1, *The Colonial Book in the Atlantic World* (Cambridge: Cambridge Univ. Press, 1999). In his review of this project (*Early American Literature*, 36 [2001], 132–36), Grantland S. Rice notes that similar multivolume national book history projects are under way in Wales, Scotland, Ireland, Australia, Canada, New Zealand, and South Africa. Two of the most brilliant analyses of the last decade that chart the interrelationships among culture, reception, politics, and national identity are Purnima Mankekar, *Screening Culture, Viewing Politics: An Ethnography of Television, Womanhood, and Nation in Postcolonial India* (Durham: Duke Univ. Press, 1999); and Louise Meintjes, *Sound of Africa! Making Music Zulu in a South African Studio* (Durham: Duke Univ. Press, 2003).

89. See Guglielmo Cavallo, Roger Chartier, and Lydia G. Cochrane, eds., *A History of Reading in the West* (Amherst: Univ. of Massachusetts Press, 1999). See also Adrian Johns, *The Nature of the Book: Print and Knowledge in the Making* (Chicago: Univ. of Chicago Press, 1998); and Kevin Sharpe, *Reading Revolutions: The Politics of Reading in Early Modern England* (New Haven: Yale Univ. Press, 2000).

90. For studies that emphasize oratory and rhetorical form, see Christopher Looby, *Voicing America: Language, Literary Form, and the Origins of the United States* (Chicago: Univ. of Chicago Press, 1996), and Nancy Ruttenburg, *Democratic Personality: Popular Voice and the Trial of American Authorship* (Stanford: Stanford Univ. Press, 1998).

91. See Elizabeth Eisenstein, *The Printing Press as an Agent of Change: Communications and Cultural Transformations in Early Modern Europe* (New York: Cambridge Univ. Press, 1979), and John Seely Brown and Paul Duguid, *The Social Life of Information* (Cambridge: Harvard Business School Press, 2002).

92. Thomas Kuhn, *Structure of Scientific Revolutions* (Chicago: Univ. of Chicago Press, 1964), and Imre Lakatos and Paul Feyerabend, *For and Against Method*, edited and with an introduction by Matteo Motterlini (Chicago: Univ. of Chicago Press, 1999).

93. Karen W. Arenson, "Job Listings Decline Twenty Percent at Colleges: Drop Is the Largest in about a Decade," *New York Times*, December 14, 2002, p. A13.

94. Evelyn Brooks Higginbotham made these comments in a presentation at the John Hope Franklin Humanities Institute at Duke University on December 11, 2002.

95. For discussions of interdisciplinarity, see Julia Thompson Klein, *Interdisciplinarity: History, Theory, and Practice* (Detroit: Wayne State Univ. Press), and *Crossing Boundaries: Knowledge, Disciplinarities, and Interdisciplinarities* (Charlottesville: Univ. Press of Virginia, 1996), and W. T. Newell, ed., *Interdisciplinarity: Essays from the Literature* (New York: College Examination Board, 1998). See also Immanuel Wallerstein et al., *Open the Social Sciences: Report of the Gulbenkian Commission on the Restructuring of the Social Sciences* (Stanford: Stanford Univ. Press, 1996). See also my "What If Scholars in the Humanities Worked Together, in a Lab?" *Chronicle of Higher Education*, May 28, 1999, p. B4.

96. Lisa R. Lattuca, *Creating Interdisciplinarity: Interdisciplinary Research and*

Teaching among College and University Faculty (Nashville: Vanderbilt Univ. Press, 2001), p. 1.

97. Kenneth Wissoker, in "Negotiating a Passage between Disciplinary Borders," argues that what one calls interdisciplinarity is governed by particular field or disciplinary assumptions. See *Chronicle of Higher Education*, April 14, 2000, pp. 4–6. This essay was reprinted in an abridged form in the Social Science Research Council's *Items and Issues*, 1 (2000), 1, 5–7, with responses by Lisa Anderson, Arjun Appadurai, Thomas Bender, Jeffrey Goldfarb, Michèle Lamont, and Joshua Guetzkow.

98. For the relationship of literacy and coloniality, see Walter D. Mignolo, *The Darker Side of the Renaissance: Literacy, Territoriality, and Colonization* (Ann Arbor: Univ. of Michigan Press, 1995).

99. Emory Elliott, in *Aesthetics in a Multicultural Age* (New York: Oxford Univ. Press, 2002), provides a retrospective assessment of the Culture Wars, looking back at the issues, assaying the results, and refuting some of the more divisive charges leveled in the Culture Wars.

100. Allan Bloom, *The Closing of the American Mind* (New York: Simon and Schuster, 1987); E. D. Hirsch, *Cultural Literacy: What Every American Needs to Know* (Boston: Houghton Mifflin, 1987).

101. See Peter Pringle, "Victims of Slavery Find Their Voice: Nobel Winner Morrison's 'Shared Honour,'" *Independent* (London), October 10, 1993, p. 18; David Streitfeld, "Author Toni Morrison Wins Nobel Prize: First African American Laureate Says Honor Is 'Shared among Us,'" *Washington Post*, October 8, 1993, p. A1; and Daniel Johnson, "Of Prizes and Prejudice," *New York Times*, October 8, 1993.

102. For an excellent analysis of many of these issues, see Christopher Newfield, "What Was Political Correctness? Race, the Right, and Managerial Democracy in the Humanities," *Critical Inquiry*, 19 (1993), 308–36.

103. See Paul Lauter, *Canons and Contexts* (New York: Oxford Univ. Press, 1991).

104. Myra Jehlen and Michael Warner, eds., *The English Literatures of America, 1500–1800* (New York: Routledge, 1997); Susan Castillo and Ivy Schweitzer, *The Literatures of Colonial America* (Malden, Mass.: Blackwell, 2001). See also Carla Mulford, Angela Vietto, and Amy E. Winans, *Early American Writings* (New York: Oxford Univ. Press, 2001).

105. Sharon M. Harris, *American Women Writers to 1800* (New York: Oxford Univ. Press, 1996); Ann Allen Shockley, *Afro-American Women Writers, 1746–1993* (Boston: G. K. Hall, 1988).

106. Deirdre Mullane, *Crossing the Danger Water: Three Hundred Years of African-American* Writing (New York: Doubleday, 1993); John Edgar Wideman, *My Soul Has Grown Deep: Classics of Early African-American Literature* (New York: Ballantine, 2001); Moira Ferguson, *Nine Black Women* (New York: Routledge, 1998).

107. Alan R. Velie, *American Indian Literature: An Anthology* (1979; rev. ed., Norman: Univ. of Oklahoma Press, 1991); Arnold Krupat, *Native American Autobiography: An Anthology* (Madison: Univ. of Wisconsin Press, 1994).

108. Emory Elliott, *Columbia History of the American Novel* (New York: Columbia Univ. Press, 1991).

109. Martin Bernal, *Black Athena: The Afroasiatic Roots of Classical Civilization*

(New Brunswick: Rutgers Univ. Press, 1987); see also Jacques Berlinerblau, *Heresy in the University: The Black Athena Controversy and the Responsibilities of American Intellectuals* (New Brunswick: Rutgers Univ. Press, 1999), and Martin Bernal and David Chioni Moore, eds., *Black Athena Writes Back: Martin Bernal Responds to His Critics* (Durham: Duke Univ. Press, 2001). The quotation about the process of intellectual change is from a talk Martin Bernal delivered at the John Hope Franklin Center for Interdisciplinary and International Studies at Duke University on February 5, 2003, entitled "The Afroasiatic Component in Ancient Greek Vocabulary."

110. Nguyen Lien and Jonathan Auerbach, eds., *Tiếp Cận Đủồng Đại Văn Hoá Mỹ/Contemporary Approaches to American Culture* (Hanoi: Nha Xuat Ban Van Hoa-Thong Tin, 2001).

111. Ibid., p. 24.

112. See Patricia M. Pelley, *Postcolonial Vietnam: New Histories of the National Past* (Durham: Duke Univ. Press, 2002), esp. pp. 1–15 and 112–60. It will also be remembered that Ho Chi Minh was an admirer and serious student of the U.S. Declaration of Independence.

Chapter 1

1. Diary of Ethan Allen Greenwood, December 23, 1807, Manuscript Department, American Antiquarian Society, Worcester, Mass. (Hereafter cited as AAS.) I am indebted to Georgia Brady Bumgardner for making available to me her paper "The Early Career of Ethan Allen Greenwood," presented at the Dublin Seminar (Essex Institute, Salem, Mass.), June 1984.

2. The caveat is not to be applied to all studies of origins by any means. On the contrary, the present work is partly inspired by Ian Watt's *The Rise of the Novel: Studies in Defoe, Richardson, and Fielding* (1957; repr., Berkeley: Univ. of California Press, 1967), still one of the finest studies of fiction by selected eighteenth-century British men. For a different account of the rise of the English novel, see Dale Spender, *Mothers of the Novel* (London: Routledge & Kegan Paul, 1986). Dale Spender generously shared many of her findings with me prior to their publication.

3. Robert Escarpit, *Sociology of Literature*, 2nd ed., trans. Ernest Pick (London: Frank Cass, 1971).

4. Robert Darnton, "What Is the History of Books?" in *Books and Society in History*, ed. Kenneth E. Carpenter (New York: R. R. Bowker, 1983), p. 3. This collection provides an excellent introduction to the discipline called, variously, *l'histoire du livre*, *Geschichte des Buchwesens*, or history of the book. See also the special issue of *Eighteenth-Century Studies*, 17 (Summer 1984), ed. Raymond Birn, and Birn's "*Livre et société* After Ten Years: Formation of a Discipline," *Studies on Voltaire and the Eighteenth Century*, 151 (1976), 287–312, as well as Darnton's "Reading, Writing, and Publishing in Eighteenth-Century France: A Case Study in the Sociology of Literature," *Daedalus*, 100 (Winter 1971), 214–56. For an excellent discussion of the relationship between *l'histoire du livre* and the study of *mentalités*, see Roger Chartier, "Intellectual History or Sociocultural History? The French Trajectories," in *Modern European Intellectual History: Reappraisals and New Perspectives*, ed. Dominick La

Capra and Steven L. Kaplan (Ithaca: Cornell Univ. Press, 1982), pp. 13–46. These ideas are applied and then combined with reader-response criticism in Chartier's "Du livre au lire," in *Pratiques de la lecture*, ed. Roger Chartier (Paris: Editions Rivages, 1985), pp. 62–87.

5. Lucien Febvre and Henri-Jean Martin, *L'Apparition du livre* (Paris: Editions Albin Michel, 1958). The book was translated into English by David Gerard as *The Coming of the Book* (London: NLB, 1976). See also G. Thomas Tanselle, *The History of Books as a Field of Study* (Chapel Hill: Univ. of North Carolina, Rare Book Collection, 1981).

6. Carlo Ginzburg, *The Cheese and the Worms: The Cosmos of a Sixteenth-Century Miller* (Baltimore: Johns Hopkins Univ. Press, 1980).

7. Susan R. Suleiman, "Introduction," *The Reader in the Text*, ed. Susan R. Suleiman and Inge Crosman (Princeton: Princeton Univ. Press, 1980), p. 35. Suleiman paraphrases Hans Robert Jauss, esp. the essay "Literary History as a Challenge to Literary Theory," repr. in *Toward an Aesthetic of Reception*, trans. Timothy Bahti (Minneapolis: Univ. of Minnesota Press, 1982), pp. 3–45. For another fine survey of reader-criticism, see Jane P. Tompkins, ed., *Reader-Response Criticism* (Baltimore: Johns Hopkins Univ. Press, 1980).

8. The term *Rezeptionsästhetic* is borrowed from Hans Robert Jauss and the other members of the Konstanz group, especially Wolfgang Iser and Jurij Striedter. See Jauss, *Toward an Aesthetic of Reception*, esp. pp. 23–24, 141–42, 171–72; and his *Aesthetic Experience and Literary Hermeneutics*, trans. Michael Shaw (Minneapolis: Univ. of Minnesota Press, 1982); also Wolfgang Iser, *The Act of Reading: A Theory of Aesthetic Response* (Baltimore: Johns Hopkins Univ. Press, 1978); and Jurij Striedter, "Introduction to Felix Vodička," *Die Struktur der literarischen Entwicklung* (Munich: W. Fink, 1976). Another important contributor to response theory (and an important influence on Jauss) is Jan Mukarovsky in works such as *Aesthetic Function, Norm, and Value as Social Facts*, trans. Mark E. Suino (Ann Arbor: Univ. of Michigan Press, 1970), and *Structure, Sign, and Function*, trans. and ed. John Burbank and Peter Steiner (New Haven: Yale Univ. Press, 1978). For an overview of *Rezeptionsästhetik*, see Richard E. Amacher and Victor Lange, eds., *New Perspectives in German Literary Criticism: A Collection of Essays* (Princeton: Princeton Univ. Press, 1979); D. W. Fokkema and Elrud Kunne-Bisch, *Theories of Literature in the Twentieth Century: Structuralism, Marxism, Aesthetics of Reception, Semiotics* (New York: St. Martin's, 1977); Peter Uwe Hohendahl, "Introduction to Reception Aesthetics," *New German Critique*, 10 (Winter 1977), 29–64; and "Interview: Hans Robert Jauss," *Diacritics*, 5 (Spring 1975), 53–61.

9. I am here, as in the title of this chapter, playing off Roland Barthes's famous distinction between a "work" (the end product of a system of artistic manufacture) and a "text" (a sign-system that is open-ended, created as much by the reader as the writer). Both aspects are crucial since works are not inspired but *fabricated* (like other forms of labor) within a specific economics, while texts are re-created (or even created) by every reader. See Roland Barthes, *Mythologies*, trans. Annette Lavers (New York: Hill & Wang, 1972), esp. his essay "Myth Today," pp. 109–59.

10. One important methodology employed by historians of the book, inspired in

part by François Furet and Jacques Ozouf, *Reading and Writing: Literacy in France from Calvin to Jules Ferry* (Cambridge: Cambridge Univ. Press, 1977), is to trace out the dissemination of books as indicated by purchase orders, account books, or lending-library rosters.

11. This issue has been addressed most forcefully by Nina Baym, *Novels, Readers, and Reviewers: Responses to Fiction in Antebellum America* (Ithaca: Cornell Univ. Press, 1984); William E. Cain, *The Crisis in Criticism: Theory, Literature, and Reform in English Studies* (Baltimore: Johns Hopkins Univ. Press, 1984), esp. pp. 51–64; and Steven Mailloux, *Interpretive Conventions: The Reader in the Study of American Fiction* (Ithaca: Cornell Univ. Press, 1982), esp. pp. 159–220.

12. Stanley Fish, *Is There a Text in This Class? The Authority of Interpretive Communities* (Cambridge: Harvard Univ. Press, 1980), and "Literature in the Reader: Affective Stylistics," *New Literary History*, 2 (Autumn 1970), 123–62.

13. Jonathan Culler, "Prolegomena to a Theory of Reading," in Suleiman and Crosman, eds., *The Reader in the Text*, pp. 46–66; and *The Pursuit of Signs: Semiotics, Literature, Deconstruction* (Ithaca: Cornell Univ. Press, 1981).

14. Janice A. Radway, *Reading the Romance: Women, Patriarchy, and Popular Literature* (Chapel Hill: Univ. of North Carolina Press, 1984).

15. A brief note on my sources is in order here. I began working with early American fiction in 1974; since then, I have tried to handle as many copies of early novels—as well as textbooks, primers, and readers, that I see as important to the development of the novel—as I could find in public and private libraries, historical societies, and bookstores. This study in no way pretends to be quantitative since I have exerted no statistical controls on my idiosyncratic perusal of almost twelve hundred copies of early American novels and approximately five thousand copies of textbooks. The only other study I know to make use of the impressionistic evidence of readers in extant copies of old books is Clifton Johnson's delightful *Old-Time Schools and School Books* (1904; repr., New York: Macmillan, 1925), pp. 155–66. Others, however, have recently turned their attention to readers. For example, in the spring of 1984 Roger Stoddard of Houghton Library, Harvard University, mounted an exhibition "Marks in Books." At Michigan State University, Jannette Fiore and Anne Tracy have begun to record and even track down readers who left inscriptions in the two thousand volumes of the Pedagogy Collection in the Russel B. Nye Popular Culture Collection. And at the AAS, the North American Imprints Program (NAIP), a computerized updating of Charles Evans's *American Bibliography* (Chicago: Printed for the author by the Blakely Press, 1903–34), includes citations of inscribers' names in AAS volumes. Special thanks to James F. Cuffe, Jr., Alan Degutis, and Richard Fyffe for making this important resource available to me before its official publication.

16. Isaiah Thomas called his edition (Worcester, Mass., 1785) of George Fisher's book *The Instructor; Or, American Young Man's Best Companion*, while the first American edition (Philadelphia: B. Franklin and D. Hall, 1748) was entitled *The American Instructor; Or, Young Man's Best Companion* and repeated the lengthy subtitle of the original British edition: "Containing Spelling, Reading, Writing, and Arithmetick, in an Easier Way than any Yet Published, and How to Qualify any Person for Business,

without the Help of a Master." Fisher's was the most popular of the many self-improvement books that Franklin published. An 1812 edition of the book (Philadelphia: John Bioren) promised "Instructions for Reading, Writing, (including English Grammar,) Arithmetic, Merchants' Accounts, Mensuration, Gauging according to the most modern and approved practice, and the Art of Dialling." Some editions also contained recipes for everything from beer to herbal medicine, astrological tables, and other features appropriated from almanacs, again suggesting that the book could be used for widely diverse purposes by readers with different interests, skills, and educational levels.

17. As will be discussed in chapter 2, rarely were publishers able to find an adequate number of subscribers for novels, and only four early novels were published bound with subscription lists: the anonymous *Humanity in Algiers; Or, The Story of Azem* (Troy, N.Y.: R. Moffitt, 1801); Herman Mann, *The Female Review; Or, Memoirs of an American Young Lady* (Dedham, Mass.: Nathaniel & Benjamin Heaton, 1797); Samuel Relf, *Infidelity, or the Victims of Sentiment* (Philadelphia: W. W. Woodward, 1797); and Susanna Rowson, *Trials of the Human Heart* (Philadelphia: Printed for the author by Wrigley & Berriman, 1795).

18. This notice appeared in the *Massachusetts Spy, or Worcester Gazette*, March 2, 1803.

19. Mathew Carey, Account Books, Manuscript Department, AAS. Few women's names are included in these account books or in those of Isaiah Thomas, which are also at the AAS. Similarly, of the 1,445 different names in account books from the Upper Valley district of rural Vermont (recorded between 1755 and 1851), William J. Gilmore has found only twenty-one female names. See his "Elementary Literacy on the Eve of the Industrial Revolution: Trends in Rural New England, 1760–1830," *Proceedings of the American Antiquarian Society*, 92 (1982), 116. Mary Silliman, in her diary, notes that her husband, a state's attorney, would not even discuss with her the mounting debts that directly affected her and their children. See Joy Day Buel and Richard Buel, Jr., *The Way of Duty: A Woman and Her Family in Revolutionary America* (New York: Norton, 1984), pp. 198–200.

20. The eight copies of *The Instructor* discussed on pp. 8–9 come, respectively, from the AAS (1800 edition), Newberry Library (1753), Newberry Library (1748), the Russel B. Nye Popular Culture Collection at Michigan State University (1812), the Leicester Public Library (1802), the AAS (1748), the AAS (1770), and Michigan State University (1812). It is virtually impossible to make a certain identification of inscribers based merely on a signature and a date. However, circumstantial evidence suggests that one recipient of the book, John Sharples (b. 1749), was a respected Massachusetts farmer and a Quaker. The book was presented to him by his uncle, John Blakey (b. 1724), who, although apparently not a Quaker, was known for presenting many books, primarily of a devotional nature, to various friends and relatives—a custom that would become widespread in the nineteenth century, fostered by a whole gift book industry. See *Genealogy of the Sharpless [sic] Family*, comp. Gilbert Cope (Philadelphia: for the family, under the auspices of the Bi-centennial Committee, 1887), pp. 179–81. My thanks to James F. Cuffe, Jr., for his help in identifying the inscriptions.

21. Clifford Geertz, *The Interpretation of Cultures* (New York: Basic Books, 1973), p. 27.

22. One of the best studies of literary influence is still Paul M. Spurlin, *Rousseau in America* (Ann Arbor: Univ. of Michigan Press, 1940). See also "Readership in the American Enlightenment," in *Literature and History in the Age of Ideas*, ed. C.G.S. Williams (Columbus: Ohio State Univ. Press, 1975), pp. 358–73. An anecdote told by Bernard Bailyn at the Conference on Needs and Opportunities in the History of the Book (Worcester, Mass., November 3, 1984) demonstrates some of the pitfalls of "influence studies." Bailyn told how, inspired by Furet and Ozouf, he determined to chart all the books actually borrowed by readers using a lending library in Hatboro, Penn., in the late eighteenth century, hoping, in the process, to document the impact of the great European intellectual tradition on American life. He gave up his study in disgust, however, when he discovered that the good readers of Hatboro borrowed not Cato's *Lives* or Locke's *Education*, but the *History of Turkey* (which included a chapter on harems), *Nuptial Dialogues*, and a host of what Bailyn refers to as "dirty novels."

23. Robert B. Winans, "Bibliography and the Cultural Historian: Notes on the Eighteenth-Century Novel," in *Printing and Society in Early America*, ed. William L. Joyce et al. (Worcester, Mass.: AAS, 1983), p. 178.

24. The best discussion of American book importation is Stephen Botein's "The Anglo-American Book Trade Before 1776: Personnel and Strategies," in *Printing and Society in Early America*, pp. 48–82. See also Giles Barber, "Books from the Old World and for the New: The British International Trade in Books in the Eighteenth Century," *Studies on Voltaire and the Eighteenth Century*, 151 (1976), 185–224; John Clive and Bernard Bailyn, "England's Cultural Provinces: Scotland and America," *William and Mary Quarterly*, 3rd ser., 11 (October 1954), 200–213; and Margaret B. Tinkcom, "Urban Reflections in a Trans-Atlantic Mirror," *Pennsylvania Magazine of History and Biography*, 100 (1976), 287–313. David Lundberg and Henry F. May, "The Enlightened Reader in America," *American Quarterly*, 28 (Summer 1976), 262–71, and app., calculate the prevalence of certain preselected European titles in a sampling of early American libraries in order to hypothesize the relative influence of both classic and popular texts. William J. Gilmore-Lehne's *Reading Becomes a Necessity of Life: Material and Cultural Life in Rural New England, 1780–1835* (Knoxville: Univ. of Tennessee Press, 1989) promises to go a long way toward providing important new findings on what books actual readers actually read, at least in rural Vermont.

25. David D. Hall, "The Uses of Literacy in New England, 1600–1850," in *Printing and Society in Early America*, pp. 2–47; John Seelye, *Prophetic Waters: The River in Early American Life and Literature* (New York: Oxford Univ. Press, 1977), pp. 3–5; and William C. Spengemann, "What Is American Literature?" *Centennial Review*, 22 (Spring 1978), 119–38; and Spengemann, "The Earliest American Novel: Aphra Behn's *Oroonoko*," *Nineteenth-Century Fiction*, 39 (1984), 384–414.

26. George Raddin, *An Early New York Library of Fiction, with a Checklist of the Fiction of H. Caritat's Circulating Library, No. 1, City Hotel, Broadway, New York, 1804* (New York: H. W. Wilson, 1940).

27. Virtually all previous studies of American fiction claim, either overtly or as an

underlying assumption, the reliance of American fiction on British models. I also wish to acknowledge that this study simply would not have been written without its important predecessors: Herbert Ross Brown, *The Sentimental Novel in America, 1789–1860* (Durham: Duke Univ. Press, 1940); Lillie Deming Loshe, *The Early American Novel, 1789–1830* (1907; repr., New York: Frederick Ungar, 1966); Terence Martin, *The Instructed Vision: Scottish Common Sense Philosophy and the Origins of American Fiction* (Bloomington: Indiana Univ. Press, 1961); and Henri Petter, *The Early American Novel* (Columbus: Ohio State Univ. Press, 1971). For a comprehensive assessment of earlier criticism, see Patricia L. Parker, *Early American Fiction: A Reference Guide* (Boston: G. K. Hall, 1984).

28. How Americans made art from native materials is the predominant theme of Kenneth Silverman's remarkable *A Cultural History of the American Revolution* (New York: Thomas Y. Crowell, 1976).

29. The continuities of the culture of the 1790s and later American culture are explored by Emory Elliott, *Revolutionary Writers: Literature and Authority in the New Republic, 1725–1810* (New York: Oxford Univ. Press, 1982).

30. Michel Foucault, *The Archaeology of Knowledge and the Discourse on Language*, trans. A. M. Sheridan Smith (New York: Harper & Row, 1976), pp. 3–17; Geertz, *Interpretation of Cultures*, p. 151; and Edward Said (esp. his distinction between beginnings and origins), *Beginnings: Intention and Method* (Baltimore: Johns Hopkins Univ. Press, 1975), pp. xi–xiii, 3–26. It should also be added, however, that even retrospectively the historian, as Dominick La Capra has argued, does "not know how it all turned out. . . . In a word, historians are involved in the effort to understand both what something meant in its own time and what it may mean for us today." See his *Rethinking Intellectual History: Texts, Contexts, Language* (Ithaca: Cornell Univ. Press, 1983), p. 18.

31. The word *genealogy* is adapted from Michel Foucault, who prefers *genealogy* to *history* since the former remains conscious of what history leaves out, what is not known, what the methodology itself cannot comprehend, or what issues simply cannot be investigated given the historical record. The absences in the record (and they are inevitable) are thus as much a part of the genealogy as what is explicated. See Foucault's "Nietzsche, Genealogy, History," in *Language, Counter-Memory, Practice* (Ithaca: Cornell Univ. Press, 1977), pp. 139–65, and for an excellent discussion on the subject, see Cain, *Crisis in Criticism*, pp. 256–77.

32. Mary Jacobus, "Is There a Woman in This Text?" *New Literary History*, 14 (Autumn 1982), 138.

33. Peter L. Berger and Thomas Luckmann, *The Social Construction of Reality: A Treatise in the Sociology of Knowledge* (Garden City, N.Y.: Doubleday, 1966), p. 116.

34. See Hayden White, *Metahistory* (Baltimore: Johns Hopkins Univ. Press, 1973), and his "The Narrativization of Real Events," *Critical Inquiry*, 7 (Summer 1981), 793–98. See also Fredric Jameson, *The Political Unconscious: Narrative as a Socially Symbolic Act* (Ithaca: Cornell Univ. Press, 1981). For a discussion of history as a "panoply of heterogeneous discursive practices," see Michel Foucault, "History, Discourse, and Discontinuity," trans. Anthony M. Nazzaro, *Salmagundi*, 20 (1972), 229–33.

35. E. P. Thompson, *The Making of the English Working Class* (New York: Pantheon, 1964).

36. Perry Miller, *The New England Mind: From Colony to Province* (Cambridge: Harvard Univ. Press, 1953).

37. For a concise and perceptive overview of the period, see William L. Hedges, "Charles Brockden Brown and the Culture of Contradictions," *Early American Literature*, 9 (Fall 1974), 107–42.

38. Mikhail M. Bakhtin, "Epic and Novel," in *The Dialogic Imagination: Four Essays*, ed. Michael Holquist and ed. and trans. Caryl Emerson and Michael Holquist (Austin: Univ. of Texas Press, 1981), esp. pp. 3–40.

39. So popular that it was read virtually into oblivion, the *New England Primer* was probably first published sometime between 1687 and 1690, although evidence of early editions remains scant and virtually no copies of the first editions of the book are extant. This quotation, however, appeared in most editions of the book, which was often retitled the *New England Primer Improved* in the later eighteenth century and which remained a steady seller until well into the nineteenth.

40. Lewis Hyde, *The Gift: Imagination and the Erotic Life of Property* (New York: Vintage, 1979), p. xii. Special thanks to Margaret Atwood for suggesting I read this book in connection with my project.

41. For theoretical discussions of taste and the politics of privileging a culture's "masterpieces," see Pierre Bourdieu, *Distinction: A Social Critique of the Judgment of Taste*, trans. Richard Nice (Cambridge: Harvard Univ. Press, 1984); and Jane Tompkins, *Sensational Designs: The Cultural Work of American Fiction, 1790–1860* (New York: Oxford Univ. Press, 1985). For excellent analyses of the politics of canonization, see Annette Kolodny, "The Integrity of Memory: Creating a New Literary History of the United States," *American Literature*, 57 (May 1985), 291–307; and Lillian S. Robinson, "Treason Our Text: Feminist Challenges to the Literary Canon," in *The New Feminist Criticism: Essays on Women, Literature, and Theory*, ed. Elaine Showalter (New York: Pantheon, 1985), pp. 105–21.

Chapter 2

1. William Charvat, "Literary Economics and Literary History," *English Institute Essays*, ed. Alan S. Downer (1949; repr., New York: Columbia Univ. Press, 1965), pp. 74–75.

2. For a sampling of different opinions on the role of the printer in fostering republican ideology, see the essays in Bernard Bailyn and John B. Hench, eds., *The Press and the American Revolution* (Boston: Northeastern Univ. Press, 1981); and those in Donovan H. Bond, ed., *Newsletters to Newspapers: Eighteenth-Century Journalism* (Morgantown: West Virginia Univ. Press, 1977); as well as Stephen Botein, " 'Meer Mechanics' and an Open Press: The Business and Political Strategies of Colonial American Printers," *Perspectives in American History*, 9 (1975), 130–211; Clyde A. Duniway, *The Development of Freedom of the Press in Massachusetts* (Cambridge: Harvard Univ. Press, 1906); Pauline Maier, *From Resistance to Revolution: Colonial Radicals and the Development of American Opposition to Britain, 1756–1776* (New York:

Knopf, 1972); Charles S. Olton, *Artisans for Independence: Philadelphia Mechanics and the American Revolution* (Syracuse: Syracuse Univ. Press, 1975); and Arthur M. Schlesinger, *Prelude to Independence: The Newspaper War on Britain, 1764–1776* (New York: Knopf, 1958).

3. Rollo G. Silver, "The Book Trade and the Protective Tariff: 1800–1804," *Papers of the Bibliographical Society of America*, 46 (1952), 33–44; and Ethelbert Stewart, *A Documentary History of the Early Organizations of Printers* (Indianapolis: International Typographical Union, 1907).

4. For an exhaustive (if controversial) study of the effects of print technology, see Elizabeth Eisenstein's *The Printing Press as an Agent of Change*, 2 vols. (Cambridge: Cambridge Univ. Press, 1979).

5. Martha Woodmansee, "The Genius and the Copyright: Economic and Legal Conditions of the Emergence of the 'Author,' " *Eighteenth-Century Studies*, 17 (Summer 1984), 433. The first epigraph to this chapter also comes from this excellent study (p. 443).

6. Lawrence C. Wroth, in *The Book in America*, 2nd ed., ed. Hellmut Lehmann-Haupt, Lawrence C. Wroth, and Rollo G. Silver (New York: R. R. Bowker, 1951), posits between three and five hundred copies as "an average figure for editions of books and pamphlets of a literary or political character in the early and middle years of eighteenth century" (p. 40). Nor was this low volume unique to America. Richard D. Altick, *The English Common Reader: A Social History of the Mass Reading Public, 1800–1900* (Chicago: Univ. of Chicago Press, 1957), notes that "single editions of the novels of Richardson, Fielding, and Smollett seldom exceeded 4,000 copies [and] . . . only when an author's star was in the ascendant did a publisher venture to order 2,000 copies in a first edition" (p. 50). Considering that almost 6 million people lived in Britain in 1750, this figure is proportionate to Wroth's figures for early American imprints. Sales figures changed dramatically by the first decades of the nineteenth century, however, when, for example, Byron's *The Corsair* (1814) sold ten thousand copies on its first day in print and twenty-five thousand copies within a month. Britain was the world leader in the production of mechanized printing operations and, by 1814, was already gearing up its technology to supply the demands of Byron's eager readers. For the parallel German history, see Rolf Engelsing, *Der Bürger als Leser: Lesergeschichte in Deutschland, 1500–1800* (Stuttgart: Metzlersche, 1974); and Albert Ward, *Book Production, Fiction and the German Reading Public, 1740–1800* (Oxford: Clarendon, 1974).

7. John Tebbel, *A History of Book Publishing in the United States*, 4 vols. (New York: R. R. Bowker, 1972), 1:210, 222.

8. For an overview of the early American book industry, see Milton Hamilton, *The Country Printer* (New York: Columbia Univ. Press, 1936); Lehmann-Haupt, Wroth, and Silver, eds., *The Book in America*; Douglas C. McMurtrie, *The Book: The Story of Printing and Bookmaking* (New York: Covici, Friede, 1937); Charles Madison, *Book Publishing in America* (New York: McGraw-Hill, 1966); Rollo G. Silver, *The American Printer, 1787–1825* (Charlottesville: Univ. Press of Virginia, 1967), and *The Boston Book Trade, 1800–1825* (New York: New York Public Library, 1949); John Tebbel, *A History of Book Publishing* and *The Media in America* (New York: Thomas Y. Crowell,

1974), esp. chap 7; Lawrence C. Wroth, *The Colonial Printer* (Portland, Me.: Southworth-Anthoensen, 1938); and Mary Ann Yodelis, "Who Paid the Piper? Publishing Economics in Boston, 1763–1775," *Journalism Monographs*, 38 (1975), 1–49.

9. Few early American publishers kept press figures, and even fewer press records survive to the present. For an excellent discussion of the problem, see G. Thomas Tanselle, "Some Statistics on American Printing, 1764–1783," in Bailyn and Hench, eds., *The Press and the American Revolution*, pp. 315–63; and Tanselle, "Press Figures in America: Some Preliminary Observations," in *Studies in Bibliography*, ed. Fredson Bowers (Charlottesville: Univ. Press of Virginia, 1966), 19:123–60. Mathew Carey's records are among the most complete. His account books are in the Manuscript Department at the AAS, and his other papers are at the Pennsylvania Historical Society, Philadelphia. See also Earl L. Bradsher, *Mathew Carey: Editor, Author and Publisher, a Study in American Literary Development* (New York: Columbia Univ. Press, 1912); Silver, *The American Printer*, app., pp. 172–74, and "Mathew Carey, 1760–1839," *Antiquarian Bookman* (February 1, 1960), p. 355. For a fascinating firsthand account of eighteenth-century publishing practices, see Mathew Carey, *Autobiography* (New York: Research Classics, 1942).

10. Frank L. Schick, *The Paperbound Book in America: The History of Paperbacks and Their European Background* (New York: R. R. Bowker, 1958), pp. 40–45. Wayne E. Fuller in *The American Mail* (Chicago: Univ. of Chicago Press, 1972) notes that by 1814 novels were already being distributed by the postal service. He quotes one postmaster general, Return J. Meigs, who attempted to forbid the mailing of books because, Meigs insisted, "the mails were . . . overcrowded with novels and the lighter kind of books for amusement" (p. 119).

11. Cooper received no financial remuneration from the English edition of *Precaution* (1820) and learned from this experience that he had to make separate arrangements with each of his publishers. He went on to become a shrewd entrepreneur of literature. His second novel, *The Spy* (1821), had, by 1825, gone through four New York editions, three British editions, two French translations, and one German translation. For a detailed account, see *The Fiction of James Fenimore Cooper: An Exhibition of American, English and Continental Editions and Manuscripts . . .* (Charlottesville: Univ. of Virginia Library, 1974), pp. 1–36.

12. Most of America's women printers such as Ann Franklin of Newport, R.I., inherited printing shops from their fathers or husbands. See Margaret L. Ford, "Ann Franklin: Colonial Newport Printer," paper presented at the AAS, August 1984; and, for a general account of these unusual women, Leona M. Hudak, *Early American Women Printers and Publishers, 1639–1820* (Metuchen: Scarecrow, 1978).

13. William Charvat, *Literary Publishing in America, 1790–1850* (Philadelphia: Univ. of Pennsylvania Press, 1959), p. 26. Further indication of how much the publishing business was decentralized can be seen in the fact that in the early nineteenth century in Massachusetts twenty-four separate printers published editions of the Bible. See Margaret T. Hills, ed., *The English Bible in America* (New York: American Bible Society, 1961); and David D. Hall, "The Uses of Literacy in New England,

1600–1850," in *Printing and Society in Early American*, ed. William L. Joyce et al. (Worcester, Mass.: AAS, 1983), pp. 8–9.

14. Novelist Samuel Woodworth compiled one of the most curious American advice books, *The Complete Coiffeur: An Essay on the Art of Adorning Natural and of Creating Artificial Beauty* (1817), which includes several plates of elegant British and French hairstyles and instructions on how such tonsorial splendors might be adapted by the American fair sex.

15. James D. Hart, *The Popular Book: A History of America's Literary Taste* (New York: Oxford Univ. Press, 1950), p. 45. A. Owen Aldridge disputes this figure in *Man of Reason: The Life of Thomas Paine* (Philadelphia: Lippincott, 1959), p. 42, although he does note that the first edition of *Common Sense*, which ran to one thousand copies, sold out in two weeks.

16. I am indebted to Elizabeth Carroll Reilly for making available to me her excellent unpublished paper "Cheap and Popular Books in Mid-Eighteenth-Century New England."

17. Paul M. Spurlin, "Readership and the American Enlightenment," in *Literature and History in the Age of Ideas*, ed. C.G.S. Williams (Columbus: Ohio State Univ. Press, 1975), p. 368.

18. Elijah R. Sabin, *The Life and Reflections of Charles Observator* (Boston: Rowe and Hooper, 1816), p. 3. Another indication of the sheer numbers of available books (even allowing for evangelical hyperbole) is the American Tract Society's report that it had distributed 13 million tracts worldwide between 1799 and 1814. See *Constitution of the American Tract Society* (Boston: Flagg and Gould for the American Tract Society, 1814), p. 5.

19. Carl Bridenbaugh and Jessica Bridenbaugh, *Rebels and Gentlemen: Philadelphia in the Age of Franklin* (1942; repr., New York: Oxford Univ. Press, 1965), p. 80; and Lewis P. Simpson, "The Printer as a Man of Letters: Franklin and the Symbolism of the Third Realm," in *The Oldest Revolutionary: Essays on Benjamin Franklin*, ed. J. A. Leo Lemay (Philadelphia: Univ. of Pennsylvania Press, 1976), pp. 3–20.

20. Charvat, *Literary Publishing in America*, p. 41.

21. See Isaiah Thomas's letter to Jeremy Belknap, November 3, 1792, Thomas Papers, Manuscript Department, AAS, where Thomas notes that he has made several (costly) revisions in his editions of William Perry's *Spelling Book* and expresses alarm that Belknap plans to publish his own version of the book: "I think you too generous, after being acquainted with the circumstances, to do anything which would be injurious to me," Thomas pleads. Only "by way of retaliation" would one reputable printer ever act in such an underhanded manner toward another.

22. Tanselle, in "Some Statistics on American Printing," notes that in Charles Evan's *American Bibliography* (Chicago: Printed for the author by the Blakely Press, 1903–34), "a great many of the . . . entries refer to items that never existed, as a result of his [Evans's] interpretation of titles announced in booksellers' advertisements" (p. 321). The practice is also discussed by Silver, *The American Printer*, p. 104; and Robert B. Winans, "Bibliography and the Cultural Historian: Notes on the Eighteenth-Century Novel," in *Printing and Society in Early America*, p. 176.

23. Parke Rouse, *The Printer in Eighteenth-Century Williamsburg* (Williamsburg: Colonial Williamsburg Press, 1958), p. 21.

24. Charles Brockden Brown, in his capacity as magazine editor, noted: "I have often been amused in observing the vast difference between writing and printing. A miserable scrawling hand, never to be decyphered but by the study of the context, ... filled with interlineations and blots, and nice adjustment of points and capitals totally neglected is metamorphosed by that magical machine, the press, into the perfection of beauty, regularity, and accuracy." *Literary Magazine and American Register*, 1 (November 1803), 83. See also Silver, *The American Printer*, p. 93; and Tebbel, *A History of Book Publishing*, 1:112.

25. It is not the province of this study to determine how much authority printers granted to the texts they published, but it might be fruitful for future researchers to compare, for example, how much textual variation existed between one edition of a novel and another versus variations between different editions of the Bible. The procedures of printing themselves embody ideologies as has been argued eloquently by French historians of *livre et société* such as François Furet et al., *Livre et société dans la France du XVII siècle*, 2 vols. (Paris et La Haye: Mouton et Cie, 1965, 1970); and Geneviève Bollème, *La Bibliothèque bleue: Littérature populaire en France du XVI au XIX siècles* (Paris: Gallimard, Juillard, 1971). See also Robert Darnton, *The Business of Enlightenment: A Publishing History of the Encyclopédie, 1775–1800* (Cambridge: Harvard Univ. Press, 1979).

26. One of the most extreme cases of a printer exerting artistic control over an early American novel is seen in the 1841 edition of Tabitha Tenney's popular novel, *Female Quixotism* (1801). Originally published by Isaiah Thomas and E. T. Andrews of Boston as two volumes bound in one, by 1825 J. P. Peaslee bound each volume separately and included a frontispiece and a vignette title page with each volume. But when George Clark republished the book in 1841, he published it in three volumes, in the manner of popular British novels. He actually renumbered the chapters in order to create the extra volume, thus violating the transition Tenney conceived in this early *bildungsroman* between volume one and two. Clark also hired an engraver to imitate the style of the earlier illustrations in two new illustrations made for the new volume.

27. The novelist Francis Hopkinson, in *Plan for the Improvement of the Art of Paper War* (Philadelphia: Mathew Carey, 1787), suggested, in a delightful satire on eighteenth-century typography, that printing could be made still more expressive if "every degree of vociferation" by a writer or character were printed in a different size and style of type.

28. Advertisement for *Emily Hamilton*, a Novel. Founded on Incidents in Real Life. By a Young Lady of Worcester County (Worcester, Mass.: Isaiah Thomas, Jr., 1803). The advertisement appeared in the *Massachusetts Spy, or Worcester Gazette* on October 20, 1802; December 1 and 29, 1802; and January 5, 1803. The advertisement also contained the full title of the novel and a portion of the preface, but no author's name and no description of the plot or contents of the book. This emphasis on the appearance of books (and especially their bindings) is also attested to by the many letters sent by Mason Locke Weems to his employer, Mathew Carey: "The Eye is every

thing—charm that and you are safe. They won't look at boards—I tell you again the eye is all, all, all!" See H. Glen Brown, "Philadelphia Contributions to the Book Arts and Book Trade, 1796–1810," *Papers of the Bibliographical Society of America*, 37 (1943), 275–92. Clearly books, then as now, had a status function as well as a literary one.

29. Bernard Bailyn, *Education in the Forming of American Society; Needs and Opportunities for Study* (Chapel Hill: Univ. of North Carolina Press, 1960), pp. 95, 93.

30. Spurlin, "Readership and the American Enlightenment," pp. 362–64; and U.S. Bureau of the Census, *Historical Statistics of the United States: Colonial Times to 1957* (Washington, D.C.: U.S. Government Printing Office, 1960).

31. Joseph Dennie to Royall Tyler, August 30, 1797, in *The Letters of Joseph Dennie, 1768–1812*, ed. Laura G. Pedder (Orono: Univ. of Maine Press, 1936), p. 165.

32. These figures come from the detailed lists of expenses at the back of Ethan Allen Greenwood's diaries, December 30, 1805, to February 9, 1806, Manuscript Department, AAS, and corroborated by Carroll D. Wright, *History of Wages and Prices in Massachusetts: 1752–1883* (Boston: Wright and Potter, 1885), p. 13. The establishment of regular steamship routes by the 1820s cut both time and cost between seaports approximately in half.

33. "Summary Account of the Book Stock and Other Property of Isaiah Thomas, Taken August 20, 1813," box 9, Isaiah Thomas Papers.

34. Charvat, *Literary Publishing in America*, pp. 17–24.

35. Tebbel, *A History of Book Publishing*, 1:240; and James M. Wells, "Book Typography in the United States of America," in *Book Typography, 1815–1965*, ed. Kenneth Day (Chicago: Univ. of Chicago Press, 1965), p. 331.

36. Cynthia Z. Stiverson and Gregory A. Stiverson, "The Colonial Retail Book Trade: Availability and Affordability of Reading Material in Mid-Eighteenth-Century Virginia," in *Printing and Society in Early America*, p. 147.

37. Reilly, "Cheap and Popular Books"; see also her "The Wages of Piety: The Boston Book Trade of Jeremy Condy," in *Printing and Society in Early America*, pp. 83–131.

38. William J. Gilmore, "Elementary Literacy on the Eve of the Industrial Revolution: Trends in Rural New England, 1760–1830," *Proceedings of the American Antiquarian Society*, 92 (1982), 124. See also Edward M. Cook, Jr., *The Fathers of the Towns: Leadership and Community Structure in Eighteenth-Century New England* (Baltimore: Johns Hopkins Univ. Press, 1976); Jackson Turner Main, *The Social Structure of Revolutionary America* (Princeton: Princeton Univ. Press, 1965); and Allan R. Pred, *Urban Growth and the Circulation of Information: The United States System of Cities, 1790–1840* (Cambridge: Harvard Univ. Press, 1973). For the relationship between literacy and the market economy, see Gilmore, "Elementary Literacy," p. 159; and David Cressy, *Literacy and the Social Order: Reading and Writing in Tudor and Stuart England* (Cambridge: Cambridge Univ. Press, 1980).

39. It is important to note in this regard that the issue is access to publishing centers, not simple population. At the time of the first census (1790), for example, 48.5 percent of the population was in the Southern states, with Virginia being the single most populous state in the Union. These figures, however, include freed blacks

and slaves to whom literacy was often denied (and even illegal). For a discussion of these figures, see Russel B. Nye, *The Cultural Life of the New Nation: 1776–1830* (New York: Harper & Row, 1960), p. 250; and Spurlin, "Readership and the American Enlightenment," pp. 364–66. Nye counts fifty booksellers in Boston in the 1770s and over thirty in Philadelphia. In contrast, a number of important studies emphasize the impediments to obtaining books in the South. See Richard Beale Davis, *Intellectual Life in the Colonial South, 1586–1763* (Knoxville: Univ. of Tennessee Press, 1978), esp. chap. 4; Joseph F. Kett and Patricia A. McClung, "Book Culture in Post-Revolutionary Virginia," *Proceedings of the American Antiquarian Society*, 94 (1984), 97–138; George K. Smart, "Private Libraries in Colonial Virginia," *American Literature*, 10 (March 1938), 24–52; Stiverson and Stiverson, "The Colonial Book Trade," pp. 132–73; and Louis B. Wright, *The First Gentlemen of Virginia: Intellectual Qualities of the Early Colonial Ruling Class* (1940; repr., Charlottesville, Va.: Dominion, 1964). The Stiverson's note that the only active bookseller in Virginia in the mid-eighteenth century had a book trade limited to approximately 230 customers per year, and, in one year, he sold only 2,028 books (excluding almanacs). For a firsthand account of the scarcity of books in the rural South, see the autobiographical *Life of the Reverend Devereux Jarratt* (Baltimore: Warner & Hanna, 1806).

40. Quoted in Reilly, "Cheap and Popular Books," from the *Acts and Resolves of the Province of Massachusetts-Bay*, 1713, 1721, and 1726.

41. For a fuller discussion, see J. R. Dolan, *Yankee Peddlers of Early America* (New York: Bramhall House, 1964); Priscilla Carrington Kline, "New Light on the Yankee Peddler," *New England Quarterly*, 12 (1939), 80–98; and Richardson Wright, *Hawkers and Walkers in Early America* (Philadelphia: Lippincott, 1927). For a comparative discussion, see Victor E. Neuburg, *Chapbooks: A Bibliography of References to English and American Chapbooks of the Eighteenth and Nineteenth Centuries* (London: Vine, 1964), and Neuburg, *The Penny Histories* (New York: Harcourt, Brace & World, 1969). And for a contemporaneous account, Isaiah Thomas, *The History of Printing in America*, ed. Marcus A. McCorison (New York: Weathervane, 1970), pp. 131, 133, 141, 153, 303, 524.

42. Tebbel, *A History of Book Publishing*, 1:111–16; and James Gilreath, "American Book Distribution," paper presented at the AAS, Worcester, Mass., November 2, 1984.

43. For a delightful account of the life of a literary agent, see Parson Weems's letters to his employer, written between 1795 and 1825, in E.E.F. Skeel, *Mason Locke Weems*, 3 vols. (New York: Random House, 1929), vols. 2, 3. Weems was the author not only of mythmaking biographies, but also of such sensational titles as *The Lover's Almanac* (1798), *Hymen's Recruiting Sergeant* (1799), *God's Revenge Against Murder* (1807), *God's Revenge Against Gambling* (1810), *God's Revenge Against Adultry* (1815), and *The Bad Wife's Looking Glass* (1823). It might also be noted that over the course of his life, Weems often appended his own name (gratuitously) to the books he sold, beginning with a 1799 pamphlet on George Washington that Weems revised only slightly. See Dean G. Hall, "Mason Locke Weems," in *American Writers Before 1800*, ed. James A. Levernier and Douglas R. Wilmes (Westport, Conn.: Greenwood, 1983), p. 1545, and Lewis Leary, *The Book-Peddling Parson* (Chapel Hill, N.C.: Algonquin Books, 1984).

44. Tebbel, *A History of Book Publishing*, 1:115. For an excellent discussion of Weems's business practices (including his methods for obtaining subscriptions to future publications), see James Gilreath, "Mason Weems, Mathew Carey, and the Southern Booktrade, 1794–1810," *Publishing History*, 10 (1981), 27–49.

45. Quoted by Earl L. Bradsher, *Mathew Carey*, p. 31.

46. Earl L. Bradsher, "Early American Book Prices," *Publishers Weekly*, 83 (March 8, 1913), 862; and Donald McKenzie, "Printers of the Mind: Some Notes on Bibliographical Theories and Printing-House Practices," *Studies in Bibliography*, 22 (1969), 1–75.

47. Wright, *History of Wages and Prices*, pp. 63–65.

48. *The History of Constantius and Pulchera* (Leominster, Mass.: Charles Prentiss for Robert B. Thomas, 1797). This unusually inexpensive version of the novel was sold by Robert B. Thomas in his Sterling, Mass., bookshop along with other inexpensive editions of popular books (chiefly British in origin if not in manufacture) such as *History of Charles Grandison* ($.25) and Edward Moore's *Fables for the Ladies* ($.37). An advertisement at the back of S.S.B.K. Wood's *Ferdinand and Elmira* indicates that another edition of *The History of Constantius and Pulchera* could be purchased in Baltimore in 1802 from the shop of Samuel Butler for $.75.

49. U.S. Department of Labor, *History of Wages in the United States from Colonial Times to 1928* (Washington, D.C.: U.S. Government Printing Office, 1929), pp. 53, 57, 133–34, 137.

50. Greenwood diaries, log at the end of the diary for December 30, 1805, to February 9, 1806. A night at the theater, however, also cost Greenwood $.75, putting it directly in competition with novels as an evening's literary entertainment.

51. Christopher Clark, "Household Economy, Market Exchange, and the Rise of Capitalism in the Connecticut Valley, 1800–1860," *Journal of Social History*, 13 (Winter 1979), 170. See also Michael Merrill, "Cash Is Good to Eat: Self-sufficiency and Exchange in the Rural Economy of the United States," *Radical History Review*, 4 (Winter 1977), 42–71. For a detailed statistical account of how printers were paid and what they published, see Yodelis, "Who Paid the Piper?"

52. This advertisement appeared throughout 1782 in the *Massachusetts Gazette and General Advertiser*, which was then being published, with little success, in Springfield.

53. Sukey Vickery, *Emily Hamilton* (1803), rear flyleaf. In 1785, Isaiah Thomas so desperately needed supplies that he paid Thomas Evans of London with a shipment of potash. This was not, however, the typical or preferred method of payment. See Clifford K. Shipton, *Isaiah Thomas: Printer, Patriot, and Philanthropist, 1749–1831* (Rochester, N.Y.: Leo Hart, 1948), p. 45.

54. Isaiah Thomas Papers, esp. box 9, "Accounts of Stock at the Walpole Store"; Mathew Carey Account Books, passim. See also Stiverson and Stiverson, "The Colonial Retail Book Trade," pp. 144–45.

55. Samuel Goodrich, *Recollections of a Lifetime*, 2 vols (New York: Miller, Orton, 1857), 1:64, 86.

56. Spurlin, "Readership and the American Enlightenment," p. 366. See Lehmann-Haupt, Wroth, and Silver, eds., *The Book in America*, pp. 50–60; and How-

ard Mumford Jones, "The Importation of French Literature in New York City, 1750–1800," *Studies in Philology*, 28 (1931), 241.

57. See Silver, "Three Eighteenth-Century Book Contracts," *Papers of the Bibliographical Society of America*, 47 (1953), 383.

58. Winans, "Bibliography and the Cultural Historian," p. 176.

59. Jesse H. Shera, "The Beginnings of Systematic Bibliography in America, 1642–1799," in *Essays Honoring Lawrence C. Wroth*, ed. Frederick Richmond Goff et al. (Portland, Maine: Anthoensen, 1951), p. 274. See also Shera, *Foundations of the Public Library* (Chicago: Univ. of Chicago Press, 1949). For a fascinating description of the first social library in Belpre, Ohio (a town settled in 1788, its library founded in 1796), see William H. Venable, *Beginnings of Literary Culture in the Ohio Valley* (New York: R. Clark, 1891), p. 135.

60. *Autobiography and Other Writings by Benjamin Franklin*, ed. Russel B. Nye (Boston: Houghton Mifflin, 1958), pp. 71–72.

61. Sarah Savage, *The Factory Girl, by a Lady* (Boston: Munroe, Francis, and Parker, 1814), esp. pp. 35–40, 54–55.

62. *Records of the Union Harwinton Library*, ed. Terry Belanger (New York: Book Arts Press, School of Library Service, Columbia Univ., 1977), pp. 5; 3.

63. George Raddin, *An Early New York Library of Fiction, with a Checklist of the Fiction of H. Caritat's Circulating Library, No. 1, City Hotel, Broadway, New York, 1804* (New York: H. W. Wilson, 1940), pp. 14–16. A bookplate listing the bylaws of the Philadelphia Circulating Library is attached to the copy of Brockden Brown's *Edgar Huntly* (Philadelphia: H. Maxwell, 1799) owned by the AAS. An advertisement in the *Massachusetts Mercury* (April 18, 1797, p. 3) includes the terms for the Pelham Library. By way of comparison, Raddin (p. 15) notes that the Samuel Berrian Library in New York charged subscribers only $4.50 a year while the Melitiah Nash Library, also in New York, charged $3.50. On the other hand, the unnamed circulating library that Greenwood joined in Massachusetts assessed its members $1 per month. In any of these cases, however, it was still far cheaper to borrow than to buy large quantities of books.

64. While lending-library rosters are notoriously incomplete, it can at least be ventured that the number of book readers in the new Republic advanced far ahead of population growth. Winans has calculated that in the five largest cities in America, the number of social libraries increased tenfold between 1770 and 1780, while the circulating libraries (for which far less data has survived) increased at least threefold and probably much more. See "The Growth of a Novel-Reading Public in Late-Eighteenth-Century America," *Early American Literature*, 9 (Winter 1975), 268–69.

65. I am grateful to Robert Gross for this information on the Concord Library.

66. Raddin, *An Early New York Library of Fiction*, pp. 35–104. See also Winans, "Growth of a Novel-Reading Public," pp. 274–75, for other figures such as the John Mien Circulating Library (Boston, 1765) that included 35 percent fiction, and W. P. & L. Blake's Circulating Library (Boston, 1800) that included 65 percent fiction. See also Winans's invaluable bibliography, *A Descriptive Checklist of Book Catalogues Separately Printed in America, 1693–1800* (Worcester, Mass.: AAS, 1981); and Thomas, *History of Printing*, pp. 151, 429.

67. John Davis, *Travels of Four Years and a Half in the United States of America During 1798, 1799, 1800, 1801, and 1802* (New York: Henry Holt, 1909), p. 204.

68. Raddin, *An Early New York Library of Fiction*, pp. 24–25.

69. *Autobiography . . . by Benjamin Franklin*, p. 72.

70. *Farmer's Weekly Museum.* This weekly advertisement ran from July 24 to October 1, 1798. Perhaps to keep himself attuned to the market, Thomas purchased two shares in the Worcester Social Library (Massachusetts) in 1813 (this at a time when his own personal library was valued at $4,000 and probably far outstripped the resources of the town collection). See Isaiah Thomas Papers, Accounts of Stock, box 9.

71. See esp. Michel Foucault, "What Is an Author?" in *Language, Counter-Memory, Practice*, trans. Donald F. Bouchard and Sherry Simon (Ithaca: Cornell Univ. Press, 1977), pp. 113–38.

72. Translated and quoted by Woodmansee, "The Genius and the Copyright," p. 425, from Georg Heinrich Zinck, *Allgemeines Oeconomisches Lexicon* (1753).

73. Silver, *The American Printer*, p. 98.

74. G. Thomas Tanselle, "Author and Publisher in 1800: Letters of Royall Tyler and Joseph Nancrede," *Harvard Library Bulletin*, 15 (1967), 135–36, 133.

75. The approximate figures here are intentional. When dealing with anonymous authors, it is often impossible to tell whether two titles represent the work of two separate anonymous authors or two books by one. Similarly, the whole definition of a "novel" was very flexible in the early national period, with some novelists pretending to be nonfiction writers and vice versa. I have intentionally retained the traditional flexible definition of what constitutes an early American novel, a practice followed by Lyle Wright in his excellent bibliography, *American Fiction 1774–1850* (1939; rev. ed., San Marino, Calif.: Huntington Library, 1948).

76. Sukey Vickery Papers, letter of February 13, 1802, Manuscript Department, AAS. For the full text of this letter and a discussion of the author and her work, see my "Female Authorship and Authority: The Case of Sukey Vickery," *Early American Literature*, 21 (Spring 1986), 4–28.

77. S.S.B.K. Wood, *Julia, and the Illuminated Baron. A Novel: Founded on Recent Facts Which Have Transpired in the Course of the Late Revolution of Moral Principles in France.* By A Lady of Massachusetts (Portsmouth, N.H.: Charles Peirce, 1800), pp. iii–v.

78. S.S.B.K. Wood, *Ferdinand and Elmira, a Russian Story* (Baltimore: Samuel Butler, 1804), p. 3. It is always difficult to know how much such statements represent merely a conventional or pro forma argument, but it does seem significant that Wood herself secured the copyright on one of her novels, *Dorval, or the Speculator* (1801), suggesting at least a passing interest in the business of authorship. See also Helene Koon, "Sally Sayward Barrell Wood," in *American Women Writers*, ed. Lina Mainiero, 4 vols. (New York: Frederick Ungar, 1982), 4:452–54.

79. Several nineteenth-century "sentimental" novelists pretended to write as an avocation but actually wrote out of necessity. Louisa May Alcott, to cite the most obvious example, supported her parents (for all his fame, Bronson was a feeble provider), her siblings, and even the children of her siblings. She wrote, "Goethe puts

his joys and sorrows into poems; I turn mine into bread and butter." Quoted in Raymond L. Kilgour, *Messrs. Roberts Brothers Publishers* (Ann Arbor: Univ. of Michigan Press, 1952), p. 113. For a sensitive and perceptive discussion of nineteenth-century women writers, see Mary Kelley, *Private Woman, Public Stage* (New York: Oxford Univ. Press, 1984).

80. Silver, "Three Eighteenth-Century Book Contracts," pp. 381–82. As a single woman, it should be noted, Hannah Adams often had to have her contracts cosigned by men, her own signature having no legal weight.

81. Hannah Adams, *A Memoir of Miss Hannah Adams, Written by Herself* (Boston: Gray and Rowen, 1832), p. 34. Adams attributes this particular observation to British author Charlotte Smith.

82. Silver, "Three Eighteenth-Century Book Contracts," p. 386.

83. Tebbel, *A History of Book Publishing*, 1:152; see also Emily E. Skeel, "Salesmanship of an Early American Best Seller," *Papers of the Bibliographical Society of America*, 32 (1938), 38–46.

84. Noah Webster to Isaiah Thomas, June 25, 1788, Isaiah Thomas Papers.

85. Quoted by William Charvat, *The Profession of Authorship in America, 1800–1870: The Papers of William Charvat*, ed. Matthew J. Bruccoli (Columbus: Ohio State Univ. Press, 1968), p. 5.

86. Tebbel, *History of Book Publishing*, 1:139–43; see also Rollo G. Silver, "Prologue to Copyright in America: 1722," *Studies in Bibliography: Papers of the Bibliographical Society of the University of Virginia*, 51 (1958), pp. 259–62.

87. For a discussion of the impact of the copyright laws, see Frederick Richmond Goff, "The First Decade of the Federal Act for Copyright, 1790–1800," in *Essays Honoring Lawrence C. Wroth*, ed. Frederick Richmond Goff et al. (Portland, Maine: Anthoensen, 1951); and Ruth Leonard, "Bibliographical Importance of Copyright Records," *College and Research Libraries*, 7 (January 1946), 34–40.

88. Silver counts only 556 copyrights granted between 1790 and 1800; see *The American Printer*, p. 113.

89. Charvat, *Profession of Authorship*, p. 5.

90. See Wallace Putnam Bishop, "The Struggle for International Copyright in the United States," Ph.D. diss., Boston Univ., 1959.

91. Letter of January 11, 1803, repr. in Silver, "The Book Trade," *Papers of the Bibliographical Society of America*, 46 (1952), 42.

92. Tebbel, *History of Book Publishing*, 1:134. Silver, "The Book Trade," p. 33, presents a somewhat more positive view.

93. *Massachusetts Centinel*, February 7, 1789. The British price of the four-volume edition was $8; Thomas promised to sell it for $5.

94. See esp. [Mathew Carey], *Wages of Female Labour* (Philadelphia: Matthew Carey, 1829), which discusses the seamstresses employed by the government to make uniforms. "This is no 'fancy sketch'—no imaginary portrait drawn to excite compassion or horror. It is a tremendous reality, revolting to every honorable or humane feeling. And will not public indignation wipe away this foul stain from the character of our city?" (n.p.).

95. Charles G. Steffen, *The Mechanics of Baltimore: Workers and Politics in the Age of Revolution, 1763–1812* (Urbana: Univ. of Illinois Press, 1984), p. 210.

96. Alfred F. Young, " 'By Hammer and Hand All Arts Do Stand': An Interpretation of Mechanics in the Era of the American Revolution," paper presented at the Organization of American Historians, San Francisco, April 1980, and discussed by Steffen, *Mechanics of Baltimore*, p. 276. See also Young's "The Mechanics and Jeffersonians: New York, 1789–1801," *Labor History*, 5 (1964), 247–76.

97. Steffen, *Mechanics of Baltimore*, 211.

Chapter 3

1. Royall Tyler, *The Algerine Captive*, ed. Don L. Cook (New Haven: College & Univ. Press, 1970), p. 27.

2. *New York Magazine*, n.s., 2 (1797), 398.

3. *Selected Writings of John and John Quincy Adams*, ed. Adrienne Koch and William Peden (New York: Knopf, 1946), p. 148.

4. Anthony Giddens, *Central Problems in Social Theory: Action, Structure, and Contradiction in Social Analysis* (Berkeley: Univ. of California Press, 1979), p. 6.

5. Giddens, *Central Problems in Social Theory*, p. 193.

6. For a survey of magazines, see William J. Free, *The Columbian Magazine and American Literary Nationalism* (The Hague: Mouton, 1968), esp. pp. 61–63; and Frank Luther Mott, *A History of American Magazines, 1741–1850* (Cambridge: Harvard Univ. Press, 1966), esp. chap. 2.

7. Jürgen Habermas, *Toward a Rational Society*, trans. Jeremy J. Shapiro (Boston: Beacon, 1968), p. 99. See also, Raymond Williams, *Marxism and Literature* (New York: Oxford Univ. Press, 1977), pp. 112–13.

8. The most interesting case is Jefferson. He praised or condemned fiction according to the status of the audience he addressed. See *The Works of Thomas Jefferson in Twelve Volumes*, ed. Paul Leicester Ford (New York: G. P. Putman's, 1905), 12:91, for a condemnation and his letter to Charles Brockden Brown, quoted in David Lee Clark, *Charles Brockden Brown: Pioneer Voice of America* (Durham: Duke Univ. Press, 1952), p. 164, for a positive evaluation. See also Jefferson's letter of August 3, 1771, to Robert Skipwith recommending that several novels be included in the young gentleman's library (repr. in Gordon S. Wood, *The Rising Glory of America, 1760–1820* [New York: George Braziller, 1971], pp. 170–74).

9. Raymond Williams, *The Long Revolution* (New York: Columbia Univ. Press, 1961), esp. pp. 41–43.

10. Williams, *The Long Revolution*, p. 113, and his *Keywords: A Vocabulary of Culture and Society* (New York: Oxford Univ. Press, 1976), esp. pp. 76–82, 145–48, 281–84.

11. Since numerous commentators have written at length on the censure of fiction, I have not analyzed that critique but have focused instead on a few telling examples of it. For a detailed discussion of the censure, see Jean-Marie Bonnet, *La Critique littéraire aux États-Unis, 1783–1837* (Lyon: Presses Universitaires, 1982), pp. 97–156; William Charvat, *The Origins of American Critical Thought, 1819–1835* (Philadelphia:

Univ. of Pennsylvania Press, 1936), esp. chaps. 2, 7; G. Harrison Orians, "Censure of Fiction in American Romances and Magazines, 1789–1810," *PMLA*, 52 (1937), 195–214; Ormond E. Palmer, "Some Attitudes Toward Fiction in America to 1870, and a Bit Beyond," Ph.D. diss., Univ. of Chicago, 1952; and Sergio Perosa, *American Theories of the Novel: 1793–1903* (New York: New York Univ. Press, 1983), p. 4.

12. William Hill Brown, *The Power of Sympathy*, ed. William S. Kable (Columbus: Ohio State Univ. Press, 1969), p. 25.

13. See Norman Grabo, *Edward Taylor* (New York: Twayne, 1961), p. 25; David D. Hall, "The Uses of Literacy in New England, 1600–1850," in *Printing and Society in Early America*, ed. William L. Joyce et al. (Worcester, Mass.: AAS, 1983), pp. 26–27; Christopher M. Jedrey, *The World of John Cleaveland: Family and Community in Eighteenth-Century New England* (New York: Norton, 1979), p. 103; and Thomas Goddard Wright, *Literary Culture in Early New England, 1620–1730* (New Haven: Yale Univ. Press, 1920). As a point of comparison, see Rolf Engelsing, "Die Perioden der Lesergeschichte in der Neuzeit," in *Zur Sozialgeschichte deutscher Mittel—und Unterschichten* (Göttingen: Vandenhoeck und Ruprecht, 1973), pp. 112–54. (Special thanks to William J. Gilmore for bringing this important essay to my attention.)

14. William Hill Brown, *The Power of Sympathy*, p. 25.

15. Dell Hymes, "Models of the Interaction of Language and Social Life," *Journal of Social Issues*, 23 (1967), 8–28.

16. "Character and Effects of Modern Novels," *Weekly Magazine*, March 10, 1798, 185.

17. Quoted in Nina Baym, *Novels, Readers, and Reviewers: Responses to Fiction in Antebellum America* (Ithaca: Cornell Univ. Press, 1984), p. 29.

18. Fredric Jameson, "Reification and Utopia in Mass Culture," *Social Text*, 1 (Winter 1979), 136.

19. Mikhail M. Bakhtin, "Epic and Novel," in *The Dialogic Imagination: Four Essays*, ed. Michael Holquist and ed. and trans. Caryl Emerson and Michael Holquist (Austin: Univ. of Texas Press, 1981), pp. 38, 37, 39.

20. Nathan O. Hatch, "Elias Smith and the Rise of Religious Journalism," in *Printing and Society in Early America*, pp. 250–77. It has also been argued, convincingly, that the first major challenge to traditional authority in America came with the Great Awakening. Although this is not the focus of my own discussion, I have certainly profited from Jay Fliegelman, *Prodigals and Pilgrims: The American Revolution Against Patriarchal Authority, 1750–1800* (New York: Cambridge Univ. Press, 1982), pp. 103–55; Alan Heimert, *Religion and the American Mind: From the Great Awakening to the Revolution* (Cambridge: Harvard Univ. Press, 1966); James A. Henretta, *The Evolution of American Society, 1700–1815* (Lexington, Mass.: D. C. Heath, 1973); and Richard Hofstadter, *Anti-Intellectualism in American Life* (New York: Knopf, 1963), esp. pt. 2, chap. 3.

21. Gordon S. Wood, "The Democratization of Mind in the American Revolution," in *The Moral Foundations of the American Republic*, 2nd ed., ed. Robert H. Horwitz (Charlottesville: Univ. Press of Virginia, 1979), pp. 102–28.

22. Rhys Isaacs, "Books and the Social Authority of Learning: The Case of Mid-Eighteenth-Century Virginia," in *Printing and Society in Early America*, pp. 248–49.

See also his *The Transformation of Virginia, 1740–1790* (Chapel Hill: Univ. of North Carolina Press, 1982).

23. "On Modern Novels, and Their Effects," *Massachusetts Magazine, or Monthly Museum*, 3 (1791), 663.

24. "An Essay on the Modern Novel," *Port Folio*, 2 (April 10, 1802), 107.

25. *New England Quarterly*, 1 (1802), 172–74. A headnote accompanying the article indicates that it was originally published in the *Monthly Mirror* (presumably, the British periodical) in November 1797.

26. William Hill Brown, *The Power of Sympathy*, p. 3.

27. The neglect of women and the inattention to the ideology of sexuality in the classical sociological literature (including most contributions by the New Left) is truly alarming. For an overview of the problem, see the excellent essay by Judith Stacey and Barrie Thorne, "The Missing Feminist Revolution in Sociology," *Social Problems*, 32 (April 1985), 301–16. For a corrective to the Marxist failure to come to terms with feminism and an excellent analysis of the relationship between gender and power, see Nancy C. M. Hartsock, *Money, Sex, and Power: Toward a Feminist Historical Materialism* (New York: Longman, 1983), esp. pp. 155–58. See also Robert Padgug, "Sexual Matters," *Radical History Review*, 20 (Spring-Summer 1979), 3–24; and Jeffrey Weeks, *Sex, Politics, and Society* (New York: Longman, 1981).

28. Patricia Murphy Robinson, "The Historical Repression of Women's Sexuality," in *Pleasure and Danger: Exploring Female Sexuality* (Boston: Routledge & Kegan Paul, 1984), p. 252.

29. See esp. Michel Foucault, *The History of Sexuality*, 3 vols., trans. Robert Hurley (New York: Pantheon, 1978), vol. 1; Sherry B. Ortner and Harriet Whitehead, "Accounting for Sexual Meanings," in *Sexual Meanings: The Cultural Construction of Gender and Sexuality* (New York: Cambridge Univ. Press, 1981), pp. 1–27; and Ellen Ross and Rayna Rapp, "Sex and Society: A Research Note from Social History and Anthropology," in *Powers of Desire: The Politics of Sexuality*, ed. Ann Snitow, Christine Stansell, and Sharon Thompson (New York: Monthly Review Press, 1983), pp. 51–73.

30. "Character and Effects of Modern Novels," *Weekly Magazine*, 1 (March 10, 1798), 185.

31. Samuel Miller, *A Brief Retrospect of the Eighteenth Century*, 2 vols. (New York: T. & J. Swords, 1803), 2:179. See also Miller's "The Appropriate Duty and Ornament of the Female Sex," in *The Columbian Preacher; or, A Collection of Original Sermons, from Preachers of Eminence in the United States. Embracing the Distinguishing Doctrines of Grace* (Catskill: Nathan Elliott, 1808), p. 253.

32. Enos Hitchcock, *Memoirs of the Bloomsgrove Family. In a Series of Letters to a Respectable Citizen of Philadelphia*, 2 vols. (Boston: I. Thomas and E. T. Andrews, 1790), 2:186–87, 184.

33. Hitchcock, *Memoirs of the Bloomsgrove Family*, 2:29.

34. For a useful discussion, and some working definitions, of "class" in the early republic, see Jackson Turner Main, *The Social Structure of Revolutionary America* (Princeton: Princeton Univ. Press, 1965), esp. pp. 197–220.

35. For an overview of the Scottish Common Sense philosophers, see Louis

Schneider's introductory essay in *The Scottish Moralists on Human Nature and Society* (Chicago: Univ. of Chicago Press, 1967). A different perspective is provided by Gladys Bryson, *Man and Society: The Scottish Inquiry of the Eighteenth Century* (Princeton: Princeton Univ. Press, 1945). The role these writers played in America has been cogently argued by both Emory Elliott, *Revolutionary Writers: Literature and Authority in the New Republic, 1725–1810* (New York: Oxford Univ. Press, 1982), pp. 30–35; and Terence Martin, *The Instructed Vision: Scottish Common Sense Philosophy and the Origins of American Fiction* (Bloomington: Indiana Univ. Press, 1961). For a quantitative survey of the availability of these writers in America, see David Lundberg and Henry F. May, "The Enlightened Reader in America," *American Quarterly*, 28 (Summer 1976), 261–62, app.

36. Timothy Dwight, *Travels in New England and New York*, 4 vols. (New Haven: T. Dwight, 1821), 1:518.

37. A number of the attacks on the novel insinuated the lowly class origins of novelists, including the anonymous "Essay on the Modern Novel" (*Port Folio*, 2 [April 10, 1802], 106) that attributed the "levity and licentiousness" of the novel to the "*Angelinas* and *Celestinas* who have exchanged a washing-tub for a writing-desk."

38. William Hill Brown, *The Power of Sympathy*, p. 5.

39. *Monima* was first published in New York by P. R. Johnson in 1802; repr. in 1803 by T. B. Jansen of New York as well as by Eaken and Mecum of Philadelphia. In 1847, J. H. Gould of Philadelphia published the novel as *Monima; or, The Beautiful French Girl in Philadelphia. A Tale of Thrilling Interest Founded on Facts. By H. Haydn.* The quotation is from the New York (1803) ed., pp. v–vi. The novel was loosely adapted from English and French sources.

40. Charles Brockden Brown, "Novel-Reading," *Literary Magazine and American Register*, 1 (March 1804), 405.

41. Helena Wells, *The Step-Mother: A Domestic Tale, from Real Life* (London: T. N. Longman and O. Rees, 1799), p. vi.

42. Dwight, *Travels in New England*, 1:516.

43. E. P. Thompson, *The Making of the English Working Class* (New York: Pantheon, 1964), p. 61.

44. Ian Watt, *The Rise of the Novel: Studies in Defoe, Richardson, and Fielding* (1957; repr., Berkeley: Univ. of California Press, 1967), esp. pp. 9–34; and Bakhtin, *Dialogic Imagination*, pp. 84–258.

45. *Autobiography and Other Writings by Benjamin Franklin*, ed. Russel B. Nye (Boston: Houghton Mifflin, 1958), p. 19.

46. James McHenry, "On the Causes of the Present Popularity of Novel Writing," *American Monthly Magazine*, 2 (July 1824), 8, 2.

47. Baym, *Novels, Readers, and Reviewers*.

48. Isaacs, *The Transformation of Virginia*; and David Reynolds, "From Doctrine to Narrative: The Rise of Pulpit Story-Telling in America," *American Quarterly*, 32 (Winter 1980), 479–98. For a concise analysis of the classic Puritan sermonic form, see Teresa Toulouse, " 'The Art of Prophesying': John Cotton and the Rhetoric of Election," *Early American Literature*, 19 (Winter 1984), 279–99. For a discussion of the contiguity of oral and print culture, see Donald M. Scott, "Print and the Public

Lecture System, 1840–1860," in *Printing and Society in Early America*, pp. 278–99. And for a different analysis of the relationship between ministerial authority and nineteenth-century culture, see Ann Douglas, *The Feminization of American Culture* (New York: Knopf, 1978).

49. Baym, *Novels, Readers, and Reviewers*, pp. 27–28.

50. Allan Cunningham, "Some Account of the Life and Works of Sir Walter Scott," *North American Review*, 36 (April 1833), 310.

Chapter 4

1. Royall Tyler, *The Algerine Captive*, ed. Don L. Cook (New Haven: College & University Press, 1970), pp. 27–28.

2. Charles Francis Adams, ed., *The Works of John Adams*, 10 vols. (Boston: Little, Brown, 1850–56), 3:456.

3. Lyle H. Wright, "Eighteenth-Century American Fiction," in *Essays Honoring Lawrence C. Wroth*, ed. Frederick Richmond Goff et al. (Portland, Maine: Anthoensen, 1951), p. 459. Wright also notes that the 1790 census counted the number of "free white males" under the age of sixteen but made "no separate tabulation of young girls" (p. 459), which also reflects who officially counted.

4. Kenneth A. Lockridge, *Literacy in Colonial New England* (New York: Norton, 1974), esp. pp. 38–42, 57–58.

5. Earlier versions of my discussion of literacy were incorporated into unpublished papers presented at the Modern Language Association conventions in Los Angeles (December 1982), New York (December 1983), and Washington, D.C. (December 1984).

6. David D. Hall, "The World of Print and Collective Mentality in Seventeenth-Century New England," in *New Directions in American Intellectual History*, ed. John Higham and Paul K. Conkin (Baltimore: Johns Hopkins Univ. Press, 1979), p. 173.

7. One of the best accounts of black education remains Carter G. Woodson, *The Education of the Negro Prior to 1861* (1919; repr., New York: Arno, 1968). See also Patricia A. Herman, *Southern Blacks: Accounts of Learning to Read Before 1861*, Reading Education Report No. 53 (Urbana: Univ. of Illinois, 1985); Bert James Loewenberg and Ruth Bogin, *Black Women in Nineteenth-Century American Life* (University Park: Pennsylvania State Univ. Press, 1976), p. 5; Philip D. Morgan, "Black Society in the Lowcountry, 1760–1810," in *Slavery and Freedom in the Age of the American Revolution*, ed. Ira Berlin and Ronald Hoffman (Charlottesville: Univ. Press of Virginia, 1983), pp. 83–141; and Mary Beth Norton, *Liberty's Daughters: The Revolutionary Experience of American Women, 1750–1800* (Boston: Little, Brown, 1980), pp. 258–59. Other analyses can be found in Daniel Perlman, "Organizations of the Free Negro in New York City, 1800–1861," *Journal of Negro History*, 56 (1971), 181–97; and Harry C. Silcox, "Delay and Neglect: Negro Public Education in Ante-Bellum Philadelphia, 1800–1860," *Pennsylvania Magazine of History and Biography*, 97 (1973), 444–64. John Hope Franklin, in *From Slavery to Freedom: A History of American Negroes*, 2nd ed. (New York: Knopf, 1956), calculates that, as late as 1870, 80 percent of all blacks above the age of ten were illiterate.

8. By surveying the *Boston Post-Boy* from 1750 to 1760, Robert B. Winans has discovered forty-two ads for runaway slaves, six of which specify that the adult male runaway can read (five of these six designating reading and writing abilities). However, by surveying ten other newspapers from Boston and Philadelphia, between 1750 and 1800, he has found that only about 5 percent of the advertisements specify reading (between 3.5 to 4 percent of that number also indicate writing ability). I am very grateful to Robert Winans for making these preliminary figures on a very important subject available to me. Important theoretical work on black literacy is being done by Hortense Spillers who finds that, historically for blacks and especially for slaves, literacy and religious conversion are synonymous experiences, and understanding the Word of God means, literally and symbolically, being able to understand words (literacy). See, for example, her "A Drama of Words: Afro-American Sermons and the Development of Community," unpublished paper presented at the Modern Language Association, Washington, D.C., December, 1984. And for a powerful firsthand account, see *Life and Times of Frederick Douglass*, rev. ed. (1892; repr., London: Collier, 1962): "[Master Hugh] forbade [his wife] to give me any further instruction, telling her in the first place that to do so was unlawful, as it was also unsafe, 'for,' said he . . . 'learning will spoil the best nigger in the world. . . . If you teach him how to read, he'll want to know how to write, and this accomplished, he'll be running away with himself' " (pp. 78–79).

9. Jackson Turner Main, *The Social Structure of Revolutionary America* (Princeton: Princeton Univ. Press, 1965), p. 156; and William J. Gilmore, "Elementary Literacy on the Eve of the Industrial Revolution: Trends in Rural New England, 1760–1830," *Proceedings of the American Antiquarian Society*, 92 (1982), 98.

10. Christopher M. Jedrey, *The World of John Cleaveland: Family and Community in Eighteenth-Century New England* (New York: Norton, 1979), pp. 102, 179.

11. Linda Auwers, "The Social Meaning of Female Literacy: Windsor, Connecticut, 1660–1775," Newberry Papers in Family and Community History, 77–4A (Chicago: Newberry Library, 1977); Ross W. Beales, Jr., "Studying Literacy at the Community Level: A Research Note," *Journal of Interdisciplinary History*, 9 (1978), 93–102; Harvey Graff, *The Literacy Myth* (New York: Academic, 1979); and Lockridge, *Literacy in Colonial New England*.

12. David D. Hall, "On Native Ground: From the History of Printing to the History of the Book," 1983 James Russell Wiggins Lecture in the History of the Book in American Culture (Worcester, Mass.: AAS, 1984), p. 23. The "Gordian knot" Hall here refers to is the statistical discrepancy among the various quantitative studies, largely a result of the different communities under study. Auwers posits, for example, almost universal female literacy before 1760 for the established and relatively wealthy town of Windsor, Conn. Yet, like the other quantifiers, she also documents a rise in both male and female literacy over the course of the eighteenth century. See also Geraldine Jonçich Clifford, "Buch and Lesen: Historical Perspectives on Literacy and Schooling," *Review of Educational Research, 54* (1984), 472–500; and Carl F. Kaestle, "The History of Literacy and the History of Readers," *Review of Research in Education*, 12 (1985).

13. Gordon S. Wood, in a review/essay in the *New York Review of Books* (Decem-

ber 16, 1982), assented to the call by eminent historians such as G. R. Elton and Oscar Handlin for a return to "old-fashioned epistemology" based on the idea that truth is "absolute as the world is real" (p. 59). Dissatisfaction with current historical praxis has also been expressed by Thomas Bender in "Making History Whole Again," *New York Times Book Review*, September 10, 1985. Bender expresses alarm over the increasing fragmentation of history and the focusing on smaller and smaller areas of investigation. He calls for a new time of "synthesis" (p. 43). And in *Class and Society in Early America* (Englewood Cliffs, N.J.: Prentice-Hall, 1970), esp. pp. 166–200, Gary B. Nash analyzes the kinds of unacknowledged assumptions that can be embedded in even the most meticulous quantitative studies. (Neither Bender nor Nash, it must be added, calls for positivism.)

14. Margaret Spufford, *Small Books and Pleasant Histories: Popular Fiction and Its Readership in Seventeenth-Century England* (1981; repr., Athens: Univ. of Georgia Press, 1982), esp. pp. 19–44.

15. Auwers, "Social Meaning of Female Literacy," p. 8. Lockridge (*Literacy in Colonial New England*, p. 127) also notes the example of modern Israeli women who have learned to fake a signature, a common enough experience among illiterates in a society that equates intelligence with literacy.

16. Linda K. Kerber, *Women of the Republic: Intellect and Ideology in Revolutionary America* (Chapel Hill: Univ. of North Carolina Press, 1980), p. 164.

17. Gilmore, "Elementary Literacy," pp. 87–88, quotes two perceptive essays by Benjamin Nelson, "Actors, Directors, Roles, Cues, Meanings, Identities: Further Thoughts on 'Anomie,' " *Psychoanalytic Review*, 51 (1964), 135–60; and "Civilizational Complexes and Intercivilizational Encounters," *Sociological Analysis*, 34 (1973), 79–105.

18. Many of these assumptions have been adapted from the work of British historian Roger Schofield. See especially "Dimensions of Illiteracy, 1750–1850," *Explorations in Entrepreneurial History*, 10 (1973), 437–54; and his "The Measurement of Literacy in Pre-Industrial England," in *Literacy in Traditional Societies*, ed. Jack P. Goody (Cambridge: Cambridge Univ. Press, 1968), pp. 311–25. Schofield argues partly on the basis of the methods of British public education, especially in the Charity Schools, where writing was not only not taught to poor children, but actually discouraged. For other studies of the British situation, see David Cressy, *Literacy and the Social Order: Reading and Writing in Tudor and Stuart England* (Cambridge: Cambridge Univ. Press, 1980); and Cressy, "Literacy in Pre-Industrial England," *Societas*, 4 (Summer 1974), 229–49; Richard Hoggart, *The Uses of Literacy* (London: Chatto & Windus, 1957); Margaret Spufford, *Contrasting Communities: English Villagers in the Sixteenth and Seventeenth Centuries* (Cambridge: Cambridge Univ. Press, 1974), chaps. 7, 8; and Lawrence Stone, "Literacy and Education in England, 1640–1900," *Past and Present*, 42 (1969), 61–139. While all of these studies illuminate aspects of English education, it is not at all clear that generalizations based on English data apply to the different tradition of American Puritan education.

19. *New England Primer Improved* (Boston: D. and J. Kneeland, 1761).

20. For a comparative discussion of literacy levels (including different interpretations of conflicting data), see Peter Burke, *Popular Culture in Early Modern Europe*

(London: Temple Smith, 1978), esp. p. 250; Bernhard Fabian, "English Books and Their Eighteenth-Century German Readers," in *The Widening Circle: Essays on the Circulation of Literature in Eighteenth-Century Europe*, ed. Paul J. Korshin (Philadelphia: Univ. of Pennsylvania Press, 1976), p. 166; and Egil Johansson, *The History of Literacy in Sweden*, Educational Reports No. 12 (Umeå: Umeå Univ. Press, 1977), esp. pp. 55–60.

21. As Abigail Adams wrote to her niece about the shortcomings of her own writing skills, "It is from feeling the disadvantages of it myself, that I am the more solicitous that my young acquaintance should excel me." Charles Francis Adams, ed., *Letters of Mrs. Adams, the Wife of John Adams*, 3rd ed., 2 vols. (Boston: Little, Brown, 1841), 2:79. Adams, it should be noted, was almost as literate as her husband, but many wealthy women were not. For example, Deborah Franklin, wife of Benjamin, was nearly illiterate. Similarly, Eldridge Gerry courted a daughter of a state legislator, Catharine Hunt, who could not even read his love letters. For other notable examples of female illiteracy even among the highborn, see Kerber, *Women of the Republic*, pp. 190–93.

22. Walter J. Ong, *The Presence of the Word: Some Prolegomena for Cultural and Religious History* (New Haven: Yale Univ. Press, 1967), esp. pp. 245–55. The first comment by Abigail Adams is quoted in *The Spur of Fame: Dialogues of John Adams and Benjamin Rush, 1805–1813*, ed. John A. Schutz (San Marino, Calif.: Huntington Library, 1966), p. 170; the second, in *Adams Family Correspondence*, 4 vols., ed. Lyman H. Butterfield et al. (Cambridge: Harvard Univ. Press, 1963–73), 3:52.

23. Raymond Williams, *The Long Revolution* (New York: Columbia Univ. Press, 1961), p. 125.

24. Stanley K. Schultz, *The Culture Factory: Boston Public Schools, 1789–1860* (New York: Oxford Univ. Press, 1973), pp. 4–5. See also George Leroy Jackson, *The Development of School Support in Colonial Massachusetts* (New York: Arno, 1969); and George Emory Littlefield, *Early Schools and School-Books of New England* (Boston: Club of Odd Volumes, 1904), p. 56.

25. Bernard Bailyn, *Education in the Forming of American Society* (Chapel Hill: Univ. of North Carolina Press, 1960); and Lawrence Cremin, *American Education: The Colonial Experience* (New York: Harper & Row, 1970). See also, Ellwood P. Cubberley, *Public Education in the United States*, rev. ed. (Boston: Houghton Mifflin, 1934).

26. Samuel Bowles and Herbert Gintis, *Schooling in Capitalist America* (New York: Basic Books, 1976); Michael B. Katz, *Class, Bureaucracy, and Schools: The Illusion of Educational Change in America*, 2nd ed. (New York: Praeger, 1975), and *The Irony of Early School Reform: Educational Innovation in Mid-Nineteenth-Century Massachusetts* (Cambridge: Harvard Univ. Press, 1968); and Michael Zuckerman, *Peaceable Kingdom: New England in the Eighteenth Century* (New York: Knopf, 1970), esp. pp. 72–83. For an excellent example of how personal ideology influences the shape of scholarship, compare the interpretations of essentially the same "data" in Katz, *The Irony of Early School Reform* (pt. 1), and in Maris A. Vinovskis, *The Politics of Educational Reform in Nineteenth-Century Massachusetts: The Controversy over the Beverly High*

School in 1860 (Washington, D.C.: National Institute of Education, 1980). While Katz sees class division in the controversy over publicly funding schools, Vinovskis argues that how one voted on the issue depended primarily upon where one lived (regardless of one's class affiliation or income level).

27. Katz, *Class, Bureaucracy, and Schools,* p. xviii; see also Kaestle, *Pillars of the Republic: Common Schools and American Society, 1780–1860* (New York: Hill & Wang, 1983), p. 35.

28. E. Jennifer Monaghan, "The Three R's: Notes on the Acquisition of Literacy and Numeracy Skills in Seventeenth-Century New England," paper presented at the American Educational Research Association, New Orleans, 1984. I am grateful to Professor Monaghan for making this paper available to me.

29. Walter H. Small, "Girls in Colonial Schools," *Education,* 22 (1902), 532.

30. Edmund S. Morgan quoted in Michael B. Katz, ed., *Education in American History* (New York: Praeger, 1973), p. 30. See also Edmund S. Morgan, *The Puritan Family: Religion and Domestic Relations in Seventeenth-Century New England,* rev. ed. (New York: Harper & Row, 1966).

31. Benjamin Rush, "Thoughts upon Female Education" (1787), repr. *Essays on Education in the Early Republic,* ed. Frederick Rudolph (Cambridge: Harvard Univ. Press, 1965), p. 28.

32. Nancy F. Cott, *The Bonds of Womanhood: "Woman's Sphere" in New England, 1780–1835* (New Haven: Yale Univ. Press, 1977), p. 103.

33. Caleb Bingham, "Oration upon Female Education, Pronounced by a Member of One of the Public Schools in Boston" (September 1791), repr. in his *American Preceptor,* 44th ed. (Boston: Manning & Loring, 1813), pp. 48–50.

34. Kerber, *Women of the Republic,* pp. 189–231; Norton, *Liberty's Daughters,* pp. 256–99. See also Carl F. Kaestle and Maris A. Vinovskis, *Education and Social Change in Nineteenth-Century Massachusetts* (Cambridge: Cambridge Univ. Press, 1980), pp. 25–26; and Thomas Woody, *A History of Women's Education in the United States,* 2 vols. (New York: Science Press, 1929), 1: chap. 4. For a contemporaneous account, see William Bentley, *The Diary of William Bentley, D.D., Pastor of the East Church, Salem, Mass.,* 4 vols. (Salem: Essex Institute, 1905–14), 2:96: "We saw at no school any girls" (July 1, 1794). Working on the Salem School Committee in 1790, the Reverend Bentley noted that "all the girls [are] unprovided for, as upon the Boston establishment" (1:188).

35. Schultz, *The Culture Factory,* p. 15.

36. Emory Washburn, *Brief Sketch of the History of Leicester Academy* (Boston: Phillips, Samson, 1855), esp. pp. 19–34. Washburn notes that increasing pressure was exerted upon the academy to teach a more standard "feminine" curriculum, pressure to which the academy partially yielded after 1815.

37. Benjamin Rush, "Plan on the Establishment of the Public Schools" (1786), repr. Rudolph, *Essays on Education,* p. 3.

38. Noah Webster, "On the Education of Youth in America." Originally published in Webster's *American Magazine* (1787–88); repr. *American Museum,* the *Hampshire Gazette,* and the *American Journal of Education,* as well as in Noah Webster, *A Col-*

lection of Essays and Fugitive [sic] Writings, on Moral, Historical, Political and Literary Subjects (Boston: Thomas and Andrews, 1790), repr. Rudolph, *Essays on Education,* p. 65.

39. For a survey of other views, see Abraham Blinderman, *American Writers on Education Before 1865* (Boston: Twayne, 1975); and Vera M. Butler, *Education as Revealed by New England Newspapers Prior to 1850* (1935; repr., New York: Arno, 1969).

40. Schultz, *The Culture Factory,* pp. 8–9.

41. Ibid., pp. 10–11.

42. Ibid., p. 23.

43. Kaestle and Vinovskis, *Education and Social Change,* p. 17. See also Albert Fishlow, "The American Common School Revival: Fact or Fancy?" in *Industrialization in Two Systems,* ed. Henry Rosovsky (New York: Wiley, 1966), esp. p. 43; and Kaestle, *The Evolution of an Urban School System: New York City, 1750–1850* (Cambridge: Harvard Univ. Press, 1973), pp. 52, 54, 89.

44. Edward Everett Hale quoted in Kaestle, *Pillars of the Republic,* pp. 52–53.

45. Charles L. Coon, *North Carolina Schools and Academies (1790–1840)* (Raleigh: Edwards and Broughton, 1915), pp. 763–64.

46. Diary of Elizabeth Bancroft, Manuscript Department, AAS; and Tyler, *The Algerine Captive,* p. 59.

47. E. Jennifer Monaghan, *A Common Heritage: Noah Webster's Blue-Back Speller* (Hamden, Conn.: Shoe String Press, 1983), p. 219. See also Harry R. Warfel, *Noah Webster: Schoolmaster to America* (1936; repr., New York: Octagon, 1966).

48. Sukey Vickery Papers, Diary entry for December 18–22, 1815, Manuscript Department, AAS.

49. These instructions were published in virtually all editions of Webster's speller and have been discussed, in depth, by Dennis Patrick Rusche, in "An Empire of Reason: A Study of the Writings of Noah Webster," Ph.D. diss., Univ. of Michigan, 1975, pp. 269–70. See also Mitford M. Mathews, *Teaching to Read* (Chicago: Univ. of Chicago Press, 1966), pp. 53–63.

50. Susanna Rowson, *A Spelling Dictionary, Divided into Short Lessons, for the Easier Committing to Memory by Children and Young Persons; and Calculated to Assist Youth in Comprehending What They Read* (1807; repr., Portland: Isaac Adams, 1815), p. iii.

51. *Juvenile Mirror, and Teacher's Manual, Comprising a Course of Rudimental Instruction* (New York: Smith and Forman, 1812), p. 24. See also, "Learning to Read," *The Ladies' Magazine,* 2, no. 1 (1829), 91. For a more conventional overview of early American textbooks than that presented here, see Butler, *Education as Revealed by New England Newspapers,* esp. pp. 402–36; Charles Carpenter, *History of American Schoolbooks* (Philadelphia: Univ. of Pennsylvania Press, 1963); John A. Nietz, *Old Textbooks* (Pittsburgh: Univ. of Pittsburgh Press, 1961), and his *The Evolution of American Secondary School Textbooks* (Rutland, Vt.: Tuttle, 1966).

52. Joseph Neef, *The Method of Instructing Children Rationally in the Arts of Writing and Reading* (Philadelphia: By the author, 1813), esp. pp. 6–19. Neef particularly advocated reform in English-language orthography in order that the mass of people might more easily become literate, and, therefore, socially activist.

53. Joshua Leavitt, *Easy Lessons in Reading for the Use of the Younger Classes in Common Schools* (Keene, N.H.: J. Prentice, 1823). Leavitt also wrote an exceptionally popular book for seamen, *Devotional Assistant and Mariner's Hymns* (1830), as well as *Cheap Postage: Remarks and Statistics on the Subject* (1848) and an antislavery tract, *Alarming Disclosures: Political Power of Slavery* (1816). In short, he, too, was an educational and social reformer.

54. William Baker quoted in Ray Nash, *Writing: Some Early American Writing Books and Masters* (Hanover, N.H.: Privately printed, 1943), p. 43. See also Nash, "Abiah Holbrook and His 'Writing Master's Amusement,' " *Harvard Library Bulletin,* 7 (Winter 1953), 88–104; Nash, *American Writing Masters and Copybooks* (Boston: Colonial Society of Massachusetts, 1959); and Nash, *American Penmanship, 1800–1815* (Worcester, Mass.: AAS, 1969).

55. John Jenkins, *The Art of Writing* (Boston: Isaiah Thomas, 1791), epigraph. In an "improved" edition published in 1809, Jenkins emphasizes the public utility of his writing system and the public gain he hopes will accrue to the author: "From the comparatively short time, and a trifling expense, necessary to attain the ART of PENMANSHIP, by the use of this system, the public may save MILLIONS OF DOLLARS" (p. 1).

56. *The Short, Plain, and Cheap Directions for Reading Books to Profit* (New York: J. Seymour, 1809), pp. 1–4.

57. Sarah Savage, *Advice to a Young Woman at Service: In a Letter from a Friend* (New York: New York Book Society, 1823), pp. 31, 4.

58. Diary of Susan Heath, September 11 and October 6, 1812, Massachusetts Historical Society, Boston. Special thanks to Elizabeth C. Reilly for this reference.

59. Elisabeth Haseltines's entry dated February 9, 1821, in *An Extract from the Journal of John Nelson: Being an Account of God's Dealing with Him from His Youth to the Forty-Second Year of His Age* (New York: John Wilson and Daniel Hitt for the Methodist Connection in the United States, 1809). This copy is in the Pedagogy Collection in the Russel B. Nye Popular Culture Collection, Michigan State University.

60. Although Uri Decker has underscored her name and the word "MINE" on the flyleaf, it has also been inscribed by Sally D [?], H. Baker, and others whose names are now indecipherable. This edition of Lindley Murray's *English Reader* was published in Canandaigua, N.Y., by J. D. Bemis in 1819, and the copy is in the Michigan State University Pedagogy Collection.

61. Quoted in G. Thomas Tanselle, "Author and Publisher in 1800: Letters of Royall Tyler and Joseph Nancrede," *Harvard Library Bulletin,* 15 (1967), 137–38.

62. In 1786, when Isaiah Thomas published a toy-book edition of *Robinson Crusoe,* no full unedited text of the novel was published at that time in America or, for that matter, in England. For an excellent discussion of some of the American editions of the novel (what was included and what was left out), see Jay Fliegelman, *Prodigals and Pilgrims: The American Revolution Against Patriarchal Authority, 1750–1800* (New York: Cambridge Univ. Press, 1982), pp. 67–81.

63. For example, in the 1794 edition of *Charlotte,* Mathew Carey advertised other books by Rowson as well as Wollstonecraft's *The Rights of Women* [sic] (for $1), sug-

gesting that he anticipated a primarily female (and feminist?) audience. In an 1811 edition of the same novel, most of the books advertised at the back are juvenile works, as are the preponderance of books in the 1815 edition of Sarah Savage's *The Factory Girl*. Conversely, in a 1793 edition of Rowson's textbook, *Universal Geography*, nearly all of the ads are for books by or about women, including some novels.

64. Rolf Engelsing, *Analphabetentum und Lektüre: Zur Sozialgeschichte des Lesens in Deutschland zwischen feudaler und industrieller Gesellschaft* (Stuttgart: Metzlersche, 1973); and *Der Bürger als Leser: Lesergeschichte in Deutschland 1500–1800* (Stuttgart: Metzlersche, 1974). The main points of Engelsing's arguments are summarized in his essay "Die Perioden der Lesergeschichte in der Neuzeit," in *Zur Sozialgeschichte deutscher Mittel- und Unterschichten* (Göttingen: Vandenhoeck und Ruprecht, 1973), pp. 112–54. It should also be noted that Engelsing's critique of extensive reading is not particularly new. The anonymous author of "Female Reading," *Boston Weekly Magazine*, 2 (March 31, 1804), condemned novels, "read with avidity, they pleasure for a moment, but in a short time after they [females] have finished them, they are forgot and another of the same kind, though gilded by the name of novelty, sought for." The reviewer, incidentally, believed women should, instead, read guidebooks to help prepare them for "rendering domestic life happy" (p. 89).

65. Engelsing's work has recently been criticized on several fronts. See, for example, Robert Darnton, *The Great Cat Massacre and Other Episodes in French Cultural History* (New York: Basic Books, 1984), pp. 249–52; and Reinhart Siegert, *Aufklärung und Volkslektüre exemplarisch dargestellt an Rudolph Zacharias Becker und seinem "Noth- und Hülfsbüchlein" mit einer Bibliographie zum Gesamtthema* (Frankfurt am Main: Buchhändler-Vereinigung, 1978).

66. The controversy over the fictionality of Charlotte Temple was revived on December 10, 1853, when a fire destroyed the Walton House in New York City (purportedly the house from which the pregnant and abandoned Charlotte had been expelled). Throughout the century, there had been public debate over the authenticity of Charlotte's grave in the Trinity Church cemetery. See, for example, the *New York Dispatch* for August 13, 1859: "[The novel's] simplicity of style and apparent sincerity has imposed upon a good many people, who made themselves believe that a mere romance was veritable history."

67. Darnton, *Great Cat Massacre*, p. 251.

68. Hannah More, *Strictures on the Modern System of Female Education*, 2 vols. (1799; repr., New York: George Long, 1813), 2:26.

69. Mary M. Ball wrote her poems in the 1821 edition (published in Exeter, N.H.); her copy is now in the Michigan State University Pedagogy Collection.

70. Margaret Smith quoted in Shirley Brice Heath, "Toward an Ethnohistory of Writing in American Education," in *Writing: The Nature, Development and Teaching of Written Communication*, ed. Marcia Farr Whiteman, 2 vols. (Hillsdale, N.J.: Erlbaum, 1981), 1:29.

71. Diary of Patty Rogers, January 10 and 11, 1785, Manuscript Department, AAS.

72. Betsey Sweet's copy of *Charlotte Temple* (New York: John Swain, 1802) is in

the AAS. Beginning with Mathew Carey's 1797 edition, virtually all later editions of the novel include the last name of the heroine in the title.

73. The 1809 copy of *Charlotte Temple* described on p. 75 (Philadelphia: Mathew Carey, 1809) was found in a bookstore in New York in 1979, whereabouts presently unknown. The others (see p. 75) are all at the AAS. Their publishing data, respectively, are: New York: Samuel A. Burtus, 1814; Hartford: Silas Andrus, 1832; Philadelphia: Mathew Carey, 1812; and Philadelphia: Benjamin Warner, 1818.

74. The publishing data for the copies of *Charlotte Temple* discussed on pp. 75–77 are: Hudson, N.Y.: Ashbel Stoddard, 1803; Chambersburg, Pa.: George Kenton Harper, 1807; New Haven: Bronson, Walter, 1808.

75. William T. Dunn's copy of *Charlotte Temple* (Boston: Charles Ewer, 1824) is a multiple monument to the power of books: It was given to me by another scholar who shares my fascination with America's first best-selling novel.

76. The AAS copies discussed on p. 77 were published, respectively, in: New Haven: Increase Cooke, 1805; Cincinnati: U.P. James, 1833; and Cincinnati: William Conclin, 1831.

77. This copy of Samuel Relf's *Infidelity, or the Victims of Sentiment* (Philadelphia: W. W. Woodward, 1797) is at the AAS.

78. E. D. Robinson signed in Rebecca Rush, *Kelroy, a Novel* (Philadelphia: Bradford and Inskeep, 1812); Harriet Wilkins Shaftsbury signed in *Charlotte Temple* (Philadelphia: Mathew Carey, 1808). Other AAS copies of *Charlotte Temple* containing especially intriguing evidence of handwriting practice and an evolution of literacy skills are: Philadelphia: Mathew Carey, 1797; Hudson, N.Y.: Nathan Elliott, 1808; New York: R. Hobbs, 1827; and Hartford: Silas Andrus, 1829.

79. This second edition of Rowson's *Spelling Dictionary* (Portland, Maine: A. & J. Shirley, 1815) is at the AAS as is the copy of the first edition of Foster's *The Coquette* (Boston: Samuel Etheridge, 1797).

80. The copy of *The History of Constantius and Pulchera* published by Edward Gray (pp. 78–79) is at the AAS.

Chapter 5

1. William Charvat, *The Profession of Authorship in America, 1800–1870: The Papers of William Charvat*, ed. Matthew J. Bruccoli (Columbus: Ohio State Univ. Press, 1968), p. 6.

2. Robert Escarpit, *Sociology of Literature*, 2nd ed., trans. Ernest Pick (London: Frank Cass, 1971), esp. pp. 55–74, and *The Book Revolution* (London: George G. Harrap, 1966), pp. 17–49.

3. Bernard Rosenthal, "Introduction" to *Critical Essays on Charles Brockden Brown*, ed. Bernard Rosenthal (Boston: G. K. Hall, 1981), p. 2; p. 18, n. 6. Charles Brockden Brown has most recently been dubbed "Father of the American Novel" (without explanation) by Philip Young, " 'First American Novel': *The Power of Sympathy*, in Place," *College Literature*, 11 (1984), 115–24.

4. Nina Baym, in "A Minority Reading of *Wieland*," in *Critical Essays on Charles*

Brockden Brown, has suggested there is "androcentricity in the idea of [Brockden Brown's] seriousness," p. 87; p. 101, n. 1.

5. For a concise summary of the whole debate, see William S. Kable, "Introduction," *The Power of Sympathy* (Columbus: Ohio State Univ. Press, 1969), pp. xi–xv. For the intriguing history of Brackenridge and Freneau's *Father Bombo's Pilgrimage to Mecca* (published for the first time in 1975), see Michael Davitt Bell's excellent introduction (Princeton: Princeton Univ. Library, 1975), pp. ix–xxxii.

6. William C. Spengemann, "The Earliest American Novel: Aphra Behn's *Oroonoko,*" *Nineteenth-Century Fiction*, 38 (1984), 384. It must also be remembered that Aphra Behn is not generally acknowledged as the "first British novelist" either, an omission which should be corrected by Dale Spender's *Mothers of the Novel* (London: Routledge and Kegan Paul, 1986).

7. See also William C. Spengemann, "What Is American Literature?" *Centennial Review*, 22 (Spring 1978), 119–38.

8. Joseph Tinker Buckingham, *Specimens of Newspaper Literature*, 2 vols. (Boston: Little, Brown, 1850), 1:323; and Francis S. Drake, *The Town of Roxbury* (Boston: Printed for the author, 1878), p. 134.

9. For a full discussion of the scandal as well as a detailed chronology of the various public and private ascriptions of *The Power of Sympathy* to Sarah Wentworth Morton (Mrs. Perez Morton), see Emily Pendleton and Milton Ellis, *Philenia: The Life and Works of Sarah Wentworth Morton, 1759–1846* (Orono: Univ. of Maine Press, 1931), esp. pp. 32–40, 109–12.

10. Arthur W. Brayley, "The Real Author of 'The Power of Sympathy,' " *Bostonian*, 1 (1894). Rebecca Valentine Thompson also reported to Brayley the story that I have used as the epigraph to this chapter. For more evidence of William Hill Brown's authorship see John R. Byers, Jr., "Further Verification of the Authorship of *The Power of Sympathy*," *American Literature*, 43 (November 1971), 421–26; Milton Ellis, "The Author of the First American Novel," *American Literature*, 4 (1933), 359–68; Ellis, "Bibliographical Note" in *The Power of Sympathy* (New York: Facsimile Text Society, 1937); Tremaine McDowell, "The First American Novel," *American Review*, 2 (November 1933), 73–81; Richard Walser, "Boston's Reception of the First American Novel," *Early American Literature*, 17 (Spring 1982), 65–74; Walser, "The Fatal Effects of Seduction (1789)," *Modern Language Notes*, 69 (1954), 574–76; Walser, "More About the First American Novel," *American Literature*, 24 (1952), 352–57; Walser, "The North Carolina Sojourn of the First American Novelist," *North Carolina Historical Review*, 29 (1951), 138–55.

11. Herbert Ross Brown, "The Great American Novel," *American Literature*, 7 (1935), 1–14.

12. *Bostonian*, 1 (1894–95); and Mrs. Perez Morton, *The Power of Sympathy*, ed. Walter Littlefield (Boston: Cupples and Patterson, 1894). Milton Ellis edited the Facsimile Text Society edition in 1937; Herbert Ross Brown also edited a reprint of the novel (Boston: New Frontiers Press, 1961). The Kable edition (Columbus: Ohio State Univ., 1969) includes such scholarly apparatus as a "Textual Introduction," "Emendations in the Copy-text," "Variants in the first Edition," and "Collation of the *Massachusetts Magazine* Passages" (pp. 185–206). The classroom paperback edition

is edited by William S. Osborne (New Haven: College University Press, 1970). See also, John R. Byers, Jr., "A Letter of William Hill Brown's," *American Literature*, 49 (January 1978), 606–11; and William Hill Brown, *Selected Poems and Verse Fables, 1784–1793*, ed. Richard Walser (Newark: Univ. of Delaware Press, 1982).

13. See, for example, Michel Foucault, "History, Discourse, and Discontinuity," trans. Anthony M. Nazzaro, *Salmagundi*, 20 (1972), 229–33.

14. My discussion of Isaiah Thomas is based on my work with the Isaiah Thomas Papers at the AAS (the fifteen boxes of papers and twenty-three volumes touch upon virtually every aspect of the book trade in the new Republic) as well as on Jacob Chernofsky, "Isaiah Thomas," in *Boston Printers, Publishers, and Booksellers, 1640–1800*, ed. Benjamin Franklin V (Boston: G. K. Hall, 1980), p. 470; Annie Russell Marble, *From 'Prentice to Patron: The Life Story of Isaiah Thomas* (New York: Appleton-Century, 1935); Charles Lemuel Nicholas, *Isaiah Thomas: Printer, Writer, and Collector* (New York: Burt Franklin, 1971); and Clifford K. Shipton, *Isaiah Thomas: Printer, Patriot, and Philanthropist, 1749–1831* (Rochester, N.Y.: Leo Hart, 1948). See also, Isaiah Thomas, *Three Autobiographical Fragments*, ed. Marcus A. McCorison (Worcester, Mass.: AAS, 1962).

15. Isaiah Thomas, *The History of Printing in America*, ed. Marcus A. McCorison (New York: Weathervane, 1970); and Marcus A. McCorison, "Isaiah Thomas, the American Antiquarian Society, and the Future," *Proceedings of the American Antiquarian Society*, 91 (1981), 27–38.

16. In *History of Printing*, Thomas describes Fowle as "a singular man, very irritable and effeminate, and better skilled in the domestick work of females, than in the business of a printing house.... Fowle could not be called an industrious man" (p. 134). Thomas's memorable anecdotes about Fowle's sloppy printing practices (arbitrary placement of punctuation, etc.) are certainly the former apprentice's best revenge against a cruel master.

17. John Tebbel, *A History of Book Publishing in the United States*, 4 vols. (New York: R. R. Bowker, 1972), 1:67.

18. Quoted by William F. Vartorella, "Isaiah Thomas," in *American Writers Before 1800*, ed. James A. Levernier and Douglas R. Wilmes (Westport, Conn.: Greenwood, 1983), p. 1450.

19. Daniel Defoe, *Travels of Robinson Crusoe* (Worcester, Mass.: Isaiah Thomas, 1786), p. 24.

20. These titles are included in the Printer's File for Isaiah Thomas at the AAS, and most can also be found in Nichols's bibliography, pp. 39–133. See also John Roger Osterholm, "The Literary Career of Isaiah Thomas, 1749–1831," Ph.D. diss., Univ. of Massachusetts at Amherst, 1978. The quotation is from Shipton, *Isaiah Thomas*, p. 43.

21. Chernovsky, *Boston Printers*, p. 470; and Shipton, *Isaiah Thomas*, pp. 43–44. However, Marcus A. McCorison has argued that Thomas could not be the American publisher of *Fanny Hill*. See McCorison, "Two Unrecorded Printings of *Fanny Hill*," *Vermont History* (1972), 64–66, 174, and his "Memoirs of a Woman of Pleasure or Fanny Hill in New England," *American Book Collector*, 1 (1980), 29–30. Although there are a number of references to clandestine publishing ventures in Thomas's diaries and letters I have found no mention of *Fanny Hill*.

22. The copy of *Emily Hamilton* from which I have quoted Thomas's ambivalent verdict on novels is at the AAS.

23. The first advertisement for *The Power of Sympathy* appeared in the *Herald of Freedom* on January 16, 1789, the second on January 23, 1789. The "First American Novel" ads ran in the *Massachusetts Spy, or Worcester Gazette* on January 29, February 5, and February 12, 1789, and in the *Massachusetts Centinel* on January 28, 1789. I have not been able to find any prepublication advertisements in newspapers outside Massachusetts. For a more detailed discussion, see also Richard Walser's excellent essay, "Boston's Reception," 65–74.

24. All references are to the Kable edition of *The Power of Sympathy*. This epigraph is from the unnumbered title page (facing p. 9 of the Kable text). Hereafter page citations will be found parenthetically within the text.

25. Walser, "Boston's Reception," pp. 68–74, and his "More About the First American Novel," pp. 352–57. Walser discovered a satirical vignette—published anonymously and reprinted in the *Herald of Freedom* on February 12, 1789—that viciously burlesques the whole Apthorp/Morton affair, including Morton's attempt to suppress *The Power of Sympathy* against his wife's advice: "You better let it alone, I think, you will only render yourself more conspicuously infamous." (The timing of the piece in the *Herald of Freedom* suggests Thomas may have had a hand in reprinting the satire for a wider newspaper audience.)

26. Clarence S. Brigham, "American Booksellers' Catalogues, 1734–1800," in *Essays Honoring Lawrence C. Wroth*, ed. Frederick Richmond Goff et al. (Portland, Maine: Anthoensen, 1951), pp. 33–34.

27. I am grateful to James Gilreath, American history specialist, Rare Books and Special Collections, for his help in investigating copies of early American novels at the Library of Congress, especially this rare copy of *The Power of Sympathy*.

28. The comments of Civil Spy and Antonia, appearing on pp. 96–97 of the text, are quoted from the following sources. The original review by Civil Spy is from the *Massachusetts Centinel*, February 7, 1789, 168; and the response by Antonia from the *Herald of Freedom*, February 10, 1789, 174; and the retort by Civil Spy from the *Massachusetts Centinel*, February 14, 1789, 179. A fourth contribution to this debate was supplied by one, Belinda, in the *Herald of Freedom*, February 20, 1789, 186. Belinda, "reports" the reactions of her aged "Aunt Antonia" upon hearing of the youthful Civil Spy's disrespectful and impudent dismissal of Lady Antonia's review. Antonia, as quoted by Belinda, insists that "the stripling who ridicules the MORAL PAGE OF INSTRUCTION will ever despise the precepts of old age," and she summarily dismisses Civil Spy as a "pupil of Chesterfield."

29. Mary Jacobus, "Is There a Woman in This Text?" *New Literary History*, 14 (Autumn 1982), 138.

30. Ross Chambers, *Story and Situation: Narrative Seduction and the Power of Fiction* (Minneapolis: Univ. of Minnesota Press, 1984).

31. *Herald of Freedom*, October 9, 1788, 51. The headline reads, "Inserted by Desire."

32. Sarah Wentworth Morton stayed with Perez until his death in 1837. During the public scandal, she stood by her husband, but undoubtedly she was deeply affected

by his affair. She bore five children in the first six years of her marriage to Perez (1781–87), her last just six months prior to her sister's delivery of Perez's illegitimate daughter, but she had no more after the scandal. Her later poetry is filled with references to a mother's obligation to protect her children no matter what the cost and the necessity of female resignation.

33. William Hill Brown returned to the Apthorp/Morton scandal in *The Better Sort or, the Girl of Spirit. An Operational, Comical Farce* (Boston: Isaiah Thomas, 1789). In January 1789, just as the scandal was dying down, Charles Apthorp, Fanny's brother, a gentleman and a naval officer, belatedly determined to uphold the family name by challenging Perez Morton to a duel. The challenge, apparently, was delivered and accepted half-heartedly, for local wits satirized how the men arrived at the appointed scene of their meeting *after* the local sheriff who conveniently forestalled the illegal encounter. Since these events occurred too late to be included in *The Power of Sympathy*, Brown included them in his farce, published in February of that year. But Brown also noted in the epigraph to the play: "Know, slander-loving readers, great and small, / We scorn on private Characters to fall—/ 'They're Knights of th' Squire, and represent you all.' " For a fuller account, see Walser, "More About the First American Novel," pp. 355–57.

34. For a fuller discussion of the ways in which the novel's social authorities are continually undercut, see my "*The Power of Sympathy* Reconsidered: William Hill Brown as Literary Craftsman," *Early American Literature*, 10 (1975), 14–29.

35. A letter/diary, half written to Perez Morton and half to herself, was composed by Fanny Apthorp shortly before her death and is now in the possession of the Massachusetts Historical Society, Boston. Herein Fanny proclaims her "guilty innocence" and her determination to die rather than face ignominy and abandonment. This missive was published in Boston newspapers as were responses, discussions, and further poems in the *Massachusetts Gazette and General Advertiser* (August 28, 1788), the *Massachusetts Centinel* (September 28 and August 4, 1788), and the *Herald of Freedom* (October 9, 13, and 16, 1788). So well known were the details of the scandal that it even became the basis for a school play performed in rural Vermont, *The Fatal Effects of Seduction, A Tragedy. Written for the Use of the Students of Clio Hall, in Bennington, to Be Acted on Their Quarter Day, April 28, 1789.* The only extant copy of the play is at the AAS. See also Tremaine McDowell, "Last Words of a Sentimental Heroine," *American Literature*, 4 (1932), 174–77; Pendleton and Ellis, *Philenia*, pp. 32–40; and Walser, "Fatal Effects of Seduction," pp. 574–76.

36. It might be noted, briefly, that William Hill Brown was the son of a mechanic— albeit one of the most skilled and prosperous mechanics of his day. Gawen Brown, an immigrant from Northumberland, was one of America's most celebrated clock-makers, a craft that allowed him to support handsomely fourteen children (several of whom died in infancy) and three successive wives (the first two of whom died young). William Hill Brown was a product of Gawen's third marriage to the widow, Elizabeth Hill Adams Brown.

37. *Diary of Sarah Connell Ayer* (Portland, Maine: Lefavor-Tower, 1910), pp. 372–73.

38. P. D. Manvill, *Lucinda; or, The Mountain Mourner. Being Recent Facts, in a*

Series of Letters (Johnstown, N.Y.: W. and A. Child, 1807). The 1810 edition published in Ballston Spa, N.Y., by William Child was the first to include the defense of the magistrates, a defense reprinted in most editions up until 1852.

39. I am grateful to Frank Shuffelton for allowing me to see his unpublished essay, "Mrs. Foster's *Coquette* and the Decline of Brotherly Watch" (forthcoming in *Eighteenth-Century Studies*), which also cites the fine article by William E. Nelson, "Emerging Notions of Modern Criminal Law in the Revolutionary Era: An Historical Perspective," *New York University Law Review*, 42 (1967), 450–82. See also, Perry Miller, *The New England Mind* (Cambridge: Harvard Univ. Press, 1953), esp. pp. 19–130.

40. Most seduction stories—whether fictional or purported to be true—included in New England magazines and newspapers between 1777 and 1794 advocate that men should be punished for their role as seducer but, as in *The Power of Sympathy*, show women actually suffering the most from illicit sexuality, a realistic rather than an idealistic portrayal. See Herman R. Lantz et al., "Preindustrial Patterns in the Colonial Family in America: A Content Analysis of Colonial Magazines," *American Sociological Review*, 33 (1968), 422–23.

41. Brown, like most of the early American novelists, was very concerned about education. For example, he vehemently championed the founding of the University of North Carolina. See Walser, "North Carolina Sojourn," pp. 148–49.

42. For a further discussion of the incest motif, see Robert D. Arner, "Sentiment and Sensibility: The Role of Emotion in the Fallen World of William Hill Brown's *The Power of Sympathy,*" *Studies in American Fiction*, 1 (1973), 121–32; and Young, " 'First American Novel,' " pp. 115–24.

Chapter 6

1. See Peter J. Rabinowitz, "Assertion and Assumption: Fictional Patterns and the External World," *PMLA*, 97 (May 1981), 408–19.

2. J. Potter, "Growth of Population in the United States, 1700–1860," in *Population in History*, ed. David Glass and D. Eversley (London: Arnold, 1965), p. 271.

3. Bernard Farber, *Guardians of Virtue: Salem Families in 1800* (New York: Basic Books, 1972), p. 41; and Robert V. Wells, "Family History and Demographic Transition," *Journal of Social History*, 9 (Fall 1975), 1–19.

4. For a perceptive discussion of the changing American attitude toward adolescence, see James Axtell, *The School upon a Hill* (New Haven: Yale Univ. Press, 1974); and Joseph F. Kett, *Rites of Passage: Adolescence in America, 1790 to the Present* (New York: Basic Books, 1977), pp. 15–50.

5. The Patty Rogers Diary, Manuscript Department, AAS, records a constant and even exhausting round of social visiting as does the Elizabeth Bancroft Diary (also at AAS). The fluid social and courtship patterns of the early Republic are discussed in Ellen K. Rothman's study of 350 women's diaries, *Hands and Hearts: A History of Courtship in America* (New York: Basic Books, 1984).

6. The story of Mrs. Anderson is told in Sukey Vickery's letter of July 19, 1799, to Adeline Hartwell, Sukey Vickery Papers, Manuscript Collection, AAS.

7. Mary Beth Norton, *Liberty's Daughters: The Revolutionary Experience of American Women, 1750–1800* (Boston: Little, Brown, 1980), pp. 3–9.

8. Linda K. Kerber, *Women of the Republic: Intellect and Ideology in Revolutionary America* (Chapel Hill: Univ. of North Carolina Press, 1980), p. 252; and Alice Kessler-Harris, *Women Have Always Worked* (Old Westbury, N.Y.: Feminist Press, 1980), pp. 6–35.

9. Nancy F. Cott, *The Bonds of Womanhood: "Woman's Sphere" in New England, 1780–1835* (New Haven: Yale Univ. Press, 1977), pp. 39–41. James A. Henretta, in *The Evolution of American Society, 1700–1815: An Interdisciplinary Analysis* (Lexington, Mass.: D.C. Heath, 1973), notes that in 1776 in Philadelphia alone over four thousand women and children earned minimum wages by "putting out" their spinning for the local textile mills (p. 194). See also, Edith Abbot, *Women in Industry* (New York: D. Appleton, 1918), pp. 66–70, 262–316; and Rolla M. Tyron, *Household Manufactures in the United States, 1640–1860* (1917; repr., New York: Augustus M. Kelley, 1966), pp. 124–33.

10. *The Diaries of Julia Cowles: A Connecticut Record, 1797–1803*, ed. Anna Roosevelt Cowles and Laura Hadley Moseley (New Haven: Yale Univ. Press, 1931), pp. 40–41; and the diary of Elizabeth Drinker, especially the entries for June 20, 1795, and February 29, 1796, Historical Society of Pennsylvania, Philadelphia.

11. Arthur W. Calhoun, *A Social History of the American Family* (New York: Barnes & Noble, 1917), 51–64; Philip J. Greven, Jr., *Four Generations: Population, Land, and Family in Colonial Andover, Massachusetts* (Ithaca: Cornell Univ. Press, 1970), pp. 113–16; Henretta, *Evolution of American Society*, p. 133; Edward Shorter, "Illegitimacy, Sexual Revolution, and Social Change in Modern Europe," *Journal of Interdisciplinary History*, 2 (1971), 237–72; Daniel Scott Smith, "The Dating of the American Sexual Revolution: Evidence and Interpretation," in *The American Family in Social-Historical Perspective*, ed. Michael Gordon (New York: St. Martin's, 1973), p. 323; and, especially, Daniel Scott Smith and Michael S. Hindus, "Pre-marital Pregnancy in America, 1640–1971: An Overview and Interpretation," *Journal of Interdisciplinary History*, 5 (1975), 537–70.

12. Catherine M. Scholten, " 'On the Importance of the Obstetrick Art': Changing Customs of Childbirth in America, 1760 to 1825," *William and Mary Quarterly*, 3rd ser., 34 (July 1977), 426–28; Daniel Scott Smith, "Population, Family, and Society in Hingham, Massachusetts, 1635–1880," Ph.D. diss., Univ. of California, Berkeley, 1972, pp. 219–25; and Robert V. Wells, "Quaker Marriage Patterns in a Colonial Perspective, *William and Mary Quarterly*, 3rd ser., 29 (July 1972), 422.

13. *The Diaries of Julia Cowles*, pp. 91–92, 94.

14. Daniel Scott Smith, "Family Limitation, Sexual Control, and Domestic Feminism in Victorian America," in *Clio's Consciousness Raised*, ed. Lois Banner and Mary Hartman (New York: Harper & Row, 1974), pp. 119–36.

15. Ansley J. Coale and Melvin Zelnick, *New Estimates of Fertility and Population in the United States* (Princeton: Princeton Univ. Press, 1963), pp. 35–36; Potter, "Growth of Population," pp. 644–47, 663, 679; Warren C. Sanderson, "Quantitative Aspects of Marriage Fertility and Family Limitation in Nineteenth-Century America: Another Application of the Coale Specifications," *Demography*, 16 (1979), 339–58;

and Robert V. Wells, "Demographic Change and the Life Cycle of American Families," in *The Family in History: Interdisciplinary Essays*, ed. Theodore K. Rabb and Robert I. Rotberg (New York: Harper & Row, 1971), pp. 85–88.

16. Alexis de Tocqueville, *Democracy in America*, 2 vols., ed. Phillips Bradley (New York: Vintage, 1945), 2:212.

17. Molly Tilghman and Abigail Adams quoted in Norton, *Liberty's Daughters*, p. 75.

18. Sanderson, "Quantitative Aspects," pp. 339–58.

19. Carl N. Degler, *At Odds: Women and the Family in America from the Revolution to the Present* (New York: Oxford Univ. Press, 1980), p. 196; Norman E. Himes, *Medical History of Contraception* (Baltimore: Williams & Wilkins, 1936); and Robert V. Wells, "Family Size and Fertility Control in Eighteenth-Century America: A Study of Quaker Families," *Population Studies*, 25 (1971), 75.

20. Kenneth A. Lockridge, *Literacy in Colonial New England* (New York: Norton, 1974); Maris A. Vinovskis, "Socioeconomic Determinants of Fertility," *Journal of Interdisciplinary History*, 6 (Winter 1976), 375–96; Tamara K. Hareven and Maris A. Vinovskis, "Patterns of Childbearing in Late Nineteenth-Century America: The Determinants of Marital Fertility in Five Massachusetts Towns in 1880," in *Family and Population in Nineteenth Century America*, ed. Tamara K. Hareven and Maris A. Vinovskis (Princeton: Princeton Univ. Press, 1978), pp. 85–125; and Wells, "Family Size and Fertility Control," p. 76.

21. Perry Miller, *The Life of the Mind in America* (New York: Harcourt, Brace & World, 1965), p. 128.

22. Marylynn Salmon, "Life, Liberty, and Dower: The Legal Status of Women After the American Revolution," in *Women, War, and Revolution*, ed. Carol R. Berkin and Clara M. Lovett (New York: Holmes & Meier, 1980), p. 85.

23. St. George Tucker quoted in Kerber, *Women of the Republic*, p. 137; Tucker, ed., *Blackstone's Commentaries: With Notes of Reference, to the Constitution and Laws, of the Federal Government of the United States; and of the Commonwealth of Virginia*, 5 vols. (Philadelphia: Wm. Birch and Abraham Small, 1803), 2:445.

24. Kerber, *Women of the Republic*, p. 140.

25. For an intriguing discussion of how changing inheritance laws may have eventually contributed to redefining the married woman's status as an individual, see ibid., pp. 140–55.

26. Harriet Martineau is quoted in Joan Hoff Wilson, "The Illusion of Change: Women and the American Revolution," in *The American Revolution: Explorations in the History of American Radicalism*, ed. Alfred F. Young (Dekalb: Northern Illinois Univ. Press, 1976), p. 419.

27. See Mary Beard, *Woman as Force in History* (New York: Macmillan, 1946). A similar view is supported by Richard B. Morris in *Studies in the History of Early American Law* (New York: Columbia Univ. Press, 1930); and Morris, ed., *Select Cases of the Mayor's Court of New York City* (Washington, D.C.: American Historical Assoc., 1935), pp. 21–25. For a revisionist view, see Norma Basch, *In the Eyes of the Law: Women, Marriage, and Property in Nineteenth-Century New York* (Ithaca: Cornell Univ. Press, 1982); Peggy Rabkin, "The Origins of Law Reform: The Social Significance

of the Nineteenth-Century Codification Movement and Its Contribution to the Passage of the Early Married Woman's Property Acts," *Buffalo Law Review*, 24 (1974), 683–760; and Marylynn Salmon, "Life, Liberty, and Dower." See also Salmon's "Equality or Submersion? *Feme Covert* Status in Early Pennsylvania," in *Women of America: A History*, ed. Carol Ruth Berkin and Mary Beth Norton (Boston: Houghton Mifflin, 1979).

28. Basch, *In the Eyes of the Law*, pp. 17, 232.

29. Judge Hertell quoted in Cott, *Bonds of Womanhood*, p. 78.

30. See especially, Norton's chapter, "As Independent as Circumstances Will Admit," which begins, "If any quality was antithetical to the colonial notion of femininity, it was autonomy" (*Liberty's Daughters*, p. 125).

31. Abigail Adams in a letter to John Adams, March 31, 1776, repr. in *The Feminist Papers: From Adams to de Beauvoir*, ed. Alice S. Rossi (New York: Bantam, 1973), pp. 10–11.

32. Grace Growden Galloway quoted in Norton, *Liberty's Daughters*, p. 45.

33. Salmon, "Life, Liberty, and Dower," p. 97; Nancy F. Cott, "Divorce and the Changing Status of Women in Eighteenth-Century Massachusetts," *William and Mary Quarterly*, 3rd ser., 33 (October 1976), 586–614; Leonard Woods Labaree, ed. *Royal Instructions to British Colonial Governors, 1670–1776*, 2 vols. (New York: Appleton-Century, 1935), 1:155.

34. Gilbert Imlay, *The Emigrants, & c., or The History of an Expatriated Family*. 3 vols. (London: A. Hamilton, 1793), 1:ix.

35. Alice Morse Earle, *Colonial Dames and Good Wives* (1895; repr., New York: Frederick Ungar, 1962), pp. 247–53; Elizabeth F. Ellet, *The Women of the American Revolution* (New York: Scribner's, 1853–54), passim; Wendy Martin, "Women and the American Revolution," *Early American Literature*, 11 (1976–77), 322–35; and Norton, *Liberty's Daughters*, pp. 195–227.

36. Sophie Drinker, "Votes for Women in Eighteenth-Century New Jersey," *New York Historical Society Proceedings*, 31 (1962), 80. See also the *Massachusetts Spy, or Worcester Gazette* (November 1, 1797) under a "Rights of Women" headline: "At the late election in Elizabethtown [N.J.], the Females asserted the privilege granted them by the laws of that state, and gave in their votes for members to represent them in the state legislature" (p. 3).

37. "Lines, Written by a Lady, who was questioned respecting her inclination to marry," *Massachusetts Magazine, or Monthly Museum*, 6 (September 1794), 566.

38. "Rights of Women, by a Lady," *Philadelphia Minerva*, October 17, 1795.

39. Alexander Keyssar, "Widowhood in Eighteenth-Century Massachusetts: A Problem in the History of the Family," *Perspective in American History*, 8 (1974), 83–119; Wells, "Family History," pp. 11–12; and Wells, "Quaker Marriage Patterns," pp. 433–34.

40. Betsey Mayhew and Sarah Hanschurst quoted in Norton, *Liberty's Daughters*, p. 241. And for hundreds of comments about the advantages of remaining unmarried and the "Cult of Single Blessedness," see Lee Virginia Chambers-Schiller, *Liberty, A Better Husband: Single Women in America: The Generations of 1780–1840* (New Haven: Yale Univ. Press, 1984).

41. Charles Brockden Brown, *Alcuin: A Dialogue*, ed. Lee R. Edwards (New York: Grossman, 1971), pp. 88; 24–25.

42. Lyman H. Butterfield et al., eds., *Adams Family Correspondence*, 4 vols. (Cambridge: Harvard Univ. Press, 1963–73), 1:87.

43. Jane Tompkins, *Sensational Designs: The Cultural Work of American Fiction, 1790–1860* (New York: Oxford Univ. Press, 1985).

44. Catherine Maria Sedgwick, "Old Maids," in *Old Maids: Short Stories by Nineteenth-Century U.S. Women Writers*, ed. Susan Koppelman (New York: Pandora, 1984).

45. Rachel M. Brownstein, *Becoming a Heroine: Reading About Women in Novels* (New York: Viking, 1982), p. 24.

46. The historiography of changing family patterns is controversial, and the picture tends to look different depending on what factors one includes. Class, regional, and racial factors all influence the interpretation in different ways. Degler, Kerber, and Norton, for example, all tend to see a changing family pattern with more options for women by the end of the eighteenth century, although Kerber, perhaps, views the situation less optimistically than the other historians. Lawrence Stone has charted a change in family structure in England during the eighteenth century, especially an increase in affectional marriages and affectional modes of child rearing. See his *The Family, Sex, and Marriage in England, 1500–1800* (New York: Harper & Row, 1977). A similar pattern is described in the United States by Jay Fliegelman, *Prodigals and Pilgrims: The American Revolution Against Patriarchal Authority, 1750–1800* (Cambridge: Cambridge Univ. Press, 1982); Daniel B. Smith, *Inside the Great House: Planter Family Life in Eighteenth-Century Chesapeake Society* (Ithaca: Cornell Univ. Press, 1980); and Ronald G. Walters, "The Family and Ante-Bellum Reform: An Interpretation," *Societas*, 3 (Summer 1973), 221–32. But Philip J. Greven, in *The Protestant Temperament: Patterns of Child-Rearing, Religious Experience, and the Self in Early America* (New York: Knopf, 1978), argues for different methods of child rearing occurring simultaneously rather than evolving. Michael Zuckerman, in "Penmanship Exercises for Saucy Sons: Some Thoughts on the Colonial Southern Family," *South Carolina History Review*, 84 (1983), 152–66, finds family patterns changing in the South by the end of the eighteenth century, while Jan Lewis, in *The Pursuit of Happiness: Family Values in Jefferson's Virginia* (New York: Cambridge Univ. Press, 1983), finds change occurring more gradually and much later. For a brief overview of the different arguments, see Thomas P. Slaughter, "Family Politics in Revolutionary America," *American Quarterly*, 36 (Fall 1984), 598–606. My own focus is not on how the family "actually" changed but how selected social commentators of the late eighteenth century presented dialectical views of the family and woman's role in the family and society.

47. Cott, *Bonds of Womanhood*, p. 202.

48. David Lundberg and Henry F. May, "The Enlightened Reader in America," *American Quarterly*, 28 (Summer 1976), 262–71; app. Lundberg and May conclude that 40 percent of all the booksellers and libraries in their sample made *Emile* available to the American reading public. See also Paul M. Spurlin, *Rosseau in America, 1760–1809* (University: Univ. of Alabama Press, 1969).

49. Jean-Jacques Rosseau, *Emilius and Sophia; or, A New System of Education*, trans. by "A Citizen of Geneva" (London: T. Becket and R. Baldwin, 1783).

50. *Boston Weekly Magazine*, 2 (May 5, 1804), 110; 2 (March 24, 1804), 36.

51. Helena Wells, *Constantia Neville; or, The West Indian* (London: C. Whittingham for T. Caddell, 1800).

52. S.S.B.K. Wood, *Amelia; or, The Influence of Virtue. An Old Man's Story* (Portsmouth, N.H.: William Treadwell, 1802), p. 103.

53. Helena Wells, *The Step-Mother; a Domestic Tale, from Real Life*, 2 vols. (London: T. N. Longman and O. Rees, 1799), 2:21–22.

54. S.S.B.K. Wood, *Dorval, or the Speculator* (Portsmouth, N.H.: Nutting and Whitelock, 1801), p. 78, and *Julia, and the Illuminated Baron* (Portsmouth, N.H.: Charles Peirce, 1800), pp. 81–82.

55. When published serially in the *Massachusetts Magazine, or Monthly Museum* from 1792 to 1794, Murray's *Gleaner* essays were signed with a male pseudonym, "Mentor." Reprinted in three volumes in Boston in 1798, however, they were signed Constantia, and earlier references suggest that, even before the collected edition, readers were aware that the Gleaner was a woman.

56. Judith Sargent Murray, *The Gleaner: A Miscellaneous Production. In Three Volumes. By Constantia* (Boston: I. Thomas and E. T. Andrews, 1798), 1:167–68, 3:220.

57. "On the Equality of the Sexes," *Massachusetts Magazine, or Monthly Museum*, 2 (March 1798), 132.

58. Murray, *The Gleaner*, 3:189.

59. For the British connection, see Dale Spender's indispensable *Women of Ideas (And What Men Have Done to Suppress Them)* (London: Ark, 1982). For a discussion of the most prominent of the American feminists of the time, see Mary Sumner Benson, *Women in Eighteenth-Century America* (New York: Columbia Univ. Press, 1935); and Wilson, "The Illusion of Change," pp. 386–93, 426–31. The "Female Advocate" became a subject of some controversy in the magazines of the time owing to an anonymous pamphlet published in New Haven, Conn., in 1801 called, simply, *The Female Advocate*. This pamphlet especially emphasized the importance of a thorough female education and suggested, whimsically, that the doors of all institutions of higher learning be shut to men and opened to women for a period of time and then it be seen just which was the smarter sex. See also Eliza Southgate Bowne, *A Girl's Life Eighty Years Ago* (New York: Charles Scribner's Sons, 1887).

60. See Charles Louis de Secondat, baron de Montesquieu, *The Spirit of Laws* (1748; repr., Berkeley: Univ. of California Press, 1977); and Marie Jean Antoine Nicolas Caritat, marquis de Condorcet, *Outline of an Historical View of the Progress of the Human Mind* (Philadelphia: Mathew Carey, 1796), esp. pp. 24–50. Condorcet's arguments on behalf of women are alluded to in Charles Brockden Brown's *Alcuin*. For a detailed discussion of Brown's feminist dialogue, see my essay, "The Matter and Manner of Charles Brockden Brown's *Alcuin*," in *Critical Essays on Charles Brockden Brown*, ed. Bernard Rosenthal (Boston: G. K. Hall, 1981), pp. 71–86.

61. James Butler, *Fortune's Foot-ball; or, The Adventures of Mercutio. Founded on Matters of Fact . . .*, 2 vols. in 1 (Harrisburgh, Pa.: John Wyeth, 1797), 1:145–46.

(The title page indicates this novel was printed in 1797, although copyright was not secured until 1798.)

62. Imlay, *The Emigrants*, pp. ii, 22–23, 66.

63. Sukey Vickery, *Emily Hamilton, a Novel. Founded on Incidents in Real Life. By a Young Lady of Worcester County* (Worcester, Mass.: Isaiah Thomas, Jr., 1803), pp. 97–98, 108.

64. Three essays perceptively discuss the American reaction to Wollstonecraft and Wollstonecraftism. See R. M. Janes, "On the Reception of Mary Wollstonecraft's *A Vindication of the Rights of Woman*," *Journal of the History of Ideas*, 39 (April–June 1978), 293–302; Patricia Jewell McAlexander, "The Creation of the American Eve: The Cultural Dialogue on the Nature and Role of Women in Late-Eighteenth-Century America," *Early American Literature*, 9 (1975), 252–66; and Marcelle Thiebaux, "Mary Wollstonecraft in Federalist America: 1791–1802," in *The Evidence of the Imagination: Studies of Interactions Between Life and Art in English Romantic Literature*, ed. Donald H. Reiman et al. (New York: New York Univ. Press, 1978), pp. 195–245.

65. Lundberg and May, "Enlightened Reader," app.

66. *New England Palladium*, 19 (March 2, 1802), 1.

67. For a fuller discussion, see also Linda K. Kerber, "Daughters of Columbia: Educating Women for the Republic, 1787–1805," in *The Hofstadter Aegis: A Memorial*, ed. Eric L. McKitrick and Stanley M. Elkins (New York: Knopf, 1974), pp. 36–59. It must be emphasized that Godwin did not expect the *Memoirs* to in any way cast his deceased wife in a negative light. Utterly bereft at her death, Godwin moved his books and papers into her study and, until his own death forty years later, continued to work in Mary's room, among her belongings, beneath the magnificent portrait of her by John Opie. For an excellent discussion of the relationship between Godwin and Wollstonecraft and a sampling of early reviews of the *Memoirs* (including those quoted here), see Peter H. Marshall, *William Godwin* (New Haven: Yale Univ. Press, 1984), pp. 189–94.

68. Samuel Miller, "The Appropriate Duty and Ornament of the Female Sex," in *The Columbian Preacher; or, A Collection of Original Sermons, from Preachers of Eminence in the United States. Embracing the Distinguishing Doctrines of Grace* (Catskill: Nathan Elliott, 1808), p. 253.

69. For an extended critique of Wollstonecraft's life and her ideas, see Benjamin Silliman, *Letters of Shahcoolen, a Hindu Philosopher, Residing in Philadelphia . . .* (Boston: Russell & Cutler, 1802), 29–32, 48. Two other novels denounced Wollstonecraft in the years immediately following the publication of the *Memoirs*, Wells's *Constantia Neville* and Wood's *Dorval*.

70. The complex and heated debate over the limits of possibilities of domesticity in the nineteenth century is outside the focus of the present study. For a survey of the basic positions, however, the reader should consult the conclusion (pp. 197–206) of Nancy F. Cott's *Bonds of Womanhood*.

71. Ruth H. Block, "American Feminine Ideals in Transition: The Rise of the Moral Mother, 1785–1815," *Feminist Studies*, 4 (1978), 101–26. See also Mary Maples Dunn, "Saints and Sisters: Congregational and Quaker Women in the Early Co-

lonial Period," in *Women in American Religion*, ed. Janet Wilson James (Philadelphia: Univ. of Pennsylvania Press, 1980), pp. 30–35; Linda K. Kerber, "Can a Woman Be an Individual? The Limits of Puritan Tradition in the Early Republic," *Texas Studies in Language and Literature*, 25 (Spring 1983), esp. 161–65; Anne L. Kuhn, *The Mother's Role in Childhood Education: New England Concepts, 1830–1860* (New Haven: Yale Univ. Press, 1947); Gerald Moran and Maris Vinovskis, "The Puritan Family and Religion: A Critical Reappraisal," *William and Mary Quarterly*, 3rd ser., 39 (January 1982), 29–63; and Peter Gregg Slater, *Children in the New England Mind: In Death and In Life* (Hamden, Conn.: Shoe String Press, 1977), esp. chaps. 3, 4.

72. William Lyman, *A Virtuous Woman, the Bond of Domestic Union and the Source of Domestic Happiness* (New London, Conn.: S. Green, 1802), pp. 22–23.

73. *Parents' Magazine* (October 1840).

74. Helen Waite Papashivly, *All the Happy Endings* (New York: Harper, 1956), pp. 31–32.

75. There were, of course, exceptions to this rule, such as Cigarette, an adventurous young woman who finds her way through several complicated adventures. See Russel B. Nye, "The Novel as Dream and Weapon: Women's Popular Novels in the Nineteenth Century," *Historical Society of Michigan Chronicle*, 11 (4th qr. 1975), 2–18.

76. Charles Brockden Brown, "Female Learning," *Literary Magazine and American Register*, 1 (January 1804), 245.

77. Samuel Relf, *Infidelity, or the Victims of Sentiment* (Philadelphia: W. W. Woodward, 1797), title page, pp. 36–37.

78. By viewing Montraville as the stock seducer and overlooking the problematic role played by Belcour, William C. Spengemann, in *The Adventurous Muse: The Poetics of American Fiction, 1789–1900* (New Haven: Yale Univ. Press, 1977), can dismiss *Charlotte* as possibly "the most rigidly programmatic sentimental novel ever written" (p. 92). But he also concedes that "certain fictive energies seem to be at work, threatening to compromise the conservative values" of this novel (p. 90).

79. For an excellent assessment of Rowson's feminism and a discussion of her fictional strengths and weaknesses, see Patricia L. Parker's *Susanna Haswell Rowson* (Boston: Twayne, 1986). I am grateful to Professor Parker for making her manuscript available to me. See also, Eve Kornfeld, "Women in Post-Revolutionary American Culture: Susanna Haswell Rowson's American Career, 1792–1824," *Journal of American Culture*, 6 (Winter 1983), 56–62; Wendy Martin, "Profile: Susanna Rowson, Early American Novelist," *Women's Studies*, 2 (1974), 1–8; and Dorothy Weil, *In Defense of Women: Susanna Rowson* (University Park: Pennsylvania State Univ. Press, 1976), esp. pp. 31–64. The quotations are from the paperback edition of the novel "edited for modern readers" by Clara M. Kirk and Rudolf Kirk (New Haven: College & University Press, 1964), p. 121. Although this is the only readily available edition of the novel, it must be emphasized that it is neither a reprint of the original edition nor a scholarly modern edition of the work.

80. *Critical Review* (London) for April 1791, repr. in Rowson's *Charlotte* (Philadelphia: Mathew Carey, 1794), n.p. For other sympathetic critical assessments, see the

Boston Weekly Magazine, 1 (January 22, 1803), 53; and Samuel L. Knapp's "Memoir," in Rowson's posthumously published *Charlotte's Daughter; or, The Three Orphans. A Sequel to Charlotte Temple* . . . (Boston: Richardson & Lord, 1828). pp. 3–20.

81. Herbert Ross Brown, *The Sentimental Novel in America, 1789–1860* (Durham: Duke Univ. Press, 1940), p. 176.

82. *Margaretta; or, The Intricacies of the Heart* (Philadelphia: Samuel F. Bradford, 1807), p. 80. The anonymous author of this novel well may be alluding to Judith Sargent Murray's earlier "Story of Margaretta." Both on the level of plot and characterization there are definite similarities between the two works.

83. See Leslie A. Fiedler, *Love and Death in the American Novel*, rev. ed. (1960; repr., New York: Dell, 1966), p. 93, and Walter P. Wenska, Jr., "*The Coquette* and the American Dream of Freedom," *Early American Literature*, 12 (1977–78), 243–55.

84. The documents pertaining to Elizabeth Whitman's life and death (right down to an inventory of all she had with her at Bell Tavern when she died) have been included in Charles Knowles Bolton, *The Elizabeth Whitman Mystery* (Peabody, Mass.: Peabody Historical Society, 1912); Herbert Ross Brown, introduction to *The Coquette* (New York: Facsimile Text Society, 1939), pp. v–xix; Caroline W. Dall, *The Romance of the Association; or, One Last Glimpse of Charlotte Temple and Eliza Wharton* (Cambridge, Mass.: Press of John Wilson, 1875); and Jane E. Locke, "Historical Preface, Including a Memoir of the Author" in *The Coquette* (Boston: Samuel Etheridge for E. Larkin, 1855), pp. 3–30. The article quoted from the *Salem Mercury* for July 29, 1788, is reprinted in Bolton, pp. 33–37.

85. Anonymous essayist quoted in Bolton, *Elizabeth Whitman Mystery*, p. 59.

86. Almost all discussions of *The Coquette* sooner or later raise the question of the real identity of Major Sanford. See Bolton, *Elizabeth Whitman Mystery*, pp. 109–32, for a summary of the early choices; and Alexander Cowie, *The Rise of the American Novel* (New York: American Book Co., 1948), p. 16; Dall, *Romance of the Association*, pp. 101–15; and James Woodress, *A Yankee's Odyssey: The Life of Joel Barlow* (New York: Lippincott, 1958), pp. 60–64.

87. Quoted in Herbert Ross Brown's introduction to *The Coquette*, p. xii.

88. Despite its being generally acknowledged as the best of the early American sentimental novels, *The Coquette* has never been published in a modern edition using modern standards of textual accuracy. The only widely available edition of *The Coquette* is that edited by William S. Osborne with punctuation and spellings silently (and not always carefully) "edited for the modern reader." But because it is available in paperback, I have taken all my references from this edition (New Haven: College & University Press, 1970), and hereafter references to this edition will be cited parenthetically within the text. Lillie Deming Loshe, *The Early American Novel, 1789–1830* (1907; repr., New York; Frederick Ungar, 1966), was one of the first critics to note that *The Coquette* "is superior to its predecessors in interest and especially in character-drawing" (p. 14).

89. Sanford does, however, allude to Laurence Sterne in the letter in which he announces his triumph over Eliza—a fitting allusion considering Foster's comments about Sterne in *The Boarding School; or, Lessons of a Perceptress to Her Pupils* (Boston: Isaiah Thomas and E. T. Andrews, 1798), warning her readers against the "licentious

wit" that is "concealed under the artful blandishments of sympathetic sensibility" in Sterne's fiction (p. 205).

90. Bolton, *Elizabeth Whitman Mystery*, pp. 39–41.

91. Ibid., pp. 59–60.

92. I have elsewhere assessed at length the inadequacy of the choices presented to Eliza. See my article "Flirting with Destiny: Ambivalence and Form in the Early American Sentimental Novel," *Studies in American Fiction*, 10 (Spring 1982), esp. 27–34.

93. Joanna Russ, "What Can a Heroine Do? Or Why Women Can't Write," in *Images of Women in Fiction: Feminist Perspectives*, ed. Susan Koppelman Cornillon (Bowling Green: Bowling Green University Popular Press, 1972), p. 13.

94. Ibid., pp. 12–13.

95. Jane E. Locke, "Historical Preface," to her edition of *The Coquette*, pp. 3–30. The novel was dramatized by J. Horatio Nichols, *The New England Coquette: From the History of The Celebrated Eliza Wharton. A Tragic Drama, in Three Acts* (Salem: N. Coverly, 1802).

96. Herbert Ross Brown, "Introduction," *The Coquette*, p. ix.

97. Locke, "Historical Preface," p. 4.

Chapter 7

1. John Cosens Ogden, *The Female Guide* (Concord, N.H.: George Hough, 1793), p. 26.

2. Thomas Paine quoted by John Fiske, *The Critical Period in American History, 1783–1789* (Boston: Houghton Mifflin, 1888), pp. 55–56.

3. Thomas Jefferson, *Writings*, ed. Merrill D. Peterson (New York: Library of America, 1984), p. 70.

4. For different analyses of Revolutionary and postrevolutionary crowd actions, see Dirk Hoerder, *Crowd Action in Revolutionary Massachusetts, 1765–1780* (New York: Academic, 1977); Pauline Maier, "Popular Uprisings and Civil Authority in Eighteenth-Century America," in *Colonial America: Essays in Politics and Social Development*, ed. Stanley N. Katz (Boston: Little, Brown, 1976), pp. 432–452, and *From Resistance to Revolution: Colonial Radicals and the Development of American Opposition to Britain, 1756–1776* (New York: Knopf, 1972); Peter Shaw, *American Patriots and the Rituals of Revolution* (Cambridge: Harvard Univ. Press, 1980); and Alfred F. Young, "English Plebeian Culture and Eighteenth-Century American Radicalism," in *The Origins of Anglo-American Radicalism* (London: Allen & Unwin, 1984).

5. For a discussion of the aristocratic assumptions about the necessity for enlightened leadership, see Bernard Bailyn, *Ideological Origins of the American Revolution* (Cambridge: Harvard Univ. Press, 1967). For a somewhat different focus, see Gordon S. Wood, *The Creation of the American Republic* (Chapel Hill: Univ. of North Carolina Press, 1969), and "The Democratization of Mind in the American Revolution," in *The Moral Foundations of the American Republic*, 2nd ed., ed. Robert H. Horwitz (Charlottesville: Univ. Press of Virginia, 1979), pp. 102–28.

6. The denunciations by the Anti-Federalists, as well as Hamilton's opposing

views, are quoted in Alfred F. Young, *The Democratic Republicans of New York: The Origins, 1763–1797* (Chapel Hill: Univ. of North Carolina Press, 1967), pp. 141–42, 58. (Young also elucidates the differences and similarities between the Anti-Federalists and the Republicans.) The final summary of each party's attacks on the other is from Ronald P. Formisano, *The Transformation of Political Culture: Massachusetts Parties, 1790s–1840s* (New York: Oxford Univ. Press, 1983), p. 108. My chapter is indebted to these two excellent studies. I also wish to note the influence of older Progressive histories, preeminently Carl L. Becker's *The History of Political Parties in the Province of New York, 1760–1776* (Madison: Univ. of Wisconsin Press, 1909), as well as more recent studies that have somewhat qualified the Progressive position (not all Democratic-Republicans were from the middling classes, nor all Federalists of the aristocracy). See, especially, Milton M. Klein, "Democracy and Politics in Colonial New York," *New York History*, 40 (1959), 221–46; Jackson Turner Main, "Social Origins of a Political Elite: The Upper House in the Revolutionary Era," *Huntington Library Quarterly*, 27 (1964), 155; and Main, "Government by the People: The American Revolution and the Democratization of the Legislatures," *William and Mary Quarterly*, 3rd ser., 23 (July 1966), 391–407. For a sampling of the documents of Anti-Federalism, see Herbert J. Storing, ed., *The Anti-Federalist* (Chicago: Univ. of Chicago Press, 1984).

7. Hugh Henry Brackenridge, *Modern Chivalry*, ed. Claude M. Newlin (New York: American Book Co., 1937), pp. 13–17. Hereafter references to this edition will be cited parenthetically within the text.

8. "To All Good People in the State of Rhode Island," n.d., Broadsides Collection, AAS. For a fuller discussion of Federalist apprehensions, see David Hackett Fischer, *The Revolution of American Conservatism: The Federalist Party in the Era of Jeffersonian Democracy* (Chicago: Univ. of Chicago Press, 1965), p. 204. See also Robert H. Wiebe, *The Opening of American Society: From the Adoption of the Constitution to the Eve of Disunion* (New York: Knopf, 1984).

9. George Washington quoted in Richard B. Morris, "The Confederation Period and the American Historian," *William and Mary Quarterly*, 3rd ser., 13 (April 1956), 139–40.

10. George Washington to James Madison, November 5, 1786, in *The Writings of George Washington from the Original Manuscript Sources*, ed. John C. Fitzpatrick, 39 vols. (Washington, D.C.: U.S. Government Printing Office, 1931–44), 39:51–52. For a fascinating discussion of Washington's own view of his role in the Republic (and, concomitantly, his view of the Republic), see Garry Wills, *Cincinnatus: George Washington and the Enlightenment: Images of Power in Early America* (Garden City, N.Y.: Doubleday, 1984).

11. Alexander Hamilton quoted in Bernard Bailyn et al., *The Great Republic* (Boston: Little, Brown, 1977), pp. 322, 342.

12. Sean Wilentz, *Chants Democratic: New York City and the Rise of the American Working Class, 1788–1850* (New York: Oxford Univ. Press, 1984), p. 26. For prerevolutionary figures, see Gary B. Nash, *The Urban Crucible: Social Change, Political Consciousness, and the Origins of the American Revolution* (Cambridge: Harvard Univ. Press, 1979), esp. pp. 125–27, 186–89, 253–56, 325–27. For an overview, see Edward

Pessen, *Riches, Class, and Power Before the Civil War* (Lexington, Mass.: D.C. Heath, 1973).

13. For further discussion, see Carl Bridenbaugh, *Cities in Revolt: Urban Life in America, 1743–1776* (New York: Knopf, 1955), esp. pp. 79, 140, 152, 281, 288; Eric Foner, *Free Soil, Free Labor, Free Men: The Ideology of the Republican Party Before the Civil War* (New York: Oxford Univ. Press, 1970), pp. 23–26, 28–29, 231–232; Susan E. Hirsch, *Roots of the American Working Class: The Industrialization of Crafts in Newark, 1800–1860* (Philadelphia: Univ. of Pennsylvania Press, 1978); Michael B. Katz, *Poverty and Policy in American History* (New York: Academic, 1983), pp. 1–16, 175–76; David Montgomery, "The Working Classes of the Pre-Industrial American City, 1780–1830," *Labor History*, 9 (Winter 1968), 3–22; Charles S. Olton, *Artisans for Independence: Philadelphia Mechanics and the American Revolution* (Syracuse: Syracuse Univ. Press, 1975), pp. 19–32; Howard R. Rock, *Artisans of the New Republic: The Tradesmen of New York City in the Age of Jefferson* (New York: New York Univ. Press, 1979), pp. 79, 155, 257, 265–268; and Charles G. Steffen, *The Mechanics of Baltimore: Workers and Politics in the Age of Revolution, 1763–1812* (Urbana: Univ. of Illinois Press, 1984), pp. 15–16, 45–47.

14. For a discussion of rural poverty, see Freeman H. Hart, *The Valley of Virginia in the American Revolution* (Chapel Hill: Univ. of North Carolina Press, 1942); James A. Henretta, *The Evolution of American Society, 1700–1815: An Interdisciplinary Analysis* (Lexington, Mass: D. C. Heath, 1973); Barbara Karsky, "Agrarian Radicalism in the Late Revolutionary Period," in *New Wine in Old Skins*, ed. Erich Angermann (Stuttgart: Klett, 1976).

15. Richard B. Morris, "Insurrection in Massachusetts," in *America in Crisis*, ed. Daniel Aaron (New York: Knopf, 1952); and Morris, "The Confederation Period," p. 142.

16. Mercy Otis Warren is quoted in Robert Allen Rutland, *The Ordeal of the Constitution: The Anti-Federalists and the Ratification Struggle of 1787–1788* (Norman: Univ. of Oklahoma Press, 1966), pp. 41–43. For a sympathetic discussion of John Adams's *Defense of the Constitutions . . .* , see Peter Shaw, *The Character of John Adams* (New York: Norton, 1976), pp. 207–23.

17. Robert Ferguson, "Ideology and Myth in the Framing of the Constitution," paper presented at the Modern Language Association, Chicago, December 1985. See also Charles A. Beard, *An Economic Interpretation of the Constitution of the United States* (New York: Macmillan, 1935); and Alfred A. Kelly and Winfred A. Harbison, *The American Constitution: Its Origins and Development* (New York: Norton, 1976).

18. Young, *Democratic Republicans*, pp. 568, 575–76. See also Formisano, *Transformation of Political Culture*, pp. 149–68, for an analysis of the relationships between class and party affiliation.

19. These representative Republican remarks are quoted in Young, *Democratic Republicans*, pp. 81, 568, 580–81, 21–22, 579. See also Benjamin Fletcher Wright, Jr., *A Source Book of American Political Theory* (New York: Macmillan, 1929).

20. Thomas Pynchon, *The Crying of Lot 49* (Philadelphia: Lippincott, 1966).

21. William Cobbett quoted in Wilentz, *Chants Democratic*, pp. 68–69.

22. All quoted in Morris, "The Confederation Period," pp. 142–43.

23. These terms (the keystones of republicanism) are analyzed by J.G.A. Pocock in "Virtue and Commerce in the Eighteenth Century," *Journal of Interdisciplinary History*, 3 (Summer 1972), 119–34, and *The Machiavellian Moment: Florentine Political Thought and the Atlantic Republican Tradition* (Princeton: Princeton Univ. Press, 1975); they are amplified by Wilentz, *Chants Democratic*, p. 14. For a different analysis of republicanism, see Joyce Appleby, *Capitalism and a New Social Order: The Republican Vision of the 1790s* (New York: New York Univ. Press, 1984).

24. Wood, "Democratization," pp. 105, 110. See also Wilbur Samuel Howell, *Eighteenth-Century British Logic and Rhetoric* (Princeton: Princeton Univ. Press, 1971); and Warren Guthrie, "The Development of Rhetorical Theory in America, 1635–1850," *Speech Monographs*, 13 (1946), 14–22.

25. James Madison quoted in Wood, "Democratization," pp. 115, 122.

26. Merle Curti, *The Growth of American Thought*, 3rd ed. (New York: Harper & Row, 1964), p. 209; and Frank Luther Mott, *American Journalism: A History, 1690–1960* (New York: Macmillan, 1962), p. 167.

27. Wood, "Democratization," pp. 120–21. For a breakdown of early American newspapers by party affiliation, see Fischer, *Revolution of American Conservatism*, pp. 413–23. Although I am quoting here from the *New York Commercial Advertiser* for July 11, 1800, this kind of virulent anti-Jefferson propaganda was commonplace both in the *Advertiser* and in numerous other Federalist papers, especially the *Gazette of the United States* and the *Connecticut Courant*.

28. The Alien and Sedition Laws, ratified on July 14, 1798, are quoted in full in James Morton Smith's excellent study, *Freedom's Fetters: The Alien and Sedition Laws and American Civil Liberties* (Ithaca: Cornell Univ. Press, 1956), pp. 441–42. My discussion of these laws is indebted to Smith's study and, to a lesser extent, to John C. Miller, *Crisis in Freedom: The Alien and Sedition Acts* (Boston: Little, Brown, 1951).

29. Wood presents both sides of the debate in "Democratization," p. 122. It must be added that Jefferson later questioned his earlier optimistic view of public opinion and noted that "nothing can now be believed which is seen in a newspaper. Truth itself becomes suspicious by being put into that polluted vehicle." Jefferson is quoted in Miller, *Crisis in Freedom*, p. 231.

30. The *Gazette of the United States*, the *Boston Centinel*, the *Connecticut Courant*, and the *New York Gazette* are quoted in Smith, *Freedom's Fetters*, on, respectively, pp. 15, 178, 179, 180.

31. Smith, in *Freedom's Fetters*, quotes John Adams's prayer (p. 181) and Thomas Jefferson's first inaugural address (pp. 432–33) and discusses Secretary of State Timothy Pickering's extraordinary measures to suppress Republican politicians and newspapers (pp. 182–87).

32. Leon Howard, "The Late Eighteenth Century: An Age of Contradictions," in *Transitions in American Literary History*, ed. Harry Hayden Clark (Durham: Duke Univ. Press, 1953), pp. 51–89. See also William L. Hedges, "Charles Brockden Brown and the Culture of Contradictions," *Early American Literature*, 9 (Fall 1974), 107–42.

33. Walter L. Reed, *An Exemplary History of the Novel: The Quixotic Versus the Picaresque* (Chicago: Univ. of Chicago Press, 1981), p. 60.

34. James Butler, *Fortune's Foot-ball; or, The Adventures of Mercutio*, 2 vols. in 1 (Harrisburgh, Pa.: John Wyeth, 1797), 1:72, 2:184, preface. See also Henri Petter, *The Early American Novel* (Columbus: Ohio State Univ. Press, 1971), pp. 281–301, for a fine discussion of the picaresque cosmology.

35. Ian Watt, *The Rise of the Novel* (1957; repr., Berkeley: Univ. of California Press, 1967), pp. 83, 65.

36. Of the myriad analyses of the self-consuming nature of capitalist society, one of the most lucid and eloquent is George Lukács's *Marxism and Human Liberation*, ed. and trans. E. San Juan, Jr. (New York: Dell, 1973). See also Lukács's *The Theory of the Novel*, trans. Anna Bostock (Cambridge: MIT Press), esp. pp. 70–93.

37. Butler, *Fortune's Foot-ball*, 1:46–47; see also, 2:140, 2:191.

38. Watt, *Rise of the Novel*, pp. 67–70; and Max Weber, *From Max Weber: Essays in Sociology*, ed. and trans. H. H. Gerth and C. Wright Mills (New York: Oxford Univ. Press, 1946), esp. pp. 349–50. Lillie Deming Loshe, *The Early American Novel, 1789–1830* (1907; repr., New York: Frederick Ungar, 1966), p. 24, notes the way in which Mercutio seems little perturbed by the demise of the women he professes to love.

39. Petter, *Early American Novel*, p. 29.

40. *The Adventures of Jonathan Corncob, Loyal American Refugee, Written by Himself* (London: Printed for the author, 1787), p. 164.

41. Umberto Eco, "Narrative Structures in Fleming," in *The Role of the Reader: Explorations in the Semiotics of Texts* (Bloomington: Indiana Univ. Press, 1976), pp. 145–72.

42. Although originally published posthumously and in bowdlerized form, *Mr. Penrose: The Journal of Penrose, Seaman* has recently been republished with an excellent introduction and notes by David Howard Dickason (Bloomington: Indiana Univ. Press, 1969).

43. Janice A. Radway, *Reading the Romance: Women, Patriarchy, and Popular Literature* (Chapel Hill: Univ. of North Carolina Press, 1984), esp. pp. 194–96.

44. The two editions of *The History of Constantius and Pulchera* that include advertisements are Norwich, Conn.: Thomas Hubbard for Simon Carew, 1796, and Portsmouth, N.H.: Charles Peirce, 1797.

45. For discussions of travel writing, see, for example, Percy G. Adams, *Travelers and Travel Liars, 1660–1800* (Berkeley: Univ. of California Press, 1962); Robert C. Bredeson, "Landscape Description in Nineteenth-Century American Travel Literature," *American Quarterly*, 20 (Spring 1968), 86–94; Percy G. Butler, *Travel Literature and the Evolution of the Novel* (Lexington: Univ. Press of Kentucky, 1984); Jane Donahue, "Colonial Shipwreck Narratives: A Theological Study," *Books at Brown*, 23 (1969), 101–34; R. W. Frantz, *The English Traveller and the Movement of Ideas, 1660–1732* (Lincoln: Univ. of Nebraska Press, 1932); G. B. Parks, "Travel as Education," in *The Seventeenth Century*, ed. R. F. Jones et al. (Stanford: Stanford Univ. Press, 1951); G. B. Parks "The Turn to the Romantic in Travel Literature of the Eighteenth Century," *Modern Language Quarterly*, 25 (1964), 22–23; and William C. Spengemann, *The Adventurous Muse: The Poetics of American Fiction, 1789–1900* (New Haven: Yale Univ. Press, 1977), esp. pp. 6–118.

46. Special thanks to John Seelye for bringing Elkanah Watson's delightful Sternean travel "novel" to my attention.

47. *Mr. Penrose*, pp. 358–59.

48. Royall Tyler, *The Algerine Captive*, ed. Don L. Cook (New Haven: College & University Press, 1970), p. 224. Hereafter references to this readily available edition of the novel will be cited parenthetically within the text.

49. Lucien Goldman, *Towards a Sociology of the Novel*, trans. Alan Sheridan (London: Tavistock, 1975), esp. pp. 1–18.

50. Robert Hemenway, "Fiction in the Age of Jefferson: The Early American Novel as Intellectual Document," *Midcontinent American Studies Journal*, 9 (1968), 91–102; and Emory Elliott, *Revolutionary Writers: Literature and Authority in the New Republic, 1725–1810* (New York: Oxford Univ. Press, 1982), pp. 191–93.

51. Claude M. Newlin, *The Life and Writings of Hugh Henry Brackenridge* (Princeton: Princeton Univ. Press, 1932), pp. 112–92.

52. James Kelleher, "Hugh Henry Brackenridge," in *American Writers of the Early Republic*, vol. 37 (*Dictionary of Literary Biography*), ed. Emory Elliott (Detroit: Gale, 1985), p. 53.

53. Newlin, *Life and Writings of . . . Brackenridge*, p. 148; and Hugh Henry Brackenridge, *Incidents of the Insurrection in the Western Parts of Pennsylvania, in the Year 1794*, 3 vols. (Philadelphia: John McCulloch, 1795), 1:54–55.

54. Newlin, *Life and Writings of . . . Brackenridge*, pp. 171, 173.

55. Ibid., pp. 205, 208; *Pittsburgh Gazette*, October 5, 1799.

56. Kelleher, "Hugh Henry Brackenridge," p. 56.

57. For a fine discussion of republican rhetoric and the novel, see Michael T. Gilmore, "Eighteen-Century Oppositional Ideology and Hugh Henry Brackenridge's *Modern Chivalry*," *Early American Literature*, 13 (Fall 1978), 181–92. Also see, C. Peter Magrath, *Yazoo: Law and Politics in the New Republic* (Providence: Brown Univ. Press, 1966).

58. For a sampling of opinion on *Modern Chivalry*, see Sargent Bush, Jr., "*Modern Chivalry* and Young's *Magazine*," *American Literature*, 44 (May 1972), 292–99; Joseph H. Harkey, "The Don Quixote of the Frontier: Brackenridge's *Modern Chivalry*," *Early American Literature*, 8 (Fall 1973), 193–203; W. W. Hoffa, "Language of Rogues and Fools in Brackenridge's *Modern Chivalry*," *Studies in the Novel*, 12 (1980), 289–300; Wendy Martin, "On the Road with the Philosopher and the Profiteer: A Study of Hugh Henry Brackenridge's *Modern Chivalry*," *Eighteenth-Century Studies*, 4 (1971), 241–56, and "The Rogue and the Rational Man: Hugh Henry Brackenridge's Study of a Con Man in *Modern Chivalry*," *Early American Literature*, 8 (Fall 1973), 179–92; Charles E. Modlin, "The Folly of Ambition in *Modern Chivalry*," *Proceedings of the American Antiquarian Society*, 85 (1975), 310–13; William L. Nance, "Satiric Elements in Brackenridge's *Modern Chivalry*," *Texas Studies in Language and Literature*, 9 (Autumn 1967), 381–89; and Amberys R. Whittle, "*Modern Chivalry*: The Frontier as Crucible," *Early American Literature*, 6 (Spring 1971), 263–70.

59. Peter, *Early American Novel*, p. 381, notes rightly that Mann's exploitation of Sampson's sexual identity is analogous to the Richardsonian prurience over a woman's virginity.

60. *The Female Review; or, Memoirs of an American Young Lady* (Dedham, Mass.: Nathaniel & Benjamin Heaton, 1797), frontmatter.

61. Percy H. Boynton, *Literature and American Life* (Boston: Ginn, 1936), pp. 195–96; Alexander Cowie, *The Rise of the American Novel* (New York: American Book Co., 1948), p. 30; and Petter, *Early American Novel*, p. 290. Special thanks to Jack B. Moore for sending me a copy of his then unpublished essay, "Our Literary Heritage: A Justly Neglected Masterpiece," which documents the magazine publishing history of this bizarre novel.

62. Robert Darnton, *The Great Cat Massacre and Other Episodes in French Cultural History* (New York: Basic Books, 1984), p. 242.

63. *The History of Constantius and Pulchera; or, Constancy Rewarded: An American Novel* (Boston: [n.p.], 1794), p. 1. Hereafter references to this edition will be made parenthetically within the text.

64. Loshe, *Early American Novel*, calls *Constantius and Pulchera* a "cheerful and animated tale" with a "cheerful conglomeration of improbabilities" (p. 64).

65. Charlotte Lennox, *The Female Quixote* (London: Oxford Univ. Press, 1970), p. 138.

66. Tabitha Tenney, *Female Quixotism: Exhibited in the Romantic Opinions and Extravagant Adventures of Dorcasina Sheldon*, 2 vols. (Boston: I. Thomas and E. T. Andrews, 1801), 2:201. Hereafter references to this edition of the novel will be cited parenthetically within the text.

67. Reed, *Exemplary History*, pp. 74–75.

68. Laurie Langbauer, "Romance Revisited: Charlotte Lennox's *The Female Quixote*," *Novel*, 18 (1984), 39. The Fielding review was recently republished in Henry Fielding, "*The Covent Garden Journal*, No. 24, March 24, 1752," in *The Criticism of Henry Fielding*, ed. Ian Williams (London: Routledge & Kegan Paul, 1970), p. 193. For a fuller discussion of Lennox, see also Gustavus Howard Maynadier, *The First American Novelist?* (Cambridge: Harvard Univ. Press, 1940); and Philippe Sejourne, *The Mystery of Charlotte Lennox: First Novelist of Colonial America* (Aix-en-Provence: Publications des Annales de la Faculté des lettres, 1967). And, for a comparison of Lennox and Tenney, see Sally Allen McNall, *Who Is in the House? A Psychological Study of Two Centuries of Women's Fiction in America, 1795 to the Present* (New York: Elsevier, 1981), esp. pp. 15–18.

69. Charles H. Bell, *History of [the Town of] Exeter, New Hampshire* (1888; repr., Bowie, Md.: Catholic Heritage, 1979), pp. 382–84; Arthur Gilman, *The Gilman Family* (Albany, N.Y.: Joel Munsell, 1869), pp. 97–98; and Mary Jane Tenney, *The Tenney Family, or the Descendants of Thomas Tenney of Rowley, Massachusetts, 1638–1890* (Boston: American Printing and Engraving Co., 1891), p. 57. The letter from Tabitha Gilman Tenney to the Honorable William Plumer (October 25, 1823) is reprinted courtesy of the Plumer Papers, New Hampshire Historical Society, Concord. My special thanks to Dr. Sally Hoople for sending me a photocopy of this letter.

70. Elizabeth Dow Leonard, *A Few Reminiscences of My Exeter Life*, ed. Edward C. Echols (Exeter, N.H.: 2 × 4 Press, 1972), pp. 46–48. Leonard also relates an amusing anecdote about how, when Washington's death was announced in Exeter,

"many ladies thought it was necessary to faint, Mrs. Tenney among the number. She had a valuable mirror in her hand when she received the terrible news of [Washington's] fate. She walked leisurely across the room, laid the mirror safely down, placed herself in a proper attitude . . . and then fainted away" (p. 48). Certainly this anecdote corroborates the rather sober, sensible Tabby Gilman portrayed by Patty Rogers in her diary. Sally Hoople, in her fine doctoral dissertation, "Tabitha Tenney: 'Female Quixotism' " (Fordham Univ., 1984, p. 291), also quotes from one other source, a letter in the Duyckinck Collection, Manuscripts and Archives Division of the New York Public Library, which notes that Tenney was "perhaps more remarkable for her domestic qualifications than for her literary performances," another sad commentary on one of the best of the early novelists.

71. Diary of Patty Rogers, Manuscript Department, AAS. See especially the entries for 1785 on January 9 and 10, May 29, June 20, August 1, 2, and 4, and September 14 and 21.

72. Hoople, *Tabitha Tenney*, p. 112.

73. G. Thomas Tanselle, *Royall Tyler* (Cambridge: Harvard Univ. Press, 1967), and "Author and Publisher in 1800: Letters of Royall Tyler and Joseph Nancrede," *Harvard Library Bulletin*, 15 (1967), 120–39. See also, Ada Lou Carson and Herbert L. Carson, *Royall Tyler* (Boston: Twayne, 1979). For a firsthand account of Tyler's family, see the memoirs by his wife, *Grandmother Tyler's Book: The Recollections of Mary Palmer Tyler*, ed. Helen Tyler Brown and Frederick Tupper (New York: G. P. Putnam's, 1925), and by his son, Thomas Pickman Tyler, "Royall Tyler," *Proceedings of the Vermont Bar Association*, 1 (1878–81), 44–62. George Floyd Newbrough has also published selections from Mary Tyler's day-to-day journal in "Mary Tyler's Journal," *Vermont Quarterly*, 20 (1952), 19–31. For the less well-known works by Tyler, see Marius B. Péladeau, *The Prose of Royall Tyler* (Montpelier and Rutland: Vermont Historical Society/Tuttle, 1972), and *The Verse of Royall Tyler* (Charlottesville: Univ. Press of Virginia, 1968). See also *Four Plays by Royall Tyler*, ed. Arthur Wallace Peach and George Floyd Newbrough (1941; repr., Bloomington: Indiana Univ. Press, 1965), vol. 15 bd. with vol. 16 (ser. title, *America's Lost Plays*, 20 vols.), and *The Bay Boy, or Autobiography of a Youth of Massachusetts Bay. Sketches from an Unpublished Eighteenth-Century Novel*, ed. Martha R. Wright (Hicksville, N.Y.: Exposition, 1978). The two contemporary editions of *The Algerine Captive* are Jack B. Moore's reproduction of the 1802 London edition (Gainesville: Scholars' Facsimiles and Reprints, 1967) and Don L. Cook's paperback edition (see n. 48) based on the first Walpole edition of 1797 and "edited for the modern reader" (meaning that the editor has silently changed spelling, punctuation, and sometimes even phrasing from the original). It must also be noted that despite the plethora of Tyler documents problems remain. Tanselle, in a review of *The Prose of Royall Tyler* (*American Literature*, 41 [March 1969], 117–19) as well as in his review essay "The Editing of Royall Tyler" (*Early American Literature*, 9 [Spring 1974], 83–95), has pointed out many of the textual problems with the contemporary editions of Tyler's work, including *The Algerine Captive*, which, "though available in a photographic reproduction, has never been properly edited; and that reproduction . . . is of the wrong edition to be of most scholarly usefulness" (*Early American Literature*, 9:93). For a list of "substantive var-

iants" in the British and American editions, see Tanselle, "Early American Fiction in England: The Case of *The Algerine Captive,*" *Papers of the Bibliographical Society of America*, 59 (1965), 367–84.

74. See Mary Tyler's Journal, box 45, Royall Tyler Collection, Vermont Historical Society, Montpelier; Newbrough, ed., "Mary Tyler's Journal," pp. 19–33; and Brown and Tupper, eds., *Grandmother Tyler's Book*, esp. pp. 76, 320.

75. Tanselle, *Royall Tyler*, pp. 19–23, provides an excellent account of Tyler's role in the rebellion.

76. Brown and Tupper, eds., *Grandmother Tyler's Book*, pp. 104–05.

77. Thomas P. Tyler, "Royall Tyler," pp. 47–48. For a fuller discussion, see the full-length version of the memoir by Tyler's son, Royall Tyler Collection, Vermont Historical Society, Montpelier.

78. Royall Tyler quoted in Tanselle, *Royall Tyler*, p. 22.

79. Royall Tyler to Joseph Pearse Palmer, February 17, 1787; quoted in Tanselle, *Royall Tyler*, pp. 21–22.

80. Brown and Tupper, eds., *Grandmother Tyler's Book*, p. 171.

81. Royall Tyler, *The Contrast* (1790; repr., New York: AMS, 1970), pp. 55–56. For an excellent discussion of the relationship between Shays's Rebellion and Tyler's first play, see Richard S. Pressman, "Class 'Positioning' and Shays's Rebellion: Resolving the Contradictions of *The Contrast*," forthcoming, *Early American Literature*. For Tyler's manipulations of an American language, see Roger B. Stein, "Royall Tyler and the Question of Our Speech," *New England Quarterly*, 38 (December 1965), 454–74.

82. Laura G. Pedder, ed., *The Letters of Joseph Dennie, 1768–1812* (Orono: Univ. of Maine Press, 1936), pp. 145–46.

83. Péladeau, *The Prose of Royall Tyler*, pp. 202–04.

84. Brown and Tupper, eds., *Grandmother Tyler's Book*, p. 185.

85. Newbrough, ed., "Mary Tyler's Journal," p. 20.

86. Tanselle, *Royall Tyler*, p. 5.

87. Brown and Tupper, eds., *Grandmother Tyler's Book*, p. xvii.

88. A detailed account of Tyler's politics and his life as a state supreme court judge can be found in Thomas P. Tyler, "Royall Tyler," pp. 51–60.

89. Newbrough, ed., "Mary Tyler's Journal," pp. 23–26.

90. Mary Palmer Tyler to her daughter, Amelia, January 19, 1825, Royall Tyler Collection, Vermont Historical Society, Montpelier.

91. James Fenimore Cooper, *Early Critical Essays*, ed. James F. Beard, Jr. (Gainesville, Fla.: Scholars' Facsimiles and Reprints, 1955), pp. 336–37. Cooper's essay originally appeared in *The Literary and Scientific Repository and Critical Review*, 4 (May 1822).

92. John Adams quoted in Peter Shaw's eloquent biography, *The Character of John Adams*, p. 311.

93. Cooper, *Early Critical Essays*, p. 370.

94. Although I disagree with a number of points raised by Larry R. Dennis in "Legitimizing the Novel: Royall Tyler's *The Algerine Captive,*" *Early American Literature*, 9 (Spring 1974), 71–80, and especially what seems to me an artificial equation

of sentimentality and women (Didn't men write sentimental novels? Didn't men read them?), his comments on the importance of Tyler's view of history are perceptive.

95. *The Algerine Captive*, ed. Don L. Cook, p. 31, n.

96. See, especially, Sacvan Bercovitch's splendid essay "How the Puritans Won the American Revolution," *Massachusetts Review*, 17 (Winter 1976), 586–630.

97. Linda Hutcheon, "A Poetics of Postmodernism?" *Diacritics*, 13 (Winter 1983), esp. pp. 40–42.

98. Carson and Carson, *Royall Tyler*, p. 60; Cathy N. Davidson and Arnold E. Davidson, "Royall Tyler's *The Algerine Captive:* A Study in Contrasts," *ARIEL: A Review of International English Literature*, 7 (July 1976), 53–67; Dennis, "Legitimizing the Novel," esp. p. 76; James C. Gaston, "Royall Tyler," in *American Writers of the Early Republic*, vol. 37 (*Dictionary of Literary Biography*), ed. Emory Elliott (Detroit: Gale, 1985), p. 283; Moore, ed., *The Algerine Captive*, p. viii; Spengemann, *The Adventurous Muse*, p. 124; and Tanselle, *Royall Tyler*, pp. 157–159.

99. Tanselle, *Royall Tyler*, pp. 153–54.

100. *The Interesting Narrative of the Life of Olaudah Equiano, or Gustavus Vassa, the African, Written by Himself*, 2 vols. (London: Printed by the author, 1789). This narrative, incidentally, also draws from others such as *A Narrative of the Most Remarkable Particulars in the Life of James Albert Ukawsaw Gronniosaw* (Bath, Eng.: 1770).

101. See, for example, the *Monthly Review* (London), 42 (September 1803): "As friends rather than as critics, we shall only beg leave to observe that the contents of the first volume are more diversified and more amusing than those of the second" (p. 93), or the *Monthly Anthology and Boston Review*, 9 (November 1810), which insists that volume 2 is "much inferiour," "common-place," and "accompanied with many trite reflections" (pp. 344–47).

102. No longer protected by the British Navy, American ships became easy prey to Barbary pirates. By one estimate, there were some twelve hundred slaves in Algiers during the 1790s. For a fuller account, see Ray W. Irwin, *The Diplomatic Relations of the United States with the Barbary Powers, 1776–1816* (Chapel Hill: Univ. of North Carolina Press, 1931); and H. G. Barnby, *The Prisoners of Algiers: An Account of the Forgotten American-Algerian War, 1785–1797* (London: Oxford Univ. Press, 1966).

103. *The Diary of William Dunlap*, 3 vols. (1930; repr., New York: B. Blom, 1969), 1:174; the *Monthly Review* (London), 42 (September 1803), 93; and *Monthly Anthology and Boston Review*, 9 (November 1810), 346.

104. Typescript of the memoir of Thomas Pickman Tyler, p. 99, Royall Tyler Collection, Vermont Historical Society, Montpelier.

105. Raymond Williams, *The Country and the City* (New York: Oxford Univ. Press, 1973), p. 93.

106. Brown and Tupper, eds., *Grandmother Tyler's Book*, pp. 258–59. A similar story is reported by William Czar Bradley, in a letter dated December 7, 1857, in the Royall Tyler Collection, Vermont Historical Society, Montpelier. Bradley notes that "an honest Westmoreland farmer" came into his father's office after *The Algerine Captive* was published and began discussing Updike Underhill's plight. When his father mentioned that the book was a novel and that the adventures were all fictitious,

"the indignation of the farmer on hearing what he called the gross imposition was almost uncontrollable and would have delighted the author."

Chapter 8

1. Royall Tyler, *The Contrast* (1790; repr., New York: AMS, 1970).

2. See especially, Claude Lévi-Strauss, *Elementary Structures of Kinship* (New York: Beacon, 1969), *The Raw and the Cooked* (New York: Harper & Row, 1970), and *The Savage Mind* (Chicago: Univ. of Chicago Press, 1969).

3. Raymond Williams, *The Country and the City* (New York: Oxford Univ. Press, 1973), p. 54.

4. Ibid., p. 83.

5. For a brief but perceptive discussion of *The Contrast* as well as a reproduction of the original frontispiece of the 1790 publication of the play, see James C. Gaston, "Royall Tyler," in *American Writers of the Early Republic*, vol. 37 (*Dictionary of Literary Biography*), ed. Emory Elliott (Detroit: Gale, 1985), pp. 280–82.

6. Quoted in Richard S. Pressman, "Class 'Positioning' and Shays's Rebellion: Resolving the Contradictions of *The Contrast*," forthcoming, *Early American Literature*. The class affiliation of early American theatergoers is also discussed perceptively by George C. D. Odell, *Annals of the New York Stage*, 15 vols. (New York: Columbia Univ. Press, 1927), vol. 1; and Kenneth Silverman, *A Cultural History of the American Revolution* (New York: Thomas Y. Crowell, 1976), esp. pp. 545–54. Silverman notes that "the postwar depression gave the theatre controversy a new note of complaining bitterness. Many railed against the theatre as a cruelly flagrant, public witness of the social inequality produced by the war. Within were Haves, outside Have-Nots" (p. 548).

7. Charles G. Steffen, review of Sean Wilentz, *Chants Democratic: New York City and the Rise of the American Working Class, 1788–1850, Journal of the Early Republic*, 4 (Winter 1984), 459.

8. Clearly the whole meaning of class must be adjusted to the American situation. For a fine theoretical introduction to social stratification, particularly as related to the American experience, see Bernard Barbar, *Social Stratification: A Comparative Analysis of Structure and Process* (New York: Harcourt, Brace, 1957).

9. Although Joyce Appleby tends to simplify trends in recent historiography of the early national period by emphasizing its antiliberal bias, her analysis on the whole is extremely astute. See "Value and Society," in *Colonial British America: Essays in the New History of the Early Modern Era*, ed. Jack P. Greene and J. R. Pole (Baltimore: Johns Hopkins Univ. Press, 1984), pp. 290–316. My discussion is also indebted to Appleby's "Commercial Farming and the 'Agrarian Myth' in the Early Republic," *Journal of American History*, 68 (1982), 833–49, and "The Radical *Double-Entendre* in the Right to Self-Government," in *The Origins of Anglo-American Radicalism*, ed. Margaret Jacob and James Jacob (London: Allen & Unwin, 1984), pp. 275–83. For a concise account of modernization in America, see Richard D. Brown, *Modernization: The Transformation of American Life, 1600–1865* (New York: Hill & Wang, 1976); and, for a critical analysis of modernization theory, Dean C. Tipps, "Modernization Theory

and the Comparative Study of Societies: A Critical Perspective," *Comparative Studies in Society and History*, 15 (1973), 199–226.

10. Gary B. Nash, ed., *Class and Society in Early America* (Englewood Cliffs, N.J.: Prentice-Hall, 1970), p. 21.

11. Crévecoeur quoted in ibid., p. 26.

12. *Selected Writings of Benjamin Rush*, ed. Dagobert D. Runes (New York: Philosophical Library, 1947), pp. 333, 331.

13. Appleby, "Value and Society," p. 308.

14. Georg Lukács, "The Old Culture and the New Culture," in *Marxism and Human Liberation*, ed. and trans. E. San Juan, Jr. (New York: Dell, 1973), p. 9.

15. Marilyn Butler, *Romantics, Rebels, and Reactionaries: English Literature and Its Background* (New York: Oxford Univ. Press, 1981), p. 11. Butler also notes that "Otranto looks uncommonly like an attempt to graft on to the novel—the modern form concerned with money, possessions, status, circumstance—the heightened passions, elemental situations, and stylized poetic techniques of the Elizabethan dramatists" (p. 21). For an account of the reactionary measures in England during the 1790s, see E. P. Thompson, *The Making of the English Working Class* (New York: Pantheon, 1964).

16. See especially the preface to the 2nd ed. of the *Lyrical Ballads* (1800) in William Wordsworth and Samuel Taylor Coleridge, *Lyrical Ballads*, ed. R. L. Brett and A. R. Jones (London: Methuen, 1963), pp. 248–49; and the Marquis de Sade's essay "Idées sur les romans" (1800) in *Oeuvres complètes du Marquis de Sade*, 16 vols. (Paris: J. J. Pauvert, 1966), 10:15. For a provocative discussion of both, see Leslie A. Fielder, *Love and Death in the American Novel*, rev. ed. (1960; repr., New York: Dell, 1966), pp. 135–36.

17. See D. Gilbert Dumas, "Things as They Were: The Original Ending of *Caleb Williams*," *Studies in English Literature, 1500–1900*, 6 (1966), 584; Gary Kelly, *The English Jacobin Novel, 1780–1850* (Oxford: Oxford Univ. Press, 1976), pp. 179–84; and Raymond Williams, "The Fiction of Reform," in *Writing in Society* (London: Verso Editions, 1984), pp. 145–49.

18. A good indication of the vast popularity of the Gothic genre, especially between 1790 and 1820, can be found by surveying Montague Summers, *A Gothic Bibliography* (London: Fortune, 1941). This popularity as well as the new narrative possibilities allowed by the Gothic form, are discussed by J.M.S. Tompkins, *The Popular Novel in England, 1770–1800* (London: Methuen, 1932). The secondary literature on the Gothic is extensive, so I will here mention only a few titles that indicate the range of interpretation to which this provocative form has been subjected: Frederick Garber, "Meaning and Mode in Gothic Fiction," in *Racism in the Eighteenth Century*, ed. Harold E. Pagliaro (Cleveland: Case Western Reserve Univ. Press, 1973), pp. 155–69; Robert D. Hume, "Gothic Versus Romantic: A Revaluation of the Gothic Novel," *PMLA*, 84 (1969), 282–90; Elizabeth MacAndrew, *The Gothic Tradition in Fiction* (New York: Columbia Univ. Press, 1979); Lowry Nelson, Jr., "Night Thoughts on the Gothic Novel," *Yale Review*, n.s., 52 (1962), 236–57; and Devendra P. Varma, *The Gothic Flame* (London: A. Barker, 1957).

19. Ronald Paulson, "Gothic Fiction and the French Revolution," *ELH*, 49 (1981), 534–35.

20. Charles Brockden Brown, *Edgar Huntly or Memoirs of a Sleep-Walker* (Kent, Ohio: Kent State Univ. Press, 1984), p. 154.

21. Margaret Atwood, *Lady Oracle* (New York: Simon & Schuster, 1976), p. 34. For an excellent discussion of the Female Gothic, see Ellen Moers, "Female Gothic," and U. C. Knoepflmacher, "Thoughts on the Aggression of Daughters," both in *The Endurance of Frankenstein: Essays on Mary Shelley's Novel*, ed. George Levine and U. C. Knoepflmacher (Berkeley: Univ. of California Press, 1979), pp. 77–87, 88–119; and also the essays collected in Juliann E. Fleenor, ed., *The Female Gothic* (Montreal: Eden, 1983).

22. For a fuller discussion of the history of the Gothic in America, see Edith Birkhead, *The Tale of Terror: A Study of the Gothic Romance* (New York: E. P. Dutton, 1921), esp. pp. 139–42, 188–200; Oral S. Coad, "The Gothic Element in American Literature Before 1835," *JEGP*, 24 (1925), 72–93; Joel Porte, "In the Hands of an Angry God: Religious Terror in Gothic Fiction," in *The Gothic Imagination: Essays in Dark Romanticism*, ed. G. R. Thompson (Pullman: Washington State Univ. Press, 1974), pp. 42–64; Arthur Hobson Quinn, "Some Phases of the Supernatural in American Literature," *PMLA*, 25 (1910), 114–33; Eino Railo, *The Haunted Castle: A Study of the Elements of English Romanticism* (London: George Routledge, 1927), pp. 300–25; Sister Mary Redden, *The Gothic Fiction in American Magazines (1765–1800)* (Washington, D.C.: Catholic Univ. of America Press, 1939); and Donald A. Ringe, "Early American Gothic: Brown, Dana, and Allston," in *American Transcendental Quarterly*, 19 (1973), 3–8. See also "The Gothic Tradition in Nineteenth-Century American Literature: A Symposium in Two Parts," ed. Richard P. Benton, *Emerson Society Quarterly*, 18 (1972), particularly the essays by Benton, Robert D. Hume, and Maurice Levy.

23. Two commentators on the Gothic have insisted that castles are a necessary and vital ingredient of the form. See Montague Summers, *The Gothic Quest: A History of the Gothic Novel* (1938; repr., New York: Russell & Russell, 1964), pp. 190–93, and Tompkins, *The Popular Novel in England*, p. 226. For a different but fascinating discussion of castle symbolism, see Fiedler, *Love and Death in the American Novel*, pp. 127–33.

24. See, especially, Michael Davitt Bell, *The Development of American Romance: The Sacrifice of Relation* (Chicago: Univ. of Chicago Press, 1980).

25. Recent critical theory has just begun to focus attention on the Gothic and to pay attention to this antimimetic strain. I am indebted to Howard Anderson for allowing me to consult his paper "Surprised by Fear: Reading the Gothic," originally presented at the Modern Language Association, San Francisco, December 1979. See also Christine Brooke-Rose, *A Rhetoric of the Unreal: Studies in Narrative and Structure, Especially of the Fantastic* (Cambridge: Cambridge Univ. Press, 1981); Shoshana Felman, "Turning the Screw of Interpretation," in *Literature and Psychoanalysis: The Question of Reading: Otherwise*, ed. Shoshana Felman (Baltimore: Johns Hopkins Univ. Press, 1977), pp. 94–207; David B. Morris, "Gothic Sublimity," *New Literary History*, 16 (Winter 1984–85), 299–319; and Eve Kosofsky Sedgwick, "The Character in the

Veil: Imagery of the Surface in the Gothic Novel," *PMLA*, 96 (1981), 255–70. For an older but equally imaginative reading of the Gothic, see André Breton, *Manifestoes of Surrealism* (1924), trans. Richard Seaver and Helen R. Lane (Ann Arbor: Univ. of Michigan Press, 1969).

26. Sigmund Freud, "The 'Uncanny'," in *The Standard Edition of the Complete Psychological Works of Sigmund Freud*, ed. James Strachey (London: Hogarth, 1953–74), 17:237–47. See also, Harold Bloom, "Freud and the Poetic Sublime: A Catastrophe Theory of Creativity," in *Freud: A Collection of Critical Essays*, ed. Perry Meisel (Englewood Cliffs, N.J.: Prentice-Hall, 1981); Brooke-Rose, *A Rhetoric of the Unreal*, esp. 309–10; Hélène Cixous, "Fiction and Its Phantoms: A Reading of Freud's *Das Unheimliche* (The 'Uncanny')," *New Literary History*, 7 (Spring 1976), 525–48; Morris, "Gothic Sublimity," pp. 306–09; and Tzvetan Todorov, *The Fantastic: A Structural Approach to a Literary Genre*, trans. Richard Howard (Ithaca: Cornell Univ. Press, 1975).

27. For a discussion of the nightmare world of Radcliffe's perceivers, see Butler, *Romantics, Rebels, and Reactionaries*, p. 95; Coral Ann Howells, "The Pleasure of the Woman's Text: Ann Radcliffe's Subtle Transgressions in *The Mysteries of Udolpho* and *The Italian*," paper presented at the American Society for Eighteenth-Century Studies, April 1985, Toronto; and Robert Kiely, *The Romantic Novel in England* (Cambridge: Harvard Univ. Press, 1972), pp. 65–77.

28. Isaac Mitchell originally published the novel in weekly installments in the *Poughkeepsie Political Barometer* from June 5 to October 5, 1804, under the title "Alonzo and Melissa." In the *Barometer* for April 17, 1811, he announced a subscription campaign for a "more ample and extended" edition of the novel, in two volumes, to be published by Joseph Nelson of Poughkeepsie and to be sold for $1.25 per volume for bound copies, $1 per volume in boards. Admitting that "novel" is "esteemed but a more courtly name for licentiousness," Mitchell assured the reader that his novel was moral, American, and true. This version also included a ten-page introduction, a fifteen-page preface, and the long first volume describing the Berghers' plight in Europe. The Jackson version (Plattsburgh, N.Y.: Printed for the Proprietor, 1811) included only the first page of the preface, omitted all of volume 1, and printed the whole of volume 2. Since both Mitchell and his publisher, Nelson, died within months after the novel's original publication, the Jackson version was issued and reprinted without protest—although also without copyright. For more information on the controversy surrounding the curious publishing history of the novel, see the *New York Times Saturday Review of Books* for June 4, 1904; June 11, 1904; September 3, 1904; September 17, 1904; January 21, 1905; January 28, 1905; and March 4, 1905. Hereafter quotations from *The Asylum* are taken from the original Mitchell edition available on microfilm (ACS reel 226.7) and are cited parenthetically within the text.

29. Lillie Deming Loshe, *The Early American Novel, 1789–1830* (1907; repr., New York: Frederick Ungar, 1966), pp. 56–57.

30. This copy of *The Asylum* (New York: Nafis and Cornish, n.d.) is the AAS collection.

31. Michel Foucault, *Madness and Civilization*, trans. Richard Howard (New York: Random House, 1965), and *Discipline and Punish: The Birth of the Prison*, trans. Alan

Sheridan (New York: Random House, 1977). See also John Bender, "The Novel and the Rise of the Penitentiary: Narrative and Ideology in Defoe, Gay, Hogarth, and Fielding," *Stanford Literature Review*, 1 (1984), 55–84.

32. Frederic Jameson, *The Political Unconscious: Narrative as a Socially Symbolic Act* (Ithaca: Cornell Univ. Press, 1981), p. 48.

33. Harrison T. Meserole, "Some Notes on Early American Fiction; Kelroy Was There," *Studies in American Fiction*, 5 (1977), 7. One copy of *Kelroy* at the Library Company of Philadelphia bears the delightful, Sternean inscription, "Presented to Miss Grace S. Itiebley [?] by her friend Corporal Trim." For new archival research on Rush correcting the National Union Catalog entry, see Dana D. Nelson's edition of *Kelroy* (New York: Oxford Univ. Press, 1992). Nelson argues convincingly that Rush did not write at least one other book attributed to her.

34. Samuel Austin Allibone, *A Critical Dictionary of English Literature and British and American Authors*, 3 vols. (Philadelphia: A. Childs and Peterson, 1855), 2: 1893.

35. For an astute discussion of both *St. Herbert* and *Kelroy*, see Henri Petter, *The Early American Novel* (Columbus: Ohio State Univ. Press, 1971), pp. 188–89, 201–05.

36. Rebecca Rush, *Kelroy, a Novel* (Philadelphia: Bradford and Inskeep, 1812), p. 13.

37. Meserole, "Some Notes on Early American Fiction," pp. 8–9, 11–12, perceptively assesses the symbolism of Mrs. Hammond's death.

38. See Petter, *Early American Novel*, p. 330, n. 39, for a list of the Brownian devices in Watterston's novels.

39. Brockden Brown's comments on the law are quoted in Harry R. Warfel, *Charles Brockden Brown: American Gothic Novelist* (Gainesville: Univ. of Florida Press, 1949), p. 29.

40. *The Diary of Elihu Hubbard Smith*, ed. James E. Cronin (Philadelphia: American Philosophical Society, 1973), p. 14.

41. David Punter, *The Literature of Terror: A History of Gothic Fictions from 1765 to the Present Day* (New York: Longman, 1980), pp. 409, 417, 414.

42. The Brown bibliography is extensive. For an overview, see Charles E. Bennett, "The Charles Brockden Brown Canon," Ph.D. diss., Univ. of North Carolina, 1974, "The Letters of Charles Brockden Brown: An Annotated Census," *Resources for American Literary Study*, 6 (1976), 164–90, and "Charles Brockden Brown and the International Novel," *Studies in the Novel*, 12 (1980), 62–64; Charles A. Carpenter, "Selective Bibliography of Writings about Charles Brockden Brown," in *Critical Essays on Charles Brockden Brown*, ed. Bernard Rosenthal (Boston: G. K. Hall, 1981), pp. 224–39; Robert E. Hemenway and Dean H. Keller, "Charles Brockden Brown, America's First Important Novelist: A Check List of Biography and Criticism," *Papers of the Bibliographical Society of America*, 60 (1966), 349–62; Sydney J. Krause with Jane Nieset, "A Census of the Works of Charles Brockden Brown," *Serif*, 3 (1966), 27–55; and Patricia L. Parker, *Charles Brockden Brown: A Reference Guide* (Boston: G. K. Hall, 1980). For additional reviews, see Evelyn Sears Schneider, "The Changing Image of Charles Brockden Brown as Seen by American Critics from 1815

to the Present," part 2 of a three-part Ph.D. diss., Rutgers Univ., 1971; and William S. Ward, "American Authors and British Reviewers 1798–1826: A Bibliography," *American Literature*, 49 (March 1977), 5–6, and "Charles Brockden Brown, His Contemporary British Reviewers, and Two Minor Bibliographical Problems," *Papers of the Bibliographical Society of America*, 65 (1971), 399–402. For Brown's estimation of his relative worth as a novelist, see the journal entry of 1799 in William Dunlap, *The Life of Charles Brockden Brown: Together with Selections from the Rarest of His Printed Works, from His Original Letters, and from His Manuscripts Before Unpublished*, 2 vols. (Philadelphia: James P. Parke, 1815), 1:107. The Dunlap biography rewords materials in the Paul Allen biography that would have been published in 1814 but for Allen's untimely death. A facsimile of the original printer's proof has recently been reissued as *The Life of Charles Brockden Brown* (Delmar, N.Y.: Scholars' Facsimiles and Reprints, 1975). An anonymous front-page editorial in the (Philadelphia) *National Gazette* for May 17, 1823, asked, "Why does not some enterprising American bookseller undertake a handsome, uniform edition of the Best Novels and Essays of the late Charles Brockden Brown? . . . It is painful to reflect upon the oblivion which the works of Brown have suffered here." (Special thanks to Peter Onuf for calling this article to my attention.) John Neal continued this theme in his "American Writers, I and II," *Blackwood's*, 16 (October 1824), 305–11, 421–26; and for Brown as a misunderstood "man of genius," see the anonymous "Brown's Novels," *American Quarterly Review*, 8 (1830), 312–37. William Hazlitt also called him a "man of genius" in "William Ellery Channing's Sermons and Tracts," *Edinburgh Review*, 50 (1829), 126–28.

43. Brown, "To the Public," in *Edgar Huntly*, p. 3. See also Brown's letter to James Brown, February 15, 1799, quoted in Dunlap, *The Life of Charles Brockden Brown*: "I find to be the writer of Wieland and Ormond is a greater recommendation that I ever imagined it would be" (p. 99).

44. Charles Brockden Brown, "To the Editor of the *Weekly Magazine*" in *The Rhapsodist and Other Uncollected Writings*, ed. Harry R. Warfel (New York: Scholars' Facsimiles and Reprints, 1943), p. 136.

45. Samuel Miller, *A Brief Retrospect of the Eighteenth Century*, 2 vols. (New York: T. & J. Swords, 1803), 2:390.

46. Charles Brockden Brown, "The Editor's Address to the Public," *Literary Magazine and American Register*, 1 (October 1803), 4.

47. The interpretations of Arthur Mervyn come from, respectively: Charles Brockden Brown to James Brown, February 15, 1799, quoted in Dunlap, *Life of Charles Brockden Brown*, 2:98; Percy Bysshe Shelly, described in *Peacock's Memoirs of Shelley*, ed. H.F.B. Brett-Smith (London: H. Frowde, 1909), p. 35; James H. Justus, "Arthur Mervyn, American," *American Literature*, 42 (November 1963), 313; Patrick Brancaccio, "Studied Ambiguities: *Arthur Mervyn* and the Problem of the Unreliable Narrator," *American Literature*, 42 (March 1970), 22, 26; Kenneth Bernard, "Arthur Mervyn: The Ordeal of Innocence," *Texas Studies in Language and Literature*, 6 (1965), 446; Warner Berthoff, "Introduction" to *Arthur Mervyn* (New York: Holt, Rinehart & Winston, 1962), p. xvii; James Russo, "The Chameleon of Convenient Vice: A Study of the Narrative of *Arthur Mervyn*," *Studies in the Novel*, 11 (1979), 381; R.W.B.

Lewis, *The American Adam: Innocence, Tragedy, and Tradition in the Nineteenth Century* (Chicago: Univ. of Chicago Press, 1955), p. 95; Petter, *Early American Novel*, p. 339; Alan Axelrod, *Charles Brockden Brown: An American Tale* (Austin: Univ. of Texas Press, 1983), p. 135; Emory Elliott, *Revolutionary Writers: Literature and Authority in the New Republic, 1725–1810* (New York: Oxford Univ. Press, 1982), p. 265; Jane Tompkins, *Sensational Designs: The Cultural Work of American Fiction, 1790–1860* (New York: Oxford Univ. Press, 1985), pp. 62–93; Russo, "The Chameleon," pp. 381–405; and Norman S. Grabo, *The Coincidental Art of Charles Brockden Brown* (Chapel Hill: Univ. of North Carolina Press, 1981), p. 86.

48. Charles Brockden Brown, *Arthur Mervyn or Memoirs of the Year 1793* (Kent: Kent State Univ. Press, 1980), p. 71. Hereafter quotations from this edition of the novel will be cited parenthetically within the text.

49. William Hedges, "Charles Brockden Brown and the Culture of Contradictions," *Early American Literature*, 9 (Fall 1974), 123.

50. Although the whole of Franklin's autobiography was not published until 1818, Brown could have read any of the paraphrases, redactions, and condensations of Part 1 that appeared as early as May 1790 in the *Universal Asylum and Columbian Magazine* and all four parts that appeared in Mathew Carey's *American Museum* in July 1790. The French translation of Part 1 (1791) was retranslated into English and published in London in 1793 in both the *Lady's Magazine* and in two separate volumes. For the complete and complex history, see *The Autobiography of Benjamin Franklin: A Genetic Text*, ed. J. A. Leo Lemay and P. M. Zall (Knoxville: Univ. of Tennessee Press, 1981), pp. xlvii–lviii; and, for a discussion, Betty Kushen, "Three Earliest Published Lives of Benjamin Franklin, 1790–1793: The *Autobiography* and Its Continuations," *Early American Literature*, 9 (Spring 1974), 39–52; and "Letter to the Editor" by P. M. Zall, *Early American Literature*, 10 (Fall 1975), 220–21.

51. Axelrod, *Charles Brockden Brown*, pp. 148, 154.

52. Grabo, *The Coincidental Art*, pp. 112–26.

53. See the following anonymous essays: "*Arthur Mervyn; or, Memoirs of the Year 1793*," *Critical Review* (London), 2nd ser., 39 (1803), 119; "On the Writings of Charles Brockden Brown, the American Novelist," *New Monthly Magazine*, 14 (1820), 609–14; and "Of Wieland and Other Novels by Charles Brockden Brown of Philadelphia," *American Monthly Magazine*, 1 (1824), 6–7. Also see Dunlap, *The Life of Charles Brockden Brown*, 2:29–30.

54. Letter of February 15, 1799, quoted in Dunlap, *The Life of Charles Brockden Brown*, pp. 97–99. In the first issue of his *Weekly Magazine*, Brown included a statement that might be construed as contradictory to the one in his letter to James: "Great energy employed in the promotion of vicious purposes, constitutes a very useful spectacle. Give me a tale of lofty crimes, rather than of honest folly" (quoted in John Cleman, "Ambiguous Evil: A Study of Villains and Heroes in Charles Brockden Brown's Major Novels," *Early American Literature*, 10 [Fall 1975], 190).

55. *Diary of Elihu Hubbard Smith*, p. 272, lamented Brown's erratic method. For other comments either by Brown or his contemporaries which suggest his own changeability, see Axelrod, *Charles Brockden Brown*, pp. 14ff.

56. Michel Foucault, "What Is an Author?" in *Language, Counter-Memory, Prac-*

tice, trans. Donald F. Bouchard and Sherry Simon (Ithaca: Cornell Univ. Press, 1977), pp. 113–38. One contemporary critic who does not privilege the author is Nina Baym in "A Minority Reading of *Wieland*," in *Critical Essays on Charles Brockden Brown*, pp. 87–125.

57. Russo, "The Chameleon," pp. 381–405, has capably documented the various openings in Brown's text—although he has also sought, unwisely in my opinion, to close them.

58. Fiedler, *Love and Death in the American Novel*, esp. pp. 150–53. Two notably careful, convincing, historical readings of *Arthur Mervyn*, those by Emory Elliott in *Revolutionary Writers* and by Jane Tompkins in *Sensational Designs*, start with the same premises about the "mood of the times," use similar literary methods and assumptions, but end up with radically different interpretations of the hero.

59. See *Arthur Mervyn*, pp. 10, 46, 72, 81, 111, 118, 122, and 154 for references to the rural life.

60. Tompkins, *Sensational Designs*, esp. pp. 62–71.

61. Elliott, *Revolutionary Writers*, p. 265; and, for a similar argument, Brancaccio, p. 25.

62. *Diary of Elihu Hubbard Smith*, p. 272.

63. "The Journal Letters," in David Lee Clark, *Charles Brockden Brown: Pioneer Voice of America* (Durham: Duke Univ. Press, 1952), p. 103.

64. Mikhail M. Bakhtin, *Problems of Dostoevsky's Poetics*, trans. R. W. Rotsel (Ann Arbor: Univ. of Michigan Press, 1973), esp. chap. 5, and "Epic and Novel," in *The Dialogic Imagination*, ed. Michael Holquist and ed. and trans. Caryl Emerson and Michael Holquist (Austin: Univ. of Texas Press, 1981), esp. pp. 3–40. See also, Jacques Derrida, "Structure, Sign, and Play in the Discourse of the Human Sciences," in *The Structuralist Controversy*, ed. Richard Macksey and Eugenio Donato (Baltimore: Johns Hopkins Univ. Press, 1972), pp. 247–73. And for a deconstructionist reading of Brockden Brown, see Michael Kreyling, "Construing Brown's *Wieland*: Ambiguity and Derridean 'Freeplay,' " *Studies in the Novel*, 14 (1982), 43–54.

Chapter 9

1. For somewhat different versions of this anecdote, see Louis O. Mink, "Narrative Form as a Cognitive Instrument," pp. 135–36, and Lionel Grossman, "History and Literature: Reproduction or Signification," pp. 18–19, both in *The Writing of History: Literary Form and Historical Understanding*, ed. Robert H. Canary and Henry Kozicki (Madison: Univ. of Wiseonsin Press, 1978).

2. For important discussions of oppositional criticism, see Frank Lentricchia, *Criticism and Social Change* (Chicago: Univ. of Chicago Press, 1983), esp. p. 15; and Raymond Williams, *Marxism and Literature* (New York: Oxford Univ. Press, 1977), esp. pp. 112–13. My discussion has also been influenced by Nicola Chiaromonte, *The Paradox of History: Stendahl, Tolstoy, Pasternak, and Others* (London: Wiedenfeld and Nicolson, 1970); Hayden White, *Metahistory: The Historical Imagination in Nineteenth-Century Europe* (Baltimore: Johns Hopkins Univ. Press, 1973); and White, "The Historical Text as Literary Artifact," in *The Writing of History*, pp. 41–62. On

a more practical level, the eminent historian William H. McNeill, in *Mythistory and Other Essays* (Chicago: Univ. of Chicago Press, 1985), has recently argued that world survival in part depends upon the recognition that one historian's truth is another's myth.

3. Thomas Paine, *The Rights of Man* (New York: Pelican Classics, 1969), pp. 140–41.

4. Charles Brockden Brown, *Arthur Mervyn or Memoirs of the Year 1793* (Kent: Kent State Univ. Press, 1980).

5. The eighteenth century's fascination with doubleness has been discussed by Sydney J. Krause, "Historical Essay," in Charles Brockden Brown, *Edgar Huntly or Memoirs of a Sleep-Walker* (Kent: Kent State Univ. Press, 1984), p. 296.

6. Moses Coit Tyler, *A History of American Literature, 1607–1765*, 2 vols. (1878; repr., Williamston, Mass.: Corner House, 1973), 1:v. These passages are quoted and discussed in Annette Kolodny's important essay "The Integrity of Memory: Creating a New Literary History of the United States," *American Literature*, 57 (May 1985), 291–307.

7. Harold Bloom, "Criticism, Canon-Formation, and Prophecy: The Sorrows of Facticity," *Raritan*, 3 (1984), 1; and Kolodny, "Integrity of Memory," pp. 291–307.

8. The relationship between pedagogy and literary theory is one of the most important issues now facing the profession. For an excellent discussion, see William E. Cain, *The Crisis in Criticism: Theory, Literature and Reform in English Studies* (Baltimore: Johns Hopkins Univ. Press, 1984), esp. pp. 67–121 and 247–77. The theoretical journal *boundary* 2 is also planning two double issues (1986–1987) devoted primarily to the topic of ideology and the politics of humanities pedagogy. See also Nancy Hoffman, "White Women, Black Women: Inventing an Adequate Pedagogy," *Women's Studies Newsletter*, 5 (Spring 1977), 21–4; and the essays in *The New Feminist Criticism: Essays on Women, Literature, and Theory*, ed. Elaine Showalter (New York: Pantheon, 1985), esp. the essays by Barbara Smith, "Toward a Black Feminist Criticism" (pp. 168–85), and Deborah E. McDowell, "New Directions for Black Feminist Criticism" (pp. 186–99). For provocative discussions of the socializing role played by the traditional humanities, see Carol Gilligan, *In a Different Voice: Psychological Theory and Women's Development* (Cambridge: Harvard Univ. Press, 1982); and Richard Ohmann, *English in America: A Radical View of the Profession* (New York: Oxford Univ. Press, 1976). For one of the starkest assessments of the function of the traditional humanities—"There has never been a document of culture which was not at one and the same time a document of barbarism"—see Walter Benjamin, "Theses on the Philosophy of History," in *Illuminations*, trans. H. Zohn (New York: Schocken, 1969), p. 253.

9. Two studies of anthologies—what is included, what excluded—have arrived at different, but not incompatible, conclusions about the politics of canonization. See the chapter " 'But Is It Any Good?': The Institutionalization of Literary Value," in Jane Tompkins, *Sensational Designs: The Cultural Work of American Fiction, 1790–1860* (New York: Oxford Univ. Press, 1985), pp. 186–201, for an analysis of the ways in which the canon changes according to the prevailing economic, literary, and political interests of the generation (although each generation insists that *it* knows what

constitutes a masterpiece). Susan Koppelman has isolated a different pattern in her survey of over a century of short story anthologies. She documents an almost un-changing percentage of both women writers (of all races) and black writers (of both sexes) in the anthologies, but she notes that each generation of anthologists tends to select *new* representatives for women and blacks. The result is a sense of historical amnesia, as if there were no tradition of women or minority writing in America. See the introduction to her anthology *Old Maids: Short Stories by Nineteenth-Century U.S. Women Writers* (New York: Pandora, 1984).

10. See Bernard Chevignard, "St. John de Crèvecoeur in the Looking Glass: *Letters from an American Farmer* and the Making of a Man of Letters," *Early American Literature*, 19 (Fall 1984), 173–90; Everett Emerson, "Hector St. John de Crèvecoeur and the Promise of America," in *Forms and Functions of History in American Literature: Essays in Honor of Ursula Brumm*, ed. Winfried Flunk et al. (Berlin: Erich Schmidt Verlag, 1981), pp. 44–55; and Albert E. Stone, Jr., "Crèvecoeur's *Letters* and the Beginnings of an American Literature," *Emory University Quarterly*, 18 (Winter 1962), 197–213.

11. Kenneth Silverman, *A Cultural History of the American Revolution* (New York: Thomas Y. Crowell, 1976), p. 513.

12. Martha Meredith Read, *Monima, or the Beggar Girl* (New York: T. B. Jansen, 1803), pp. 434, 436, 440–41.

13. The ways in which purportedly aesthetic judgments are actually founded upon ideological (and often tautological) arguments has been perceptively analyzed by Nina Baym in "Melodramas of Beset Manhood: How Theories of American Fiction Ex-clude Women Authors," *American Quarterly*, 33 (Summer 1981), 123–39.

14. Raymond Williams, *The Country and the City* (New York: Oxford Univ. Press, 1973), p. 72.

15. Dominick La Capra, *History and Criticism* (Ithaca: Cornell Univ. Press, 1985), p. 126. For additional comments on the relationship between literature and history, see also La Capra's *Rethinking Intellectual History: Texts, Contexts, Language* (Ithaca: Cornell Univ. Press, 1983), esp. pp. 13–22. For an analysis of the politics of literature by a social historian, see Steven Watts, *The Republic Reborn: War and the Making of Liberal America, 1790–1820* (Baltimore: Johns Hopkins Univ. Press, 1987). Two jour-nals concerned with literary theory have recently addressed themselves to the rela-tionships between literature and history. *Poetics*, 14 (1985), is devoted to the related issues of the empirical sociology of cultural production and the politics of writing the history of literature, and *New Literary History*, 16, no. 3 (1985), has similarly explored the politics of literary history.

16. Borges quoted in Walter L. Reed, *An Exemplary History of the Novel: The Quixotic Versus the Picaresque* (Chicago: Univ. of Chicago Press, 1981), p. 265.

17. Ibid., p. 264.

18. Margaret Atwood, *Surfacing* (Don Mills, Ontario: Paperjacks, 1972), p. 129.

Index